Aviation in Perthshire – People, Places and Planes

A historical exploration of awe-inspiring aviators, their wartime contribution, Perthshire airfield history, facts, and memorable events

A special edition of the aviation stories with links to Perthshire, written by Kenneth Bruce. Produced in support of Take Off, an independent aviation focused youth charity founded and run by members of the Scottish Aero Club

Kenneth Bruce

www.take-off.org.uk   www.scottishaeroclub.org.uk

Text Copyright © Kenneth James Bruce 2023

All Rights Reserved

Kenneth James Bruce has asserted his right under the Copyright, Designs, and Patents Act, 1988 to be identified as the author of this work.

This book is distributed subject to the condition that it shall not by way of trade or otherwise, be lent, sold, hired out, or otherwise circulated without the publisher's prior consent in any form of binding or cover other than that in which it is published and without a similar condition including this condition being imposed on the subsequent publisher.

No part of this work may be reproduced, stored in a retrieval system, or transmitted in any form or by any means, electronic, mechanical, photocopying, recording or otherwise, without prior permission of the author.

Copyright © 2023 Ken Bruce

All rights reserved.

ISBN: 9798865450047

Cover image by Josef Svoboda – www.vecteezy.com

Forewords

I have long had a fascination with the history of aviation in Perthshire. The airfields, the events, and the war time aviators who were born, lived in and around, or were trained at RAF Perth, now Perth Airport, and other local airfields (most now long gone) can be found in this book.

The book contains the full collection of my Perthshire aviation history and aviator stories written for the madeinperth.org website, the Perthshire Advertiser newspaper, and my book, *Where Sky and Summit Meet*, published by Tippermuir Books in Perth.

Perthshire has a long history of involvement in aviation, from the early attempts to fly at Errol in 1903 and later at Blair Atholl in 1907 and Forgandenny in 1909, through to the Second World War where thousands were trained at what I call the 'Pilot Factory' at RAF Perth. I have included the stories of the very Early Aviators in Scotland at the beginning of the book for interest.

This volume tells the stories of 15 First World War aviators and over 90 from the Second World War, including 7 Battle of Britain heroes. All of Perthshire's airfields over the years are included along with notes of where German bombs were dropped and the aircraft that were lost. Also included is some other local aviation history that I thought you might find interesting.

Ken Bruce, Author

November 2023

Take Off

I am deeply indebted to Ken, for his generosity in making available his vast body of work in this special edition from which all the profits go directly to Take Off. Our charity was founded in 2013 by three members of the Scottish Aeroclub and continues to be managed by a group of trustees who are members there.

The aim of our charity is to promote the education of young people in the field of aviation through,

1. The provision of flying opportunities for young people in Scotland to promote self-confidence, self-belief, and motivation.
2. Raising awareness of the opportunities in aviation related careers to help young people see where they might develop their potential, bringing benefits to all areas of their lives and thereby, society as a whole.
3. Working in partnership with other bodies to achieve these purposes.

Over the years we have been successful in giving several deserving young people from schools in the

Perth area the opportunity to undertake flight training. In the coming years we intend to continue this core activity and also to expand our reach across Scotland, developing and delivering materials that can be used in Schools to promote a deeper awareness of the vast array of careers that the Aviation and Aerospace Industries can offer. Your purchase of this book helps us to fund this important work,

Thank you!

Howard Duthie,

Chair, Take Off, (Scottish Charity 043716).

The Scottish Aeroclub

The Scottish Aeroclub is the oldest and largest sports aviation club in Scotland. As we head towards our centenary in 2027 with an ever-increasing age profile, we know that we must encourage a much stronger active engagement with young people across the country. We want to do everything that we can therefore to support the work of Take Off.

I echo Howard's words above in thanking Ken for his remarkable generosity in supporting Take Off in this way,

So, sit back, relax, and enjoy this rich and detailed history of aviation and aviators with links to Perthshire. Keep an eye out too for the appearance of other interesting characters, contemporaries of those whose story is being told, like Captain W.E. Johns of Biggles fame. There is also much to give us pause for thought, on the ultimate sacrifice made by so many in this book.

Chocks away!

William Scott,

Chair, The Scottish Aeroclub.

Dedication

To Tippermuir Books, and their madeinperth.org website and especially Paul Philippou who supported me on my writing journey, without them, these amazing stories may have never been told. Also, to the Perthshire Advertiser for publishing some of my stories over the last few years.

Contents

Table of Contents

Text Copyright © Kenneth James Bruce 2023	2
Forewords	3
Dedication	5
Contents	6
A Selection of Abbreviations	12
The Early Aviators	15
Flying Father	15
James Tytler	16
Vincenzo Lunardi	17
Percy Pilcher	19
Hiram Maxim	22
Samuel Franklin Cody, Wild West Cowboy and Kite Builder	24
Preston Albert Watson & the Power Necessary for Flight	28
John William Dunne	31
Barnwell Brothers	36
Andrew Blain Baird	39
First World War Aviators	40
Sergeant Alexander Stewart Allan	40
Ian Dermid Campbell	43
Robert Alexander Duff	48
David Ogilvie Duthie	51
Group Captain Robert Halley DFC & 2 bars, AFC	59
Second Lieutenant Herrick Peter Gladstone Leyden & Second Lieutenant Robert William Gladstone Leyden	74
Lieutenant Courteney Patrick Flowerdew Lowson	79
Lieutenant John Watson McCash	82
Lieutenant Peter MacFarlane	88
Second Lieutenant Alexander McKenzie	91
Second Lieutenant John Ross	93
Robert Leonard Grahame Skinner	95
Andrew Beattie Sneddon	97
Second Lieutenant Howard Watson	99
Lieutenant Cyril Williams	100
Airships and Zeppelins	103
Extracts from local Newspapers.	104
Zeppelin facts	106
Zeppelin raids	106
The (first) London aircraft bomber Blitz of WW1	108
Invasion Preparations	110
The airship mystery continued	113

Further Speculation	114
Air Circuses	115
Blackburn R.B.3A Perth Flying Boat	118
The Kay Gyroplane (Autogyro)	121
RAF Airfields in (& close) to Perthshire during the Second World War	124
RAF Balado	124
RAF Buttergask	126
RAF Errol	126
RAF Findo Gask	133
RAF Grangemouth	136
RAF Methven	137
RAF Perth	138
RAF Tealing	148
RAF Whitefield	149
Scone Park	149
South Kilduff Airfield	149
Murie Cemetery Errol, Fairey Swordfish, and the river Tay	150
Arthur A. J. Roberton	150
Bertram Henry Prance	151
John Roland Hobday	153
Charles Muirhead	154
Winston Veron Stark.	154
William (Billy) Edmonstone Woodington	155
John Weatherhead	155
Tay Estuary during WW2	159
Bombs Over Perthshire	161
Locations of Bombs dropped in Perthshire during the Second World War	164
Gas Attack Expected	170
Bourne End Rail Crash	171
Civilian Bombing Casualties Across Scotland & in particular Dundee & the Counties of Angus, Fife, & Perthshire During the Second World War	175
Royal Naval Stores Depot at Almondbank	176
Ice Rink Heinkel	178
Strathallan Airfield	180
Jean Millar Valentine	183
Ethel Cassidy	188
William Deuchars	189
John Neil Campbell Denholm	193
Nan Menzies Roberts	195
Margaret Cunnison & the ATA	196
Margaret Watson-Watt	203
Aircraft Crashes Within Perthshire in the 1930s	207
8 February 1936	207

18 February 1939	207
5 July 1939	207
Aerial Activity Within & Close to Perthshire Airspace during the Second World War	208
16 October 1939	208
7 December 1939	208
18 December 1939	208
13 January 1939	208
29 January 1940	208
30 January 1940	208
9 February 1940	208
7 May 1941	208
28 August 1943	208
Aircraft Crashes Within & Close to Perthshire - During WW2	209
24 November 1940	209
10 March 1941	209
15 April 1941	209
1 August 1941	209
18 August 1941	210
4 September 1941	210
5 September 1941	210
20 October 1941	210
19 January 1942	210
2 March 1942	211
24 March 1942	211
16 April 1942	212
21 April 1942	212
14 August 1942	212
15 August 1942	212
17 September 1942	213
6 October 1942	213
23 December 1942	213
3 June 1943	214
13 June 1943	214
31 May 1944	214
8 November 1944	215
Battle of Britain Heroes	216
Neil Cameron	217
John King 'Jack' Norwell	218
Forgrave Marshall Smith	224
William Nairn Gardiner	234
Andrew Smitton Darling	236
Alexander Henry Thom	239
Sir Alan Smith	243

Notable mentions	247
Second World War Aviators	249
David Taylor Adams	249
Peter Gordon Anderson	251
Ronald Scott Baillie	254
Alan Reid Beveridge and Robert Graham Webster Beveridge	260
Colin David Brough	262
Douglas Cameron	264
Patrick Cameron	271
Archibald Campbell	273
David Ferguson Sharpe Campbell	275
James Cameron Campbell	276
John Archibald Campbell	278
Douglas Carr	279
Joseph MacCrae Chambers	284
Eric Cooke	285
James William Crow	286
Allan Dickson	288
Douglas James Morrison Dunn	290
John Tyndel Farquhar	293
James Roy Fenwick	294
Duncan Cameron Findlay	296
William Fraser	298
Henry Anselm de Freitas	300
James Victor Gardiner	305
Gilbert Cameron Gibson	307
William James Gilchrist	309
Denholm Gow	312
Alastair Donald Mackintosh "Sandy" Gunn	314
Charles Grant	323
James Crawford Halley	326
William John Henderson	328
David Hodge	329
Ernie 'Sherl-E' Holmes	330
James Harper Greig Horne	336
Edward Peter William Hutton	338
Herome Alexander Innes	343
Thomas Kaye	349
Thomas Kennedy	350
William Knaggs	352
John Laidlay	354
David Maxwell Laing	356
Alexander Little	357

John Littlejohn	359
Ian Neil MacDougall & David Ormond MacDougall	362
Charles MacFarlane	365
John George Mackay	367
Colin Mackenzie	370
James McCash	371
William J J McDougall	374
William Henderson McDougall	376
Alistair Stuart McLaren	378
Ian (Graham) Miller	379
John William Charlton Moffat	381
John Alexander Morrison	386
William Blair Morrison	392
Thomas Ralph Morton	393
Andrew McKenzie Munn	394
Thomas Nicholson	402
Ronald Staples Ogg	404
Alex Thomson Patterson	407
Charles Duncan Powrie	408
David Douglas Pryde, George Pryde, William Symington Pryde, John Marshall Pryde	409
Charles Rankin	413
Colin 'Robbie' Robertson	417
Gilbert Ferguson Sage	420
James Shaw	423
Roderick Forbes Sim	425
Derrick Barrie Simpson	427
Alfie Smith	430
Crichton Alexander Smith	431
Gavin Strang Smith	433
Leonard Albert Soutar	439
Robert Stewart	442
Peter Straiton	444
Ian Taylor	445
Benjamin Thomas	447
William Thomson	448
Antony Verdon Verdon	452
Flight Lieutenant William Walton DFC and Alexander McInnes	454
William Alexander Watson	455
James Milton Whitehead	462
David Wood	465
James Currie Wood	466
William James Young	469
Victoria Crosses	482

John Manson Craig VC	483
Hugh Gordon Malcolm	485
Flight Lieutenant William Reid VC	486
Flight Sergeant George Thomson VC	492
Polish 309 Squadron	494
No. 309 Squadron Commanders	497
No. 309: Squadron Operational Locations	497
No. 309: Squadron Aircraft Flown	498
Polish Airforce Graves at Wellshill Cemetery, Perth	499
Lieutenant Colonel Gwido Karol Langer	500
A selection of RAF jargon	501
About the Author	502

Abbreviations

AACU Anti-aircraft Co-operation Unit

AFC Air Force Cross

ALG Advanced Landing Ground

AFM Air Force Medal

AFU Advanced Flying Unit

ATA Air Transport Auxiliary

BEA British European Airways

BEF British Expeditionary Force

CANS Civil Air Navigation School

DARA Defence Aviation Repair Agency

DFC Distinguished Flying Cross

DFM Distinguished Flying Medal

DSC Distinguished Service Cross

EFTS [RAF] Elementary Flying Training School

EGS Elementary Gliding School

ERFTS [RAF] Elementary & Reserve Flying Training School

FIS Flying Instructor School

FRAeS Fellowship of the Royal Aeronautical Society

FTU Ferry training Unit

GPI Ground Position Indicator

HE High Explosive Bomb

HCU Heavy Conversion Unit

IFF Identification, Friend or Foe

IY Incendiary Bomb

MB Mine Bomb

MGDA [RAF] Maintenance Group Defence Agency

MSAA Moscow Special Assignment Airgroup

MU Maintenance Unit

NARO Naval Aircraft Repair Organisation

RNAW Royal Naval Aircraft Workshop

OL Oil Bomb

OTU Operational Training Unit

PRU [RAF] Photographic Reconnaissance Unit

RAAF Royal Australian Air Force

RAF Royal Air Force

RAFO Reserve of Air Force Officers

RAFVR Royal Air Force Volunteer Reserve

RCAF Royal Canadian Air Force

RFC Royal Flying Corps

RLG Relief Landing Ground

RNAW Royal Navy Aircraft Workshop

RNFAA Royal Navy Fleet Air Arm

RNSD Royal Naval Stores Depot

RNZAF Royal New Zealand Air Force

SAR Search & Rescue

SLAIS Specialised Low attack Instructors' School

SLG Satellite Landing Ground

TBR Torpedo Bomber Reconnaissance

TDS Training Depot Station

TEU Tactical Exercise Unit

TFS Tactical Fighter Squadron

TFW Tactical Fighter Wing

USAF United States Air Force

UXM Unexploded Mine

VC Victoria Cross

WRAFVR Women's Royal Air Force Volunteer Reserve

WRNS Women's Royal Naval Service

The Early Aviators

Flying Father

Father John Damien (Giovanni Damiano de Falcucci) was an Italian priest and alchemist at the court of King James IV of Scotland. There he practised alchemy, medicine and flying! Not much is known about Father Damien bar that he lived from about 1470 to about 1530, he was a firm favourite of James IV, and was also known as the 'French Leach'. (Leach, Leech, Leche, and Leich being old Scots names for a physician.) Father Damien was nonetheless regarded by many as in fact a bit of a charlatan and a fraudster.

Father Damien prepared court entertainments for the king and he directed the building of alchemical furnaces at Stirling Castle and Holyrood House, Edinburgh. He arranged for the building of these furnaces to produce the *Quinta Essentia*, the fifth pillar of life, a substance alleged to exist alongside the 4 classical elements: air, earth, fire, and water.

James IV seems to have been impressed with Father Damien as he promoted him to the position of Abbot of Tongland (1504-9) (near Kirkcudbright). There are however no confirming records that Father Damien took up the residency. Father Damien hung up his wings and decided to retire when he received a large pension from James IV in 1509, but he may have continued to live at the court until 1513.

Some accounts suggest that a failure to produce gold through alchemy was the catalyst for Father Damien attempting human-powered flying. Conversely, there are accounts of significant amounts of money lost by the king playing cards and betting on shooting matches with Father Damien. So, it is a possibility, boasting of an ability to achieve human flight was an attempt to get back in the king's favour after falling out with him over money or perhaps a result of arrogant boasting gone too far. Whatever the reason, Father Damien attempted to fly.

In September of 1507, a meeting was convened by Pope Julius II in Paris at which Father Damien was requested to attend. He announced that he would use a pair of wings made from bird feathers to fly from Stirling Castle all the way to France. He launched himself from the castle walls and an account stated that he fell straight down into a dunghill, 70 feet below. Father Damien survived but had broken his hip.

Father Damien blamed his failure to fly on the fact that he had used hen feathers instead of eagle feathers as recommended by Leonardo Da Vinci in 1485 (hens don't fly!). A late seventeenth century carpenter's bill for work at Stirling Castle refers to a now unknown location as where 'the Devil flew out'.

The Balloons Go Up, After Father Damien's dismal effort, no other powered-flight endeavours are chronicled in Scotland until the era of the hot-air and hydrogen-filled balloons which commenced at the end of the 1700s. Scotsman James Tytler is assumed to be the first person in the UK to fly by virtue of a hot-air balloon.

James Tytler

James 'Balloon' Tytler as he became better known, was born in the small hamlet of Fern in the county of Angus, that lies some 40 miles north-east of Perth. He was born there in 1745, the fourth child of George Tytler, Church of Scotland minister in the Presbytery of Brechin, and his wife, Janet Robertson.

James Tytler lived a varied life that included being a surgeon on a whaling ship and having to move to Newcastle for a while to escape the debtors' prison. He was appointed editor of the second edition of Andrew Bell's and Colin Macfarquhar's Encyclopaedia Britannica. Under Tytler's exceptional editorship, the collection was enlarged from 3 to 10 volumes (many of the contemporary entries were penned by Tytler). It was in circulation between 1777 and 1784.

In 1783, at the royal palace of Versailles, the Montgolfier brothers, Joseph-Michel, and Jacques-Étienne, exhibited a flying balloon to the king and queen of France – Louis XVI and Marie Antoinette. The balloon carried a duck, rooster, and sheep, all of which survived their ascent to the lower heavens. The animals' survival gave the impetus to attempt a human flight and the go-ahead to do so was given by King Louis. On 21 November 1783, the first balloon flight by a human was made by scientist Jean-François Pilâtre de Rozier and army officer The Marquis, François Laurent d'Arlandes.

The successful piloted flights using balloons developed by the Montgolfier brothers in France fired Tytler with an enthusiasm for ballooning. In June of 1784, he exhibited the 'Grand Edinburgh Fire Balloon' in the partially completed dome of Robert Adam's Register House. The 'Fire Balloon' was barrel-shaped, 40 feet high and 30 feet in diameter. Lift was generated by employing a stove to heat the volume of air contained in the balloon.

On 25 August 1784, after several stabs at balloon ascent, Tytler lifted off from ground close to Holyrood Park. His first attempts saw him rise but a few feet off the ground. A couple of days later, Tytler ascended to a height of 350 feet and drifted a kilometre in land distance – from Comely Gardens – before landing near Restalrig. The slopes of Arthur's Seat and Calton Hill were crowded with a paying audience (of some 100,000) fervently witnessing the momentous occasion.

Comely Gardens does not exist today. It was roughly in the district of Waverly Park, just east of the Palace of Holyrood. Mind-bogglingly, Tytler's flight took place 5 years before the French Revolution and the Declaration of Independence, which founded the USA, had been signed just 8 years earlier.

In 1792, Tytler fled Edinburgh for Ireland after being charged with producing anti-government pamphlets. Three years later, he emigrated to Salem, Massachusetts. There, on a stormy night in January 1804, the first Scottish aviator drowned whilst walking home.

Vincenzo Lunardi
The distinction of being the second person to soar gently through Scottish air space, goes to **Vincenzo Lunardi**, the 'Aeronaut'. In October of 1785, a sizeable and passionate throng of aero nautical enthusiasts crammed the grounds of George Heriot's School in Edinburgh to witness a Lunardi flight – his first in Scotland – in a hydrogen-filled balloon. The 46-mile voyage crossed the Firth of Forth and terminated at Coaltown of Callange in the Parish of Ceres, Fife, roughly 30 miles east of Perth (towards Cupar and St Andrews).

A month later, Lunardi delighted the masses of Glasgow with a balloon flight from St Andrews Square. That flight lasted over 2 hours, took in Hamilton, before its descent caused some distress to the shepherds of Hawick. A subsequent ascent which began at Glasgow narrowly avoided calamity, when a dissenting preacher known as 'Lothian Tam' was caught in the mooring ropes of Lunardi's balloon and hoisted one score feet into the air before being freed and tumbling at speed down to *terra firma* – without serious injury it must be added. Due to bad weather, the flight lasted only 20 minutes, landing in Campsie Glen, about 10 miles away.

On his next flight, Lunardi ditched in the North Sea but luckily for him, he was (after some time) rescued by a fishing boat and taken to North Berwick. In all, Lunardi made 5 flights in and above Scotland with his 'Grand Air Balloon', flights that took place but 2 years after the world's very first balloon voyage had occurred in France. Ballooning was making rapid strides and Scotland was at the leading edge.

Scotland had not been the start of the Lunardi grand tour. Before coming to Edinburgh, he had made successful balloon exhibitions in London and Liverpool. In London, a 24-mile flight had brought Lunardi instantaneous notoriety and launched the ballooning fad that inspired fashions and styles of the day. 'Lunardi Skirts', for example, were decorated with balloon ornamentation. And, in Scotland, the 'Lunardi Bonnet' was named after the epic aerial adventurer – it was balloon-shaped and stood around 60 centimetres tall.

Sardonic talk at the time claimed that Lunardi had "flown to the moon", deduced in part no doubt by his having a 'lunar' sounding name. However, in 1786, a mishap in Newcastle-upon-Tyne caused the death of one of Lunardi's assistants who was holding a restraining cord. Following critical reactions from the public, Lunardi was obliged to take leave of Britain. He did nonetheless take to the skies again – over Mount Vesuvius in 1789 and Sicily in 1790, demonstrating perhaps a penchant for volcanoes (Arthur's Seat an extinct variety).

NOTES: In 1786, Lunardi published An Account of Five Aerial Voyages in Scotland in a succession of correspondences to his guardian, Chevalier Gherardo Campagni. The book was much sought after. A signed first edition of Lunardi's book was once owned by Charles Dickens.

In his poem, 'To a Louse, On Seeing One on a Lady's Bonnet at Church', Robert Burns makes mention of the 'Lunardi Bonnet'. Composed in 1786, Burns's poem which features the well-known lines, "O wad some Power the giftie gie us – To see oursels as ithers see us!" is contemporaneous with Lunardi's aerial exploits.

"I wad na been supris'd to spy

You on an auld wife's flainen toy;

Or aiblins some bit dubbie boy,

On's wyliecoat; But Miss' fine Lunardi! fye! How daur ye do't?"

Percy Pilcher

Percy Sinclair Pilcher was born on 16 January 1866 in Bath, the son of a Scottish mother and English father. Pilcher joined the Royal Navy when he was 13 years old. He served for seven years as a naval cadet before becoming an apprentice at the Govan shipbuilders of Randolph, Elder and Company. In 1891 he was an assistant lecturer in the naval architecture and marine engineering department of Glasgow University.

Pilcher had a deep and passionate interest in aviation and began building a glider in 1891. Altogether, he built at least 4 piloted gliders and one (almost) powered aircraft. He can be rightly considered the first person in the UK to fly using a heavier-than-air machine. Pilcher tested his first glider, 'The Bat', at Cardross, near Helensburgh, during 1895, making repetitive flights. Importantly, he had acquired an engine and was arranging to use it with the glider.

Towards the end of 1895, Pilcher went to Germany to meet Otto Lilienthal, then the world's foremost expert on gliding. Lilienthal had begun to appreciate the essential scientific principle of flight, the force of lift, i.e., how the geometric character of a wing influences the movement of air over it. This comprehension helped determine the design of Percy's next trio of gliders. (Lilienthal, whose influence on Percy's work was enormous, died in 1896 when he lost control of one of his gliders.)

By 1897, Pilcher and his sister Ella had built their most effective (fourth) glider. It was designated 'The Hawk'. With it, Pilcher broke the world distance record by flying 250 metres at Stanford Hall, a stately home in Leicestershire, England, near the village of Stanford on-Avon. A replica of 'The Hawk' forms part of the holdings of National Museums Scotland Airfield at North Berwick in Scotland. Pilcher's other gliders were styled 'The Beetle' and 'The Gull'.

Pilcher was however unwavering in his desire to achieve powered flight. By 1899, he had developed a triplane winged aircraft to be powered by a 4-horsepower engine. Building the triplane was costly and Pilcher ran out of funds causing him to seek commercial support. He set up a company with Walter Gordon Wilson, later a successful motor engineer, subsequently acknowledged by the 1919 Royal Commission on Awards to Inventors as the co-inventor of the latest weapon of war, the tank. Sir William Tritton had in 1915 constructed the first tank prototype, 'Little Willie'. It was Wilson who came up with the rhomboidal design of the iconic tank, the Mark 1.

On 30 September 1899, Pilcher had his triplane prepared and arranged an authentication flight in the countryside near Stanford Hall where many spectators had congregated to witness the first piloted and powered flight. Unfortunately, the engine suffered a broken crankshaft. So as not to disappoint the crowds and any would be sponsors among them, Pilcher resolved to fly his back up, 'The Hawk'. Although the weather was poor, Pilcher took off despite the rainy and stormy weather conditions. During the flight, 'The Hawk's' tail broke off causing Pilcher to fall some 10 metres to the ground. This was a fall which he did not survive: Pilcher perished from his injuries a couple of days later, 2 October 1989

Scotland's pioneering aviator and second Icarus, Percy Pilcher, is buried in Brompton Cemetery, West London. A monument at Stanford Hall acknowledges Pilcher's achievement in the development of the aeroplane and marks where the early aviator crashed.

NOTES: Notably, Pilcher is one of the unsuccessful aviation pioneers mentioned in the 1946, Marc Blitzstein music composition, The Airborne Symphony. This work was officially dedicated to the US Eighth Army Air Force. (Blitzstein served with them in the in the US Army Air Corps Film Division during the Second World War.)

In 2003, research undertaken at the School of Aeronautics at Cranfield University, demonstrated that Pilcher's aircraft design was workable and could have been flown. Had he been able to develop the engine, it is conceivable Pilcher may have succeeded in being the first person to fly a heavier-than-air powered aircraft with a reasonable amount of control. An astonishing feat, which was properly accredited in 2011 when Pilcher became one of the 7 inaugural inductees to the 'Scottish Engineering Hall of Fame'.

Bill Brookes, an aircraft designer, achieved a flight of 1 minute 25 seconds in a reproduction aircraft. Brookes' time competes well with the Wright Brothers' best flight time of 59 seconds at Kitty Hawk. While Brookes undertook his flight in dead calm air conditions as a matter of health and safety, the Wright Brothers (in December 1903) undertook their flight in wind speeds of 20 mph or more to achieve the necessary airspeed for take-off. (The Wright Brothers' Flyer is recorded as the first successful heavier-than-air powered aircraft. It flew 4 times on 17 December 1903.)

Sir William Tritton who was knighted 21 February 1917 for his part in the development of the tank, died age 71 on Tuesday 24 September 1946. It was reported in newspapers upon his death that he married in Willesden, North London in 1916, to Isobel, born in 1895, the daughter of Graeme Gillies of Perth. Isobel died in Lincoln on 15 November 1950. (I have not been able to find a record of her birth in the Perth area).

> He married, in 1916, Isobel, daughter of Grahame Gillies, of Perth.

The Mercury and Guardian Wednesday 2 October 1946

Sir Hiram Maxim collaborated with many aeronauts, including Percy Pilcher. (See Hiram Maxim)

Percy Pilcher, The Hawk, Kelvingrove Park, Glasgow 1896 (top image Percy's sister)

Hiram Maxim

Sir Hiram Maxim, (see also The Early Aviators - Percy Pilcher), an American inventor and businessman was best known for the first automatic machine gun but was also an avid enthusiast of flying. Back in 1894, Maxim built a huge, hundred-foot combined wingspan, multi winged machine powered by two lightweight 180-horsepower steam engines. Maxim did not build an airship himself, but did build a Captive Flying Machine, a fun fair attraction that he hoped would stimulate human flight. One working example still exists and continues to run to this day at Blackpool's Pleasure Beach.

Sir Hiram Maxin also developed a myriad of other inventions including an incandescent light bulb, hair-curling tongs, mousetraps, and steam pumps. He was a keen aviation enthusiast who also claimed to be the inventor of the first machine that rose from the earth. An assertion he made in a lecture to the Scottish Aeronautical Society delivered in Glasgow in November 1913 and in an interview to the Glasgow Herald. Percy Pilcher came to assist Maxim with flying machines and develop his own.

The Hawk (Percy Picher) and Hiram Maxims hangar at Upper Austin Lodge, near Eynsford in Kent 1896

Maxim 1894 – **Steam** Powered aircraft! Test began 1894, on the third attempt it flew about 200 feet, and crashed.

Blackpool Pleasure Beach, Hiram Maxim's Captive Flying Machine 1904 (still operating)

Samuel Franklin Cody, Wild West Cowboy and Kite Builder

'Colonel' Samuel Franklin Cody (not to be confused with William F. Cody, aka Buffalo Bill – see next story) was born 6 March 1867. He was a flamboyant self-publicist, a Wild West showman, a cowboy, a gambler, a sharpshooter, a Klondike gold prospector, and a passionate kite builder. If there was a Nobel Prize for self-publicity, Cody would have equalled Marie Curie in achieving it twice. After his demise, Cody was given a full military funeral in Britain making him the first civilian and the only cowboy to lie alongside some of the greatest heroes of British military history.

Cody is most famous for his own aircraft accomplishments. His spectacular 'Flying Cathedral' was perhaps his most celebrated design. Cody came to the aircraft construction world through his passion for piloted kite flying. During the First World War, man-lifting 'Cody War-Kites' were used as a smaller alternative to balloons for artillery spotting.

In about 1901, Cody succeeded in interesting the British military establishment in his kites. By 1906, he was the chief instructor of kiting at the Balloon School in Aldershot and soon after joined the new Army Balloon Factory at Farnborough. On 5 October 1907, Britain's first powered airship – British Army Dirigible No. 1 Nulli *Secundus* – flew from Farnborough to London in 3 hours 25 minutes, with Cody and his commanding officer Colonel J. E. Capper on board (see - John William Dunne).

Cody's first appearances in Scotland were 5-13 August 1910 at Springbank Farm Aviation Ground at the **Lanark Scottish International Aviation Meeting**. Twenty-two competitors took part in competition around a circuit of 1¾ miles.

Over 250,000 people came to Lanark to observe the spectacle. A railway terminus was constructed for the event at the racecourse. Fourteen special trains a day helped move around 50,000 people a day who were attending.

Some £8,060 was awarded in prizes to the competitors – a value today of about £900,000. Cody, it appears, did not take part in the competition, preferring to remain on *terra firma*. His huge 1¼-ton biplane was severely underpowered. Cody explicated that he wanted to get used to the single engine before fitting a twin-engine configuration. - Cody's 'Flying Cathedral' having outside the Farnborough failed to take off at Lanark received a new name, 'The Hedge Trimmer'.

During the event, when fire broke out in an adjoining hangar, Cody bravely rushed in with a fire extinguisher, just in time to prevent any serious damage and save the day. (Hangars in those days were known as garages.)

It was after Lanark that the British military establishment put in an order for 60 planes that went on to form the Royal Flying Corps (RFC), which in 1918 became the Royal Air Force (RAF).

Circuit of Britain Air Race, Cody also took part in the 1911 Daily Mail Circuit of Britain air race. This was a contest for the fastest completion of a course around Britain during which competitors had to land at Edinburgh, Stirling, and Glasgow. Cody, flying his 'Cody Circuit of Britain' biplane, landed at Paisley Racecourse on 25 July 1911, just after 08:00 hours. An enthusiastic audience of 20,000 had gathered. Cody finished the race, coming in fourth (and last of the finishers) out of 30 competitors.

The cowboy aviator died in a flying accident 2 years later whilst testing his latest seaplane design for the 1913 Circuit of Britain. His funeral procession attracted a crowd of more than 100,000. Cody was buried with full military honours at Aldershot Military Cemetery. Cody's only son, Samuel Franklin Leslie Cody, born in Basel, Switzerland, is also remembered on the grave memorial. He was killed whilst serving with the RFC in Belgium on 23 January 1917.

Contestants at The Lanark Scottish International Aviation Meeting

1	Ogilvie – British – Biplane – Wright Brothers – ENV 40 horsepower and Bollee 40 horsepower, 4 cylinders.

2	Barnes – British – Monoplane – Humber – Humber 40 horsepower, 4 cylinders.

3	Chavez – Peruvian – Monoplane – Bleriot – Gnome 50 horsepower, 7 cylinders.

4	Vidart – French – Monoplane – Hanriot – Clerget 40 horsepower, 4 cylinders.

5	Champel – French – Biplane – Voisin – ENV 65 horsepower, 8 cylinders.

6   Cattaneo – Italian – Monoplane – Bleriot – Gnome 50 horsepower, 7 cylinders.

7   Tetard – French – Biplane – Sommer – Gnome 50 horsepower, 7 cylinders.

8   Blondeau – French – Biplane – Farman – Gnome 50 horsepower, 7 cylinders.

9   Gibbs – British – Biplane – Farman – Gnome 50 horsepower, 7 cylinders.

9   Gibbs – British – Monoplane – Sommer – Gnome 50 horsepower, 7 cylinders.

10   Cockburn – British – Biplane – Farman – Gnome 50 horsepower, 7 cylinders.

11   Dickson – British – Biplane – Farman – Gnome 50 horsepower, 7 cylinders.

12   Gilmour – British – Monoplane – Bleriot – JAP 35 horsepower, 8 cylinders.

13   Radley – British – Monoplane – Bleriot – Gnome 50 horsepower, 7 cylinders.

14   Cody – British – Biplane – Cody – Green 50-60 horsepower, 4 cylinders and ENV 65-80 horsepower, 8 cylinders.

15   Audemars – Swiss – Monoplane – Tellier – Panhard 40 horsepower, 4 cylinders.

15   Audemars – Swiss – Monoplane – Demoiselle – Clement 35 horsepower, 2 cylinders.

16   Hanriot – French – Monoplane – Hanriot – Clerget 40 horsepower, 4 cylinders.

17   Colmore – British – Biplane – Short Brothers – Green 50-60 horsepower, 4 cylinders.

18   Grace – British – Biplane – Short Brothers – ENV 65 horsepower, 8 cylinders.

19   Grace – British – Monoplane – Bleriot – Gnome 50 horsepower, 7 cylinders.

20   Edmond – French – Biplane – British & Colonial – Gnome 60 horsepower, 7 cylinders.

21   Edmond – French – Biplane – British & Colonial – ENV 65-80 horsepower, 8 cylinders.

22   Drexel – American – Monoplane – Bleriot – Gnome 50 horsepower, 7 cylinders.

23   McArdle – British – Monoplane – Bleriot – Gnome 50 horsepower, 7 cylinders.

24   Kuller – Dutch – Monoplane – Antoinette – ENV 65 horsepower, 8 cylinders.

Note: Samuel Franklin Cody should not be confused with William F. Cody (Buffalo Bill as he is better known). While both were flamboyant Wild West showman, Samuel Franklin had taken the surname 'Cody' as a young man in tribute to his hero Buffalo Bill. His real surname was Cowdery. Interestingly, the 'Buffalo Bill Wild West Show' visited Scotland twice in 1892 and 1904. It performed in Dundee, 18-20 August 1904 and visited Perth on 4 August 1904 where a power cable was damaged during the installation of lighting for the show causing a power cut in the city and disrupting the show.

Cody at the controls of Cody aircraft mark II with a Native American man as a passenger © IWM

S F Cody demonstrates the passenger carrying capabilities of the Cody Aircraft Mark IIE (nicknamed Omnibus). Cody built this aircraft in 1910 and modified it to develop the ability to carry passengers. With an Austro-Daimler engine fitted, the aircraft could carry four passengers and was the first aircraft to do so in this country. It was eventually crashed by Lieutenant J N Fletcher whilst Cody was teaching him to fly on 5 April 1912 © IWM.

Preston Albert Watson & the Power Necessary for Flight

Preston Watson was born in 1880 into the family of the powerful Dundee merchant Thomas Watson of the firm Watson & Philip. The company still exists to this day, they have a distribution centre on Riverside in Dundee, just west of Dundee Riverside Airport. Young Watson was a keen sportsman. He is documented as a Scottish long jump and hurdles titleholder and was a member of Panmure Rugby Club when they won the Scottish championships. There is a street in Errol, a village neighbouring the fields where Watson did a lot of his 'flying', named after him. The fields are now part of Errol Airfield (11 miles to the west of Perth). Watson also flew in fields by Forgandenny (5 miles to the south of Perth). At Errol, Watson's 'flight' fields lie east of the Leys farms towards Muirhouses; at Forgandenny; they are by Dovecot Park, near Rossie House. Watson later flew at The Haughs, Forgandenny Station, and possibly at Belmont, near Meigle. (For Errol airfield, see also-Murie Cemetery, Fairey Swordfish, and the river Tay)

It has been suggested that as a young man, Watson would occasionally sit observing the river Tay and watch seagulls in flight. *"One day too, we will be able to fly"*, he is said to have pronounced prophetically, only to be chided by his brother, James, and friends for an idea that they said was *"just daft"*.

The Philip side of the Watson-Philip enterprise derived from a Perthshire family and both families were good friends who would vacation with each other. In the rather agreeable Kinclaven Church (close to the Beech Hedges on Murthly Road), Watson family (graffiti) inscriptions could be seen on pew 17 – one of which read *"P. W. AVIATOR"*. Pew 21 has inscriptions from the Philip family – including *"B. M. Philip"*. This is Beatrice Philip who was espoused to Watson in 1906. The dedications are dated 1899 and 1900.

It was whilst studying engineering at the University College of Dundee that Watson's curiosity in aeronautics flourished and in June or July 1903, in the aforementioned fields near Errol, he made a number of investigational flights using a full-scale glider that he had built, which it is believed may have been powered by an engine.

In recent years, a lively discussion has arisen vis-à-vis the notion that Watson may have flown in his own powered aircraft, 5 or 6 months before the Wright Brothers accomplished theirs at Kitty Hawk, North Carolina. Probably not or possibly yes, were the various deductions. Watson it seems, was not a self-publicist and was not absorbed with fame and fortune, and this may account for his failure to be recognised as pre-dating the Wright Brothers in the development of powered flight. The issue deserves additional deliberation.

The first issue is whether Watson did indeed leave the ground in a powered aircraft? The answer is most definitely, yes. Watson (and his younger sibling James) was viewed flying above the hedgerows at Errol by several witnesses – 'hopping' above the ground for 100 to 200 yards. The second issue is what constitutes 'flight'? How long is the minimum adequate flying distance? And, how prolonged should a 'flight' be? Are a few yards sufficient? or perhaps a few hundred? It seems that with some certainty the Watson Brothers flew for a few minutes. The third issue relates to whether Watson's aircraft was controllable. Could it go up and down and turn with some degree of acceptable realisation. Watson had developed an upper wing that could be pivoted, a 'rocking wing' as it was called, providing some rudimentary turning capability, so the answer again must be yes. Fourthly, had Watson an engine powerful enough to lift his aircraft into the air and sustain flight for a practical period? Watson is known to have acquired his first aircraft's engine from celebrated Brazilian aviator Alberto Santos-Dumont, who too was trialling heavier-than air flying machines. It was a 4-cylinder horizontally opposed engine manufactured in very small numbers by Dutheil Chalmers & Cie, Paris, France.

The air-craft had an uncommon arrangement in that the propeller was affixed between a pair of horizontally opposed banks of cylinders. Was that engine powerful enough to allow Watson to fly? Some witnesses have argued it was. Lastly, just exactly when did this first powered controllable flight take place? Eyewitness have said that they saw Watson take off several times during the summer of 1903. But are their memories reliable? Were they mistaken? Do these constructive answers prove that Watson beat the Wright Brothers into the air? We will never know for certain, but it is nice to think that, possibly, in a Perthshire field, the first ever human controlled flight took place.

Watson went on to utilise 3 other aircraft, all of them achieving flight. He had hoped to enter the 1910 Lanark Scottish International Aviation Meeting (See – Samuel Franklin Cody), but a fractured propeller experienced during earlier tests meant Watson missed out on competing.

With the declaration of the Great War in July 1914, Watson endeavoured to enter the Royal Flying Corp (RFC). He already had a commission as a volunteer with the Royal Forfarshire Yeomanry. The application to the RFC was refused. It seems that his having not attended a public school and his age, 34, regarded as too old to fly, were the impediments to entry. It is hard to believe that the RFC would turn down someone with Watson's knowledge and experience. Unperturbed, and at his own expense, Watson undertook official flying training at Hendon and on 16 March 1915, he joined the Royal Naval Air Service (RNAS).

At 05:00 hours on 30 June 1915, Sub-Lieutenant Watson was ready to start a cross-country flight that would complete his training requirements at RNAS Eastchurch, on the Isle of Sheppey in Kent, England. The weather conditions were not good, and it was decided to reschedule the take-off. At 07:00 hours, the weather improved. The flight route was due to take Watson from Eastchurch to RNAS Eastbourne on the South Coast of England, a flying distance of about 60 miles.

Less than an hour later, and less than 20 miles from his destination, Watson's plane, a Cauldron GIII, was heard to emit an unexpected loud noise. The engine stopped abruptly, and parts fell from the aircraft, which then hurtled towards the ground. In the ensuing crash, Preston Watson was killed. He was just 35 years old. Watson was buried on 5 July 1915 in Dundee's Western Cemetery. The grave obelisk bears the design of a dove in flight.

AUGUST 1910 AT ERROL

James Yeaman Watson, Preston's brother, continued to fly and was a member of the Strathtay Aero Club at Scone Airport. He died at age 78 on 17 October 1957 at his home in Blairgowrie; only a few weeks before his death, he had flown an aircraft out of Scone Airport. Beatrice Watson (Preston's widow) died in 1971. The couple's son, Ronald Watson, was killed on active service at sea in 1941 whilst serving as a lieutenant in the Royal Navy Volunteer Reserve (RNVR).

Power Necessary in Flight by Preston Watson is a very rare and significant pamphlet on early flight. A copy of the original 1st Edition 20-page pamphlet published in Dundee by John Leng in 1908 will set its buyer back around £1,000, if one can be found.

NOTES: The war memorial at Kinclaven Church is situated within its lychgate. The church is also notable for its stone belfry of 1848 that houses a bell (with a diameter in excess of 50 centimetres) cast in 1656 at the Middleburg Foundry in Holland by Johannes Burgerhuys.

Eastchurch airfield had played a distinguished role in early aviation history: aviation pioneers John Moore-Brabazon, Cecil Stanley Grace, Charles Stewart Rolls, and Eustace and Oswald Short, all tested aircraft there. Wilbur and Orville Wright visited Eastchurch in 1909.

Watson at Rossie, Forgandenny

John William Dunne

Those Magnificent Men in their Flying Machines, yes, they went up tiddly up up, and down tiddly down down, in would you believe it the Highlands of Perthshire. It may surprise you to learn that the War Office had to put out a statement in 1907 dismissing rumours that the Balloon Factory near Farnborough Common was to be transferred to some remote spot in the vicinity of Dunkeld. The reason being, that during tests of new military airships at the Royal Aircraft Establishment, Farnborough, the crowds were so great, and the photographers so persistent, that some quieter spot was imperatively necessary, if indiscreet and secret revelations were not to be made.

On 5 October 1907, the first British flight by a powered airship, British Army Dirigible, *Nulli Secundus* flew from Farnborough to Crystal Palace in London. It was piloted by Samuel Franklin Cody with Colonel J. E. Capper on board.

A small working party of Royal Engineers from the Army Balloon Factory was sent northwards to conduct certain work in connection with the fitting of machinery to a new airship, but not to Dunkeld, the out-of-the-way spot was in fact on the Duke of Atholl's estate at Blair Atholl. These top-secret tests they hoped would lead to the first engine powered British military aeroplane.

A delicate aircraft was put in a railway carriage at Farnborough in July 1907 and transported under great secrecy up to Blair Atholl, then carted from the station up to Glen Tilt, just north of the village. Here the aircraft was assembled and camouflaged from inquisitive eyes by having white stripes and dark patches painted on the upper surfaces.

The aircraft design was of a swept back arrowhead planform design with no movable vertical surfaces. Starting with the glider, Dunne D.1-A, the aircraft configuration was tested at Glen Tilt, launched from a 4-wheel trolley, and flown by Colonel Capper, it achieved some success, but was heavily damaged on landing, hitting a wall. Repaired and brought closer to Blair Atholl, power was added to it with two 12hp Buchet engines. The now modified John William Dunne designed aircraft; the D.1-B, piloted by Lieutenant Lancelot Gibbs, first for one successful 8-second flight on 29 September 1907. It was again damaged on landing wrecked when it rolled off the chassis of the trolley gear. This was not an uncommon event in the early days of flying.

THE EVENING TELEGRAPH 23 SEPTEMBER 1907

Certain parts of the test aeroplane were sent the next day by train to Farnborough for minor alterations and repairs. They were packed at daybreak and loaded onto two railways wagons ready to be attached to the afternoon express from Inverness.

These experiments had validated the stability Dunne considered so indispensable to flight. Dunne had concentrated his efforts on tailless designs, and he produced inherently stable aircraft, capable of flying steadily, even with the controls locked on a straight course, all by itself.

In 1905, Dunne had been appointed to the Army Balloon Factory at South Farnborough, England, then under the competent leadership of Colonel John Edward Capper. Capper was the pilot of the Dunne aircraft and was slightly injured in the glider flight.

The Marquis of Tullibardine (heir to the Duke of Atholl) told the press in an interview that everything pointed to success. "Even if people like myself, who are sceptical concerning the utility of these things as fighting machines, have been convinced. Personally, and in common with many other soldiers, I would rather they were unnecessary, but while other nations are at work on them it would be poor tactics for Great Britain to lag behind. Lieutenant Dunne wishes his inventions to be at the disposal of the British Government, he is actuated purely by patriotic motives. I have ascertained that the model tested in the valley of the Tilt will glide, drive, or hover, and that stability in a marvellous degree has been attained."

The Marquis also spoke of the loyalty of his retainers, "the gillies have been without sleep night after night and have questioned everyone who lingered on the road. They are trained men, and even the shepherds can signal by semaphore." The popular recounting of Dunne's flying episode asserts that such great clandestineness was observed that "the [Duke's] tenants were enrolled as a sort of bodyguard to prevent unauthorized persons from entering".

John William Dunne was born at the Curragh Camp in County Kildare, Ireland, on 2 December 1875. He became a soldier at the outbreak of the Second Boer War and volunteered for the Imperial Yeomanry as an ordinary Trooper fighting in South Africa. In 1900 he was caught up in an epidemic of typhoid fever and was invalided home. He recovered and was commissioned as a Second Lieutenant in the Wiltshire's. He went back to South Africa in March 1902, and he again fell ill, diagnosed with heart disease. He was again invalided home.

It was then that Dunne instigated his study of the science of aerodynamics and flight in earnest, commencing with observations of avian flight and the *Alsomitra Macrocarpa*, the seed of the Javan cucumber, also known as the Zanonia. A Zanonia seed is swept-winged and displays an inherent stability when dispersed by the wind. He became convinced that a safe aeroplane needed to have inherent aerodynamic stability.

Dunne growing up was inspired by a Jules Verne story at the age of 13, he envisaged a machine that could fly, one that did not require steering, that would right itself irrespective of wind or weather. Fortified by the encouragement of a family friend, the writer of science fiction H. G. Wells, Dunne designed and built several prototypes based on a 'tailless' design. At that time when Dunne first took up the study of aviation, no one had yet flown in Europe, and he could therefore receive little benefit from the results achieved by other pilots and constructors.

In the spring of 1909, the War Office support for Dunne's airplane development was withdrawn. Dunne left the Balloon Factory, taking the D.4 with him. He continued his work under the aegis of the Blair Atholl Aeroplane Syndicate Ltd., formed in 1910 by the Marquis of Tullibardine. Like its predecessor, the D.4 was camouflaged, it was fitted with two 15hp Buchet engines and later a single 25hp R.E.P. engine. Dunne regarded the D.4 as 'more of a hopper than a flier'. The best flight of the D.4 was 120 feet (36.58m) on 10 December 1908.

In 1910 the Dunne designed aircraft D.5, built by Short Brothers, was demonstrated on a flying field at Eastchurch, Isle of Sheppey. The same airfield that five years later, 30 June 1915, Preston Watson took off from on his final flight. He crashed and died 20 miles from his destination at Eastbourne. Charles Richard Fairey became the General manager of the Blair Atholl Syndicate at Eastchurch, working with Dunne on his tailless aircraft. A Fairey Gannet, carrier-borne aircraft sat outside at Errol airfield for many years. The Gannet featured a tricycle undercarriage, a feature pioneered by John William Dunne and others in that early pioneer era of aviation.

John William Dunne was not only a pioneering aeronautical engineer, but he was also a philosopher and the author of, An Experiment with Time in 1927. A treatise on precognition, consciousness, and the concept of time. Dunne argued that past, present, and future were in fact simultaneous and only experienced sequentially because of our mental perception of them. Dunne also published a book on dry-fly fishing: Sunshine and the Dry Fly in 1924, discussing a new method of making realistic artificial flies.

Dunne vision of tailless aircraft design was finally realised with the construction of 'flying wings', such as the 1920s' Westland Pterodactyl, which Dunne helped design, the 1929 Waldo Waterman Whatsit, the 1940s' Northrup Flying Wing, and the modern stealth aircraft like the Northrop Grumman B-2. This aviation legend also pioneered many other aircraft features which were not destined to reappear for many years. John William Dunne FRAeS (1875–1949) died at Banbury in England on 24 August 1949, aged 74.

NOTES: The test flying at Blair Atholl was five years, almost to the day, since the Wright Brothers' epic flight travelled almost the same distance at Kill Devil Hills, Kitty Hawk, North Carolina USA. Preston Watson had also been attempting to get off the ground with his designs since the summer of 1903 at Errol, and later in 1909 at Forgandenny. Frank and Harold Barnwell were experimenting at the same time at Causewayhead. They managed to achieve a flight of just 80 yards on 28 July 1909, this was regarded as the first successful powered flight in Scotland. A year later they flew for one mile, again at Causewayhead. In France, Santos Dumont, the Brazilian aviation innovator, had been astonishing the world in 1906 with his flying feats at the Château de Bagatelle near Paris and on 25 July 1909, Louis Charles Joseph Blériot crossed the English Channel, landing at Northfall Meadow, close to Dover Castle.

Experimental Aircraft Designed by John William Dunne

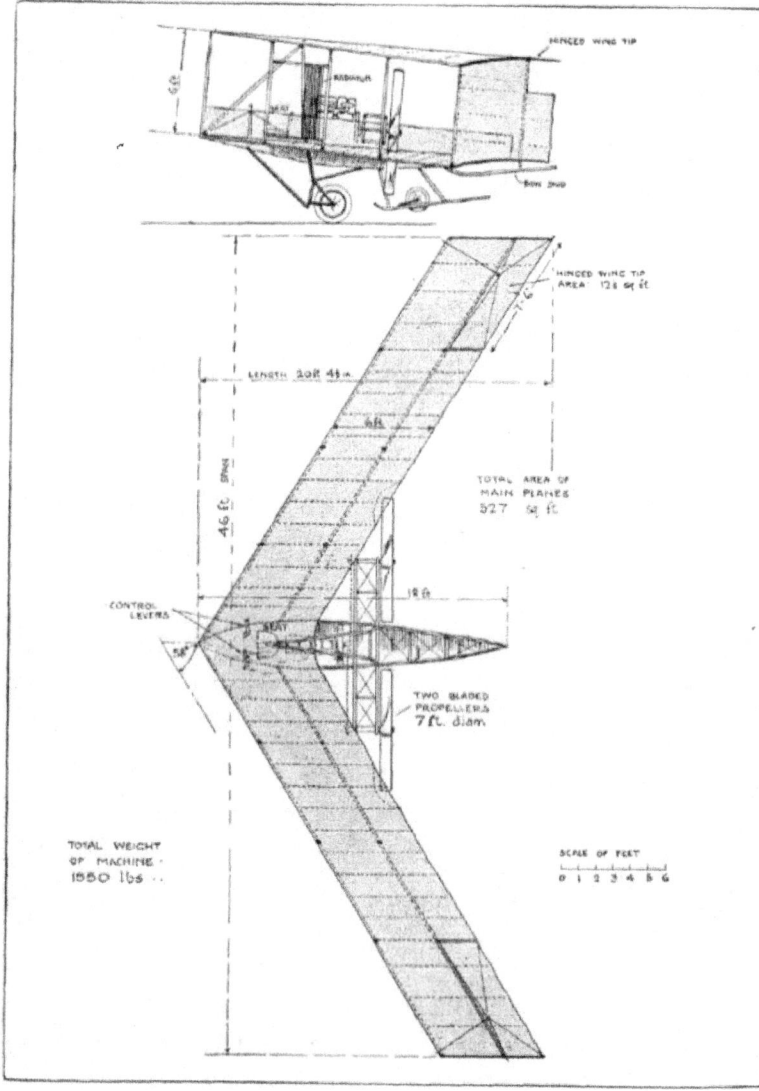

D.5, published in Flight magazine June 1910

D.1-A Glider. Built in 1907 – limited success in a single flight.

D.1-B Powered Airplane (modified D.1-A). Built in 1907 – crashed during its first flight.

D.2 Training Glider. Designed in 1907 – never constructed.

Dunne-Huntington. Gas Powered Triplane.

Designed in 1907/8 - flown successfully in 1911.

D.3 Person-carrying Glider. Flown successfully in 1908.

D.4 Powered Airplane. Flown in 1908 – partially successful.

(In Dunne's words, "more a hopper than a flyer").

D.5 Powered tailless biplane. Flown successfully in 1910.

D.6 Monoplane. Built in 1911 – never flown.

D.7 Monoplane. Built in 1911 – flown successfully.

D.8 Biplane. Several built and flown in 1912-13.

D.9 Sesquiplane. Begun in 1913 – never fully constructed.

D.10 Biplane. Built in 1913 – a complete failure.

John William Dunne, D.5, Eastchurch 14 June 1910

Dunne D.1-A/ D.1-B, 1907 Glen Tilt

Barnwell Brothers

At Causewayhead, Stirling, two celebrated brothers made early Scottish aviation history and one of them went to design some of the most iconic aircraft of World War I and II.

Just above Causewayhead, on a volcanic crag called Abbey Craig, stands the National Wallace Monument commemorating our thirteenth-century Scottish hero, Sir William Wallace. Below at the Causewayhead roundabout, there is a memorial to the Bramwell Brothers.

The brothers travelled abroad for two years starting in 1903 and during that time met with the Wright Brothers who had undertaken the first heavier-than-air flight that year. They built their first glider in 1905 and later built three powered aircraft. They opened the Grampian Engineering and Motor Company in 1906 and this gave them the funds and facilities to pursue their passion for aviation.

Frank and Harold made the first successful powered flight in Scotland on 28 July 1909. This flew for just 80 yards at a height of 13 feet. In 1910, they built a mid-wing monoplane and flew it to win a prize of £50 from the Scottish Aeronautical Society for a flight of over a mile at Causewayhead. It was powered by a Grampian 40hp, twin cylinder engine.

Frank and Harold's family home was Elco House in Balfron. They were educated at Fettes Academy, Edinburgh and their father was the managing director at Fairfields Shipyard, Govan.

Harold Barnwell became the chief test pilot in 1912 at A V Roe, based at Brooklands. He was killed in 1917 whilst flying a new model of a Vickers fighter aircraft.

Captain Frank Sowter Barnwell OBE AFC FRAeS BSc had a very successful career as an aeronautical engineer. As a noted aircraft designer from 1911 with the Bristol and Colonial Aeroplane Company, he designed such aircraft as the Bristol Fighter, the Bristol Bulldog and the Bristol Blenheim. The Bristol F2 (Fighter) was a two-seat biplane fighter and reconnaissance aircraft of the First World War. It is often just called the Bristol Fighter or by its popular names, the 'Brisfit' or 'Biff'.

Frank S. Barnwell, The Bristol Aeroplane Company,

Experimental Designer 1911 – 1914,

Chief Designer 1915 – 121,

Chief Engineer 1936 – 1938

Some artefacts were uncovered before the Grampian Engineering and Motor Company closed in 2003. An original wing strut and a 1/16th scale model of the Barnwell monoplane is on display at the Stirling Smith Art Gallery & Museum, Dumbarton Road.

Frank and Marjorie Barnwell had three sons who all lost their lives in the Second World War:

Flight Lieutenant Richard Antony Barnwell, RAF, 102 Squadron, died age 24, 29 October 1940.
Pilot Officer John Sandes Barnwell, RAF, 29 Squadron, died age 20, 19 June 1940
Pilot Officer David Usher Barnwell DFC, RAFVR, 607 Squadron

Stirling Council Archives

Canard Biplane that was damaged after flying 80 yards, 1909 *at Causewayhead, Stirling*

Barnwell Brothers memorial Causewayhead roundabout, Stirling

Frank Barnwell

Andrew Blain Baird

Andrew Blain Baird was born in the village of Sandhead on the west side of Luce bay in Dumfries and Galloway. Baird was apprenticed to a Blacksmith in Sandhead, then worked as a Lighthouse Keeper on the island of Lismore, as an iron worker in the Clyde shipyards before setting up his own smiddy workshop at 113 High Street, Rothesay, Isle of Bute. Andrew Baird made many innovative improvements to the plough and also built a unique triple expansion engine powered by electricity.

Andrew Baird is said to have corresponded with Louis Blériot and Samuel Franklin Cody. In October 1909, he visited the Aviation Week in Blackpool and came home to Rothesay to design and build his own aircraft.

With a monoplane design similar to Louis Blériot's 1909 English Channel crossing aircraft, it was powered by a 24hp, 4-cyclinder, air cooled with water cooled valves, the engine being built by the Alexander Brothers in Edinburgh. Once completed in the Summer of 1910 it went on show at an exhibition in the Esplanade Flower Garden and subsequently at the Bute Highland Games on 20 August 1910.

In the very early morning of 11 September 1910, the Baird monoplane was taken to Ettrick bay. Flight Magazine on 24 September 1910, described his attempt at flight as follows:

"Mr Baird was seated in the machine and on the engine being started the plane travelled along the sands at good speed. Naturally, on clearing the ground, the swerving influence of the axle ceased, and the influence of the steering wheel brought the machine sharply round to the right causing it to swoop to the ground. The contact was so sharp that the right wheel buckled, and the right plane suffered some abrasion by scraping along the beach."

Baird's monoplane engine was given to the Museum of Transport in Glasgow, the two-blade propeller was in private ownership until it was presented to the Museum of Flight in 2010 (Museum reference EF.2010.379). Baird's designs were incorporated into an aircraft designed by Tommy Sopwith and Baird continued to advise other aviation pioneers. Andrew Baird was one of the original members of the Scottish Aeronautical Society. He died age 89 on 9 September 1951 in Rothesay.

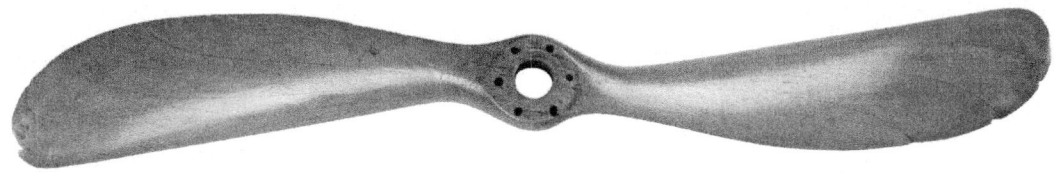

Image © National Museums Scotland

First World War Aviators

Sergeant Alexander Stewart Allan

RAF Sergeant Alexander Stewart Allan, 406711, *Medaille Militaire*, died of wounds on 27 August 1918. Alexander was the fourth son of Andrew Allan and Jemima Stewart, 1, South Muirton Cottages, Perth.

Alexander was born on 27 March 1894 at 6 Mill Close, Perth (Mill Close was at 281 High Street). The Census of 1911 shows the family (9 children) living in Tibbermore with Alexander recorded at 17 years old as an Apprentice Clerk.

On 14 December 1917, Alexander was serving in France with the Royal Flying Corps, 55 Squadron. On 13 January 1918 he qualified as an Aerial Gunner and was promoted on 7 February 1918 to Sergeant. On 1 April 1918, the Royal Air Force (RAF) was formed with the amalgamation of the Royal Flying Corps (RFC) and the Royal Naval Air Service (RNAS), and Alexander transferred over as a Sergeant Mechanic.

Gazetted on 16 July 1918, RAF Sergeant Alexander Stewart Allan was awarded the French Medaille Militaire. The Médaille Militaire is a military decoration of the French Republic for other ranks for meritorious service and acts of bravery in action against an enemy force. It is the third highest award of the French Republic. It is possible that this medal was awarded for his action during a raid on Mannheim, 24 March 1918. Sergeant Allan and his pilot, 2nd Lieutenant William Legge, were credited with an Albatross Scout Aircraft out of control.

On 24 August 1918, Sergeant Alexander Allan was the Observer in Airco DH.4 (The Aircraft Manufacturing Company Limited), B3967 flying from Azelot in France when he was wounded by machine gun fire on a bombing raid over Luxembourg. The name of the pilot is unknown or whether it was from an enemy aircraft or ground fire. The original target for the raid was Köln, but over Trèves (Trier) strong winds meant they would not reach their allotted targets and the flight leader decided to bomb Luxembourg instead.

Sergeant Alexander Stewart Allan, age 24 years, succumbed to his wounds and passed away 3 days later, 27 August 1918 and is laid to rest in Charmes Military Cemetery, Essegney, Vosges, France (44 km south of Nancy.)

NOTES: The Airco DH.4 was nicknamed 'The Flaming Coffin' due to aircraft's propensity to catch fire. The main fuel tank was situated between the pilot and the observer. Despite this, the DH.4 was highly advanced for its time.

William Earl Johns (who wrote as Captain WE Johns) was a DH.4 pilot with RAF 55 Squadron in 1918.

Johns created a fictional character named *Biggles*. His stories were in the 1950s and 60s very popular. Surprisingly, the very first Biggles stories were not intended for children, but for an adult readership. Second Lieutenant W. E. Johns was shot down on the 16 May 1918 but survived. A pre-war Territorial in the Norfolk Yeomanry, William Johns was, in 1915, posted to Gallipoli, and sailed on *HMT Olympic* (a sister ship to the *Titanic*). The regiment landed at ANZAC cove on 10 October 1915. After contracting malaria, Johns applied to join the Royal Flying Corps and was accepted, gaining a temporary commission in September 1917. Johns gave his opinion of the Airco DH.4:

"At the time of its introduction, no faster machine flew in France, and it was not until 1918 that the enemy produced fighters which surpassed it in speed and climb... It was one of the few [bombers] that dared operate on long distance shows without an escort, and its manoeuvrability was on a par with many single seat fighters of the period." – 'The Day's Work', Wings: A Book of Flying Adventures, 1931 (By Jove, Biggles, page 53)

Johns described his first reaction to aerial warfare:

"The first dog fight I was ever in...we were sailing along all merry and bright, and the next minute the air was full of machines, darting all over the place...I looked around nervously at my gunner but he was an old hand and merely gave me a pitying glance...Then he sent a stream of tracers in the direction of the rapidly approaching scouts to let them know he was ready for them... I didn't see where they came from or where they went. I didn't see where my formation went either. By the time I had grasped the fact that the fight had started and was looking to see who the dickens was perforating my plane, the show was all over. Two machines lay smoking on the ground and everybody else had disappeared. Whilst I was considering what the dickens, I should do I suddenly discovered that I was flying back in formation again! The fellows had come back to me pick me up and formed up around me...The leader gave the signal for the bombs to be dropped, and we turned for home. I knew I should get it in the neck when we got back for behaving so foolishly – and I did." – Passage combined from pieces in The Modern Boy, 5 December 1931 and 'Adventures in the Air' The Modern Boy's Annual 1934 (By Jove, Biggles, page 55)

The three RAF Squadrons at Azelot, France, 55, 99 and 104, were part of **Major General Hugh Trenchard's Independent Force.** The Independent Force of the RAF was an early attempt at a strategic bombing campaign. The force was made up of both day and night bombing squadrons and was based in the Metz-Nancy region, well to the south of the British sector of the Western Front. Its main targets were strategically important railway and industrial centres on the Rhine between Strasbourg in the south and Koblenz in the north. Attacks were made on the German cities of Frankfurt, Mannheim, Cologne, Coblenz, Duren and Mainz. These bombing raids were highly dangerous and subject to constant attack by the German air force.

Blacklunans, Blairgowrie born 2nd Lieutenant Alexander McKenzie was also an observer in RAF 55 Squadron. McKenzie also flew with and was killed alongside Lieutenant William Legge.

Perth born Group Captain Robert Halley DFC & 2 Bars, AFC was a member of Royal Naval Service 16 Squadron which operated out of Autreville, 35 km to the west of Azelot, during that summer of 1918. Flying Handley Page 0/100 and 0/400 aircraft, they carried about five times the bomb load of the Airco

DH.4, although at a slower speed and lower altitude.

BRITISH AIRCRAFT OF THE FIRST WORLD WAR (Q 69257) Airco DH.4 two-seat light bomber biplane. Copyright: © IWM.

Record of Sergeant A. S. Allan award for the Miltary Medal for his gallantry and devoution to duty, gazzetted 16 July 1918

Ian Dermid Campbell

Ian Dermid Campbell was born 12 October 1898 to John Stuart Campbell, South African Merchant, and Mary Ann Campbell. Ian's birth certificate states that he was born at 13 Lonsdale Terrace, Edinburgh, but his birth was registered in the parish of Dunning, the family home being, Innerdunning House. Ian was educated at Dollar Academy, boarding with a Dr. Butchart from 1909 to 1913. In the supplement to the London Gazette, 29 May 1917, under the General List for the Royal Flying Corp, Cadet Ian Dermid Campbell was promoted to 2nd Lieutenant (on probation).

On the morning of 30 November 1917, 24 Squadron Royal Flying Corps had nineteen Airco D.H.5 aircraft on charge. Second Lieutenant Ian Dermid Campbell of 24 Squadron, Royal Flying Corp, took off at 12.15pm in an Airco DH.5, A9509. Having moved down from the coast, Royal Flying Corp 24 Squadron had just commenced patrols over the Cambrai salient.

Captain Bernard Paul Gascoigne Beanlands 24 Squadron's Counter Offensive Patrol was attacked by Jagdstaffel 11 east of Bourlon. Second Lieutenant Ian Dermid Campbell was shot down by Leutnant Hans-Georg von der Osten of Jagdstaffel 11 at 12.45pm, who claimed this as his fourth victory. Captain Beanland was seen engaged with an enemy aircraft over Bourlon Wood at 13.00pm. Captain Beanland was killed in a flying accident on 8 May 1919 at Northolt.

Second Lieutenant Ian Dermid Campbell is commemorated at the Arras Flying Services Memorial in the Faubourg d'Amiens Cemetery and at Dollar Academy. Ian's father and mother are buried in St. Serf's Church graveyard, Dunning (F 358) Inscription: "In loving memory of JOHN STUART CAMPBELL who died 10th Dec. 1909 aged 52 years and his wife MARY ANNE BREWSTER who died 9th Oct. 1912 aged 54 years. Also, their son 2nd Lt. IAN D. CAMPBELL, R.F.C., missing 30th Nov. 1917 aged 19 – Erected by the family".

Ian Dermid was killed during the Battle of Cambrai (20 November 1917 – 7 December 1917). This was the first large-scale, effective use of tanks in warfare. The Tank Corps deployed its entire strength of 476 machines, of which more than 350 were armed fighting tanks. One day after the battle began, church bells in England were ringing for the great breakthrough at Cambrai. Initially it was very successful with large gains of ground being made, but with no fewer than 179 tanks being destroyed, disabled, or broken down. By the afternoon, the attack had already lost its early impetus and German reserves eventually brought the advance to a halt. Ten days later (30 November 1917), a counter-attack by the Germans regained much of the ground. British forces during the period of the Battle of Cambrai suffered 75,681 casualties, 10,042 killed or died of wounds, 48,702 wounded and 16,987 missing or prisoners of war. The stalemate of trench warfare was to continue.

Statement issued by General Headquarters, 1st December 1917:

"On November 30th, clouds were at a height of 2,000 ft. all day, but our aeroplanes were out continuously co-operating with the other arms in the counter-attacks against the enemy south-west of Cambrai. Our artillery machines, in addition to registering our guns, located, and reported over 200 hostile batteries. The bombing machines concentrated their efforts on troops and transport collected in the villages in rear of the battle, dropping over 200 bombs. The enemy's troops and transport moving on roads behind the fighting also offered good targets to our scout pilots, who fired over 15,000 rounds at them from their machine guns. The fighting in the air was very severe and resulted greatly in our favour. Fifteen hostile machines were brought down, and three others were driven down out of control. Seven of our machines are missing."

Royal Flying Corp Communiqué number 116:

"Very hard fighting took on the ground all day. Machines of the 3rd Brigade co-operated with our troops by carrying out reconnaissance's, contact patrols, bombing and firing at ground targets all day, although clouds were very low.

Machines of the 3rd Brigade carried out 19 contact patrols and the 2nd Brigade one counter-attack patrol."

In all, 20,000 rounds were fired from the air, 4,000 being by Corps machines of the 3rd Brigade and over 11,000 by Scout Squadrons, which dropped 88 25-lb bombs, while Corps machines dropped 23 25-lb bombs.

With aeroplane observation, seven hostile batteries were successfully engaged for destruction and four were neutralised, three-gun pits were destroyed, two damaged, six explosions and a fire caused. 276 active hostile batteries were reported by zone call, 203 of these being by the 3rd Brigade.

Twenty targets were registered by balloons, 18 being by the 2nd Brigade, while balloons of the 14th Wing located three active hostile batteries and reported ten trains opposite their front.

In addition to the bombs dropped by the 3rd Brigade, No 2 Squadron dropped four 25-lb bombs on billets; the 2nd Brigade dropped 39 25-lb bombs on various targets; No 48 Squadron dropped four 25-lb bombs on various targets and No 25 Squadron attacked Oisy-le-Verger on which 10 112-lb bombs were dropped from 2,000 feet, while one pilot went down to 500 feet before releasing his bombs. No 27 Squadron dropped seven 112-lb bombs on Marquion from about 6,000 feet. The raids by Nos 25 and 27 Squadrons were carried out by machines flying singly or in pairs through clouds.

NOTES: Second Lieutenant Ian Dermid Campbell's aircraft, Airco DH.5 was a presentation aircraft. During WW1 individuals and groups around the Commonwealth were invited to contribute a nominal sum towards the war effort in return for which an aircraft would be inscribed with a name of their choice. Ian's DH.5 was donated by North China residents and marked on the fuselage, North China Aeroplane.

The Royal Prussian Jagdstaffel 11 or Jasta 11 became the most successful fighter squadron of the Deutsche Luftstreitkräfte (German Air Force). Manfred Albrecht Freiherr von Richthofen, the Red Baron became the commanding officer of Jasta 11 on 16 January 1917. One 26 July 1917 Jasta 11 became part of Jagdgeschwader 1 ("The Flying Circus" (German: Der Fliegende Zirkus)), a collection of four Jasta's into one administrative and highly mobile tactical force. Leutnant Hans-Georg August von der Osten took Acting Command of Jagdstaffel 11 from 19 January 1918 to 16 February 1918. He was given command of Jagdstaffel 4 on 26 March 1918. Osten was shot down and wounded on 28 March 1918 and finished the war as an ace credited with five victories. During World War II he commanded all the Luftwaffe bases in Germany. Jagdstaffel 11 were based at Avesnes-le-Sec, Cambrai from 22 November 1917 to 19 March 1918. The pilots of Jasta 11 included Manfred's brothers, Lothar and Wolfram, Kurt Wolff, Ernst Udet and Hermann Göring. Leutnant Hans-Georg August von der Osten passed away on 27 March 1987.

Manfred Albrecht Freiherr von Richthofen, the Red Baron in an Albatross D.V (4963/17) shot down near Mœuvres at 14.30pm on 30 November 1917, Lieutenant Donald Argyle Douglas Ian MacGregor from Leith, RFC 41 Squadron who was on an unknown 'special mission' flying a Royal Aircraft Factory S.E.5a (B644). This was Richthofen's 63rd victory. The shooting down on this day of Captain R T Townsend in a S.E. 5a by Richthofen on this day is incorrect. He was shot down by Leutnant Josef Mai at 15.48pm near Le Pave (possibly Le Pavé Gourmand about 40Km north of Cambrai).

Lieutenant Cornell in Airco DH5 (A9532), of RFC 68 squadron left the aerodrome at Baizieux at 8:40am on a 'special mission' over Bourlon Wood. His machine was shot down by enemy aircraft and was unsalvable. His aircraft was reported missing for a day until he turned up at the aerodrome, after spending an exciting 24 hours in a heavily shelled position.

Royal Flying Corp 24 Squadron was formed on 1 September 1915 at Hounslow Heath, they moved to France in February 1916. They were the first squadron to operate the Airco DH.2 fighter. The 'pusher' design of the DH.2 meant that its fixed forward firing machine gun was unobstructed by a propeller, and it therefore played a large part in defeating the 'Fokker Scourge'. Airco DH.5s arrived in May 1917 and the following December these were replaced by the Royal Aircraft Factory S.E.5a, which they operated until the end of the war.

The Airco DH.5 was a single-seat biplane fighter aircraft. It was designed and manufactured at British aviation company Airco. Development was led by aircraft designer Geoffrey de Havilland. The DH.5 was one of the first British fighters designed with the improved Constantinesco gun synchronizer, which allowed a forward-firing machine gun to fire through the propeller faster and more reliably than the older mechanical systems.

Earlier that day Captain James Thomas Byford McCudden, VC, DSO & Bar, MC & Bar, of 56 Squadron, a flying ace of the First World War and among the most highly decorated airmen in British military history, was also flying above Bourlon Wood in a Royal Aircraft Factory S.E.5. On 30 November 1917, McCudden with other pilots drove away enemy machines from over Bourlon and then attacked two German two-seater aircraft: "At 11.15 saw 2 enemy aircraft two-seaters coming West over Fontaine (Fontaine-Notre-Dame). I secured a good position behind front enemy aircraft and fired a good burst from both guns. Enemy aircraft's engine stopped, and water streamed from radiator. As enemy aircraft glided West, I let him land O.K. and then landed myself, as enemy aircraft gunner had hit my engine with explosive bullet. Enemy aircraft landed Southeast of Havrincourt intact with exception of bullet holes. The pilot badly wounded. Placed guard on enemy aircraft."

British Flying Ace Major Lanoe George Hawker VC, DSO (30 December 1890 – 23 November 1916) was in command of RFC 24 Squadron from early 1916 until his death when he was shot down by Leutnant Manfred von Richthofen of Jasta 2.

Sopwith Camel pilot Lieutenant John Watson McCash from Perth, 3 Squadron RFC was killed on 20 November 1917 also over Bourlon Wood during the Battle of Cambrai.

ACES OF THE FIRST WORLD WAR AND THEIR AIRCRAFT (Q 67598) Captain Lanoe George Hawker VC DSO of No. 24 Squadron RFC. Copyright: © IWM.

Major J B McCudden, VC, DSO, MC, MM (Art.IWM ART 2979) image: A half-length portrait of McCudden in uniform sitting in a wooden armchair. Copyright: © IWM.

THE BATTLE OF CAMBRAI 20-30 NOVEMBER 1917 (Q 47963) An aerial photograph of part of the battle area from the British Front to Bourlon Wood where the British advance was halted. It shows the intact condition of the countryside in the wake of the British advance. Copyright: © IWM.

Robert Alexander Duff

Robert Alexander Duff, T4/083084 Royal Flying Corp was son of Mr Duncan Duff, farmer, and Mary Ann Douglas Duff, Woodend, Logierait, Ballinluig. Before his attachment to 22 Squadron of the Royal Flying Corps, Robert had joined the 8th Royal Highlanders in 1908. The following year his battalion changed to become the 8th Royal Highland Cyclist's which later became merged with the 6th Black Watch (Perthshire's Own). Shortly after WW1 commenced, he joined the Scottish Horse and because of an accident was given a discharge. He again enlisted for the third time and was a driver for over two years in the 3rd Army, Auxiliary Horse Transport Company, part of the Army Service Corps.

Robert was a well-known rifle shot in the Atholl area, being equally expert with the service miniature rifle and fowling piece, the winner of many prominent prizes during his time with the 8 Royal Highland Cyclists and Mid-Atholl Rifle Club.

On Wednesday 30 January 1918, Royal Flying Corp Bristol Fighter F2b C4832 took off at 10.35am from the airfield at Auchel, Hauts-de-France, France. The pilot was New Zealander 2nd Lieutenant Godfrey Gleeson Johnstone, age 22 and the Observer was Air Mechanic 3rd Class Robert Alexander Duff, age 25.

Their mission was listed as an offensive patrol. They were seen to fall in flames about 12.45pm during an aerial engagement. The pilot, 2nd Lieutenant Johnstone was killed, and Air Mechanic 3rd Class Duff died from his injuries later that day.

Oberleutnant Harald Auffarth (Auffahrt), of the Royal Prussian Jagdstaffel (Jasta) 29 flying from Militärflugplatz Bellincamps claimed the shooting down of the Bristol Fighter C4832 near Neuve Chapelle, about 25kms northeast of Auchel.

Just eight days before, RFC 22 Squadron, part of the 10th Army Wing, 1st Brigade had transferred to the aerodrome at Auchel (they moved on again on 2 February 1918). Robert Duff had been attached to the Royal Flying Corp for only two months, it is probable that his time flying on active service with RFC 22 Squadron lasted only eight days, possibly this was his first and only mission.

Mr Duncan Duff, his father in the Perthshire Advertiser, 27 March 1918 said *"that his son and a Flight Officer had volunteered for duty, during which they engaged an enemy plane, which was successfully downed. But it was surmised that in the deadly combat both the officer and Observer Robert Duff were wounded seriously, and their aircraft damaged."*

The inscription on Robert's grave at Merville Communal Cemetery Extension reads *'Reared beside the Tummel and the Tay – He lived simply and died bravely'.*

NOTES:

Merville is a town 15 kilometres north of Béthune and 20 kilometres south-east of Armentières. Auchel Aérodrome Britannique was 12 km à l'ouest de (West of) Béthune, in the Département, Pas-de-Calais.

Corporal Hope Duff, the elder brother of Robert, prior to his enlistment with the Cameron Highlanders in May 1915, was a gamekeeper in the employment of The MacIntosh of Mackintosh at Moy Hall, Inverness-shire. Lance Corporal Duff was first wounded at Delville Wood in July 1916 and was back in the fighting line by November 1916.He was with the Machine Gun Corps when he was awarded the Distinguished Conduct Medal for conspicuous bravery and devotion to duty during the great German offensive of April 1917. Many forebearers of Hope and Robert served in the army. Private Hope Duff of the Black Watch after who he was named was said to be the first to fall at the battle of Tel el Kebir in 1882 during the Anglo-Egyptian War.

Bristol Fighter F2b C4832 was a presentation aircraft donated on 6 November 1917 with funds raised by Udaipur No.1, India.

The Bristol Fighter was known as the "Brisfit", or "Biff" was developed by Frank Barnwell at the Bristol Aeroplane Company. Frank Sowter Barnwell along with his brother Harold, established the Grampian Motors & Engineering Company at Causewayhead, Striling in 1907. On 30 January 1911 they won a prize for the first flight of over a mile in Scotland at Causewayhead, just outside Stirling University and under the Wallace Monument.

Harald Auffarth scored his first victory with Jagdstaffel 18 on 16 September 1917. By the end of that month, he had become an ace. He then transferred to Jagdstaffel 29 and was appointed Staffelführer (commanding officer) in November 1917. By the end of the war, he had scored 29 victories. Auffarth's personal aircraft colour scheme was of yellow nose and green fuselage with a stylized eight-pointed comet on the side. Auffarth served as an Oberstleutnant (Lieutenant Colonel) during WW2 and died 12 October 1946.

On 5 October 1918, Harald Auffarth shot down an Airco DH.9 piloted by Clayton Knight who although hurt survived and was made a prisoner of war in a German clinic. Auffarth was also downed during this encounter. Clayton Knight OBE (30 March 1891 – 17 July 1969) was an author, aviation artist and illustrator, one of the founders of the Clayton Knight Committee (along with Billy Bishop) and best known as the illustrator of the comic strip *Ace Drummond* published in 135 newspapers. The comic strip and movie serial *Ace Drummond* was scripted by Captain Eddie Rickenbacker, the most decorated US flying ace during WW1.

Harald Auffarth was awarded: Knight's Cross with Swords of the Royal House Order of Hohenzollern, Iron Cross 1st and 2nd Class, Hanseatic Cross and Silver Wound Badge. On 3 September 1918 when his victory count reached 20, he was recommended for the *Pour le Merite* (The Blue Max).. It was not approved before the abdication of Kaiser Wilhelm II.

The Army Service Corps, the ASC was jokingly referred to as *Ally Sloper's Cavalry*. Alexander "Ally" Sloper was the eponymous fictional character of the British comic strip *Ally Sloper*. First appearing in 1867, he is considered one of the earliest comic strip characters and he is regarded as the first recurring character in comics. Sloper has also been cited as an influence on W. C. Fields and Charlie Chaplin's "little tramp" character.

During the First World War, the Army Service Corps (ASC) operated the transport systems that delivered ammunition, food, and equipment to the Front Line. At its peak, the ASC numbered 10,547 officers and 315,334 men.

Oblt. Harald Auffarth of Jasta 29 in front of a Pfalz D.VIII with one piece, four-bladed Wotan propeller.

Pfalz D.VIII 193/18 of Jasta 29 with one piece, four-bladed Wotan propeller and another D.VIII in the background, late 1918. Fifth from left is Oblt. Harald Auffarth.

David Ogilvie Duthie

Second Lieutenant David Ogilvie Duthie, 79334, Royal Air Force was reported killed age 25 years just 80 days before the end of the First World War on 23 August 1918. He was born on 12 August 1893 and was the son of William and Betsy Duthie, of 38, Causewayend, Coupar-Angus, Perthshire. David Duthie before joining up, worked as a clerk with the Caledonian Railway Company in railway offices at Coupar Angus, Alyth, and Crieff.

Second Lieutenant Duthie was a member of RAF 2 Squadron, serving as an Artillery Observer and Air Gunner. He joined the Royal Flying Corps on 14 May 1915 attending Observer School on 13 August 1917, was promoted to 2nd Lieutenant on probation, with effect the same day. This was confirmed on 11 September 1917. David Duthie was posted overseas on 16 September 1917 and wounded in France on 23 November 1917. When he recovered and was declared fit for service, he returned to duty as an observer on 22 March 1918, passing out of Wireless Observer School, Brooklands on 30 April 1918. At Brooklands he re-trained in Artillery Observation and Aerial Gunnery. Brooklands was requisitioned by the War Office and closed to motor racing during World War I, it continued its pre-war role as a flying training centre, although it was now under military control.

The sector of northern France where David Duthie was now to be stationed was attacked as the second part of the 1918 German Spring offensive, the Lys offensive. The Battle of the Lys, also known as the Fourth Battle of Ypres, was fought from 7 to 29 April 1918. The German Spring Offensive or Kaiserschlacht ("Kaiser's Battle") began on 21 March 1918. The Germans realised that this was their last remaining chance of victory before soldiers of the United States could fully deploy on the battlefields. The Russian withdrawal from the war following the Treaty of Brest-Litovsk freed up 50 German divisions to join the offensive.

The Kaiserschlacht was masterminded by General Erich Friedrich Wilhelm Ludendorff (9 April 1865 – 20 December 1937). Ludendorff was convinced that an attack in Flanders, the region stretching from Belgium to the north of France, was the best route to a German victory in the war and decided to first launch a sizeable diversionary attack further south to lure Allied troops away from the main event.

The final offensive push of the war by the Germans started on 15 July 1918, the 2nd Battle of the Marne. The Germans began their advance after an initial artillery bombardment and found that the French had set up a line of false trenches, manned by only a few defenders. The real front line of trenches lay further on and had scarcely been touched by the bombardment. The German infantry subsequently advanced too far from its supply bases and railheads which slowed their advance and allowed the Allies to reinforce their positions. On 8 August 1918, the Germans were completely surprised at Amiens when British tanks broke through their defences and intact formations surrendered. To Ludendorff it was the "black day in the history of the German Army".

On 12 August 1918, Lieutenant Edward Oscar Drinkwater (Pilot) & 2nd Lieutenant David Ogilvie Duthie (Observer) of RAF 2 Squadron were flying in Armstrong Whitworth FK8, F4264. The mission was for a photographic reconnaissance over German held territory. Take-off was at 11.45am and they were reported engaged by anti-aircraft fire (ack-ack) at 12.56pm between Givenchy and La Bassée. They were shot down and seen to spin into the ground from 500 feet to the southwest of La Bassée.

RAF 2 Squadron were based on 30 June 1915 to June 1918 at Hesdigneul-lès-Béthune, to the south of Béthune and about 15 km to the east of La Bassée.

2nd Lieutenant David Duthie's place of burial remains unknown, he is commemorated on the Arras Flying Services Memorial and at the former Coupar Angus, North U. F. Church. (Memorial names were transferred to brass plaques in the Abbey Church Halls.) His RAF record reports that he was *'buried at the ?????? of the canal'*, - (Possibly percée, meaning breakthrough or opening), north of Auchy by Copenhagen, German. - (Auchy-les-Mines and Copenhagen is not marked on the trench maps of that time)

Lieutenant Edward Oscar Drinkwater (Pilot), the husband of Ruby F. Drinkwater, of "The Firs," Labumham Rd., Maidenhead, was subsequently re-buried in Brown's Road Military Cemetery, Festubert. Enquiries made with Berlin in September 1918, revealed his grave was also north of Auchy, at the bend of …. (The Canal D'Aire?).

NOTES: On April 1, 1918, the Royal Air Force (RAF) was formed with the amalgamation of the Royal Flying Corps (RFC) and the Royal Naval Air Service (RNAS). The second half of 1918 saw the air war on the western front reach a bloody crescendo with 4,300 casualties, a third of them RAF. New tactics of integrating fighters and bombers into a powerful strike force and through exploiting their numerical supremacy saw success, but at a great cost.

RAF 2 Squadron was the first to fly across the English Channel to France during WW1. The squadron mostly spent WW1 on reconnaissance duties in France. They were formed at Farnborough, Hampshire on 13 May 1912 and from 26 February 1913, the squadron was based at Montrose Air Station in Angus, the first operational Royal Flying Corps base in the UK. Montrose was established on the instructions of the First Lord of the Admiralty, Winston Churchill, to protect the Royal Navy.

The Armstrong Whitworth F.K.8 was a British two-seat general-purpose biplane built by Armstrong Whitworth. They were equipped with wireless telegraph equipment to adjust artillery guns onto enemy targets. In June 1918, FK8's with radio transmitters were assigned to the Tank Corps to coordinate air-to-ground operations. The noise inside the tanks made it near impossible to hear the radio messages. The 'Big Ack' as the FK8 was commonly known, was strong and well-liked by its crews. Two Victoria Crosses were awarded to pilots of the FK8 during WW1.

Cuinchy lies to the south of Givenchy, by the south side of the Canal d'Aire, both right where the Allied trenches met the German trenches. Robert von Ranke Graves (24 July 1895 – 7 December 1985), the English poet, historical novelist, and critic, served with the 3rd Battalion of the Royal Welch (correct spelling) Fusiliers and was friends with another famous poet, Siegfried Sassoon who served in the same regiment. Regarding trench conditions and Cuinchy-bred rats, Graves stated in his 1929 autobiography, Good-Bye to All, "They came up from the canal, fed on the plentiful corpses, and multiplied exceedingly." On 11 November 1985, Graves was among sixteen Great War poets commemorated on a slate stone unveiled in Westminster Abbey's Poets' Corner.

At the start of the war, the 8th (Jullundur) Brigade of the 3rd (Lahore) Division relieved the French and held the Cuinchy sector on 11 December 1914. The 1st Manchester Regiment being first British regiment into the defensive trench line, relieving the French 256th Régiment d'Infanterie. From that time onwards the Cuinchy sector was always in Allied occupation. The front line in mid-1915 settled to the east of Cuinchy. A brick yard on the German side was notorious for close-in fighting and was known as the "Brickstacks". Cuinchy was gradually reduced to rubble by German artillery. The position of this front line scarcely moved until the very last months of the war.

In August 1918, 847 aircraft of the RAF were lost and on one day alone (8 August), 100 aircraft were lost. At the commencement of the war Britain had some 113 aircraft in military service, France had 160 aircraft and Germany 246. When the RFC deployed to France in 1914 it comprised some four Squadrons (No's 2,3,4 and 5) with 12 aircraft each, which together with aircraft in depots, gave a total strength of 63 aircraft supported by 900 men. The 2nd Battle of the Marne saw the largest air battle of the Great War involving 2,700 (900 German & 1,800 Allied) aeroplanes.

Sir John Denton Pinkstone French was chief of the Imperial General Staff and commander of the British Expeditionary Force (BEF) at the start of World War I, he was dismissed from his role in late 1915, subsequently commanding the Home Forces and then became Lord Lieutenant of Ireland. King George V wrote to his private secretary on 25 October 1915, *"The troops here are all right but…several of the most important Generals have entirely lost confidence in [Sir John] and they assured me it was universal and that he must go, otherwise we shall never win this war. This has been my opinion for some time."*

King George V visited Hesdigneul aerodrome on 28 October 1915, to inspect the 1st Wing of the Royal Flying Corps. A sudden cheer from the men there frightened the horse of King George V. The horse, reared up and slipped on the muddy ground, falling, and pinning the King underneath. His pelvis was fractured in two places, leaving the King in great pain. The King's doctors were unsure of the extent of the injuries and did not want to risk transporting him any considerable distance. Concern was also for the King's safety so near the front line, especially if the Germans were to discover where he was. Sir John French attempted to convince the doctors to evacuate the King, and, when this failed, he sent a message to the King himself. The King, at this point under heavy sedation, responded brusquely: *"Tell Sir John to go to hell."*

General Erich Ludendorff contributed significantly to the Nazi's rise to power during the 1920's and 1930's, a promoter of the stab-in-the back conspiracy myths that treasonous Marxists, Freemasons and Jews were responsible for Germany's defeat during WW1.

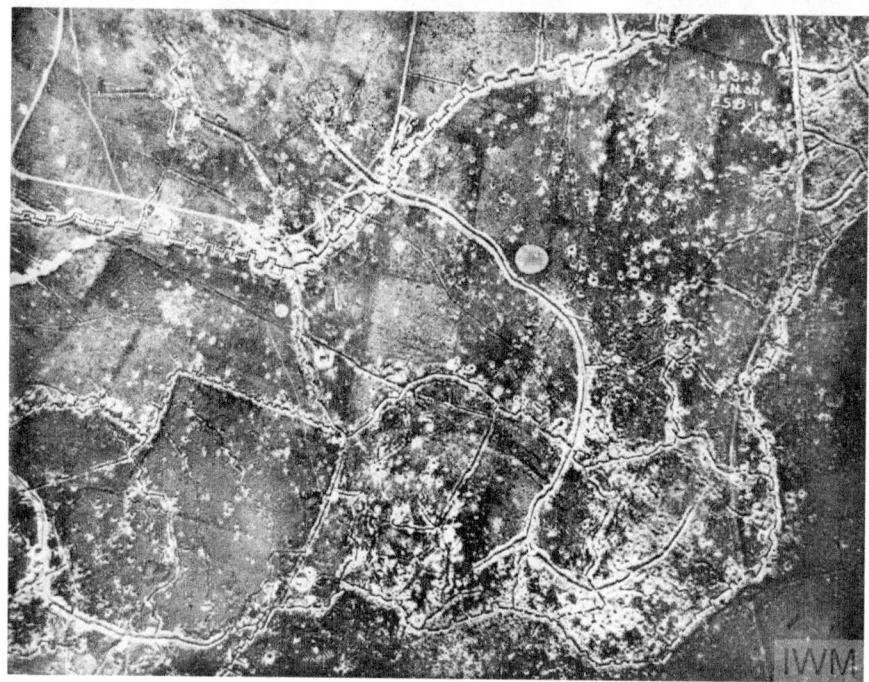

AERIAL PHOTOGRAPHY ON THE WESTERN FRONT DURING THE FIRST WORLD WAR (Q 85216) Aerial view of the Ypres-Comines Canal to La Bassee Canal area, showing the first- and second-line trenches at Spanbroekmolen, northeast of Messines. Copyright: © IWM

MINISTRY OF INFORMATION FIRST WORLD WAR OFFICIAL COLLECTION (Q 17862) *Ruins in the Rue d'Estaires, La Bassee, 1919. Copyright: © IWM*

MINISTRY OF INFORMATION FIRST WORLD WAR OFFICIAL COLLECTION (Q 17869) *Concrete observation post built by the Germans, La Bassee. Copyright: © IWM.*

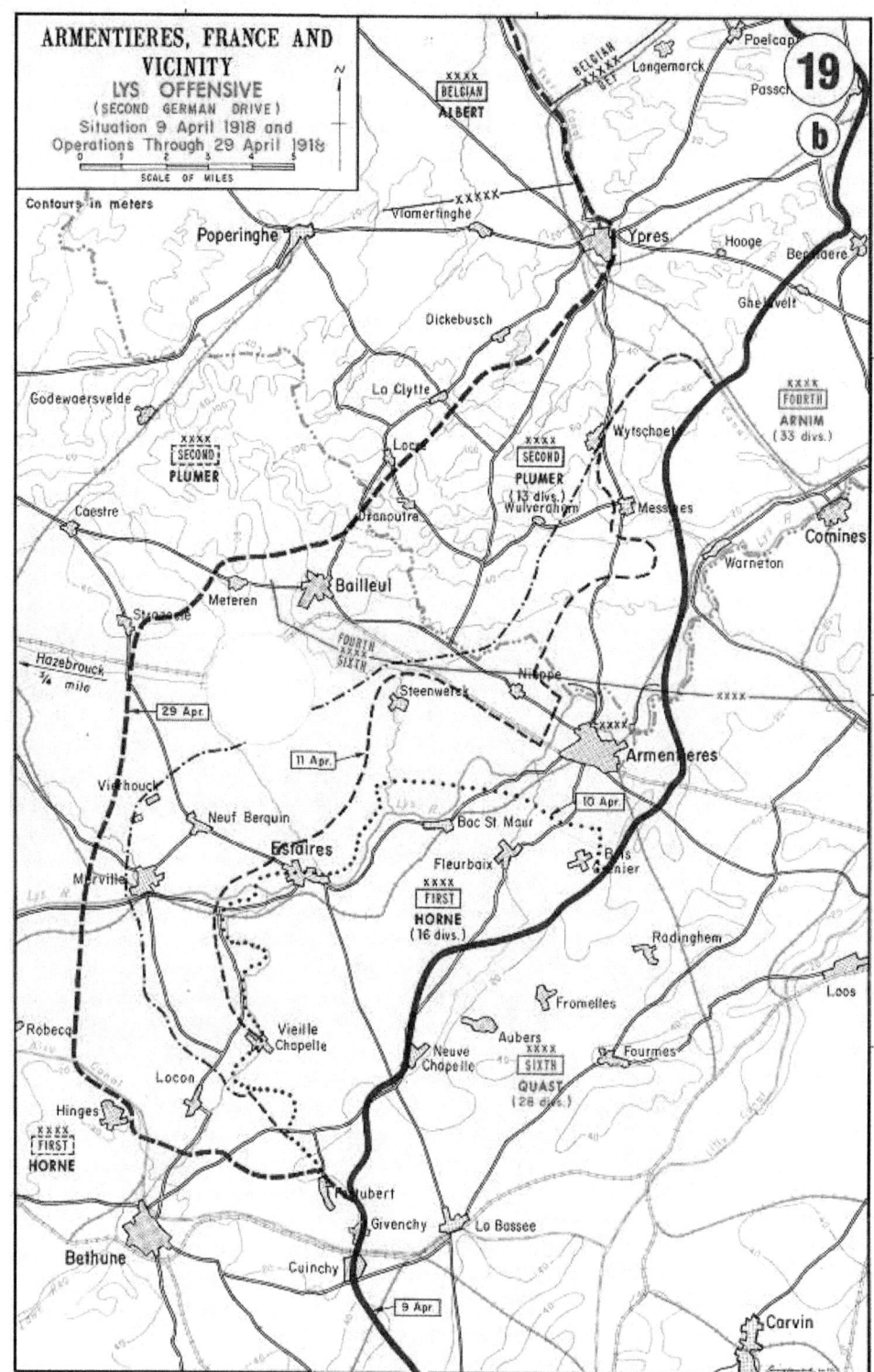

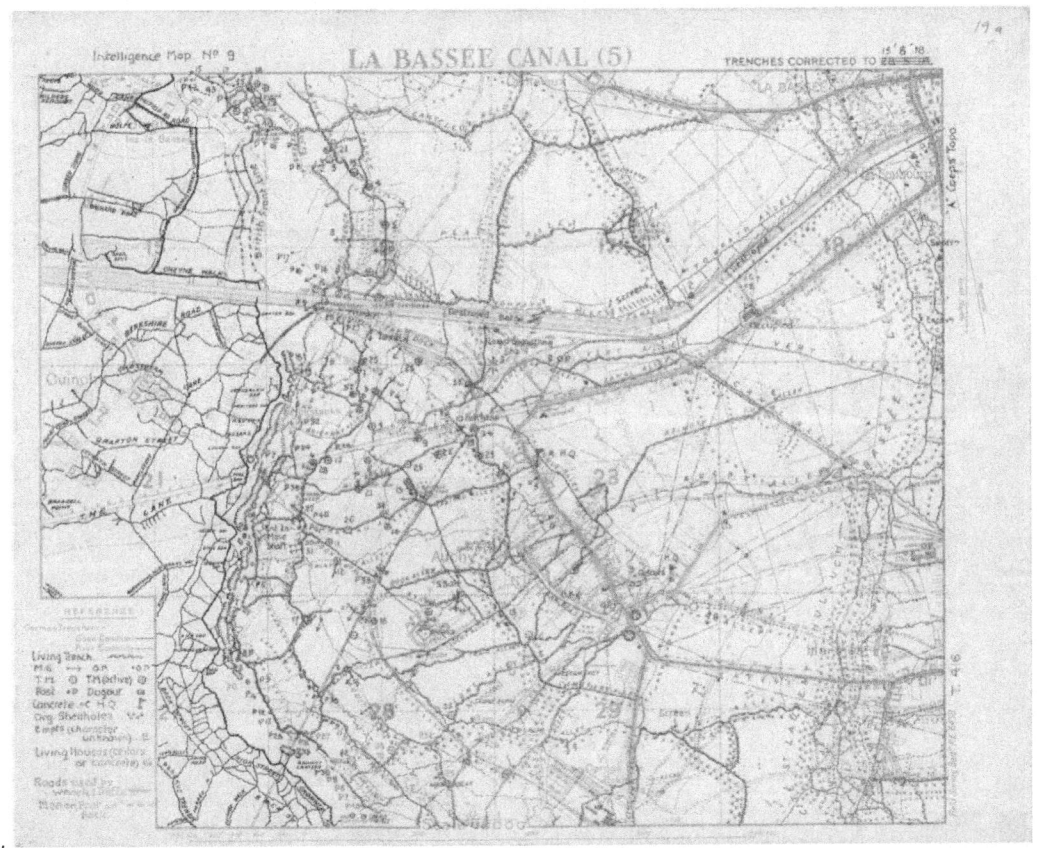

Printed map sheet (1:10,000) showing the La Bassee Canal Basin, with the British and German trenches between Givenchy/Cuinchy and La Bassee/Auchy from which the British attacked in August 1918

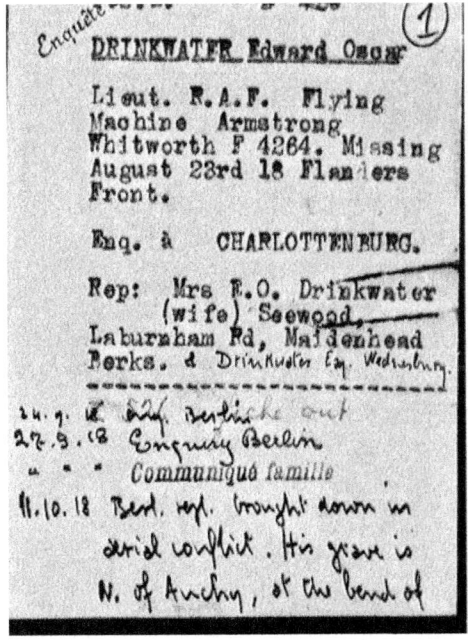

Pilots and observers studying maps in front of an Armstrong-Whitworth F.K.8. Poperinghe Aerodrome, 12 April 1918. Image, David McLellan, Public domain, via Wikimedia Commons

Air mechanics affixing bombs under the lower plane of an Armstrong-Whitworth F.K.8. Poperinghe aerodrome, 12 April 1918. Image, David McLellan, Public domain, via Wikimedia Commons

Group Captain Robert Halley DFC & 2 bars, AFC

It is not well known that a young 24-year-old Perth aviator played a key role in bringing a period of peace to Afghanistan by bombing the city of Kabul in 1919. His bombing of Kabul had a considerable psychological effect, impacting on the morale of the Afghan citizens, and contributed to the quick bringing about of an armistice, thus ending the Third Afghan War or the British-Afghan War of 1919.

On 8 August 1919, the war weary British and King Amanullah for the Afghans, jointly signed the Treaty of Rawalpindi, the fighting ending on August 19. The British relinquished their control over Afghan foreign affairs and Afghanistan became an independent country. Afghans celebrate their Independence Day to this day on the 19 of August.

Afghanistan has been a strategically important location throughout history. It was a gateway to India from the west and benefited handsomely from trade along the Silk Roads to China. Afghanistan was described as the 'Central Asian roundabout' where routes converged from the Middle East, the Indus Valley, through the passes of the Hindu Kush, the Eurasian Steppe and from China via the Tarim Basin. Many conquerors have come and went through this land including Alexander the Great and the Mongols. Many costly wars have been fought for control of this country.

The story of Perth born, Robert 'Jock' Halley is one of a man who was incredibly courageous and heroically determined to successfully target and attack the enemy. Halley was awarded the Distinguished Flying Cross (DFC) on three occasions.

Group Captain Halley was born in Perth in November 1895. He was the second son of Ballie and Mrs Robert Halley, 5 Barossa Place, Perth. He was educated at Perth Academy and was following out agricultural work at Ardoch of Gallery, near Montrose when on reaching military age, he enlisted. Halley was a prominent member of Perthshire Cricket Club, second eleven and was regarded as a very good slow bowler.

He joined a cyclist unit of the Royal Highlanders (HCB) in February 1915 at Montrose. In February 1917, he transferred to the Royal Naval Air Service (RNAS) at RNASTE Vendôme, France taking his officers commission as a Probationary Flight Officer. The airfield operated over 100 Caudron G.III tractor biplane trainers and some Maurice Farman S.7 Longhorn pusher biplanes.

On graduation, he was posted to Naval 'A' Squadron (later 16 Naval Squadron and 216 Squadron R.A.F.), flying twin-engine Handley Page 0/100 (H.P.11) bomber aircraft. His observer was usually the American millionaire, Bobbie Reece.

Halley undertook as verified by his Flying Logbook, over 20 night-bombing, open cockpit, biplane aircraft missions in all weathers before the end of the war. These were very daring long-distance strikes against targets in Köln (Cologne), Frankfurt, Stuttgart, and Mannheim (6 times). Naval "A" Squadron had been hurriedly formed at Manston in 1917, the Germans had been bombing London and cities in the southeast and civilians were crying out for reprisals. They were initially equipped with Handley Page 0/100-night bombers and sent out to Ochey aerodrome in France to bomb the German Rhine towns.

The first aircraft crash of the squadron occurred when Flight Lieutenant (later Captain) Halley came down in the middle of a wood at Chancenay, near Saint-Dizier. The machine (3140) practically buried itself in the mud and slush, only the engines being saved. All the occupants were uninjured.

One bombing mission of Robert Halley shows how he won his first bar to his DFC. And gives an indication of the challenges faced during such sorties. This account is from Peter Chapman's article for the 1914-18 Journal, "Frankfurt – By Night and By Day":

'In late August 1918, 216 Squadron were based at Autreville, France and were equipped with Handley Page 0/100 and Handley Page 0/400 twin-engined heavy bombers. These aircraft normally carried a crew of three – pilot, observer/navigator and gunner – and with a bomb load of up to 1650lbs were able to reach targets as far afield as Cologne, Stuttgart or Frankfurt.

The weather outlook on 24 August 1918 was not good, with a strong south-east wind blowing across much of eastern France and a weather forecast of severe thunderstorms approaching later that evening. Despite this, orders were received at the squadron to mount a maximum effort that night, the main target being the railway station and sidings at Frankfurt am Main, with the Burbach works at Saarbrucken as an alternative target, should a raid on Frankfurt not be possible.

Shortly after dusk the squadron's six serviceable aircraft took off individually, with a time lapse of a few minutes separating each take off, each aircraft being given the go ahead by the aerodrome officer via signal lamp. Soon after they had all departed, however, it became apparent to many crews that they would be faced with an almost impossible task to reach Frankfurt in the prevailing weather, and gradually all but two aircraft returned to their aerodrome with their bombs. One of the remaining two chose to bomb Boulay aerodrome, an alternate target, before also returning to Autreville.

The sixth aircraft that night was Handley Page 0/100 No. 3138, crewed by Captain Robert Halley, D.F.C. (pilot), Lieutenant Robert H. Reece, D.F.C. (observer/navigator) and 2nd Lieutenant C. W. Treleaven, a relatively new pilot in the squadron, who went along as their gunner. An experienced pairing, Halley and Reece had already undertaken a number of long-distance bombing sorties to targets such as Mannheim and Stuttgart, and both had been decorated with the Distinguished Flying Cross for their exploits.

After taking off and gaining height over their aerodrome, they steered a course to D lighthouse, one of a number of automated signalling lights on the Allied side of the lines which continually flashed a predetermined Morse Code letter as a guide to the night bombers. By figuring their ground speed and drift en route, the two men calculated that they could reach Frankfurt and return safely, despite the wind, if they steered a direct course there and back. Even then, their margin for error was almost nil, as they calculated they would have no more than five minutes over Frankfurt itself if they were to regain their own lines safely afterwards, and then with only 10 minutes of fuel to spare.

Steering a 039-degree course from D lighthouse, at an average altitude of 6000 feet, they encountered no more than sporadic flak from each town as they flew north of Saarburg, Bitsche and Pirmasens, then south of Kaiserslautern before crossing the Vosges mountains. They then crossed the Rhine River valley north of Oppenheim and flew on to Mainz. Here they followed the Main River to Frankfurt, arriving at their target at midnight. They were greeted by a heavy anti-aircraft barrage and numerous searchlights, but switching off engines briefly, Halley quickly glided their aircraft down and Reece dropped their bomb load, comprised of a single 550lb and four 112lb bombs, as close as possible to the Hauptbahnhof, or main railway station.

All of their bombs missed the intended target, falling in a ragged line across the properties alongside the river front, near the Westhafen. One bomb that landed on the Westhafen itself caused considerable damage to material stored there. This was likely the 550lb bomb. The rest of the bombs damaged private property. Overall damage was considerable, however, amounting to 100,000 German marks (£50,000).

Having dropped their bombs, Halley and Reece hastily steered the most direct course for their own lines, over 100 miles away against a strengthening headwind. To add to their problems, they were approaching a storm ahead, which they dared not climb above as they did not have the fuel to spare. They elected instead to fly right underneath it and found themselves being tossed about by fierce winds while being illuminated by lightning flashes and soaked by driving rain for hours. They were also being caught periodically in searchlights and their aircraft received numerous shrapnel hits from the accurate anti-aircraft fire, although none of these were serious enough to bring them down.

They finally cleared the first storm as they passed over Kaiserslautern, only to fly straight into another storm on the other side of the town. This storm too was cleared briefly, sufficient for them to again check their course and make a course correction before they flew into a third and even more violent storm than those before. Fortunately, this storm was over quicker than its two predecessors, as Halley was unable to do more than keep the aircraft flying while it lasted, with no chance to follow a compass course. They arrived south of the Marne-Rhine canal as dawn was breaking, and steered for the nearest aerodrome, but shortly after crossing into friendly territory their engines stopped through lack of fuel, and the exhausted crew were forced to make a safe landing in a field near Luneville, eight and a half hours after they had set out.

Having striven against almost impossible weather, this brave crew had succeeded in reaching Frankfurt and dropping their bombs there, causing some considerable damage, albeit in the wrong place. They had then returned to a safe landing on their own side of the lines.

Their chief enemy this night was not the Germans however, but the weather, which may well have caused a less experienced crew to fail in their mission. They did not encounter enemy fighters during the entire flight but had been subjected to accurate anti-aircraft fire from various towns en route, as they were forced to fly low in a storm and were being illuminated by lightning flashes as well as searchlights from the ground.'

After this mission, Halley was awarded Bar to his DFC for this effort and he was selected to be one of only four pilots for a top-secret mission to attack 'the right spot', to bomb the German capital of Berlin. This would involve for the first time, non-stop flying by bomber aircraft all the way from England and back again.

Next Stop Berlin

Asleep in bed one night following another long night bombing raid on Mannheim, Halley was awoken and told he had to leave for England the following morning. A destroyer was waiting for him at Dunkirk and a car would meet him at Dover to take him to London. Halley was to fly the new Super Handley V/1500', very large, four-engine biplane designed to carry a 3,000 lb bomb load and fly from airfields in East Anglia, the distance to Berlin and back. The V/1500 was the very first aircraft to feature a gun turret in the tail and its size was not surpassed until the Boeing Super Fortress arrived in WW2. The Handley Page V/1500 had a wingspan of 126 ft and four Rolls Royce Eagle engines, between them developing 1,400hp.

Before these Berlin raids could be carried out, the war ended, the Armistice was agreed with Germany and World War One ended.

The following message was received by RAF 216 squadron at the termination of WW1 hostilities:

D.S.O.

To O.C. No. 216 Squadron

Sender's Number G.O.C./211.

AAA On the Armistice being singed I would like to congratulate you on having materially assisted in bringing about this desirable result by creating demoralisation in Germany AAA It was only by the determination of the Ground Personnel in keeping the machines in an efficient condition and of the Pilots and Observers in getting the distance that this result was brought about AAA I hope to be able to come and thank you personally shortly AAA I would like you all to remember however that although the Armistice has been signed we must keep our weapons ready for instant use in case the enemy shows any signs of negligence to carry out the conditions AAA

From General Trenchard, H.Q., I.F.

(AAA was standard telegram-ese for a full stop)

Flying to India

A few weeks later, in December 1918, Halley with Major A C S McLaren as co-pilot (and Maltese Terrier, 'Tiny'), Flight Sergeant Smith, Sergeant Crockett, and Sergeant Brown as the crew set off to fly to India from Ipswich in Handley Page V/1500 J1936, 'HMA Old Carthusian '. They also carried a passenger, Brigadier General Norman D K McEwen who was to take over as AOC (Air Officer Commanding) in India. The planned route was via Paris, Rome, Malta, Cairo, Bagdad, and Karachi – 5,560 miles, accomplished in a time of 72 hours and 41 minutes, at an average speed of 77 mph. Only once did they land at their designated aerodrome on the flight plan. When they arrived in Delhi, the Viceroy, and a crowd of 30,000 greeted them.

The London *Daily Mail* was keenly interested in the great adventure. The following account was published:

"A British Aeroplane left England today, Friday (13 December 1918) for a flight to India.

At 9.30 a.m., a giant Handley Page, of V/1500 type, carrying six members of the Royal Air Force, rose from the aerodrome at Martlesham, near Ipswich, and headed for the Channel and France on a flight to Karachi, and hence to Delhi.

The huge craft crossed the Channel but ran into a bank of thick fog and was compelled to land at a small town near the French coast. It is hoped that the weather tomorrow morning will allow a continuance of the journey, and that Miramas, near Marseille, may be reached to-morrow night.

On the front of the engines was "H.M.A. Old Carthusian." She was named by chief pilot, Major Archibald Stuart McLaren, M.C., A.F.C., who was a Charterhouse boy, as was one of the passengers, General McEwen.

If everything goes well and the most sanguine of hopes are realised the journey may be made in seven stages.

A.F.C. – Pioneering Through Flight to India

As Halley later recalled in his lively account of the flight for Aeroplane Monthly (December 1978):

'It was indeed a great moment. MacLaren and I had a lot in common, except that he was 6ft. 2in. and I 5ft. 3in wearing my thick socks! He was also a Scot and had already flown to Egypt in an O/400 with General "Biffy" Borton. Our considerable experience on heavy aircraft had brought us together ... A day or two later we were at Martlesham Heath, as it was from there that we were going to start, and Rolls-Royce mechanics were working on the aircraft. All the crew were now assembled there. Flight Sergeant Smith and Sergeant Crockett, fitters, and Sergeant Brown, rigger, had been selected as maintenance

crew. Going with us as a passenger was General Norman McEwan, who was to take over as A.O.C. in India on arrival. As General MacEwen and MacLaren were both at school at Charterhouse, the aircraft was named H.M.A. Old Carthusian. We also had another passenger, "Tiny", a little Maltese Terrier belonging to MacLaren that had already flown to Egypt earlier in the year. He was mad keen on flying and whenever the engines started, he ran to the bottom of the ladder to be taken up into the cockpit!'

Thus ensued an extraordinary journey, via Paris, Rome, Malta, Cairo, Baghdad, and Karachi, the whole enacted between 13 December 1918 and 15 January 1919, a journey 'full of incidents, some of them not easy to cope with', not least the final flight into Karachi – Christopher Cole and Roderick Grant take up the story in But Not in Anger:

'To reduce weight only one of the N.C.O.s could travel – he was in fact needed in the tail cockpit to give the correct trim for take-off – and Smith won the toss. While Halley dashed back to get their kit and pay the bills, MacLaren taxied his way between the dunes as fast as he dared to avoid getting stuck in the soft sand. The tide was right out leaving a two-mile strip of firm, damp beach. There was a slope across its width, but the pair of sound engines was on the side to counteract any tendency to swing. Today, a three-engine ferry take-off by a four-engine aircraft from a concrete runway is a routine piece of operating procedure, and with the substantial power reserves of a modern jet transport presents no hazard. The crew of Old Carthusian were – as far as is known – doing it for the first time in aviation history, in a hot climate, from wet sand in an aircraft considered underpowered even by 1919 standards.

MacLaren opened up the three Eagles and at 17.45 the aircraft slowly rolled away, gradually picked up speed and was airborne after a run of about a mile. Twenty minutes later they had reached 1,000 feet and were passing the Britomart on their starboard side. Her smoke was still a smudge on the horizon when their justifiable elation was rudely shattered as both starboard engines gave a few splutters and then stopped, leaving them to defy gravity by the sole efforts of the front port. The crew's immediate diagnosis was the right one – the wind driven pump for transferring fuel from the main tank to the starboard gravity tank had finally shed all its miserable little vane cups and given up the struggle. Halley dived back to the engineer's station and strenuously attacked the emergency pump with both hands, wondering how he could attract Smith's attention. The engines picked up again and Halley hastened back to the cockpit. He had just managed to get through to Smith – 60 feet to the rear – by sign language when the engines again stopped, and again Halley rushed to the pumps. As the engines picked up for the second time, Smith came crawling down the fuselage and thereafter they took turns to man the pumps.

At 18.45, just as the last light had faded, and with about 35 miles to go the rear starboard engine began to lose revolutions, its temperature shot up and there was no alternative but to throttle it right down, then switch off completely. The seizure was due to a broken oil pipe, and nothing could be done in flight. Since they were providentially left with an engine on each side, they retained reasonable control though it was impossible to maintain height. The next half hour seemed like an eternity. With both remaining engines at full throttle and their temperatures reading only 5 degrees C below boiling point, MacLaren held the aircraft barely above the stall, and with the airspeed indicator showing 52 m.p.h. she staggered along, losing about 10 feet of vital altitude with every minute that passed. They just scraped over the ridge of hills to the west of Karachi, but very soon they must hit the ground and there was no possibility of circling around looking for the city's temporary aerodrome.

By some happy chance, the priority departure signal despatched by Brown from Ormara had not only arrived but was sent straight away by runner to the senior Royal Engineer officer who was playing hockey. He immediately appreciated the need for urgent action, grabbed some men and hastily improvised flares from petrol and rags, and for good measure fired off a few pyrotechnics as soon as the faint drone of engines was heard to the west. From the flight deck of *Old Carthusian*, the crew peered at the myriad lights of Karachi still some miles away and wondered where they could safely put down. Then Halley gave a wild shout and pointed straight ahead. He had spotted one of the signals, and faintly twinkling on the ground almost dead in line with their heading was an obvious flare-path. They were now frighteningly low down and the straight in approach had to be exactly right, first time. It was precisely so and when the Handley Page rolled to a halt at 19.15 the pilots climbed out, grabbed one another by the arms and literally danced for joy.

"Until that moment I thought that dancing for joy was just a figure of speech", recalls Halley, "but we did it – though since we were such an oddly sized couple, the onlookers probably thought we were quite mad. They had seen us make a good and apparently normal landing but knew nothing of our harrowing experience."

That night Halley underlined the impression that flyers were eccentric people by arriving for dinner with the Governor of Sind half an hour late and wearing a dinner suit nearly a foot too long in the sleeves and leg. He had fallen asleep in his bath from sheer fatigue – and was not the easiest to fit when it came to borrowing clothes.

When McEwen arrived and heard the full story, he promptly forestalled any criticism of the pilots by signalling Air Ministry, saying that he could not speak too highly of their enterprise, grit and determination for successfully completing the flight in the face of so many difficulties, particularly during the final 170 miles – over 50 of which there was no possibility of landing.

Despite only once being able to land at the aerodrome designated on their flight plan, the crew had nearly always managed to notify some authority of their whereabouts before anxiety was aroused. The aircraft was for a short time posted as missing after the forced landing in Egypt, since it had not been sighted after passing Sollum, and H.Q. Middle East was about to launch a major search when the message reporting its safety was received.'

The Viceroy of India later asked Halley to carry out a daring bombing strike on **Kabul**, Afghanistan. At 03.00 hours on 24 May 1919, *Old Carthusian* took off. The route was northwest towards the Khyber Pass, on up the Kabul River and followed a rough road to Jalalabad just as the sun was coming up. Then west another 90 miles to Kabul. They pressed on despite a starboard engine water leak coming from the second cylinder. The precipitous mountains ahead were the next concern, they just managed to clear the gap where the road went through the 8,000 feet ridge of Jagalak Pass.

Kabul Raid

Halley takes up the story:

'Having then flown on to Delhi, where a crowd of 30,000 and the Viceroy greeted the Old Carthusian, and undertaken some V.I.P. flights, I was summoned by General McEwan in lieu of the mounting troubles on the frontier and, to cut a long story short, was ordered to carry out a daring bombing strike on Kabul.

Four 112lb. bomb racks from No. 31 Squadron's B.E.2Cs were attached to the lower wing main spars and connected to the front cockpit where an Observer would release the bombs. We put sixteen 20-pounders in the rear cockpit, and they would be dropped by the crew once the 112lb. bombs had been released. We had to true up the wings and tighten the fabric. We also fitted two laminated four-bladed propellers fashioned from a local wood called padouk.

We took off at about 3 a.m. on 24 May 1919 – Empire Day. An L-shaped flare path was laid out, consisting of seven flares made from empty five-gallon oil drums filled with oil-soaked cotton waste. These proved effective for take-off and would have been useful if it were found necessary to land in the dark in case of emergency.

The route lay towards the Khyber Pass, and as the clearing height was about 3,000 feet this meant flying around for about an hour to gain height before going over a ridge of hills. The Khyber was only dimly visible, as were a few lights at Jamrud Fort and Landi Kotal. From there we flew over the Kabul River and a rough road running parallel up to Jalalabad, the only town of any size on the route. As we were approaching Jalalabad and daybreak was coming up, I was checking the starboard rev. counter when to my horror I saw water leaking from the base of the second cylinder. I got Flight Sergeant Smith up beside me and, with engines throttled back to aid hearing, we hurriedly conferred as to what should be done.

The leak was caused by a defective rubber connection fitted between the water jacket and the collecting pipe running along the base of the six cylinders. Drops of water were being blown by the slipstream, making it impossible to estimate the extent of the leakage. Kabul was still about 90 miles ahead, and there was the return time to think about. I was in the middle of a steep turn, and on looking down noticed smoke from a fire being blown in the direction of Kabul and stretching out parallel with the ground, indicating a favourable wind of some force.

Villiers got Flight Sergeant Smith alongside me again, and after some shrugging of shoulders and other signs of an even chance, we decided to continue.

Oh, God – somewhere ahead there was that ridge to cross, with Kabul still further on. Much went through my mind at this stage of the journey. I was continually looking at the leakage and the frightening appearance of the precipitous mountains around. The Jagfalak Pass, through which the road went at nearly 8,000 feet, was not yet visible. It was quite thrilling threading one's way between high peaks. Suddenly on making a turn, the road appeared on a crest of the ridge ahead, but to my horror it was some height above the aircraft's nose.

Remembering the smoke, we had just left behind, I wondered whether we could gain enough up-lift to take us over the hills ahead. At about two miles away we were definitely below the ridge, so I said to myself "here goes" and, holding the nose up and with the four engines running full out we went sailing over the top and down on the other side. It was unbelievable – even now I can see the look Villiers had on his face! He quickly took to looking downwards from his side of the cockpit and with a grin gave me a "thumbs up"! Afterwards he told me that, on passing over the ridge, he saw a camel convoy of over 100 animals on its way to Kabul or the Khyber stampede in all directions, quite a number falling down the precipitous mountain side.

On getting over the ridge and regaining my breath I saw our target ahead, spread out over a vast area on a lush green fertile plateau; a marked change from the barren and mountainous terrain that we had just come across. With a population of 300,000, it was not surprising that Kabul covered such an area. It was also reputed to have the busiest and finest Bazaar in the East.

Owing to the risk of starboard engine failure, we had to cut our time over Kabul to a minimum. Nevertheless, the bombing achieved good results, and if that didn't frighten a city that had never seen an aircraft before, the sight and sound of the Old Carthusian roaring over the city at a few hundred feet with four engines fitted with stub exhausts certainly did!

On the return journey we again headed for the Jagdalak Pass, and believe it or not, had the benefit of a slightly following wind, which had veered through 180 degrees! As we were now relieved of our bombs, we flew over the ridge with height to spare.

The return flight seemed interminable, and we were all very conscious of the water leakage on the starboard engine. My eyes were glued to the temperature gauge in the nacelle, and we had nearly reached the Khyber when I saw the pointer rise slowly above normal; there was nothing to do but switch off the engine and carry on with three running full out to keep height. This we were able to do and landed at Risalpur after six hours in the air. It would be an understatement to say we were all greatly relieved!

The main object of bombing Kabul was to alarm King Amanullah, a result so successfully attained that a message came to the Viceroy immediately afterwards to the effect that the Afghans wanted peace. This was the end of the Old Carthusian's career, which had been bedevilled by misfortune from first to last. Nevertheless, the old V/1500 had accomplished something unique in history – it had ended a war on its own! So finished the Third Afghan War, terminated by a strategic bombing raid at a negligible cost which must have saved hundreds of lives and the cost of an extensive land campaign. It also restored peace to a large slice of India.

The raid had one or two amusing angles to it. For example, when Amanullah's uncle, a keen golfer, died suddenly under rather questionable circumstances, Amanullah had him buried under the first tee. As one of our twenty-pounders, carelessly thrown out by the crew, had landed near the grave, Amanullah complained to the Viceroy that we had bombed the tomb of his ancestor! Another comic episode appeared in The Aeroplane of 22 April 1942. The founding editor, C. G. Grey wrote, 'The raid on Kabul was made with decisive effect – that was when Jock Halley blew out the walls of the King's Harem and started the fashion of female emancipation in Afghanistan!'

A few years after the Afghan War, King Amanullah visited England as a guest, and was given an air display at Hendon. Being in Scotland at the time I was unable to attend. However, I received a letter from C. G. Grey: 'Dear Jock, I noticed you were conspicuous by your absence at Hendon on Saturday. Had you been there no doubt you would have had a knife in your back!'

There is one final comment that I would like to make concerning the raid. As the pilot and captain of the aircraft I was given a Second Bar to my Distinguished Flying Cross. However, my stalwart N.C.O.s, Flight Sergeant Smith and Sergeant Crockett, fitters, and Sergeant Brown, rigger, who accompanied me quite voluntarily and who had supervised the rebuilding of the aircraft, received no official recognition in spite of all my recommendations. They had all won the Air Force Medal for their efforts on the flight to India. Now, we know that the D.F.C. and D.F.M. are awarded for 'distinguished flying in the face of the enemy,' and the A.F.C. and A.F.M. for 'distinguished flying in the face of Providence!' Surely these brave men had earned some recognition in the former category and Lieutenant Villiers also.

Here, belatedly, let me pay my respects to them' (Aeroplane August 1979, refers).

'Old Carthusian 'dropped 20 bombs, one 112-pound and three 20-pound on the Amir's palace sending the ladies of the royal harem into the streets screaming in terror, this caused a great scandal. Another three 112-pound and seven 20-pound bombs hit the royal arsenal at Arg causing a large explosion. Six hours later they landed at Risalpur, now in Pakistan.

King Amanullah had declared Jihad on 3 May 1919 and sent the 50,000 strong Afghan army supported by 120,000 frontier tribesmen into British India to start the Third Afghan War, known in Afghanistan as the War of Independence. The Treaty of Gandamak in 1879 had held for 40 years, but now they wanted to be free and independent of existing treaties with British India.

The purpose of the Halley raid was to alarm King Amanullah and it did so successfully, attaining an immediate message to the Viceroy in India that the Afghans wanted peace. Halley later claimed to have 'ended the war on his own'. An armistice was signed on 8 August 1919.

D.F.C. London Gazette 3 August 1918:

'A gallant and determined leader in long distance night bombing raiding. He has been most successful in many of these raids, generally under adverse weather conditions and intense anti-aircraft fire from the enemy and having had to fly by compass owing to density of mist. In his last raid the flight outward and homeward lasted eight hours.'

Later Years

Gaining steady promotion between the Wars, Halley enjoyed varied employment, including stints with the Fleet Air Arm in *HMS Eagle* and *HMS Glorious.* in the 1920s and 1930s. He was Assistant Commandant at RAF Cranwell when WW2 started. He was posted to Gibraltar as Commanding Officer of No. 200 Group, Coastal Command in 1941. Halley pressed the Governor, Lord Gort, to back his plan for extending the runway to deal with "modern aircraft", a plan which in fact the Governor refused to support, instead complaining to the C.-in-C. Coastal Command about Halley. He was ordered back to RAF Silloth in Cumbria as Station Commander. Inevitably, the Gibraltar runway was extended in time for "Operation Torch", the North African landings on 8 November 1942.

Group Captain Robert Halley DFC & 2 Bars, AFC (Air Force Cross) was made a Wing Commander on 1 July 1933 and Group Captain on 1 July 1938. He retired from the RAF on 6 May 1945. Group Captain Robert Halley died on 13 December 1979, exactly 61 years since his departure to India. His obituary stated that he was 'one of the aviation 'greats' of all time, a man cast in the 'heroic mould'.

Awards:

Bar to D.F.C. London Gazette 1 January 1919.

Second Bar to D.F.C. London Gazette 12 July 1920 (Afghanistan).

A.F.C. London Gazette 22 December 1919.

First and Second D.F.C.s – Night Bomber Pilot

Medals

In September 2011, the medals of Group Captain Robert Halley were sold by auction. Established in 1990, Dix Noonan Webb Ltd are the UK's leading specialist auctioneers and valuers of banknotes, coins, tokens, medals, and militaria staging regular auctions throughout the year.

The following information is from the information provided by Dix Noonan Webb at the time of sale of the medals.

Robert Halley's medal were sold by auction with a quantity of original documentation, including the recipient's original Royal Naval Air Service Pilot's Flying Logbook, covering the period February 1917 until September 1919, and two or three portrait photographs, together with a letter opener fashioned from wood taken from one of the Old Carthusian's propellers, with ink inscription and Halley's signature:

copies of Aeroplane Monthly for December 1978 (with Halley's account of the U.K. to India flight), August 1979 (with his account of the Kabul raid), and November 1979 (with his account of Hendon displays in the 1920s); and bound photocopies of the A.O.C. India's official report on the U.K. to India flight and the text of a speech given by Halley on the same subject; so, too, a CD from the Royal Air Force Museum's film and sound archive, with an interview with Halley.

Dix Noonan Webb Ltd.

LONDON SPECIALIST AUCTIONEERS

Lot 912

Date of Auction: 23rd September 2011

Sold for £24,000

Estimate: £18,000 – £20,000

The unique Great War and Afghan War D.F.C. and 2 Bars, A.F.C. group of eleven awarded to Group Captain R. "Jock" Halley, Royal Air Force, late Royal Naval Air Service: having won a brace of D.F.C.s for his gallantry in daring long-distance night bombing raids to Germany in 1918, he was awarded the A.F.C. for the epic flight of the Super Handley V/1500 Old Carthusian to India – where he promptly won a third D.F.C. for a remarkable raid on Kabul in May 1919.

Distinguished Flying Cross, G.V.R., with Second and Third Award Bars, unnamed as issued; Air Force Cross, G.V.R., unnamed as issued; British War and Victory Medals, M.I.D. oak leaf (Capt. R. Halley, R.A.F.); India General Service 1908-35, 1 clasp, Afghanistan N.W.F. 1919 (Flt. Lieut. R. Halley, R.A.F.); 1939-45 Star; Africa Star; Defence and War Medals, M.I.D. oak leaf; Jubilee 1935; Coronation 1937, mounted court-style as worn, very fine and better – £18000-22000

NOTES: RNASTE (Royal Naval Air Service Training Establishment) Vendôme was located between Le Mans and Orléans.

Bobby Reece originally served with the *La Lafayette Escadrille*. The escadrille of the *Aéronautique Militaire* was composed largely of American volunteer pilots flying fighters. Bobby Reece came over from the USA and joined the "Lafayette" in 1915. Reece apparently crashed so many planes that they let him go. Halley described Reece as 'ham-handed' as a pilot but had managed to wrangle his way into becoming his observer in RAF 216 Squadron. Bobby Reece was awarded the DFC at the same time as Robert Halley during a bombing mission to Germany, one of the few Americans to hold this award. Reece was part of the Reece Buttonhole Manufacturing Company, Sewing Machine Manufacturers, Boston Massachusetts, USA. The company is still in business, merging with AMF Sewn Products Inc. in 1991 to form AMF Reece.

Robert Halley was the nephew of Group Captain Robert Halley, see Second World War Aviators

The airfield at Risalpur was created in 1910 by the Royal Flying Corp. RFC/RAF No. 31 Squadron flew B.E.2c and Farman biplanes in a ground support role from Risalpur. In 1947, it became the airfield of the Pakistan Air Force (PAF). In 1967 it was upgraded to the Pakistan Air Force Academy Asghar Khan.

On 17 May 1919, a Handley Page Type O/400, D5439 of RAF 58 Squadron carrying Thomas Edward Lawrence (Lawrence of Arabia) on a flight to Cairo, Egypt crashed at the airport of Roma-Centocelle. T E Lawrence had been attending the 1919 Peace Conference in Paris and had hitched a ride in order to collect from Cairo documents relating to his service in the Middle East during the Great War. The pilot and co-pilot were both killed; Lawrence survived the incident with a broken shoulder blade and two broken ribs. The latter injury troubling him for the rest of his life.

Captain John William Alcock DSC and Lieutenant Arthur Whitten Brown of the RAF aboard Vickers Vimy F.B.27A Mk. IV biplane bomber made the very first successful non-stop trans-Atlantic crossing by air on 14-15 June 1919

A Bristol Fighter, **BF4626** aeroplane of RAF 20 Squadron was lost on 30 July 1919 during the conflict. Acting Captain George Eastwood was shot through the chest by a party of tribesmen concealed on the hillside. The observer, 2nd Lieutenant David Lapraik was also injured. A rescue mission was undertaken by the Kurram Militia from the post at Badama. Both airmen survived, George Eastwood was discharged from the RAF in December 1919 and David Lapraik in May 1920.

In December 1978, **Aeroplane Monthly** published the first-hand account of Group Captain Robert Halley's trail-blazing journey to India at the end of 1918. This magazine article is still under copyright, but a back issue may still be available to purchase and some of the text was reprinted when Halley's medals were auctioned in 2011.

Titled: **Per Ardua Ad India**

Subtitle: Sixty years ago, on December 13, 1918, the third prototype Handley Page V/1500, J1936, took off from Martlesham Heath for a flight to India. GP CAPT ROBERT HALLEY, AFC now aged 63, was one of the pilots, and he recalls this trail-blazing through flight from England to India, a journey bedevilled by bad weather and mechanical failures.

Opening Text: *'On Friday, December 13, 1918, the second aircraft to fly to India from this country took off from Martlesham Heath in Suffolk. As I happened to be the co-pilot, along with Maj. Stuart MacLaren, on that early pioneer flight, and this year – 1978, a record of some of the amusing things that happened, together with some of the rather frightening occurrences with which we had to cope, might be of interest.'*

Closing Text: *'We had left on Friday, December 13th, 1918, and arrived on January 15, 1919 – and we never once landed at out intended destination! Up to this time I had never been a superstitious man, but after all we went through, I am still inclined to look a little askance on Friday the 13th.'*

Picture – Ron Eisele

Aerial view of part of Kabul taken from Handley Page V/1500, J1936, "HMA Old Carthusian", during its bombing raid on the Afghan capital, 24 May 1919. Attribution: British Air Force RAF, Public domain, via Wikimedia Commons

AIRCRAFT OF THE ROYAL AIR FORCE 1918-1939 (H(AM) 194) A Handley Page V/1500 bomber, which made the first flight from England to India in January 1919. In May 1919 it bombed rebel Afghans in Kabul and was thus the only V/1500 to see action. Copyright: © IWM.

Group Captain Robert Halley

Second Lieutenant Herrick Peter Gladstone Leyden & Second Lieutenant Robert William Gladstone Leyden

Lieutenant Herrick Peter Gladstone Leyden was the son of Patrick Peter and Margaret Florence Gladstone Leyden, of Beechwood, 9 Pitcullen Terrace, Perth. Herrick was born on 24 March 1898 at Pontardawe in the Swansea Valley. His father was a Customs and Excise and Old Age Pensions Officer in Tay Street. He attended Swansea Grammar (Bishop Gore Grammar) from September 1912 to July 1915, Sharp's Institution in South Methven Street and Perth Academy from September 1915 to June 1916.

Herrick who was employed as a motor driver, enlisted in The Black Watch, 3rd Battalion (Royal Highlanders), on 10 January 1917 he signed his service paper, he was aged 18 years and 10 months. Herrick went to The Black Watch army camp at Nigg, Ross-shire for six weeks training and then joined the Royal Flying Corp, 7 March 1917. As a trained flying officer pilot, he went on the RFC list on 5 July 1917. He was promoted on 31 March 1918 on the understanding it was to be confirmed. It was made effective the following day; 1 April 1917 and he was officially gazetted as 2nd Lieutenant on 2 May 1918.

He was again gazetted on 26 July 1917 as Lieutenant, but his CWG (Commonwealth War Graves) entry shows him at time of death as still a 2nd Lieutenant.

Herrick's pilot training took him first to:

Officers Cadet Wing at Denham Aerodrome on 8 March 1917.

No. 2 School of Military Aeronautics at Oxford on 11 May 1917.

39 T S (Training Squadron) on 5 July 1917 at Montrose (Note: 39 T.S. is recorded as not coming into operation until 26 August 1917).

61 T S (Training Squadron) of 23 Wing on 20 September 1917 at Cramlington.

51 T S 27 Wing at Filton.

36 T S on 31 October 1917 at Beverley.

58 Squadron, 19th Wing on 8 November 1917 at Cramlington.

75 T S on 28 November 1917 at Waddington. Possibly just for further instruction and returned to 58 Squadron.

No.1 School of Flying and Gunnery at Turnberry on 13 June 1918. Three-week course in the art of aerial gunnery and combat.

Herrick Leyden, age 20, was told he was to be operational in France with 104 Squadron on 28 June 1918, effective 6 July 1918. However, it is possible that he was already posted to France; 58 Squadron departed Dover on 22 December 1917, were based at St Omer, Trézennes, Clairmarais, Auchel, Fauquembergues and Alquines through the first half of 1918. These airfields would have been covering the battlefields in the Nord-Pas De Calais area during the German Spring Offensives of 1918. As the allies were pushed back, they would have moved back west from 23 April 1918 and through the summer to Fauquembergues and Alquines.

He may have been held in reserve, still under training in England, or was perhaps rested. He could have returned for further gunnery training at Turnberry, but we know he was re-assigned to 104 Squadron who were at Azelot near Nancy.

On 13 August 1918, he was piloting a Geoffrey de Havilland designed Airco DH. 9, single engine, two seat, biplane bomber. The aircraft designation, D7229 was seen to be hit by anti-aircraft fire, fold up and then fall on to another DH.9, crewed by pilot, 2nd Lieutenant Francis Henry Beaufort (from New York) and Observer, 2nd Lieutenant H O Bryant.

On his RAF Casualty Card, Herrick was reported missing the next day, along with his observer, Sergeant Alan Lacey Windridge age 20, and the two other airmen.

Herrick's Casualty Card and his service records sheets contain other information. A letter was sent on 20 August 1918, to his next of kin, which was listed as his father, informing him that Herrick was missing. There is a pencil note saying that Herrick was buried in a church cemetery and another that he was reported as possibly having crashed at Arnaville. A memo from the Imperial War Graves Commission on 5 March 1921 confirms that he was initially buried close-by in the nearby Array Churchyard, Lorraine – Grave 4.

Arnaville would have been in German held hands at the time, the frontline was near Pont-à-Mousson just to the south, on the Moselle River. His squadron was based at Azelot, about 60 km from Arnaville, again to the south, just below Nancy.

Herrick's bereaved father later received a letter from Major J C Quinell, the officer commanding RAF 104 Squadron in which he referred to Lieutenant Leyden as 'a most excellent officer who did splendid work and would have made a name for himself in the Royal Air Force. Please accept on behalf of his fellow-officers with the squadron my deepest sympathy in your loss'.

Another note on Herrick's Casualty Card states that 'according to inf. from German Red X this officer was killed on 13 August, buried at Ehrenfriedersdorf'. This is most probably a mis-identification error, an Airco DH.9a had the range to reach Ehrenfriedersdorf but would not have the fuel to fly back. Ehrenfriedersdorf is approximately 650Km east of Azelot.

The list of aircraft flown by Herrick Leyden from his service record:

Farman S11 Shorthorn (MF S.H.)

Armstrong Whitworth (possibly a F.K.3)

Royal Aircraft Factory B.E. (possibly a B.E.2)

Airco DH.6

Royal Aircraft Factory R.E.8

Airco DH.9

After the war, Second Lieutenant Leyden and the other three who died were reinterred and buried together in one grave at the Perreuse Chateau, Franco British National Cemetery, 60 km east of Paris. Leyden is commemorated on the war memorials of Perth Academy and the St John the Baptist RC Church, Melville Street, Perth, and on the Bishop Gore School War Memorial, Sketty, West Glamorgan.

Robert William Gladstone Leyden, born 21 April 1900, followed his brother into the RAF. He joined on 8 April 1918 after being declared fit as pilot. There is a note to say that he transferred from Army School to 32 TDS (Training Depot Squadron) at RAF Montrose, RAF 20 Group, effective 14 September 1918. This was less than two months from the end of the war. He was sent to Edinburgh Castle for dispersal back to civilian life on 4 January 1919.

NOTES: The de Havilland Airco DH.9 was first flown in July 1917. They suffered heavy losses due to their unreliability and the poor performance of the 230 hp Armstrong Siddeley Puma 6-cylinder engine. Alternative engines were sought and eventually the US 400hp V-12 Liberty engine was adopted and a redesigned aircraft, the DH.9a was put into service.

During the Great War, 3,024 DH.9s and 2,300 DH.9as were built. They were armed with a forward firing Vickers machine gun and one or two rear firing Lewis guns on a Scarf ring. The DH.9as could carry up to 740 lb of bombs under the wings and on fuselage racks.

RAF 104 Squadron was formed on 4 September 1917 at Wyton, England. It moved to Andover and then to France in May 1918. When the war ended, the Squadron returned home, first to RAF Turnhouse, Edinburgh and was disbanded on 30 June 1919, at RAF Crail, Fife. 104 Squadron was part of the Independent Force (RAF) of the British Expeditionary Force (BEF). The Independent Air Force (IAF) was a First World War strategic bombing force which was part of the RFC/RAF that could strike against German railways, aerodromes, and industrial centres without co-ordination with the Army or Navy.

Also on 13 August 1918, USAF Pilot, Field Eugene Kindley shot down Lothar von Richthofen, the brother of the late great German war ace Manfred von Richthofen. Lothar had 40 confirmed air-to-air victories at the time, he suffered serious wounds when he crashed and never flew in combat again.

RAF Turnberry was used for the testing of Barnes Wallis's 'Highball' bouncing bombs by RAF 618 squadron during the Second World War. An old French Battleship, the Courbet and later the HMS Malaya were anchored in Loch Striven (above Rothesay) and were used as practice targets for the bouncing bombs. The loch was also used for the training of X-craft midget submarines. Both these weapons were to be used against the German Battleship Tirpitz, anchored in a Norwegian Fjord. The Tirpitz was later sunk on 12 November 1944 by Avro Lancaster bombers using the Barnes Wallis *'Tallboy 'bombs*.

The day before Herrick Leyden was killed marked the end of the Battle of Amiens (8-12 August 1918), and the start of the Allied counteroffensive known as the 'Hundred Days Offensive'. This led to the end of the war with the Armistice being signed in a railroad carriage at Compiègne on 11 November 1918. It had all started on 21 March 1918 with the last effort, the 'German Spring Offensives', a series of large-scale surprise attacks against the Allied lines along the mostly northern length of the Western Front. By the end of August 1918, the Germans had been driven back and greatly weakened by the loss of men and morale. At 11 am on 11 November 1918 – 'the eleventh hour of the eleventh day of the eleventh month' – a ceasefire came into effect.

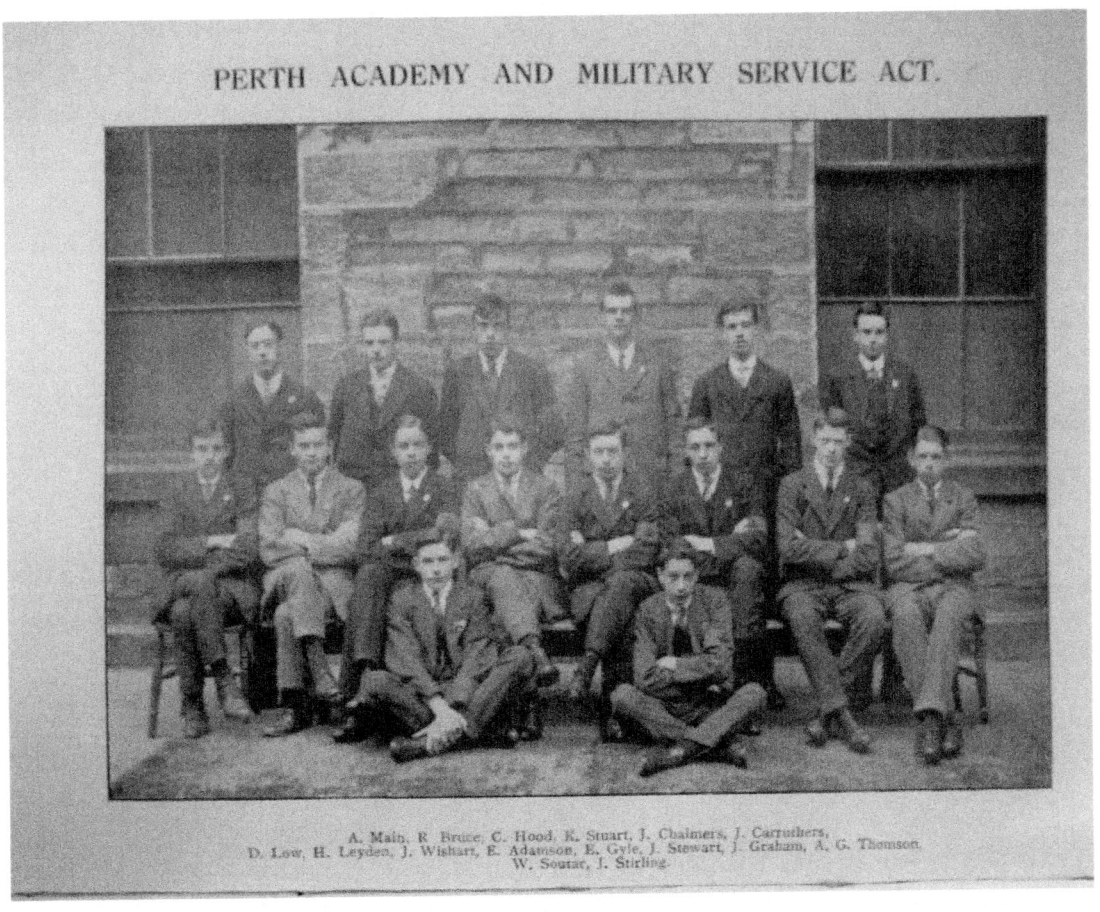

Image courtesy of the Perth Academy Flowers of the Forest First World War commemorative project - Herrick Leyden, 2nd from left, middle row - William Soutar (Perth Poet) 1st on left, front row

157 Extracted from WO file Perth Cl a / 228
9DE/17/165 R Weeding
20/6/50

Army Form B. 2513.

RECORD OF SERVICE PAPER **A.**

For men deemed to be enlisted in H.M. Regular Forces for General Service with the Colours or in the Reserve for the period of the War, or Ex-Soldiers recalled for Service with the Colours, under the provisions of the Military Service Acts, 1916.

No. S/18816 Christian Names: Herrick Surname: Leyden
Corps: 3rd B.W.

Questions to be put to the Reservist on Joining.

1. What is your Name? — 1. Christian Names: Herrick Surname: Leyden
2. What is your full Address? — 2. 9 Pitcullen Tce, Perth
3. Are you a British Subject? — 3. Yes
4. What is your Age? — 4. 18 Years 10 Months
5. What is your Trade or Calling? — 5. Motor Driver
6. Are you Married? — 6. No
7. Have you ever served in any branch of His Majesty's Forces, naval or military? If so, which? — 7. No
8. Have you any preference for any particular branch of the service, if so, which? — 8.
9. Are you desirous of serving in the Royal Navy, if so, state your qualifications. — 9.

I, Herrick Leyden do solemnly declare that the above answers made by me to the above questions are true.

Christian Name: Herrick Surname: Leyden SIGNATURE OF RECRUIT.
Date: 10 1 1917
Place: Perth   W M Inlace Signature of Witness.

EXEMPTION FROM COMBATANT SERVICE ON CONSCIENTIOUS GROUNDS.

If the Recruit has been exempted by a Tribunal on conscientious grounds from serving as a combatant it should be so stated here.

MEDICAL CLASSIFICATION AS TO FITNESS FOR SERVICE ON JOINING.

Classification:

*To be filled in by the Recruiting Officer after Classification by the Medical Board.

† Certificate of Approving Officer.

I approve the acceptance of the above-named man, and appoint him to the The Black Watch
Date: 16 JAN 1917 19
Place: PERTH
Colonel, Commanding Depot, The Black Watch. Approving Officer.

Lieutenant Courteney Patrick Flowerdew Lowson

Lieutenant Courtenay Patrick Flowerdew Lowson was born at Hollycot, Lasswade, Midlothian on 4 April 1897. His father was James Gray Flowerdew Lowson, Paper Manufacturer, and member of the King's Bodyguard for Scotland. His mother was Adelaide Louisa Scott, the daughter of Colonel Courtenay Harvey Saltron Scott (1833–1925) of the Bengal Staff Corps and Highland Light Infantry, the son of General Sir Hopton Scott, veteran of the Crimean War and Indian Mutiny.

Lieutenant Lowson's grandfather was William Fullerton Lowson (1814 – 1893) born in Arbroath, who in 1865 purchased Balthayock Estate, near Kinfauns. He also maintained a house at Upper Pleasance, Dundee and his business interests were located at Cowgate and St. Andrew's Street, Dundee.

Lieutenant C P F Lowson was 20 years old when he died. His ashes were originally interred in the family mausoleum at Kinfauns Parish Churchyard. In 1926 they were removed and placed in the church wall behind the tablet to his memory, which was designed by Lorimer and Matthew, Architects, Edinburgh. Recorded at the time of his death his father was Dr. James Gray Flowerdew Lowson, Ph.D., of Quarwood, Stow-on-the-Wold, Gloucestershire.

Lieutenant Lowson was educated (from September 1910 to 1915) at Boxgrove Preparatory School, Winchester, and the Royal Military Academy Sandhurst. Due to the outbreak of war, he did not take up a place at Christ Church College, Oxford University. He was recorded as being a good horseman, having passed the Cavalry School Course at Tidworth. He was also much interested in mechanics.

2nd Lieutenant C. P. F. Lowson

In December 1915, Lieutenant Lowson was gazetted Second Lieutenant in the Rifle Brigade and was promoted Lieutenant in July 1916. After leaving Sandhurst he was attached as an Observer to the Royal Flying Corp and was posted to France with RFC 22 Squadron. Lieutenant Lowson flew as observer on many hazardous missions taking photographic images during the Battle of the Somme (1 July 1916 – 18 November 1916).

Lieutenant Lowson obtained his Pilot's Certificate and was gazetted Flying Officer on 4 July 1917 with seniority from 21 March 1917. He was then attached to RFC 81 Squadron at Scampton, Lincolnshire.

Lieutenant Lowson was killed in a flying accident on 3 November 1917 when his aircraft was in mid-air collision whilst carrying out banked turns, with another aircraft flown by Lieutenant Owen Ellis Augustus Allen. Lieutenant Courtenay Patrick Flowerdew Lowson (instructor) was flying Avro 504J, B3224,

Lieutenant Owen Ellis Augustus Allen was flying Avro 504J, B3194. Lieutenant Allen was still alive when he reached the ground but died later in the 4th Northern General Hospital in Lincoln. He was 24 years old and is buried in Cambridge (Histon Road) Cemetery. A passenger in Lieutenant Allen's Avro 504j, 2nd Lieutenant Edward James Gallagher was injured but survived. The subsequent investigation put this crash down to pilot error.

Lieutenant Allen was previously with the 9th Battalion Suffolk Regiment, flew as an observer with "A" flight RFC 22 Squadron and posted to 37 Training Squadron on 6 August 1917. RFC 37 Training Squadron operated out of RFC Scampton between November 1916 and September 1917, equipped with Avro 504, FK3 and DH6 aircraft.

NOTES: The author, Margaret Julia Scott (1843–1913) (Alternate Name(s): Colquhoun (maiden name); M.J. Colquhoun (pseudonym)) was born in 1843 in Calcutta, India, the daughter of James Colquhoun. In 1862 she married Colonel Courtenay Harvey Saltron Scott (1833–1925) of the Bengal Staff Corps and Highland Light Infantry, the son of General Sir Hopton Scott and veteran of the Crimean War and Indian Mutiny. Margaret Julia Scott lived most of her first thirty years in India and returned to England in the 1870s when her husband retired. Her first book was The Invasions of India from Central Asia (1879) which she followed with three novels: *Under Orders (1883)* set in India; *Primus in Indis (1885),* a historical novel about India and Clive; and *Every Inch a Soldier (1888)* about the mutiny. She died in 1913 in London. References: British Census (1881); Burke; Times (11 February 1925)

The only brother of Lieutenant Courteney Patrick Flowerdew Lowson, Denys Colquhoun Flowerdew Lowson was Lord Mayor of London from 1950-51 and was made a Baronet.

The first battle for Kitchener's new volunteer army, the Battle of the Somme, the British suffered 400,000 casualties for negligible gains. The 57,000 casualties of the first day of the battle is the most ever suffered in one day.

An Avro 504 aircraft was the first British aircraft to be shot down by the Germans, on 22 August 1914. It became obsolete as a frontline aircraft coming into its own as a trainer aircraft with thousands being built during WW1. Twenty-four companies are recorded as manufacturing the Avro 504 under licence and they were operated by thirty-nine countries.

The Polikarpov Po-2 (also known as U-2), a 1928 development of the Avro 504 was in production with the USSR until 1978. The U-2 became best known as the aircraft used by the 588th Night Bomber Regiment, during the Second World War, composed of an all-woman pilot and ground crew complement. The unit was notorious for daring low-altitude night raids on German rear-area positions.

The pilots earned the nickname *"Night Witches"* and earned numerous Hero of the Soviet Union and Order of the Red Banner medals.

The Sphere 19 December 1917 (Courteney Lowson, third row, left)

Lieutenant John Watson McCash

The Royal Flying Corp squadron of a young incredibly brave young pilot from Perth was equipped with the new outstandingly manoeuvrable Sopwith Camel aircraft in October 1917, just in time for the Battle of Cambrai one month later where in a dogfight with the Red Baron's Flying Circus, he was shot down.

Towards the end of the year 1917, the First World War, the war to end all wars, was to see the first large-scale effective use of tanks at the Battle of Cambrai (20 November 1917 – 7 December 1917) in France. Rittmeister Manfred Freiherr von Richthofen, the Red Baron, was returning to command his flying circus after convalescent leave following a serious head wound that he received on 6 July 1917.

Lieutenant John Watson McCash of The Black Watch, attached to the Royal Flying Corps (RFC), was reported as missing in the Perthshire Advertiser on Wednesday 5 December 1917. He was the 24-year-old son of William F McCash (Grain Merchant, J McCash & Son) and Alice H McCash, Cornhill House, Jeanfield Road, Perth. Lieutenant McCash was the nephew of J B McCash, Solicitor, Perth. The firm of J. McCash & Sons of Dovecotland, Perth have been supplying animal feed since 1746.

John Watson McCash was educated at Clifton Bank School, St Andrews, and later the University of St Andrews. He studied civil engineering and worked for the Caledonian Railway Company in Perth. He enlisted in the Scottish Horse, a Yeomanry regiment of the British Army's, Territorial Army. The Scottish Horse fought as the 13th Battalion of The Black Watch during the First World War. McCash was promoted to corporal and was commissioned in October 1913 into The Black Watch, 6th Battalion, as an officer. He was then attached in April 1917 to the RFC as a pilot serving with No. 3 Squadron of the RFC. At the time of his death was flying from an Advanced Landing Ground (ALG) at Bapaume. In October of 1917, his squadron was equipped with Sopwith Camel aircraft which were just being introduced to the fighting on the Western Front in France.

On 20 November 1917, at dawn, approximately 6.20 am, the British launched an attack at Cambrai (Schlacht von Cambrai) in the département of the Nord, Hauts-de-France region. Six British infantry divisions led by 320 tanks created on the first day a hole in the German defences ten kilometres wide and six kilometres deep. The town of Cambrai was an important supply point for the German Hindenburg Line (Siegfriedstellung), and it's capture along with the nearby Bourlon Ridge would threaten the rear of the German line to the North. The British infantry carried forward the momentum of the attack, they reached a point five kilometres from the *Luftstreitkräfte* (Imperial German Air Service) (Flying Circus) Jasta 11 base at Boistrancourt where they began shelling the airfield, the Jasta retreated to an improvised base at Valenciennes.

On 22 November 1917, the weather prevented flying except at extremely low height, but on 23 November, bitter air combat took place. Just after noon, Jasta 5 Flying Circus aircraft engaged Sopwith Camels over Bourlon Wood. Three Camels got on the tail of Jasta 5's commander, Oberleutnant Richard Flasher, who was saved by the intervention of Vizefeldwebel, (Leutnant der Reserve), Fritz Rumey and Leutnant Otto Könnecke. Both pilots were reported to have shot down one Sopwith Camel each. In fact, only Fritz Rumey received credit for both.

The Sopwith Camels, B5153 & B2369, shot down were piloted by:

Lieutenant Frederick Henry Stephens, 3rd Squadron RFC & Canadian Infantry, age unknown (Canadian).

Lieutenant John Watson McCash, 3rd Squadron RFC & 6th Battalion, Black Watch (Royal Highlanders), age 24.

The body of John Watson McCash was not found. He is commemorated at the Arras Flying Services Memorial (Commonwealth Graves Commission) which is in the Faubourg d'Amiens Cemetery, Arras, France. McCash is also remembered on the War memorial in the parish church at Tibbermuir and the book of remembrance at St Andrew's University.

Second Lieutenant W F McCash, a son of Mr and Mrs McCash of Queen Street, Craigie, Perth, educated at Perth Academy and a member of the firm of James McCash & Sons, Grain Merchants, was awarded in early 1917 the Military Cross. Lieutenant McCash was 29 years of age enlisted in the Black Watch at the start of the war. He had been at the front for eight months when he received his commission in The Gordon Highlanders. When he returned to the front he was severely wounded in November 1917. The Gordon Highlanders also took part in the Battle of Cambrai.

NOTES:

During the Second World War another member of the McCash family, Pilot Officer James McCash, was killed ferrying a Bristol Blenheim to Tunisia on 18 June 1940. (See Second World War Aviators - James McCash)

Jagdgeschwader 1 (JG1) had been rushed from Ypres to Cambrai by 23 November 1917, following the launch of the British offensive, and did much to stabilise the air war over the battlefield when the bad weather permitted. Perhaps John McCash's Squadron was unaware of or not expecting to come up against the Flying Circus over Cambrai.

Vizefeldwebel, (Leutnant der Reserve), Fritz Rumey. Rumey was one of the Flying Circus pilots of Jasta 5 which was one of the four squadron wings (Jasta's) in Jagdgeschwader 1 (JG1) under the command since 26 July 1917, of Rittmeister Manfred Freiherr von Richthofen, known as the 'Red Baron', (in German as the 'Der Rote Kampfflieger'). Fritz Rumey was one of the very best aces, if you take away the number of reconnaissance aircraft shot down and look at just the number of combat fighter aircraft shot down, his tally was 45, Richthofen's only 35.

A replica of Rumey's Albatross aircraft was built in 2016 by The Vintage Aviator Ltd in Wellington, New Zealand. They have built several full-scale, 100% accurate reproductions of WW1 German Albatros D. Va fighters. It may have been re-painted since then.

On the side of the aircraft, there is a picture of his demon head motif, this was how his aircraft was re-painted when Richthofen took over command in July 1917 at Boistrancourt airfield (French: Aérodrome de Boistrancourt-Suererie, german: Feldflugplatz Boistrancourt).

Perhaps in my view, the two best aircraft at this time during WW1 were the German Albatros D. Va and on the British side, the Sopwith Camel. You had to be good to fly either, both were extremely deadly in the right hands as fighter aircraft.

Rittmeister Manfred Freiherr von Richthofen was flying in his red Albatross D.V. above Bourlon Wood that day, about an hour later. He forced the pilot of a No. 64 Squadron, Airco D. H. 5 aircraft to make an emergency landing. His next victim was Lieutenant J A V Boddy flying D. H. 5, A9299, his gun had jammed, and he was trying to clear it when Richthofen's red Albatross opened fire on him. A bullet fractured his skull but somehow, he manged to land his aircraft near the northeast corner of the wood, additionally breaking his thighs. Boddy recovered from his injuries, but his flying days were over. No. 64 Squadron lost six D.H. 5's that day. None of the pilots were killed, but two were wounded.

The Royal Flying Corp losses for 23 November 1917 was 14 with 15 enemy aircraft claimed shot down. In the air that day over Cambrai, were several other notable 'Aces', Manfred's brother. Lothar Richtohfen, and Captain James T B McCudden, VC, DSO & Bar, MC & Bar, MM (57 victories). McCudden first served with 3 Squadron RFC as a mechanic and then observer (June 1913 – January 1916) before becoming a pilot. On the ground, Private Archie McMillan of the Argyll and Sutherland Highlanders was one of many thousands killed on the ground, he was a footballer with Glasgow Celtic.

The Royal Flying Corps was established in 1912, just three years after Louis Bleriot had flown across the English Channel. The RFC during 1914 and 1915 the recruits were mainly professional soldiers who had already seen some action in the trenches. By 1916, many of the new recruits were volunteers and those who were technically skilled railwaymen, such as John McCash were much favoured by the RFC.

JG1 were the first squadrons to receive the new Fokker DR.1 triplane, as famously associated with the Red Baron. The first two were received on 21 August 1917. The German Ace pilot, Werner Voss was perhaps the greatest exponent, scoring ten victories in just 21 days before he died in combat. Rittmeister Richthofen left on convalescence leave on 6 September, returning on 23 October 1917. Richthofen spent time hunting on the estate of the Duke of Saxe-Coburg-Gotha (German: Sachsen-Coburg und Gotha), visiting his family at Schweidnitz and going to Adlershof for more consultations about aircraft design. Adlershof was the headquarters of the German Experimental Institute for Aviation

(Deutsche Versuchsanstalt für Luftfahrt – DVL). During Richthofen's time away, several fatal crashes involving the new Fokker DR.1 saw it withdrawn for modifications. They were grounded from 23 October 1917 until early December 1917.

Fritz Rumey was a German 'Ace', credited at the time of his death with 45 victories. He was a holder of the Pour le Mérite (Blue Max) and the Goldenes Militär-Verdienstkreuz (Golden Military Merit Cross). He was only one of five pilots to receive both these awards. There are two accounts of Rumey's death on 27 September 1918, that following a mid-air collision with a Royal Aircraft Factory S.E.5a of 32 Squadron flown by Captain G E B Lawson, his parachute failed to open, and he threw it away. The second account, that during a full throttle pursuit of the S.E.5, it caused the fabric to peel off from his upper wing and this caused his aircraft to fall from the sky and crash. Lawson survived and was awarded a DFC, Lawson later died in a flying accident in 1922. Parachutes were also used in limited numbers by the Germans in the last months of the war. Famously, Flying Circus 'Ace' Ernst Udet used one on 29 June 1918 following a mid-air crash with a French Breguet aircraft.

Leutnant Otto Könnecke survived the war, he died 25 January 1956, age 64. During the Great War he received the Pour le Mérite (Blue Max), the Goldenes Militär-Verdienstkreuz, Knight's Cross with Swords of the Royal House Order of Hohenzollern and the Iron Cross. His tally was 35 victories.

Manfred von Richthofen's death was to come on 21 April 1918 when he was killed following an attack by the Canadian, Captain Arthur "Roy" Brown (23 December 1893 – 9 March 1944) in his Sopwith Camel. Brown died of a heart attack just after posing for a photograph with the WW2 Canadian flying ace, George Frederick "Buzz" Beurling (known as "The Falcon of Malta" and the "Knight of Malta"). Cedric Bassett Popkin (20 June 1890 – 26 January 1968) is considered the likely person to have killed Richthofen. Popkin was an anti-aircraft (AA) machine gunner with the First Australian Imperial Force (AIF).

At the Battle of Cambrai, the German artillery and infantry defences exposed the frailties of the Mark IV tank. By the second day of the battle only half the tanks were still operational. The Sopwith Camel first appeared over the third Battle of Ypres (also known as Passchendaele, 31 July 1917 – 10 November 1917), it lasted over 100 days. In that time, the Allies advanced about 5 miles for the loss of over 250,000 soldiers killed, wounded or missing. The overall average life expectancy during the Great War of a pilot was 92 flying hours. There was nonetheless no shortage of volunteers for aircrew training. The Sopwith Camel with its outstanding manoeuvrability made it deadly in the hands of a good pilot. It dominated the skies over the trenches and became the RFC/RAF's main fighter until the Armistice, on the 11th hour of the 11th day of November 1918.

The 2008 movie, The Red Baron starring Matthias Schweighöfer, Joseph Fiennes, Til Schweiger and Lena Headey is the best to watch. The music is also excellent, with a couple of haunting tracks by Dirk Reichardt and Stefan Hansen that linger in your brain.

Bourlon Wood Reconnaissance Photograph

Lewis Gun being used for AA defence

Jagdgeschwader 1 pilots

Fritz Rumey Manfred von Richthofen

Lieutenant Peter MacFarlane

Lieutenant Peter MacFarlane was part of an RAF 32 Squadron offensive patrol of 40 aircraft, when, on 10 August 1918 he was shot down whilst escorting 12 bombers of RAF 27 and RAF49 Squadrons to attack Péronne railway station, 50 km east of Amiens. Lieutenant Peter MacFarlane was flying a Royal Aircraft Factory S.E.5a, aircraft, C8838 from his squadron airfield at Warlincourt-lès-Pas, Letiště, La Bellevue Aerodrome [1916-1919]. La Bellevue Aerodrome is 38 km north of Amiens.

The most probable account of what happened to Lieutenant MacFarlane was that between 11.30am – 11.45am on 10 August 1918 three RAF 32 squadron S.E.5a's of the lowest flight escorting the bombers, were attacked by nine German Fokker aircraft. Some of the RAF 32 Squadron S.E.5a's covering above the bombers were brought down into the dogfight resulting in four Fokkers being shot down out of control.

One of the pilots involved in the dogfight, a Lieutenant Donaldson (US) had to evade the attention of four more Fokker's and about his combat wrote: *'Pilot observed Lieutenant MacFarlane fire at one EA (Enemy Aircraft), and saw it fall side by side with EA shot by pilot at 10,000ft.'*

An opinion is that the enemy aircraft had been fighting with the S.E.5a of Lieutenant MacFarlane and was at the same time shot at by Lieutenant Donaldson – his report further reads, *'Pilot observed 9 Fokker Biplanes, at 13000 feet, over PERONNE, at 11.30 am dive on 3 SE5a. Pilot coming to their assistance, fired 150 rounds into first EA at close range, EA turned over on its back, and went down in a flat spin, and was observed to spin, out of control, about 10000 feet…'*

It appears that Lieutenant MacFarlane engaged and fired at an enemy aircraft and was subsequently shot down by that aircraft (Berthold). Lieutenant Donaldson then shot down the enemy aircraft. The enemy aircraft was a Fokker D.VII, painted with a scarlet engine cowling and a royal blue fuselage with a winged sword emblem. It was flown by the German flying ace (44 victories) and commander of *Jagdgeschwader II* (Fighter Wing 2), Hauptmann Oskar Gustav Rudolf Berthold (24 March 1891 – 15 March 1920) *Pour le Mérite; Iron Cross: 2nd class; Iron Cross: 1st class*.

On 10 August 1918, the German flying ace, Rudolf Berthold led 12 of his pilots into battle and claimed he shot down a Royal Aircraft Factory S.E.5a fighter for his 43rd victory (Lieutenant MacFarlane) and an Airco DH.9 bomber for his 44th. When he tried to pull away from the Airco DH.9 at 800 meters (2,625 ft) altitude, his controls came loose in his hand. His attempt to use a parachute failed because it required the use of both hands. His Fokker D.VII crashed into a house in Ablaincourt-Pressoir (40 km west of Amiens) with such force that its engine fell into the cellar. German infantrymen plucked him from the rubble and rushed him to hospital. His right arm was rebroken at its previous fracture. Rudolf Berthold would never fly again. On 12 August 1918, Berthold checked himself out of hospital and returned to take command of *Jagdstaffel 15* (Fighter Squadron 15). On the 14th, Kaiser Wilhelm II personally ordered the ace to take sick leave, the war ended whilst he was covalescing.

Berthold had earlier on 10 October 1917 hit in the arm by a ricocheting British bullet. This then should have meant the amputation of his arm, but his sister Franziska arranged specialist care and after months of being bedridden he returned to command one of the world's first air combat fighter wings in February 1918. Berthold spent his convalescent leave learning to write with his left hand. He believed, *"If I can write, I can fly."* His right arm remained paralyzed, painful and he was dependent on narcotics to continue flying.

Peter MacFarlane was the son of Daniel and Isabella MacFarlane of Nether Obney, Bankfoot. McFarlane was appointed as a Civil Service assistant clerk on 14 October 1912. He was 23 years old when he was killed and is commemorated at the Arras Flying Memorial, Faubourg-d'Amiens Cemetery, Boulevard du General de Gaulle in the Pas de Calais, France and on a memorial plaque of the Scottish Insurance Commission (Scotland Office) in Edinburgh.

NOTES:

On an offensive patrol over Fimes on 25 July 1918 RAF 32 Squadron engaged 7 enemy aircraft (probably from Jasta 27) part of a larger formation at different heights. Lt. Callender claimed a Fokker DVII destroyed and Capt. Green, Lt. Donaldson, Lt. MacFarlane, Lt. Trusler and Lt. MacBean each claimed Fokker DVII's out of control. Lt. Struben was missing after this combat and later confirmed as a POW.

The S.E.5 was described as a nimble fighter and the 'Spitfire' of World War One. It was one of the fastest (138 mph) aircraft of the war, while being both stable and relatively manoeuvrable. Together with the Sopwith Camel, the S.E.5 was instrumental in regaining allied air superiority in mid-1917 and maintaining it for the rest of the war. Royal Aircraft Factory S.E.5a, aircraft, C8838 was accepted for allotment to the Expeditionary Force at Brooklands Aircraft Acceptance Park on 25 May 1918. It was allocated to RFC 32 Squadron on 28 June 1918. It appears to have had an engine failure, a Wolseley W.4a Viper liquid-cooled 8 -cylinder V-engine 203 hp (149.3 KW) No. 2167 two days later and was flying with engine no. 2487 when it was struck off charge on 10 August 1918.

In February 1919, Rudolf Berthold put out a call for volunteers to form a Freikorps militia to stave off communist insurrectionists. Freikorps were irregular German and other European military volunteer units, or paramilitaries. The Freikorps also fought against communists and Bolsheviks in Eastern Europe, most notably East Prussia, Latvia, Silesia, and Poland. On 13 March 1920, Berthold and his men took part in the Kapp Putsch, an attempted coup against the German national government. By late afternoon ammunition was running low, Berthold called a truce and tried to negotiate safe passage for his men. He exited a back door of a Hamburg schoolhouse they occupied and a mob overpowered Berthold. His handgun was taken from him and used to shoot him twice in the head and four times in the body as the mob mauled him. Two of his old flying comrades who lived in Hamburg rushed to the hospital. They stayed with Berthold's body until his sister Franziska arrived from Berlin. Berthold's *Pour le Merite, Iron Cross First Class, and Pilot's Badge* were retrieved from a rubbish dump before she arrived.

The German air service introduced in the summer of 1918, becoming the world's first air service to introduce a standard parachute to airman. Out of the first 70 German airmen to bail out, around a third died, mostly caused by the chute or ripcord becoming entangled in the airframe of their spinning aircraft. A parachute saved the life of the German flying ace Ernest Udet on 29 June 1918. He returned to flying later that day and chocked up another 27 victories before the end of the war. The RAF started issuing parachutes to airmen in September 1918.

A group of pilots and Royal Aircraft Factory S.E.5As of No. 32 Squadron at Humieres aerodrome, 6 April 1918. © IWM

Royal Aircraft Factory S.E.5As of No. 32 Squadron at Humieres aerodrome near St. Pol, 6 April 1918. © IWM

Second Lieutenant Alexander McKenzie

Over the Western Front on Thursday 13 June 1918, during World War One, 2nd Lieutenant Alexander McKenzie, 16939 was flying as an Observer in Airco DH.4, A7466 of RAF 55 Squadron. His pilot was Lieutenant William Legge (see Sergeant Alexander Stewart Allan), and they were last seen under control during a bombing mission over their intended target, near Trèves. They were then engaged by enemy aircraft and shot down in flames.

RAF 55 squadron was the first squadron to be equipped with the new Airco DH4's before moving to France in the spring of 1917. Their first major action was at the Battle of Arras (9 April to 16 May 1917) bombing the Valenciennes railway station on 23 April 1917.

RAF 55 Squadron was based initially at Fienvillers (north of Amiens) and then Boisdinghem (just west of Saint-Omer) where 55 Squadron patrolled over Flanders and the Belgian coast. They were transferred south to Ochey (west of Nancy) and then Tantonville (south of Nancy and west of the Vosges mountains). On 5 June 1918, just 8 days before Alexander McKenzie's last flight and the day of his promotion and posting to the squadron, the squadron moved 17 km north to Azelot, sharing the aerodrome with 99 & 104 Squadrons. From here RAF 55 Squadron raided deep into Germany itself, hitting such targets as Mannheim and Kaiserslauten (east of the USAF Ramstein Air Base) in the German Rhineland-Palatinate.

Their intended target was not Trèves in France, which lies 400km south, just south of Lyon, but the German city of Trier, 150 km north on the river Moselle, just to the east of the Luxembourg border (15 km). Trier was formerly known in English as Trèves. (Karl Marx was born in Trier.)

At the age of 21, Alexander McKenzie enlisted in the Royal Flying Corps on 27 December 1915. In civilian life, Alexander was a chauffeur and the son of Mr and Mrs Simon Peter McKenzie, of Borland, Blacklunans, Blairgowrie, Perthshire. (Blacklunans is north of the Bridge of Cally, halfway to the Glenshee Ski Centre, on the road west over to Bridge of Brewlands and Kirkton of Glenisla, parish of Glenshee.) Alexander according to his official record was Presbyterian, 5 feet 8 ¾ inches tall, had a chest size of 36 ½ inches, fair hair, grey eyes, and fresh complexion.

On 20 April 1918, Alexander was promoted to Flight Cadet, confirmed on 29 April 1918. It is probable that at the same time he was promoted, he was immediately posted to the British Expeditionary Force in France to join the Royal Air Force 55 Squadron on 5 June 1918. Sadly, he was shot down and killed only 8 days later. (On April 1, 1918, the Royal Air Force (RAF) was formed with the amalgamation of the Royal Flying Corps (RFC) and the Royal Naval Air Service (RNAS).)

Lieutenant William Legge, age 23, was the son of William R. and Annie Legge, of 3, Fingzies Place, Leith, Edinburgh. Both 2nd Lieutenant Alexander McKenzie and Lieutenant William Legge are buried in Cologne Southern Cemetery, Nordrhein-Westfalen, Germany

NOTES: On 15 October 1917, the British War Cabinet made a decision regarding the strategic bombardment of Germany. The military in France were told that *"immediate arrangements should be made for the conduct of long-range offensive operations: against German towns where factories existed for the production of munitions of all kinds."* Two days later, eight Airco DH.4 out of eleven launched- from RAF 55 Squadron dropped 1,792 pounds: of bombs on the Burbach works at Saarbrücken.

RAF 55 Squadron was the first to frequently raid deep into Germany, one of its first raids to attack the railway station at Mannheim. They narrowly missed bombing, by one hour, Kaiser Wilhelm II, the last German Emperor and King of Prussia who was visiting Manheim. The Allies did attempt on an earlier occasion to deliberately kill Kaiser Wilhelm II, taking off from Ruisseauville Airfield (45 km east of Le Touguet) at 4.50 am on Sunday 2 June, 12 RAF de Havilland-4 bombers (Squadron unknown) reached the Kaiser's secret Western Front residence at Trelon (160 km, near the Belgium border) at 5:25am. They dropped around a dozen 50kg bombs and two dozen 11kg ones.

RAF 55 Squadron developed tactics of flying in wedge formations, bombing on the leader's command and with the massed defensive fire of the formation deterring attacks by enemy fighters. The squadron flew 221 bombing missions during the war, dropping approximately 141 long tons (143,000 kg) of bombs.

The Airco DH.4 (The Aircraft Manufacturing Company Limited) was a British two-seat biplane day bomber. It was designed by Geoffrey de Havilland for Airco and was the first British two-seat light day- bomber capable of defending itself. Following a chance meeting at the Royal Aircraft Factory, Farnborough, Captain Geoffrey de Havilland joined the company in May 1914 as Chief Designer – his machines (denoted DH) accounted for 30% of all British and US aircraft in the WW1 years. The Airco DH4 day bomber was easily the best day bomber of WW1, usually fitted with a Rolls Royce Eagle engine, the predecessor of the Merlin (although due to shortages, the Beardmore Halford Pulinger, Puma and Royal Aircraft Factory, 3a were also often used), with a Pilot, Observer, strong defensive armament, a very good bomb load and using an oxygen system owing to the high altitudes at which the aircraft could operate at.

Perth born Sergeant Alexander Stewart Allan, 406711, Medaille Militaire, was also an observer in RAF 55 Squadron. Allan also flew with Lieutenant William Legge.

Perth born Group Captain Robert Halley was a member of Royal Naval Service 16 Squadron which operated out of Autreville, 35 km to the west of Azelot, during that summer of 1918. Flying Handley Page 0/100 and 0/400 aircraft, they carried about five times the bomb load of the Airco DH.4, although at a slower speed and lower altitude.

Second Lieutenant John Ross

On 8 August 1918, the Battle of Amiens offensive opened at 4.20 am with a deafening artillery barrage by over two thousand guns. Moments later a combined assault by infantry and tanks commenced along a twenty-mile front between Morlancourt and La Neuville-Sire-Bernard (on the river Ayre to the south).

The advance went well, there was a heavy ground mist which helped conceal the advancing Allied armies. The German army was taken by surprise and offered only slight opposition. By the end of the day the front line had been pushed back between seven and eight miles in places.

For the Royal Air Force (RAF) it was one of the most important and complex of days, with an unprecedented level of liaison with ground troops, artillery, and tanks, in addition to offensive patrolling, bombing and low attack work. Allied aircraft were already in the air by the time the offensive began. Gloomy conditions hindered their effectiveness, but as conditions cleared around 9.00 am, the RAF dominated the air throughout the morning. The afternoon saw a major change of plans, it was now to attack and destroy bridges. It was hoped that this would cause chaos and hinder the German army's retreat. Two hundred and five attacks were made on the bridges with twelve tons of bombs dropped, with limited success.

German air reinforcements, including Jagdgeschwader I (JG I) *"The Flying Circus"* (Der Fliegende Zirkus) were called in to assist and it soon became apparent that they need to defend the bridges in the river Somme area. Titanic struggles ensued in the air throughout the day with heavy losses incurred on both sides. The Allies lost 105 aircraft in the many air battles on 8 August 1918. The German JG 1 fighter wing was reduced from fifty to eleven serviceable aircraft and was withdrawn from the fighting.

Second Lieutenant John Ross was the son of Robert and Mary Ross, 4 Clinton Street, Newburgh, Fife. John Ross was the Observer in an Airco DH.9 C2195, single engine biplane bomber of RAF 49 Squadron based at Beauvois (50 km west of Lens, 57 km north of Amiens), France. The pilot of the DH.9 was Lieutenant M D Allen who survived.

At 4.45pm, on a bombing mission near Amiens, they were hit by ground anti-aircraft fire ('Archie' was the RFC vernacular name). The DH.9 was shot through with nineteen-year-old Second Lieutenant Ross being killed in action. Second Lieutenant Ross had previously survived several crashes and forced landings with Lieutenant Allen, 30 June 1918, and 1 July 1918.

Second Lieutenant John Ross is buried and commemorated at the Roye New British Cemetery, 42 km southwest of Amiens.

NOTES: Jagdgeschwader I (JG I) had been subjected to intensive operations over the Amiens battle in August 1918, by mid-September an exhausted Jagdgeschwader I (JG I) was withdrawn from the British part of the front, having lost all four Jasta commanders by the end of August; Erich Lowenhardt of Jasta 10 was killed, Jasta 6's Leutnant de Reserves Paul Wenzel (Acting) and Oberleutnant Lothar von Richthofen of Jasta 11 both wounded and hospitalised, and Oberleutnant Ernst Udet (Jasta 4) exhausted and sent on leave. Jagdgeschwader, I scored just 17 claims during September, despite the month seeing the highest losses for the Allied Air Forces of the war. From June 1917 until November 1918, JG I claimed 644 Allied aircraft destroyed, while losing 52 pilots killed in action and 67 wounded.

The RAF had in operation at the end of the war on 11 November 1918, over 20,000 aeroplanes, over 30,000 aviators and over 200,000 mechanics and other personal.

On 29 June 1918, Oberleutnant Ernst Udet was one of the early fliers to be saved by parachuting from a disabled aircraft, when he jumped after a clash with a French Bréguet aircraft. Oberleutnant Lothar von Richthofen was the younger brother of Manfred Albrecht Freiherr von Richthofen, the Red Baron (Der Rote Baron) who was killed just after 11:00 am on 21 April 1918. During May of 1917, Lothar von Richthofen shot down Captain Albert Ball, the top scoring English ace at that time. Albert Ball mentioned here: Lieutenant Cyril Williams

Colonel Thomas Edward Lawrence CB DSO (T. E. Lawrence – Lawrence of Arabia) (16 August 1888 – 19 May 1935) enlisted in the Royal Air Force as an aircraftman, under the same name – John (Hume) Ross in August 1922. At the RAF recruiting centre in Covent Garden, London, he was interviewed by recruiting officer Flying Officer W. E. Johns, later known as the author of the Biggles series of novels. (See also - Sergeant Alexander Stewart Allan)

Closing Up- a Bombing Formation of British Biplanes (dh9a s) Closing Up to Beat Off an Enemy Formation of Fokker triplanes Art. © IWM This image was created and released by the Imperial War Museum on the IWM Non-Commercial Licence.

Robert Leonard Grahame Skinner

Second Lieutenant Robert Leonard Grahame Skinner was a pilot with RAF 46 Squadron attached to 1st/2nd Battalion, Black Watch (Royal Highlanders). Robert Skinner was the son of the Rev. Henry Leonard Skinner and Susanna Maria Skinner, of The Rectory, Callander. Perthshire.

Most of this personal information below was researched by 'The Ellesmerian Club', the alumni organisation for Ellesmere College where Robert was a pupil. Robert Leonard Grahame Skinner went to Ellesmere College from the McLaren High School, Callander in Perthshire, Scotland. He arrived in May 1911 and stayed until July 1914. His father, the Reverend Henry L. Skinner, lived at the St. Andrews Rectory, Callander with his mother Susannah. From the Scottish Census of 1901 it seems that Robert had a twin, Helen.

Robert was allocated a bed in the 'Arthur' dormitory and placed in Form Upper II under the instruction of Mr. J. G. Sinclair. There were 158 on the nominal roll. During his time at Ellesmere, Robert represented his dormitory in all the major sports, cricket, rugby, football, and hockey. In his senior years, he was a frequent speaker from the floor in the Debating Society and took the part of 'the widow' in the Shakespearian Society production of "The Taming of the Shrew" (1913), the last such play before the outbreak of war.

He passed Arithmetic, Divinity, History, English, Geography, Drawing and Chemistry in the Oxford Local Examinations of 1913, the same year that he was confirmed. He was awarded the Vth Form Science prize in his final term.

As soon as he was able, he enlisted in the 8th Battalion, the Cameron Highlanders, serving with them in the trenches for five months. Afterwards he received a commission in the 1/2nd Battalion, the Black Watch. He was then commissioned to the Royal Air Force and soon obtained his Royal Aero Aviators Certificate # 5374 (his "wings") on 27th October 1917 at the Graham-White Flying School, Hendon.

Second Lieutenant Robert Skinner returned to France at Easter time 1918, as a pilot with RAF 46 Squadron which was part of the 22nd (Army) Wing, the 5th Brigade, based at Busigny, southwest of Cambrai. Within five weeks, on 3rd May 1918, he was reported missing over German lines when flying with five others. At 1.00pm he was last seen entering a cloud in his Sopwith Camel, single seater fighter bi-plane, B7357.

When his British War Medal was put up for auction in 2012 the documentation accompanying it stated that he was shot down by Leutnant Paul Billick, Staffelführer (Commanding Officer) of the Royal Prussian Jagdstaffel 52. Robert Skinner was the 14th of his 31 'victories'.

News came through on 31st May that Robert was a prisoner of war. His wounds and injuries, however, were too great and he died very soon after age 20 years.

Robert Skinner has no known grave but is remembered on the Arras Flying Services Memorial and on the War Memorials at Ellesmere College and at Callander. His sacrifice is also commemorated on a cairn on Dounmhor (Dunmore), erected by Callander Scouts in 1921 to commemorate the sacrifice made by past members of their local group.

The Flight-Commander of No. 46 Squadron wrote of him: *Although he had been with us such a short time, he had endeared himself to us all and proved a very brave boy, who was always there when he was wanted.*

NOTES:

Leutnant Paul Billik commanded Jagdstaffel 52 from 27 December 1917 to 10 August 1918 (POW). He died in a landing accident in Staaken, Berlin, on 8 March 1926 while piloting one of the world's first passenger liners, the Junkers F.13.

Paul Billick was the highest 'scoring' German ace not to be awarded the "pour le Merite" (known as the Blue Max during the war). His capture and interment as a prisoner of war prevented him being awarded the medal.

At the same time as Robert Skinner was shot down, 1.00pm, 2nd Lieutenant Victor Maslin Yeates also of RAF 46 squadron claimed his first victory, shared with Captain D R McLaren (also 46 squadron). Yeates is best known for his book, Winged Victory, widely regarded as a classic description of aerial combat and the futility of war. Captain Donald Roderick McLaren was a WW1 ace, credited with 54 victories. McLaren helped found the Royal Canadian Air Force.

Second Lieutenant Robert Leonard Grahame Skinner

Andrew Beattie Sneddon

Andrew Beattie Sneddon RFC born in 1898 was the son Andrew M (Solicitor) and Sophie E Sneddon of Bellwood Park, Perth. On Wednesday 3 October 1917 he lost his life when he flew his Royal Aircraft Factory B.E.2e, A8641, aircraft out over the North Sea and did not return.

Sneddon attended Sharp's Institution in Perth, which merged with Perth Academy in 1915, and he is commemorated on the school bronze plaque memorial. Sneddon then attended St Bees School – Old St Beghian's in the west of Cumbria where he is also commemorated on the school brass plaque. Sneddon is officially remembered at the Hollybrook Memorial in Southampton.

Second Lieutenant Sneddon (66396) enlisted in 1916 and eventually joined RFC Squadron No. 65. The squadron was first formed at Wyton, near St Ives on 1 August 1916. In early May 1917, they moved to Sedgeford and were renamed as 65 Training Squadron.

Sedgeford aerodrome in the north of Norfolk, was a Royal Navy Air Force (RNAS) training base and an airfield that was used for aircraft attacking German Graf Zeppelin airships. The airfield was also a Class 1-night landing ground for pilots unable to locate their home aerodrome or who were forced to make an emergency landing. It was the only airfield in the area to have lit flares along its landing strip enabling the pilots to land safely in the dark.

Two nights before Sneddon was killed, the night of 1/2 October 1917, when there was a full 'harvest' moon, 18 Gotha aircraft bombers of Kagohl 3, dropped their bombs on Sheerness (350 kg), Harwich (980 kg), Ramsgate and Margate (1050 kg). Two or just one bomber may have also attacked London (1325kg) (425 kg and 900 kg). The official German air service information bulletin stated that only a single Zeppelin-Staaken VI R.39/16 aircraft attacked London that night. German records for this attack are incomplete.

NOTES: The first Zeppelin airship attacks in 1915 were made along the North Norfolk coast, from Great Yarmouth to Kings Lynn. By late 1916, Sedgeford aerodrome had been taken over by the Royal Flying Corp (RFC) and the reserve No. 65 squadron arrived in early May 1917. It was renamed 65 (Higher) Training Squadron, dedicated to turning out Corp pilots. They flew at that time, Royal Aircraft Factory B.E.s, Royal Aircraft Factory R.E.8s, and some Armstrong Whitworth F.K.8s. (See also Airships and Zeppelins)

German bombing during World War 1 started in January 1915 using Zeppelin and Schütte-Lanz airships. Most of the Schütte-Lanz airships were not usable due to their wooden construction which could not cope with damp conditions. About 51 raids were made during the war by airships, the effect was minimal, but they caused widespread alarm and the diversion of essential war resources to combat their threat.

In May 1917, German Gotha heavy bomber biplane aircraft began daylight attacks on England. By August 1917, when the British increased their air defences, they were forced to switch to night attacks. The Gotha's were later joined by four-engine biplane strategic bombers, the Zeppelin-Staaken R.VI.

The Staaken was known to the British as an R-planes, these aircraft were German *Riesenflugzeug* (German for giant aircraft) biplane strategic bombers. They were powered by four engines, two pusher, and two tractors housed in nacelles between the wings.

The last Zeppelin airship raid on England was on 6 August 1918 and one Zeppelin, L.70 was shot down over the North Sea, near Wells-next-the-Sea on the north Norfolk coast. The pilot of the de Haviland DH4 who intercepted and destroyed L.70 was Major Egbert Cadbury (of the Cadbury Chocolate family). Cadbury was attending a charity concert at which his wife was performing. An RAF orderly found him, and they drove back to the airfield. Three Zeppelins had been reported about 50 miles off the coast and the weather was bad. Cadbury along with another pilot attacked a Zeppelin which promptly turned and headed for home. Cadbury, his gunner, Captain Robert Leckie, and the second pilot, Lieutenant Ralph Edmund Keys all received the Distinguished Flying Cross for their actions. (Cadbury had been recommended for a Victoria Cross for this action.) He later recounted:

'At 22.20 we had climbed to 16,400 feet and I attacked the Zeppelin ahead slightly to the port so as to clear any obstruction that might be suspended from the airship. It was a most fascinating sight – awe inspiring – to see this enormous Zeppelin blotting the whole sky above one. The tracers ignited the escaping gas, the flames spreading rapidly and turning the airship into a fireball in less than a minute. The L.70 dived headlong into the clouds. It was one of the most terrifying sights I have ever seen to see this huge machine hurtling down with all those crew on board'. (Handford, Paul (3 July 2014). "The story of Egbert 'Bertie' Cadbury and his remarkable achievement during WWI".)

The B.E, R.E. and F.K aircraft were two-seater machines carrying one pilot and one observer, who were chiefly used for artillery observation, correcting by observation from the air, the fire of batteries on the ground. They were tractor biplanes, the engine and propeller were in front, while the observer and pilot sat tandem in two cockpits, or nacelles, in the fish-shaped body.

The Royal Airforce was formed from the RFC and the RNAS on 1 April 1918. Later in October 1917, the Russian Revolution took place. In July 1919, Winston Churchill, the UK's first Secretary of State for Air was almost killed while taking flying lessons at Beddington (Surrey), one of the locations for home defence in response to the Zeppelin raids. His aircraft stalled and tumbled out of the sky. On impact, it did not catch fire, and Churchill and his tutor, A J L Scott escaped with cuts and bruises. Churchill never again took flying lessons.

Second Lieutenant Howard Watson

Howard Watson was the son of Robert and Margaret Irons Chalmers Watson, Birnam View, Coupar Angus. His father was the Town Clerk of Coupar Angus. Watson was formerly engaged in the Bank of Scotland and enlisted in 1917.

Watson died age 18 whilst training with RAF 64 Training Squadron at RAF Harlaxton Prior to 1 April 1918 RFC Harlaxton), southwest of Grantham, Lincolnshire. He is buried at Coupar Angus Parish Churchyard.

Three training squadrons were based at RAF Harlaxton in 1918: 20, 53 and 64 Squadrons – all part of No. 40 Training Depot Station RAF.

On 8 May 1918, during formation flying practice, Royal Aircraft Factory R.E.8, B7728 collided near Stamford, Lincolnshire with R.E.8, A4546 of RAF 53 Training Squadron. The crew were:

Lieutenant Arthur Burrell Thorne, age 23, R.E.8, B7728

Second Lieutenant Howard Watson, age 18, R.E.8, B7728

Second Lieutenant Myer Levine, age 18, R.E.8, A4546

Lieutenant Cyril Williams

Lieutenant Cyril Williams was an Observer on a Morane BB (5193) aircraft, Royal Flying Corps (RFC) Squadron No. 60 in France during WW1.

Cyril was born on 5 June 1986 at Argyll Place, Edinburgh, the elder son of George Thomas Williams, Civil Engineer, and Elizabeth Fenton, of Fenton's Shipbuilder and Wood Merchants, Perth. Cyril had two sisters, Doris born in Edinburgh and Winifred, born in Shimla, Himachal Pradesh, India. Cyril also had two brothers, Alan McGregor born in Perth and Donald Murray born in Udaipur, India.

Cyril's father was the state engineer of Rajasthan in India. The family lived in Udaipur, also known as the "City of Lakes". When the family returned home to Scotland, they lived at Craigie Park, Craigie, Perth. Cyril went to Perth Academy and in 1910 they moved back to Edinburgh where Cyril attended the High School as a day boy. The career chosen for Cyril was the Army, he had served in the Edinburgh University Training Corps as a cadet and in 1914, he passed the competitive Sandhurst Entrance Examination. He attended the Royal Military College, Sandhurst in January 1914 and joined the Highland Light Infantry as a second Lieutenant in September 1914 and was posted to France.

During the Battle of the Somme (21 June 1916 – 18 November 1916) on 30 July 1916, at about 4.10pm, 4 Morane Saulnier Type BB and Type N biplanes of RFC 60 Squadron took off from Vert Galand aerodrome, 20 kms north of Amien. They were on reconnaissance patrol over the area of Saint-Quentin (80 km west) when they were attacked by German LVG two seaters. The weather was slightly clear, and the German fighters came out in force. Some twenty-five attacked crossing over the lines of the British fourth army. From midday the fighting was ceaseless for some hours.

The aircraft of Captain Lesley Stafford Charles age 21 years and Lieutenant Cyril Williams age 20 years was a French made Morane Saulnier Type BB, no. 5193. It was seen going down, smoking, and was forced to land over Estrées, to the south of Douai. Cyril Williams was killed in the air fight and Captain Charles was taken prisoner, he later died of his wounds.

Lieutenant Cyril Williams was at the time of his death was the son of Mrs. Williams of 3 Abbey Road, Eskbank, Midlothian, and the late G. T. Williams, State Engineer, Meywar, Rajputana, India. Lieutenant Williams is commemorated at the Arras Flying Services Memorial, France.

Captain Charles had only graduated as Flying Officer on 2 June 1916. He was the son of Mr. and Mrs. R. Stafford Charles, of Woodside House, Chenies, Bucks. He was born at Stanmore, Middlesex and before joining the RAF served with the 6th Battalion Worcestershire Regiment. He is commemorated at Roisel Communal Cemetery Extension, France

NOTES: Major Robert Smith-Barry, (later to revolutionise British pilot training), was a flight commander with RFC 60 Squadron from July to December 1916. During that month of July 1916, the squadron had suffered twelve casualties. He informed Lieutenant Colonel Hugh Dowding; the Commanding Officer of 9th Wing that he would not send new pilots over the lines with less than 7 hours flying time. Dowding agreed and informed Field Marshal Douglas Haig, 1st Earl Haig of his decision to temporarily withdraw the squadron from active duty.

The squadron re-equipped with Nieuport 17 C.1 Scouts and soon acquired a first-class reputation. On 2 June 1917, Captain W. A. "Billy" Bishop (Canadian) received the Victoria Cross for his solo attack on a German aerodrome destroying three enemy aircraft in the air and several 'probables' on the ground before returning unhurt in a damaged aircraft. A month later, Royal Aircraft Factory S.E.5 fighters arrived, and these remained with the squadron until it was disbanded on 22 January 1920

Haig commanded the British Expeditionary Force (BEF) on the Western Front from late 1915 until the end of the war. During WW2 Air Chief Marshal Hugh Caswall Tremenheere Dowding, 1st Baron Dowding was Air Officer Commanding RAF Fighter Command during the Battle of Britain and is credited with playing a crucial role in Britain's defence, and hence, the defeat of Adolf Hitler's plan to invade Britain. Dowding was born in Moffat, Dumfriesshire.

The Battle of the Somme was a battle fought by the armies of the British Empire and French Third Republic against the German Empire. It took place between 1 July and 18 November 1916 on both sides of the upper reaches of the river Somme, France. More than three million men fought in the battle and one million men were wounded or killed, making it one of the deadliest battles in human history. On 30 July 1916, the Allies advanced north of Somme, from Delville Wood *(Bois d'Elville)* to the river. The British made progress east of Waterlot Farm and Trones Wood; the French reached the outskirts of Maurepas and the German attack on left bank of Meuse was repulsed.

Shimla was the summer capital of British India, and it was at the terminus of the famous narrow-gauge Kalka-Shimla railway which was completed in 1903.

The LVG German two-seat reconnaissance biplanes were designed at the Luft-Verkehrs-Gesellschaft for the *Luftstreitkräfte* (German Air Force, known before October 1916 as the *Fliegertruppen* (Flying Troops). Introduced in late 1915, the LVG C.II had the pilot and observer positions reversed, a top speed of 130 km/h (81 mph, 70 kmh) with a fixed, forward-firing 7.92 mm (.312 in) and a flexible 7.92 mm (.312 in) ring-mounted machine gun to the rear. The LVG C.IV was the first fixed-wing aircraft to bomb London, when six bombs were dropped near Victoria station on 28 November 1916 (The first air raid on London was by the Zeppelin LZ 38, in the early hours of 1 June 1915).

Perhaps the most famous British air ace of the First World War was posted to RFC 60 Squadron three weeks after the death of Cyril Williams. **Captain Albert Ball** already had 11 victories whilst with 13,11 and 8 Squadron RFC. He was the RFC's highest scoring pilot at the time. He went on to add another 20 victories with RFC 60 squadron. Ball increased his tally to 17 by the end of the month including having shot down three aircraft on 23 August 1916. Albert Ball was not a conventional type of pilot, he was innovative and developed many new combat techniques. For example, in the evening of 15 September 1916 he fitted to his wing struts, 8 Le Prieur rockets (Fusées Le Prieur) deigned to fire electronically. His intention was to shoot down an observation balloon, but he spotted a formation of 3 German LFG Roland C.II aircraft. He fired the rockets at them, breaking up their formation and then proceeded to shoot them down one at a time with his machine gun. Albert Ball was the winner of a Military Cross and a Distinguished Service Order and Bar, he was shot down on 7 May 1917 also near Douai and was buried at Annœullin by the Germans with full military honours. Ball was last seen by fellow pilots pursuing the red Albatros D.III of the Red Baron's younger brother, Lothar von Richthofen. His final tally was 45 victories. Albert Ball was posthumously awarded, by France, the Croix de Chevalier, Legion d'Honneur and the Victoria Cross was presented by King George V to his parents.

 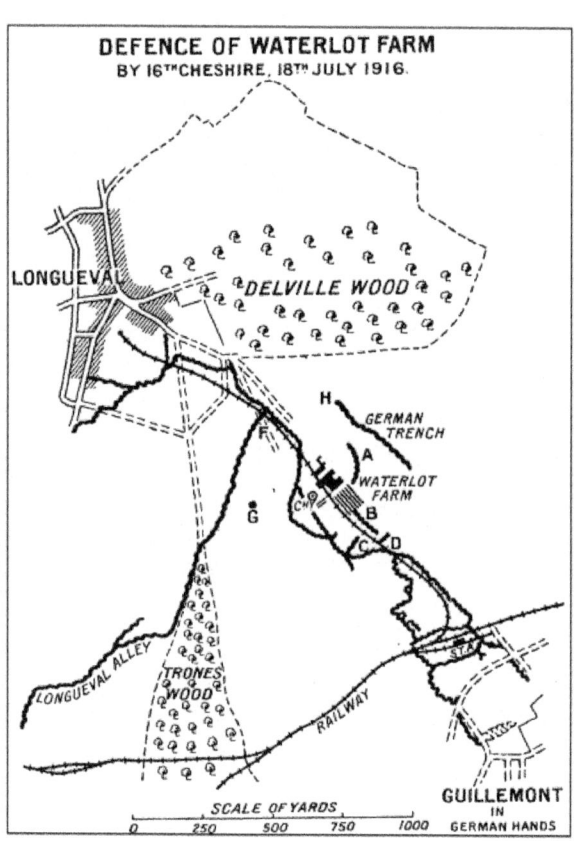

Lieutenant Cyril Williams

Airships and Zeppelins

I came across some interesting newspaper stories about mysterious unexplained happenings in the sky above Perthshire. I did investigate these reported occurrences and found nothing conclusive or logical to explain them. I even thought, only for just a moment, that there might have been UFOs over Scotland 100+ years ago. So, what were these strange lights in the sky and was there perhaps the irrational fear of being bombed from above whilst you slept at night by a German Zeppelin airship?

What was it that worried our ancestors, was it a reasonable fear? Was it a justified fear of being bombed without warning? Did they just imagine what they saw in the sky, or was there some genuine explanation for what they claimed they saw?

During October of 1914 in Pitlochry many observers of the western sky wondered for the fourth night in a row what were the mysterious various coloured light flashes in the sky. It was first reported by Pitlochry Police Sergeant Cameron, and ex-Sergeant Grant. This visitant, it was widely conjectured might be the long-threatened Zeppelin airship raid. The unusual light shows in the sky usually lasted for about thirty minutes, then receded northward. This exact same light show event was also reported in a newspaper further south in Cheshire, England.

This was not the first occurrence of strange objects in the sky above Pitlochry, in March of 1913 a bright light described as being *"like the moon with a haze over it."* This incident went unreported at the time, not until later was the report published and it was suggested that it was the northward flight of some mysterious phantom aircraft. Again, a similar sighting was reported in a newspaper on the same night, in Kirkcaldy and Montrose.

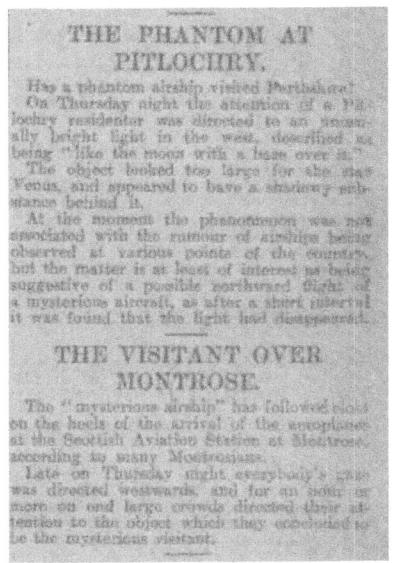

THE COURIER 1 MARCH 1913

Perhaps the strangest happening I found was reported in Perth, this took place on the opposite bank of the river Tay, at Bridgend. It was reported in the Perthshire Advertiser of 15 August 1906. The report was headlined –

MYSTERIOUS AFFAIR IN BRIDGEND – STRANGE AERIAL VISITOR – SPECULATIONS OF THE CROWD

"Bridgend was last night plunged into the vortex of curiosity, not that the good people there are more susceptible to its allurements than those who reside ayont the bridge, but on this occasion, there was a grand muster of the collective curiosity of a section of the community."

"Towards six o'clock there appeared in the sky far away to the North a phenomenal elongated looking

object. At first sight it looked for all the world like a gigantic bird, but no one in the crowd had a sufficient knowledge of the diversities in feathered life to hazard an opinion as to which family it was a member of.

As the mysterious object grew in volume on approaching the point of observation, theorising on dogmatic lines passed into a state of suspended animation, while those hazarded had perforce to undergo slight change. At the outset it is well we should state it was no bird at all. To all appearance it was an air-ship, although those who viewed it with the aid of the naked eye only could not at the time have on their soul and conscience sworn it was part and parcel of an aerial fleet."

Passing from the north to the north-east, it gradually sank and as suddenly rose to its former altitude; sank again and rose once more. There could now be no doubt as to its identity as the instrument of aerial navigation, for by the aid of a powerful telescope one could see the movement of its giant wings as they flapped rhythmically against its ponderous sides. The telescope has its limitations, and so you will search in vain among the notes of observers for the number or the personality of the crew who stood upon the deck.

The most obvious answer to many as to what torpedo shaped air ship flew over Perth that night was a German Zeppelin. But no, it was not any kind of airship, it was not a dirigible or a balloon. None of them were recorded as being even anywhere near Scotland at that time and airships had not developed sufficiently to achieve such a wonderous achievement of flying like a *'gigantic bird.'* They that were not even somewhat capable of in 1906 flying just a short distance under power, none could flap their wings, and none were known to be even under construction anywhere near Scotland.

It is possible that something was in the sky that night in August 1906 above Perth, but the most probable answer to me anyway is that the writer of that elegantly composed Bridgend article had just read Jules Verne, probably Robor the Conqueror (Master of the World) and some vivid imagination, alcohol and/or dreams had got in the way of writing a factual newsworthy article for the paper the next morning.

Extracts from local Newspapers.
This was not the only instance of these observations happening, the Dundee Courier of 1 March 1913 reported two stories of Mysterious lights seen in the sky:

Mysterious Airship is seen hovering over Kirkcaldy – Exhibiting a focussed light.

The "mysterious airship" whose appearance has been more pronounced in other parts of the country, hovered over Kirkcaldy on Thursday night and yesterday morning.

Information is scant, for only those whose occupation kept them out of doors in the "wee sma' oors" saw the mysterious visitor, yet it agrees with the statements of those who witnessed the "phantom" airship in other parts of the country.

Seen by a Policeman.

A member of the police force, too, while in the course of his rounds, speaks of seeing the peculiar sight which during the time that it attracted him seemed to be revolving on a pretty wide area.

The light suddenly faded. That was about three o'clock yesterday morning, and it was travelling in a south-easterly direction.

The Phantom at Pitlochry

Has a phantom ship visited Perthshire?

On Thursday night the attention of a Pitlochry residenter was directed to an unusually bright light in the west, described as being "like the moon with a haze over it.

The object looked too large for the star Venus and appeared to have a shadowy substance behind it.

The Visitant over Montrose

The "mysterious airship" has followed close on the heels of the arrival of the aeroplanes at the Scottish Aviation Station at Montrose, according to many Montrosians.

Late on Thursday night everybody's gaze was directed westwards, and for an hour or more on end large crowds directed their attention to the object which they concluded to be the mysterious visitant.

(Similar stories circulated around the population of Blair Atholl during 1914.)

Following the Edinburgh Zeppelin raid on 2 April 1916 (see below), the people of Scotland's imagination ran wild, and many rumours were started. This from the Perthshire Advertiser of 8 April 1916:

Those "Lights"

Remarkable rumours have been circulating in the city during the week as to mysterious and suspicious lights having been seen at various points. Spies or traitors are, of course, suggested. It is understood that the police have received many reports on the matter. It is, indeed, alleged that signalling by a certain code system has been distinctly observed. All, however, have thus proved wills-o'-the-wisp, though searching investigation has been made. Imagination may be inclined to get a little out of hand in these strange times.

There were developments and reports made of sightings in other countries, earlier on 12 January 1906, the sighting of a 'phantom ship', a shuttle-sized airship caused the alarm to be raised in Toul, France (near Nancy). On 26 March 1906 a balloon crossed from Berlin to Sweden, travelling in a fierce snowstorm, it came down in a Swedish forest. (This balloon did not drift unmanned and cause panic in Scotland.) Later that year in France, the first Gordon Bennet Race took place on 30 September 1906, from Tuileries, Paris, the winning distance was 641km. Sir Charles Rolls (Rolls-Royce) landed in the night near Hull. Incidentally, James Gordon Bennett's father was Scottish, and his name is the idiomatic phrase used to express surprise, contempt, outrage, disgust, or frustration. It is said to have come from his controversial reputation.

So, did the Zeppelin's ever fly over Scotland? The answer is yes, quite a few times and they caused a fair bit of damage and one occasion at 13 deaths. They started flying above us in 1916, until the last one visited our shores just before the start of the Second World War in 1939.

Zeppelin facts
Some facts about Zeppelin's. The Zeppelin company was based in Friedrichshafen on Lake Constance (Bodensee in German) which borders Germany, Austria, and Switzerland. The company Luftschiffbau Zeppelin GmbH was founded in 1908. Count Ferdinand von Zeppelin's research was up until then financed by the count himself. The German army numbered their airship aircraft starting with LZ - standing for "Luftschiff [airship] Zeppelin". The most famous Zeppelin was LZ 129, the *Hindenburg* which came to a dramatic end in New Jersey, USA on 6 May 1937.

The first Zeppelin rigid airship constructed LZ 1, flew on 2 July 1900 and the second LZ 2 departed its hangar on 30 November 1905, but failed to lift off the ground. It did however fly on the second attempt but was damaged beyond repair. The third, the one to be truly successful, was LZ 3, it first flew on 9 October 1906, two months after the Perth airship sighting. Disaster stuck LZ 4 in 1908 when it caught fire after landing to conduct engine repairs. None of them to my knowledge flew anywhere near Scotland in their early days.

Zeppelin raids
It would not be until the night of 2/3 April 1916 for the first Zeppelin raid on Scotland. It caused the deaths of 13 and injured 24 residents of the City of Edinburgh. Until then the German Zeppelin's had monthly raided the Eastern and South-Eastern counties of England. By the end of 1915 in the south of England, 203 people had been killed and 711 injured.

The Edinburgh impending air raid warning was received at 7pm on Sunday 2 April 1916. The electric power of street lighting was lowered. Police in Leith and Edinburgh stopped all traffic and instructed lights on vehicles to be extinguished. The first report of bombs being dropped was around midnight. Zeppelin L 14 came in from the sea at St. Abbs, about 45 miles to the east, on route for Rosyth and the Forth Railway Bridge but instead decided to bomb shipping in Leith docks. Zeppelin L 22 came in further south about Newcastle and headed for the south of Edinburgh where it dropped its bombs.

Four of the latest P-class Zeppelins L 13, L 14, L 16 and L 20 had taken off from the Nordholz Naval Airbase, about 25kms north of Bremerhaven. L 13 developed engine trouble and went back. Zeppelin L 16, due to a northerly wind made for its secondary target of Tyneside and dropped its bombs 11 miles off target.

Lasting approximately one hour, scores of bombs were dropped across Leith and Edinburgh. Zeppelin L 14 first bombed Leith Docks and landed a direct hit on a whiskey bond on Commercial Street. The fire from the warehouse lit up the area and the Germans proceed inwards following the Water of Leith towards Edinburgh city centre. At Bonnington an explosion killed a baby boy who was asleep in his cot. In the next 40 minutes, L 14 dropped 18 High Explosive and 6 incendiary bombs killing 11 people and destroying several buildings, mostly tenements.

On the night of 2/3 May 1916, Zeppelin airship's set out to bomb the UK. Bad weather, a moderate gale had sent two German Navy Zeppelins much further north than where there intended targets were in the north of England or Firth of Forth. They dropped just three high explosive bombs, Zeppelin L 14 (Kapitänleutnant Böcker) let go one bomb just west of Arbroath and two bombs just north of Carnoustie. The bombs caused a horse take fright, it was injured when it jumped a fence at Bonhard Farm, Arbirlot. A single pane of glass was also broken at Penlathy Farm, near Muirdrum.

The other attacking Q Class Marine Luftschiff Zeppelin L 20 (Kapitänleutnant Franz Stabbert) then proceeded north hoping to find a shipping target in the Cromarty Firth. Coming ashore at Lunan Bay it went up by Glen Clova and managed to get itself lost in the bad weather until they found themselves over Loch Ness. They then reversed course until it was over Aberdeenshire where it released six, high explosive bombs on Craig Castle, a mansion house near Rhynie, they had mistaken it for a coal mine. The owners had innocently neglected to turn off their newly installed electric lights and the Germans though it was the mine lift shaft. A few more bombs were dropped before it made its way out to sea. Not having enough fuel to return to Germany, it headed for neutral Norway. It landed off the coast near Stavanger on 3 May 1916. The crew destroyed the airship, 16 were captured and interred, and 3 died.

The Aberdeen Evening Express reported on 3 May 1916 reported:

SCOTLAND RAIDED BY ENEMY AIRCRAFT

NORTH-EAST VISITED

OVER AN AREA FOR FULLY ONE HOUR

(Official Press Bureau)
The following communique was issued by the Field-Marshall Commanding-in-Chief the Home Forces at 12.20 a.m. this morning: -
Five hostile airships attacked the north-east cost of England and the south-east coast of Scotland last night.
The movements of the raiders appear uncertain.
A few bombs were dropped in Yorkshire, but no details are yet to hand as to the casualties and damage caused thereby.
Bombs Dropped.

Early this morning the following message was submitted to the Press Bureau, and it was passed for publication: -

Hostile aircraft also visited the north-east coast of Scotland and hovered over a certain area for over an hour. Bombs are reported to have been dropped, but as yet it is not known what, if any, damage was done.

NOTES: Kapitänleutnant Franz Stabbert escaped six months later.

Zeppelin L 20 was tactically renumbered from LZ 59 for this raid.

On the night of 31 January 1916 LZ 59 carried out the first bombing raid of the war on England, 7 high explosive bombs on the railway junction at the Bennerley Viaduct and steelworks near Awsworth, 6 miles northwest of Nottingham.

In response to bombing raids by German Zeppelin airships. RFC 77 Squadron was made responsible for the defence of the Firth of Forth and the coastline from Berwick-upon-Tweed northwards. One airfield that they used was between Balado and Crook of Devon at the farm of South Kilduff. (See RAF Airfields)

The (first) London aircraft bomber Blitz of WW1
On 13 June 1917, 14 German **Gotha** GIV aircraft bombed all over the east end of London with 162 dead and 432 injured. One 50Kg bomb hit the Upper North Elementary School, 18 children were killed. It penetrated three storeys before exploding in an infants' class on the ground floor of the building. Desperate rescuers pulled the lifeless, mangled bodies of 18 children from the wreckage: another 28 emerged bearing cruel injuries.

It was the deadliest air raid on London during WW1 with no German aircraft being lost. The raid was led by Hauptmann Ernst Brandenburg who was subsequently summoned to Berlin to be awarded the Pour le Mérite (Blue Max), Germany's highest military honour. On his return from Berlin his aircraft crashed, he lost a leg.

'Diplomatically' it is said, 5 weeks later on 17 July 1917, the royal family name, Saxe-Coburg und **Gotha,** which had come into the British Royal Family in 1840 with the marriage of Queen Victoria to Prince Albert, son of Ernst, Duke of Saxe-Coburg & Gotha', was changed when King George V issued a proclamation declaring, *"Our House and Family shall be styled and known as the House and Family of Windsor, and that all the descendants in the male line of Our said Grandmother Queen Victoria who are subjects of these Realms...shall bear the said name of Windsor."*

The Manchester Guardian reported that, *"The King has approved of the following titles being adopted": Duke of Teck: Marquis of Cambridge, Prince Alexander of Teck: Earl of Athlone, Prince Louis of Battenberg: Marquis of Milford Haven, Prince Alexander of Battenberg: Marquis of Carisbrooke."*

The 1930 Visit

The Dundee Courier on 12 July 1930 reported:

ZEPPLIN VISITS SCOTLAND

CRUISES OVER EAST COAST PORTS

WAR-TIME AIR RAIDS RECALLED

The German airship Graf Zeppelin flew down the East Coast of Scotland yesterday.
She had been cruising over Scandinavia, and was sighted over Tromsoe (Tromsø), in Norway on Thursday.
The Zepplin then steered a course for North Cape, the northernmost point in Norway.
The next news of the airship was received from Stromness. Here she was seen at 09.30 a.m. yesterday coming from the west.
When passing over Scapa Flow, those on board must have got a view which would be received with mixed feelings, for at the time salvors were busily trying to raise the German battleship Hindenburg.
Over Aberdeen
The Zeppelin reached Aberdeen a few minutes before eleven o'clock. The citizens and thousands of holidaymakers got a splendid view of the vessel, gleaming like silver in the sunshine. The Zeppelin was flying so low that her number DLX 127, was plainly visible, while her name "Graf Zeppelin" stood out distintly on her bow.
As the Graf passed over the harbour the skipper of a German vessel blew a long blast of welcome to the pride of his country. The airship continued via Stonehaven, Montrose, and Arbroath to the Tay, where it was easily seen from Dundee.
Visit to Edinburgh, *the Zeppelin passed over St. Andrews about 11.45 and, still flying to the south, visited Edinburgh. After passing close to the castle, the airship turned east down the Firth of Forth.*
When sighted near North Berwick it was still following a coastal route.
Note: Directly underneath this report, someone had taken the advantageous opportunity to advertise their product, the lines read:

ON THIS FLIGHT, RECENT WORLD FLIGHT
AND PREVIOUS ATLANTIC CROSSINGS
GRAF ZEPPELIN HAS BEEN EXCLUSIVELY
LUBRICATED BY VEEDOL MOTOR OILS.

Invasion Preparations

When Germany was preparing to invade Britain, their military preparations included the production of a series of military/geographical assessments, showing what might be found by their invading army. This material was to be used in a military evaluation of the regions of the British Isles and considered each from the viewpoint of invasion.

The image below is taken from the northeast side of Perth. The North Inch is on the right with Smeaton's Bridge, Victoria Bridge, and the Railway Bridge down the river towards the harbour. The photograph shows a scheduled passenger aircraft, de Havilland DH.89A, Dragon Rapide G-AFEY owned by Scottish Airways Ltd., Renfrew. Scottish Airways was formed on 12 August 1937 with investment amongst others, from LMS Railway and David MacBrayne, the ferry company. In 1947, the British scheduled airlines were nationalised, and they became part of British European Airways (BEA). The route they operated via Perth (Scone Aerodrome) was Glasgow -Perth – Inverness (Longman) – Wick (Hillhead) – Kirkwall (Wideford) – Lerwick (Sumburgh) (daily except Sunday) (see RAF Perth)

*Image from **The David Rumsey Historical Map Collection**, David Rumsey Map Center, Stanford Libraries. It is a free resource available to all. Permitted for non-commercial use. Short Title View: 119. Perth. Publisher Generalstab des Heeres, (Military High Command). Publisher Location: Berlin Publication Author: Oberkommando der Wehrmacht (OKW) (Nazi German Supreme Command of the Armed Forces) Pub Date: 1940 Pub Title: Unternehmen Seelöwe (Operation Sea Lion – the Original Nazi German Plan for the Invasion of Great Britain).*

During the war, civil operations came under the control of the Air Ministry, National Air Communications (NAC) based at Whitchurch in Shropshire, England. Camouflage was applied to many NAC aircraft; many had their windows blacked out so passengers could not see things outside they shouldn't. The carrying of cameras was forbidden.

On 18 March 1940, whilst approaching Kirkwall Airport, Dragon Rapide G-AFEY hit a hill in Wideford, about five miles northwest of the airfield. All six occupants were injured, and the aircraft was damaged beyond repair.

This was not the only surveillance trip the Germans made before World War Two started. The *Cambridge Daily News* of 4 August 1939 reported:

'An airship which was sighted off the Kincardineshire and Aberdeen shire coasts yesterday afternoon was identified as the Graf Zeppelin by two aeroplanes of No. 612 Squadron, Auxiliary Air Force, stationed at Dyce, near Aberdeen. The Zeppelin was about 20 miles east of Aberdeenshire and was traveling in a north-easterly direction when it was identified by the two aeroplanes from Dyce. The airship was first seen off Stonehaven travelling slowly in a north-easterly direction.'

The Graf Zeppelin (Deutsche Luftschiff Zeppelin #130 D-LZ 130) was on an 'espionage trip' from the 2 - 4 August 1939. It was in the air for over 48 hours and travelled 2,612 miles, the longest trip LZ 130 had made. The mission of the Graf Zeppelin was to secretly collect information on the British Chain Home radar system. On board was radio-listening and radio transmission location equipment. A radio-measuring spy basket was used to try and determine the wavelengths the British were using. The results turned out to be negative for two reasons, the British radar was switched off and the strong German transmissions disturbed their extremely sensitive receivers making it impossible to investigate the British wavelengths.

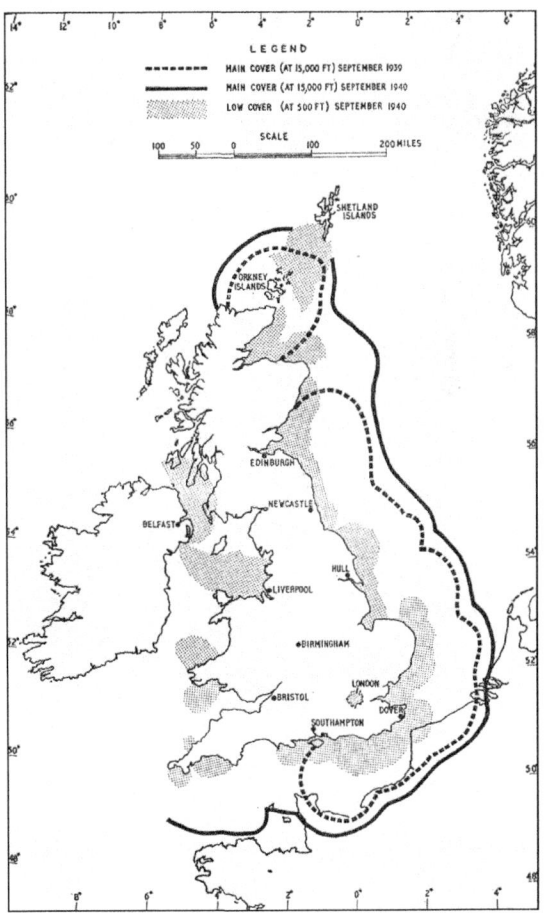

Right: Chain Home coverage WW2

Over Aberdeen, they stopped their engines, pretending that they had engine failure, to investigate the strange British Antenna masts. As they drifted westwards over land, they thought they saw (and later reported back to Germany), two

Spitfires which they 'apparently' photographed. The RAF reports say that Squadron Leader Finlay Crerar in a Miles Magister and his adjutant, Flying Officer A E Robinson in an Avro Anson intercepted the raider. Another RAF aircraft, piloted by Flying Officer N S F Davie in a Tiger Moth also took off later to try and get a closer view.

When they returned to Germany, they were told that they could not land because the British had lodged a diplomatic protest over their actions. A British delegation was at the airfield and wanted to inspect the airship. The British were told that due to the weather the airship had landed at another part of the airfield. By the time the British got to LZ 130, the spy crew had been whisked away to a hotel and a search found nothing suspicious on board.

The Cambridge Daily News of 04 August 1939 reported (war broke out on 1 September 1939):

An airship which was sighted off the Kincardineshire and Aberdeen shire coasts yesterday afternoon was identified as the Graf Zeppelin by two aeroplanes of No. 612 Squadron, Auxiliary Air Force, stationed at Dyce, near Aberdeen. The Zeppelin was about 20 miles east of Aberdeenshire and was traveling in a north-easterly direction when it was identified by the two aeroplanes from Dyce. The airship was first seen off Stonehaven travelling slowly in a north-easterly direction.

LZ130 flew three more times and was grounded on 1 September 1939 when war broke out. Hermann Göring, the head of the Luftwaffe ordered the last two remaining Zeppelins and an unfinished Zeppelin framework to be scrapped. The metal (Aluminium) was needed for building other aircraft. He also ordered the enormous airship hangars levelled by explosives on 6 May 1940, three years to the day after the airship Hindenburg LZ129 disaster in New Jersey, United States.

LZ 130 Graf Zeppelin *in flight (from a postcard) The copyright of this image has expired in the European Union because it was published more than 70 years ago without a public claim of authorship (anonymous or pseudonymous), and no subsequent claim of authorship was made in the 70 years following its first publication.*

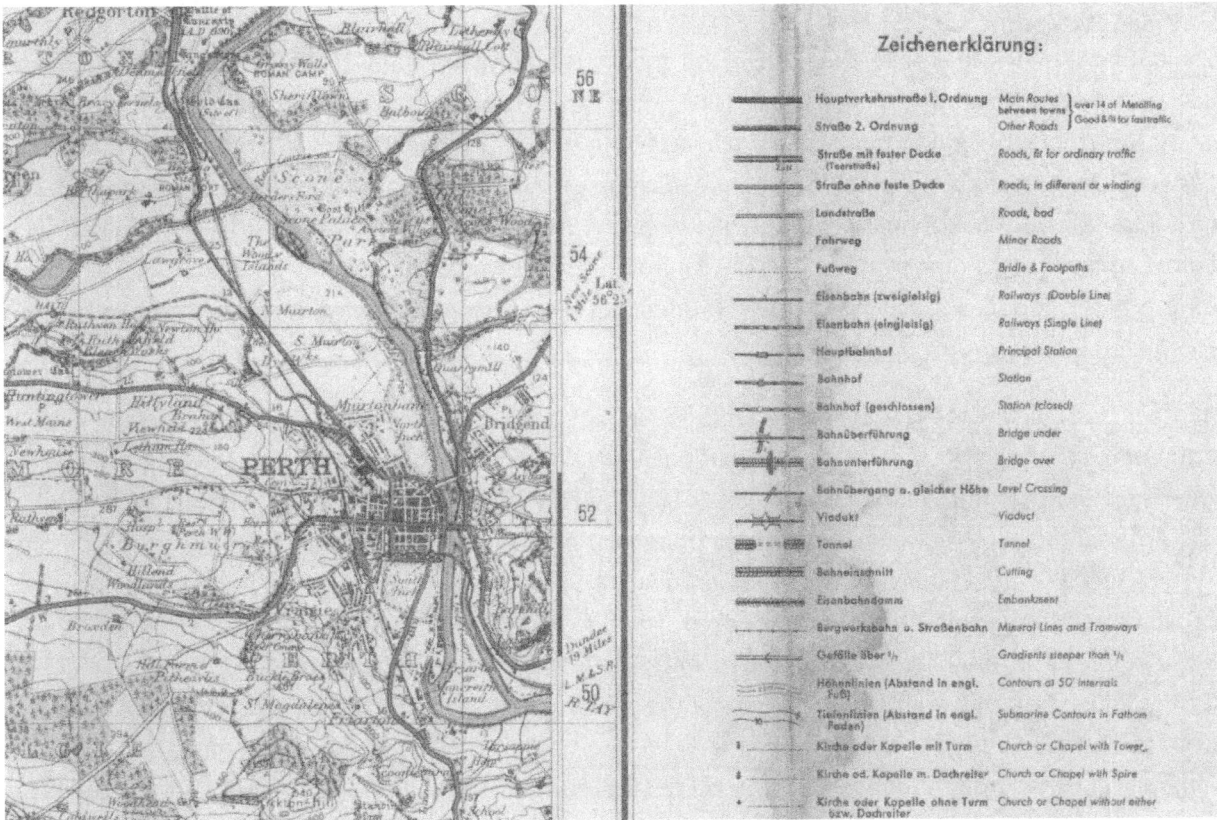

Sample of an Ordnance Survey map, version produced and to be used by - German Army, Karte von Schottland, 1:50,000 – 1941 - Reproduced with the permission of the National Library of Scotland.

This was from is a set of Ordnance Survey Quarter-Inch to the mile maps, captured by the Germans and reprinted in 1939-40, as part of their Second World War intelligence preparations. There was no revision of topographic detail, but the sheets were metricated, enlarged from 1:253,440 to 1:250,000, with updated German titles, marginalia and legends. The series was primarily intended for aeronautical purposes. The original maps at quarter inch to the mile (1:253,440) were reduced from larger-scale mapping at the half-inch and one-inch to the mile scales, primarily dating from the third national revision of 1912-1923.

The airship mystery continued

So, who else could possibly have been responsible for the Perth/Bridgend sighting in 1906, Britain's first airship British Army Dirigible No.1 *Nulli Secundus* did not fly until 10 September 1907. The Dr Francis Alexander Barton's dirigible airship flew from Alexandria Palace on 22 July 1905 for 14 miles, coming down dramatically at Heaton Grange, Havering in Essex. In progress on the ground was a garden party. Another contender would be the William Beedle airship. He conducted trials on 3 November 1903 at Alexandria Palace in north London. Further scheduled flights were made for the following April but he ran out of money. The airship was put in storage for two years in hope of continuing his experiments. Two years later, Beedle took his airship to E. T. Willows in Cardiff, Wales. They worked together for the next two years from 1906 to 1908 building airship gondolas for the Balloon Factory at Farnborough. What happened to his airship is unknown, possibly he tried again.

Further Speculation

Could it have been the French, the *Patrie*? The answer is no, the first semi-rigid airship built for their army was not completed until November 1906. The *Patrie* did break away from its temporary moorings on 30 November 1907 from her base in Southesmes in the Meuse department in Grand Est of north-eastern France. It crossed the English Channel passing through English airspace during the night and was next spotted over Wales and Ireland the following day. The *Patrie* made a brief landfall near Belfast before rising again to be blown out into the Atlantic Ocean towards the north of Scotland. A steamship off the Outer Hebrides spotted it for the last time. The sister ship to the *Patrie*, the *République* was completed in June 1908.

Another possibility was the Wellman Expedition airship *America* on 20 August 1906. This was to be an attempt to reach the North Pole via Spitzbergen, it was conveyed by ship, not flown, to Danes Island (Wellman Camp) in the Svalbard archipelago of northern Norway. With no expense spared, Wellman had ordered the construction of his airship, *America*, a steerable dirigible airship built by Mutin Goddard at the Eugène Godard family factory in Saint-Ouen-sur-Seinne, in the Île-de-France region, just north of Paris. It was 50.3m in length with a diameter of 16m. It was powered by three 75hp engines capable of lifting a weight of 16,000lb. It was equipped with 5 hp engine motor-sledges and dog-dragged sledges for the final part of the journey. When testing the airship's engines, they self-destructed. The *America* was rebuilt that winter but would not be ready for another failed attempt until September 1907. The *America* launched from Atlantic City in the United States on 15 October 1910, attempting to be the first to cross the Atlantic. After 38 hours the engine failed, and the crew were rescued by the Royal Mail steamship RMS *Trent* not far from Bermuda.

Water E. Wellman was a US journalist, explorer, and aeronaut. His newspaper provided funds of US$75,000 for the Wellman Chicago Record-Herald Expedition. This was not his first attempt to get to the North Pole, he led a polar expedition in 1894 and again 1898 where he slipped on the ice and broke his leg. The expedition of 1889 greatest success was the finding of Graham Bell Island which he named after the famous Scottish inventor of the telephone. The second in command of the 1898 expedition was Captain Evelyn Briggs Baldwin, a character named after him appeared in the Max McCoy novel, Indiana Jones and the Hollow Earth published in 1997.

An Alberto Santos-Dumont airship flew in France № 14. This airship was 41 meters long, 3.4 meters in diameter, 186 square meters in cubic footage, and with a 14 HP engine. It made a short flight on June 12, 1905. It was modified due to lack of stability and renamed № 14-b (airship). It was only 20m long, but now 6 meters in diameter and with a 16 HP engine. It was tested between 21-25 August 1905

Air Circuses

Scone Aerodrome was not the first airfield in the Perth area. It may astonish the reader to be informed that fields at the uppermost section of Necessity Brae – Woodhead of Mailer Farm and Windyedge Farm – hosted in the early 1930s at least 4 impressive 'Air Circuses' by competing air display businesses.

The first of the aerial circuses to call on Perth is likely to have been Captain C. D. Bernard's Air Tours, which performed at Woodhead of Mailer on 26 and 27 September 1931. The company had over 100 other presentations under its belt when it came to Perth. Bernard himself was an aviation celebrity having broken several world records: England to India and back in 7½ days, Cape Town in 20½ days – both in a Fokker F. VIIa, and the first non-stop flight from England to Africa (Tangier) – the 2,480-mile return journey in a DH.80A Puss Moth was accomplished in 21½ hours.

Bernard's Air Tours offered trial flying lessons under the tutelage of James Allan Mollison, who in 1932 married one of the most eminent female pilots of her day, Amy Johnson. Like his partner, Glasgow-born Mollison was an aviation record breaker, often flying with Johnson.

Aviation displays also thrilled the crowds assembled at Woodhead of Mailer, Bernard himself providing the leading edge of the company's 8-plane presentation in his record-breaking Fokker that he dubbed 'The Spider'.

Bernard's flying circus utilised the following aircraft, some of which would have been seen in Perth.

1927 Fokker F. VIIa G-EBTS 'The Spider'.

1931 Spartan 3-Seater I G-ABJS.

Cierva C.19 Autogiro G-AAYP.

1930 Avro 616 Sports Avian G-AAXH belonging to Henlys Ltd.

1930 Desoutter, a licensed Dutch Koolhoven F.K.41 design, manufactured by Desoutter at Croydon Aerodrome.

1931 Potez 36.17 'Ladybird' F-ALJC/G-ABNB.

The Cierva autogyro was also flown for the first time in Perth, it was said to look as if it was hanging practically motionless in the air before landing on a literal pinhead.

The autumn of 1931 was a busy time of year for air circuses in Perthshire. Not long after the visit of Bernard's Air Tours – 16-17 October 1931 – *"the world-famous"* Berkshire Aviation Tours Ltd came to Woodhead of Mailer. Their advertisements for the display are rather fascinating for they not only pronounced the air circus as providing *"the most exciting display of flying ever given and a roar from beginning to end"* and *"selections of music and announcements by loudspeaker"*, but also offering a novel attraction, *'Bombing the Bridal Pair'*.

To coincide with the air circus, the Perth Alhambra [movie] Theatre in Kinnoull Street showed *Hell's Angels*, Howard Hughes's *"Epic of the Air starring Jean Harlow"*. As well as directing and producing this multi-million-dollar WWI aviation action film, Hughes had made forays himself into the world of early aviation. His most famous flying project was the Hughes-H4 Hercules (NX37602), known to all as the 'Spruce Goose', a 111-ton wooden troop-carrying 8-engine beast of a plane that was a complete failure. The largest flying boat ever constructed, 'The Goose' only managed a short test flight (piloted by Hughes himself near Long Beach, California) of only 26 seconds – rising to just 70 feet in the air.

Bernard and his team might have been good pilots, but their sense of navigation was poor. An intended September visit of Bernard's Air Tours to the Auchterarder area was advertised by posters announcing an air circus to be held at West Mains, Gleneagles – the wrong place. This location had been confused with West Mains Farm on the Strathallan Estate, also the wrong place. The circus finally took place at Easthill Farm, Auchterarder on 18 October 1931. Easthill Farm is at the west end of Auchterarder, at the end of the Tullibardine Road where it meets Easthill Road.

Another aviation circus, that of the Scottish Motor Traction Co. Ltd (which had run a garage on Perth's Dunkeld Road for several years, SMT), took place on Tuesday, 22 August 1933. Advertised as "Scotland's Own Air Circus…the most comprehensive, spectacular, and daring display of Scotland's progress in aviation", the event offered flights to the public at 5 shillings, flying performances with Dragons, Fox Moths, Tiger Moths, and Avro Cadets, which included 'stunting', 'crazy flying', and 'bombing', a race around nearby landmarks, and exhilarating parachute plunges by parachutist A. C. Fairley.

The following year saw another air display company in Perth, that run by the ground-breaking aviator Sir Alan Cobham. Cobham's flying air circus toured Britain during the summer months. Between 1932 and 1935 upwards of 4 million spectators visited their aerial exhibitions, and almost a million passengers were treated to aerial experiences known as '5-bob flips'.

Cobham's foremost competitor was the British Hospitals Air Pageant company whose retinue included famous female pilots, including Pauline Gower, who during the Second World War set up the women's division of the Air Transport Auxiliary; Mary Bruce, a record-breaking aeroplane, motor car, and powerboat racer; and the pioneering aeronautical engineer Dorothy Spicer. During her time of employment by Cobham, Gower utilised her own modified Fairey Fox (G-ACAS) to take some 6,000 paying customers for airborne joyrides. British Hospitals Air Pageant came to Perth on 12 September 1933 and despite it being but a few weeks since the Scottish Motor Traction Co. Ltd event, large crowds were present. The display included several innovative aspects including 'bottle shooting', 'crazy flying', and 'wing walking'.

Having such large crowds in this part of Perth created transport difficulties. On Sunday, 27 September 1931, with large numbers of vehicles amassing on the air circus, a Perth Corporation omnibus taking locals out to the air show collided with a motor car on Needless Road – fortunately, no one was injured in the crash.

British Hospitals Air Pageant returned to Perthshire on 19 July 1934 with a show at Aldour, Pitlochry in which they presented the newly-named 'Sky Devils' air circus. As the company's name suggests they might do, monies raised from the air circus were given to local hospitals. One feature of the Aldour event was the exhibition of Charles William Anderson Scott's record-breaking aircraft that he had piloted from England to Australia in 8 days and 20 hours. Scott's de Havilland DH.88 Comet had won the London to Melbourne Air Race, considered the most prestigious air race of all. Another feature of the event was the presence of the biggest 'air liner' ever seen at a touring air display, the 'City of Glasgow' Armstrong Whitworth A.W.154 Argosy (G-EBLF) of Imperial Airways. Fitted with a 1,500 horsepower Argosy engine, the aircraft could carry 26 passengers. For air shows, the Argosy was stripped of its cloakroom and luggage areas thus allowing 4 additional travellers per flight. Aldour in Pitlochry is on the left as you enter from the south. Now a small industrial estate and private housing, one street being named Aldour Gardens.

Note: Amy Johnson had first made a name for herself with her solo flight to Darwin, Australia in a de Havilland DH.60 Gipsy Moth (G-AAAH), 'Jason'. Alongside her husband, Johnson set several long-distance flight records in the 1930s. She served as a pilot with the Air Transport Auxiliary during the Second World War transporting aircraft across the UK. On 5 January 1941, enroute – in bad weather – from Prestwick Airport to RAF Kidlington, in an Airspeed Oxford, First Officer Johnson found herself off course. She bailed out before her plane crashed into the Thames Estuary. The reason for her crash is unclear. Two theories dominate the debate: that she ran out of fuel or was shot down by a British anti-aircraft battery. Her parachute deployed and Johnson landed in the sea. An attempt to rescue her was made by Lieutenant-Commander Walter Fletcher who manoeuvred his ship HMS Haslemere to aid her, but this failed. Fletcher, during the rescue attempt, dived into the icy sea. He perished a few days later due to his exposure to the intense cold.

Blackburn R.B.3A Perth Flying Boat

Designed and built by the Blackburn Aeroplane & Motor Company, Brough, West Yorkshire, the R.B.3A biplane flying boat named after the City of Perth undertook its first flight in 1933. Four of the then largest aircraft of its type, entered RAF service the following year. It was armed with 3 Lewis Machine Guns and a single Coventry Ordnance Works (COW) 37 mm (1½ lb) canon. Powered by three 825hp Rolls Royce "Buzzard IIMS" water cooled engines giving it a speed of 132 miles per hour. The aircraft had a range of 1,500 nautical miles and a top speed of 132 mph (115 knots) and a cruising speed of 109mph (95 knots).

The COW gun was capable of firing 100 shells a minute in bursts of six with a range of one mile. Its maximum gross weight was 38,000lb (19 tons). The crew compliment was five, two pilots sitting side by side with dual controls, immediately aft the navigator's compartment, a wardroom with sleeping berths, a canteen, more sleeping berths and living quarters, the wireless cabin, the engineer's station and in the cockpit in the tail with machine gun mounting, an air gunner. It could carry up to 2,000 pounds of bomb ordnance and the dimensions were: Span 97ft, length 70ft, height 25ft 5½ inches.

One of the four Perth aircraft, K3851 took part in a formation fly-past of flying boats at the Hendon RAF Display at Hendon in 1934. The other flying boats were a Supermarine Scapa, Short Singapore, Short Sarafand, Short S18 (Knuckleduster) and a Saunders-Roe Saro Cloud.

K3580 had a float torn away by heavy seas on 14 September 1935 whilst attempting to take off from Stornoway. It was driven towards shore where there was danger of it breaking up. Rocket signals were answered by a drifter fishing boat and a lifeboat which took off the crew. The aircraft was taken in tow and safely beached. The Blackburn Perth was on its way to Oban having just refuelled.

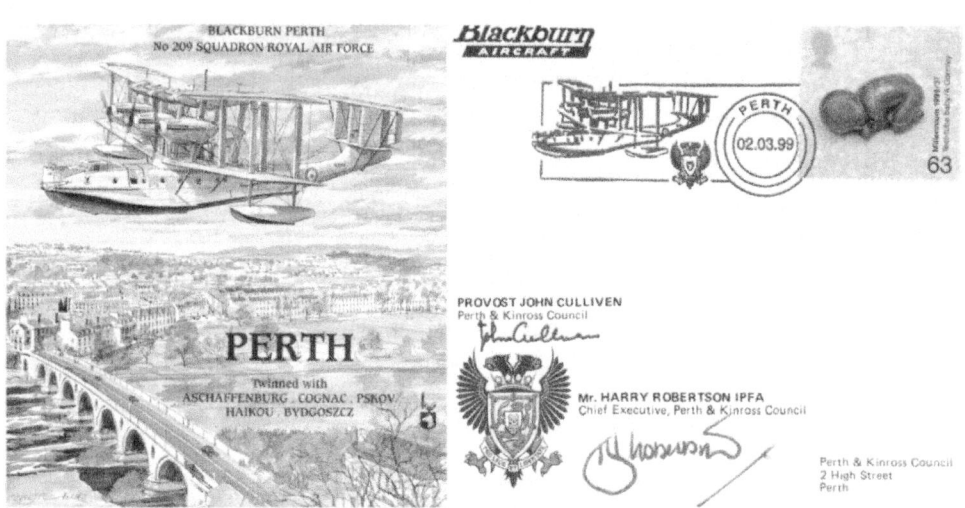

Blackburn Perth Commemorative First Day Cover

Cigarette Card

GERMANS INDIGNANT

Britain's "Flying Battleship" and Disarmament

BERLIN, Monday.

The launching of the new Blackburn-Perth flying-boat near Hull is greeted with bitterness in the German press this evening.

This new "flying-battleship," it is stated, speaks for itself, coming as it does on the heels of recent accusations by Germany that others have been arming throughout the disarmament talk.

A London correspondent expresses the greatest admiration for the aeroplane's performance, but asks, "If the Perth No. 1 can do such wonders with her new 1½-pounder quick-firing gun, what will Perth No. 12 be able to do?"

He suggests that the aeroplane should be re-named "The Spirit of Disarmament."—Reuter.

Western Mail & New South Wales News 24/10/1933

The Kay Gyroplane (Autogyro)

The First Kay Gyroplane (Type 32/1) was designed by David Kay of Blackford and John Grieve of Scone. (Kay was, with his brother Andrew, partners in Kay's Garage, located in Moray Street, Blackford.) The gyroplane was built at Shields Garage on Perth's Dunkeld Road and was powered by an ABC Scorpion engine. Testing of the aircraft began in August 1932 at RAF Leuchars. In April 1933, Kay's Type 32/1 gyroplane was damaged during a heavy landing. Kay Gyroplanes Ltd was formed as a commercial concern at Edinburgh in 1934 and Oddie, Bradbury & Cull Ltd of Southampton, England (with previous experience of Cierva Autogiro rotor construction) was ordered to construct 2 airframes, c/n 1002 and 1003. Both were conveyed to Kay for finishing, however, only G-ACVA was completed and registered (26 June 1934).

The newly constructed Kay Gyroplane (Type 33/1) flew for the first time on 18 February 1935 taking off from Eastleigh (Southampton) Airport. It was driven by a 75 horsepower, 7-cylinder Pobjoy 'R' engine driving a coarse-pitch 4-bladed wooden propeller: its body, a welded tubular steel fuselage. The design of the Kay Type 33/1 was way ahead of its time. It was the first rotorcraft to use variable incidence rotors, a feature that would become orthodox for all helicopters. The increased lift added by fitting a 4-bladed rotor was an additional significant feature.

Testing of the aircraft was undertaken by Flight Lieutenant A. H. C. Rawson whose flights corroborated the usefulness of the Kay's variable incidence arrangement for take-off and landing.

Although the aircraft impressed Air Ministry officials, no orders were placed for a production version. Film footage of the Kay gyroplane at Southampton in 1938 can be viewed on the British Pathé website.

In 1935, the Lord Provost of Perth, Thomas Hunter, indicated that discussions were in progress between Perth Town Council and David Kay with the view to the establishing of a gyroplane manufacturing plant as an adjunct to Scone Aerodrome. The company subsequently stored their gyroplane at Perth Aerodrome for many years, where it was latterly refurbished. The restoration was concluded in 1967 and the Kay Gyroplane was loaned to Glasgow Museums. It was afterwards sold to National Museums Scotland and is today on display at the National Museum of Scotland. Regrettably, the first 1932 prototype is no longer in existence.

Kay was called up to serve with the RAF during the Second World War and sent to Canada as a flight instructor. During this time, Kay's invention patents ran out so that others were freely able to capitalize on his ideas. It is alleged that Igor Ivanovich Sikorsky asked to see Kay's patents for his variable pitch rotor head. Following the war, Kay returned to Scone where he continued as a flight instructor.

Note: I must confess that as a fanatical young lad, I often deliberately walked up and down the Lade path into town, just so I could get a glimpse of a Kay's gyroplanes through the back door of Shields Garage. I don't recall exactly when this was – probably in the late 1960s, early 1970s.

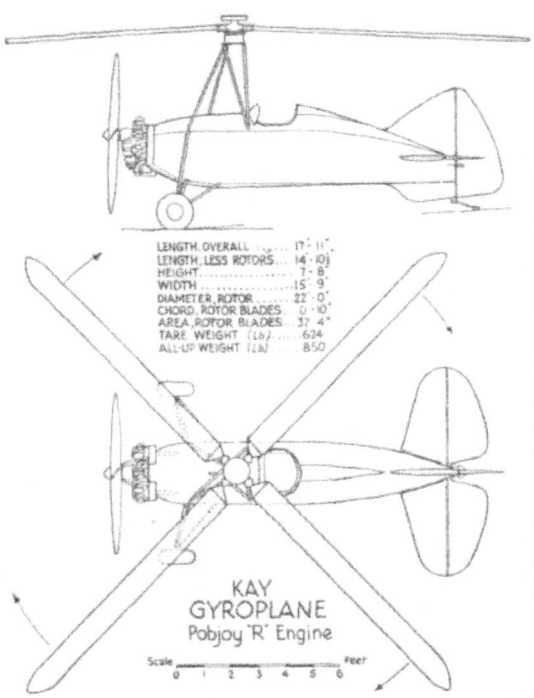

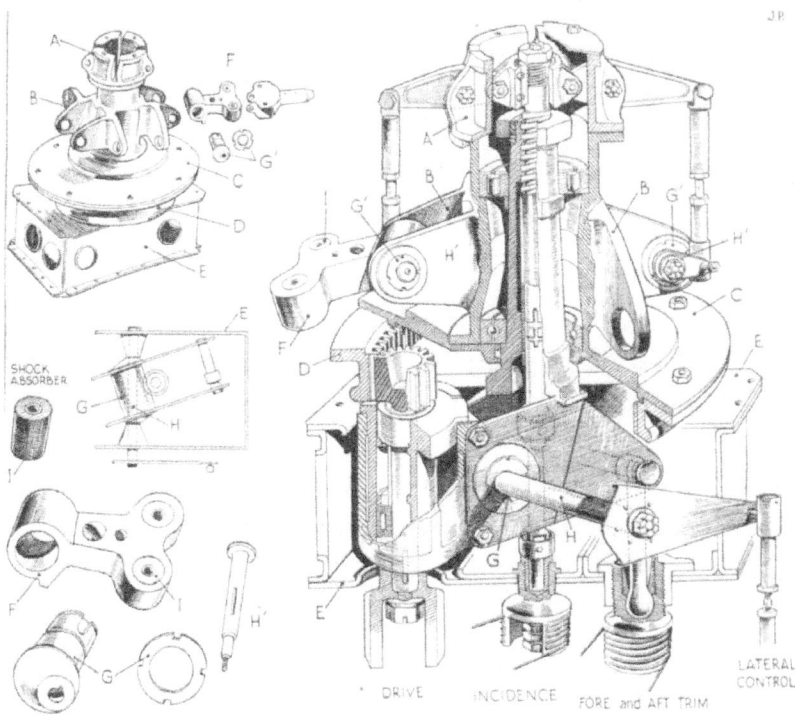

Patent drawings for the rotor head that allows for cyclic and collective variation of the blade pitch as they rotate.

RAF Airfields in (& close) to Perthshire during the Second World War

RAF Balado

Originally named RAF Balado Bridge, this airfield, 2 miles west of Kinross was utilised for training Polish Spitfire and Hurricane pilots. It was established on 30 March 1942 as a Satellite Landing Ground (SLG) supporting RAF Grangemouth and remained operational until 25 June 1944. Among other uses, RAF Balado was the base for No. 58 OTU RAF (later renamed No. 2 Tactical Exercise Unit – disbanded in June 1944) and was briefly used as an SLG by No. 9 (Pilot) Advanced Flying Unit (PAFU) based at RAF Errol. The runways (1,650 and 1,400 yards long) were constructed of hardcore and concrete. There were 25 hard-standings for aircraft. The station's RAF complement included 24 officers, 83 SNCOs, and 616 ORs – its WAAF complement included 8 officers, 20 SNCOs, and 180 ORs.

Simulated night flying at RAF Balado commenced on 5 August 1942 with pilots sporting special goggles to replicate dark conditions. To assist with take-off and landing, the runway was marked by 8 sodium flares.

In the post-war period, RAF Balado became an 'aircraft graveyard' where the McDonnell Aircraft company (Milnathort) dismantled hundreds of superfluous and unwanted RNFAA naval aircraft. The work peaked in 1946/1947 and lasted at least until 1955.

Between 1985 and 2006, part of the RAF Balado site functioned as a NATO SATCOM SLG Listening Station. Many will remember the radio station here with the aerials housed inside the large 'Golf Balls'. In 2002, a de-commissioned Jet Provost T3A XM412 was delivered to RAF Balado to undergo preservation work. The popular T-in-the Park music festival took place at the former RAF station between 1997 and 2014.

A US civilian aircraft, Vultee Valiant BT-13A trainer aircraft (NX54084) named 'Next Thursday's Child' was parked at Balado aerodrome in March 1952. This was a plane used by Miss Richarda Morrow-Tait, a 24-year-old aviator who on 18 August 1948 became the first woman to fly around the world. Thursday's Child (from the popular children's song, 'Monday's Child', in which "Thursday's child has far to go …") Following several mishaps, minor damage, and an engine change in Calcutta, Morrow Tait had to make an emergency landing in Alaska. The aircraft was not repairable and after some fund raising, she continued her journey by purchasing the Vultee Valiant (Next Thursday's Child). She landed back at Croydon, one year and one day later 19 August 1949.

NOTES:

Between 1985 and 2006, part of the RAF Balado site functioned as a NATO SATCOM SLG Listening Station. The radio station housed its aerials housed inside what looked like a large 'golf ball', this can still be seen from the A977. In 2002, a de-commissioned Jet Provost T3A (XM412) was delivered to RAF Balado to undergo preservation work. The popular (and now defunct) T-in-the Park music festival took place at the former RAF station between 1997 and 2014.

An SLG generally included 1-2 grass runways blended into their natural surroundings from aerial observation to disguise their usage and potential target value. Typically, SLGs were also utilised by maintenance units – aircraft being dispersed on site to reduce the damage in an attack.

Other units using RAF Balado during the Second World War include No. 2 Combat Training Wing, No. 2 Tactical Exercise Unit (TEU), and the civilian firm of T. McDonald & Sons.

Balado Airfield "Golf Ball" 2008

RAF Buttergask

Situated at Saucher, near Kinrossie and Collace, RAF Buttergask was an SLG used by 1 Group, RAF No. 11 EFTS. It was officially operational between 1 December 1942 and 28 November 1948.

RAF Buttergask was essentially just a large field, but it did see thousands of circuits by pilots in de Havilland Tiger Moths. It was probably used by No. 11 EFTS from as early as 1941 and was still in use by them until late 1945.

Buttergask has 2 associations with Shakespeare's Macbeth. The first is Macbeth's Law, a 15 feet high mound near Lawton House.

The second is Dunsinane Hill (Fort of Macbeth) that lies a mile south of the airfield made famous in Act 4, Scene 1 of Macbeth:

"Macbeth shall never vanquished be until

Great Birnam Wood to high Dunsinane Hill

Shall come against him".

Dunsinane Hill can be accessed by a path that begins close to the village of Collace.

RAF Errol

The RAF opened an airfield by the village of Errol, within the Carse of Gowrie, midway between Dundee and Perth, on 1 August 1942. Operations at RAF Errol commenced with the transfer of No. 9 (P)AFU from RAF Hullavington in Wiltshire and No. 21 AFU, which was posted there on 9 August 1942.

The station's RAF complement included 67 officers, 116 SNCOs, 1682 ORs – its WAAF complement included 10 officers, 15 SNCOs and 405 ORs. There were 6 Type 1 hangars and 13 blister hangars, 17 concrete hard standings (circular), 3 runways arranged in an 'A' orientation of lengths 1,600 yards, 1,180 yards, and 1,170 yards. No. 21 AFU maintained a complement of 37 pilots, 9 of whom were from New Zealand.

Units using RAF Errol during the Second World War include:

No. 9 EGS (Elementary Gliding School).

No. 9 (P)AFU (Navy pilot training unit relocated from

RAF Hullavington, Wiltshire).

No. 260 MU, No. 271 Squadron RAF.

No. 810 Squadron RNFAA.

No. 1544 BAT Flight (Blind (later Beam) Approach Training Flight).

No. 1680 (Transport) Flight RAF

Training at Errol was initially for naval pilots though it remained an RAF unit (see also - **Murie Cemetery, Fairey Swordfish, and the river Tay).** Miles Master and Hawker Hurricane aircraft were mainly used, supplemented later by Fairey Swordfish and Fairey Albacore, both single-engine (carrier-borne) biplane torpedo bombers. In mid-1942 the aircraft on strength were: 36 Miles Master, 10 Hawker Hurricane 5 Fairey Swordfish and 5 Fairey Albacore. In addition, in May 1943, a pair of Fairey Barracuda (carrier-borne) torpedo and some Fairey Albacore dive bombers were allocated to No. 9 PAFU for conversion purposes. As the training increased at RAF Errol, they were allocated the use of SLGs at RAF Findo Gask, RAF Balado, RAF Tealing and RAF Kinnell (near Friockheim, Angus). By March 1944 the establishment training aircraft increased to 126 Miles Master and 14 Fairey Albacore/Swordfish. By August 1944 the unit had converted to using 96 North American Harvard trainer aircraft. Later several Hawker Hurricanes, Airspeed Oxford, and de Havilland DH.89 Dominie aircraft were also acquired and the Glider School from May to November 1945 utilised the Slingsby T.6/T.23 Kirby Kite, single seat sport glider.

Early in 1943, 3 Supermarine Walrus single-engine, amphibious biplane reconnaissance aircraft were loaned to RAF Errol. Despite remonstration that at least one Walrus should be retained for rescuing downed pilots in the river Tay, they were assigned elsewhere in April 1944.

Between 25 January 1944 and 30 August 1944, RAF No. 1544 BATF was formed at RAF Errol flying Airspeed Oxfords. The unit flew in from RAF Scampton in June 1944, the original intention was to be affiliated to No. 14 PAFU at RAF Banff, the unit disbanded in August 1944. The Beam Approach Training Flight Oxfords carried distinctive yellow triangles to warn other aircraft to keep clear as the pilot was frequently flying on signal and instruments with the cockpit window screened off.

The Western Isles Communication Flight, no. 1680, had a detachment at RAF Errol from April to May 1944.

The station's RAF complement included 67 officers, 116 SNCOs, 1682 ORs – its WAAF complement included 10 officers, 15 SNCOs and 405 ORs. There were 6 Type 1 hangars and 13 blister hangars, 17 concrete hard-standings (circular), 3 runways arranged in an 'A' orientation of lengths 1,600 yards, 1,180 yards, and 1,170 yards. No. 21 AFU maintained a complement of 37 pilots, 9 of whom were from New

Zealand.

Although initially utilised for the advanced training of RAF pilots, RAF Errol is best known as the base of No. 305 Ferry Training Unit (FTU), a specialist training entity commissioned to provide crossover training in the twin-engine Armstrong Whitworth A.W.41 Albemarle transporter for Soviet aircrew of the Moscow Special Assignment Airgroup (MSAA) – later given the prestigious accolade of being named the 10th Guards Air Transport Division. Two hundred Albemarle aircraft were ordered by the Soviet Air Force in October 1942 although only 14 were provided: P1455, P1477, P1562, P1567, P1590, P1595, P1636, P1637, P1638, P1640, P1642, P1645, P1647, and V1598. The air groups mission was to fly the contracted 200 Albemarle back to the Soviet Union.

The first group of Soviet pilots and engineers (3 of each) landed at RAF Prestwick on 11 January 1943. Two weeks later they began the first Albemarle transporter flights. Despite the cancellation of the order in May 1943 due to technical faults and suitability issues with the aircraft, between 14 December 1942 and 30 April 1944, the FTU at RAF Errol trained 60 Soviet engineers, navigators, and pilots. The training undertaken by Soviet personnel included a limited amount of de Havilland Mosquito fighter-bomber training. It is likely that in 1944 a few Mosquitos were flown from RAF Errol to the Soviet Union. No. 305 (FTU) stopped training at RAF Errol in March 1944 and disbanded the following month.

There is a somewhat tragic story associated with the MSAA. An Albemarle ST1 (P1503) crewed by Major Aleksander Gruzdin (pilot), Vasily Drjamin (navigator), Alexander Alexeev (flight engineer), and Staff Sergeant Frantisek Drahovzal crashed during a training run. Their plane came down on 29 May 1943 near to the village of Fearnan that sits close to Loch Tay and a few miles from Kenmore, Perthshire, killing all on board.

Gruzdin's ashes were taken back to Moscow where he was awarded the accolade, 'Hero of the Soviet Union'. He lies next to his wife who also was a pilot. To commemorate and venerate the bravery of the MSAA and the sacrifice made by the 4 who perished at Fearnan, a memorial has been raised on the ground formerly occupied by RAF Errol. In a symbolic gesture to the Soviet Union, the memorial includes several birch trees, a national icon of Russia.

Another notable MSAA pilot based at RAF Errol within No. 305 FTU is Peter Kolennikov who trained with the unit between 1 January 1943 and 30 April 1944. Kolennikov's war record saw him awarded several medals for bravery and gallantry including 2 Orders of the Red Star. The medals were well deserved: Kolennikov, as part of the Special Moscow Airgroup, carried out many daring missions including the evacuation of civilians from Leningrad, evacuating casualties from Sevastopol under dense artillery fire, and flying behind enemy lines to provide supplies to partisans during the Rzhev campaigns.

Units using RAF Errol during the Second World War include:

No. 9 EGS (Elementary Gliding School). No. 9 PAFU (Navy pilot training unit relocated from RAF Hullavington, Wiltshire).

No. 260 MU, No. 271 Squadron RAF.

No. 810 Squadron RNFAA.

No. 1544 BAT Flight (Blind (later Beam) Approach Training Flight).

No. 1680 (Transport) Flight RAF.

Two Armstrong Whitley A.W.38 twin-engine bombers, each towing a glider, landed at RAF Errol from RAF Kirkbride (Cumbria) on 6 August 1943. The outmoded Whitley had been removed from frontline service but nonetheless attested to be useful as a glider tug. In addition, RAF Errol was used as a base for packing and air-dropping supplies to advancing troops. Six Douglas C-47 Skytrain transport aircraft, (aka Dakotas) of No. 271 Squadron RAF were used at RAF Errol for this purpose. A pair of Airspeed As.51 Horsa 1 troop-carrying gliders are listed on the manifest of RAF Errol. These gliders were towed into flight by the station's Dakota complement. Although RAF Errol had been photographed by Luftwaffe reconnaissance aircraft in April 1943, the later additions to the airbase remained unknown to the German military.

The Allies tried to deceive the German high command that an invasion of Norway was planned. 'Operation Tindall' was conceived to suggest that the main goal of the Allies was a sea and air landing in mid-September 1943 at Stavanger – to capture the city and Sola Airfield, which could be used as a base for forward operations well beyond the range of Scotland-based fighter squadrons. RAF Errol was a player in 'Operation Tindall'. Operation Tindall' was one of 3 'fake' invasion stories under the overall name of Operation Cockade, the other 2 being 'Operation Wadham', an invasion at Brest, and 'Operation Starkey', an invasion at Boulogne.

There were a series of three deception operations designed to deceive the Germans that an invasion might occur in areas such as Brest and Boulogne in France or at Stavanger in Norway. The Germans kept back twelve army divisions in Norway to counter the potential threat. This weakened their defences in Sicily which the allies invaded 9 July 1943 – 17 August 1943 and reduced the forces available for the German Operation Citadel, the encircling attack at the Battle of Kursk, July 1943 which was repulsed by the Soviet Red Army. Adolf Hitler eventually cancelled further attempts to break through the Soviet defences during this offensive, in part due to the news of the Allied invasion of Sicily. The soviets suffered 800,000 casualties at Kursk. These deception plans also weakened the German defences at Normandy where the D-Day landings took place in June 1944.

Two Armstrong Whitley A.W38 twin-engine bombers, each towing a glider landed at RAF Errol on 6 August 1943. RAF Errol at the time was a base for packing and air-dropping supplies to advancing troops using six Douglas C-47 Skytrain transport aircraft, (aka Dakotas) of RAF 271 Squadron. A pair of Airspeed As.51 Horsa I troop-carrying gliders were listed on the manifest of RAF Errol in 1943. The various activities at Errol worried the Germans, a Luftwaffe reconnaissance aircraft of Luftwaffen-Führungsstab Ic (Command Staff) was detailed to photograph the Flugplatz (airfield) in April 1943.

RAF Errol went into maintenance mode on 26 June 1945 when 800 RAF and WAAF personnel left for

Shropshire. One hundred men entrained at 2.00pm at Inchcoonans and about five hundred personnel left by train at 6.00pm from Errol Station. Perth Black Watch Pipe Band piped them on the 2½ miles from the aerodrome. The remainder flew directly to Shropshire. The daily transport service plane to RNAS Hatston (HMS Sparrowhawk) in Orkney was maintained until the RAF left the aerodrome.

NOTES:

RAF 'Flights' were fully independent flying units of less than squadron size.

The Supermarine Walrus which was first flown in 1933 was designed by R. J. Mitchell, he of the legendary Spitfire design fame.

The last aircraft to use RAF Errol was probably a Vickers Wellington from RAF Dalcross (Inverness Airport) that landed there in August of 1945.

Drahovzal was a 34-year-old cook in the Czechoslovakian Army who wished to take an aerial excursion before the end of his tour in Scotland. He lies in Murie Cemetery, Errol, a section of which was reserved for airmen who died while based at RAF Errol.

No. 271 Squadron RAF became part of the newly formed No. 46 RAF (Transport) Group in February 1944. They trained extensively with the 1st and 6th Airborne Divisions and the 1st (Polish) Independent Parachute Brigade.

Frantisek Drahovzal-cook, Aleksandr-Alexeev-flight-engineer, Vaslily-Dryamin-navigator-radio-operator & Aleksandr-Gruzdin-Pilot-Commander

Gannet & Vampire at Errol

Armstrong Whitworth Albemarle

Nur für den Dienstgebrauch

GB 10477 b

Bild Nr. F 15/43 SG 109 (Lfl. 5)

Aufnahme vom 10. 3. 43

Errol

Flugplatz

Länge (westl. Greenw.): 3° 11' 00" Breite: 56° 24' 09"

Mißweisung: — 12° 36' (Mitte 1943) Zielhöhe über NN 10 m

Maßstab etwa 1 : 21 500

500 0 500 1000 m

Lw. Fü. Stab Ic April 1943

Karte 1 : 100 000

GB/S 23

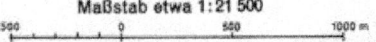

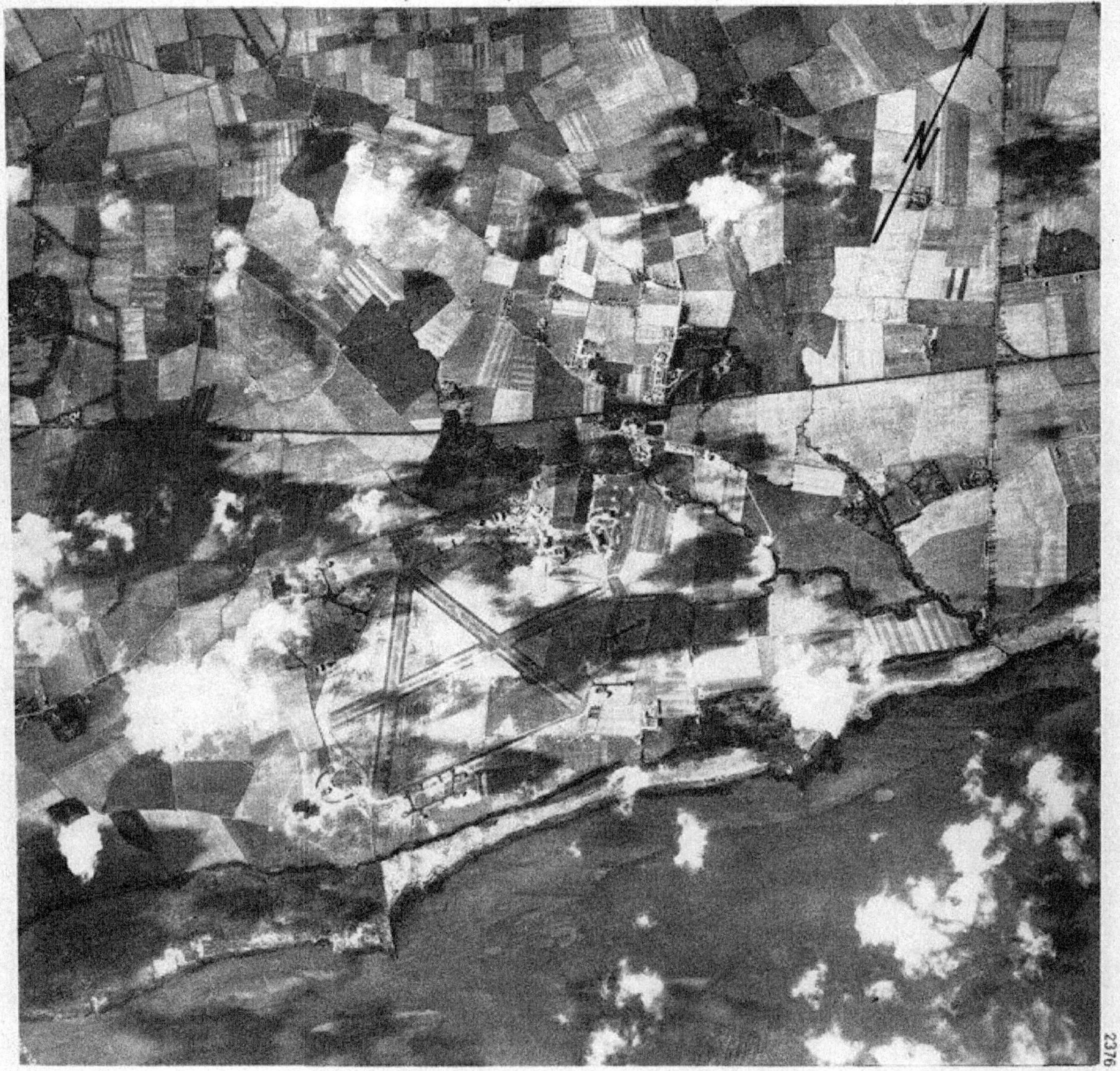

RAF Findo Gask

RAF Findo Gask was located at Clathymore, near Findo Gask, some 8 miles west of Perth. it was operational between 14 June 1941 and 12 September1948. it was, however, abandoned as an airfield in 1944 due to problems with flooding, mud, and poor drainage. the complex comprised3 grass runways (1,100, 1,250, and 1,950 yards) fabricated with Sommerfeld wire mesh tracking, a type t2 (13-bay) hangar, 7 blister hangars (portable arched of corrugated steel sheeting), a technical area, dispersal areas, 16 hard- standings for aircraft, and accommodation facilities. The airfield's complement included 59 officers, 70 SNCOs, 538 ORs, and 196 WAAF personnel. Pilots using RAF Findo Gask used Dupplin Lake on the grounds of the Dupplin Estate (east of the airfield) as a flying landmark.

RAF Findo Gask operated as a flight training airfield for personnel joining Polish squadrons. Flights A and C of No 309 Squadron operated out of RAF Findo Gask between 26 October 1942 and 8 March 1943 (Westland Lysanders); Flight 'B' of No. 309 Squadron between 15 December 1942 and January 1943 (North American Mk I P-51 Mustangs). Flight 'B' was subsequently redeployed to RAF Gatwick as Findo Gask's runways proved too short for the Mustangs. These were sent south to conduct to conduct English Channel patrols and reconnaissance missions. They were then reallocated up to RAF Peterhead, where the 309 Squadron Polish airmen in their Mustangs, flew protection cover for very many Russia bound convoy patrols in the North Sea.

In addition, the airfield operated as an SLG for the RNFAA's Miles M.9 Masters of No. 9 PAFU (RAF Errol) (28 March 1943 – 12 September 1944) – No. 25 SLG. Other units using RAF Findo Gask during the Second World War include No. 11 EFTS, No. 44 MU, and No. 260 MU.

One consistent comment recorded in reports regarding the field at Findo Gask was that it suffered poor draining, with the runways becoming waterlogged and muddy. The grass runways were constructed using Sommerfeld steel tracking, which used steel mesh pinned to the ground and reinforced with steel bars, but continued flooding led to the eventual abandonment of the airfield.

RAF 309 Squadron Mustangs at RAF Drem (near North Berwick)

309 Squadron "Land of Czerwien" Lysanders

Findo Gask

Wellshill Cemetery & General Władysław Sikorski, Polish Commander-In-Chief. The stone is inscribed with the words: "Eternal glory to the Polish soldiers who died in 1939-1945 for our freedom and yours."

RAF 309 Squadron Mustangs at RAF Peterhead

RAF Grangemouth

Not quite in Perthshire, RAF Grangemouth lay just to the south of Perthshire across the River Forth. It played a primary role in the instruction of hundreds of RAF, Polish Force, and other international pilots within No. 58 OTU RAF.

Air

In 2008, a memorial garden was opened on land that stood within the perimeter fence (Abbotsinch Road, by the Powdrake Roundabout) of the former RAF Grangemouth to memorialise the 71 trainee pilots (from 11 different countries) who died while training at the station. Their names are inscribed on a wall within the garden. On 9 May 2013, a full-size replica of a Spitfire Mk 1 (upon a plinth) was added to the memorial garden. The replica bears the code PQ-N, the plane flown by Sergeant Pilot Eugeniusz Lukomski (23), who died in an accident during training in November 1941. His plane crashed in the Avondale Estate, Polmont.

A typical flight training course delivered by No. 58 OTU RAF at RAF Grangemouth is detailed below.

14 July-25 August 1941

Flying Miles Masters – 2 hours 50 minutes dual, 6 hours 25 minutes solo.

Flying Supermarine Spitfires – 36 hours 10 minutes.

Link – 6 hours 50 minutes.

Instrumentation – 3 hours.

Formation Flying – 12 hours.

Flying aptitude was listed under several headings:

Natural Aptitude - Skill in Landing

Airmanship - Aerobatics and Dog Fight

Cockpit Drill - Instrument Flying

Formation Flying - Air Firing Map Reading.

RAF Methven

Situated to the east of Methven Castle (close to where Loan Leven Quarry is located today), RAF Methven operated as No. 24 SLG RAF. Operational units based at RAF Methven included No. 652 Squadron RAF (28 March 1943 – 2 July 1943) equipped with de Havilland Tiger Moths and later Taylorcraft Auster observation aircraft, No. 44 Maintenance Unit RAF, and an Air Observation Post. The station was established in 1940.

The airfield that covered 3 fields in area included accommodation buildings made of wood and those of Nissen design hidden among a wooded area (on the south side of the A85 close to the minor road to Tibbermore). Aircraft sent to RAF Methven for repair were hidden in 'cut-out' areas among the trees. Aircraft repaired there included Bristol Beaufort torpedo bombers, Hawker Hurricanes, Vickers Wellington medium bombers, and Westland Lysanders. On 30 July 1943, a Short Stirling 4-engine heavy bomber landed at RAF Methven. By the end of the year, Stirling bombers were a regular sight at the airfield.

By the end of the war, RAF Methven had been converted into an 'open' camp for Italian and later German prisoners of war. Camp life was not harsh, and many prisoner accommodation huts had their own small gardens.

NOTES: No. 652 Squadron RAF moved with the Second Army from the breakout at Normandy, through France, Belgium, and the Netherlands and into Germany. The 'C' flight of the squadron has been recognized as responsible for discharging the last British gunshots of the war in Europe while guiding artillery at the siege of Dunkirk – 7 May 1945 – alongside No. 665 Squadron RCAF.

Vickers Wellington bombers were predominantly designed by Barnes Wallace, he of the 'bouncing bomb' and 'Dambusters' renown. (Wallace also designed the de Havilland DH.98 Mosquito.) There is a good chance a few Mosquitos were repaired at RAF Methven. Along with RAF Findo Gask, RAF Methven was used for warehousing light non-operational aircraft such as the 3-seater dual-control Percival Proctor monoplane (formerly stored at RAF Perth).

The Short Stirling was renowned for its challenging flight characteristics during take-off and landing. It is striking that such a large aircraft was landed at all on RAF Methven's single runway.

RAF Perth

Early Days

The idea of an aerodrome at Perth was first mooted in the early 1930s by Thomas Hunter, Lord Provost of Perth (later the local Member of Parliament) but received scant backing from the inhabitants of the Fair City. It was anticipated an airfield near Perth would attract several air operations, including domestic scheduled flights, and airmail services.

In late 1934, the British Government announced an expansion of the RAF and Councillor Ure Primrose revived Hunter's plans for an aerodrome. This time there was an expectation that a small aerodrome might attract pilot training work to Perth and in turn draw business to the area. A year later, tenders were put out for the planned aerodrome.

In December 1936, Airwork Limited, a firm based in Middlesex, England, commenced its lengthy connection with Scone Aerodrome being contracted to deliver RAF flying training. This was RAF No. 11 ERFTS, a flight preparation facility for RAF personnel.

For the construction of the airfield, a relatively fog-free site 400 feet above sea level was nominated just beyond Scone village. Work began in June 1935. Flying training commenced on the frozen airfield on 14 January 1936 with the first recorded landing – a DH.85 Leopard Moth (G-ACHD) piloted by W. Gardiner. Landing was suspended as the thaw came, to allow the newly sown grass to establish. A direction-finding tower was soon installed.

Perth initially enjoyed four daily civilian passenger services, two to Glasgow and two to Inverness. In 1936-7, North Eastern Airways began regular services between Perth and Newcastle, Leeds, Doncaster, and London, northwards to Aberdeen, and westwards to Renfrew using Airspeed AS.6 Envoys, and later de Havilland DH.89 Dragon Rapide's. A service was established in September 1939 by British Airways between Perth and Stav anger and Oslo, Norway) using Lockheed Model 14 Super Electra's and German Junkers JU 52s of Swedish registration. This was not to last very long as war hostilities had commenced on the first of that month with Germ any's attack on Poland. The service was closed on 9 April 1940 with the invasion of Norway.

Wartime

During the Second World War, RAF Perth (based at what was then called Newlands Aerodrome, subsequently Scone Aerodrome and now Perth Airport) maintained a complement of 28 officers, 37 SNCOs and 326 ORs – a total of 391. There are no records of the WAAF personnel at RAF Perth. The grass runway length was listed as 1,300 yards, extendible and in a direction, NE to SW. As well as a large hangar whose construction pre-dated the war, the RAF made use of two civil buildings – one 160 x 90 feet, the other 120 x 110 feet. Six blister type buildings were added alongside (at least) four defensive pillboxes. No hard standings for aircraft are detailed in the available archival records.

At the end of December 1940, RAF Perth was the base for 90 de Havilland Tiger Moths of a total of 367 training aircraft assigned to RAF No. 11 ERFTS at RAF Perth. As well as Tiger Moths, the training school operated Airspeed Oxford, Avro Anson, Hawker Audax, Hawker Hart, Hawker Hind, Hawker Hurricane, Miles Magister, Miles Master, North American Harvard, and Fairey Battle aircraft. The 41 aircraft of No. 5 FIS included Airspeed Oxfords, Miles Magisters, Miles Masters, and Tiger Moths.

Overall, during World War Two, the total number of aircraft assigned to the main units at RAF Perth was:

318 Tiger Moths, types I & II

164 Miles Magister, type I

2 Hawker Audax, type 1

5 Hawker Hart, type I (1), Trainer (2), Special (1)

3 Hawker Hind, type Trainer (2)

1 Fairey Battle, type I

1 Avro Anson, type I

4 Airspeed Oxford, type I (3) & II (1)

1 North American Harvard, type IIB

I Hawker Hurricane.

The Hawker Hurricane N2325 was only assigned for 3 days from 1 August 1940 to 3 August 1940. It was originally sold 2 February 1940 to the Gloster Aircraft Company for delivery to Finland. It crashed however at RAF Wick (Pilot Ensign Tapio Taskinen); when its right main gear collapsed. After its short stint at RAF Perth, it was passed on to RCAF 1 Squadron and may have taken part in the Battle of Britain flying out of RAF Croydon and RAF Northolt. N2325 was later assigned to RAF 59 OTU, at RAF Millfield on 3/2/1941.

Flight Sergeant Henry Anselm de Freitas (Wellshill Cemetery, Perth) was a ground attack instructor at RAF Millfield with RAF 59 OTU in 1943.

A trainee pilot reminisces.

Trainee pilots were expected to fly solo on a Tiger Moth after typically 10 to 12 hours training in the aircraft. Alternate days were spent in lectures and flying. The 'wanabee' pilots would receive between 30 and 40 hours flying per week, the flying day lasted between seven and nine hours. The odds of success of becoming a pilot and being posted for further pilot training were 33%. Those who did not qualify went on to be observers, wireless operator/gunners, navigators, bomb aimers and air gunners.

Stephen P L Johnson one of the early trainees at Perth recalled:

"Everybody has a tremendous respect for the man who teaches him to fly an aeroplane. You have a lasting sense of gratitude and admiration for your first Flying Instructor. It is unlikely that you will forget entirely your first girlfriend, but you don't remember her with anything like the same affection and respect as you do the man who says, 'Well off you go,' on your first solo flight.

I expect Sergeant Winning was really quite an ordinary little man but to me he was simply wonderful because he could handle a Tiger Moth with such unconcerned skill. On my first flight with him I was scared to death and thought, 'God, I shall never be able to do this by myself.' But gradually I became used to it all and even became accustomed to stalling and spinning, which we had to do before we went solo. We were grounded for four days from October 18th to 22nd by bad weather and I was terrified lest I should have forgotten all I had learnt: but luckily I hadn't and on October 24th I was given my solo test by another instructor. I didn't think that I was nearly good enough but after doing a circuit with him he climbed out and said, 'Well off you go and do one circuit.

There I was without a familiar figure in the front cockpit. The green of the aerodrome stretched away towards the distant hills. After the cockpit checks, I eased the throttle gradually open and went bumping away across the grass. Soon there were no more bumps and I was climbing away at the correct speed with only the familiar sound of the Gypsy engine and the buffeting of the slipstream on my helmet for company. Then I had a feeling that there was something missing. For a moment, I couldn't place it till suddenly I realised that it was the fact that I wasn't feeling at all frightened. I had always imagined that I should be scared absolutely to death on my first solo. I was quite amused to find that I wasn't. I managed quite a reasonable landing and was as proud of myself as is everyone when he or she achieves a first solo flight.

Naturally this called for a terrific celebration that evening and we repaired as usual to the Salutation (Hotel) where there was plenty of alcohol and some extremely attractive girls'.

I don't think that I have ever in my life enjoyed a month more than the one I spent in Perth. We flew about over the wonderful countryside on clear October days. The hoar-frost glistened in the shade and the sun shone on golden bracken and stubble with the mountains in the distance. The Tay twisted its way through woods and fields. It was all something that I shall never forget.

Even flying one of those ancient aircraft, which were designed before people fully realised why an aircraft stayed aloft, one experienced an elementary thrill which is denied to the pilot of the present day. He sits in an enclosed heated and pressurised cabin. His speed may be many hundreds of miles an hour, but it gives him no thrill. Our speed was only eighty miles an hour, but we were fully aware of every single one of those mph as the air rushed and whistled past our faces. If we glanced up at the ancient wings and the rusty bolts where they were attached to the fuselage, we saw that they moved up and down in an alarming way as the wind buffeted them. It is quite remarkable that these very, very old aeroplanes are still used today to teach people to fly. One might just as well expect to see a pterodactyl flying around.

We didn't have time to do many aerobatics for I only did twenty hours solo the whole-time I was at Perth. I did get as far as looping the loop and felt very brave about it. The first one I did by myself, I thought was rather good. I was just coming nicely out of it feeling somewhat relieved to be the right way *up again when the aircraft gave the most horrible shudder. I glanced back anxiously around to see whether any essential piece had fallen off, but all seemed to be well. Eventually I realised that my loop had been altogether too accurate, and that I had flown through my own slipstream.*

We were very much spoilt in Perth. The carefree attitude and friendship between instructors and pupils was too good to last."

Units Based at RAF Perth During the Second World War

Main Units

RAF No. 11 ERFTS (27 January 1936 – 3 September 1939).

No.7 Civilian Air Navigation School (9 January 1939 – 1 November

1939). The school was run by civilians until the start of the Second World War at which point it became part of the RAF and was renamed as No. 7 Air Observer & Navigation School (1 November 1939 – 1 June 1940).

No. 11 EFTS (3 September 1939 – 18 March 1947).

Other Units

Wireless Development Flight (12 September 1939 – 24 October 1939). 'D' Flight,

Aeroplane & Armament Experimental Establishment (15 September 1939 – Unknown).

No. 7 Air Observer & Navigation School (AONS) (1 November 1939 – 1 June 1940).

No. 5 Flying Instructors School (FIS)

(8 October 1940 – 23 November 1942). No. 5 FIS (Elementary).

No. 5 FIS (Supplementary)

No. 9 Gliding School (November 1945 – Unknown).

No. 9 EGS.

No. 11 RFS (18 March 1947 – 20 June 1954).

No. 11 EFTS.

No. 666 Squadron RAF (1 May 1949 – 10 March 1957).

No. 1966 Reserve AOP Flight (1 May 1949 – 1 January 1957) – associated with Taylorcraft Auster observation (artillery spotting) aircraft.

No. 1967 Reserve AOP Flight (2 February 1954 – 1 September 1955) – associated with Taylorcraft Auster observation (artillery spotting) aircraft.

Glasgow University Air Squadron (1 December 1950 – 1 January 1965). No. 1 Civilian Fighter Control Co-operation Unit (8 March 1957 – 31 January 1961). Universities of Glasgow & Strathclyde Air Squadron (1 January 1965 – 1992).

No. 309 Squadron (March 1941 – May 1941) – the squadron was based at RAF Perth until RAF Findo Gask was available. The training undertaken by the squadron at RAF Perth included night flying.

No. 12 Air Experience Flight (1 April 1996 – Unknown).

Experimental Flight. No. 7 CANS.

Detachments

No. 6 AACU (2 May 1940 – 20 November 1940). No. 7 AACU (27 December 1940 – 1941).

The Villa "Durn"

The Royal Air Force Volunteer Reserve (RAFVR)used the villa Durn, Isla Road Perth as it headquarters during World War Two. Listed as Commandant was Wing Commander (Retired) G. H. Hall AFC and the Assistant Commandant Flight Lieutenant W. C. Wilson OBE (RAFO).

In use during WW2 at Durn was a Link Trainer flight simulator. These trainers were built from 1934 up to the early 1940s. They had a colour scheme that featured a bright blue fuselage and yellow wings and tail sections. The wings and tail sections had control surfaces that moved in response to the pilot's movement of the rudder and stick. Many of the trainers built during mid to late war did not have these wings and tail sections due to material shortages and critical manufacturing times.

It was reported in the Dundee Courier and Advertiser, Monday, June 6th, 1938: *"Flyers will learn Bombing indoors, RAF Buys Perth residence.' It Said 'One of the most picturesquely-situated houses in Perth – The Durn, Isla Road – has been sold to the R.A.F. Volunteer Reserve. It is to be used as an instructional and recreation centre, and one of the latest devices for training is to be incorporated in two of the rooms. This consists of a cockpit, complete with all controls, in which the pilots learn, among other things bombing. 'Synchronised with the controls is a projector that casts the picture of a moving landscape, showing churches, houses, and factories, etc. Should the pilot deviate from the course that has been set him this deviation is at once indicated. "Hits", by bombs on this landscape are also calculated, the effect being that the potential pilot receives "flying training" without leaving the ground. Actual flying experience is carried out at Newlands Aerodrome during daytime.'*

'Wing Commander Hall, town commandant told the "Courier and Advertiser" reporter 'that the Durn was to be used as town headquarters. We have an establishment of 50 trainees" he said. "I hope that in the very near future the establishment will be increased to at least 100". The building will also incorporate mess rooms and rooms for recreation, while tennis courts are also to be constructed. The house, which belonged to Mr A. E. Pullar, stands on the banks of the river Tay, opposite the North Inch.'

Stephen P L Johnson, described his training: -*'In charge at the 'Durn', and responsible for seeing that we got into the bus each morning to go to Scone Aerodrome, was the dirtiest, scruffiest, idlest Flight Sergeant any Airman ever had the good fortune to meet. Never once during our stay did he polish his own boots or buttons and he didn't care in the least whether we did or not.*

Scone Aerodrome had been a peace-time flying school. To convert it to a war-time RAF aerodrome the instructors were issued with uniforms, but little appeared to have been done to alter their habits. We went there to learn to fly and if it was humanly possible to teach us to do so they did: but they never minded whether we arrived clean and tidy or not. Mark you we were all extremely keen.

The preliminary training, when we never saw an aeroplane and sometimes doubted whether we ever should, had been somewhat frustrating. To us the few disintegrating and ancient Tiger Moths with which Scone was equipped were a wonderful sight. The one terrible fear which we all had was that we should be unable to make the things perform their evolutions sufficiently well to satisfy our instructors."

Flying Schools like RAF Perth No. 11 ERFTS were run by civilian contractors who mainly employed instructors who were members of the Reserve of Air Force Officers (RAFO). They had previously completed a four-year service commission as pilots in the RAF.

Hundreds of pilots were trained at RAF Perth during the war. There must have been at least 100 training aircraft in use every day. The airfield was a 'pilot factory' producing the large numbers of pilots required by the war effort. When you read about some of the Second World War pilots who were trained at Scone (RAF Perth), you will further understand the impressive contribution of this aerodrome to the war effort.

The post-war period

In the post-war period, the RAF underwent major changes. On 20 June 1954, RAF No. 11 EFTS was renamed as an RFS and was reequipped with de Havilland Chipmunks. And, in 1960, Airwork acquired the Aeronautical Engineering College in Hamble, and relocated it to its existing training operation at Perth/Scone Aerodrome where it became known as Airwork Services Training. Scone Aerodrome's pair of runways were laid with asphalt in 1969. The company added an English language school to the facilities in 1971 to fulfil an Imperial Iranian Navy training agreement. The Flying School and the Aeronautical Engineering College became part of Air Service Training. Air Service Training ceased pilot training at Scone in 1996 but a popular and successful AST engineering training school continues at Perth College, which forms part of the University of the Highlands & Islands.

Today, the main entrance road from the A94 into the airport is called Spitfire Avenue. Perth Airport at Scone is now owned by the Morris Leslie Group. The airfield operations are managed by ACS Aviation who also run a commercial pilot training school. The Scottish Aero Club, a private recreational flying club with its own microlight training organisation Alba Airsports are also based at the airport. Take Off, c/o The Scottish Aero Club at Scone Airport is a charitable trust set up to increase opportunity, education, and awareness in the field of aviation in Scotland. Scotland's Charity Air Ambulance Service (SCAA) was formed in 2012 and launched a helicopter air-ambulance service in May 2013 using Perth Airport as its central base. There are currently no scheduled commercial flights from the airport.

There is an interesting short film of the first post-war flying display at the aerodrome viewable on the British Pathé website – Around Britain (1947).

As part of the US government lend-lease programme, Britain received aid, military equipment, and aircraft. Some of the aircraft that had long-distance capability were flown over the Atlantic via Newfoundland, Greenland, and Iceland before landing at either RAF Prestwick or RAF/USAAF Burtonwood in Lancashire, whereafter they were delivered to where they would be in service. Shorter-range aircraft, such as the Republic P-47 Thunderbolt, were shipped to British ports, including that at Govan. From Govan, the crated aircraft were transported to RAF Renfrew and RAF Perth for assembly. They were then flown to operational units by the ATA (Air Transport Auxiliary).

Author's Notes:

Ostensibly a civilian operation, the ATA included 168 female pilots (of a pilot complement of over 1,300). Its unofficial motto was 'Anything to Anywhere'.

Airwork Service Training at Hamble purchased several Airspeed Oxfords after the war, some of which ended up at Scone Aerodrome. In total, 750 Airspeed Oxfords (Mk 1) were manufactured by the Standard Motor Car Company Limited, Coventry.

Former Second World War flying instructor Ian Rae served with No. 11 RFS in the 1950s. His time there and earlier experiences in the RAF are the subject of his collection of poetry - A Pilot's Notes (2011).

Information regarding Stephen P L Johnson pilot training taken from Ken Fenton's War - https://kenfentonswar.com/raf-training/

PERTH AIR CADETS AT CHURCH.—On Sunday the Perth Air Cadets paraded and attended divine worship at Trinity Church. The picture shows them marching past the Old Academy buildings after their inspection on the North Inch by Brig.-Gen. J. H. W. Becke, C.M.G., D.S.O., A.F.C. The smart appearance of the boys was commented upon.

("P.A." Photo.)

Postcard showing the DH 82 Tiger Moth Trainer, notes on the reverse state 'Flown at Perth E.F.T.S. 28 Hours Dual, 19 Solo.'

Taken in 1947 and shows a number of Tiger Moths still on Scone Aerodrome.

PERTH
Lat. 56° 26' 23"N. Long. 3° 22' 8"W.   385 FT. A.S.L.

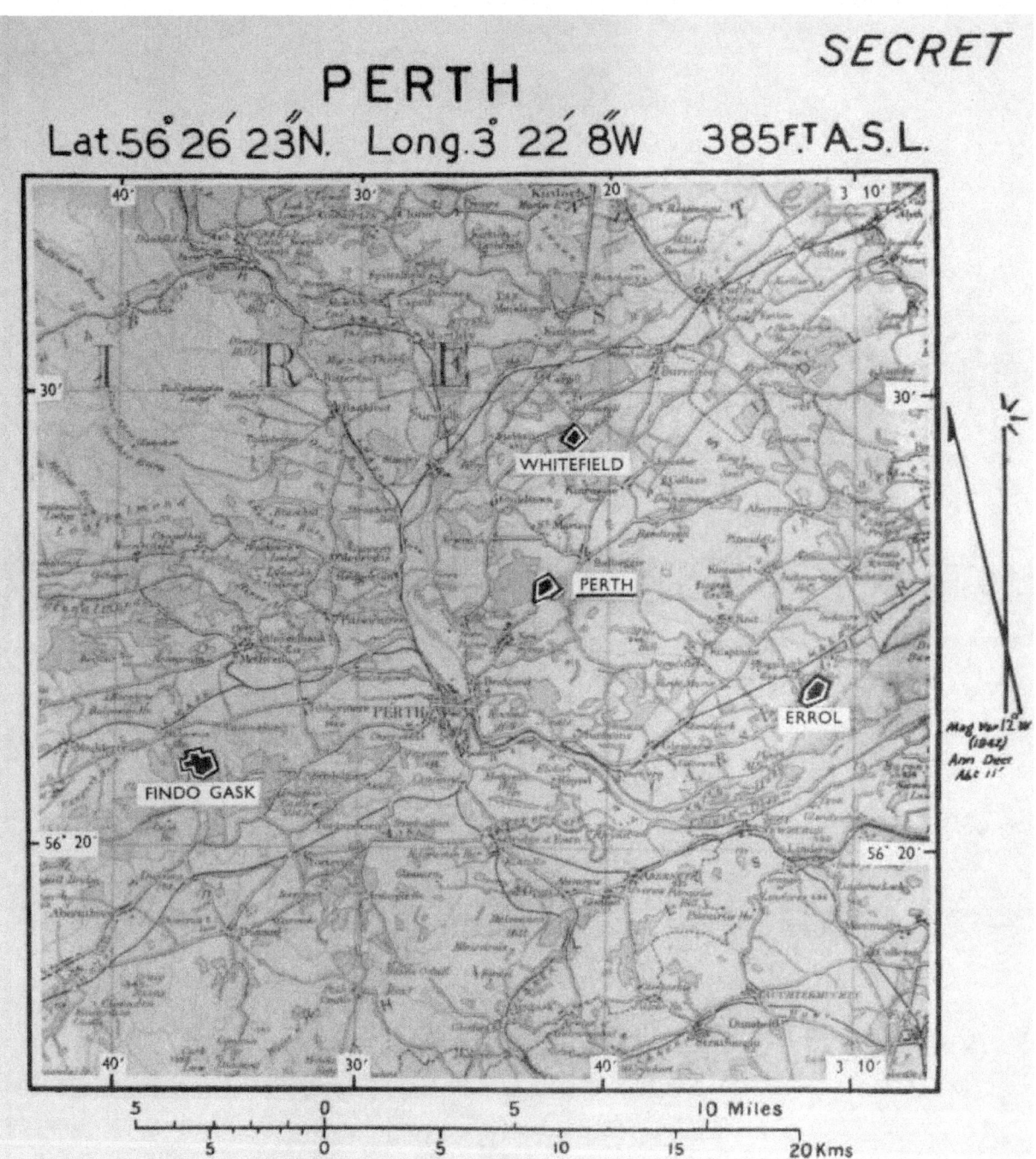

BLOTTER
AIRWORK SERVICES TRAINING.
BRITAIN'S AIR UNIVERSITY.
FLYING EXERCISES.

1. Preparation for, and action after, Flight.
1A. Engine Starting and Propeller swinging.
2. Air Experience.

EMERGENCIES.

3A. Fire in the Engine in the Air.
3B. Fire in the Engine on the Ground.
3C. Fire in the Cockpit in the Air.
3D. Fire in the Cockpit on the Ground.
3E. Engine Failure after Take-off.
3F. Engine Failure en route and action taken.
3G. Precautionary Landing en route and action after.
3H. Procedure when Lost.
3J. Action with Brake Failure.
4. Effect of Controls.
5. Taxying.
6. Cruising Flight.
7. Climbing and Descending.
8G. Stalling from a Glide and Recovery.
8S. Stalling in a Turn and Recovery.
9N. Turns Normal.
9C. Turns on to Compass Courses.
9S. Steep Turns.
9G. Steep Gliding Turns.
10G. Spinning from a Glide, and Recovery.
10F. Spinning, further Recovery Action.
10T. Spinning from a Turn, and Recovery.
11N. Take-off Normal.
11S. Short Take-off.
11X. Cross Wind Take-off.
12G. Glide Approach and Landing.
12E. Engine Assisted Approach and Landing.
12F. Flapless Approach and Landing.
12X. Cross Wind Landing.
12W. Wheel Landing.
12S. Short Landing.
12O. Overshooting.
12A. Asymmetric Approach and Landing.
13. First Solo in Type.
14. Circuit Rejoining.
15F. Instrument Flying — Full Panel.
15L. Instrument Flying—Limited Panel.
15R. Instrument Flying — Radio Aids.
15A. Instrument Flying — Airways Flying.
16. Precision Flying Practice.
17. Sideslipping.
18. Aerobatics.
19. Night Circuits and Landings.
19N. Night Navigation.
20M. Local Map Reading.
20X. Cross Country Flying. (Always enter Turning or Landing Points.)
20R. Radio Navigation.
21. Asymmetric Flight.
22. Familiarisation on New Type. (Minimum of Take-off, Stall, Overshoot, Landing, any peculiarities of Equipment or Handling.)

D. LESLIE, Printer & Stationer, **PERTH.** Works - 42-48 CANAL ST. Retail Shop — 20 ST. JOHN ST.
Telephone: PERTH 22231.

Pre-war photograph of Scone Aerodrome

RAF Tealing

Like RAF Grangemouth, RAF Tealing lay just beyond the borders of Perthshire, some 6 miles north of Dundee and 25 miles east of Perth. It deserves inclusion in this book as it was the home of No. 56 OTU RAF and operated for a time as an SLG for No. 9 PAFU (RAF Errol).

Flight instruction at RAF Tealing employed Hawker Hurricanes, Westland Lysanders, and Miles M.9 Masters. With the deployment of No. 527 Squadron, the Hurricanes were swapped for Supermarine Spitfires. The squadron's operational role was radar station calibration. Given the proximity of University College, Dundee, where Robert Watson-Watt, who played a pioneering role in the development of radar, held a professorship, he may have been the reason that No. 527 Squadron was sited at RAF Tealing.

One important episode associated with RAF Tealing is the visit to Britain in May 1942 of Vyacheslav Molotov, the Minister of Foreign Affairs of the Soviet Union, to deliberate with the British Government the opening of a second front against Nazi Germany. Molotov's secret flight in a high altitude 4-engine Petlyakov Pe-8 bomber from the Soviet Union took him over Luftwaffe dominated airspace. None the less, his plane landed at RAF Tealing safely.

Molotov's onward flight to meet Vyacheslav Molotov, Winston Churchill might well have been his last. Two, de Havilland DH.95 Flamingo airliners were provided for the passage, one of which crashed near to the village of Great Ouseburn in the Harrogate district of North Yorkshire killing all its passengers (senior RAF personnel and Soviet staff) and crew. Molotov had been given the choice as to which plane to take. By pure fortuitousness he was not on the plane that crashed. At his meeting with Churchill, Anthony Eden, the British Foreign Minister, and other government members, Molotov formally signed the Anglo-Soviet (mutual assistance) Treaty of 1942 that created a military and political alliance between the 2 great political powers.

The Imperial War Museum is the depository of several films showing the arrival of Molotov at RAF Tealing and his later departure from RAF Prestwick.

Note: Considered one of the inventors of radar, Robert Watson-Watt whose first wife was from Perth, is buried in the graveyard of Holy Trinity Episcopal Church, Pitlochry (see **Margaret Watson-Watt**).

RAF Whitefield

RAF Whitefield situated near Wolfhill, some 7 miles north-east of Perth, opened late in 1939, primarily as a Relief Landing Ground (RLG) to RAF Perth. It comprised a small (1,050-yard-long) grass runway with 8 blister hangars and temporary accommodation (possibly tents). To assist night landings, the airfield utilised a 'Gooseneck Flarepath', which comprised several short, oval watering-can-style paraffin lamps, with wicks protruding from their spouts, placed along the runway. They were later replaced by small electric Glim Lamps and Chance Floodlights powered by a generator mounted on a trailer.

RAF Whitefield closed on 9 July 1945, the land reverting to farmland. Today, only the flight office survives as evidence of the former airfield. Records detail a staffing complement of 36 in 1944. Units using RAF Whitefield during the Second World War include No. 11 EFTS and No. 5 Flying Instructor School (FIS). The airfield was employed to ease the load at RAF Perth and was very busy in this task. As would be expected from a busy flight training school, there were many recorded accidents, most due to poor landings especially those involving night flying. Fortunately, no one was seriously injured in any known incident. In one case, a de Havilland Mosquito FBV1 (HP856) out of RAF No. 8 OTU was forced to land at RAF Whitefield due to its cockpit filling with smoke because of a faulty radio. The aircraft underwent repair and continued in service until being scrapped in July 1947.

Scone Park

Scone Park was an SLG of RAF Perth. It is not listed as a separate RAF airfield; it was regarded as being part of RAF Perth at Scone. Scone Park is today occupied by Scone Racecourse.

South Kilduff Airfield

Between Balado and Crook of Devon lies the farm of South Kilduff. It was described as a '3rd class landing ground' by the NW Area of the Royal Flying Corps, 46th Wing of No. 77 Home Defence Squadron – one of the home defence squadrons formed in 1916 in response to bombing raids by German Zeppelin airships. No. 77 Squadron was responsible for the defence of the Firth of Forth and the coastline from Berwick-upon-Tweed northwards.

Such landing grounds were created in case of engine failure or if bad weather prevented an aircraft from returning to its main base. When the squadron was flying, the farmer, on whose land the strip lay, was telephoned to remove any of his animals that might be grazing on the landing area.

RFC South Kilduff landing strip measured 440 metres by 247 meters (11 hectares). There are no traces of its existence left. Where it was exactly is unknown, there are two or three fields to my knowledge that are possibilities. The airfield was notified for relinquishment at the end of WW1.

Royal Aircraft Factory, BE2 and BE12 fighters were allocated to RFC 77 Squadron. In 1918, they switched to Avro 504ks. The BE 12 was the single-seat version of the BE 2. The Avro 504k was a two-seat training aircraft, some were converted for anti-zeppelin work and converted for night fighting. The Avro 504 was used by 38 countries and more than 10,000 were built until production ended in 1940 in Japan (Yokosuka K2Y).

Murie Cemetery Errol, Fairey Swordfish, and the river Tay

Arthur A. J. Roberton

Arthur A. J. Roberton was born on 12.03.14, in Westmount, Quebec, Canada to Lewis Alexander Roberton (of Govan, near Glasgow) and Mary (nee Pearson), also born in Scotland. Arthur's parents were married in Montreal on 17.05.06 and Arthur was the third child (and second son), all of whom were born in Canada.

Arthur was baptised (as a Presbyterian) in Montreal on 19.03.14. His father, Lewis Snr, was a chartered accountant, who died on 30.03.16 aged 49 years, shortly after Arthur's second birthday. Mary and her three children arrived back in Glasgow, on board the Athenia, on 29.10.16. Arthur's mother remarried in 1933, when Arthur was 19, to Douglas Graham in Hillhead, Glasgow.

Arthur spent much of his schooldays at Hillhead High School except for a short period at Liverpool Collegiate. He attended the Universities of both Edinburgh and Glasgow, studying the Arts at Glasgow from 1931 – 34 and 1937 – 39, then decided – according to the honour roll of Glasgow University – to enter the Church, though there was no further evidence to substantiate this. Towards the end of 1941, Arthur joined the Fleet Air Arm and was trained at Kingston, Ontario, Canada, where he won his "wings" and was commissioned. He became a temporary acting Sub-Lieutenant on 30.12.42. Also in 1942, in Hillhead, Glasgow, Arthur married Sarah Beattie McNaughton Tait, from Kirkintilloch, who was aged 19 at the time of their wedding (Arthur was 28).

After training, Arthur was posted on 22.02.43, for further instruction and flying duties to Errol in Scotland, then to Crail Aerodrome.

Royal Naval Air Station Crail, or RNAS Crail (HMS Jackdaw) was located 4.9 miles (7.9 km) east of Anstruther, Fife and 8.8 miles (14.2 km) south of St Andrews. The Royal Navy had commissioned the Crail airfield on 1 October 1940 as HMS Jackdaw for use as a TBR (Torpedo Bomber Reconnaissance) base. Many units, at least 32 Squadrons, visited Crail for varying lengths of time including brief stays from aircraft carriers and longer durations of training. Crail's location gave quick accessibility to the sea ranges in the Firth of Forth and Navy ships with which to train, making the airfield ideal as a base for torpedo training especially. When HMS Jackdaw became overcrowded another grass runway airfield at RNAS Dunino (HMS Jackdaw II) about 5 miles northwest and was also used as a satellite field. Its main role was to support the 309 Polish Squadron (See Findo Gask).

Arthur is listed as being part of RAF 9 (Pilots) Advanced Flying Unit and, at this stage of WW2, his training (after having received his wings) could have been expected to last 4 – 6 weeks. Tragically, he would appear to have been only about 4 weeks into this advanced training, whilst on an exercise from HMS Jackdaw that he met his death. The University of Glasgow memorial site records that he was flying in close formation over the Firth of Tay when his aircraft came into contact with another, and both crashed, with fatal results to the occupants. The aeroplane Arthur was reported at the time as flying in was a Miles Master two-seater training aircraft.

Royal Navy Reserve Sub-Lieutenant **Arthur Allan Jackson Roberton** is in fact cited in conjunction with Royal Navy Volunteer Reserve Sub-Lt Bertram Henry Prance on several reports, as both having died on the same day. Sub-Lt Roberton and Sub-Lt Prance were in fact the pilots of two Fairey Swordfish biplane torpedo bombers on 19 March 1943 which collided and interlocked above the River Tay near Longforgan. No other individuals were listed as having died on that date on the graves' registration record. Sub-Lieutenant Arthur A.J. Roberton was flying Fairey Swordfish I V4380, Sub Lieutenant Bertram H. Prance was flying Fairey Swordfish II DK781.

It should be noted that whilst Arthur was listed as serving with the RAF 9 (Pilots) Advanced Flying Unit, Sub-Lt Prance was reported as having been serving with the Fleet Air Arm, in 834 Sqn. Both were still officially listed at the time of their death as assigned to HMS Jackdaw. Whilst Arthur was listed on the Royal Navy casualty lists – Sub-Lt Prance was not.

Arthur was survived by both his siblings, despite his brother – a lieutenant in the Royal Artillery – having had to survive the rigors of a Japanese P.O.W. camp. Brother Lewis died in Montreal in 1994 and sister Mary in Glasgow in 1990. No reliable evidence of a date of death for Arthur's mother could be located. Arthur's wife Sarah died in Kelvin on 23.08.61 and no evidence of her re-marrying or of any children could be located.

Bertram Henry Prance
Sub-Lt Bertram Henry Prance, age 24, was the son of Henry Aylett Prance and Cissie Elizabeth Prance and the husband of Maude Evelyn Prance of Colney Hatch, Middlesex, England. Bertram Henry Prance was born on 31st March 1918, the first (and only) son of Harry Aylett Prance and his wife, Cissie Elizabeth (nee Elsdon). Bertram was the youngest of four children. Bertram was five years old when his father died in 1923, at aged 40. His mother remarried (to Henry Snell) in 1928, when Bertram was around ten years old, and Henry was fifty-three.

On 28th October 1935, Bertram joined the police force, aged 17 years (though one site lists him as having joined on 7th February 1938). His warrant number was 126666 and he appears to have served in both G and Y Divisions, which accounts for the anomaly in dating, if 1938 was the time at which he transferred divisions. One set of police records identifies him as having left on 19th March 1943 (his passing), so it is feasible that he remained "on the books" of the police force until that time (see below).

In 1939, Bertram was recorded as living at 40 Beak Street, London W1. His occupation was given as 'police constable'. On the same register, two of his three sisters (Katie and Marjorie) were listed as living in Orchard Cottages, Richmond in the North Riding of Yorkshire. Both Katie and Marjorie were married at this time; Katie's husband was a 'farm pig man' and Marjorie was recorded as living with them.

On the eve of the war there were some 60,000 police officers in England and Wales divided between 182 separate police forces. The largest force was the Metropolitan Police in London with just under 20,000 men; there was a separate force for the City of London (1,100 men). There were fifty-eight county forces and 122 forces patrolling cities and boroughs. (There were fewer than three hundred women in the total of 60,000. Policing was seen as a man's job. Women police officers were largely confined to dealing with family problems and particularly with women and children.)

The advent of war meant that young men were required to fight in the conflict, but the situation also required reservists – men who had recently been soldiers – to return to the army or navy since trained men were essential. Many police officers were reservists, and many more were young enough to serve in the armed forces. This meant that, at the outset of the war, police numbers were reduced as reservists returned to their units and as young police officers volunteered for military service. The government and the police authorities sought to limit the reduction in police officers by restricting the numbers who might volunteer. Police ranks were made up by recruiting reserve policemen, special constables, and more women officers. In the closing months of 1939, 3,000 reservists left the police forces to serve in their former military units. Over the course of the war another 16,500 policemen volunteered for the army, navy, or air force; of these 1,275 were killed or died while on active service.

Policemen who were military reservists had been called up at the start of the war. The more formal use of 'reserved occupations' in the Second World War did include policemen. However, manpower shortages by 1942 meant policemen under twenty-five were conscripted. As Bertram did not leave the police force (to enlist) till 10th July 1942, aged 24 years. It is therefore possible that he had been conscripted.

Bertram married Maude (elsewhere spelt 'Maud') Evelyn Elizabeth Stonehouse (also incorrectly cited as 'Storehouse' on one occasion) in 1940. Maude had been born in Edmonton, Middlesex on 29th October 1915. The couple were married in the same locale. There is no evidence of children from this marriage.

All three of Bertram's sisters outlived him, dying in the 21st century. His mother Cissie also outlived him, dying in 1974 in Brixworth, Northamptonshire; her second husband having passed away in 1948 also in Brixworth. This would appear to suggest that at least most of the family had moved to the north of England at some stage. (His sister Ivy died in Enfield, Middlesex.)

Bertram's probate record, registered on 6th September 1943 in Llandudno, leaves a total of £832.11.2d to his widow, Maude Prance. At the time of that deposition, his address was cited as 39 St Ivian Court, Muswell Hill, Middlesex. Maud remarried, to Geoffrey D. Kay, in 1945.

Bertram was reported as having been serving with the Fleet Air Arm, in 834 Sqn at the time of the incident in which he lost his life, having been seconded to No.9 (Pilots) A.F.U. Course RAF Errol for further training.

Bertram Prance's, Fairey Swordfish DK781 was delivered from Fairey's Blackburn factory on 25 April 1942, one of a batch of four hundred made. It was assigned to 834 Squadron from July 1942 to September 1942 when it was transferred RAF 9 (P)AFU at Errol. 834 Squadron was formed at RNAS Palisadoes (HMS Buzzard), Jamaica 10 December 1941 as a torpedo bomber reconnaissance Swordfish squadron. They embarked with four Fairey Swordfish aircraft on the Long Island Class escort carrier, HMS Archer which was commissioned into the Royal Navy on 6 May 1942 at Brooklyn, New York. After sailing to South Africa, HMS Archer was detailed to convoy duties to the USA and Gibraltar.

Fairey Swordfish DK781 was marked as written off following the crash on 19 March 1943. Ten numbers after DK781 were designated, a surviving Swordfish from the Blackburn factory batch, DK791 is now on display at the Museum of Transport and Technology in Auckland, New Zealand.

Bertram Henry Prance is interred in Murie cemetery, beside his comrade (Sub-Lt Roberton), in a section designated for those who served with HMS Jackdaw.

NOTES:

Two days before Arthur and Bertram's mid-air collision, a Miles Master T8768 belly-landed at Errol.

John Roland Hobday

John died 30 March 1944, at the age of nineteen. Various sources report that he was flying a Miles Magister T8559 from RAF 9(P)AFU Errol at RAF Errol when the aircraft became "iced up" during a night flight exercise and had to be abandoned, subsequently crashing into the river Tay near Newburgh in Fife. John bailed out before the crash but did not survive. His body was recovered from the river on 11 May 1942.

John was born on 12 July 1924, in Walsall, Staffordshire, England to Harold and Sarah (nee Wootton). John's mother died in April 1936, a few months before John's 12th birthday. John's father appears to have remarried within three months of his mother's passing, to Joan (nee Cullerne) and it is Joan who is memorialised on his gravestone. John's half-brother, Peter, was born in 1940.

John attended Moseley Grammar School, near Birmingham from 1935 till 1940. No information could be found about his life from then until 12 January 1944, when John – as a member of the Royal Naval Voluntary Reserve – became a Temporary Acting Sub-Lieutenant, serving with H.M.S. Macaw (Wellbank Hostel), as part of the Fleet Air Arm.

The Wellbank Hostel was had been built in 1941-42 on land requisitioned by the Ministry of Supply near Bootle Station, to house five hundred workers engaged in the construction of the Royal Ordnance

Factory at Hycemoor. It was transferred to the Admiralty in November 1943 and work began to adapt the site as a transit camp where new Fleet Air Arm Pilots were to assemble on their return to the UK after completing their preliminary flying training in the Service Flying Training Schools in Canada. The hostel was commissioned on 17 November 1943, as H.M.S. Macaw and, initially, the ship's accounts were carried by the Naval Air Station at Inskip, H.M.S. Nightjar, before becoming an independent command on New Year's Day 1944, less than a fortnight before John was commissioned.

Although no records were discovered of John's service prior to him joining H.M.S. Macaw, it would not seem unreasonable to assume that his career path followed the "standard route". Trainee pilots left the UK for Canada as Leading Naval Airmen, having completed their preliminary, non-flying training at HMS St Vincent in Gosport. On arrival back in the UK, those qualified as pilots reported to HMS Macaw where they attended the Admiralty Interview Board, which comprised a panel of senior naval officers, to decide their suitability to become an officer in Royal Navy Volunteer Reserve (Air Branch). Those under 19½ would become a Temporary Acting Midshipman RNVR, whilst those over 19½ – like John – would become a Temporary Acting Sub Lieutenant RNVR. The newly commissioned officers were then sent on two weeks leave, during which time they would attend a Naval Tailors and to be fitted for uniforms. On return to HMS MACAW any deficiencies in their flying equipment or other kit would be rectified from stores held on site in preparation for appointment to their next stage of flying training in the UK.

In John's case, he began his documented service with HMS Macaw on 07.02.44 and was sent to 9 (Pilot) Advanced Flying Unit based at Errol, Perth, where he died just over a month later.

John is interred in Murie Cemetery, where his headstone states he is "remembered with honour". (On this stone, as previously mentioned, Joan is recorded as his mother, though her name is recorded as 'Joan Pease Hobday', whilst her middle name is Pearl).

John was survived by his father, stepmother, and brother.

Charles Muirhead
RAF Sergeant Pilot (Instructor) 1345409 Charles Muirhead, 9 (P)AFU RAF Errol, was reported as killed on active service on 25 January 1943. Age 21 he was the only son of Mr and Mrs Douglas Muirhead, Palacehill, near the village of Ancrum in the Borders. It is not confirmed but is suggested that he was the pilot of Miles Master Mk. I T8398 which flew into high ground at Balluderon Hill near Auchterhouse, north of Dundee. Balluderon Hill is beside the popular Balkello Community Woodland Park managed by the Forestry Commission. Sergeant Muirhead is buried in Murie Cemetery, Errol.

Winston Veron Stark.
Sub-Lieutenant Winston Veron Stark, Royal New Zealand Reserve, HMS Macaw, age 20, died on 7 March 1943. He was the son of George Harry and Eliza Stark of Havelock North, Hawke's Bay, New Zealand, formerly of Leicestershire, England. After training at HMNZS Philomel, Devonport Dockyard, Auckland, New Zealand, Winston left New Zealand in October 1941 to join the Fleet Air Arm. On arrival in the UK, he transferred to HMS St. Vincent, shore establishment in Gosport and was sent on to 9(P)AFU at Errol.

After advance flight training, he was posted to HMS Jackdaw at Crail. Winston was flying Hawker Hurricane V6786 when on 7 March 1943 it crashed into Loch Leven near Kinross. The crash was recorded as 'unauthorised low flying'. Sub-Lieutenant Stark is buried in Murie Cemetery, Errol. Winston's parents George and Eliza Stark did later visit his grave and Loch Leven.

William (Billy) Edmonstone Woodington

Sergeant Pilot William (Billy) Edmonstone Woodington, R/112242, Royal Canadian Air Force, age 19, was killed on 29 December 1942. He was the son of Leslie and Jean Woodington of Kensington, Prince Edward Island, Canada. Sergeant Woodington was born in Scotland; they went to Canada in October 1942 where he was a student. Billy Woodington was killed when his Miles Master monoplane advanced trainer aircraft from 9 (P)AFU at RAF Errol crashed near Rossie Priory, Inchture. He is buried in Murie Cemetery, Errol.

John Weatherhead

Sub-Lieutenant John Weatherhead from Pitlochry flew Swordfish K8586 at RAF Errol in 1943. After completing basic flying training, he was sent to 9 (P)AFU at RAF Errol to convert to the Fairey Swordfish. On the first occasion on 24 June 1943, he flew K8586 for one hour and 10 minutes, on the second occasion two days later for 35 minutes when he brought it back from RNAS Crail (Jackdaw). He moved on to RNAS Crail for weapons training, followed by a spell at East Haven (HMS Peewit, between Carnoustie and Arbroath) for carrier deck landing. HMS Peewit was commissioned on 1 May 1943 and closed in July 1946. During WW2, John Weatherhead flew 375 hours in Fairey Swordfish, 108 of those on anti-submarine hours with Fleet Air Arm 836 Squadron. He notched up sixty-seven deck landings (four at night) flying from Merchant aircraft carrier (MAC) ships. These were converted grain or tanker ships with a makeshift flight deck installed. They could carry up to four Swordfish aircraft or six Hawker Hurricane fighters whilst still maintaining its cargo-carrying capacity. John Weatherhead stayed in Bonnethill Road, Pitlochry, when he retired.

NOTES:

Although they may not have seen active service per se, Arthur, John and Bertram's volunteering spirit is deserving of honour and respect. These two brave men, both of whom had lost their fathers at an early age, may have been buried at a distance from their homes and loved ones but they are not forgotten. Lest we forget.

Fairey Swordfish K8407 collided with a Tiger Moth BB685 on 23 December 1942 at Balhepburn Farm, near Elcho Castle, Rhynd. Swordfish K8407 was delivered to the packing depot at RAF Sealand, south of Liverpool on 29 December 1936. This was where aircraft were crated before (usually) being sent overseas. It was then assigned to 824 Squadron in April 1937 until October 1941. It spent some time at RAF White Waltham and RNAS Lee (on Solent) until was transferred to 9 (P)AFU at Errol in April 1942.

Swordfish K8407 is not listed as being lost due to the accident, one report suggested the pilot was killed, this is unconfirmed. The assumption must be that this aircraft survived the crash and returned to its base, probably RAF Errol.

RNAS 824 Squadron took part in Operation Judgement, the Battle of Taranto on 11 November 1940, 5 aircraft being transferred to new HMS Illustrious from the elderly HMS Eagle (launched 1918) which was having its leaking aviation fuel system repaired. 824 along with 813, 815, and 819 squadrons were involved in the battle.

Fairey Swordfish P4267 from 9 (P)AFU at Errol on 14 November 1942 had an engine failure and force landed at Balhelvie Farm just east of Newburgh. The aircraft nosed over at speed; Sub-Lieutenant P. T. Gifford was unhurt. This was near the location where William Wallace fought in a skirmish with the English, Earl of Pembroke in 1298, at the battle of Black Earnside.

Fairey Swordfish Mk. I, W5856 which was at RAF Errol in 1943 and 1944 was restored to fly again from a badly corroded condition at Sir William Roberts Strathallan Aircraft Museum near Auchterarder. Swordfish W5856 is the oldest surviving in the world. She first flew on 21 October 1941 and was delivered to 82 MU (Maintenance Unit) at RAF Lichfield for overseas transport to Gibraltar on board the SS Empire Morn. After a year she returned to Fairey's Stockport factory for refurbishment in the winter of 1942/43. On 14 April 1943, W5856 was assigned to 9 (P)AFU at RAF Errol. After a temporary short loan in February 1944 to RAF Manston for tactical trials, she returned to join C Flight at 9 (P)AFU and suffered an engine failure on take-off from RAF Errol on Sunday 5 March 1944. W8586 crashed through the road on the north side of the aerodrome. The pilot was Sub-Lieutenant S. T. Brand who was unhurt. It was repaired at 76 MU RAF Wroughton on 11 July 1944, and it was known to be in transit between Hamble and Eastleigh on 18 July 1944. On 15 October 1944 it went to 1 Naval Air Gunners School at RCAF Yarmouth on the Isle of Wight. It was taken on strength by Canada on 15 December 1944. She was sent to storage in April 1945 at RCAF Mount Hope (Hamilton Ontario), where she was again used in the training role. Struck off charge on 21 August 1946, W8586 was sold as war assets. It was bought by an Ontario man and stored on a farm until it was re-sold to a J. F. Carter from Monroeville, Alabama, USA, for use as a crop duster. It was next bought by the Strathallan collection and arrived there in crates on 7 August 1977. British Aerospace at Brough acquired W8586 for reconstruction in 1991 and following a successful test flight in 1993 she was gifted to the Royal Navy Historic Flight. Three years later was adopted by the City of Leeds, in tribute to the local companies that built Swordfish components during WWII. She now wears the City's coat of arms and name on her port side just forward of the pilot's cockpit. Grounded with corrosion in her wing spars in 2003, a new set of wings were delivered in 2012 and W8586 re-joined the display circuit in 2015. It now carries a new paint scheme depicting a Swordfish of 820 Naval Air Squadron during the attack on the Bismarck in 1941.

Arthur Roberton's Fairey Swordfish V4380 was delivered from Fairey's Blackburn factory on 26 April 1941 to 812 Naval Air Squadron, one of a batch of three hundred made. It took part in Operation EF, the Raid on Kirkness and Petsamo, on 30 July 1941. During the German Operation Barbarossa, Fleet Air Arm aircraft from the aircraft carriers HMS Victorius and HMS Furious attacked merchant vessels in the northern Norwegian port of Kirkness and the north Finnish port of Liinakhamari in Petsamo. Swordfish V4380 was one of nine Swordfish along with nine Fairey Albacores that attacked Petsamo. V4380 was transferred to 779 Squadron Fleet Requirements Unit at Gibraltar which was form on 1 October 1941. In February 1942 it was back with 812 Squadron and on 8 September 1942 a tail wheel was broken on landing at RAF Docking (Norfolk). An engine failure occurred on 13 October 1942 on take-off from RAF Coltishall (Norfolk) and it appears it was then transferred up to 9 (P)AFU – (Pilots) Advanced Flying Unit) at Errol. Marked as written off following the crash at Longforgan on 19 March 1943. A notable Coltishall fighter pilot was Douglas Bader, appointed as leader of No. 242 Squadron, a mostly Canadian pilot Hurricane squadron.

Liinakhamari, Petsamo was in part of the Finnish territory that was ceded to the Soviet Union in 1944 at the conclusion of their Continuation War. Following their armistice and with pressure put on the Finns by the Soviets to actively remove the occupying German forces in Lapland, the retreating Germans adopted a scorched earth policy and laid waste to the entire Northern half of the country. 100,000 people lost their homes. The main strategic interest to the Germans was the nickel mines in the Petsamo region.

Early in 1943, three Supermarine Walrus single-engine, amphibious biplane reconnaissance aircraft were lent to RAF Errol. Despite remonstration that at least one Walrus should be retained for rescuing downed pilots in the river Tay, they were assigned elsewhere in April 1944.

Malcolm (Callum) Mitchell a resident of Kinnoull, Perth was born in 1923 and joined the Fleet Air Arm at the age of seventeen. He was commissioned as a Sub-Lieutenant a year later. In 1943 he spent five months at RAF Errol, RNAS Crail and RNAS Arbroath (HMS Condor) learning to fly the Swordfish, torpedo, and land on aircraft carrier decks. In 1944 he sank a U-boat during Russian convoys operations. He left the navy with the rank of Lieutenant Commander in 1946.

The surname Roberton was first found recorded in Lanarkshire. The village of Roberton is in South Lanarkshire, where it was the seat of the Roberton's until their dispossession by Robert the Bruce in 1296 for Stephen de Roberton's signing of the Ragman Roll (their allegiance to the English King Edward I)

Murie Cemetery

Fairey Swordfish Mk. I on a training flight from Crail 1940

Tay Estuary during WW2

Seven paratroopers drowned on 13 June 1943 at Wormit Bay during a training exercise. They were aboard two Armstrong Whitely bombers approached from the south at about 4.00pm. Winds were gusting up to 30 mph and 18 fully laden paratroopers of the 8th Battalion (Midland Counties) The Parachute Regiment landed in the river, instead of on land as planned. RAF air sea rescue launches, and the Broughty Ferry RNLI lifeboat took part in the rescue. One of the two planes contained Polish troops who landed in shallow water and survived.

These two aircraft were part of a ten Armstrong Whitley parachute drop exercise, carrying in total 130 troops were about 10 miles west of their intended drop zone at Tentsmuir, near Leuchars. One paratrooper at Wormit Bay refused to jump and was later court-martialled. At Tentsmuir, a paratrooper was struck during the jump by an ammunition box and killed.

In the River Tay Estuary opposite Dundee between Woodhaven, Newport and Tayport on 6 October 1938, the Short Brothers-Mayo (Maia & Mercury) composite flying boat/seaplane aircraft (piggy-backed aircraft, see image below) set off to establish a record seaplane flight to South Africa. The two aircraft comprised the Short S.21 Maia (G-ADHK) and the Short S.20 Mercury (G-ADHJ). They separated over the Dundee Law and Captain Donald C.T. Bennett (later to be founder of the Pathfinder bomber force) and his co-pilot Ian Harvey, proceeded to fly 6,045 miles in Mercury in 42 hours 26 minutes to the estuary of the Orange River, just short of their destination at Cape Town.

Sunderland Flying Boats of 210 Squadron arrived at Tayport around the same time being transferred as a precaution during the Munich Crisis. They did not stay long and transferred on to Wales on 8 October 1938.

In February 1942, No. 333 (Norwegian) Squadron RAF, a detachment of No. 1477 (Norwegian) Flight arrived at Woodhaven equipped with Consolidated PBY-1b (Catalina) seaplanes. This was a mixed squadron; in May 1943, a full squadron was formed from this flight, equipped with de Havilland Mosquito's Mk. II and Mk. V, based at RAF Leuchars and later RAF Banff. The Catalinas carried out anti-submarine patrols and search and rescue. They also operated in the 'Special Duties' role assisting the Norwegian Resistance. They landed agents, transmitters and even are said to have dropped Christmas presents to the Norwegian population. The squadron is still operational today and is currently based at Andøya Air Station in Nordland, Norway.

Maia & Mercury

Bombs Over Perthshire

There are a number of half-truths and myths about how the city of Perth fared during the Luftwaffe's bombing campaign against the British Isles. A common account claims that Perth was bombed but once and the fragments of that bomb are to be found in Perth Museum & Art Gallery. A friend of the author has recounted how, during the Second World War, he and his wife were awoken one night by the sound of that very bomb exploding. They stayed in the Craigie area, a mile or so to the south of Perth city. It is also suggested that a local search took place the next morning to find where the bomb dropped. Another tale depicts the Germans as attempting to bomb the railway tunnel entrance at Craigend, by the Hilton Railway Junction, but were instead fooled by a decoy target further to the west.

Perth was defended during the Second World War. An anti-aircraft battery was stationed further along the Kirkton of Mailer to Aberdalgie Road, and it is suggested that the location of the battery acted as a decoy. (Another battery operated from a position on Moncrieffe Hill, close to where the motorway at the Friarton Interchange is today.) A third story claims that 6 bombs landed on the Perth to Stanley Road. They seemingly caused no damage apart from craters that required filling. Then there is a version of the Moncrieffe Tunnel bombing involving an entire squadron of aircraft flying between the River Forth and Montrose attempting to hit a train before it entered the tunnel.

The truth is that there were 2 bombing incidents affecting the city of Perth, 3 if Whinniemuir Farm, which lies a few miles from the city centre, is included. Perth Museum & Art Gallery is in possession of bomb fragments from the Moncreiffe Tunnel bombings (as well as those from the 6 high explosive bombs dropped at Whinniemuir Farm, Scone) though none are on display. These include:

1977.6.1 Vane of an incendiary bomb collected from the crater near the centre airshaft of Moncrieffe Tunnel, 26 June 1940 Craigend, Moncrieffe. Size 120 x 50 mm - Credit Perth Museum

1977.6.2 Fragment of shrapnel collected as above. Size 200 x 80 x 15 mm. of shrapnel Incendiary, 24 October 1940 Whartlawhill Farm and Gelvan Farm, south of Carnbo, west of Tillyochie - Credit Perth Museum

As to the tales, well they can perhaps be put down to local legends, incorrect history telling, poor memories, or memories embroidered over the passing years. A factor in all this poor recall and disinformation may have been the wartime campaign, 'Carless Talk Costs Lives' – the discouragement of conversation about anything that might be said as intelligence to help the enemy and that of morale-sapping rumours.

All told, 56 aerial bombing incidents occurred in the county of Perthshire during the Second World War, 3 of which occurred before the start of the Battle of Britain of 10 July 1940 to 31 October 1940. These involved some 450 explosive devices – mostly high explosive bombs – and many incendiaries. (Fife experienced 300-400 high-explosive bombs.) In almost all the bombings across Perthshire, the likely rationale for the area's targeting can be put down to 'the jettisoning of payload before returning home' from a 'failure to find an intended target', rather than the deliberate bombing of Perthshire.

In most cases, targets such as airfields and opportunistic targets, like ships and railways, were attacked by lone raiders. Most of the raids across Perthshire caused little or no damage and few casualties. Bombing incidents reduced considerably in and after 1941 due in part to the invasion of the Soviet Union and consequent transfer of Luftwaffe resources to the Eastern Front and in part to improvement in RAF defences and interception rates.

Perth itself was on the flight path of German bombers heading for Clydebank, Greenock, and Glasgow, who were likely using the Tay Estuary and Strathearn to guide them. This would be particularly so on 13-16 March 1941 when Clydebank was devastated by over 200 bombers – 650 lives were lost in the raids, and some 11,350 people made homeless. The following year witnessed the 'Clydebank Blitz' in which 528 were killed.

Note: People who lived in Dunning during the war, recounted numerous Luftwaffe bombing raids flying over their village. The villagers of Fearnan (near Kenmore) witnessed the night sky and loch surface illuminated by reflections of fiery explosions from the Luftwaffe's bombing of Clydebank, some 50 miles away. Waves amounting to around 200 bombers (predominantly Heinkel HE. 111s and Junkers Ju 88s) flew over Fearnan between 21:00 and 04:00 hours on the night of 13-14 March 1941. The route was likely to have been chosen to evade detection by radar, barrage balloons and/or Observer Corps observation, and interception by fighters from Central Scotland RAF bases.

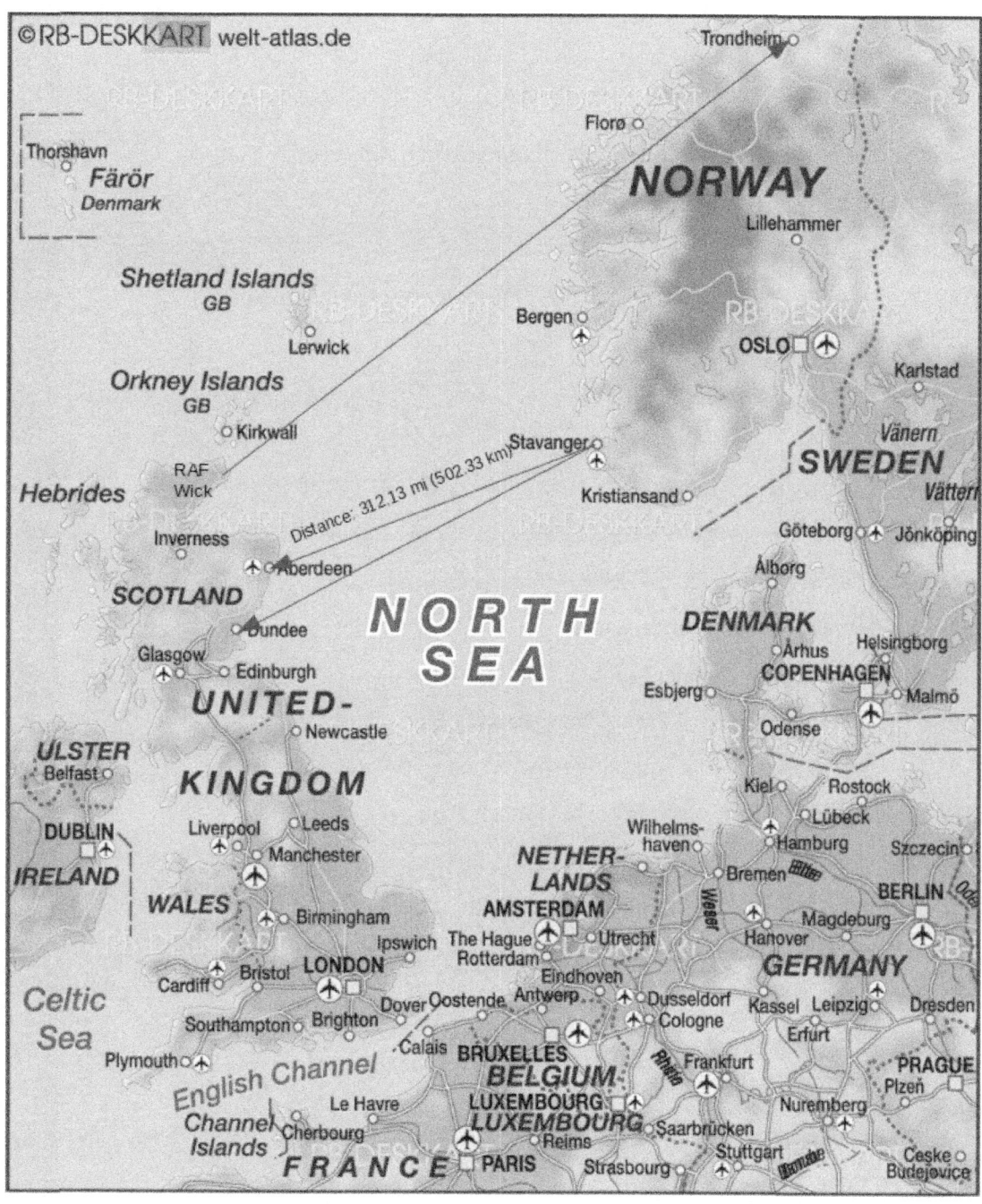

Locations of Bombs dropped in Perthshire during the Second World War

Key/Notes

HE – High Explosive Bomb.

OL – Oil Bomb.

IY – Incendiary Bomb.

UXM – Unexploded Mine.

MB – Mine Bomb.

Borlick (or Borelick) Farm lies about halfway between Dunkeld and Amulree.

Whinniemuir Farm lies between Perth and Scone.

Dirnanian Hill lies north of Kirkmichael, near Enochdhu.

Auchenglen Farm lies on the southern side of the River Earn, opposite Innerpeffray.

(Date Location Bomb Number/Type)

25 June 1940 Craigend, Moncreiffe 5 HE

26 June 1940 Craigend, Moncrieffe 30 IY

26 June 1940 Kirkmichael District 8 HE

13 July 1940 Kirkton Wood, Rossie Priory 4 HE

17 July 1940 Borelick Farm, Strathbraan 14 HE

4 August 1940 Three miles south of Grandtully 3 HE

4 August 1940 Whinniemuir Farm, Scone 6 HE

28 August 1940   Links Farm, just east of Meikleour 2 HE

28 August 1940   Grandtully Hill and Laidneskea Wood 6 HE/2 OL

28 August 1940   Loch Ericht, north of Loch Rannoch 2 HE

16 October 1940 Near Glen Quaich, Aberfeldy 6 HE/2 OL

24 October 1940 Whartlawhill Farm and Gelvan Farm, south of Carnbo, west of Tillyochie 1 HE/70 IY

24 October 1940 North Kilduff Farm, near the above 1 HE

24 October 1940 Mawmill Farm, southwest of Kinross 1 HE

24 October 1940 Coldon Farm, south of Kinross 1 HE

24 October 1940 Near Braco 1 HE

24 October 1940 Dirnanian Hill, north of Kirmichael 4 HE

1 November 1940 Kintillo, Bridge of Earn 1 HE

1 November 1940 Muir of Durdie Hill, Kilspindie (Pitroddie) 2 HE

1 November 1940 Tillywhally, Milnathort 2 HE

1 November 1940 Between Red House and Lochend, south of Scotlandwell, near Portmoak Airfield 2 HE

3 November 1940 Airleywright and Sunnybrae Farms, Bankfoot   13 HE

5 November 1940 Blamuick, just north of Comrie 8 HE

14 November 1940 Between Keilour Castle and the Sma' Glen 6 HE

7 April 1941 Loch Tummel 1 HE

7 April 1941 Vicinity of Lethendy, Essendy House 9 HE

7 April 1941 Westown No. 1 Holding, north of Middlebank, on the A90 150 IY

7 April 1941 Between Moreland and Muckhart 1 HE

7 April 1941 Middlebank, on the A90 20 IY

7 April 1941 Newmill Road, Stanley 9 HE

7 April 1941 Lambhill, southwest of Powmill, near Pitfar 2 MB

7 April 1941 Rednock House, Port of Menteith 2 MB

7 April 1941 Ardonachie, north end of Five Mile Wood, near Bankfoot 13 HE

7 April 1941 East of Mains of Dounie Farm, Kirkmichael 1 HE

7 April 1941 Between Hatchbank (just south) and Kinross (unknown no.) IY

7 April 1941 West of Milnathort at Thormanean Farm 50-100 IY

7 April 1941 north side of Easter Coldrain Farm, south of Balado 1 HE

7 April 1941 West and East Bowhouse Farms, east of Scotlandwell 4 HE

7 April 1941 Cambusmichael and Loanfold Farms, west of Guildtown 3 HE

8 April 1941 Medownhead Farm, west of Cleish, south of Powmill 1 HE

8 April 1941 Torrie Moor, North of Thonhill, on road to Callander, near Braes of Greenock. 3 HE

8 April 1941 Balnabroich Hill, south of Kirkmichael 1 HE

16 April 1941 Boreland Farm, Cleish 1 HE

21 April 1941 North of Callander 1 HE

26 April 1941 Beinn Ghlas, Ben Lawers 2 HE

6 May 1941 South east of Earnyside Farm, nr. Dollar 2 HE

7 May 1941 Lintibert Farm, Muthill 2 HE

7 May 1941 West Part, Gartwhinzean, near Powmill 1 HE

8 May 1941 North of Auchenglen Farmhouse, Muthill 1 HE

10 May 1941 Dalreach Hill, Enochdhu, Kirkmichael 5 HE

12 May 1941 Fathan Glen, Balquhidder (south of Loch Voil) 3 HE

20 August 1941   Cleish Hill 1 HE

20 August 1941   Loch Nan Eun, about 5 miles north of the Spittal of Glenshee 1 HE

October 1941 Loch Nan Eun, about 5 miles north of the Spittal of Glenshee 1 HE

10 September 1942 Laighwood, Clunie 1 HE

25 March 1943 Pitlochry (unknown no.)

6 May 1943 East of Milton of Edradour 1 UXM

NOTES: Mine Bombs were fitted with impact fuses and had a high charge ratio of 60-70 per cent explosive. They had a slow parachute retarded descent, and they created considerable blast damage in built-up areas. Oil Bombs comprised a combination of a high-explosive charge and an oil admixture. Due to their frequent failure to detonate, they were withdrawn at the start of 1941.

Looking for bomb fragments at Moncrieffe 1942

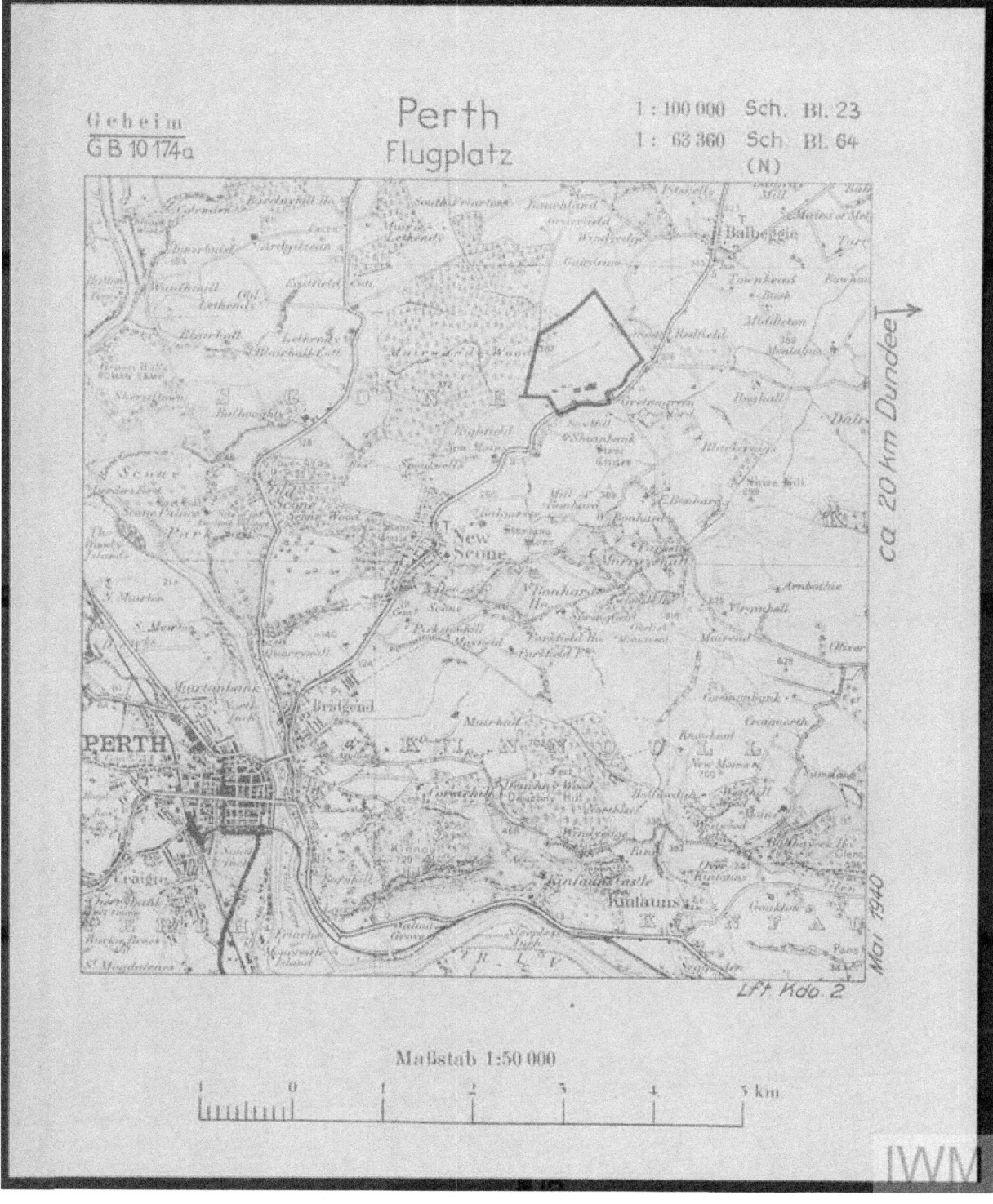

© IWM LBY LUFT 994

© IWM LBY LUFT 994 - WW2 German Luftwaffe Komando 2 published, details of RAF Perth and surrounding area.

It is hard to read, a few things I think it states:

Zivilflugplatz – civil airport

Rollfeld = Runway, details of runway lengths, funkestation = radio station, lubhaus = club house, several (mehrere) accommodation - possibly at the S. edge of the place?, feste tankstllen = fixed gas station, reparaturwerkstatt – repair station

Fliegerhorstflieg Leuchars = Air Base Leuchars 26 km

at 23 km possibly übungsplatz see = training ground lake.?,

nearest falk-garrison Dundee 23km

Uterlauf = underflow Kinfauns 6.5km (possibly bend in river)

Sidlaw Hills 2km

Gas Attack Expected

The Perthshire Advertiser of 14 April 1943, a few weeks after Pitlochry was bombed, reported that a Home Guard and Civil Defence exercise was to take place the following Sunday:

The enemy have accused the defenders of Pitlochry of using gas, and it is expected that this is a preliminary to their using it and that will probably come in the form of gas bombs dropped from aeroplanes. The enemy however are neither German, Italian nor Japanese. They are Home Guardsmen wearing Balmorals or forage caps who are expected to invade Pitlochry during the latter stage of a Home Guard and Civil Defence exercise to be help on Sunday first from 2.5pm, and the gas will be quite harmless.

After the gas attack, an enemy plane will machine gun Pitlochry and district, and the public, although their full cooperation is requested, are advised to make no attempt to deal with causalities when infantry action is taking place in the streets.

Ways in which they can help are by wearing gas masks during the exercise or staying indoors if they do not wish to take part: withholding food, information, or any other help to the enemy, and helping to make the exercise as realistic as possible. The defenders, it should be added, will wear steel helmets.

The exercise seems to have gone well, the PA reported on 25 April 1943; *the operations as being of a thoroughly realistic character. Boys and girls who were entrusted with the role of messengers between the various groups entered cheerfully into the spirit of the occasion. A rest centre was located at the High School for "blitzed" families, communal feeding was provided by Fisher's Hotel and housewives in several sectors dealt with casualties.*

Bourne End Rail Crash

Perhaps the most tragic event to befall the people of this area happened just one month after the end of World War Two. The rail crash in 1979 at Invergowrie (5 dead and 51 injured) was not the worst to affect the people of Perth and Perthshire. The Bourne End crash was truly tragic, newlyweds, soldiers being de-mobbed, just released POW's, many who had served in combat and not been home for years. To them, it was all over, and they were looking forward to life returning to peaceful and happy normality.

On the night of 30 September 1945, the overnight train to London Euston Station left Perth packed with over 700 people on board, many of them servicemen and women. It was a 15-coach express train hauled by The London, Midland and Scotland, Royal Scot Class 4-6-0 No. 6157, The Royal Artilleryman. Due to engineering work being carried out on the Watford Tunnel, the train was diverted from the fast lanes to the slow lanes at Bourne End, near Hemel Hempstead in the Borough of Dacorum. The morning was fine and sunny, and the train driver was highly experienced.

At 8.20pm the driver of the train failed to slow down in response to the cautionary signals on the approach to the diversion. The train entered the 15 miles an hour section at nearly 60 miles per hour. The train derailed and the first 6 carriages overturned and fell down an embankment. Only the last three carriages remained on the rails.

The alarm was raised by a U.S.A.A.F. pilot, Captain McCallum who had just taken off from Bovingdon Aerodrome and observed the accident. He notified his control tower, and they notified the railway authorities. American personal at the aerodrome and local people helped significantly with assistance to the injured. Medical aid was forthcoming at once, a doctor who was a passenger rendered immediate assistance and was joined by another doctor at 9.20pm and two more at 9.30pm. The first casualty was admitted to the West Hertfordshire Hospital, three miles away at 9.30pm.

Local St. John's ambulance crews arrived at the horrific crash within 20 minutes and were soon joined by ambulances from further afield. The residents of the hamlet of Bourne End were having a VJ (Victory over Japan) party as the train derailed. The uneaten sandwiches and sausage rolls were welcomed by the survivors. The Berkhamsted Woman's Voluntary Service quickly provided urns of hot tea.

The first carriage, a luggage van was completely crushed by the second carriage and flung at right angles above it. The floor of the third carriage was ripped out and it was left pointing into the air at 45 degrees. The fourth carriage lay alongside the third.

43 people were killed and 124 injured, 64 seriously. Among the dead and injured were members of the Services who had fought on many battlefields and had just returned from the war safely.

Perthshire Casualties:

Former Leading Aircraftwoman Lillian Mary Bennett Edwards, 462073, Women's Auxiliary Air Force, Age 25. Mrs Lillian Edwards died on 1st October 1945 at the West Hertfordshire Hospital. Lilian was stationed at RAF Leuchars until her demobilisation three weeks previously. A guard of honour of W.A.A.F.'s from Leuchars escorted the hearse from her parents' home at 11 Park Crescent, Scone to Scone Cemetery. Helen was travelling with her new husband, Corporal Leslie Edwards from Coulson in Surrey. He was uninjured in the crash.

Corporal Helen Ann Taylor (Nicky) Grassie, W/156152, Auxiliary Territorial Service (ATS), age 24. Helen was the daughter of Captain J.T. Grassie, D.S.O., M.B.E., Sports Master at Perth Academy and formerly of the Black Watch, and Mrs Grassie of Atholl Bank Cottage in Perth. Helen was formerly employed in the art department of Munro Press Ltd., Perth.

Sergeant David MacBeth, Black Watch, Age 29 son of Mr George MacBeth, Blackford Estate.

Sergeant William Lumgair, Black Watch, Age 40, formerly a piping instructor at Glenalmond College and a well-known soccer referee and swimmer.

Trooper William Albert Toy, 316888, Royal Armoured Corps, Age 34. His wife lived at 8 Crieff Road, Perth. Trooper Toy was wounded twice in North African and Italian campaigns.

Guardsman Alexander Lachlan Bruce, 2699533, Scots Guards, Age Unknown. Guardsman Bruce was from the Central Hotel in Errol. He was on compassionate leave to attend to the business of his father-in-law who was seriously ill. Guardsman Bruce is buried in Murie Cemetery, Errol.

Leading Aircraftman Henry Albert Frost, 1611304, RAFVR, Age 42, stationed at RAF Errol.

Leading Aircraftman Harry Albert Harris, 1216387, RAFVR, Age 37, stationed at RAF Errol.

Gunner John Smith, 1562772, Royal Artillery, age 32, son of Mary Smith, 31 Darnhall Drive, Craigie, Perth. Gunner Smith was to report to The Royal Arsenal at Woolwich after having served in Italy.

The Perthshire Injured:

Wren Rose Donaldson, age 18 from Ainslie Gardens, Perth.

Wren Catherine West, age 22 from Charlotte Street, Perth

David Grieve, Ainslie Gardens, Perth

Wing Commander Robert Napier, Burnbank Terrace, Perth

David Phillips and Mrs Phillips, George Street, Perth

Chief Petty Officer Douglas Clark, age 29, was going south to take part in a course.

Driver David Birrell, Ballantine Place, Perth was a P.O.W. in Germany for five years and was on his way to re-join his unit.

Able Seaman David Guthrie, Abbot Street, Perth, on route to Plymouth.

Private Alex Miles, age 26, Park Terrace, Perth. Served three years in the Middle East and was returning home after his first leave home in four years.

Thomas Ferrell, 13 George Street, Dunblane.

George Strathdee, 72 George Street, Dunblane.

William, Mrs Betty and Miss Betty Munro, Invergowrie

Lance Corporal Sadgrove, Rosebank, Bankfoot.

Private David Philp, Lance Corporal Ronald Seagrave, Private Peter Francis McFarlane, and Corporal James Meek, all stationed at the Queen's Barracks, Perth.

Perthshire Uninjured:

Lieutenant Colonel A. V. Holt, Guildtown.

Buchanan Dunsmore, Comely Bank, Perth.

Flight Lieutenant W. G. Wood, MurrayVille, Kinnoull, Perth.

Eddie Robertson, Black Watch, Ainslie Place, Perth.

Images credit: The Dacorum Heritage Trust Ltd

Civilian Bombing Casualties Across Scotland & in particular Dundee & the Counties of Angus, Fife, & Perthshire During the Second World War

Perth had made some preparations for the onset of hostilities in 1939 and the air war that was likely to follow. In January 1938, a meeting was held in Perth Council Chambers to plan what might be needed. Similar meetings took place in council chambers across Scotland. One of the outcomes of this early work was the establishment of first aid stations around Perth and across Tayside, responsibility for which was with the local St Andrew's Ambulance Association. (During the war, specially modified hospital trains ferried wounded service personnel to Perth for onward transfer by ambulance wagon to Bridge of Earn Hospital.)

The first civilian victim of the air war over Britain was 27-year-old James Isbister, at Brig o' Waithe, Stenness, Orkney, on March 16, 1940. After a raid on the Royal Navy Home Fleet Scapa Flow base, a German bomber returning home ditched its residual bombload over the Orkney Islands. The high explosive and incendiary bombs caused devastation to the cottages they landed on resulting in Isbister's death.

After London, Peterhead experienced one of the highest level of bombings with 28 recorded raids. Elsewhere in Scotland, Aberdeen was raided 24 times, Fraserburgh 23, Edinburgh 18, Montrose 15, and Glasgow 11. All told, during the war, some 2,500 people were killed in Scotland because of the bombings and around 8,000 were injured.

In total, at least 779 bombs were dropped on Dundee and on the counties of Angus, Fife, and Perthshire. These caused 31 civilian deaths, 37 seriously injured civilians (requiring hospital treatment), and 57 slightly injured civilians (not requiring hospital treatment). Of note is the attack on Dundee docks in July 1940 and the city's Blackness Road, 5 November 1940, that resulted in 3 deaths and 7 injuries.

Royal Naval Stores Depot at Almondbank

By 15 January 1946, all naval stores had been transferred from Perth Ice Rink to a new depot at Almondbank, where they had been temporarily kept following their dispersion from Coventry,

The decision to move all naval stores was taken following the devastating German bombing attacks on the city, especially during the evening of 14 November 1940 in which around two-thirds of building were damaged. Coventry Cathedral was left as a ruin and is today still the principal reminder of the bombing.

By the end of 1946, the Almondbank depot had extended to 7 sites for the repair, maintenance, manufacture, and storage of all categories of naval air supplies – for fixed-wing aircraft and helicopters. In the early 1970s, the RAF took over the repair and overhaul of fixed-wing aircraft. A new body, the Naval Aircraft Repair Organisation (NARO) was instituted to undertake helicopter repair and service for the Navy, Army, and the RAF. The Royal Naval Aircraft Workshop (RNAW) at Almondbank was created in June 1973 with all remaining activities located in the main on the chief workshop site (Site 2).

The main tasks carried out at RNAW Almondbank included manufacture and repair of helicopters: transmissions, gearboxes, general engineering components, hydraulics, avionics, search/rescue equipment (winches and stretchers), modification sets, aircraft seats and covers, electrical cable looms, avionic test sets, engine stands, and ground support equipment. It also saw to the repair of Westland Lynx main rotor blades and glass fibre reinforced products. In addition, tools were manufactured to be used in the repair and maintenance of helicopter engines; components of fixed-wing McDonnell Douglas F-4 Phantoms and Blackburn Buccaneer aircraft were also repaired.

In the 1990s, RNAW Almondbank had a work force of over 400, 175 of whom, due to the nature of the work, were (very) highly skilled. It was vital that the helicopters were maintained to the utmost standard. A breakdown of a gearbox, transmission, or rescue winch during an air-sea rescue in the Scottish mountains would have potentially deadly results. Helicopters would land within RNAW Almondbank on a regular basis – they included Sea King, Scout, Puma, Merlin, Lynx, Gazelle, and Chinook models. Due to the size of the Chinook helicopter, a nearby football ground was used for landing. Helicopters based on aircraft carriers undergoing re-fit at Rosyth were flown to RNAW and aircraft such as the Sea Venom, Sea Hawk and Sea Vixen were transported to Almondbank by road for servicing and storage.

Helicopters would land within RNAW Almondbank on a regular basis—they included Sea King, Scout, Puma, Merlin, Lynx, Gazelle, and Chinook models. Due to the size of the Chinook helicopter, a nearby football ground was used for landing. Helicopters based on aircraft carriers undergoing re-fit at Roysth were flown to RNAW and aircraft such as the Sea Venom, Sea Hawk and Sea Vixen were transported to Almondbank by road for servicing and storage. (Not every helicopter arrival at RNAW was for 'live' servicing, quite often they were transport for visiting officials and high-ranking officers.)

The Royal Naval Stores depot at Almondbank, was a 'stone frigate' i.e., land-based naval establishment, it went on in the post-war period to play an important role in aircraft repair and support.

NOTES: In April of 1999, the UK Government brought together the RAF Maintenance Group Defence Agency (MGDA) and the Naval Aircraft Repair Organisation (NARO) to form DARA, the Defence Aviation Repair Agency. DARA Components at Almondbank had the capability to repair, modify and test an extensive range of hydraulic and transmission components found in both air and land systems for the Ministry of Defence and civilian operators.

For several years, a decommissioned Westland Whirlwind helicopter was used as a static display representatively defending the entrance gates. The Almondbank site was served by an 'Electric Mineral Railway' linked to the main railway line at Lochty Station until its closure – to passengers on 6 July 1964 and freight in September 1967. The 'Electric Mineral Railway' was in its early years used by the Huntingtower and Pitcairnfield Bleachworks.

Westland Lynx landing at Almondbank, image courtesy of Ian Mathewson

RNAW Almondbank was sold off to Vector Aerospace in 2008 which was taken over by EuroCopter (now Airbus) and is today part of StandardAero.

On 9 January 1946, a fire broke out in a hangar at the Royal Naval Stores at Almondbank caused damage of well over £200,000 in value. (Equivalent to just over £7½ million today.) Chief Officer Duncan and his men from the Perth division of the National Fire Service tackled the blaze for over 3 hours. Dundee and Kirkcaldy fire brigades were also called out to assist. Despite an enquiry, no evidence was found as to the fire's cause.

In May of 1942, a naval officer from RNAS Donibristle (east of Rosyth) visited RAF Methven, which lay adjacent to the Royal Naval Stores Depot at Almondbank, to investigate the option of using the airfield for the conveyance of naval stores. This was approved but was limited to flights by smaller aircraft like the Percival Proctor and de Havilland Dominie.

Ice Rink Heinkel

The old Ice Rink on Dunkeld Road was used as a temporary store for the Royal navy until the RN stores at Almondbank opened, it also was used to display a German bomber. I am taking a guess here that this may have been the famous "Humbie Heinkel" which was shot down on 28 October 1939 by RAF 602 Squadron (City of Glasgow) based at RAF Drem. Humbie is about 15 miles south of Edinburgh.

A Nazi bomber, which was shot down in Scotland, is now on view to the public at Perth. The proceeds of the exhibition are to be devoted to war funds.

The German Nazi bomber was put on show in the Central Scotland Ice Rink, Perth on 2 October 1940. It was a badly damaged Heinkel HE 111. It arrived on 1 October 1940 and was exhibited in a marquee adjoining the rink. It had been shot down in Scotland as was on view to the public to raise funds for the war effort. It had been obtained from the RAF by the agency of Mr. A. M. Mackay, secretary of the Strathtay Aero Club and the display is being organised by Mr. Adam Alexander, secretary-manager of Perth Ice Rink. The charge was 6d for adults and 3d for children. It was so big (fuselage 54 feet) that even though the doors of the ice rink were taken off, it could not be gotten into the rink.

From the Perthshire Advertiser, Saturday 5 October 1940:

"To the managers of the cinema houses in Perth, editors of the "Perthshire Advertiser" and "Perthshire Constitutional" for so willingly cooperating with us to advertise our exhibition we also convey our warmest thanks. This is the first German bomber to be exhibited in this part of Scotland, and everybody

is urged to try and see it. Besides seeing it for yourself what massive machines these bombers are, you also see how devastatingly our gallant airmen in Spitfires and Hurricanes deal with them. See for yourselves the bullet holes and smashed engine. Together they tell a thrilling story of the heroism, daring and dauntless courage of the men of the R.A.F., and your contributions are for good causes, parcels for our prisoners of war through the Red Cross, Spitfires to bring more of these monsters crashing to earth, and funds to help in the initial training of budding pilots to man the Spitfires."

Much interest has been taken in the damaged Heinkel bomber, brought to the city by the Perth Air Cadet Defence Corps, which has been on view at Perth Ice Rink this week and will again be available for inspection to-day. The proceeds are to be devoted to the Prisoners of War Fund, the Air Cadet Spitfire Fund, and the funds of the Corps. Picture gives an idea of the interest taken in the Nazi machine by the young people. ("P.A." Photo.

Strathallan Airfield

Strathallan Airfield lies some 14 miles west of Perth near the village of Auchterarder. It was established in 1966 by brothers William and David Roberts as the base for their aviation company, Strathallan Air Charter Ltd. (Strathair), which provided private charter, air freight and aircraft maintenance services. (Strathallan Air Services est. 1963 and renamed Cirrus Aviation in 1970)

An earlier landing strip had been established by their father, Sir James Roberts (1904-73) in the 1930s next to the family home, Strathallan Castle. Sir James Roberts had used his own Gipsy Moth to travel between Strathallan and his property in Kent. David Roberts was killed in 1971 when his aeroplane crashed on approach to Strathallan.

A large and internationally important collection of historic aircraft was amassed here from the early 1970s by the elder brother, Sir William, who gained credit as an early pioneer of the preservation of aircraft. The collection was auctioned off in 1981. An aircraft museum was maintained at Strathallan until 1988. The bulk of the collection was, however, sold in the early 1980s. Today, Strathallan is used by Skydive Strathallan (est. 1960), parachuting, the biggest and oldest skydiving centre in Scotland.

Among the aircraft collection at Strathallan was a Westland Lysander V9367 that was built in 1938 and had been part of Polish 309 Squadron before being allotted to the RCAF (Royal Canadian Air Force) to function as a 'target tug'. The Lysander returned to Scotland in 1971 and was restored to flight worthiness at Strathallan. Today, dressed to represent an aircraft of 161 Squadron, which flew clandestine operations over enemy territory (1942-5), the Lysander V9367 is part of the Shuttleworth Collection in Biggleswade, Bedfordshire. Another 309 Squadron aircraft once on display at Strathallan (main hangar) was a Lysander (V9441) that bore the code letters AR-A signifying service before 1944 when the squadron changed its code letters to WC.

Westland Lysander IIIa 'V9367 MA-B' (G-AZWT) via licensed under the Creative Commons Attribution-Share Alike 2.0 Generic license.

Avro Shackleton T4 at Strathallan, the stripes on the propellers were to stop you walking into them. Strathallan's Shackleton was broken up eventually, although its nose is now in the Midland Air Museum in Coventry. Image taken by Ken Bruce

Former BOAC de Havilland Comet XK655 at Strathallen, broken up for scrap metal, in 1995 its nose was sold to Gatwick Airport for display purposes on the Spectators Terrace Image taken by Ken Bruce

V9941 in hangar at Strathallan - Credit: David Kirkwood

Jean Millar Valentine

Jean Millar Valentine was born 1924 in Perth, Scotland, the only child of Mr and Mrs James Valentine of Wilson Street. Jean was an operator of the Bombe decryption device in Hut 11 at Bletchley Park in England. This was the machine designed by Alan Turing and others during World War II to break the German Enigma Code. Station X at Bletchley Park was run by Mi6, the British Secret Intelligence Service.

Jean was a member of the "Wrens" (Women's Royal Naval Service, WRNS) and was one of 8,000 women who worked at Bletchley Park. This represented about 75% of the workforce at Bletchley. During this time, she lived in Steeple Claydon in Buckinghamshire.

Following an interview in Carnoustie, Jean at the age of eighteen started working at Bletchley on 15 shillings (75 pence) a week. Along with all her co-workers, she remained quiet about her war work until the mid-1970s. Jean Valentine mentioned during an interview, how moving down to London was a new experience for her, as she had never been out of Scotland up to that point.

More recently, Jean Valentine had been involved with the reconstruction of the 'bombe' at Bletchley Park Museum, it was completed in 2006. She said that: *"Unless people come pouring through the doors, a vital piece of history is lost. The more we can educate them, the better."* She still demonstrated the reconstructed bombe at the Bletchley Park Museum and lead tours there. She participated in a major reunion at Bletchley Park in 2009.

On 24 June 2012, Jean Valentine spoke on her wartime experiences at Bletchley Park and else-where as part of a Turing's Worlds event to celebrate the centenary of the birth of Alan Turing, organised by the Department for Continuing Education's Rewley House at Oxford University in co-operation with the British Society for the History of Mathematics (BSHM).

Jean Valentine worked for eight hours during the day at Bletchley Park and mentioned how no one would ever talk about what they have done or would be doing when outside of Bletchley Park. She worked in Hut 11 and recalled how there would be *"five machines within the hut, ten girls and one Petty Officer that would be in charge of the telephone"*.

Summary of Jean's war time service:

Adstock - Manor September 1943 - March 1944. Bombe operator.

Colombo - April 1944 - 1945. Breaking Japanese meteorology codes.

After several years at Bletchley, Jean Valentine unexpectedly obtained her father's consent for her dispatch to Ceylon for more war work. He gave it in a letter addressed 'to whom it may concern'.

The cramped trip through U-boat bobbing seas was exhaustingly long and carefully circuitous. Jean decided she'd never travel by P&O again. In Ceylon she was to meet her future husband, only marrying this almost complete unknown after receiving another carefully worded 'to whom it may concern' letter from her father.

With a smattering of Japanese and the Japanese version of Morse code, she worked painstakingly, decrypting Japanese weather reports. Jean spent 15 months in Ceylon breaking the Japanese cypher. She said that she didn't have a machine to do all that, we were breaking the Japanese meteorological code which was all in figures, and it was really a case of getting down and working it out.

During this time, she met only one former pupil of Perth Academy, Alex Torrance who was stationed at the same Fleet Air Arm base as Clive Ingram Rooke, who was to become her husband. Clive was a Fleet Air Arm pilot flying Supermarine Seafires, the naval version of the Spitfire.

In fact, when Alex left his aircraft in somewhat of a hurry Clive drove him to the Rest Camp at a hill station called Diyatalawa. He subsequently attended their wedding on 7 June 1945 in the Scot's Kirk and afterwards at the Galle Face Hotel in Colombo.

Leading Wren, Jean Millar Rooke (née Valentine) passed away on Friday 17 May 2019 at Henley-on-Thames. Jean is commemorated on the Codebreakers Wall at Bletchley Park.

Jeans photograph was used on a postage stamp issued in 2004 to commemorate the 60th Anniversary of D-Day, issued by the St. Vincent & Grenadines Islands.

Rejewski monument Bydgoszcz, Poland (twinned with Perth)

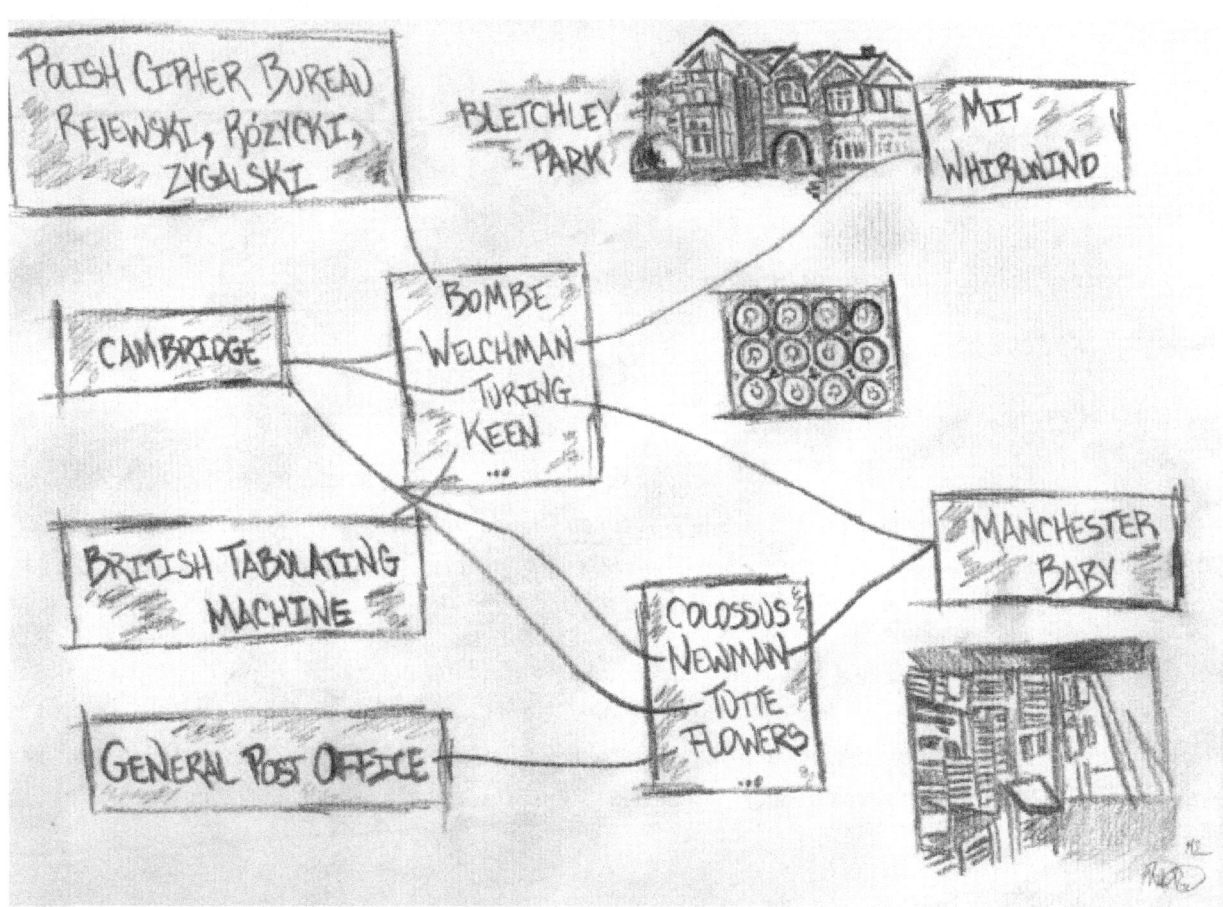

Diagram showing the links from the Polish Codebreakers, Marian Rejewski, Henryk Zygalski and Jerzy Różycki through to Gordon Welchman, Alan Turing Harold Keen, Max Newman, Bill Tutte, and Tommy Flowers who designed and built Colossus, the world's first programable computer.

Ethel Cassidy

Leading Aircraftwoman Ethel Cassidy 896633 WAAF (Women's Auxiliary Air Force) was tragically killed whilst walking with another Aircraftwoman along a road shortly before 11 pm on Saturday 28 March 1942.

The Cornishman newspaper of 2 April 1942 reported the following:

REDRUTH TRAGEDY

Girl Dies Following Car Accident

A tragedy occurred outside Redruth on Saturday night, when 20-year-old W.A.A.F. Ethel Cassidy, was knocked down by a passing car and killed. She was taken to a nearby house, where she received medical attention. Later she was removed to the Miners' and General Hospital at Redruth, where she died in the early hours on Sunday Morning. She was a native of Perth.

Ethel was the daughter of Mr and Mrs Frank Cassidy of 17 Cutlog Vennel, Perth. Frank Cassidy was the Janitor at St John's RC School, which Ethel had attended. Ethel Cassidy had been in the service for 18 months and was the first servicewoman from Perth to die in active service in the Second World War. She was previously employed in Brydson & Co, Drapers, St John Street, Perth. She is buried in Wellshill Cemetery, Perth.

Ethel Cassidy, Perthshire Advertiser 01 April 1942

William Deuchars

Leading Aircraftman William Deuchars was killed in one of the largest non-nuclear explosions in history and the largest in the UK. Only three other larger blasts were recorded during World War Two, those at Hiroshima, Nagasaki, and the US New Mexico desert nuclear bomb test.

In 1937, 450,000 square feet of disused gypsum workings in Staffordshire, England were purchased by the Air Ministry for weapons and ordnance storage. On Monday 27 November 1944, at 11.11am, an explosion occurred at RAF Fauld, No. 21 Maintenance Unit Bomb Storage Dump. Up to 4,500 tonnes (4.4 million kg) exploded, including 3,500 tonnes of bombs packed with high explosives. It created a crater with a depth of 30m and 230m diameter. A nearby reservoir containing 450,000 cubic metres of water along with several buildings including a complete farm were obliterated in the incident. Flooding caused by the destruction of the reservoir added to the damage. In addition, an open dump of incendiary bombs caught fire and it was allowed to burn itself out without further damage or casualties.

It is estimated that 70 to 78 people died because of the explosion. The rescue work took months and was hindered by pockets of gas, 6 million gallons of water and 10,000 tons of rubble. The entire mine completely disappeared, seismographs recorded the shock waves at Casablanca, Morocco.

A court of inquiry found that the likely cause of the explosion was due to a site worker removing a detonator from a live bomb using a brass chisel, rather than a wooden batten, resulting in sparks. This was in direct contravention of the regulations in force at the time.

Leading Aircraftman William Deuchars, RAFVR, 1341152 was 38 years old and the son of Mr John and Mrs Christina Deuchars, King Street, Crieff. William was a painter before he joined the RAF and a keen member of Crieff Bowling Club. He is buried in Crieff Cemetery.

CRIEFF AIRMAN KILLED IN ACCIDENT

Intimation has been received by Mrs Deuchars, King Street, Crieff, that her son, A/C. W. Deuchars, R.A.F., has been killed in an accident in England. Employed as a painter before he joined the R.A.F. three years ago, Deuchars was a keen member of Crieff Bowling Club.

Perthshire Advertiser 2 December 1944

IN MEMORY OF THOSE WHO LOST THEIR LIVES IN THE FAULD EXPLOSION
27th NOVEMBER 1944

THE FIRST EIGHTEEN PEOPLE NAMED HAVE NO KNOWN GRAVE AND THIS CRATER IS THEIR RESTING PLACE

	G.A. Mahon	
J. Brassington	A.W. Mellor	T. Sanders
F. Campbell	J.R. Miles	A.A. Shipley
F. Cartwright	E. Nicklin	Miss E. Smith
L.D. Frow	J. Redfern	B.H. Stanley
C.E. Hogg	F.G. Rock	R. Wagstaffe

L.A.C. J.T. Bailey   L.A.C. H.C. Fairbanks

	E. Fell	
J.H. Appleton	Mrs. N. Ford	P. Page
E. Barker	W. Ford	A. Patterson
J. Beard	W. Gent	S. Pickering
J. Bell	A.O. Gilbert	G. Powell
F.C. Bowring	M. Goodwin	G. Priestley
H. Carter	Mrs. M. Goodwin	H. Shepherd
R. Cartwright	A. Harris	W. Shepherd
S. Chawner	F.W. Harrison	J. Skellett
L.G. Cokayne	H.J. Hill	F.W. Slater
J. Cooper	Mrs. S.L. Hill	G. Smith
P. Cooper	T. Hudson	J.W. West
Mrs. L.E. Crook	W. Kidd	S. West
E.W.G. Daniels	E.A. Page	E. Woolley
B. Fell	G.E. Page	N. Worthington
Sgt. S.G. Game	Cpl. L. Scuto	Pte. R. Novello
Cpl. A.S. Durose	Pte. E. Di Paolo	Pte. S. Ruggeri
L.A.C. W. Deucharas	Pte. A. Lanzoni	Pte. S. Trovato

WE WILL REMEMBER THEM

A close-up of the memorial plaque at the Fauld Crater by Humphrey Bolton, CC BY-SA 2.0 via Wikimedia Commons

ROYAL AIR FORCE MAINTENANCE COMMAND, 1939-1945. (CH 20852) Oblique aerial view of the crater caused by the detonation of 3,500 tons of high explosive in the New High Explosive Bomb Area at No. 21 Maintenance Unit at Fauld, near Hanbury, Staffordshire, at 11.11 am on 27 November 1944. RAF Fauld, situated in a former gypsum mine, was the main repository of HE ordnance in the country. The explosion, calculated at some 4 kilotons, constitutes the world's … Copyright: © IWM.

ROYAL AIR FORCE MAINTENANCE COMMAND, 1939-1945. (CH 3043) Storemen stack 250-lb MC bombs in one of the tunnels at No. 21 Maintenance Unit at Fauld, near Hanbury, Staffordshire. RAF Fauld, situated in a former gypsum mine, was the main repository of high explosive ordnance in the country. Part of the MU blew up on 27 November 1944, – the World's largest non-nuclear explosion, – and 70 servicemen and civilian workers were killed or declared missing. Copyright: © IWM.

ROYAL AIR FORCE MAINTENANCE COMMAND, 1939-1945. (HU 93007) A light railway train loaded with 500-lb GP bombs outside the entrance of No. 21 Maintenance Unit, Fauld, Staffordshire. The wagons are being given a final check before travelling up to the mainline link at Scropton, roughly one mile to the north of the underground storage depot. Copyright: © IWM.

ROYAL AIR FORCE MAINTENANCE COMMAND, 1939-1945. (CH 3046) 250-lb MC bombs being transported out of No. 21 Maintenance Unit at Fauld, near Hanbury, Staffordshire, by light railway. Copyright: © IWM.

John Neil Campbell Denholm

Captain John Neil Campbell Denholm, (63451) 1st Battalion, the Cameronians (Scottish Rifles), seconded to The Glider Pilot Regiment, Army Air Corps, was the only son of John and Gertrude Denholm of Boatland, Isla Road, Perth, and Bo'ness, Linlithgowshire. It was officially reported to his parents that he had been killed in action in North Africa.

John Denholm was educated at Charterhouse from 1928 to 1932 and then went on to Cambridge University. He was married in March of 1943 to Sheila Spiers Alexander from Kensington, London. Denholm was a keen sportsman and as an accomplished skier had frequently visited Switzerland. He joined the army in 1937 and was seconded to the Glider Pilot Regiment to train as a glider pilot. He was in India when war broke out.

Denholm was killed in action on 10 July 1943 when his glider crash-landed near the Porte Grande, Siracusa, Sicily. He was taking part in Operation Ladbroke, a glider landing by British airborne troops that began on 9 July as part of Operation Husky, the Allied invasion of Sicily. The objective was to secure the Ponte Grande Bridge and then move on to take control of Syracuse.

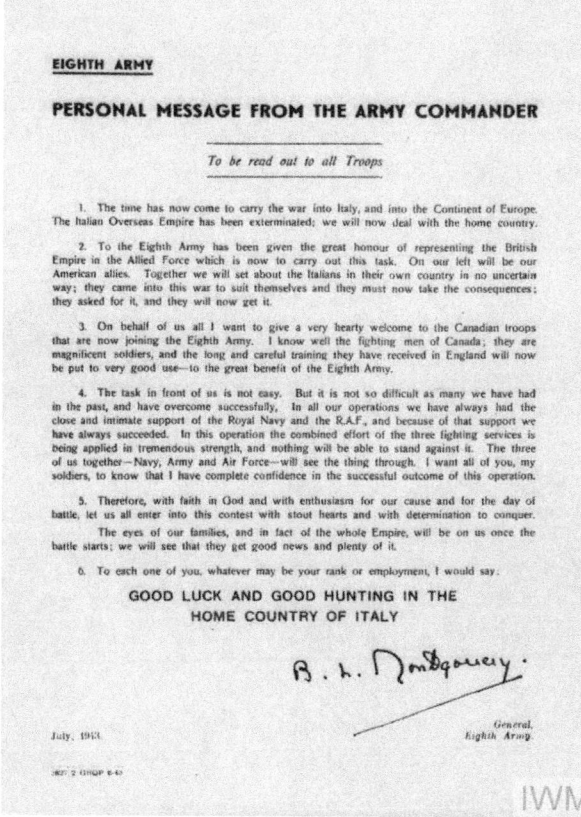

On route, 65 gliders were released too early and crashed into the sea and approximately 252 men drowned. Only 87 men, from 12 of the 147 gliders landed in the target area. They made it to the Ponte Grande Bridge, which they successfully captured. They held on beyond the time they were to be relieved, but with their ammunition expended and only 15 men remaining unwounded, they surrendered to the Italian Forces.

Denholm, who was 28 years of age at the time of his death is buried in the Syracuse War Cemetery.

On the North Inch in Perth, by the river Tay stands the obelisk shaped memorial, the Lynedoch Monument which honours the Cameronians (Scottish Rifles). They were disbanded in 1968. The memorial is across the river from the houses on Isla Road and Denholm House at Boatlands.

THE CAMPAIGN IN SICILY 1943 (NA 5543) Operation Husky: The Sicily Landings 9 – 10 July 1943: An Airborne Division Horsa glider, after landing off course nose down in a field near Syracuse. Although unsuccessful in achieving their primary objectives, the Airborne forces did cause considerable disruption behind the lines. Copyright: © IWM.

THE CAMPAIGN IN SICILY 1943 (CNA 1002) Planning and Preparations January – July 1943: British airborne troops wait to board an American WACO CG4A glider. Copyright: © IWM.

Nan Menzies Roberts

Leading Aircraftwoman Nan Menzies Roberts 2116233, Women's Auxiliary Air Force was the daughter of David and Annie Duncan Menzies from Perth and the wife of Albert Pearson Roberts of Glasgow.

On 25 March 1945 a Hawker Typhoon Mk. Ib MN236 of RAF No. 55 Operational Training Unit at RAF Aston Down, piloted by Warrant Officer Robert Thomson RAFVR, crashed into a dispersal hut whilst making a forced landing and exploded.

Warrant Officer Thomson was instantly killed along with two others on the ground, Leading Aircraftman Robert Henry Gunn 1537902 RAFVR, age 24 and Leading Aircraftwoman Nan Roberts, age 20.

Two others died in the RAF Hospital at Cosford, Aircraftman 1st Class John Wightman 2214447 RAFVR, on 2 April 1945 and LACW Minnie Nicholson WAAF 2111620, age 21 on 7 April 1945. In addition, 17 others required hospital treatment for serious injuries, 8 were on the dangerously ill list.

Leading Aircraftwoman Nan Menzies Roberts is buried in Wellshill Cemetery, Perth.

Margaret Cunnison & the ATA

Margaret Cunnison was born on 29 May 1914, the second daughter of James and Isabella Cunnison (nee Inverarity). There appears to be some dubiety around the location of Margaret's birthplace: one Wikipedia site names it as Haddington, East Lothian, whilst census records state it to be King's Norton, Warwickshire. (her Royal Aero Club Aviator's Certificate, dated 1933, identifies the place of birth as Bournville, Birmingham.)

The family (on both sides) originated in the Blairgowrie area of Perthshire over several generations and made many prestigious contributions to the broader local communities. However, Margaret's parents were recorded as living in Bournville, Birmingham in the 1911 census and her elder sister Kathleen was born in Birmingham in 1912. James was noted to be a lecturer in Social Economics at Glasgow University in 1919.

Margaret gained her private "A" pilot's licence in 1933, at the age of 19, whilst living in Milngavie, apparently after having entered a competition to win an "air scholarship" sponsored by the "Evening News" newspaper; the prize being lessons with the Scottish Flying Club. Later, Margaret travelled to Lympne in Kent, where she gained her "B" licence, enabling her to pilot commercial aircraft. Margaret was the second woman in Scotland to gain a commercial licence.

In 1937, Margaret was appointed the chief instructor at Strathtay Aero Club in Perth. She was only the second woman in the whole of the UK to qualify as an instructress at a flying club and – at the time of her appointment – was the only female flying instructor in Scotland. No mean feat for a lass who had only learned to fly four years before!

The ATA itself began with a suggestion proposed by Gerard d'Erlanger, the director of British Airways, in 1938, when he foresaw a problem. A war with Germany would lead not only to the suspension of many overseas routes, but also to the impounding of civil aircraft by the British government. The result would inevitably be – in his opinion – that commercial airline pilots would have no planes to fly and nowhere to go. Some of these commercial and civilian pilots could, and would, be absorbed into the Royal Air Force, but many capable and experienced pilots, because of their ages and in some cases because of physical limitations, would not be considered suitable for operational service in the Royal Air Force.

But d'Erlanger believed that war would create a demand for the service these pilots could provide, such as transporting dispatches, mail, supplies, medical officers, ambulance cases, not to mention the occasional VIP. He proposed the creation of a pool of peacetime civil pilots who could employ their aviation skills in service of their country.

As he was the one with the idea, d'Erlanger was given the job of contacting holders of "A" (private) licenses with at least 250 hours of flying time, and making arrangements to interview and flight-test these candidates, with the goal of incorporating them into this newly created organization, which was given the working name "Air Transport Auxiliary."

In preparation for a wartime standing, the ATA was given the urgent task of ferrying trainers, fighters, and bombers from storage units to RAF squadrons. Before the war, the RAF had thought it could handle all its own ferrying duties, but it was becoming apparent, from an early stage, that more aircraft would be required to have a viable air force. The resultant workload was beyond the capacity of the RAF ferry pilots. With its ever-increasing demand for ferrying services, the Under Secretary of State for Air proposed that the ATA open its ranks to women. There was a snag, though. The ATA was now operating out of RAF ferry pools, its pilots working alongside RAF transport pilots, and the Air Ministry was opposed to the posting of women pilots to RAF units.

Politically and culturally, there was opposition, as well, the arguments falling broadly along two lines:

1. *Aviation was an unsuitable profession for a woman.*

2. *Women pilots would be taking flying jobs away from men.*

The view taken by C. G. Grey, editor of "Aeroplane" magazine was typical of the sentiment of the time: *"there are millions of women in the country who could do useful jobs in war. But the trouble is that so many of them insisting on wanting to do jobs which they are quite incapable of doing. The menace is the woman who thinks that she ought to be flying in a high-speed bomber when she really has not the intelligence to scrub the floor of a hospital properly, or who wants to nose around as an Air Raid Warden and yet can't cook her husband's dinner. There are men like that so there is no need to charge us with anti-feminism. One of the most difficult types of man with whom one has to deal is that which has a certain amount of ability, too much self-confidence, an overload of conceit, a dislike of taking orders and not enough experience to balance one against the other by his own will. The combination is perhaps more common amongst women than men. And it is one of the commonest causes of crashes, in aeroplanes and other ways."*

Despite this somewhat widely held perspective, Pauline Gower – a commercial pilot with over 2000 hours' experience and a commissioner in the Civil Air Guard – was charged in November 1939 with the unenviable task of forming a female contingent of the ATA, consisting of a pool of eight women pilots to ferry Tiger Moths, which were small, slow single-engine open cockpit trainers. Pauline was appointed commander of this first batch of women flyers, and, like d'Erlanger, she would hold the post throughout the war.

The women would be based at Hatfield, just north of London and would fly their planes from the nearby de Havilland factory to training airfields and storage units. As it turned out, these destinations would be located for the most part in northern England and Scotland. As it also turned out, this task would be done in the middle of winter. There were two reasons why the women were given this task:

1. *Nobody else wanted it.*

2. *Light trainers would be cheapest to replace if broken by a woman. As Pauline herself remarked on this attitude, "("It's assumed) that hand that rocked the cradle wrecked the crate."*

Margaret joined the Air Transport Auxiliary (ATA) in 1940 with the other initial seven ladies who formed the First Eight (Joan Hughes – the youngest of the group at aged 21; Mona Friedlander, Rosemary Rees, Marion Wilberforce, Margaret Fairweather, Gabrielle Patterson and Winifred Crossley Fair). They were appointed by Pauline Gower, now officially the Commandant of the ATA's women's section. All these women were highly experienced, each having more than six hundred hours of flying time, and all were rated flying instructors. This was the first time in history (in England, or anywhere else in the world) that women would be officially employed in ferrying military aircraft. As with the men, they came from all walks of life. Several were mothers (and there was one grandmother!), including the world-famous record-setting endurance pilot Amy Johnson, who was killed on a ferry trip in January 1941. At this time, the women pilots were not allowed to ferry operational aircraft. Flying fighter planes was considered beyond a woman's physical and psychological capabilities, though some of the non-operational single-engine planes they flew were almost as powerful, and their handling almost as complex, as the Hurricanes and Spitfires they dreamed of flying.

Margaret was the leading instructor at Hatfield Aerodrome, with responsibility for evaluating and training the new pilots. She signed off on the American women pilots at Luton. As a result of this role, Margaret mostly flew light aircraft. Margaret trained most of the women in the A.T.A.

In the meantime, Pauline worked tirelessly to get her women recognized as competent to ferry more advanced aircraft, and finally the decision was made to allow women to fly Lysanders, which were light Army Co-op planes designed for short take-offs and landings, and twin-engine non-operational aircraft, such as Oxfords and Dominies.

Eventually, the ATA would have twenty-two ferry pools. Some pools, like Hamble, Cosford, and Hatfield (which in 1942 moved to Luton) were all-women ferry pools. Most of the others were "mixed," with men and women pilots working side-by-side.

With aircraft factories under constant attack, it was vital to get planes out of harm's way as soon as they were flyable. So, maintenance units, or MUs, were built, where the fine work (installing armament and radios, and making other minor modifications) could be carried out under safer conditions. MUs were smaller units and could be easily hidden around the countryside. The use of MUs followed on a grander scale, the general principle of "dispersal" as practiced at RAF bases: scattering aircraft around as much as possible and camouflaging them, to minimize losses in the event of aerial attack. This protection came at a cost to ATA resources: A plane needed to be ferried twice in its journey from factory to RAF base, so ATA movements were doubled from the start. If the planes were damaged in combat and could not be repaired at squadron workshops, they were ferried back to the MUs, or in some cases factories, for repair (if the planes were flyable, that is, and often they were barely airworthy, another challenged to ferry pilots). [1]

Margaret married Major Geoffrey Ebbage in 1943, at which time she left the Air Transport Auxiliary. The couple were married at Glasgow University Chapel, possibly because of her father's connection to the university.

Geoffrey, twelve years older than Margaret, was a doctor – following in his father's footsteps – and the author of several works in areas of his clinical field. Geoffrey had previously been awarded the Freedom of the City of London in 1924 and served during the war as an ophthalmic surgeon with the Royal Army Medical Corps. The couple lived in or around the Highgate area of London from 1946 to at least 1965 and Geoffrey died 05 September 1971 in London.

Margaret and Geoffrey had one child, Ian, born in 1948. Margaret herself passed away on 04. January 2004, in Haddington, leaving a son, daughter-in-law and granddaughter. Her legacy is, however, an extensive one.

A bus company in Hatfield, Hertfordshire named its eight buses after the "First Eight" of the Tiger Moth pilots in the ATA, including Margaret.

In 2008, four years after Margaret's death, the fifteen surviving women members of the ATA (and one hundred surviving male pilots) were given a special award by Prime Minister Gordon Brown.

In 1953, five women (Jackie Moggridge; Jean Bird; Benedetta Willis; Freydis Leaf and Joan Hughes) were the first women to be awarded their wings. Jackie Moggridge (nee Dolores Theresa Sorour) had been recruited by Pauline Gower – see above – into the ATA at the age of 18, not that long after Margaret, making her the youngest female pilot at that time. The next female pilot to be granted her wings was Julie Ann Gibson – in 1991. Without the ground-breaking achievements of the First Eight, none of this may have been possible.

Research by Sue Gibson and Ken Bruce

Reference:

[1] Much of this information was garnered from the British Air Transport Auxiliary site ATA History (airtransportaux.com)

Connie Leathart, Lois Butler, Margaret Cunnison, Pauline Gower, Jackie Sorour, Honor Pitman, Ann Douglas, Anna Leska, Stefania Wojtulanis, Winnie Crossley, Lettice Curtis, Pat Beverley (at the time she was a Driver), Audrey Sale-Barker, Audrey Macmillan, Rosemary Rees & Kitty Farrer

THE AIR TRANSPORT AUXILIARY, 1939-1945. (C 382) The first pilots of the ATA Womens' Section pilots walking past newly-completed De Havilland Tiger Moths awaiting delivery to their units at Hatfield, Hertfordshire. They are, (right to left): Miss Pauline Gower, Commandant of the Women's Section, Miss M Cunnison (partly obscured), Mrs Winifred Crossley, The Hon. Mrs Fairweather, Miss Mona Friedlander, Miss Joan Hughes, Mrs G Paterson and Miss Ros... Copyright: © IWM.

Pauline Gower, Winnie Crossley & Margaret Cunnison as 2nd Officer

THE AIR TRANSPORT AUXILIARY, 1939-1945. (C 389) Pauline Gower (far left), Commandant of the Women's Section of the ATA, stands with eight other founding female ATA pilots at Hatfield, Hertfordshire, by newly-completed De Havilland Tiger Moths awaiting delivery to their units. The other pilots are; (left to right), Mrs Winifred Crossley, Miss M Cunnison, The Hon. Mrs Fairwhether, Miss Mona Friedlander, Miss Joan Hughes, Mrs G Paterson, Miss Rose... Copyright: © IWM

Margaret Cunnison, Rosemary Rees, and Gabrielle Patterson, 1940. (Photo Credit: Keystone / Getty Images)

L to R Winifred Crossley, Margaret Cunnison, Margaret Fairweather, Gabrielle Patterson, Mona Friedlander, Joan Hughes, Rosemary Rees.

Margaret Watson-Watt

'The Mother of Radar', Margaret Robertson was born in St Catherine's Road, Perth. Her father, David, was a draughtsman and her mother was employed in Campbell's Dyeworks. Her father was a partner for a few years, along with Alexander Robertson in the Perth Foundry business, Paul Street, off the Old High Street. Margaret was educated at Perth Academy where she showed an aptitude for languages. She worked for a brief time in the office at Perth Foundry. In 1904, she left Perth to go to London where her father had taken up a position as draughtsman. Her grandfather, Mr. D Robertson, was the founder of the stationery and booksellers' business at 95-97 High Street, Perth.

Shortly after being married, Margaret returned to Perth for a visit – in 1916 – along with her husband Robert Alexander Watson Watt. Watt was born in Brechin, 13 April 1892, and is regarded as the 'Inventor of Radar'. At the very least, he was a significant contributor to its development. Watson was not the only person to have thought about the possibilities in this area, but he was the first to produce a workable solution. Watson Watt added a hyphen between his last names to become 'Watson-Watt' in the 1940s. In his autobiography 'Three Steps to Victory' he introduced the unsubstantiated fact that he was a descendant of James Watt of Greenock, the inventor of the first practical steam engine in 1776.

Watson-Watt attended University College in Dundee, where he was introduced to wireless telegraphy, radio frequency oscillators and wave propagation while assisting Professor William Peddie, the Chair of Physics at Dundee. At the age of eighteen, Robert won a prize in Chemistry and graduated with a BSc in Engineering in 1912.

Margaret was a teacher in Dundee and had studied at University College. She attended evening classes where her future husband was the lecturer. She also went to evening classes in metalwork and learned to make jewellery. Watson-Watt and Margaret Robertson married on 20 July 1916 in Hammersmith, London. That year he joined the Meteorological Office which was interested in his ideas for using radio to detect thunderstorms.

They started their married life living in a wooden hut between Aldershot and Farnborough, the Wireless Station of Air Ministry Meteorological Office. A second hut was used for their joint research work. Margaret used her jewellery-making skills to repair Robert's devices, soldering connections and making repairs to the apparatus. At the time, Watson-Watt described his radio apparatus as little more than lengths of wire. Margaret's other duty was that of recorder and observer of the radio experiments. Every two or three days, she would cycle into Aldershot to buy supplies for the home.

During the Great War, Margaret had another useful skill, she transcribed messages from Paris in Morse-Code and passed them on the British High Command in Aldershot. She also listened to the time signals from Berlin and Paris, with a stopwatch in one hand and a telephone in the other, and at precisely the correct moment gave the word 'Go' to the command HQ. They then sounded three 'pips' on a siren. This was the forerunner of the BBC Time Signal.

In 1923, Watson-Watt set sail for the Indian Ocean and the Red Sea for three months to study atmospherics. Margaret later joined him in Alexandria, and they set up tents on the outskirts of Cairo full of equipment for further experiments. Armed Bedouins carried off the tent with the apparatus.

Without the apparatus, they moved further up the Nile to the Helouan (Helwan) Observatory. The government of Sudan then invited them to Khartoum and provided them with a house. Here they conducted more experiments into atmospherics with some of the best thunderstorms they had ever seen.

Back in Britain, Margaret became a homemaker again until nine years later when she once again became the assistant to Watson-Watt in his research work. This time they were off to Tromsø, Norway, two hundred miles within the Arctic Circle.

Watson-Watt joined the Meteorological Office, which in 1927 was amalgamated with the National Physical Laboratory (NPL) – with Watson-Watt at the head. In 1933, he became Superintendent of the NPL in Teddington. By 1934, he was the head of Radio Research at Ditton Park near Slough. He was approached by the Air Ministry who asked him whether a radio wave could be used to produce a death-ray. The Germans had claimed that they had invented a device that could do this. Working with Arnold Wilkins at the time he assured the Air Ministry that this was, of course, impossible, but it did give him the chance to put forward the idea of using radio to detect aircraft. Soon Watson-Watt and Wilkins demonstrated to the Air Ministry official and physicist, A P Rowe (also known as Jimmy Rowe).

On 2 April 1935, Watson-Watt was granted a patent for radar and by June was detecting aircraft up to fifteen miles away. By the end of the year, this had risen to up to sixty miles. What Watson-Watt eventually produced was the highly effective Chain Home radar system. This proved to be invaluable during the air battles that were to come.

Initially, the work of the Telecommunications Research Establishment (TRE) was carried out at Bawdsey near Felixstowe. This was felt to be a bit unsafe as it was just a short German E-boat run over the English Channel should war break out. The name of the unit changed in 1936 to the Air Ministry Experimental Station (AMES). When the war broke out the team rushed to Dundee University where the Rector was only dimly aware of an earlier conversation with Watson-Watt about them working there.

Part of the team, now at Dundee, which was working on Airborne Interception Radar (AI), was sent along to RAF Perth (Scone) airfield to work. This was not entirely suitable and later in the year, the main part of the team was moved down to RAF St Athan in the Vale of Glamorgan, Wales. This also was found to be unsuitable, and the team was moved again to Worth Matravers in Dorset near Swanage. By May 1940, the distance between the teams proved unworkable and the AMES team left Dundee to a new location near the AI team at Worth Matravers.

Watson-Watt managed to cut through red-tape and have the Radar stations staffed by Women's Auxiliary Air Force (WAAF) members who did the calculations and passed on the enemy raid information by telephone to Fighter Command. The first five coastal radar-manned stations were up and running by July 1938, By the time the Second World War started on 1 September 1939, there were nineteen operational radar stations.

Watson-Watt filed patents in 1935 and 1936 on a system to identify friend or foe (IFF) aircraft. The first active IFF transponder was first used experimentally in 1939. Watson-Watt had an assistant, Edward Bowen, who came up with an airborne radar system to help pilots detect enemy planes beyond visibility. Watson-Watt also helped develop the use of radar for use by the Royal Navy against German U-boats.

In 1942, Watson-Watt was knighted becoming Sir Robert Alexander Watson-Watt, KCB, FRS, FRAeS. In 1952, Watson-Watt was given £50,000 by the British Government for his work on radar. Margaret filed a divorce petition against Robert on grounds of adultery, and they divorced that year. Margaret returned to Perth, purchasing Dunalistair, Muirton Bank, Perth. Watson-Watt moved to Canada where he set up an engineering consultancy. In Canada, he married his second wife, Jean Wilkinson. Whilst in Canada, he ironically received a speeding ticket from a policeman using, a radar gun. Robert wrote an ironic poem ('Rough Justice') afterwards:

Pity Sir Robert Watson-Watt,

strange target of this radar plot

And thus, with others I can mention,

the victim of his own invention.

His magical all-seeing eye

enabled cloud-bound planes to fly

but now by some ironic twist

it spots the speeding motorist

and bites, no doubt with legal wit,

the hand that once created it.

Jean Wilkinson died in 1964 and Watson-Watt returned to Scotland and in 1966 at the age of seventy-four, he married for the third time, Dame Katherine Jane Trefusis Forbes who was sixty-seven at the time.

Watson-Watt lived in the winter in London with Dame Katherine Forbes and in the summer at 'The Observatory', the home of Dame Katherine in Pitlochry. Dame Katherine was the first director of the Women's Auxiliary Air Force (1939-1943). She died in 1971.

Watson-Watt died two years later – in 1973 – in Inverness, age 81, and is buried along with Forbes in the churchyard of the Episcopal Church in Pitlochry.

Margaret, Lady Watson-Watt, passed an Italian 'A' level course in 1972, only one of six to pass the exam and while in her eighties. She celebrated her 102nd birthday on 3 May 1988 with a sherry party and specially made cake at St Johnstoun Nursing Home, Perth. She passed away peacefully on Wednesday 7 September 1988 at St Johnstoun Nursing Home. A funeral service was held in St Stephen's Parish Church, Muirton and she was interred thereafter in Dunning Cemetery.

Watson Watt once paid tribute to the value of Margaret Robertson Watson-Watt's contribution:

'The technique we worked out in those years has been extended over the whole field of radio research, and in that sense was the forerunner of the experiments that led to radio location '.

The couple had no children.

NOTES: Campbell's Dyeworks was in St Catherine's Road. It was destroyed by fire on 20 May 1919 and then amalgamated with Messrs. J Pullar & Sons, Limited. John Pullar who established Pullar's was apprenticed to Peter Campbell in 1814/16.

Perth Foundry was in Paul Street. An iron steamship, the *'Eagle'* was built by Perth Foundry in 1836.

Margaret and Robert Watson-Watt

Aircraft Crashes Within Perthshire in the 1930s

8 February 1936
Whilst undertaking a training exercise at Scone Aerodrome (with Airwork Ltd), Acting Pilot Officer James Beck (22) was killed when his de Havilland DH.82A Tiger Moth (G-ADVO) collided with another Tiger Moth (G-ADOK). Those onboard G-ADOK escaped without injury.

18 February 1939
Newly commissioned Auxiliary Pilot Officer Ingram Edward Pease (24) of No. 603 Squadron RAF, was killed when his Hawker Hind Mk. 1 (K6819) crashed in poor visibility (due to mist) in the Lomond Hills. The crash site is at Bishop Hill, east of Wester Balgedie (not far from Loch Leven's Larder farm shop/restaurant).

This was not the first 'death in uniform' to befall the Pease family. Captain Christopher York Pease died during the Great War (9 May 1918) when Ingram was but 3 months of age; Arthur Peter Pease, Ingram's cousin, perished during the Battle of Britain flying with No. 603 Squadron RAF. Ingram Pease is buried at St Oswald's Church Graveyard, Newton under Roseberry, North Yorkshire.

5 July 1939
A de Havilland DH.82A Tiger Moth (L6931) of No. 11 EFTS (RAF Perth) collided with a hillside at Craigvinean, Dalguise, near Dunkeld while flying during a thunderstorm and in very poor visibility. The plane's pilot, Allan Gardiner of Cheadle Hume, near Manchester, was later found dead in the burned wreckage by 2 local policemen who had formed part of a substantial search effort. He was 19 years old. Despite having spent 10 hours finding the missing plane, the 2 police officers remained at the crash site until the next morning when the body was removed. After Gardiner's plane went missing, 20 aircraft were scrambled to search for it. The search was extremely difficult and hazardous due to the conditions with very low visibility (as low as 50 to 100 feet above ground level). So bad were the conditions that 2 of the search aircraft – one piloted by Hugh Black (who landed by Alyth) and the other by Pilot Officer Winning (who landed by Meigle) – were forced to make emergency landings.

Aerial Activity Within & Close to Perthshire Airspace during the Second World War

16 October 1939
Junkers 88A-1 4D+AK, 1/KG.30 shot down by RAF 602 Squadron (City of Glasgow) Supermarine Spitfires off Elie, west of Crail, East Neuk of Fife at 14.45/55pm. Three of the four crew were killed. This was the second JU 88 to be brought down during the Battle of the River Forth. The survivor Helmut Pohle later helped Franz von Werra to escape for the first time from No. 1 POW Camp, Grizedale Hall Lake District (The One That Got Away, 1957 movie starring Hardy Krüger).

7 December 1939
2 Heinkel He 111-H3 bombers part of an armed reconnaissance mission of 3 Heinkel's were shot down over the Tay Estuary by Spitfires from RAF 603 Squadron (City of Edinburgh) out of RAF Montrose and RAF 72 Squadron out of RAF Leuchars.

18 December 1939
RAF 603 squadron intercepted a raid of seven enemy aircraft heading for the Tay and chased them out to sea.

13 January 1939
Heinkel He 111 shot down of Fife Ness, one survivor.

29 January 1940
Heinkel He 111 attacked a trawler in the Firth of Tay and was driven off by Spitfires.

30 January 1940
German aircraft attacked shipping waiting to enter the Firth of Tay. Four bombs dropped and one ship, the *SS Stancourt*, was strafed by a Heinkel which made repeated passes.

9 February 1940
The hopper barge Foremost 102 was bombed and strafed. The crew of the Arbroath Lifeboat took off the crew for which they received gallantry awards from the RNLI. Foremost 102 was towed to Dundee with an unexploded bomb in her hold.

7 May 1941
A Junkers Ju 88 was shot down over the Tay Estuary by No. 43 Squadron RAF.

28 August 1943
A Junkers Ju 88 was shot down by anti-aircraft fire over the Firth of Tay.

Aircraft Crashes Within & Close to Perthshire - During WW2

24 November 1940

Whilst assigned to convoy escort duties in the Atlantic, an Armstrong Whitley V (P5090) Y(G-L) of No. 502 Squadron, RAF Coastal Command, out of RAF Limavady, Derry, crashed into a hillside at Bealach Stacach, in the Trossachs, just west of Fathen Glinnie. The crash site is located about 2 miles south of Loch Doine and some 6 miles west of Strathyre. Pieces of burned wreckage still lie there today and the crash site is easily spotted.

The aircraft had become lost in bad weather and had considerably overshot RAF Limavady. Only one crew member, Sergeant William Stanley Hamilton, RAFVR (an air gunner), survived the crash. The other crew members died and are buried in Grandsable Cemetery, Grangemouth:

Sergeant William John Barnfather (754627) RAFVR, pilot.
Sergeant John James Westoby (741729) RAFVR (21), pilot.
Pilot Officer John Whitsed (758109) RAFVR, observer.
Sergeant James Gerrard Curtis (22) (943020) RAFVR, wireless operator/air gunner.
Sergeant Jack Perfect (19) (942632) RAFVR, wireless operator/air gunner.

10 March 1941

A Mk 1 Spitfire (X4647) being ferried from RAF Northolt to RAF Grangemouth crashed in a snow-covered inaccessible location in the proximity of Loch Tay, near Ben Ledi. The burned-out aircraft was spotted 2 days after the crash. The body of Sergeant Kenneth Ernest Frank Purcell (22) of the RAFVR was recovered the day after. Purcell is buried in Ford Park Cemetery, Plymouth.

15 April 1941

Whilst on patrol from No. 233 Squadron RAF, a Lockheed Hudson Mk. III (T9432) out of RAF Alder grove Coastal Command (Antrim) crashed in bad weather on Ben Lui, near Tyndrum. All 4-crew members died in the crash:

Flight Sergeant Douglas Eric Green, (742597) RAFVR, buried in Milton Cemetery, Portsmouth.
Sergeant Frederick Victor Norman Lown (21) (748548) RAFVR, buried in Hither Green Cemetery, London.
Sergeant Leonard Alfred Aylott (32) (747979) RAFVR, buried in St John the Baptist Churchyard, Buckhurst Hill, Essex.
Sergeant Wilfred Alan Rooks (28) (759349) RAFVR, buried in Tiverton Cemetery, Devon.

1 August 1941

A Mk 1A Supermarine Spitfire (X4777), of No. 58 OTU RAF out of RAF Grangemouth, piloted by Pilot Officer R. F. Minnick (22) (J/5340) of the RCAF, collided in mid-air just outside Dunblane with a second

Spitfire (R2076), piloted by Sergeant J. W. Walton. Minnick was killed; Walton was unhurt. Minnick is buried in Grandsable Cemetery, Grangemouth.

18 August 1941
Sergeant Bohumil Sima (25) (787535 – L-375), a Czechoslovakian national assigned to and training with No. 58 OTU RAF, was killed during a training exercise. Flying his Spitfire (N3099) out of RAF Grangemouth, while undertaking 'direction finding homing' practice, Sima spun out of cloud before crashing his aircraft near to Ballinluig. Sima is buried in Grangemouth Grandsable Cemetery.

4 September 1941
Sergeant David Colburn Johnston (24) from Birmingham, an RAFVR pilot flying a Spitfire (R6789) crashed at Callander, near to the River Teith. He had imperfectly made a right-hand roll resulting in him crashing the aircraft, which came down near the A81 road (opposite Callander Primary School). Johnston is buried in Grangemouth Grandsable Cemetery.

5 September 1941
Sergeant R. Brady (21) (1066638) RAFVR crashed his Spitfire (X4254) near Auchterarder. Brady had descended within cloud to determine his position and crashed into high ground. He is buried in St Bridget's churchyard, Moresby in Cumberland (Cumbria).

20 October 1941
Sergeant Ronald Joseph 'Digger' Gardiner (RAFVR 932502) crashed his Spitfire (R6760) at around 12:15 hours near Strathallan Army Camp. Gardiner had been undertaking practice in aerobatics, low flying, and low-level landing when his aircraft went into a shallow dive and crashed killing Gardiner. He is buried in Cheshunt New Burial Ground (Waltham Cross).

11 November 1941

Sergeant Alison Boyce McKie of the RCAF (R72679) flying a Spitfire (L1083) was engaged in a formation-flying exercise with another Spitfire (piloted by Sergeant Argue). During the exercise, McKie's Spitfire disappeared from view. McKie's body was later discovered at Loch Tay. He is buried in Grangemouth Grandsable Cemetery.

19 January 1942
During a training flight from RAF 20 OTU (RAF Lossiemouth), a Vickers Wellington Mk. 1C (R1646) crashed into a hill south of Braemar at a location about 2 miles north of the Glenshee Ski Centre. The winter of 1941/2 was a particularly bad one and has been described as one of the coldest of that century. Inclement conditions were difficult, temperatures low, and snowfall heavy, which meant it took several weeks to locate the downed aircraft. It was finally found by a gamekeeper from the Invercauld Estate on 19 February 1942. Six of the Wellington's complement of 8 are buried in Dyce Old

Churchyard (near RAF Dyce – today Aberdeen Airport) on 2 March 1942. Thomson's and Jackson's bodies were not recovered until 15 April 1942 and were buried alongside the rest of the crew on 17 April 1942:

Flight Officer James Williamson Thomson, DFC (25) (40667) RNZAF.
Sergeant Robert James Jackson (21) (R83904) RCAF.
Flight Sergeant Harry Joseph Kelley (23) (R/76125) RCAF.
Sergeant John Bernard Riley (23) (995062) RAFVR.
Sergeant Beaumont Churchill Dickson (22) (404634) RAAF.
Sergeant Roy Alistair Milliken (22) (404637) RAAF.
Sergeant Michael Henry John Kilburn (19) (1380631) RAFVR.
Sergeant William Morphet Greenbank (20) (1029811) RAFVR.

In November 1943, Greenbank was reinterred in his hometown, in St Mary's Cemetery, Windermere. In January of 1943, Kilburn was also reinterred – in Green Lane Cemetery, Farnham, Surrey.

Andy Brown (15), who was a participant in the first search party that looked for the Wellington, never forgot about those who lost their lives in the crash. In later life, he organised the retrieval of the aircraft's 2 Bristol Pegasus engines, one of which was to be used as part of a supplementary war memorial at Braemar. It was unveiled on 23 August 2003.

2 March 1942
First Officer William Silver Edgar was ferrying an Airspeed Oxford Mk I (L4597) of No. 4 Ferry Pilots' Pool in poor weather from Cambridge to No. 45 Maintenance Unit (MU) at RAF Kinloss. Over Rannoch Moor, the aircraft's starboard engine failed, which meant Edgar was unable to preserve altitude. He force-landed the Oxford on Loch Laidon, to the west of Rannoch (near Glencoe). Due to its momentum, the aircraft only came to a complete halt upon reaching the loch's southern shoreline. At this point, the aircraft caught fire and was consumed by the blaze. Edgar himself was unharmed and traversed the moor on foot, arriving a day later at Rannoch Station. Sadly, Edgar was killed on 2 April 1942 when his Spitfire Mk Vb (BM358) en route from Prestwick to Kinloss crashed in Aberdeenshire. Edgar, a citizen of the USA, is buried in Cambridge American Cemetery.

In 1978, the 2 Armstrong Siddeley Cheetah engines of the Airspeed Oxford were retrieved from the moor. The engines were restored, and one was put on display at Bamburgh Castle, Northumberland.

24 March 1942
An Armstrong Whitworth Whitley (Z6933) of RAF 19 OTU out of RAF Forres crashed during a navigation exercise. The aircraft came down on Finalty Hill, Angus, just north of Glen Isla and Glen Prosen killing all 7 on board, all of whom are buried in Sleepyhillock Cemetery, Montrose:

Pilot Officer Robert Eric Wheatley, DFM (28) (110568) RAFVR.
Sergeant Donald Frank Drake (24) (R/88694) RCAF.

Sergeant George Kenneth MacRae (21) RCAF.
Pilot Officer Ronald Renshaw Flint (24) (111936) RAFVR.
Sergeant Frank Jennings (20) (994287) RAFVR.
Sergeant Alan Blackman (20) (917077) RAFVR.
Sergeant Jack Sutcliff (29) (1060163) RAFVR.

16 April 1942

Sergeant Lloyd Livingstone Armour (R/101320) (21) and Sergeant James Richard Waclaw Derzona (R/101835) (20), both RCAF, perished when their Miles M.9 Master 2-seater advanced monoplane trainer crashed near Kirriemuir, Angus. Armour from British Columbia had been undertaking a 'special instructors' course at RAF Perth (RAF No. 11 EFTS) at the time of his death. Fellow Canadian Derzona hailed from Winnipeg. Both are buried in Wellshill Cemetery, Perth.

21 April 1942

Just above Dron Hill, by Bridge of Earn, 2 Mk 1A Spitfires from 58 OTU RAF based at RAF Grangemouth engaged in 'dogfighting' exercises collided. N3100, piloted by Pilot Officer Richard Frederick Short (69480) cut off the tail of P9545, piloted by Sergeant Mel L. Tushingham (1071855), who quickly bailed out of his disabled aircraft. Both pilots survived the incident and went on to further service, Tushingham with No. 111 Squadron RAF at El Alamein, and Short with No. 152 Squadron RAF.

14 August 1942

De Havilland DH.82A Tiger Moth, N6841 MSN 82090 (Gipsy Major #81022) was written off when it stalled at 300 feet and crashed at Dunning. Pilot Officer R F Humphries was injured, and Leading Aircraftman Chasney was uninjured.

The aircraft was from RAF Perth (Scone), No. 11 Elementary Flying Training School and was struck off charge on 20 August 1942 as FACE (Flying Accident Cat. E). Previously it was taken on charge at No. 10 MU (Maintenance Unit), RAF Hullavington, Chippenham, Wiltshire on 23 May 1939. It was transferred to RAF 612 Squadron (County of Aberdeen) at RAF Dyce on 13 November 1939 and operated by No. 1 Coastal Patrol Flight. From there to No. 46 MU, RAF Lossiemouth on 3 July 1940 and the No. 11 EFTS at RAF Perth on 23 April 1941.

RAF 612 Squadron used unarmed Tiger Moth's to patrol the coast on anti-invasion patrols and 'scarecrow' patrols against enemy submarines in the North Sea. U-Boats sighting these aircraft dived without waiting to discover whether they were capable of attack. It was a bluff tactic used in the early days of the war when there was a shortage of combat capable aircraft and undoubtedly saved much shipping.

15 August 1942

A de Havilland DH.82 Tiger Moth out of RAF Perth crashed after entering a flat spin from which the pilot could not recover. Both the aircraft's occupants bailed out successfully and survived.

17 September 1942

Flight Lieutenant David Fergus Hamilton (28) (37933) RAFO died when his Hawker Hurricane Mk. 1 (Z4180) dived into the ground at high speed. The crash site is by Castle Law, near Culteuchar Hill, Forgandenny. The Hurricane was part of a section of RAF 56 OTU which had relocated to RAF Tealing (near Dundee) from RAF Sutton Bridge in March 1942.

Prior to the commencement of the Second World War, Hamilton had served as a civilian instructor of the Reserve of Air Force Officers (RAFO) having undertaken at least 4 years as a commissioned pilot in the RAF. It is surmised that Hamilton lost consciousness due to anoxia (deficient supply of oxygen to the tissues) with the failure of his supplementary oxygen system during a climb to 25,000 feet. He is buried in Southgate Cemetery, London.

6 October 1942

Within the archives of the de Havilland aircraft company is the record of a DH.82A Tiger Moth (T7361) being abandoned (by its trainee pilot and their instructor) after its port wing collapsed during an aerobatics routine at RAF Methven.

Note: Abandoning a Tiger Moth in mid-air was a rather unusual occurrence.

23 December 1942

Above Bathepburn Farm, by Elcho Castle (Rhynd), 4 miles southeast of Perth, a Fairey Swordfish (K8407) of No. 9 PAFU (RAF Errol) collided with de Havilland DH.82 Tiger Moth (BB685) of RAF No. 11 EFTS (RAF Perth). Both Tiger Moth's crew – Sergeant (Pilot) Robert Baxter Neilson (27) (1370210), instructor, and Leading Aircraftman (pilot under training) Kenneth Bell Hunter (26) (1672053), were killed in the collision. The fate of the Swordfish pilot is unconfirmed, though he is listed as also killed in the accident. Neilson is buried in Motherwell Dalziel (Airbles) Cemetery; Hunter at Harrogate (Stonefall) Cemetery.

16 January 1943

King's Seat Hill, near Dollar, was the scene of an accident involving 3 Spitfires from 58 OTU RAF based at RAF Grangemouth. Flying Officer 'Bud' Hugh Gordon Reynolds (20) (J/9465) and Sergeant

'Gordie' Gordon Murray Duda (20) (R/128862), both RCAF, and Sergeant 'Vin' Vincent Patrick Daly (21) (AUS/408634) of the RAAF, were taking part in formation-flying training exercises above the Ochils. Reynolds in AR254 was flight leader that day and at about 11:45 hours led the other 2 Spitfires – Duda's X4614 and Daly's P8276 into cloud. As the aircraft emerged from the cloud 5 minutes' later, they found themselves moving rapidly towards a hill and despite attempts to climb, all 3 Spitfires crashed into the 648-metre-high King's Seat Hill. Only Daly survived. He managed to clamber to Duda's Spitfire but found his fellow pilot dead. Australian born Daly suffering horrendous injuries to his back, face, right tibia, scalp, and lacerations to many parts of his body, dragged himself down the hill. Some 48 hours later, he was found suffering with frostbite by a shepherd. Reynolds and Duda are buried in Grangemouth Grandsable Cemetery. Daly required specialist medical care and plastic (re-constructive) surgery and spent time at Larbert Naval Hospital, the Queen Victoria Hospital, East Grinstead, and Princess Mary's RAF Hospital, Halton, before repatriation to Australia where he lived until his death in 1969. On the eastern side of the hill, a memorial cairn has been raised in recognition of the tragic triple Spitfire crash.

RAF 58 OTU triple aircraft crash crews Courtesy Patricia Katherine Svinth Brammer

3 June 1943
On this day, a Taylorcraft Auster Mk III (MZ124) observation aircraft attached to No. 652 Squadron RAF was making its approach to RAF Methven when it got into difficulties entering an area of thermal currents. The aircraft crashed into a wood.

13 June 1943
Flight Sergeant Mark Charles Burton and Sub-Lieutenant W. G. Claque died when the Miles Master II (Dl966) crashed during a flight training exercise (No. 9 PAFU (RAF Errol)) by Jordanstone House, south of Alyth. Burton hailed from Redcar, Claque from Douglas, Isle of Man.

31 May 1944
A Handley Page Halifax (LL414) 4-engine heavy bomber out of RAF Sandtoft, Lincolnshire, taking part in night-time cross-country training came down in the vicinity of Glen Isla, about 16 miles north of Blairgowrie. It is believed that the aircraft suffered one or more engine failures causing it to spiral out of control. On board were 8 crew, 6 of Canadian birth. All lost their lives in the tragedy:

Pilot Officer Leslie Llewellyn Williams (22) (J/85856) RCAF.
Sergeant Sidney William Doughty (20) (933062) RAFVR.
Sergeant John Arthur Treby (19) (1867730) RAFVR.

Flight Officer William Campbell (22) (J/35226) RCAF (born to Scottish parents).
Flight Sergeant Robert Trevor Dean (22) (R/181350) RCAF.
Warrant Officer Class 1 James Stewart MacDonald (28) RCAF.
Sergeant Thomas Goldie (21) (R/215319) RCAF.
Sergeant Vernon Thomas Sherven (20) (R/211938).

Doughty is buried in Rippleside Cemetery, Barking, Campbell at Uphall Cemetery, West Lothian, and the others at Sleepyhillock Cemetery, Montrose.

8 November 1944
Another Handley Page Halifax (LK901) out of RAF Sandtoft, Lincolnshire, also undertaking a night-time cross-country training exercise broke apart in mid-air and came down close to Glenshee Post Office, 20 miles north of Blairgowrie. All 7 crew members perished, 6 of whom were Australian, and are buried in Sleepyhillock Cemetery, Montrose:

Flight Officer Arthur Wallace Spencer-Maggs (24) (439657) RAAF.
Pilot Officer William Alexander Edmonds 26) (19882) RAAF.
Flight Sergeant Arthur Wallace Cooke (33) (1510) RAAF.
Flight Sergeant Jeffrey James Grieve (26) (419307) RAAF.
Flight Sergeant Keith Edward Jeffrey (24) (38363) RAAF.
Flight Sergeant Charles Bede Mackay (19) (439896) RAAF.
Flight Sergeant Walter Picton (3000833) RAFVR, the flight engineer, is buried in Hertford Road Cemetery, Enfield.

Battle of Britain Heroes

The Battle of Britain ran from 10 July to 31 October 1940. It is regarded as the first military campaign fought entirely by air forces. The success of the RAF in defending Britain prevented Nazi Germany from launching an invasion across the English Channel. Many pilots from Perthshire and Kinross-shire as well as many who came to live in these counties after the war took part in the battle. To pay tribute to 'the few', I would like to tell you about some of the Battle of Britain pilots who once walked amongst us.

In the early 1930s, the Lord Provost of Perth, Thomas Hunter, first mooted the idea of an aerodrome for Perth. In 1934, the government announced an expansion of the RAF so that Perth Councillor Ure Primrose decided to revive Thomas Hunter's plans for an aerodrome, hoping it would draw business to our area. Work began in June 1935 and in December 1936, Airwork Limited undertook the delivery of RAF and civilian flying training at Scone Aerodrome. By December 1940, RAF No. 11 Elementary and Reserve Flying Training School at Scone was equipped with 367 training aircraft.

With Perthshire having one of the main pilot training facilities on its doorstep, it naturally attracted its young people who dreamed of 'spiffing' aerial adventures and the glamourous 'Brylcreem boy' image. Throughout the county, Air Training Corps units were formed and the Royal Air Force Volunteer Reserve (RAFVR), established in 1936, became the recruitment pathway for civilian entry in the RAF.

The turning point of the Battle of Britain took place on 15 September 1940, when the Luftwaffe launched a significant bombing attack on the City of London. They were met by a large group of defending fighters. Fifteen hundred aircraft engaged in air battles which lasted until dusk, and which resulted in 56 aircraft being shot down. The Luftwaffe felt at the time that they were close to victory, but that decisive day for the RAF showed that they had clearly not gained the air superiority they needed for invasion. Winston Churchill visited RAF Fighter Command Headquarters on 15 September 1940 and saw first-hand the development of the struggle on this crucially important day.

The most highly awarded Perth-born pilot who flew in the Battle of Britain was Marshal of the Royal Air Force:

Neil Cameron

Neil Cameron, Baron Cameron of Balhousie, KT, GCB, CBE, DSO, DFC. was born at 32 Pitcullen Terrace, Perth, on 8 July 1920. Cameron's father was a Company Sergeant Major in the Seaforth Highlanders; he died when Neil was only three weeks old. Neil's mother moved in with his grandparents who lived at 33 Balhousie Street, Perth.

Neil Cameron joined the RAFVR in May of 1939 and as a fighter pilot took part in the later stages of the Battle of Britain when he was posted to RAF 17 Squadron at RAF Martlesham Heath in Suffolk. He later took part in the Battle of Alam el Halfa, the First Battle of El Alamein, and the Second Battle of El Alamein. As a squadron leader, Cameron served in actions over Burma flying the Republic P-47 Thunderbolt.

Cameron became a military thinker and strategist, and, in August 1977, the Chief of the Defence Staff. He later became Principal of King's College, London, and was awarded an honorary Doctor of Law degree. In 1983, he was created a life peer as Baron Cameron of Balhousie and later that year appointed a Knight of the Order of the Thistle. Marshal of the Royal Air Force Neil Cameron, Baron Cameron of Balhousie, KT, GCB, CBE, DSO, DFC died in London on 29 January 1985.

John King 'Jack' Norwell

Sergeant John King 'Jack/Jock' Norwell, AFC, Second World War fighter ace was born in Perth on 4 September 1917.

Sergeant John King Norwell, RAF 740233, began his military flying with the Royal Air Force Volunteer Reserve in May 1937. Initially he trained at Scone Aerodrome, and in early 1939 he was offered six months training with the regular RAF, he joined RAF 74 Squadron at RAF Hornchurch.

Norwell returned to civilian life on 15 August 1939, but war was to break out two weeks later and he was called up on 1 September 1939. He was posted to RAF Evanton, then the RAF 11 Group Pool at RAF St. Athan.

The first of Norwell's 7 fighter pilot 'victories' occurred 2 days before the evacuation of the British Expeditionary Forces from Dunkirk (26 May 1940-4 June 1940) when on 24/25 May 1940, he downed a Messerschmitt Bf 109 and shared in the downing of another.

Other aerial martial events followed including damage to a Dornier Do 17 light bomber (3 July 1940); the shared downing of a Messerschmitt Bf 110 and damage to 2 Messerschmitt Bf 110s (both 18 August 1940); the downing of a Messerschmitt Bf 109 (22 August 1940); a possible downing of a Messerschmitt Bf 109 (28 August 1940); and a shared downing of a Messerschmitt Bf 109 (31 August 1940).

On 11 September 1940, Norwell was assigned to RAF 41 Squadron with which he is credited as having damaged 2 Messerschmitt Bf 109s (17 September 1940) and shot down 2 other Messerschmitt Bf 109s (27 and 30 September 1940).

The following month, Norwell had a lucky escape when his Supermarine Spitfire (X4545) collided with a parked Spitfire. Fortunately, he suffered only minor injuries and was back on operational duty a week later, 9 October 1940.

As the Battle of Britain was reaching its conclusion, Norwell chose overseas service in Malta, which was then under siege (11 June 1940-20 November 1942) and on 11 November 1940 he made the passage to the Mediterranean island that then sat amid Axis shipping lanes on board HMS Argus. The ship's cargo included 12 Hawker Hurricanes and 2 carrier-borne Blackburn B-24 Skuas destined for active service on the island.

The plan was for the aircraft to take off from HMS Argus and land on Malta. The first wave of 6 Hurricanes and a single Skua, with Norwell as one of the Hurricane pilots, left in the early hours of 17 November 1940. A second wave left an hour later.

The mission was a complete disaster: every aircraft in the second wave ditched into the sea, and of the first wave only 4 Hurricanes reached the island. Norwell put his plane down on Malta with only 2 gallons of fuel remaining in his reserve. At the end of the war, only Norwell of the 4 pilots who reached Malta that fateful day was still alive.

On Malta, Norwell became part of RAF 261 Squadron based initially at RAF La Luqa and after 20 November 1940 at RAF Ta Kali.

From April 1941 onwards, it is highly likely that Norwell took no part in operational service, instead he was involved in test flying aircraft in Ghana. There, he was promoted to pilot officer on 2 July 1942, flying officer on 2 January 1943, and flight lieutenant on 2 July 1944.

For his "acts of exemplary gallantry while flying, though not in active operations against the enemy", Norwell was awarded the AFC on 1 January 1945.

Post-war, Norwell left the RAF (in 1946) although he rejoined the RAFVR a year later. He became a partner in Norwell's Perth Footwear Ltd, part of his family's shoemaking business that dated back a century and a half and which included a shoe shop in Perth's High Street. Additionally, Norwell ran the Cherrybank Inn for 26 years. Sergeant John King 'Jack/Jock' Norwell, AFC died on 28 May 2003 in the town of his birth.

Aircraft Jack Norwell was known to have flown in 1939:

Supermarine Spitfire 1a K9882 3 March 1939 (later lost in combat on 26 September 1940)

Supermarine Spitfire 1a K9880 9 November 1939 (later lost in combat on 20 July 1940)

Supermarine Spitfire 1a K9883 13 November 1939

Supermarine Spitfire 1a K9900 17 November 1939

Jack's Hawker Hurricane JS290 (WN-P) of RAF 527 squadron on the ground at RAF Digby (Lincolnshire) in 1945. Flight Lieutenant Norwell was the Flight Commander of the Radar Calibration Unit stationed there. There were detachments of RAF 527 squadron based at RAF Longman (Inverness) and RAF Tealing during that time. Its motto was 'Silently We Serve'.

The aircraft above is in the standard Day Fighter paint scheme with an 18" Sky (colour) band (added to aircraft in December 1940) to indicate it was a day fighter. The leading edges of the wings were yellow, and a good guess is that the propeller spinner was red.

54 Squadron, picture taken at the time of Dunkirk, Jack seated on the left.

```
                                                        24721
   NORWELL      John King
               "Ardenlea", Perth, Scotland.



   Born 4th Oct. 1917.           at Perth.
   Nationality      British
   Rank, Regiment, Profession    Director
   Certificate taken on
   At                     Qualified Service Pilot.
   Date    13th July 1948.
```

Hawker Hurricane V7795. It is shown being ferried to Greece on 9 April 1941 and at the controls is Sergeant Norwell. It was passed over to RAF 80 Squadron and just hours later piloted by Pilot Officer Bill Vale, it destroyed a Junkers JU87 over Bulgaria. 24 hours later Bill Vale shot down two Junkers JU88's. After evacuating to Crete, Bill Vale claimed five more. It was destroyed at Maleme on 18 May 1941, two days before the German invasion of Crete.

54 Squadron Picture -back row -Sgt. JK Norwell, F/O DAP McMullen, F/O CF Gray, F/Sgt. PH Tew - front row - P/O JL Allen, F/O AC Deere, F/Lt. JA Leathart, F/O BH Way, F/O DG Gribble

THE HURRICANE OF THE BATTLE OF BRITAIN FLIGHT

Personally signed by
Flt Lt John K Norwell
AFC Ae 54 Spitfire
Squadron RAF Hornchurch
Battle of Britain 1940

FLOWN IN HAWKER HURRICANE LF363 WHICH CARRIES
No. 242 SQUADRON'S WARTIME MARKINGS OF LE-D
Gp. Cpt. Douglas Bader's Aircraft
Pilot : Sqdn. Ldr. R. M. RAW, A.F.C., R.A.F.
Battle of Britain Memorial Flight
Display Flight Time : 10 minutes

SCOTTISH AIR DISPLAY RAFA
14 JUNE 1975

SIEGE OF MALTA
'OPERATION HALBERD'
24-30 September 1941

FLIGHT LIEUTENANT JOHN KING NORWELL AFC

On 17th November 1940 Sergeant Jack Norwell took off in his Hurricane from HMS 'ARGUS' in the Mediterranean and landed on Malta with but two gallons of fuel left. He joined No.261 Squadron at Ta Kali and operated in defence of the Island until April 7th 1941

CHIEF ENGINE ROOM ARTIFICER ALBERT DENIS SAUNDERS

Engine Room Artificer Sandy Saunders served aboard submarine HMS REGENT during 1941 and took part in the extraordinary Kator incident in Yugoslavia after which REGENT returned to Malta for repairs. There he experienced the heaviest bombing of the Siege of Malta

Officer Commanding
Royal Air Force
Akrotiri

A.F.C. For Perth Airman

F./Lt. Jack Norwell, A.F.C., and companion—a lion cub.

Flight-Lieutenant Jack Norwell, Ardenlea, Perth, was awarded the Air Force Cross in a recent list of R.A.F. honours

Flight-Lieutenant Norwell, who is 27, joined the R.A.F.V.R. in 1939, undergoing his preliminary training at Perth Aerodrome. He took part in the Battle of Britain, and, subsequently, served abroad for four years—in Malta, Greece, and Crete, and at various stations in Africa and the Middle East. He is now stationed in this country.

In civil life Flight-Lieutenant Norwell is a partner in Norwells Perth Footwear, Ltd.

Forgrave Marshall Smith

Wing Commander Forgrave Marshall (Hiram) Smith, D.F.C. was a resident of Dunning for many years, Hiram (as he was known) was born in Victoria, Alberta, Canada on 17August 1913, to Thomas and Margaret (nee Marshall), both born in Canada. Thomas and Margaret were married in 1904 in Montreal. Thomas died on 31 October 1967 aged 90; his wife having passed away in April 1965, aged 91. Both had been living in Edmonton, Canada at the time of their deaths. Hiram was their only child and was educated at Oliver & Westmount High School and Victoria High School. Hiram joined a local militia unit when he turned 20 and spent three years learning all about the Canadian Army. He was, however, at the same time pursuing his private pilot's licence at the North Alberta Aero Club. In 1935, Hiram was documented as a civil servant with the Attorney-General's Department, living with his parents and sister at 11033, 86th Avenue, Edmonton, Alberta.

In late 1935, Hiram decided that a life in aviation was what he wanted. His first flight in the January of 1935was over snow in an aircraft equipped with skis. By considerable effort including working as a cattle miner on a freight train, he raised the money to qualify to fly on Cirrus Moth aircraft at the Edmonton Aero Club. He appeared before a selection board in December 1935 and made his way to England.

He was accepted into the Royal Air Force (RAF) and commenced instruction with RAF 1 EFTS at RAF Hatfield. On 11 March 1936, Hiram, RAF No. 37613 was granted a short service commission as an acting pilot officer on probation, with effect from – and with seniority of – 2 March 1936. He reported to RAF No. 3 Flying Training School at RAF Grantham, Lincolnshire on 14 March 1936 where he got his wings. At RAF Grantham he flew the Hawker Hart and the Hawker Fury.

In December 1936, the newly promoted Pilot Officer Smith was posted to RAF 1 (Fighter) Squadron at RAF Tangmere flying the Hawker Fury, and on 22 February 1937, Hiram's 'B' flight was detached to the nucleus of a new unit, RAF 72 (Fighter) Squadron at RAF Church Fenton, which was equipped with Gloster Gladiator aircraft.

In April 1939, No. 72 Squadron was re-equipped with brand-new Supermarine Spitfire Mk. 1 aircraft. Smith was one of the first Canadians to fly this potent fighter.

During the opening months of the war, the squadron flew convoy and defensive patrols, only occasionally coming to grips with the enemy. In the northern part of England and in Scotland, the weather was often atrocious. At the end of a long patrol over the water, returning pilots were often greeted with rain and fog. More than once Smith just managed to make a 'blind' landing or was forced to divert to another airfield with mere 'fumes' remaining in his gas tank. It must have seemed to the aviators of RAF 72 Squadron that meeting the Luftwaffe in combat was a safer proposition then dealing with English and Scottish weather.

Flight Lieutenant F. M. 'Hiram' Smith claimed the first victory for RAF 72 Squadron on 4 September 1939. Taking off from RAF Church Fenton at 12.05 hrs, he was to intercept a barrage balloon that had broken away from its moorings. Forty minutes later he brought the balloon down near Pateley Bridge about 40 miles northwest. Flying Officer's Sheen and Eldson of RAF 72 Squadron whilst patrolling the East Coast of England on 21 October 1939 encountered fourteen Heinkel He 115, 3-seat seaplane torpedo bombers attacking a convoy and shot down two of them.

RAF 72 Squadron was temporarily stationed at many other airfields before the Battle of Britain began, sometimes just for days, or a week or two. These temporary stays were used to rest and re-group. RAF Leconfield in the East Riding of Yorkshire was taken over in October 1939 by RAF Fighter Command and the Spitfires of RAF 72 Squadron were the first squadron to arrive, though not for long: they were sent up to RAF Drem in East Lothian that same month. In January 1940, they were recalled to RAF Leconfield and then assigned to RAF Church Fenton where they remained until March 1940.

On 1 June 1940, RAF 72 Squadron were ordered south and saw five days of flying over the beaches at Dunkirk, Operation Dynamo covering the evacuation of the British Expeditionary Force and other allied troops. On one occasion Hiram Smith's Spitfire had a failure of the engine coolant pump. He landed with the cockpit filled with, as he noted in his log "a cloud of Glycol steam". Another note is his log for this time states that he returned to RAF Shoreham (Brighton) "by the Grace of God, with 2½ Gallons left".

Despite fog so thick that they could not see the top of the hangars, on 4 June 1940 they were demanded to take-off 'at any cost' from RAF Gravesend. Returning to the airfield was hair-raising, a section landed at RAF Manston, an attempt narrowly missing at church steeple. Two Spitfires landed in a farmer's field. Hiram Smith landed 60 miles further west at RAF Shoreham near Sevenoaks with only fumes left in his petrol tank.

Flight Lieutenant Smith (by now a section leader) dealt with increasing German attention throughout June and July as the Luftwaffe (night-time) attacked their airfield at RAF Acklington on a regular basis. Several aircraft were dispersed to satellite fields to avoid being bombed. At RAF Woolsington pilots had to sleep on chairs in the Flying Club longue as no other accommodation was available.

Flight Lieutenant Ronald Alexander Thomson from New Zealand on 26 June 1940 shot down a Junkers Ju 88 which had been caught in searchlights, one of the few night victories gained in a Spitfire. Thomson began his training on 16 November 1936 at No. 11 E&RFTS (Elementary & Reserve Flying Training School), RAF Perth (Scone).

Hiram Smith on 29 June 1940 (with two other members of the section) was credited with one-third of an enemy aircraft being destroyed. Hiram Smith, leading three Spitfires of Yellow Section, scrambled from RAF Arklington and intercepted a solitary Dornier Do 17 which had been spotted about 10 miles from Holy Island. After flying for 40 minutes, they overtook the Dornier at 23,000 feet and Smith flashed a recognition signal at it. They received no response; the aircraft was then recognized as a 'Flying Pencil'. Hiram circled the Dornier and closed to point-blank range from astern. He raked the Dornier with his machine guns. He was hit by defensive fire from the bomber and broke off his attack. Two other members of the section took their turn and then Hiram attacked from the enemy's port quarter from about 50 yards away. The Dornier went into a spiralling dive and crashed into the sea.

Back at RAF Arklington it was discovered that an armour piercing bullet had just missed his Glycol tank, smashed into the engine rocker box, and had bounced along the rocker arms without breaking anything. Hiram was given the bullet as a souvenir by the aircraft mechanics. It was later learned that the Dornier was on a reconnaissance mission and was carrying a senior member of the German Meteorological Service.

Hiram was in the thick of things again on 15 August 1940 when RAF 72 Squadron was part of an RAF response to numerous German attacks throughout the day. Heinkel He 115's made a feint attack towards Edinburgh, hoping to draw the defending RAF fighters north. German reports were that the RAF had suffered heavy losses in the south and the north would only be lightly defended. In fact, there were six Spitfire squadrons, a squadron of Boulton Paul Defiant's and a squadron of Bristol Blenheim's waiting for them. Most of the pilots in these squadrons were experienced, having fought in the previous two months over France and Dunkirk. They were now well rested and re-equipped. The Germans were also unaware that a 28-ship convoy was due to sail at noon from Hull, and all radars stations had been warned to be particularly alert. Anstruther Radar was first to report two formations of enemy aircraft approaching, one of which turned back about 40 miles from the coast of Scotland.

At eight minutes past noon radar stations began to plot a formation of 20+ enemy aircraft opposite the Firth of Forth. An hour later, the estimates rose to 30, in three sections, heading south-west towards Tynemouth. At Watnall, Fighter Command for the Midlands, they noted the approach of 13 Group's first daylight raid. Scrambled in the afternoon at 12.15pm, RAF 72 Squadron and two other squadrons encountered more than one hundred Luftwaffe aircraft of Luftflotte 5 from bases in Denmark and Norway.

With an hour's warning the fighter controller was able to put squadrons in an excellent position to attack. RAF 72 Squadron Spitfires were placed in the path of the enemy off the Farne Islands, about 25 miles to the north. They climbed to 18,00 feet and were the first to attack. It came as a bit of a shock to them when the 30 enemy aircraft materialised, 65 Heinkel He 111's and 34 Messerschmitt Bf 110's. Squadron Leader E. Graham led RAF 72 Squadron straight into the attack from the flank with one section attacking the Bf 110 fighters and the rest the He 111 bombers. Hiram Smith was leading four aircraft of Red Section. The Me 110s formed defensive circles whilst the He 111s split up. Some jettisoned their bombs in the sea and headed back to Norway.

A Messerschmitt Bf 110 streaked past Hiram, he saw a circle of six close and locked onto the last one. He emptied his guns into it noticing some effect. Aircraft were criss-crossing the sky in all directions with plumes of smoke marking the departure of several enemy aircraft. The fight lasted just five minutes. The surviving German aircraft were set upon again five minutes later by Hawker Hurricanes of RAF 605 Squadron followed ten minutes later by Hurricanes of RAF 79 Squadron. Pressing on the surviving

Germans met Spitfires of RAF 41 Squadron. When they arrived at the coast, they found unbroken cloud from 10,000 feet to the ground making it impossible to bomb any of their intended targets. They jettisoned their bombs and headed for home, still harassed by newly refuelled and re-ammunitioned RAF fighters. Hiram recalled the event as:

"Turning in behind a formation of bombers, I opened fire at one hitting its starboard engine, which started to smoke and large pieces flew off the main plane. I swung quickly behind another bomber firing a short burst into its port engine. I then transferred the attack to the third Heinkel, closing to point-blank range and I could see the incendiary bullets flash as they ricocheted on contact. I was close astern when the aircraft blew up with a tremendous explosion and disintegrated in a ball of fire, which I narrowly avoided flying into."

The Luftwaffe lost eight bombers and seven fighters with several more damaged, all without any RAF losses. Further south, another unescorted raid of 50 Junkers Ju 88s from Aalborg in Denmark resulted in more losses for the Luftwaffe. In all, the northern attacks resulted in the loss of 16 bombers out of a serviceable Luftflotte 5 force of 123, and additionally seven fighters out of a force of 34 that were available. Luftwaffe reports indicated that 20% of the aircraft sent, had not returned.

When the Battle of Britain started, RAF 72 Squadron was based at RAF Acklington, Northumberland (6 June 1940 to 31 August 1940), but urgently they were transferred on 31 August 1940 to the frontline at RAF Biggin Hill. Biggin Hill suffered severe damage on 30 August 1940. At 1.30 pm successive waves of German bombers started coming in over southern Kent; the third and largest raid began around 4 pm. One of the last remaining hangers was destroyed and most telephone, gas, electricity, and water supplies were cut.

The following afternoon, RAF Biggin Hill was attacked again by high altitude bombers – the damage had meant that two of the three squadrons based there had to be put under the control of nearby control sector stations. The temporary telephone lines installed after the previous day's raid at Biggin Hill were destroyed. RAF 72 Squadron operated from the following day, (1 September 1940 to 12 September 1940) out of RAF Croydon.

It was from this airfield on 31 August that Smith's part in the Battle of Britain came to an abrupt halt. During the last two weeks of August 1940, the life expectancy of RAF frontline fighter pilots has dropped to just two weeks. After little more than three hours after arriving at their new home, squadron members were scrambled to engage German raiders. Somehow, Hiram Smith and the three other pilots of his section became separated from the rest of the squadron and found themselves alone in the sky, they had climbed to 20,000 feet over the port town of Rye. More than 100 enemy aircraft were a few thousand feet below them. The four airmen did not hesitate, and dived into them, each man for himself. Smith was immediately challenged by a Messerschmitt Bf 109 making a head-on pass, cannons, and machine guns blazing. His first thought was "missed me", but then a 20mm cannon shell exploded with a bang near the left earphone of his flying helmet, fragments of steel penetrated his head, neck, shoulders, and arm. More shells smashed into his Spitfire sending it plunging vertically. Smith's Spitfire was mortally damaged.

With his aircraft spiralling down out of control, the dazed and bloody Canadian, but still conscious, he jettisoned the cockpit canopy and attempted to climb out of the aircraft. The slipstream pinned Smith to the rear of the cockpit, hanging half in and half out of the Spitfire. Later, Smith recalled:

'Every effort having been made to no avail and having gone through the full range of emotions – embracing emergency, frustration, consternation, fear, panic, and supplication, it was clear to me that owing to the speed at which I was approaching the ground, it could only be a matter of moments before I hit it. I then became completely relaxed and resigned to imminent extinction.'

Then suddenly, unexpectedly and for no reason, he found himself clear of the aircraft. Hurriedly pulling the ripcord of his parachute he drifted down to a hard but satisfying landing. In his weakened state, he could not grab the lines of his parachute to collapse it. He was dragged by a strong wind across a field.

After convincing a member of the Home Guard pointing the barrel of a .303 rifle at him, that he was indeed an 'English' airman and not eligible for shooting, he was taken to No. 7 Casualty Clearing Station. Smith survived his extensive injuries, the pieces of steel, according to the surgeon had missed "all the important pipes and things".

Amongst his fellow patients in the RAF hospital at Halton was an old friend, Flight Lieutenant Eric James Brindley 'Nick' Nicolson, VC, DFC. Nicholson was a former member of RAF 72 Squadron; he was awarded the Victoria Cross on 16 August 1940 whilst flying a Hawker Hurricane. He was fired upon by a Messerschmitt Bf 110 injuring him in one foot and the eye. As he struggled to leave his blazing Hurricane, he saw another Messerschmitt. He got back in and continued firing until he saw it dive away to destruction. Then he bailed out and upon landing was fired upon by the Home Guard who ignored his cry of being an RAF pilot. When the pair of them were transferred to the Palace Hotel, Torquay, Flight Lieutenant E. J. B. Nicolson, VC, promptly wrote Hiram out a cheque for £1 in payment for a bet they had taken earlier in the war. The bet was for the first man to be credited with a confirmed kill. Hiram takes up the story:

" We met at the R.A.F. Hospital, Halton, about the end of December 1940. I had sustained 109 cannon shell injuries to my head and neck, and Nick had severe burns to his face and hands. At that time treatment for burns involved liberal coatings of gentian violet, which, added to their injuries, resulted in burns patients not being a pleasant sight ... Sometime later I met Nick again at Torquay. Once again, we had been to town at lunch time and, upon returning to the Palace Hotel and entering the front door, Nick was called over to the desk in the hall. I sat down on a settee at the opposite side of the room. A few moments later, a completely shattered Nicolson collapsed beside me and thrust a piece of paper into my hand. It was a telegram and the message started off 'His Majesty King George VI ...', and I thought it must be a joke, but reading on it promulgated 'the award of the Victoria Cross to Flight Lieutenant J. B.

Nicolson.' As I finished reading the message, Nick turned to me and said, "Now I have to go and earn it."

After three months in hospital, Smith returned to RAF 72 Squadron. Hiram was promoted to Squadron Leader and posted to command RAF 603 (City of Edinburgh) Squadron at RAF Turnhouse on 1 April 1941. On 16 May 1941 Hiram and his squadron moved to RAF Hornchurch, back into the front line of the battle. Conditions had changed, the RAF were now taking the fight to the Germans with fighter sweeps and bomber escorts over enemy held territory.

Hiram wrote in his logbook, "on almost every occasion, the formations of Messerschmitt Bf 109's were waiting high in the sun, often well above the RAF raiding aircraft: and they dived down at will on them when they were in a favourable position. They used dive and climb tactics, almost dog-fighting at will with their Bf 109 f's which were slightly superior to the Spitfire V used by No. 603 Squadron, and most other units on the Channel Front in the summer of 1941".

Hiram's first success with No. 603 Squadron came on 12 June 1941 when he shot down a Messerschmitt Bf 109 from a range of about 40 yards whilst it was attacking another Spitfire. Two days later, 14 June 1941 he thought he had just damaged another Bf 109 between Dunkirk and Dover in the English Channel. He did not claim this one as he did not see it crash, however other pilots confirmed that the aircraft attacked by Hiram plunged into the sea.

Hiram Smith was rested after two operational tours, 86 sorties and flying time close to 1,000 hours. He left the squadron on 24 July 1941 and on 14 August went to 52 OTU (Operational Training Unit) as Chief Flying Instructor. It was formed at RAF Debden and moved to RAF Ashton Down on 31 August 1941.

Smith formed and then briefly commanded RAF 175 Squadron at RAF Warmwell, Dorset, from 3 March 1942, flying Hawker Hurricane IIB aircraft. Hiram then flew with RAF 145 Squadron flying Spitfire Vb's out of RAF Helwan in Egypt and them RAF Gambut in Libya. The Spitfire's key role was to provide high-altitude cover against Messerschmitt Bf 109's and Italian Macci C.202 Foglore (Italian "thunderbolt").

Promoted to Wing Commander, he was posted to India as Chief Flying Instructor at Risalpur. After a course at the Middle East RAF Staff College, Haifa, Palestine, he returned to India and became Wing Commander Operations at Air HQ, New Delhi. Smith returned to the UK for a course at the Fighter Leaders' School and again returned to India, this time to command RAF 902 Wing.

In March 1942, he formed RAF No. 175 Squadron and in August 1942 he went to India where he became Chief Flying Instructor at 151 OTU, Risalpur. In 1944, he attended RAF Staff College at Haifa, Palestine, returning to India in June to become Wing Commander Operations at Air HQ, New Delhi.

He returned briefly to the UK to attend the Fighter Leaders' School and then back to India as Wing Commander, Flying, 902 Wing. He was Joint Assault Commander for the invasion of Ramree Island, on the Arakan coast, Burma. The Battle of Ramree Island (Operation Matador) took place from 14 January 1945 to 22 February 1945. In May 1945, Smith was detached for the invasion of Rangoon, with the task of establishing an airfield. Hiram Smith remained with 902 Wing until the end of the war, following which he led RAF 11 and RAF 75 squadrons off the deck of HMS Trumpeter in the planned but never fully executed Operation Zipper, designed to recapture Singapore. At the end of the war in the Pacific, the Japanese garrison in Penang surrendered (2 September 1945) – the formal Japanese surrender was held in Singapore on 12 September 1945. A Commonwealth force reached Kuala Lumpur on the same day.

During this period, Hiram rose to the rank of wing commander and was awarded a Distinguished Flying Cross, gazetted 30 October 1945. Public Records Office Air 2/9287 has original recommendation by G/C G.P. Marvin dated 27 July 1945 when he was credited with 346 hours operational flying time and was Wing Commander (Flying) of No.902 Wing, No.224 Group:

Wing Commander Smith is in his fourth operational tour and has carried out 280 operational sorties involving 346 hours flying.

This officer's first and second tours were carried out during the Battle of Britain and consisted of interception, convoy patrols, day and night air cover over Dunkirk and sweeps over France and Belgium during which time he carried out 236 operational sorties involving 300 hours flying. During the Battle of Britain, he was wounded in the head by a cannon shell. His third tour was carried out in the Middle East and consisted of bomber escorts and fighter sweeps over Alamein involving 16 sorties totalling 17 hours flying. This tour was terminated on his posting to India.

During the above operational tours, he has destroyed three Ju.88s, one Do.17, one Me.109 and damaged one Me.110 and three Me.109s.

Wing Commander Smith is now in his fourth operational tour and has carried out 28 operational sorties involving 30 hours flying in the Burma theatre of operations. He has taken part in escort to bombers, bombing and ground strafing Japanese positions and sampans over the worst type of country to be found in any theatre of operations. His record shows that he has been almost continuously on operational flying throughout the present hostilities.

As Wing Commander Sweep Leader during his present tour, he has displayed exceptional keenness and has at all times set a very high example to the pilots of the squadrons in the wing.

To this, the Air Officer Commanding, No.224 Group, adds on 4 August 1945:

During his appointment as Wing Commander Flying in the Burma campaign, Wing Commander Smith has displayed a fine sense of leadership and his courage and devotion to duty have been largely responsible for the offensive spirit of this wing. This and his previous operational record make him worthy of the award of the Distinguished Flying Cross for which he is strongly recommended.

Wing Commander Forgrave Marshall Smith took part in 280 operational sorties during the war. Hiram retired from the RAF on 13 October 1957 as a wing commander and went to work for British Petroleum as a departmental personnel manager. He was recorded, along with his wife June, in the 1958 and 1959 electoral rolls, as both living at Meadow Croft, Tilthams Corner, Godalming, Guilford, Surrey. (The 1955 and 1956 rolls recorded June at this address, but not Hiram). On the 1960 and 1961 electoral rolls, both Hiram and June were listed as living at Byways, Ridgley Road, Farnham, Surrey, England.

Following his retirement from B.P., and at the time of his death, Hiram, and his wife June, resided at Glebe House, Dunning. Hiram is reported to have liked fishing for salmon in the River Earn and his wife June, painting landscapes of the surrounding area. Hiram died of natural causes on 9August 1994, at Hillside Hospital, Perth, Scotland, shortly after his 81st birthday. His death was reported in The Courier and Perthshire Advertiser on 12 August 1994. He was survived by his wife June, two sons (Ian and David) and two daughters (Fiona and Katherine).

Hiram's WW2 1940 to 1941 known tally:

29 June 1940, Dornier Do17 (1/2 claim),

(Spitfire Mk. 1 P9438, 100m East of Isle of May Island, Firth of Forth, RAF 72 Squadron)

15 August 1940, Heinkel He 111 (2 destroyed)

15 August 1940, Heinkel He 111 (probable)

15 August 1940, Messerschmitt Bf 110 (damaged)

(Spitfire Mk. 1 P9438, 300m East of Farne Islands, off Bamburgh, Northumberland, RAF 72 Squadron)

12 June 1941, Messerschmitt Bf 109 (destroyed)

(Spitfire Mk. Va, W3130, 10 miles of Ostend, Belgium, RAF 603 Squadron)

14 June 1941, Messerschmitt Bf 109 (destroyed),

(Spitfire Mk. Va, W3130, between Dunkirk/Dover (10 miles west of Calais), RAF 603 Squadron)

NOTES: Accounts of aircraft shot down by Hiram on 15 August 1940 have been recorded as 2 x Junker Ju 88 with 1 x Ju 88 probable. His D.F.C. recommendation tally states 5 shot down including Ju 88's, the northern raid he encountered was Bf 110 and Bf 111 aircraft. Junkers Ju 88's from Denmark did attack further south and were met by RAF 73 and RAF 616 Squadrons off Flamborough Head.

Hillside Hospital at Barnhill, Perth closed on 31 December 1997. Glebe House, Dunning, was the former manse of St. Serf's Church.

The attack by the Luftwaffe of 31 August 1940 was Fighter Command's heaviest day of losses. Thirty-nine RAF fighters were shot down with 14 pilots killed. The Luftwaffe lost 41 aircraft in the whole 24-hour period. It was advised at 6.35 pm that all telephone lines to Biggin Hill Fighter Control sector were dead and urgently required was the frequency and call signs of RAF 72 and RAF 79 squadrons. A despatch rider had to be sent to fetch the information. A fourth attack was delivered at 5.30 pm by

Junkers Ju 88s and Messerschmitt Bf 110s which further cratered runways, mainly at RAF Hornchurch. RAF Hornchurch and RAF Biggin Hill were, nonetheless, serviceable the next morning.

RAF 72 Squadron nickname, "Basutoland", is derived from the fact that during both world wars, the Basutoland Protectorate, now Lesotho, donated aircraft to RAF, which were assigned to No. 72 Squadron

RAF 54 Squadron was caught in the act of taking off on 31 August 1940. Two sections had got airborne, but the last was blown into the air by explosions. All three pilots emerged shaken and injured but were back on operations the next morning. Thirty Dornier Do 17s dropped about 100 bombs on the airfield; four were later shot down.

The Messerschmitt Bf 110, often known unofficially as the Me 110, was a twin-engine Zerstörer, fighter-bomber.

Flight Lieutenant Ronald Alexander Thomson on 1 September 1940 was shot down in Supermarine Spitfire P9448 by Messerschmitt Bf 109's. Wounded in the chest, lungs, stomach, hands and one leg by shell splinters and with a dead engine he manged a belly landing outside Leeds Castle. He re-joined RAF 72 Squadron at Biggin Hill on 11 October 1940.

Luftflotte 5 at the time of the northern raids was under the command of Generaloberst Hans-Jürgen Stumpff, (10 May 1940 – 27 November 1943). Stumpff served as the representative of the Luftwaffe at the signing of the unconditional surrender of Germany. He was released from captivity in 1947 and died in 1968.

Although lightly armed and with several other design flaws, during mid-1942, in North Africa, the underrated Macci C.202 Folgore achieved a ratio kill/loss better than that of the Messerschmitt Bf 109.

The first prototype of the Vickers Supermarine Spitfire (K5054) made its maiden flight at Eastleigh aerodrome on 5 March 1936 with Joseph 'Mutt' Summers at the controls.

Supermarine Spitfire Mk. 1 K9942 which was flown by Hiram Smith and Flying Officer J. B. Nicholson VC, was restored and is in the collection of the RAF Museum, (hangar 3) at RAF Cosford, north-west of Birmingham.

As a wing commander, E. J. B Nicolson, VC, DFC was killed on 2 May 1945 when a RAF B-24 Liberator from No. 355 Squadron, in which he was flying as an observer, caught fire, and crashed into the Bay of Bengal. His body was not recovered. He is commemorated on the Singapore Memorial. Hiram remained good friends with Nick Nicholson until his death, and back in 1940 he became godfather to his son, James.

Flight Lieutenant James Brindley Nicolson VC playing a 'Jew's harp' while recovering in hospital, 1940. Forgrave Marshall Smith playing the washboard (authors guess) R.A.F. FIGHTER V.C. (CH 1697) Original wartime caption: The Swanee whistle. Copyright: © IWM.

William Nairn Gardiner

Sergeant William Nairn Gardiner was a Battle of Britain pilot. William was born in Perth on 26 January 1921. He joined the RAFVR at the age of 18 in August 1939 as an under-training Pilot (754858). When war broke out, he was immediately mobilised on 1 September 1939 and completed his flying training with RAF 3 Squadron at RAF Castletown.

RAF Castletown is located just east of Thurso and was one of the bases that provided fighter cover for the Royal Navy at Scapa Flow. William Nairn Gardiner flew his first operational sortie with the squadron on 27 October 1940. The previous day the Luftwaffe had attacked Wick, RAF Lossiemouth and Aberdeen and a twin-engine Heinkel He-115 seaplane was shot down by RAF 603 Squadron off Fraserburgh.

On 25 December 1940 he was posted to RAF 96 Squadron at RAF Cranage in Cheshire. The squadron was just being formed to serve in the night air-defence role. They were equipped with Hawker Hurricane Mk 1's and Boulton Paul Defiant's. The Boulton Paul Defiant was found to be very effective at night against the bombers of the Luftwaffe. It had a powered dorsal turret equipped with four 0.303 Browning Machine Guns; it had no forward firing weapons. In combat it would attack from below or alongside the German bombers. When it was introduced to the public the British government put out disinformation that it had 21 guns, 4 in the turret, 14 in the wings and 3 cannons in the nose.

COURTESY OF AUDREY WYPER (DAUGHTER)

By this time, the Battle of Britain was over, and the Luftwaffe had turned its attention to bombing cities and trying to destroy the British war industry. The Blitz as it was known lasted from 7 September 1940 through to 11 May 1941. The focus was London, in daylight to begin with, the Luftwaffe changing its main effort to night attacks from October 1940 onwards.

RAF 96 Squadron received new aircraft throughout the war, in May 1942, the Bristol Beaufighter, in June 1943 the de Havilland Mosquito, in December 1944 the Handley Page Halifax and in March 1945 the Douglas Dakota. They operated from many RAF stations in England and for two months from 3 September of 1943 in Scotland at RAF Drem (East Lothian). From December of 1944 they were a RAF Transport Command flight. In March of 1945 they were in Cairo and in May 1945 they had relocated to Bilaspur in India.

William Nairn Gardiner was commissioned as a Pilot Officer on 22 March 1942, Flying Officer on 1 October 1942 and Flight Lieutenant on 22 March 1944. In the London Gazette of 5 August 1947, William Nairn Gardiner (121234) was recorded for his appointment to commission as flying officer in the reconstituted RAFVR on 30 June 1947.

Bill Gardiner lived on Burghmuir Road in Perth and passed away on 5 November 1998. His newspaper obituary described him as a Hydroelectric Engineer, Former Town Councillor and RAF Fighter Pilot. He is listed on the Battle of Britain War Memorial Wall at Chapel-le Ferne near Folkestone.

NOTES: As the war progressed, No. 96 Squadron RAF received other aircraft including the Bristol Type 156 Beaufighter (May 1942), de Havilland Mosquito (June 1943), Handley Page Halifax (December 1944), and Douglas Dakota (March 1945). The squadron also found its operational base shifted around several RAF stations in England and was briefly at RAF Drem. In December 1944, the squadron were an RAF Transport Command flight; in March 1945, they were deployed in Cairo; by May 1945, they were at Bilaspur, India.

At the start of the Second World War, RAF 3 Squadron were stationed at RAF Biggin Hill and briefly deployed to France as part of the British Expeditionary Force. It was forced to withdraw after 10 days. They were based at RAF Wick from 30 May 1940, moving to RAF Castletown on 30 October 1940. On 14 September 1940 detachments were based at RAF Turnhouse, RAF Montrose, and RAF Dyce.

Andrew Smitton Darling

TAKEN DURING TRAINING EARLY 1939

Battle of Britain fighter pilot Andrew Smitton Darling (740544) was the son of Peter and Mary Ann Greig Darling of 64 Feus, Auchterarder, the husband of Margaret Robertson Darling, Ayr. After taking a commercial course in Perth, he was employed on the clerical staff of Scottish Agricultural Industries Limited, Crieff. Later, he was a grain traveller with a company from Lanark. Darling was a member of his local dramatic society and the Scottish Horse Territorials. He had been keenly interested in flying and joined the RAFVR in August of 1937, training at RAF Perth with No 11 EFRTS. He gained his wings at RAF Prestwick with No 12 EFRTS.

Darling was called up on 1 September 1939. He completed his training as a recruit at RAF 12 Group Pool at Sutton Bridge, near King's Lynn in Lincolnshire. On 3 February 1940, he joined RAF 611 Squadron at Digby, not far away, just south of Lincoln. 611 Squadron became fully operational in May 1940 just in time to help by flying 'sweeps' over the beaches at Dunkirk during the evacuation. During the Battle of Britain, the squadron was part of the Duxford Wing, 12 Group's 'Big Wing' formations.

Darling shared in the destruction of two Dornier Do 17s off the Lincolnshire coast on 21 August 1940. He was flying Supermarine Spitfire MK IIa P7305 that day. On landing after combat with Dornier Do 17s over Mablethorpe, the Spitfire hit a wheel chock that had been left on the runway and nosed over at 2.05 pm. Spitfire P7305 was back in action two days later.

Darling was posted to 603 (City of Edinburgh) Squadron on 17 September 1940 at RAF Hornchurch, near Romford. Ten days later, he probably destroyed a Messerschmitt Bf 109. He damaged another Bf 109 on 5 October 1940 and on the 20 October 1940, he added another probable Bf 109 to his score. On 28 October 1941, he had another probable Bf 109 and a damaged Bf 109. Over the Straits of Dover, Darling destroyed two Italian Fiat Cr42s on 23 November 1940. On 29 November 1940, he shared in the destruction of a Dornier Do 17, east of Ramsgate.

Darling was posted to RAF 91 (Nigeria) Squadron at RAF Hawkinge on 3 March 1941 and promoted to Flight Sergeant. Whilst flying Spitfire P7615 on a shipping reconnaissance patrol, Darling was acting as 'weaver' to F/O Robert H. Holland on 26 April 1941. They were attacked by two Messerschmitt Bf 109s. Darling was able to warn and save his flight commander before being shot down by Oberleutnant Schumann of II/JG 51. His burnt-out Spitfire aircraft was found close to Reindene Wood, Hawkinge, with his body still in the cockpit.

Darling had been flying Spitfires since February 1940 and was instrumental in bringing down seven enemy aircraft without having sustained so much as a single bullet hole damage to his own plane. Members of Auchterarder Home Guard, family and personal friends of Darling carried his remains to his final resting place at Auchterarder Cemetery. The committal service was perhaps strangely, punctuated temporarily by the noise of low flying aircraft overhead. He was 28 years old.

NOTES: The funeral service was attended by the entire Town Council and many off duty serviceman who were home on leave also attended.

His mother, Mary lived on till the grand age of 102 and when she finally passed away in 1972, her remains were also laid to rest with her beloved husband and their boy Andrew.

Although Flight Sergeant Andrew Smitton Darling, RAF VR was never granted any gallantry awards, his accredited Air Combat Claims speak for themselves of his excellent flying and fighting abilities.

The 'Big Wing' was commanded by Wing Commander Douglas Bader until he was shot down and captured on 9 August 1941.

The Dornier Do 17 was referred to as the Fliegender Bleistift (Flying Pencil). It was a light bomber produced by Claudis Dornier's company, the Dornier Flugzeugwerke.

RAF 603 Squadron shot down the very first enemy aircraft during the war, a Junkers Ju88 over the Firth of Forth on 16 October 1939.

It is not well known that the Corpo Aereo Italiano of the Italian Royal Air Force (Regia Aeronautica Italiana) bombed Britain during the Second World War. Benito Mussolini insisted that his air force assist the German Luftwaffe during the Battle of Britain. They were based at Melsbroek, Ursel and Flugplattz in Belgium. Attacks by the Italians continued until 10 January 1941.

Squadrons attacking Italian raiders, some example raids:

24 October 1940, Harwich, 2 Squadrons deployed, 16 Fiat Br.20 medium bombers.

29 October 1940, Ramsgate.

11 November 1940, Harwich, 10 Fiat Br.20 escorted by 40 Fiat CR.42 Biplane Fighters attacked by Hawker Hurricanes, 7 BR.20's and 3 CR.42 fighters shot down.

The Fiat Cr.42DB single seat fighter aircraft held the distinction of being the fastest biplane to have ever flown (440+ km/h). It was a sesquiplane type of biplane, where the lower wing is smaller than the other, the word literally means, 'one-and-a-half-wings'. It had an open cockpit and a fixed undercarriage. They were also painted inappropriately for this task, pale sand yellow with green and brown mottling.

PERTHSHIRE ADVERTISER 3 MAY 1941 (THE COFFING BORNE BY THREE OF HIS BROTHERS AND LOCAL HOME GUARD WHO WERE ALL RELATIVES. FOLLOWED BY HIS WIDOWED MOTHER)

Downed Fiat Cr42 'Falco' guarded by the Home Guard, somewhere in Essex

Alexander Henry Thom

Battle of Britain pilot, Sergeant Alexander Henry Thom 114075 RAFVR was born in Perth on 29 May 1919. He was educated at Perth Academy and Dundee Technical College; and later trained as a quantity surveyor. Thom was the son of George Thom and his wife, 44 Crieff Road, Perth. Prior to enlisting, Thom served a five-year apprenticeship with J. Nairne Campbell, Methven Street, Perth. Thom, who was married in August 1942 to Cynthia Wilson, Bath, was well known in Perth as a skilled violinist. He gained many certificates at musical festivals in Perth, Dundee, and Arbroath.

On 24 June 1939, Alex Thom joined the RAFVR and started flying at the weekends with No. 11 EFTS at RAF Perth as an airman under training pilot. This was just over two months before the outbreak of the Second World War.

Alex was called to full-time service at the outbreak of World War two and posted to RAF No. 3 ITW (Initial Training Wing) at Hastings on 2 October 1939. Alex moved next to No.15 EFTS at RAF Redhill, just north of Gatwick Airport and then on to RAF No. 15 FTS at RAF Brize Norton. By 29 September 1940 he was at RAF No. 6 OTU at RAF Sutton Bridge in Lincolnshire where he trained on Hawker Hurricanes. Alex joined RAF 79 Squadron at RAF Pembury in Carmarthenshire for a very short period and was then transferred to RAF 87 Squadron who moved to at RAF Exeter on 30 October 1940.

During the Battle of Britain, Alexander Thom's first victory was not until 21 July 1941, whilst the Squadron was stationed in the Scilly Isles, Alex had a share in the destruction of a Heinkel He 11, twin-engine medium bomber. Three days later, he shared in the destruction of another Heinkel He 111. On 20 October 1941 he shot down a Heinkel He 111 and on 21 October 1941 he shot down yet another Heinkel He 111.

RAF 87 Squadron had returned from active duty in Northern France in May 1940, just before the fall of France and the evacuation of allied forces from the beaches at Dunkirk. They had been In France since September 1939, part of the air component of the BAF (British Expeditionary Force). On the day of the German invasion, the squadron moved forward to Lille, but after ten days it was forced back to Merville and then falling back some more until they were sent back over the U.K., to RAF Debden, near Safron Walden.

Thom made his first sortie with 87 Squadron on 10 November 1940. On 18 July 1941, two Hawker Hurricanes of RAF 87 Squadron were scrambled to intercept enemy aircraft reported 30 miles to the south of the Scilly Isles. A detachment of the squadron was stationed in the Scilly Isles at RAF St Mary's. Thom was the first to attack the lone Heinkel He111, his windscreen being sprayed with oil as his rounds tore into the Heinkel's starboard engine. Flying Officer Roscoe took over the chase, but the Heinkel was finished and came down on the sea. The Heinkel crew took to their lifeboats just minutes before their aircraft sank. Thom circled their life raft until a motor launch came to rescue them. He later met the crew and was given as a thank you the flying helmet of the German pilot.

On 21 July 1941, Thom had a share in the destruction of a Heinkel He 111, twin-engine medium bomber. His first solo 'kill' came on 20 October 1941 when he shot down another Heinkel He 111. The following day he shared in the destruction of yet another Heinkel He 111, which crashed into the sea southeast of the Scilly Isles.

Thom was appointed Flight Commander of B Flight on 10 July 1942 and awarded the DFC on 14 August 1942 and promoted to acting flight lieutenant. During this period, he shot down two enemy Heinkel He111 aircraft and claimed another probable.

Citation for the Distinguished Flying Cross:

This officer has been engaged on operational flying for a long period, both by day and by night. Throughout he has displayed great keenness and devotion to duty. He has destroyed two enemy aircraft both of which he shot down after pursuing them out to sea for more than 50 miles. On one occasion, he engaged a Heinkel 111 in extremely hazardous flying weather and probably destroyed it. Recently, Pilot Officer Thom has completed several successful intruder operations. He has invariably displayed initiative and courage.

Operation Jubilee was an allied amphibious attack on the French coast at Dieppe. One of the pilots providing fighter cover that day, 19 August 1942, was Thom. During the attack, Thom's Hawker Hurricane (LK-M) was hit by ground fire causing a loss of oil pressure. Thom coaxed his Hurricane back making a forced landing at East Dean, near Eastbourne. It was reported that Thom managed to get back to his airfield as a passenger in a Miles Master. He immediately took off again, this time in another Hurricane (LK-A) and returned to Dieppe where he continued to strafe enemy positions.

Operation Jubilee was an allied amphibious attack on the French coast at Dieppe. One of the pilots providing fighter cover that day, 19 August 1942, was Thom.

During the attack, Thom's Hawker Hurricane (LK-M) was hit by ground fire causing a loss of oil pressure. Thom coaxed his Hurricane back making a forced landing at East Dean, near Eastbourne. It was reported that Thom managed to get back to his airfield as a passenger in a Miles Master flown by a Flight Sergeant Lowe. He immediately took off again, this time in another Hurricane (LK-A) and returned to Dieppe where he continued to strafe enemy positions.

On 2 November 1942, RAF 87 Squadron was on-route to Gibraltar and North Africa. From 7 November 1942, they were based at RAF Gibraltar, Phillipville, Setif, Djedjelli and Taher in Algeria. The squadron was tasked to support the allied invasion of French North Africa, Operation Torch (8 November 1942-10 November 1942).

Thom returned to Britain on 27 September 1943 as a flight lieutenant. He became a flight instructor with RAF 55 OTU at RAF Annan, Dumfries, and Galloway on 17 November 1943. On 12 March 1944, he moved to RAF 53 OTU at RAF Kirton in Lindsey, Lincolnshire. He was appointed Flight Commander Fighter Affiliation Flight at 84 OTU at RAF Husbands Bosworth, Leicestershire on 19 May 1944, and remained there until 10 October when he was posted to RAF Peterhead as Adjutant. His final posting was to RAF 13 Group, RAF Inverness on 8 May 1945, as a staff officer. Thom retired from the RAF on 4 December 1945 as a flight lieutenant.

Thom returned to his profession as a quantity surveyor; his last position was as Regional Quantity Surveyor for the Western Region Hospital Board, Scotland. Flight Lieutenant Alexander Henry Thom passed away on 10 January 2016 and is commemorated on the Battle of Britain Monument, Victoria Embankment, London.

NOTES: RAF 85 OTU was formed from an element from No.14 OTU and was tasked with training crews to undertake night bombing operations utilising a bombing range just to the north of the airfield. An intensive training programme of navigation and fighter affiliation exercises, air firing (usually over the Wash or open sea), and practice bombing. Frequently this latter exercise was carried out on a range situated in open country near Mowsley to the north of the Husbands Bosworth airfield.

During the Dieppe Raid, Air Chief Marshall Sir Trafford Leigh-Mallory reported losses of 70 pilots and 10 crew killed or missing; aircraft destroyed as 88 fighters, 10 Army Co-operation aircraft, one from 2 Group and seven of the smoke laying aircraft.

RAF Bone is now Rabah Bitat Airport, formerly also known as Les Salines Airport, and popularly as El Mellah Airport.

Pilot Officer Alex Thom, Perthshire Advertiser 15 August 1942

DISTINGUISHED FLYING CROSS FOR RAFVR PILOT OFFICER (CH 4255) Original wartime caption: Pilot Officer Alexander Henry THOM, RAFVR., No.87 Squadron, (image above) who has gained the DFC has been engaged on operational flying for a long period, both by day and night. Throughout he has displayed great keenness and devotion to duty. He has destroyed two enemy aircraft shot down after pursuing them out to sea. On one occasion, he engaged a Heinkel III in extremely hazardous flying weather and probably destroyed it. Recently, has completed several successful intruder operations. He has invariably displayed initiative and courage, states the Air Ministry citation. Copyright: © IWM

Sir Alan Smith

Sir Alan Smith, CBE, DFC and Bar, DL was a Battle of Britain hero. Alan Smith also took part in RAF Fighter Command's offensive over northern France in the spring and summer of 1941. Smith, however, is better known as the wingman of legendary Spitfire pilot Douglas Bader. (A wingman's duty is to protect the leader of an element of fighter aircraft. In dangerous dog fights with enemy aircraft, the wingman always stays close, flying 'on his leader's wing'. They support and protect the leader, watching out for enemy attacks from behind.)

During the Battle of Britain, Alan Smith, was converting over to fly Supermarine Spitfire's. Alan Smith joined Royal Air Force Volunteer Reserve on the eve of the start of the Second World War. In October 1940 he was posted to RAF 610 squadron at RAF Acklington. He was next posted to RAF 616 Squadron as a sergeant pilot in early January 1941, just as the squadron moved south to RAF Tangmere (near Chichester). He was very soon in action over northern France, conducting offensive sweeps against the enemy. On 18 March 1941, Wing Commander Douglas Bader (who had lost both legs in a pre-war flying accident) arrived from RAF Duxford to take command of the 3 Spitfire squadrons that comprised the Tangmere Wing, which was subsequently nicknamed the 'BBC' ('Bader's Bus Company').

Douglas Bader immediately selected Smith to be his wingman. Bader's only comment on choosing Smith being, *"God help you if you let any Hun get on my tail"*. Two of the squadron's most charismatic pilots, Johnnie Johnson, and 'Cocky' Dundas, were chosen to form Bader's section of 4 aircraft, which used the call sign 'Dogsbody'. Bader always led RAF No. 616 Squadron in his personal Spitfire marked with his initials, 'DB'.

Sergeant Pilot Alan Smith described how he was selected and what Bader was like as a leader: - *"We had just come back from an operation and were at readiness, refuelling and such like, when a single Spitfire flew across the airfield, and performed aerobatics, the like of which you had never seen. He did three slow rolls, flick rolls and side slipped down to a perfect landing beautifully like a butterfly. He switched off and the prop stopped. The hood slid back and out got this legless guy we had heard about. He came into the dispersal hut and said,' I am Douglas Bader and I have come to take over the wing, I have decided to fly with 616 Squadron'. All other Wing Commanders took turns to fly with all their squadrons, but Douglas looked around those standing in the hut, and he saw Billy Burton, Cocky Dundas and spoke to each of them in turn. Then he spoke with Johnnie Johnson who he had obviously heard off. He looked at me and said 'who are you' I replied I'm Sergeant Smith sir. He said to me' you'll do you can fly as my number two'. Needless to say, I was taken aback. I was just an ordinary Sgt pilot; I can't say that I flew with him on all trips but most. He was a great leader. He always flew after that with 616."*

Johnnie Johnson later described Smith as "leech-like", and "a perfect number two who never lost sight of his leader". Due to a bout of influenza, Smith was not with Bader when the latter was forced to bail out of his Spitfire after a dogfight over France on 9 August 1941. Bader spent the rest of the war as a prisoner of war, eventually being sent to the 'escape-proof' Colditz Castle.

Alan recalled that Bader being shot down had a serious effect on morale: *"My job was to watch Bader's tail and watch out for the hun in the sun. I was to cling to him like a limpet. No one can describe what it's like to be in the middle of an air combat. One minute flying along in perfect formation, blue sky and peaceful and sun shining then all of a sudden, all hell breaks loose, I called it a Beehive, aircraft going in all directions. Then all of a sudden nothing, everything vanishes. We didn't have time to be frightened, but in the middle of all this action, aircraft exploding and parachutes opening all around. In the middle of all this Bader called up Group Captain Woodhall, the Tangmere controller and say 'Woody old chap, Douglas here. I quite forgot to book a squash court for 7 o'clock, can you book one for me'. All of a sudden, there was an aura of peace around you, as you digested the fact that if Douglas was not afraid, what was I doing afraid?*

Bader always flew as often as he could and he was never out of the cockpit, he was such a great pilot, I think eventually he was getting tired and could have done with a rest. He always insisted on flying on every operation. I always enjoyed flying with him and I always managed to stay with him in combat. I was too scared to leave him! He drove himself very hard harder than he expected anyone else to work. I learned all my skills from him. As we crossed the coast on the way back from France, he would get you to tuck in close in formation, you felt safe with him as he was the Wing Commander. He would often beckon me closer, very close in behind his wing. You could see him in the cockpit sucking on his pipe as we crossed back over the English coast.

He was quite a colourful character, it used to be amusing that once a week that he would get a signal asking for him to 'moderate his language in the air' as the WAAF's were refusing to write down what he said! On one occasion, I wasn't there but the story goes that he went to the cinema and asked the ice cream girl. 'Miss, can you get me a screwdriver' she promptly did, he undid a few screws and took his legs off and she subsequently fainted!"

With Bader captured, Alan Smith was posted to RAF Balado (near Kinross), to train new pilots. It was here that he met Margaret Todd, a local girl who was aiding the war effort in the Women's Voluntary Service.

Alan Smith later joined RAF 93 Squadron and took part in *Operation Torch* (the Anglo-American invasion of French Morocco and Algeria during the North African Campaign 8 Nov 1942 – 16 Nov 1942). Flying from Algeria he shot down four Focke-Wulf Fw 190 fighters. After service as a flying instructor in Florida he left the RAF in December 1945 as a Flight Lieutenant.

> On 4 November 1941, the then Pilot Officer Alan Smith, Royal Air Force Volunteer Reserve, No. 616 Squadron is awarded the Distinguished Flying Cross in recognition of gallantry displayed in flying operations against the enemy: *Throughout the 44 operational sorties in which, he has participated, this officer has shown the greatest keenness to 'engage the enemy and has destroyed at least four of their aircraft. In combat, he has been of great support to his leader on numerous occasion* — London Gazette

On 16 February 1943, Flight Lieutenant Alan Smith DFC, Royal Air Force Reserve, No. 93 Squadron is awarded a Bar to the Distinguished Flying Cross in recognition of gallantry displayed in flying operations against the enemy: *During the campaign in North Africa, Flight Lieutenant Smith has destroyed 4 enemy aircraft. His great skill, and fine example have inspired the formation he leads.* — London Gazette

Alan Smith survived the war and ended up with at least 20 confirmed kills during more than 1,500 combat hours flying time. He married his Scottish sweetheart and settled in Kinross where he became a highly successful businessman, mostly in the textile trade with his company Dawson International. Alan Smith was a former director of the Scottish Cashmere Association and served as chairman of the Perth-based Tay Foundation, a charitable trust which seeks to help the river Tay, its tributaries, fish, and environment. (The Tay Foundation aims to conserve and enhance the area's fish species and their ecological cycles.) He also served as Chairman of Quayle Munro, merchant bank, in Edinburgh.

Alan Smith was awarded the DFC on 4 October 1941. A bar was added on 16 February 1942, and he was appointed CBE on the 1 January 1976. On 12 June 1982, Smith was appointed Knight Bachelor as chairman and chief executive of Dawson International, becoming Sir Alan Smith.

Smith's description of his early flight training in a Tiger Moth is telling: *"The instructor merely pointed out the levers, patted me on the back and said, 'best of luck'."*

Alan Smith remained friends with Johnnie Johnson after the war and described him with affection: - *"Johnnie was everyone's pall, Johnnie enjoyed life and he was a bloody good pilot. In all the war, he only once had a bullet hole in his aeroplane. He was a damn good shot because he had spent much of his youth shooting partridges. He knew deflection, far better than townsfolk like me who had never fired a gun in his life. Johnnie used to visit me at my Mill after the war in Scotland."*

Alan Smith was born on 14 March 1917 in South Shields, County Durham, he left school at 14 after the death of his merchant navy captain father to work in his mother's ironmongery business. Alan Smith passed away in Perth Royal Infirmary on 1 March 2003, aged 95.

NOTES: Johnnie Johnson was the fifth greatest British fighter pilot of all time – the 4 above him all being First World War pilots – credited with 34 individual victories, 7 shared, 3 shared probable's, 10 damaged, 3 shared damaged, and 1 destroyed on the ground. Twenty of the enemy aircraft he shot down were the formidable Focke-Wulf Fw 190s. In fact, he was the highest scoring British fighter ace of the Second World War.

Alan Smith was one of the pilots who escorted six Bristol Blenheim's on a mission to drop by parachute a new false leg for Douglas Bader which he had lost when he bailed out: *"I can still remember seeing the box dropping under the parachute; it was one hell of a day, low broken cloud and rain. We had six Blenheims, the weather was appalling, and the bombers could not drop their bombs on the target at Lille, but the leg was dropped over St Omer."*

Left to right, Johnnie Johnson, Cocky Dundas, Douglas Bader, Alan Smith

Alan Smith with Johnnie Johnson

Notable mentions

(More details in individual stories under Second World War Aviators)

One Perth pilot who should have taken part in the battle is RAF 603 Squadron, Spitfire pilot, **Squadron Leader Colin Robertson DFC** from Graybank House, Perth. Robertson suffered a fractured skull in a horse-riding accident in June 1940 and as a result, was stood down from flying. After a time in Canada, he returned to fly de Havilland DH. 98 Mosquito's, recording 325 hours flying time.

On 12 December 1943, his squadron was tasked with proving cover for bomber aircraft attacking the V-weapons facilities at Peenemünde, Germany. His aircraft after take-off pitched up and dived into the ground near Filey in Yorkshire. He is buried in Camelon Cemetery, Falkirk.

The fighter pilots who took part received much of the glory, but it was not without the backing of the ground crews who kept them in the air, fighting. Once such hero was Corporal Colin Mackenzie, aircraft fitter with RAF 222 Squadron at RAF Hornchurch during the battle.

Colin Mackenzie was injured when he fell off an aircraft after an engine was wrongly started. This was the start of a lengthy illness from which he died in Perth Royal Infirmary on 25 November 1942, age 22. He is buried in Scone Cemetery.

Four other local airmen had their names inscribed in the official Roll of Honour of the Battle of Britain in 1947.

Sergeant Derrick Barrie Simpson from Balvaird Place, Perth

Pilot Officer John Littlejohn from Charlotte Street, Perth

Sergeant David Neill from Blairgowrie

Sergeant William Thomson from Dupplin Brae, Perth

But they were from squadrons who were subsequently denied the right to the 'Clasp' to the 1939/45-star award, the Battle of Britain bar (if they had flown at least one operational sortie during that time).

On 9 November 1960, the RAF issued a revised list of those squadrons considered to qualify for the Battle of Britain bar (single-engine fighters). Those airmen who previously had been issued this award were instructed to take down the bar immediately and return it to the RAF medals branch. One such was RAF 59 Squadron, a Coastal Command Squadron but was under the control of Fighter Command during the Battle of Britain. Another, RAF 235 Squadron, a Bristol Blenheim squadron, took part in similar operations and were recognised as Battle of Britain participants. As one RAF 59 Squadron pilot later put it when writing of the withdrawal of the award: *'...the feelings about this change ran pretty high at the time, I can tell you!'.*

Four of "The Few"

The names of four Perthshire men are among those which have been inscribed in the official Roll of Honour of the Battle of Britain.

The men—Sgt. Derrick Barrie Simpson, of Perth, Pilot Officer John Littlejohn, of Perth, Sgt. David Neill, of Blairgowrie, and Sgt. William Thomson, of Gannochy—all died in action during the period of the Battle of Britain between July 10 and October 31, 1940. Their memory will be preserved in the Battle of Britain Chapel in Westminster Abbey, where H.M. the King will unveil the Roll of Honour on July 10.

Arrangements have been made for relatives of the "Immortal Few" to attend the unveiling ceremony, but many have not yet applied for tickets. Next-of-kin, who have not already done so, are therefore asked to apply as soon as possible for tickets to S.4 (f), Air Ministry, King Charles Street, S.W.1. Applications must be made before May 31. Demobilised aircrew who fought in the Battle may also apply for tickets to the same address.

Perthshire Advertiser 17 May 1947

Second World War Aviators

David Taylor Adams

Sergeant David Taylor Adams was killed in a Lockheed Hudson Mk VI accident on 7 January 1943 during take-off from RAF Takoradi in Ghana, West Africa. He was from 10 Keir Street, Bridgend, Perth, the son of Mr and Mrs D T Adams and was a wireless air gunner with 200 Squadron RAF.

450 Lockheed Hudson Mk VIs were supplied to the RAF under the Lend-Lease scheme with the United States. It is possible that this was a new aircraft and was being ferried from RAF Takoradri to begin operations in Gambia. RAF 200 squadron would go on to operate marine patrol aircraft from RAF Bathurst, Jeswang Airfield, The Gambia, from March 1943 until July 1943.

The accident report stated that the aircraft struck rising ground approximately 400 yards south of the runway. The four crew on board were killed:

Sergeant Reginald Charles Payne RAAF (408135) captain/pilot – age 23

Sergeant William James Thomas Watson RAAF (401179) navigator – age 25

Sergeant Frank Edward Guy RAAF (4050407) wireless operator/air gunner – age 23

Sergeant David Taylor Adams RAF (1067899) wireless operator/air gunner – age 20

The crew are buried in the Takoradi European Public Cemetery, Ghana.

The squadron they were replacing was RAF 126 fighter squadron flying Hawker Hurricane Mk1 and MK IIb. RAF 126's role had been to defend Gambia from attack by Vichy French forces operating from Dakar in the neighbouring Senegal. The Vichy French forces in Africa eventually came under Allied control following the Anglo-American invasion of North Africa in November 1942 (code named Operation Torch).

Note: The capital of The Republic of The Gambia is now Banjul – it was renamed from Bathurst in 1973.

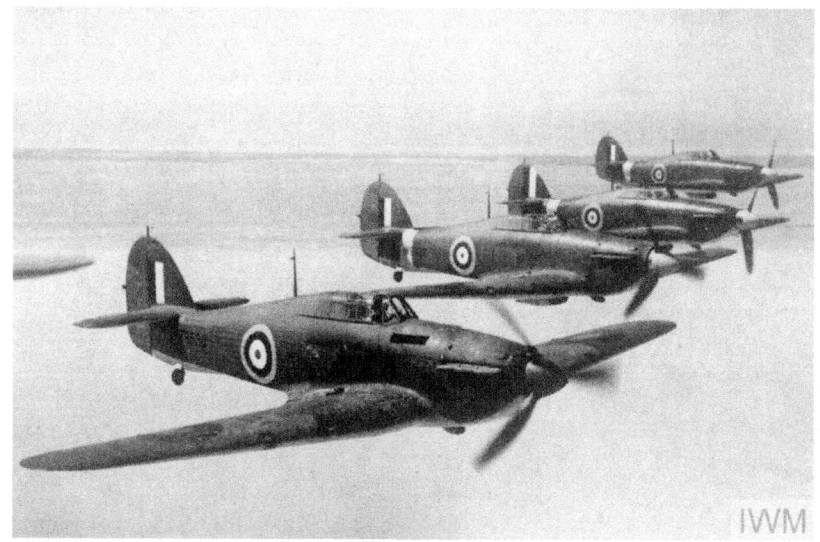

AIRCRAFT OF THE ROYAL AIR FORCE 1939-1945: HAWKER HURRICANE. (CM 849) Four untropicalised Hurricane Mark Is, T9530, W9320, W9349 and Z4095, in port echelon formation during a test flight from Abu Sueir, after arriving in Egypt via the West African Air Reinforcement Route from Takoradi, Gold Coast. T9530 was one of a small batch of aircraft built by the Canadian Car & Foundry Company Copyright: © IWM

ROYAL AIR FORCE TRANSPORT COMMAND, 1943-1945. (CH 15968) Douglas Dakotas of Transport Command and other aircraft parked at Takoradi, Gold Coast, during the rainy season. Copyright: © IWM.

ROYAL AIR FORCE: WEST AFRICA COMMAND, 1941-1945. (CM 3022) Hawker Hurricanes being assembled for despatch to the North African and Mediterranean theatres, at Takoradi, Gold Coast. In the foreground Hawker Hurricane fuselages are pulled by civilian labourers from their packing crates for assembly, after being shipped from the United Kingdom. Behind them are parked aircraft in various stages of assembly. In the background, a line of completed Hurricanes, Copyright: © IWM..

Peter Gordon Anderson

Pilot Officer Peter Gordon Anderson RAFVR (88023) of 20 Balhousie Street, Perth, the only son of Margaret Crawford Logan Anderson and the late Peter Anderson, agent of the Commercial Bank of Scotland Ltd. Peter Anderson was 22 years of age, he was educated at Perth Academy and Strathallan School. Prior to joining the RAF shortly after the start of the war, he was employed in the York Place branch of the Commercial Bank. Peter was well known in Rugby circles and was a playing member of the Perthshire Club.

Peter Anderson died when his aircraft was shot down and crashed at Ploudalmézeau just north of Brest, France, on 24 July 1941. The aircraft was a Handley Page Hampden Mk I, AE225 of RAF 144 Squadron flying from its base at RAF North Luffenham, Rutland, England.

The day before a PRU (Photographic Reconnaissance Unit) Supermarine Spitfire had brought back photographs showing the German battleship *Scharnhorst* moored at La Rochelle on the French Atlantic coast. On the other side of the Atlantic, a convoy with 30,000 Canadian troops was preparing to sail. If the *Scharnhorst* and other battleships sailed and attacked that convoy, many lives would have been lost, she had to be stopped.

The *Scharnhorst* and *Gneisenau* had docked at Brest on 22 March 1941, they had been at sea for 60 days in which they had sunk 22 merchant ships. The heavy cruiser *Prinz Eugen* arrived on 1 June 1941. During the weeks between March and July the port of Brest was attacked many times by the RAF. The *Gneisenau* was badly damaged, but the 'lucky ship' *Scharnhorst* always seemed to escape anything serious.

The French Resistance informed London on 20 July 1941 that an order for provisions had been placed for the *Scharnhorst*. That could only mean one thing, she was getting ready to sail. On the morning of 23 May 1941, the *Scharnhorst* slipped out of Brest and a Photographic Reconnaissance Unit aircraft spotted her berthed at a pier in La Pallice, La Rochelle later in the day.

PERTHSHIRE ADVERTISER 2 AUGUST 1941

An all-out effort was called for. The main *Scharnhorst* attack force of 24 July 1941 was comprised of Handley Page Halifax bombers, 15 aircraft in total, nine from RAF 35 Squadron and six from RAF 76 Squadron. This was a dangerous daylight raid without fighter cover, due to the distance. To avoid enemy radar, they flew below 1,000 feet. The *Scharnhorst* was badly damaged from several direct hits and had to return to Brest for four months of repairs. One RAF 35 Squadron Halifax and three RAF 76 Squadron Halifax aircraft were shot down. Four German fighters were also shot down.

Total bombers taking part that day over Brest and La Rochelle: three Flying Fortress, 18 Hampdens, 79 Wellingtons and the 15 Halifax aircraft who were specifically targeting the *Scharnhorst* – 16 bombers were lost. The *Gneisenau*, *Prinz Eugen* and a large tanker were hit at Brest. Several Bristol Blenheims attacked Cherbourg as a diversion. The night before the *Scharnhorst* had also received one direct hit from a Short Stirling bomber.

Three of the crew in Anderson's Hampden died and two became prisoners of war – Flight Lieutenant R B Barr and Sergeant J E Wiggall; they seemed to have survived the war.

The three crew who were killed are buried together at Ploudalmézeau Communal Cemetery, Finestere, Row 14 Coll. Grave 179-180:

Pilot Officer Peter Gordon Anderson RAF (88023) pilot, age 22

Sergeant Albert Bertram Cooper RAF (944245) wireless air gunner, age 22

Sergeant Donald Parking RAF (989144) wireless air gunner, age 21

NOTES:

Following the 'Channel Dash' in February 1942 in which the German Battleships *Scharnhorst* and *Gneisenau* and the heavy cruiser *Prinz Eugen* managed to break the British blockade and sail through the English Channel to Germany, RAF 144 Squadron was one of two squadrons converted to anti-shipping role as torpedo bombers. They moved to RAF Leuchars in July 1942 and then in September they were assigned to Operation Orator and temporarily transferred to Murmansk to protect the Allied Arctic convoy PQ 18. The squadron lost five Hampden bombers en-route to Russia. Only three examples of the Hampden survive today. One is in the RAF Museum at Cosford, P1344. It was recovered from a crash site on the Kola Peninsula, Northern Russia, in 1991.

Another local RAF officer who passed away at Milburn Court, Craigie, Perth, Wing Commander Gerald A Lane OBE, DFC was a member of RAF 35 Squadron.

ROYAL AIR FORCE BOMBER COMMAND, 1939-1941. (C 4109) Vertical aerial photograph taken during a daylight attack on German warships docked at Brest, France. Two Handley Page Halifax's of No. 35 Squadron RAF fly towards the dry docks in which the battlecruisers SCHARNHORST and GNEISENAU are berthed (right), and over which a smoke screen is rapidly spreading. Copyright: © IWM

Ronald Scott Baillie

Authors Note: Please note that this is the account of an Avro Lancaster bomber crew incident during World War Two that which I have been unable to find definitive evidence to confirm that it actually happened, as was claimed. The account below was obtained from squadron operational records.

On board the Lancaster flight that took place in February 1945, was a Perth lad from Barossa Place, Flying Officer Ronald Scott Baillie. He was the mid-upper air gunner. The crew upon return from their bombing mission, claimed to have shot down, not just one but two German jet Messerschmitt Me 163 aircraft.

I have questioned some other knowledgeable people about this claim, and all are sceptical as to its validity. However, it was officially reported in the squadron operational records, and their story was reported by several newspapers.at the time, including the Perthshire Advertiser. I personally have only heard about German jet fighters or guided missiles such as the V1 Flying Bomb 'Doodlebug's' being shot down by fast allied aircraft, such as the Supermarine Spitfire, Yakaloev Yak 9, Lavochkin La-7, North American P51 and Republic P47, never any jet powered aircraft being downed by any allied bomber crew during WW2.

F./O. R. S. Baillie.

My personal deduction is that it is possible that this happened, they were an experienced crew, and it was during the last confused days of Nazi Germany. It was perhaps a last gasp effort by some suicidal Luftwaffe pilots. The German Luftwaffe records do not show any jet aircraft losses for that night. It is also possible that the Lancaster crew misidentified the jet aircraft. It is even possible that they were some sort of unmanned rocket fuelled guided projectile fired from attacking aircraft or the ground, but none are shown operational in that area by February 1945. I did consider that it was a friendly fire incident, 4 de Haviland Mosquitoes were lost that night on that same raid and possibly many more allied fighter aircraft were also in action in the area.

Ronald Baillie was 23 years old when he helped shoot down the two claimed Me 163's, he started his RAF career with the Perth Academy Air Defence Cadet Corp, Perth Squadron of the Air Training Squadron (A.T.C.). Before joining he was in his second year at Dundee Art College and was formerly a member of the 10th (Academy) Boy Scouts. By May 1941 he was a gunner in a RAF night fighter squadron, Ballie by February 1945 had nearly four years air gunnery experience. Flying Officer Ronald Scott Baillie was the son of Major and Mrs James Bailie of 23 Barossa Place, Perth.

On the night of 7/8 February 1945, in his position as mid-upper gunner in Avro Lancaster BI, NG 380, Flying Officer Ballie of RAF 61 Squadron was returning from bombing the Dortmund-Ems Canal in Germany. That night, 177 Avro Lancaster and 11 de Haviland Mosquito of RAF 5 Group attacked the canal section near Ladbergen, northeast of Münster, Germany. They were equipped with delayed action bombs which landed harmlessly in nearby fields. The intended target, the banks of the canal were not damaged.

Twelve aircraft of RAF 61 Squadron were detailed to be part of the attack. The meteorological report was 7/10 to 9/10 cloud cover with tops at 8,000 to 9,000 feet. Pathfinder aircraft marking was by Red and Green T. I.'s (Target Indicator flares). Flying Officer H. R. Smith, the captain of the Baillie's aircraft had identified the target and bombed at the M.P.I. (Main Point of Impact) of Red T. I's. at 00.01 hours at 9,500 feet. All aircraft successfully bombed the target, but the results could not be observed owing to the cloud cover.

Ten minutes after they had dropped their bombs, Lancaster NG 380 was attacked by jet fighter, they identified it as a Messerschmitt Me 163. Flying Officer H. R. Smith noticed a white-hot glare racing astern of their aircraft. The Lancaster NG380's rear gunner, Flying Officer G. Bobenic thought it was a flare dropped by an enemy fighter, but Flying Officer Ronald Baillie identified it as an Me 163 jet fighter. Baillie could not use his guns as the Me 163 had passed under the Lancaster. Bobenic opened fire and saw some of the tracer rounds from his four Browning machine guns strike home. The Me163 came round for another pass and both Bobenic and Baillie fired. Thousands of feet below they saw the Me 163 explode.

Five minutes later, another Me 163 attacked from the starboard quarter. The guns of Bobenic and Baillie now jammed at the same moment. The Lancaster could do two things, to try and get away in a hurry, or turn or face the Me 163 jet so that the bomb-aimers guns in the nose could be brought to bear. Flying Officer Bobenic stated that "Smitty threw us into a stall turn so fast that we turned over on our backs, we damaged our aircraft, but we brought it back and we got the German fighter."

The bomb-aimer, at the front of the Lancaster, Sergeant Harris did manage to score strikes on the Me 163. By this time Baillie had cleared his guns and was pouring lead into the circling enemy. Bobenic hand-cocked his two right guns and took over from Baillie. The jet fighter fell to earth, heat coming from the flames and firing his guns into the ground. The Me 163's tracer rounds were seen by Bobenic to be ricocheting off the fields below.

Thirty minutes later, two of Lancaster NG 380's, 1,000 lb MC (Medium Capacity) bombs that had been hung up were jettisoned. One of the Me 163 jets was reported by Flying Officer Smith as seen destroyed at 50.02N, 00.25E at 2.10am, about 50 kms east of Ladbergen near Legden. Three Avro Lancaster's from 5 Group were lost that night.

To shoot down two Me 163's is quite a unique achievement for the crew of Avro Lancaster NG380. The attacking Me 163's would have flown at three times their speed, around 600 mph. The deflection angle, shooting ahead of the target, calculating the lead time and the angle at which they fired, so that the Me 163 would fly through your bullets was an act of incredible gunnery skill. Flying Officer Baillie was awarded the Distinguished Flying Cross (DFC) in December 1945. His citation describes Ronald as possessing "fine fighting spirit and outstanding efficiency."

NOTES: No night-time claims against any type of jet- or rocket-propelled aircraft/projectiles were officially recognised by Bomber Command Head Quarters at the time because of the sheer number of such claims and BCHQ believed that most, if not all such claims were against non-piloted projectiles other than aircraft. Only one Messerschmitt Me 163 is recorded in one British source I have found as being maybe shot down by Lancaster NG 380 that night. The shooting down of two on the night of 7/8 February 1945 is recorded in the RAF 61 Squadron Operational Record Books and was reported in the Perthshire Advertiser on 4 April 1945.

The Messerschmitt Me 163 jet operated and were tested at the largest Luftwaffe airbase in Northern Germany, the "Adlerhorst" (Eagles Nest) military airport in Rostrup, near Bad Zwischenahn by Erprobungskommando 16 (Testing-command 16). This unit was disbanded on 14 February 1945 and almagamated into Jagdgeschwader (Fighter Wing) 400 and sent to Brandis, near Leipzig, to provide additional protection for the Leuna synthetic gasoline works. South of the airfield, on the banks of Lake Zwischenahn, mooring places for floatplanes were built at E-Hafen (E-Harbour) for the Seefliegerhorst (Naval Flying Base). On 1 May 1945 Canadian troops captured the airfield.

Bad Zwischenahn, is about 150 kms northwest of where Lancaster NG 380 was attacked by jet aircraft. The Messerschmitt Me 163 Komet was a rocket powered interceptor piloted aircraft capable of exceeding 620 mph in level fight but had only fuel enough for 7.5 minutes endurance. It is more likely that the Me 163's operated from airbases along the route home of NG380. Two air bases are the most likely candidates, Twente, and Deelen in the Netherlands. Deelen is just north of Arnhem where an allied military operation to outflank the German Defences and seize strategic bridges using paratroopers and glider born troops, took place between17 September 1944 and 26 September 1944. Twente is about 58 kms east of Deelen and 21 kms from Legden. To the south of Legden, in the Ardennes (280 kms), the Battle of the Bulge, the last German offensive campaign on the Western Front had just taken place, 16 December 1944 to 28 January 1945.

In July 1944 the German Me 163 test pilot, Heini Dittmar reached a speed of 700 mph, a speed unmatched until 1953. Mach 1, the speed of sound, at sea level is approximately 768 mph. The Me 163 was powered by Hellmuth Walter Kommanditgesellschaft HWK 109-509A-2 bi-propellant liquid-fuelled rocket motors. The fuel used was a dangerous highly volatile mix of C-Stoff (fuel – methyl alcohol, mixed with hydrazine hydrate) and T-Stoff (oxidiser – hydrogen peroxide). By the end of 1944, 91 aircraft had been delivered, but a lack of fuel kept most on the ground. The Me 163 Komets attacked singly or in pairs a typical tactic was to fly vertically upward through the bombers at 9,000 m (30,000 ft), climb to 10,700–12,000 m (35,100–39,400 ft), then dive through the formation again, firing as they went. This approach afforded the pilot two brief chances to fire a few rounds from his cannons before gliding back to his airfield. The pilots reported it was possible to make four passes on a bomber, but only if it was flying alone.

The fuel is what is known as a hypergolic propellant, a rocket propellant combination used in a rocket engine, whose components spontaneously ignite when they make contact with each other.

Three days before NG380 shot down the Me 163's, on 4 February 1945, the Red Army made a request at the Yalta conference for air action to hinder the enemy from moving troops to the Eastern Front. Churchill, Stalin, and Roosevelt met 1945 in the ballroom of the Livadia Palace, the summer residence of the Tsars near Yalta in Crimea. This led to the increased RAF and USAF bombing of cities in Germany to disrupt the movement of German troops. Intelligence had suggested that dozens of German army divisions were moving to the Eastern Front to try and stop the Soviet advance which by now was approaching the River Oder, Germany's border with Poland, and only 90 kms from Berlin. One of the cities to be attacked was Dresden and in 4 raids between 13 and 15 February 1945, 650,000 incendiaries bombs, and 3,900 tons high explosive were dropped. The bombing resulted in a firestorm which destroyed 1,600 acres of the city centre. It is estimated that between 22,700 and 25,00 people were killed in Dresden.

		W/O. FISHER.	A.G. 2.			
	LANCASTER 1. NG.380½	F/O. SMITH.	CAPTAIN.	20.52	03.25	Sortie Completed. F/O. SMITH identified and bombed M.P.I. of Red T.I's. at 00.01 hours 19,500 ft. No results were seen. Attacked by Jet fighters and two destroyed. 50.02N 00.25E. 02.10 hours 4,000 ft. 2 x 1000 MC ½ hour delay jettisoned owing to hang-up.
		SGT. GIBSON.	FLT/ENG.			
		F/S. WILLIAMS.	NAV.			
		SGT. HARRIS.	A/B.			
		W/O. SCHMIDT.	W/OP. AIR.			
		F/O. BORENIO.	A.G. 1.			
		F/O. BAILLIE.	A.G. 2.			

R.G. of Lancaster "O" observed E.A. which was identified as a M.E.163 because the jet unit was switched on and off during the attack and E.A. fired so proving it was an aircraft and not a projectile. M.E.163 was dead astern at 1000 yards and as he closed in R.G. and M.U. opened fire and when E.A. got to 780X Range he started firing and continued to do so until fire from gunners forced him to break-off. E.A. circled and attacked from port quarter down and R.G. kept firing until E.A. burst into flames. Pilot, W/Op and both Gunners confirm that aircraft hit the ground and exploded.

Claim destroyed.

.... F/LT
GUNNERY LEADER No. 61 SQUADRON

.... W/C
COMMANDING No. 61 SQUADRON.

.... G/CAPT.
COMMANDING R.A.F. STATION SKELLINGTHORPE.

Me262 pack attacking Avro Lancasters, ©Julio Arróspide

Alan Reid Beveridge and Robert Graham Webster Beveridge

Flight Sergeant Alan Reid Beveridge RAFVR (748353), served with RAF 10 Squadron. On 13 March 1941, he was the second pilot of an Armstrong Whitley type V, serial Z6496 bomber. The aircraft took off from RAF Dishforth at 2035 hours to bomb Hamburg, Germany. The aircraft was struck by flak and considerably damaged but managed to return safely to RAF Leeming at 0335 hours. The squadron records described the damage to the aircraft as considerable.

On the night of 27/28 May 1941, Beveridge was the pilot of Armstrong Whitley P5055 tasked with bombing Köln (Cologne). Take off was from RAF Leeming at 2217 hours. They bombed the target from a height of 15,000 feet at 0239 hours. They sustained minor damage and safely returned at 0609 hours.

On 1 July 1941, whilst returning from a mission to bomb Duisburg, Germany, the aircraft that Beveridge was piloting, Armstrong Whitley type V, serial Z6584 was shot down by a Luftwaffe intruder aircraft of I./NJG near Thetford, Norfolk.

Records of the crash of Z6584 suggest only two crew members were killed:

Sergeant Alan Reid Beveridge RAFVR (748353) pilot, age 21

Sergeant Graham Aeron Alcock RAFVR (978333) wireless operator/air gunner, age 20

Beveridge was a former pupil of Dundee High School and Perth Academy. He was 21 years old and the second son of John Graham and Grace Webster Beveridge, Rowanbank, 44 Camphill Road, Broughty Ferry. They ran the Panmure Hotel, Monifieth, after having been in business in Perth. Flight Sergeant Beveridge is buried in the family grave at Dunbarney Cemetery, Bridge of Earn.

His brother, Flight Lieutenant Robert Graham Webster Beveridge RAFVR (86337) was also killed in action on 14 April 1942 whilst serving with RAF 39 squadron in Malta.

Robert Beveridge also attended Perth Academy and Dundee High School and stayed at 44 Camphill Road, Broughty Ferry. He was an apprentice-chartered accountant with Messrs Henderson & Loggie, Dundee.

Robert Beveridge flying his Bristol Beaufort N1169 twin engine torpedo bomber was shot down at 1745 hours by enemy aircraft after attacking an Italian convoy:

Flight Lieutenant Robert Graham Webster Beveridge RAFVR (86337) pilot, killed, age 25.

Lieutenant Peter Laverick Royal Navy observer, missing believed killed, age 22.

Sergeant George Stanley Fox RAFVR (1152586) wireless operator/air gunner, missing believed killed, age 22.

Sergeant Norman Austin Payne RCAF (R/56073) air gunner, missing believed killed, age 31.

The crew of N1169 were all lost, it was just one of six Bristol Beaufort's that were lost on that mission.

Alan Beveridge is interred at the Malta Capuccini (Kalkara) Naval Cemetery, plot E, grave 20. The other crew members are believed to have gone down into the sea with the aircraft about two miles off the island of Malta. It was reported that four bodies were seen in the water, but by the time a high-speed boat got there only Beveridge's body was found.

NOTES: Laverick served at HMS *Grebe*, a Fleet Air Arm shore base in Alexandria used for aircraft flown ashore from aircraft carriers. HMS *Grebe* was the pre-war Alexandria airport, known as Dekhelia.

Whitely Z6496 was built to contract 106962/40 by Armstrong Whitworth Ltd at Baginton and was ready on 27 January 1941 for collection to be delivered to RAF 10 Squadron. It was damaged on 9 May 1941 when engine issues forced it to return. During landing at 0105 hours, the right undercarriage gave way and it skidded to a halt with no casualties. It was repaired once more on 10 July 1942 due to a forced landing and written off on 1 September 1942 following an engine failure, crashing on undershooting the runway and catching fire.

Whitely P5055 was built to contract 75147/38 at Babington and was ready on 18 June 1940. It was slightly damaged on the night of 20/21 September 1940 and quickly repaired. Again, it was damaged again by flak on 25 September 1940 and on 28 May 1941. On 28 June 1941, it was lost on an operation to bomb Bremen and its crew of five where killed.

Colin David Brough

Flight Sergeant Colin David Brough RAFVR (1570574) was the observer of the six-man crew on board a Douglas C-47 Skytrain (Dakota DC-3) KG747 when it crashed on 8 June 1946 in Nigeria. The aircraft was on route from Kano Airport (now Mallam Aminu Kano International Airport), Nigeria to Lagos/Ikeja Airport (now Murtala Muhammed International Airport), Nigeria.

The weather was poor with low visibility and turbulence in cumulonimbus cloud. To avoid the low-pressure area, the pilot reduced his altitude and descended below the clouds. The aircraft hit treetops and crashed in a wooded area a mile northeast of Oni, Abeokuta Ogun, about 85 miles north of Lagos. All 22 on board (civilians, medical staff and engineers included) perished. An African civilian on the ground was also killed.

The six crew were:

Flight Lieutenant James Henry Gilfillan RAFVR (153036) pilot, age 22

Warrant Officer Cecil Brian Morgan RAFVR (1412375) pilot, age 22

Flying Officer Colin Henry Lynch RAFVR (167984) navigator, age 20

Flight Sergeant Colin David Brough RAFVR (1570574) observer, age 22

Aircraftman 1st Class Raymond William Peden RAFVR (1901334) position unknown, age 22

Flight Sergeant Roy Pitt RAFVR (1817246) U/T (Under Training) air gunner, age 21

It was reported that the navigation charts used by the crew were partially wrong. The altitudes marked were incorrect.

Colin David Brough is buried at Yaba Cemetary, Nigeria, Plot 4, Row 1, Grave 4. He was the son of Colin and Margaret Ross Brough, Milnathort.

OpenStreetMap © OpenStreetMap contributors OpenStreetMap is open data, licensed under the Open Data Commons Open Database License (ODbL) by the OpenStreetMap Foundation (OSMF).

A Royal Air Force Douglas Dakota C.III VIP transport aircraft (serial KG770) of No. 24 Squadron RAF based at Hendon, Middlesex (UK), in flight carrying King George VI and Queen Elizabeth on a visit to the Channel Islands, 1945. Credit: Wikimedia Commons https://commons.wikimedia.org/wiki/File:Dakota_24_Sqn_RAF_with_King_George_VI_in_flight_1945.jpg – Unknown author / Public domain This work created by the United Kingdom Government is in the public domain

Douglas Cameron

Flight Lieutenant Douglas Cameron DFM completed four tours of operations, 122 flight bomber missions over enemy territory as a rear gunner during the Second World War. He flew with three VC recipients and bailed out of two aircraft.

Two of those pilots were both awarded the Victoria Cross for their actions when they were shot down: Flight Sergeant R H Middleton VC and Squadron Leader Ian Bazalgette VC.

Douglas Cameron was born in Kenmore in 1909 and was a Perthshire gamekeeper with Major J Falconer-Stewart, Feddal, Braco. Before the war, he lived with his wife and father at The Kennels, Feddal Estate.

His occupational skills helped him avoid capture the second time he bailed out, in daylight, landing on the edge of a German forest, with soldiers spraying machine-gun bullets and dogs baying at his heels.

Cameron enlisted in September 1939 volunteering for flying duties. Two tours followed in Armstrong Whitely bombers, the first tour with RAF 58 Squadron, RAF 5 group at RAF Linton-on-Ouse: the second with RAF Coastal Command at RAF St. Eval, Cornwall.

During this period as an air gunner, Cameron shot down a Focke Wulf FW190 fighter. A third tour followed immediately, this time flying with RAF 149 Squadron out of RAF Lakenheath, Suffolk. This time the aircraft were Short Stirling's, and he was on Flight Sergeant Middleton's crew. They transferred for a short while to RAF 7 PFF (Pathfinder Force) Squadron, but some of the crew did not meet the required standards. They returned to RAF 149 Squadron to complete their tour.

On the night of 27/28 November 1942, Cameron and Middleton took off to attack the Fiat Works, Turin; they took off at 18.14 hours. Their Short Stirling, I BF372 (OJ-H) was badly damaged by flak and Middleton was severely wounded. He had lost an eye and the bone above his eye was exposed. The co-pilot, Flight Sergeant Leslie Hyder was wounded in the head and the legs and could not immediately take over. The aircraft dived to just 800 feet before Hyder managed to regain control. Flying Officer Skinner, the wireless operator, was also injured. They were further hit many times by light flak..

Middleton was given a shot of morphine and somehow managed to fly the aircraft back to base. With the windscreen shattered and the biting wind rushing in, for four hours he kept the Stirling on course. There was also barely enough fuel left for the return trip, everything that could be, was jettisoned, even the guns, anything that would save fuel and allow the aircraft to climb back over the 12,000 feet Alps. The possibilities of abandoning the damaged aircraft or landing in Northern France were discussed as options. Middleton expressed the intention of trying to make the English coast so that his crew could leave the aircraft by parachute and be safe. Owing to his wounds and diminishing strength, he had little hope of accomplishing this himself.

After four hours, they eventually crossed the French coast, flying at 6,000 feet and again they were hit by intense light and anti-aircraft fire. Middleton mustered enough strength to take evasive action. Fuel ran out as they crossed the English Channel and Middleton gave the order to bail-out. Four of the crew successfully bailed out, but Middleton and two crew members who remained to help him were killed when the aircraft crashed into the sea near Dymchurch, Kent.

The bodies of the front gunner, and the flight engineer were recovered the following day. Middleton's body was not found.

Middleton was awarded, on 13 February 1943, a posthumous VC for his efforts, given the rank of a pilot officer and buried with full military honours, in the Military Cemetery of St John's Church, Beck Row, near RAF Mildenhall. His citation in part read:

'His devotion to duty in the face of overwhelming odds is unsurpassed in the annals of the Royal Air Force'.

Cameron and two other crew were given the DFM.

From the Operations Record Book of RAF 149 Squadron, November 1942:

28.11.42, Stirling I, BF372, "H".

F/Sgt. Middleton, R. A. Captain, F/Sgt. Hyder, L.A. 2nd Pilot, P/O Royde, G. R., Navigator, P/O Skinner, K. E., W/Operator, F/Sgt. Cameron, D., M/Upper, Sgt. Mackie, S. J., F/Gunner, Sgt. Gough, H. W., R/Gunner, Sgt. Jeffrey, J. E., F/Engineer.

Time up, 1814. Time Down, 0255.

Target TURIN. Aircraft crashed into sea of Dymchurch. Crew bailed out. Captain, Wireless Operator and F/Engineer killed. (Strikethrough replaced with Front Gunner in records)

Cameron was taken off operations for a rest, commissioned as an officer and transferred to RAF 20 OTU at RAF Lossiemouth as a gunnery leader. His next posting was to RAF Milltown, near Elgin. Here he was recruited by Squadron Leader Bazalgette for his fourth tour of bomber operations and with the help of another heroic flyer from Leith, Group Captain Thomas Gilbert 'Hamish' Mahaddie (born Leith), they were assigned to the Pathfinder Force at RAF 635 Squadron.

On 4 August 1944, during a target marking mission at Trossy Saint-Maximin, just north of Paris, Lancaster III ND811 (F2-T) was hit by severe anti-aircraft fire. Both starboard engines were put out of action causing a serious fire. Despite the damage to the aircraft, they pressed on with the attack, the master bomber had been put out of action and they took over, marking the target accurately. After their bombs had been dropped: the Lancaster dived almost out of control. Then the port inner engine also failed, and the starboard main-plane caught fire.

Bazalgette ordered the crew who were able to, to bail-out. He then attempted to land the crippled aircraft near Senantes, about 70 km to the northeast. Unfortunately, it exploded killing Bazalgette and two remaining crew members.

Five of the crew including Cameron successfully bailed-out and evaded capture. Cameron managed to hide in a forest and eventually contacted the French Resistance. Cameron joined them and became a saboteur, helping to attack the Germans. Dressed in civilian clothes and armed with a revolver and a grenade, he would have been executed if captured. For that ultimate emergency, he had been given a pill. Several times he had close calls; once a whole German Panzer Division arrived at the place where he and his resistance group were hiding.

Mission details:

3rd August 1944 – Forêt-de-Nieppe Lancaster III NE123 MG-J (2.35) Craig as Master Bomber 7/10th Cloud Area G – Good Results
1,114 Aircraft – 601 Lancasters, 492 Halifax's, 21 Mosquitos – carried out major Raids on the Bois de Cassan, Forêt de Nieppe & Trossy St Maximin V1 Flying-Bomb Stores. The weather was clear, and all Raids were successful. 6 Lancasters lost, 5 from the Trossy St Maximin Raid & 1 from the Bois de Cassan raid. 1 Lightning & 1 Radar Counter Measures Aircraft accompanied the Raids. The Unit's role was Radar Countermeasures (RCM), and this entailed the identification of Enemy Radar patterns & wavelengths.

Bazalgette and his crew flew 25 operations between 6 May 1944 and 3 August 1944 against railway marshalling yards, synthetic oil factories, V-1 Rocket storage depots, coastal batteries (on D-Day) and tanks and troops after the invasion. On a night raid to Hamburg on 28 July 1944, described as 'a hot one', German fighters attacked and had a field day. Bazalgette flew the violent corkscrew evasive manoeuvre all the way back to avoid the fighters. This made for a wild ride for the rear gunner, Doug Cameron who remarked: *'I've never had a trip like that. I don't know how I stood it'.*

Barely one month previous on 6 June 1944, the allies had landed on the beaches at Normandy. Cameron took part in resistance actions near the Falaise Pocket, 12-21 August 1944 and in the 'Bocage' (thick hedgerows). When the British Army eventually broke through the German lines, Cameron, the navigator, and the wireless operator from Lancaster ND811 were reacquainted near Bayeux and flown home.

After the war, Cameron joined the Royal Observer Corps then went back home to resume his life as a gamekeeper. He christened his daughter, Margaret Middleton Bazalgette Cameron. Cameron lived quietly in his later years with his wife and widowed sister in the house where he was born, Kenmore, Feddal Road, Braco. He passed away on 16 February 1994. The grave of Douglas Cameron DFM is in Ardoch Parish Churchyard, Braco

NOTES: The French Resistance had informed the Allies that Cameron was with them, but his wife was not informed for security reasons. She was in her native Stornoway when a policeman arrived to tell her the good news.

Bazalgette's grave is at Senantes Churchyard, France. His Victoria Cross is displayed at the Royal Air Force Museum in Hendon. Nanton Lancaster Society Air Museum, now the Bomber Command Museum of Canada (located in Nanton, Alberta, south of his hometown Calgary), is home to an Avro Lancaster, FM159, which, after a lengthy period of reconstruction and repair, was painted in the colours and markings of Bazalgette's aircraft.

'Hamish' Mahaddie had a very successful career as a consultant to the movie and television industry after the war. He worked on films such as *633 Squadron*, *You Only Live Twice* (which includes an autogyro sequence with Ken Wallis), and *Battle of Britain*.

Only 35 Avro Lancasters out of an estimated 6,500 in service, were successful in flying 100 or more operational missions during the Second World War (0.54%). The most successful was Lancaster ED888, which flew 140 operations.

The Lancaster when empty could climb below 9,000 feet on one engine and maintain level flight above that altitude. It could carry a full bomb load and maintain speed on three engines. A Squadron Leader from RAF 635 Pathfinder Squadron once lost an engine on take-off, rather than return, he carried on to the target, marking it successfully and on his return, he buzzed the airfield control tower before landing safely.

The Pathfinder Force flew a total of 50,490 individual sorties against 3,400 targets. The cost was the loss of 3,727 Pathfinder aircrew.

BADGES OF R.A.F. SQUADRONS (CH 15890) Original wartime caption: Badge of No.149 Squadron 'FORTIS MOCTE' (Strong by Night). Copyright: © IWM. **And** R.A.F. SQUADRON BADGES (CH 16672) Original wartime caption: The badge of No.635 Squadron R.A.F. 'NOS DUCIMUS CETERI SECUNTER' (We Lead - the Rest Follow) Copyright: © IWM

ROYAL AIR FORCE 1939-1945: BOMBER COMMAND (CH 12677) A Stirling of No 149 Squadron at Lakenheath being loaded with 1,500lb sea mines, March 1944. Copyright: © IWM

THE ROYAL AIR FORCE IN BRITAIN, JANUARY 1942 (TR 135) A seven-man crew from No 149 Squadron, Royal Air Force under the nose of Short Stirling W7455/`OJ-B' at Mildenhall, Suffolk, while the aircraft is being bombed-up. Copyright: © IWM.

ROYAL AIR FORCE 1939-1945: BOMBER COMMAND (CH 8167) Flight Sergeant Leslie Hyder of No 149 Squadron chats with a nurse while recovering from wounds received over Turin on the night of 28-29 November 1942. Hyder was second pilot in a Stirling which was hit by flak over the target. Copyright: © IWM.

THE BRITISH ARMY IN NORTH-WEST EUROPE 1944-45 (BU 5892) Liberated POWs walk out to Lancaster bombers of No. 635 Squadron at Lubeck aerodrome, waiting to fly them home to Britain, 11 May 1945. Copyright: © IWM.

The grave of Douglas Cameron DFM in Ardoch Parish Churchyard, Braco.

Patrick Cameron

Sergeant Patrick Cameron RAF (573311) was an air gunner aboard Consolidated B-24 Liberator VI EW277. His squadron was part of the RAF 205 group consisting of US (daytime) and British (primarily night-time) long-range heavy bomber units under the command of Major General James H Doolittle. On 14 June 1944, age 22, he was reported as missing in action over Germany.

On the night of 13 June 1944, some 90 planes of 205 group took off from Foggia airfields (24) in Italy to bomb the railway yards at Munich:

32 Wellingtons of 231 Wing

13 Wellingtons of 236 Wing

22 Wellingtons of 330 Wing

10 Pathfinder Halifax's of 614 Squadron

13 Liberators of 178 Squadron from the airfield at Foggia No 1, Celone, Italy (including number EW277)

RAF 178 Squadron spent the entire Second World War operating in the Mediterranean Command area. It was formed at Shandur, Egypt on 15 January 1943. They moved with the advancing allied armies through Hosc Raui airbase, Terria, El Adem in Libya, and then onto Celone and Amendola in Italy.

Apart from normal bombing missions, the squadron was also used to drop supplies to partisans as far as Poland on occasion. Number 178 was actively involved in dropping supplies to the besieged Polish Home Army in Warsaw in 1944.

The RAF crew of EW277 were as follows:

Sergeant Stephen Thomas Geraint Gill, RAFVR (1452957) pilot, age unknown

Sergeant Patrick Cameron, RAF (573311) air gunner, age 22

Sergeant Robert McLean RAFVR (1671314) air bomber, age 20

Sergeant Malcolm Charlish, flight engineer RAFVR (2202796), age 19

Sergeant Frank Cooney, wireless operator/air gunner, (1684744) RAFVR, age 21

Two members of the crew it is believed were captured and interred in the POW Camp Stalag Luft 7, (Bankau, Nr. Kreulberg) Upper Silesia, Poland):

Camp L7 POW No. 146 A W Billing 1355714

Camp L7 POW No. 155 P H Craig 1578239

The five crew members who lost their lives were buried as US airmen by the Germans in Friedhof Fürstenfeldbruck to the west of Munich. This confusion arose due to the fact they were flying a (normally flown by) US-built Liberator aircraft. When the occupying force of the American Army found their graves, they transferred the bodies to the US Military Cemetery in St Avoid in France. When this mistake was finally realised, the bodies were again recovered and they were buried in Commonwealth Graves at Choloy War Cemetery, East of Nancy, France.

Cameron was the son of Dr Patrick Cameron, MB, CH B, and Jenny Cameron, Perth.

NOTES: One of the other airfields at Foggia was Ramitelli, it was the home of the legendary 99th Pursuit Squadron and the 332nd Fighter Group of the United States Army Air Force. The 99th and 332nd deployed to Italy in early 1944 and were equipped with what they became more commonly associated with, North American P-51 Mustangs. When they painted the tails of their aircraft crimson red, the first African American aviators became famously known as the 'Red Tails' or 'Red Tail Angels'. They were also known, after the training airfield in the United States, as the 'Tuskegee Airmen'. The 'Red Tails' combat record was distinguished, and they became some of the best pilots in the US Army Air Forces, despite being subject to restrictive pilot training requirements, negative predictions, harassment, and racial segregation and discrimination.

Archibald Campbell

Flight Sergeant Archibald Campbell RAFVR (1371720), age 29, was the son of Archibald and Isabella Campbell of 5 Kincarrathie Crescent, Perth. Archibald Campbell was the pilot of a de Havilland Mosquito Mk IV Series II, DZ368 of RAF 540 Squadron. At this time RAF 540 squadron was based at RAF Leuchars but kept a flight down south at RAF Benson.

DZ368 was built at a private airfield and aircraft factory owned by the de Havilland Aircraft Company at Hatfield Aerodrome in Hertfordshire, England. It was built between 12 October 1942 and 30 December 1942 under the order number, 555/C.23(a). It was equipped with two Rolls Royce Merlin 21/23 engines, four 20mm cannons and four .303 in Browning machine guns. Given the model type and number, it is likely that this Mosquito aircraft was built as a fighter and photo-reconnaissance type.

Sergeant Campbell and his navigator/wireless operator, Sergeant James (Jimmy) Arkle 1109187 RAFVR, age 21, were not on operations. They are listed as being en-route from their base at RAF Benson in South Oxfordshire. They crashed on 20 May 1943 following an engine failure four miles south-west of Newbury in Berkshire. Both were killed.

Archibald Campbell for nine years was a partner in the firm of Campbells, McLagan & Co, wholesale grocers in North St John's Place. He attended Perth Academy, was well-known as an artist and turned out on many occasions for Mayfield Cricket Club. Archibald Campbell joined the RAF in 1941, he had just returned to his squadron from a spell of leave four days earlier. He is buried in Wellshill Cemetery, Perth.

Several salvaged items from this crashed aircraft have been sold online over the past few years.

NOTES: RAF 540 Squadron are believed to have taken part in a very daring Cold War mission in late August 1953 to photograph a suspected Soviet missile base called Kapustin Yar, 60 miles east of Stalingrad. The request had come from the US who had received intelligence of a Soviet missile construction programme. At the time the US had no aircraft capable of a long-range photo-reconnaissance flight, the famous Lockheed U-2 spy planes had not yet come into service and this was long before satellites existed.

The British solution was to use an RAF English Electric Canberra B.2 bomber. Stripped of excess weight, fitted with a 100-inch focal length camera and with its bomb bays filled with extra fuel tanks, the Canberra WB726 took off from Giebelstsadt Army Airfield (USAF) in West Germany to fly to Kapustin Yar and then south to land in friendly territory. The 'Project Robin' Canberra flew at an altitude of between 46,000 ft and 48,000 ft and had a cruising speed of 540 miles per hour. The Soviets tracked the Canberra and attempted to intercept using their Mikoyan-Gurevich MiG-15 jet fighters. It was difficult to see the Canberra above them in the dark and the MiGs found it difficult to maintain altitude. As the sky grew lighter, they finally did get off a burst of cannon fire which hit the Canberra. The Canberra was not seriously damaged, but it did cause a vibration in the aircraft, and this blurred the photographs they took as they over-flew the missile base. The Canberra flew on and landed safely in Iran.

ROYAL AIR FORCE: OPERATIONS BY THE PHOTOGRAPHIC RECONNAISSANCE UNITS, 1939-1945. (HU 1634) Three De Havilland Mosquito PR Mark IXs of No. 540 Squadron RAF based at Benson, Oxfordshire, flying in loose echelon formation. Copyright: © IWM.

V1 FLYING BOMB (CL 1055) Aerial reconnaissance view of the V1 launching ramps at the Luftwaffe Test Installation, Peenemunde West, Usedom Island, Germany, showing a Fiesler Fi 103 flying bomb positioned on its ramp (arrowed). This was the photograph from which Flight Officer Constance Babington-Smith, a photographic interpreter at the Allied Central Interpretation Unit, RAF Medmenham, Buckinghamshire, confirmed the existe... Copyright: © IWM

David Ferguson Sharpe Campbell

South of Bergen and North of Stavanger in Norway lies the cemetery of Haugesund (Rossebo) Var Frelsers in which lies the war grave of Sergeant David Ferguson Sharpe Campbell.

Campbell, 74301, RAFVR was the observer on a Bristol Blenheim Mk IV, N3604, (QY-R), a twin-engine light bomber from RAF 254 Squadron on 25 June 1940. All three on board were killed, the pilot was Flight Sergeant Percival Gordon Cory, 564105, RAF, age 26, and wireless operator/air gunner Sergeant Francis George Kinhan, 535306, RAF, age 23.

They took off at 12.48 hours from RAF Sumburgh in the Shetland Islands on a mission to attack targets of opportunity. Whilst attacking a ship off Stavanger at 14.25 hours, they were shot down by Oberfeldwebel Hans-Jakob Arnoldy from the Luftwaffe 77 Jagdgeschwader, (II/JG77) flying a Messerschmitt Bf 109. The Blenheim crashed near Osthuvik, Rennesoy in Norway.

Campbell was the son of Andrew and Catherine Campbell from 52 Queen Street, Craigie, Perth. To his friends he was known as Fergus Campbell. He joined the RAFVR in February 1938. He had the distinction of being the first to pass his test as an air observer at Perth Aerodrome. He was formerly employed in the foreign department of the General Accident Fire and Life Assurance Corporation in Perth. Six months after his death, his mother told the Perthshire Advertiser that she steadfastly refuses to abandon hope that her son is still alive.

NOTES: Oberfeldwebel Anrnoldy was later killed on 15 April 1941 in Greece after an emergency landing in a Greek controlled area near Larissa. He is buried at the Kriegsgräberstätte of Dionyssos-Rapendoza (Greece). There is some controversy as to his fate. A report states that he engaged RAF 33 Squadron Hurricanes as they were taking off from an airfield at Larissa. He was wounded in the chest by fire from the Canadian ace, Flight Lieutenant John McKie. He bailed out and as he came down by parachute, he was fired on by Greek soldiers. His aircraft, Messerschmitt Bf 109 E (W.Nr. 5277) 'White 5' made an almost perfect belly landing and was virtually undamaged, except for two bullet holes in the cockpit hood, in line with the pilot's chest. However, a picture taken of his aircraft later, showed that the cockpit canopy had been opened in the normal fashion, not blown off by explosive bolts he would have fired before bailing out. Earlier in the war, JG 77 took part in the invasions of Poland and Norway.

AIRCRAFT OF THE ROYAL AIR FORCE 1939-1945: BRISTOL TYPE 149 BLENHEIM IV. (CH 2992) Six Blenheim Mark IVFs of No. 254 Squadron RAF, flying in formation over Northern Ireland shortly after the unit's arrival at Aldergrove, County Antrim. Copyright: © IWM

James Cameron Campbell

At Shalloch, on Minnocha Corbett, at the north end of the 'Awful Hand' range in the Southern Uplands, part of Galloway Forest Park, Leading Aircraftman James Cameron Campbell was a member of an Avro Anson crew that was lost on 2 July 1942.

Perthshire Advertiser 8 July 1942

L.A.C. J. C. Campbell.

Campbell, 1346334, RAFVR was the husband of Catherine Mason Campbell of 32 Viewlands Terrace, and the eldest son of Mr and Mrs Campbell, Thistlebank, 185 Glasgow Road, Perth.

James Campbell had been in service with the RAF for about a year, formerly working for Alex Thomson & Sons, grocers and wine merchants of 255 High Street, Perth. James and Catherine had two sons, he is buried in Wellshill Cemetery, Perth.

Avro Anson Mk. I of No 2 (O) AFU from RAF Millom in Cumbria was on a cross country navigation training flight with a crew of five, a staff pilot and a wireless operator and three trainees. The aircraft was spotted by the ground Observer Corps flying northwest of Dumfries at 3,000 ft. It is thought that they flew into the hill which was obscured by cloud. Two days later, a shepherd discovered the wrecked aircraft on the eastern summit. The crew bodies were removed the following day.

Flight Sergeant William Thomas Gale, R/84247, RCAF, pilot, age 22

Leading Aircraftman James Cameron Campbell, 1346334, RAFVR, observer (u/t), age 30

Leading Aircraftman Joseph Arthur Wild, 1576055, RAFVR, observer (u/t), age 31

Sergeant John Benson Hall, 1354005, RAFVR, wireless operator/air gunner, age 22

Aircraftman 2nd Class, Ernest Everall, 1126654, RAFVR, wireless operator/air gunner (u/t), age 21

Note: Catherine Mason, his wife died 4 January 2012, age 97 years.

BRITISH AIRCRAFT IN ROYAL AIR FORCE SERVICE, 1939-1945: AVRO 625A ANSON. (C 2117) Two Anson Mark Is, K6285 and N9742, of No. 321 (Dutch) Squadron RAF based at Carew Cheriton, Pembrokeshire, in flight north-west of Tenby. K6285 still bears the unit code letters ('MW') of No. 217 Squadron RAF, to which it formerly belonged. (Port three quarter front view). Copyright: © IWM.

ROYAL AIR FORCE: 1939-1945: COASTAL COMMAND (MH 33968) An Anson of No 502 Squadron undergoing a major inspection at Aldergrove, near Belfast, April 1940. Copyright: © IWM.

John Archibald Campbell

On 22 July 1943, Sergeant John Archibald Campbell RAFVR (1690312) age 20, lost his life in an aircraft accident at RAF Stradishall in the Borough of St Edmundsbury in the English county of Suffolk (between Cambridge and Ipswich).

Campbell was flying in a Short Stirling Mk1, W7586 four-engine heavy bomber from RAF 1657 Heavy Conversion Unit (HCU) at RAF Stradishall. Heavy Conversion Units were formed in late 1941 to qualify crews trained on medium bombers to operate heavy bombers. They took off, detailed to carry out practice circuits and landings. An attempt was made to practice a three-engine approach; the aircraft overshot the runway and they tried to go around again for another go. The aircraft stalled and crashed at 17.46 hours. All on board were killed:

Pilot Officer Leonard Gerrard Sellars RAAF (409454), pilot, age 31

Sergeant John Archibald Campbell RAFVR (1690312), flight engineer, age 20

Flying Officer Robert Henry Rutherford RAFVR (133718), navigator, age 20

Flight Sergeant Raymond Henry Murdock RCAF (R/128432), bomb aimer, age31

Sergeant Richard George Kings RAFVR (1185185), air gunner, age 27

Sergeant George Frank Albert Wix RAFVR (1804500), air gunner, age 20

Flight Sergeant Ernest Henry Benjamin Saker RAAF (425224), age 20

Campbell was the son of May D Campbell formerly of 177 Glasgow Road, Perth, and latterly Pitlochry. He was a member of Pitlochry ATC before joining the RAF ten months prior. He was cremated at the Golders Green Crematorium, London.

NOTES: Some Heavy Conversion Units did, if their help was needed, take part in operational bombing missions over Germany.

RAF Stradishall –see also William Alexander Watson and John Reginald James Laidlay.

Also cremated at Golders Green Crematorium – Marc Bolan, Sir Kingsley Amis, Keith Moon and Sigmund Freud

Douglas Carr

Comrie airman Douglas Carr was reported missing at sea in late July 1941. His mother, 9 Glebe Cottage, Comrie was informed he was missing on the same day that she received a letter from him saying that he was well. (See also John Tyndel Farquhar)

Leading Aircraftman Douglas Carr RAFVR, 981525, was 24 years of age and was previously employed at Abertuchill estate, two miles west of Comrie before being called up. Douglas Carr's father, Corporal John Carr, R.A.S.C. died in service during World War One.

Leading Aircraftman Douglas Carr was onboard SS *Anselm* when it was torpedoed by the German U-boat, U96 on 5 July 1941, about 300 miles north of the Azores. The SS *Anselm* was on passage from Gourock on the River Clyde to Freetown, Sierra Leone, and was carrying 1,200 troops.

HMS *Challenger* and SS *Anselm* were in line ahead formation being screened by three Flower-class corvettes, HMS *Lavender*, HMS *Petunia* and HMS *Starwort*. The Asdic (anti-submarine detection equipment) on HMS *Starwort*, was out of order, so it was stationed astern. All the escorts were keeping a listening watch in thick fog, but at 03.50am, the fog cleared.

HMS *Lavender* and HMS *Petunia* took up screening positions on either bow of HMS *Challenger* and commenced zigzagging on a course just east of south and at a speed of 11 knots. At 04.26am, in the approximate position of 44 30N, 28 30W, not far from the Canary Islands, the SS *Anselm* was stuck by a torpedo on the port side amidships. (German U-boat records show the position as 44°25'N 28°35'W)

The SS *Anselm* went down rapidly by the head, sinking 22 minutes after being hit. All the lifeboats got away except for one, No.6. By skilful manoeuvring HMS *Challenger* placed her bow alongside SS *Anselm's* port quarter and rescued 60 men. Unfortunately, 254, including 175 RAF personnel were killed. It is probable that many of these were killed by the explosion of the torpedo which stuck the ship just below their accommodation space.

HMS *Lavender* and HMS *Petunia* counter attacked U96 with depth charges. The U-boat was seriously damaged and forced to curtail its patrol, arriving back at Saint Nazaire after 21 days at sea.

Leading Aircraftman Douglas Carr is commemorated on the Runnymede Memorial.

Aircraftman 1st Class John Tyndel Farquhar of Perth was also on-board SS *Anselm* and killed on 5 July 1941.

NOTES: The SS *Anselm* was built in 1935 by Denny W. & Bros. Ltd in Dumbarton and owned by the Booth Steamship Co. (Booth Line) of Liverpool. SS *Anselm* was converted into a troop ship at the start of WW2. Powered by three Parsons steam turbines, it had a top speed of 12 knots and a weight of 5,954 grt (Gross Register Tonnage). (Gross register tonnage uses the total permanently enclosed capacity of the vessel as its basis for volume)

Kapitänleutnant Heinrich Lehmann-Willenbrock (Knights Cross) was the captain of the Type VIIC U-boat, *U-96* which sank the SS *Anselm*. The fifth patrol of U96 started on 19 June 1941, departing from Saint

Nazaire on the west coast of occupied France. Two weeks later, U96 made contact with the convoy and sank the SS *Anselm*.

The keel of *U96* was laid down on 16 September 1939, by Germaniawerft, of Kiel as yard number 601. She was commissioned on 14 September 1940, with Kapitänleutnant Heinrich Lehmann-Willenbrock in command. After active service during WW2, *U96* from 8 February 1943 spent the rest of the war as a training vessel. *U96* was decommissioned on 15 February 1945 in Wilhelmshaven and sunk in the Hipper basin at Wilhelmshaven by the US Eighth Air Force in a bombing attack on 30 March 1945. The remains were broken up after the war.

On 27 October 1941, for the seventh patrol of *U96*, the journalist (official artist), Lothar-Günther Buchheim joined the submarine to provide impressions of the German Navy and to take photographs which were to be used for propaganda purposes. U-Boat, *U96* joined the Wolfpack Stosstrupp (30 October – 4 November 1941) and three days later. On 31 October 1941, *U96* attacked convoy OS 10. At long range, a torpedo stuck the Dutch ship, SS *Bennekom* which sank. *U96* was forced to dive and attacked underwater by twenty-seven depth charges. The next day *U96* encountered more convoy escorts and managed to escape once more.

U96 entered the neutral port of Vigo in Spain on 27 November 1941 to be resupplied by the interned German MV *Bessel*. After leaving Vigo, *U96* made for the Straits of Gibraltar where late on 30 November 1941 she was spotted by Fairy Swordfish aircraft of 812 Naval Squadron. Two bombs were dropped by the aircraft, unable to reach her destination, U96 returned to Saint Nazaire.

If much about the seventh patrol of *U96* sounds familiar, it will be because Lothar-Günther Buchheim authored a short story about his experience on board *U96*, "Die Eichenlaubfahrt" (The Oak-Leaves Patrol) and then in 1973, wrote a novel which was to become an international best-seller, Das Boot (The Boat). *U96* was the number of the U-boat used as the fictional basis of the 1981 classic claustrophobic thriller movie based on the Das Boot book. The movie script was written by Wolfgang Petersen and starred Juergen Prochnow. The movie Das Boot was nominated for 6 Oscars, Best Director, Best Writing, Best Cinematography, Best Film Editing and Best Effects. It was nominated for a Golden Globe for Best Picture. The BBC also ran it as a miniseries in 1985. The replica of *U-96* used in Das Boot, was also used in Steven Spielberg's 1981 film, Raiders of the Lost Ark, but had the number *U-26*.

On the night of the 3rd or 4th of February 1914 Aberuchill Castle was one of three properties in the Comrie area targeted by suffragettes (the others being the House of Ross and Allt-an-Fhionn at St Fillans). A fire was started in an arson attack and was discovered in a drawing room by six maids who had been asleep in the castle. Several sources differ on the extent of the damage. All seem to agree that numerous paintings, antiques, and pieces of furniture were destroyed but some state that the castle was gutted while others say that the fire was quickly extinguished, the thick walls of the castle seemingly preventing the fire from spreading. (Source http://www.stravaiging.com)

The name Anselm is a male given name: from Germanic words meaning "divine" and "helmet.". Or composed of the elements - 'god' + helm 'protection helmet' (God's Helmet) See also Henry Anselm de Freitas.

RMS Anselm

RMS Anselm

U96 Image taken by Lothar-Günther Buchheim

U96 returning from patrol. The Laughing Swordfish Cartoon was the insignia of the 9th Flotilla (U-boat)

U96 Image taken by Lothar-Günther Buchheim

Joseph MacCrae Chambers

Sergeant Joseph MacCrae Chambers was the son of Dr Walter Duncanson Chambers and Eva Annabella Chambers, Murray House, Perth. Dr Chambers was well known as the superintendent of James Murray's Royal Asylum in Perth.

Sergeant Chambers completed his training with RAF 56 OTU at RAF Sutton Bridge in Lincolnshire, England at the age of 19. He was a former pupil of Hurst Grange Preparatory School, Stirling, Edinburgh Academy, and Trinity College, Glenalmond. At Glenalmond, he was a crack rifle shot and was in the team that won the public schools' trophy – the Ashburton Shield at the National Rifle Association at Bisley Camp, Brookwood, Woking in Surrey. He joined the RAF in October 1939.

Chambers had just finished a course on Hawker Hurricanes when he was killed in a flying accident – 25 February 1941. No information is available regarding the aircraft type or how the accident occurred. There are unconfirmed records that it was possibly a Hawker Hurricane he was flying and that it crashed near Wiggenhall St Mary Magdelen, just south of King's Lynn and RAF Sutton Bridge.

Chambers is remembered on a plaque on the wall in the dedicated Air Force Memorial Chapel of St Matthew's Church in Sutton Bridge, Lincolnshire, and is buried in St Mathews Church, Sutton Bridge.

Between January and September 1941, there were 11 incidents at RAF Sutton Bridge involving aircraft from RAF 56 OTU with one pilot killed (Chambers not recorded). During an air raid on 12 May 1941, one was destroyed, and another 6 others were severely damaged.

Eric Cooke

Twenty-five-year-old Flight Sergeant Eric Cooke from Grimsby came to Perth when war broke out to train at RAF Perth 11 EFTS. Cooke was employed in the Admiralty chart department when war broke out. On 26 July 1941, he married Daphne May Ferris, 8 Stanley Place, Perth. Daphne and her twin sister Betty joined the Auxiliary Territorial Service at the age of 17 when war broke out. After many hours of flying over enemy territory as an air gunner, Cooke became an instructor at the RAF Central Gunnery School at RAF Sutton Bridge, Lincolnshire.

On 10 April 1943, Vickers Wellington Mk Ia N2865 took off from the Central Gunnery School, detailed to carry out an exercise with a Supermarine Spitfire Mk IIa P7677 doing various quarter attacks. During the exercise (at 1035 hours), the two aircraft collided just southwest of Wyton, near Huntingdon, Cheshire.

Perthshire Advertiser 17 April 1943

All six crew on board Wellington N2865 were killed:

Flight Lieutenant Terence Cathcart Stanbury RAF (42271) pilot, age 30

Flying Officer Reginald Ross Hely RAAF (403811) 2nd pilot, age 22

Flight Sergeant Eric Cooke RAFVR (742967) air gunner instructor, age 25

Flying Officer John Alfred Town RCAF (J16172) air gunner, age 25

Flight Sergeant Clifford Harrison RAAF (1000251) air gunner, age 28

Sergeant Charles Ronald Archer RAFVR (1113141) air gunner, age 40

The pilot of the Spitfire P7677, Pilot Officer E H Griffith, bailed out with minor injuries.

Cooke was buried at Grimsby (Scatho Road) Cemetery with full military honours. Exactly one week before he died, Cooke was home in Lincolnshire after having a spell of leave in Perth with his wife.

Note: Pilot Officer E H Griffith died a few months later – 29 September 1943 – when his Mosquito Mk. II DZ690 spun and crashed after a high-speed stall during which the engine detached.

James William Crow

Petty Officer James William Crow, Airman Royal Navy was born on 27 September 1924, the son of James R Crow and Annie Crow of 31 Dupplin Road, Perth. Before joining the Fleet Air Arm, James Crow was on the staff of John Dewar & Sons Limited, Whisky Distiller. He was also a member of the Perth Air Training Cadets.

James Crow did his initial training at Dartmouth and was sent to RCAF (Royal Canadian Air Force) Station Hamilton, Ontario, Canada for flying training. Whilst in Canada he spent leave time in Boston, USA where he told his family he had met Corrinne, fallen in love, and intended to marry her after the war. On return to Scotland, he was posted to RAF Errol where he learned to fly the Miles Martinet.

After 250 hours of flying time experience, he was posted to Fleet Air Arm (FAA) 772 Squadron at HMS *Landrail* at RNAS Machrihanish, near Campbeltown on the Kintyre peninsula. Here he teamed up with his telegraphist/ air gunner.

On 17 January 1944, Crow was flying Miles Martinet M25, MS757, two-seat, target tug aircraft. The Martinet was towing a drogue when the aircraft crashed into the sea near the Iron Rock Ledges buoy just off the coast of Corriecravie on the Isle of Arran. Both on board were killed:

Petty Officer Airman James William Crow, Royal Navy (FAA/FX.95515), age 19.

Leading Airman John Millan Martin, Royal Navy (FAA/JX.401581), age 20.

The aircraft was seen by the crew of the escort-carrier *HMS Activity* to make a turn at the end of its run and then dive vertically into the sea. The cause of the crash appears to be that the tow-line fouled the tail-plane of the aircraft, causing an irrecoverable stall.

Today, just to the north of Corriecravie, on the Isle of Arran, at the top of a small rise stands a memorial to the two airmen. In August 1998, his sweetheart from the time of his training in North America, returned to put up the memorial was set up, it reads *"In Memory of James – 'Scottie' – From Winston and Corrinne Wood WV USA 1998".*

James Crow and John Martin are also remembered on the Royal Navy memorial at Lee-on-Solent, Hampshire.

Research assisted by Donald Scott and Mike Hardie

NOTES: Machrihanish at one time laid claim to the longest military runway in Europe at 3,059 metres (1.9 miles).

HMS Activity was built in 1940 at the Caledon Shipyards in Dundee. *HMS Activity* had just embarked 819 Naval Air Squadron on 12 January 1944, to begin active service performing escort duties on 29 January as part of the Second Escort Group (Atlantic and Artic convoys). Along with No. 815 Squadron, 819 Squadron performed the successful night attack on the Italian fleet at Taranto on 11 November 1940.

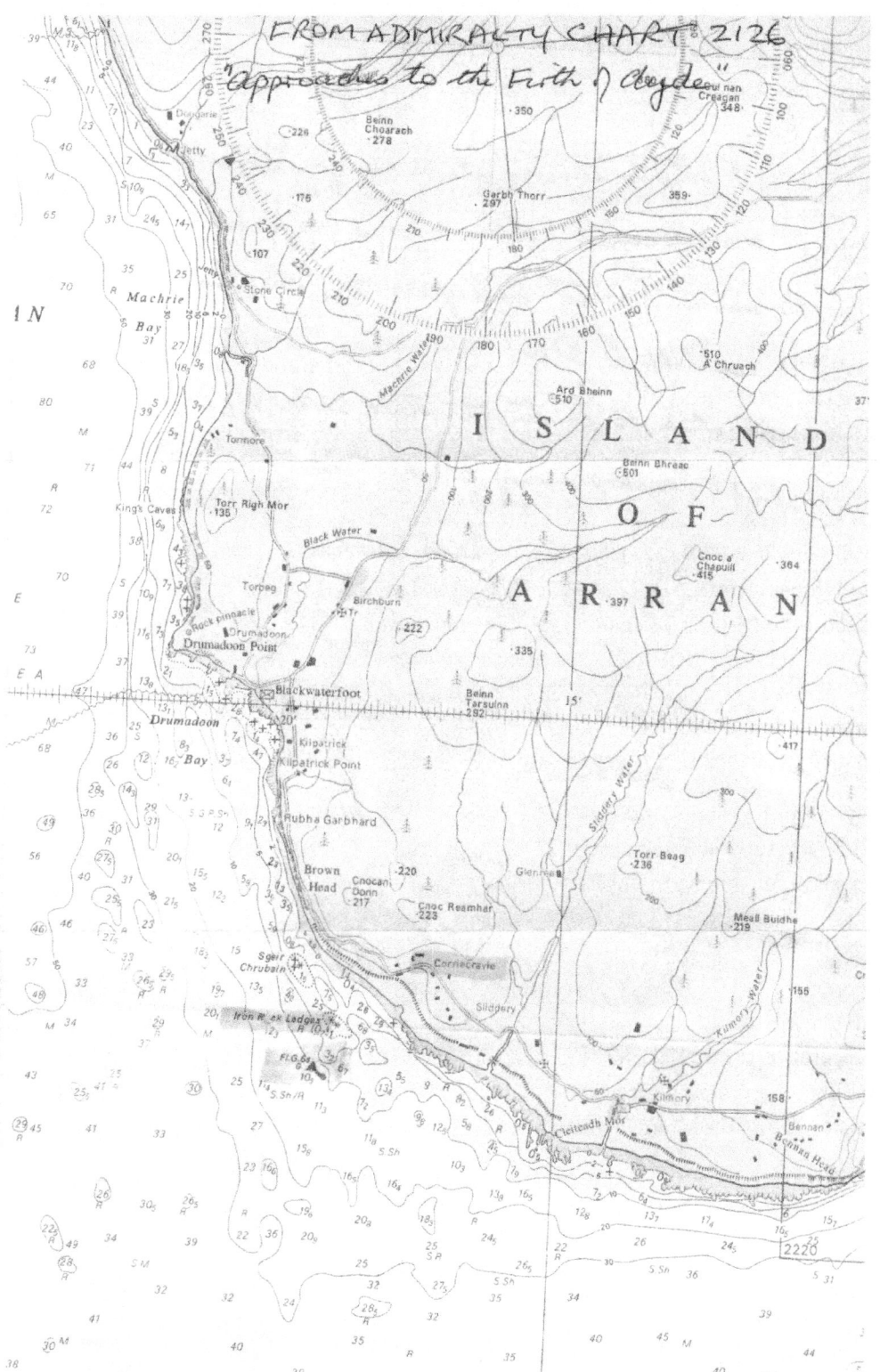

Allan Dickson

Sergeant Allan Dickson RAF 1564075 was the son of George Dickson, Hay Street, Coupar Angus. Before joining up Sergeant Dickson was employed with Messrs William Stewart Ltd. Coupar Angus as a baker.

On Sunday 23 July 1944, Allan Dickson was part of the crew of Avro Lancaster III PB208 PG-S of RAF 619 Squadron. Take off from RAF Dunholme Lodge, Lincolnshire, England was at 23.00 hours. The target for that night was Kiel, Germany.

Avro Lancaster PB208 is believed to have crashed southwest of the island of Sylt but may have crashed slightly further north. Pilot Officer Allan Daniel Aumell washed ashore at Thorsminde Beach, in the area of Nissum Fjord. He was laid to rest in Søndre Nissum Cemetery by the German Wehrmacht on 12 September 1944.

Avro Lancaster PB208 crew:
Flying Officer John Parker RAFVR (173134), Pilot, age unknown
Pilot Officer Allan Daniel AUMELL RCAF (J/89210), Air Bomber, age 21
Flight Sergeant James Broll RAFVR (1690453), Air Gunner, age unknown
Sergeant Allan Dickson RAFVR (1564075), Air Gunner, age unknown
Pilot Officer George Alan Grigg RAFVR (176583), Navigator, age 22
Sergeant Norman Mackenzie Rice RAFVR (1821876), Flight Engineer, age 20
Flight Sergeant William Arthur SHARP (1575581), Wireless Operator/Air Gunner, age unknown

The bodies of the other members of the crew were found after the war and concentrated in a grave at Neumunster Civil Cemetery on 9 September 1946: John Parker, George Alan Grigg, William Arthur Sharp, James Broll, Allan Dickson and Norman MacKenzie Rice.

All the crew of Lancaster PB208 are remembered on the Runnymede Memorial.

NOTES: A German night fighter piloted by Leutnant Heinz Rudolf Molowitz of 9.NJG 3, claimed his only known, two four-engine bombers (4 mots) that night, one at 01:45 hours and the other at 02:00 hours, west of Westerland/Sylt. Leutnant Heinz Rudolf Molowitz was killed later that same day during aerial combat at Bockhorn, near Vaerl, west of the Jade Bight. He bailed out at too low an altitude for his parachute to deploy. Leutnant Molowitz flew Messerschmitt Bf110 and Junkers Ju88 aircraft.

On 31 March 1944, John Parker, George Alan Grigg, William Arthur Sharp, Allan Dickson, Norman MacKenzie Rice, and John Harold Woodcock were on a mission to bomb Nuremburg, Germany (James Broll replaced John Woodcock for the 23 July 1944 mission). Their aircraft, Avro Lancaster III LM418 sustained heavy damage. Flying Officer John Parker brought home the Lancaster on only two engines. They crash-landed at RAF Woodbridge, Surrey. The aircraft was subsequently burnt out, no injuries were reported.

RAF 619 Squadron were stationed at RAF Coningsby from 9 January 1944 and at RAF Dunholme Lodge from April 1944 through to September 1944.

Nachtjagdgeschwader 3 (NJG 3) was a Luftwaffe night fighter-wing. Two aircraft that served with NJG 3 are displayed together at the Royal Air Force Museum London. They are a Messerschmitt Bf 110 G Werk Nr. 730301, which was surrendered to the British at the end of the war in 1945, and a Junkers Ju 88 R-1, Werk Nr. 360043,[2] which came into British hands in 1943. Both aircraft are unique – each is one of only two intact survivors of their type.

AIRCRAFT OF THE ROYAL AIR FORCE 1939-1945: AVRO 683 LANCASTER. (CH 21128) Almost head-on view of Lancaster B Mark III, LM449? PG-H?, of No. 619 Squadron RAF based at Coningsby, Lincolnshire, in flight over the North Sea. Copyright: © IWM.

Douglas James Morrison Dunn

Flight Sergeant Douglas James Morrison Dunn RAFVR (1554921) navigator, age 23 was killed in an aircraft accident whilst landing at Foggia Main airfield in Italy on 9 June 1944. Dunn was the son of Andrew and Jeanie Dunn of Rosefield Farm, Balbeggie, Perthshire.

Extracts from AIR 27/822, RAF 104 Squadron Operations Record Book, June 1944.

Detail of Work Carried Out:

Target: *Szolnok, Hungary, June 1st Aircraft Vickers Wellington X, LN754*

Crew: Sgt. Baleey M.W., F/S Dunn D.J., Sgt. Silor F.A., F/S Flenk G.J., Sgt. Mitchell R.F.

Up: 22.00, Down: 03.50

Details of Sortie or Flight: Bombs dropped 1st Burst seen right in middle of the railway, remaining bombs of the stick fell on open ground.

Target: *Aircraft despatched to attack bridge over the River Tiber, June 3rd, Aircraft Vickers Wellington Y-LP 201*

Crew: Sgt. Baleey M.W., F/S Dunn D.J., Sgt. Silor F.A., F/S Flenk G.J., Sgt. Mitchell R.F.

Up: 00.50, Down: 03.35

Details of Sortie or Flight: Two bombs hung up and were jettisoned North of river near coast. Bursts seen- low cloud obscured the target on the run up, bombs were seen to overshoot by about 20 yards and fell in the river and also on the bank.

Target: *Aircraft despatched to attack marshalling yards at Niš, Yugoslavia (Serbia), June 8th, Aircraft Vickers Wellington Z-LN899*

Crew: Sgt. Baleey M.W., F/S Dunn D.J., Sgt. Silor F.A., F/S Flenk G.J., Sgt. Mitchell R.F.

Up: 00.25, Down: 04.45

Details of Sortie or Flight: Aircraft blew up on landing, presumed due to a hang up of a 500 lb bomb. Pilot and Bomb Aimer Escaped, the Rear Gunner was killed, Navigator seriously wounded and died shortly after admittance to hospital, Wireless Operator was seriously wounded.

Sergeant Robert Fairbairn Mitchell RAFVR (1592422), age 19, was the rear Air Gunner on LN899. He is buried at the Bari War Cemetery, a port city on the Adriatic Sea in Italy.

Flight Sergeant Douglas James Morrison Dunn was 23 years old and is also buried at Bari War Cemetery and is commemorated on the St Martins War Memorial.

From the Perthshire Advertiser, 21st June 1944:

"DEATHS – On Active Service

"DUNN. - 1554921 Flt. / Sgt. D. J. M. Dunn, age 23, youngest son of the late Mr Andrew Dunn and Mrs Dunn, Rosefield Farm, Balbeggie, has died of wounds in Italy."

NOTES: Foggia is located near the Adriatic Sea in Italy, opposite Naples. By 9 June 1944, the Allied armies have advanced north of Rome which had fallen 4 days earlier. The Soviets were getting ready to start Operation Bagration, attacking the German Army Group Centre and advancing to the Vistula River and Warsaw. In the west, the Allies had landed in Normandy on D-Day and were pushing inland. In the Pacific, US forces were about to commence air strikes on the Marianas Islands, as a prelude to invade Saipan. In Burma, the Battle of Kohima was nearly won, ending the Siege of Imphal.

Since August 1943, the Allies had been bombing the oil fields and installations in Romania (Rumania), mainly around Ploiești (formerly Ploesti). The German army was being starved of fuel to run their war effort. The bombing of marshalling yards and railway infrastructures forced the German to travel more often by road, forcing them to use up their remaining precious petrol and diesel fuel stocks.

AIRCRAFT OF THE ROYAL AIR FORCE, 1939-1945: VICKERS WELLINGTON. (ME(RAF) 6297) Wellington Mark II, Z8524 U? of No. 104 Squadron RAF, about to be loaded with 500-lb GP bombs for a sortie, on a landing ground in North Africa. The front turret has been removed from this aircraft, which also carries 52 operation symbols on its nose. Copyright: © IWM

ROYAL AIR FORCE: OPERATIONS IN THE MIDDLE EAST AND NORTH AFRICA, 1939-1943. (CM 3927) Vickers Wellington B Mark IIs of No. 104 Squadron RAF await their bomb loads at LG 224/Cairo West, Egypt, before undertaking night operations against enemy columns retreating after the Battle of El Alamein. Copyright: © IWM

John Tyndel Farquhar

Aircraftman 1st Class John Tyndel Farquhar RAFVR (1107691) of RAF 200 Squadron was a passenger onboard the SS *Anselm* on route from Gourock on the Clyde to Freetown, Sierra Leone, when it was torpedoed by the German submarine U-96, 300 miles off the Azores on 5 July 1941. (See also Douglas Carr) The SS *Anselm* was built in Dumbarton in 1935 and owned by the Booth Steamship Company, Liverpool. It was a coal-fired passenger ship that was converted to a troop ship in 1940 The warship HMS *Challenger* and the SS *Anselm* were in line ahead and were being screened by HMS *Lavender* and HMS *Petunia*. HMS *Starwort* was stationed astern, the HMS *Starwort's* Asdic (anti-submarine detection equipment) was out of order at the time.

A listening watch was kept by the escorts due to the thick fog. At 03.50 the fog lifted. HMS *Lavender* and HMS *Petunia* took up screening positions on either bow of HMS *Challenger*. They commenced a zigzag course at a speed of 11 knots. At 04.26, not far from the Canary Islands, the SS *Anselm* was stuck by a torpedo on the port side, amidships. The SS *Anselm* settled rapidly by the head and sank 22 minutes after being hit. All the lifeboats got away except for No.6 lifeboat which was damaged by the explosion. HMS *Challenger* placed her bow alongside the SS *Anselm's* port quarter and rescued 60 men.

On board the SS *Anselm* were 1,200 troops. 250 (including 175 RAF personnel) and four crewmen were lost. Many of those who were killed were probably killed by the explosion of the torpedo which struck the ship immediately below the accommodation space. Aircraftman 1st Class John Tyndel Farquhar, age 31 was the youngest son of John T and Isabella Farquhar of Rockville, Letham Road, Perth. He was married with a son to Elizabeth Webster Farquhar, Far Row, Kinnaird Bank, Craigie, Perth. Farquhar was a junior partner in the city firm of Farquhar & Son, Stationers, and Bookbinders, 7 Atholl Street, Perth. His father was head of the business. Farquhar was educated at Balhousie Boys School and Perth Commercial School. Aircraftman 1st Class John Tyndel Farquhar was married with one child. He was home on leave about a month before setting sail on the SS Anselm.

John Tyndel Farquhar joined the RAF in 1940 and is commemorated at the Runnymede Memorial in Surrey.

Note: Leading Aircraftman Douglas Carr from Comrie was also killed when the SS Anselm was torpedoed, see extra details - U-Boat U96

The cargo and passenger liner SS Anselm, 5,954 gross tons of the Booth Steamship Company. Item is held by John Oxley Library, State Library of Queensland. Image identified as out of copyright, and available can use without requesting permission.

James Roy Fenwick

At 1630 hrs on Wednesday, 14 January 1942, Vickers Wellington IC X9742 took off on a mission to bomb the city of Hamburg in Germany. Most of the squadron, RAF No 40 had transferred to Malta where they operated as night bombers, attacking targets in Italy and North Africa. The part of the squadron that stayed in the UK at RAF Alconbury, later became RAF 156 Squadron (14 February 1942). RAF Alconbury was an active air force station, south of Peterborough. Since 1942, it has been the home of the US Air Force although flying operations are no longer carried out, the land and runways having been sold for housing in 2009.

At 1932 hours, X9742 was heard on the radio asking for help. Somewhere over the North Sea, the aircraft was lost. All the crew are commemorated on the Runnymede Memorial:

Pilot Officer Edgar George Broad RAAF (402849), pilot, age 23

Sergeant James Roy Fenwick RAFVR (1052485), age 30

Sergeant Christopher Donaldson Russell, RAFVR, age 25

Sergeant John Priestley RAFVR (916519), age 25

Sergeant Patrick Joseph Timmons RAFVR (997190), age unknown

Sergeant Thomas Hugh Thomas RAFVR (1284757), age 20

(Crew assignments are unknown)

James Roy Fenwick was the son of James Roy and Margaret Roy Fenwick of Sunnybrae Cottage, Scone, and the husband of Margaret Cameron Fenwick, 10 Barnton Street, Stirling, who formerly resided at 44 Verena Terrace, Perth.

Fenwick was expected home on leave on the day that word was received that he was missing. He was expecting to be commissioned as an officer within a few days.

Fenwick volunteered for the RAF in November 1940. He was in business as a tobacconist and confectioner and had shops in Stirling and Falkirk. He played for Perthshire Rugby Club and was a member of Kinnoull Tennis Club.

Timmons was the son of John Timmons who became MP for Bothwell in 1945.

WELLINGTON Ic. (CH 1425) Original wartime caption: 2 x 1000 h.p. Bristol PEGASUS 18 engines. No.214 Squadron. Copyright: © IWM.

Duncan Cameron Findlay

Sergeant Duncan Cameron Findlay, RAF, (565318) died when his aircraft crashed and burned out in woods near Saint Hiliare-le-grand, Moronvilliers, three miles south of Bétheniville, to the west of Reims, France.

On 26 March 1940, Fairey Battle Mk.1, P2256 from RAF 103 Squadron hit trees on take-off from their airfield at Bétheniville at 10.15 pm. They were on a night bombing exercise over the ranges at St-Hilaire-le-Petit.

The crew of Fairey Battle P2256:

Pilot Officer Ian Percival Hinton, RAF, (40592), pilot, age 23

Sergeant Duncan Cameron Findlay, RAF, (565318), observer, age 25

Aircraftman 2nd Class John Alexander Sharpe, RAF, (617513, wireless operator/air gunner, age 20 (from Kingstown, County Dublin, Eire)

All are buried at the Terlincthun British Cemetery, Hameau de Terlincthun, Wimille, Pas de Calais, France. Findlay was the third son of William Nevay Porter Findlay and Annie Cameron Findlay of 14 Gray Street, Perth. He is remembered by name on a stained-glass War Memorial window in St Mathew's Church in Tay Street and the Bétheniville Memorial.

Sergeant Findlay was killed within 48 hours of returning to duty from a short leave at home.

From the Perthshire Advertiser of Saturday 30 March 1940 –KILLED IN 'PLANE CRASH IN FRANCE – *"Official notification of the death of Sergt-Observer Duncan Cm Findlay has been received by his parents, Mr and Mrs W Findlay 14 Gray Street, Perth.* **He is the first Perth man serving with the forces to be killed in action since the outbreak of war.**

Sergt-Observer Findlay was a member of the crew of a 'plane which crashed in France. He had just returned to his station only on Monday, after being home on leave. He was 25 years of age and had been in the R.A.F. for about eight years."

Note: The so-called 'phoney war' ended on 10 May 1940 when Germany invaded France, the same day Winston Churchill was appointed as Prime Minister. The Fairey Battle squadrons were thrown in on that day to try and stop the advancing German troops. Without fighter escort, 13 out of 32 aircraft were lost and all the others were damaged. The next day 7 out of 8 were lost and on the next day, 5 out of 5 were lost whilst attacking the Albert Canal. Further losses came on the 14 May 1940 when 35 out of 63 Fairey Battles did not return. The Fairey Battles were withdrawn, ending its career as a day bomber.

ROYAL AIR FORCE: FRANCE, 1939-1940. (C 1071) Bomb-trolleys loaded with 250-lb GP bombs and attendant armourers being towed out by tractor to Fairey Battles at Betheniville prior to a sortie to the bombing practice range at Moronvilliers. Behind them, Battle, K9408 'PM-N', of No. 103 Squadron RAF is prepared for a flight. Copyright: © IWM.

ROYAL AIR FORCE: FRANCE, 1939-1940. (C 1061) Three Fairey Battles of No. 103 Squadron RAF overfly Betheniville, watched by ground crew servicing K9408 'PM-N', another aircraft of the Squadron. Copyright: © IWM.

William Fraser

Flight Lieutenant William (Bill) Simpson Fraser (sometimes spelt Frazer) was born on 5 June 1908 to the Alexander family of 12 Pitcullen Crescent, Perth. The family business was Messrs Frazer & Sons, Clothiers (merchant tailors and complete outfitters) which was located at 55-59 High Street, Perth, with branches in Pitlochry, Kingussie and Aberfeldy. Alexander Frazer, his father, was the Lord Dean of Guild in Perth.

William Fraser attended Strathallan School, worked in a bank as a clerk in Perth and was well known as a moving spirit in local dramatic circles. In 1930, he received a theatrical appointment in London. The first few months were spent in Calcutta, India. He did not have a great start to his career and was often penniless, sleeping rough on the Embankment in London. Just before the Second World War, Fraser was running the Connaught Theatre in Worthing. He was there for seven years and in that time had acted in approximately 300 plays.

During the war, he was called up and served with the RAF in a RAF Special Liaison Unit reaching the rank of flight lieutenant. During this time, he met Eric Sykes and after the war, he met him again and gave him his first work as a writer for radio comedy. They worked together many times over the following years. Fraser is also credited with giving Peter Cushing his first acting job.

In 1942, Fraser married Betty Bowden, grand-daughter of the late rear Admiral Edward Kellyin, St Martin-in-the-Fields, London.

Fraser first appeared on television is The Tony Hancock Show (1956). He later joined The Army Game which led to a sequel for which he is probably best known and remembered, **Bootsie and Snudge**. There were very many roles in which he appeared on stage and TV over the years, many of them comedic parts. He appeared in 50 movies from 1938 through to 1987. In 1986 he won the Laurence Olivier Award for Best Comedy Performance for his stage role in the play, When We Are Married. In 1981, he was the subject of Eamonn Andrews, This Is Your Life.

When he was not acting, Fraser ran a sweetshop and tobacconist in Ilford Lane, Ilford. He later married again; to Pamela Cundell in 1981. Fraser died at the age of 79 on 9 September 1987 in Bushey, Hertfordshire. Pamela Cundell played Mrs Fox in the long-running TV comedy series, Dad's Army.

Special Liaison Units were connected to the Government Code and Cypher School at Bletchley Park, they oversaw the distribution of ULTRA intelligence.

Perth Man Weds Leading Lady

Mr W. S. Frazer and Miss Rosemary Elizabeth Bowden, after their wedding in St Martin's-in-the-Fields. *"Worthing Herald" Photo.*

In St Martin's-in-the-Fields, London, took place the marriage of Mr W. ("Bill") Simson Frazer, son of ex-Dean of Guild Alexander Frazer, late principal of Frazers of Perth, Ltd., and Mrs Frazer, Normandene, Christchurch Road, Worthing, to Miss Rosemary Elizabeth ("Betty") Bowden, London.

"Bill" Frazer was a well-known personality in Perth amateur dramatics before going south to take up professional stage work. After appearing in the London show "New Faces," and for a time with Ambrose and his band, he joined up as an aircraftman in the R.A.F. When he can the Worthing Repertory Company with Mr C. W. Bell, Miss Bowden was leading lady at the Connaught Theatre, Worthing. She is now leading lady with the Birmingham Repertory Company.

Daughter of Mr and Mrs W. E. Bowden, Prince of Wales Mansions, London, the bride was given away by her father. She was becomingly attired in a hyacinth blue two-piece costume.

Her mother wore a pink and black dress with a long black coat and black hat. The bridegroom's mother had chosen navy georgette and matching hat.

The ceremony was conducted by the bride's cousin, the Rev. Guy Bowden, Chaplain, R.A.F. Mr Robert Page was best man.

Guests at the reception in the Adelphi Theatre included Major Eric Mashwitz and Dame Sybil Thorndike. About 150 gifts were received.

XMAS AT FRAZER & SONS
SPLENDID STOCK OF USEFUL GIFTS.
Travelling Rugs, Dressing Gowns, Smoking Jackets, Ladies' Cashmere Jerseys, Scarves and Caps, Shetland Spencers, Shooting and Fancy Vests, Knicker Stockings and Socks, Trousers Pressers and Stretchers, Umbrellas, Kilt Outfits, &c.

FUR COATS

Burberry Coats, Ladies' or Gent.'s 45/-, 55/-, 63/-

FRAZER & SONS of PERTH,
Merchant Tailors and Complete Outfitters,
Also Pitlochry, Aberfeldy, and Kingussie.
'PHONE 436.

---

within TWENTY-ONE DAYS *after its occurrence;* of a MARRIAGE *within* THREE DAYS *after its celebration;* and of a DEATH *within* EIGHT DAYS *after its event.* *If these rules are not complied with* PENALTIES *are exigible.*

BIRTHS.
BEATON—June 1, at Murthly, the wife of James Beaton, Haugh of Meikleour, of a daughter.
FRAZER—June 5, at 12 Pitcullen Crescent, Perth, Mrs Alexander Fraser, of a son.

MARRIAGES.
DODS — ANDERSON — June 8, at the County Hotel, Edinburgh, by the Rev. Thomas R. Rutherford, M.A., Dunkeld Cathedral, John, son of the late William Dods, Lugton, Dalkeith, to Lily Douglas,

Perthshire Advertiser 10 December 1913

Henry Anselm de Freitas

Of all the war graves of Perthshire's aviators that I have researched, the grave of Henry Anselm de Freitas, AFM (1917–1943) is one I often revisit and have in a way adopted. Henry is unique in being buried in Perth, so very far away from his home in Trinidad where he was it is clear held in the highest regard with deep love and respect by his wife and family. Henry is buried in Wellshill Cemetery in Perth, in a Commonwealth War Graves Commission grave, Section O, Grave 15 (nearer to the Rannoch Road, and close to the cemetery's war memorial).

This is the story of how a top WW2 Hawker Hurricane pilot came to be buried in Perth, 4,500 miles away from his home.

Henry Anselm de Freitas was one of 8 children. Born on 21 April 1917 in Trinidad, West Indies, to Alderman, Henry Alexander de Freitas MBE, and Jessimina de Freitas of Port of Spain. During WW2, 5 of their children served and 3 sons would be lost to accidents by 1946.

Henry was, by all accounts, an intelligent, charismatic, and active boy. He attended a prominent Roman Catholic School, St Mary's College and was awarded the Jerningham Medal for being the top student in the Island Scholarship examinations. Henry left Trinidad in 1935 to attend the Royal School of Mines at London University. Henry did well, he was President of the School of Mines Student Union, Captain of their rowing club and President of the Imperial College Riding Club. As a talented oarsman he represented the Thames Rowing Club at the 1939 Belgian International Regatta in Dinant, Belgium.

Henry de Freitas demonstrated both his humanity and bravery when in June 1937 he dived into the river Thames, near Putney, and successfully saved the life of 11-year-old Cyril Basil Smith who had gotten into difficulties and was being carried away by a strong ebb tide. He also saved 16-year-old typist, Margaret Bunker who had been first to attempt to rescue Smith.

Just before the Second World War started, Henry was awarded a scholarship for the 1939-1940 school year to study Petroleum Engineering at the University of Birmingham. He instead joined the RAF, and we know that on 1 July 1940, Leading Aircraftman "Henry Anslem de FREITAS (81695) was granted a commission for the duration of hostilities as Acting Pilot Officer on Probation". By 3 November 1940 he was promoted to Pilot Officer on Probation. For some unknown reason on 20 June 1941 his commission as an officer was terminated, he did however continue flying as a Flight Sergeant and in July of 1943 was awarded the Air Force Medal.

Henry was the first West Indian to be so honoured. Henry became a top flying instructor at the RAF Flight Leaders' School and served with RAF No. 59 Operational Training Unit (O.T.U.). The indications from my research are that he was a very skilled pilot.

Henry married Helen Janice Begg of Charles Street, Perth, in September 1941 at Kensington, London. They could have met while they were both students at university in London or possibly when Henry was undertaking flying training at 59 OTU at RAF Turnhouse, now Edinburgh Airport. The couple had 2 children, Alexandra Jacqueline, born March 1942, followed by his namesake, Henry Anselm, in July of 1943.

During 1943, de Freitas was serving as a Flight Sergeant, RAFVR (RAF Volunteer Reserve) (1393818) with RAF No. 59 Squadron OTU (Operational Training Unit) at airfields in the Northumberland area of England. Henry was killed, aged just 26, in a training accident when his Canadian built, Hawker Hurricane Mk X (AG111, HK-G) crashed at 15:00 hours on 5 May 1943. De Freitas is reported as crashing onto Horton Moor near Doddington, Northumberland, just north of Wooler. His aircraft collided with a Supermarine Spitfire IIA P7902 just over Wooler and it crashed into a bog, close to a dry-stone wall at Doddington Hill. The Spitfire was piloted by Sergeant F. T. L. Futon, RNAZ 416496, aged 19, he was also killed.

The accident happened after a flight of Hurricanes from 59 OTU 'bounced' from above, a formation of Spitfires from 57 OTU in a mock combat attack. De Freitas's Hurricane AG111 had earlier been passed from No. 59 OTU RAF (at RAF Turnhouse) to No. 57 OTU RAF at RAF Eshott, Northumberland. RAF 57 OUT was primarily a Spitfire-equipped unit but used Hurricane's in a support role. Henry was still listed as being from No. 59 OTU at the time of the accident. RAF Eshott during WW2 was the home for between 77 and 100 Mk1 & Mk2 Spitfires, with pilots receiving about 60 hours combat training. No 57 OTU was established at Eshott in November 1942. De Freitas I believe may have been instructing on courses at RAF Eshott and nearby RAF Milfield at the time of the accident.

RAF Millfield was located just northwest of Wooler in Northumbria, it was formed there on 7 December 1942, operating until 26 January 1944 when it was absorbed into the Fighter Leaders School. The unit provided ground attack practice for pilots from operational squadrons based elsewhere. Goswick Sands, about 15 miles to the east, was the location of the ground attack range. Pilots were also ground attack training at the time with the relatively new Hawker Typhoon and the USAF Republic P-47 Thunderbolt.

This happened at a time in 1943 when the intensive training of pilots was finally possible and was now extremely well organised. The Luftwaffe had turned their attention away to the attack on the Soviet Union, 22 June 1941, and the United States had joined the war following the day of infamy attack by the Japanese on Pearl Harbour, 7 December 1941.

Unfortunately, the RAF records for 57 & 59 Operational Training Unit have not been digitised, this is all I can find out about Henry. Where he was from 1941 to 1943 is not known. To be an instructor, Henry must have been an excellent pilot, and must have been involved in brave action at some point.

The Air Ministry announced on 2 April 1943 the award of the AFM to De Freitas – the first West Indian to be awarded the AFM:

"ROYAL AIR FORCE. The KING has been graciously pleased to approve the following awards: Air Force Medal to Sergeant Henry Anselm de FREITAS."

(The AFM was a military decoration, awarded to personnel of the Royal Air Force and other British Armed Forces, and formerly to personnel of other Commonwealth countries, below commissioned rank, for 'an act or acts of valour, courage or devotion to duty whilst flying, though not in active operations against the enemy.)

De Freitas is commemorated on a memorial to honour those who served and died at RAF Milfield between 1941 and 1946. The memorial was unveiled in 2002 and is located outside the Borders Gliding Club.

After his death, Henry's parents arranged for Henry's wife, Helen de Freitas's B.Sc., and their children to relocate to Trinidad. Helen lived in Trinidad for 38 years and died in Nashville, Tennessee in 1998. Helen's older sister Jessie, who died in 1941, age 24 is buried with Henry in Wellshill Cemetery.

NOTES: Notably, De Freitas's Hurricane is not listed as a Specialised Low Attack Instructors' School (SLAIS) allocated aircraft which was based at RAF Milfield. The Imperial War Museum picture of Hurricane AG111 (Source: © IWM (CH 9222)– **See Below** – shows his aircraft on the ground at RAF Milfield, and it bears the unit codes of the Fighter Leaders School based at Charmy Down, Wiltshire. It was common for pilots as it looks like in Henry's case to bring with them their personal mount. I believe that unknown pilot in the picture is in fact Henry Anselm de Freitas.

De Freitas's Hurricane AG111 was one of a batch of 140 Canadian built Mk. 1 Hurricanes produced at the Fort William (Thunder Bay) plant, arriving in the UK from June 1940. They were built by Canadian Car & Foundry and when powered by a 1,300 horsepower (969 kilowatts) Packard Merlin 28 engine, they were redesignated the Mk. X Hurricane. They were initially fitted with 8 Browning.303 machine guns, later Mk. X variants had 12 guns. If used for ground attack would have been fitted with 2 Vickers Class 'S' 40 mm cannons. Later, aircraft were fitted with 8 unguided 60 pounder RP-3 rockets.

The name Anselm is a male given name: from Germanic words meaning "divine" and "helmet.". Or composed of the elements - 'god' + helm 'protection helmet' (God's Helmet).

Hurricane Mark X, AG111 HK-G, of No. 59 Operational Training Unit, on the ground at Milfield Hurricane Mark X, AG111 HK-G, of No. 59 Operational Training Unit © IWM (CH 9222), Northumberland (Henry's personal mount)

1943 Milfield airfield. Ground crew refuelling a Hurricane IID from 1 Specialised Low Attack Instructors School

James Victor Gardiner

Sergeant James Victor Gardiner RAFVR 656465 was the only son of Mr and Mrs John Gardiner, The Crescent, Luncarty. He was 23 years old, formerly a pupil at Perth Academy and was studying in London when World War Two broke out.

James served for a year with the South Wales Borderers before transferring to the RAF and obtained his pilots certificate in December of 1941. He was training on 9 March 1942 with RAF 15 OTU (Operational Training Unit) RAF Hampstead Norris, south of Oxford when he was killed in an aircraft accident.

Vickers Wellington Mk IA DV576 was on a night training flight which failed to gain sufficient height on take-off with 15% degrees of flap. It hit trees, after failing to avoid a slight hill one mile from the end of the runway.

The crew **killed** were:

Sergeant Dennis Albert Flemming RAFVR 1212046, Pilot, age 20

Sergeant James Victor Gardiner RAFVR 656465, Pilot, age 23

Sergeant Harold Medley RAFVR 1113468, Wireless Operator, age 28

Injured:

Sergeant P K Briggs,

Sergeant J A Saunders,

Sergeant C Hirst.

James Victor Gardiner is buried in Kirkhill Cemetery, Luncarty.

LUNCARTY PILOT KILLED.
Sergt. Pilot James Victor Gardiner, only son of Mr and Mrs John Gardiner, Crescent, Luncarty, has been reported killed on service. Sergt.-Pilot Gardiner, who was 23 years of age, is an ex-pupil of Perth Academy and was studying in London when war broke out. He served for over a year in the South Wales Borderers before transferring to the R.A.F., in which he got his pilot's certificate about four months ago.

Perthshire Advertiser 14 March 1942

NOTES:

RAF Hampstead Norris was bombed on 16 September 1940 by the Luftwaffe during the battle of Britain, 3 bombs fell on the runways. On 4 March 1941, a Vickers Wellington bomber was attacked by a German fighter aircraft as it approached to land on the airfield.

On 12 May 1941, the airfield was gain attacked, 10 High Explosive and 100 Incendiary bombs destroyed some aircraft and damaged the flare path and southern runway.

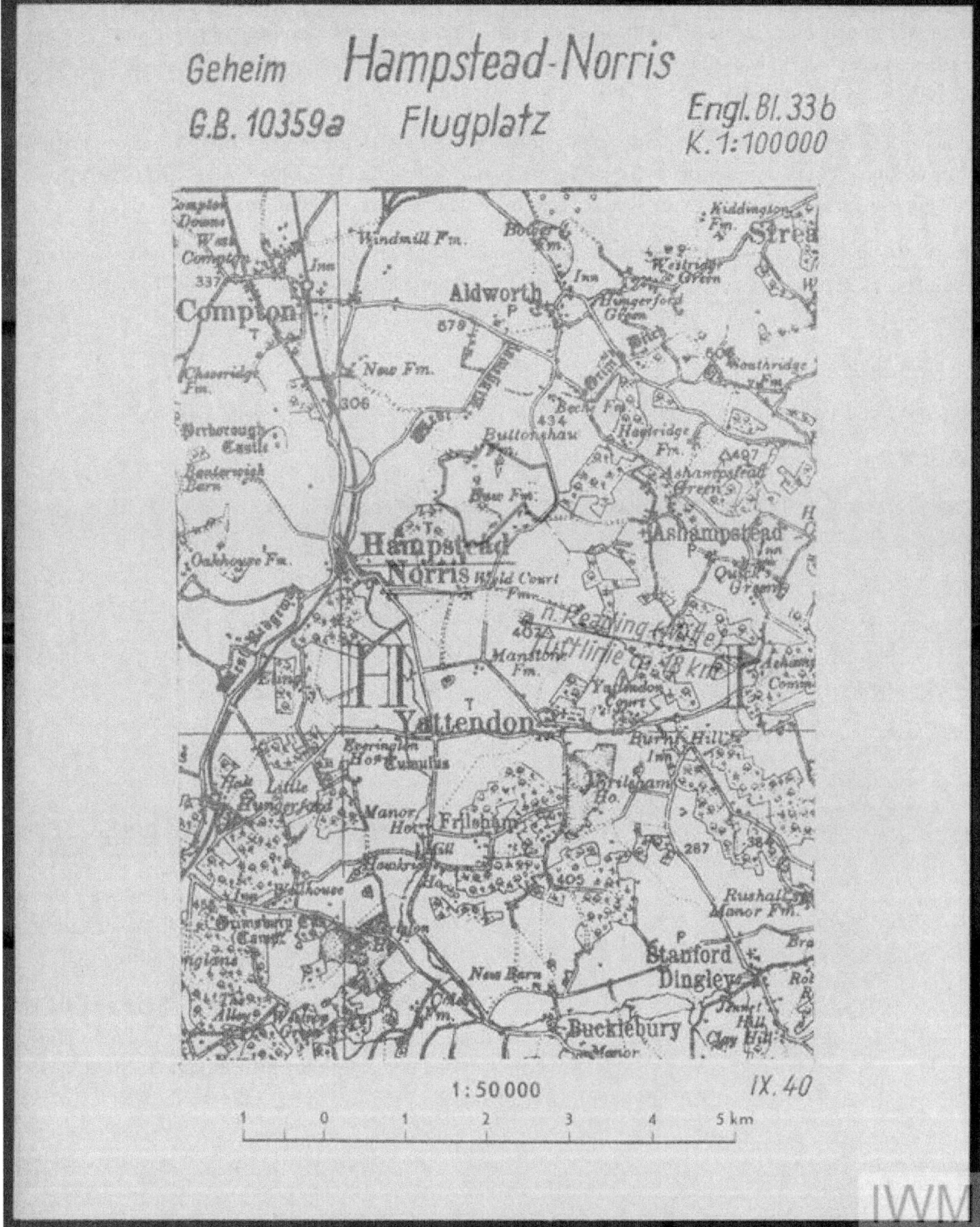

Hampstead Norris Flugplatz: [Luftwaffe Target Folder] (LBY LUFT 1116) Copyright: © IWM.

Gilbert Cameron Gibson

Sergeant Gilbert Cameron Gibson was in the Gambia with RAF 95 Squadron flying in Short Sunderland Mk.III DW105. Shortly after take-off at 11.05 hours on 5 January 1944, the aircraft was seen returning to base with smoke emitting from it and losing height. The starboard inner engine had developed a fault and caught fire filling the cabin with smoke and fumes making it impossible for the pilot to see. The aircraft failed to make a landing, exploding, and crashing into the water just south of Cansado Point at 11.15 hours.

RAF 95 Squadron were based at Bathurst (Banjul) in The Gambia, about 700 miles south of Port Étienne (Nouadhibou) in Mauritania. The squadron had set up an operation base at Port Étienne working in co-operation with the French to launch attacks on U-Boats and to escort troopships and convoys in the Atlantic.

Crew of Short Sunderland DW105:

Flying Officer L. K. J. Spinney RAFVR, 2nd Pilot, admitted to hospital, discharged 12 January 1944, survived.

Flying Officer Selwyn Guy Phillips RAFVR (142240), Controller (acting as Wireless Operator (Air Gunner, age unknown, missing believed killed

Flying Officer Kenneth Gilbert Mullett RAFVR (139714), Navigator, age 23, killed

Flying Officer Derek Anthony Roper RAFVR (142478), Wireless Operator/Air Gunner, age 23, killed

Pilot Officer Thomas Willoughby Sadleir, RAFVR (171950), age unknown, missing believed killed.

Sergeant Thomas William Ewen RAFVR (10046464), Air Gunner, age unknown, killed.

Sergeant Gilbert Cameron Gibson RAFVR (1369021), Air Gunner, age 29, missing believed killed.

Sergeant David Mason Campbell RAFVR (1343817), age 22, missing believed killed.

Sergeant Charles Ernest Norris RAFVR (1280880), age 31, missing believed killed.

Corporal Roy Stuart Crate RAFVR (753247), Mechanic, age 23, killed.

Flying Officer Phillips was acting as WOP/AG in place another crew member on sick leave, as also was Corporal Crate who volunteered to fly as mechanic.

Four of the crew of the crashed Sunderland DW105, F/O Roper, P/O Phillips, Sgt Ewen, Cpl Crate, were buried in the Port Étienne Chapel Cemetery (Nouadhibou). The others are commemorated on the Malta Memorial.

Sergeant Gilbert Cameron Gibson was the son of Robert and Cissie Gibson, King Street, Crieff. Gilbert played for Earngrove FC and was employed as a joiner by W B Dodd's of Crieff.

Note: The prototype Short Sunderland S.25 K4774 flying boat was first flown on 16 October 1937 at Rochester on the River Medway, about 30 miles southeast of London, England. The Germans are reputed to have nicknamed the Sunderland as the *'Fliegendes Stachelschwein'* ('Flying Porcupine') due to its defensive firepower. During the Berlin Airlift (June 1948–August 1949), ten Short Sunderland's and two transport variants (known as Hythe's) were used to transport goods from Finkenwerder on the Elbe, near Hamburg to Berlin, landing on the Havel River near RAF Gatow.

Photo of the crew from David Campbell's niece from the RAF 95 Squadron Coastal Command website: http://www.95squadron.co.uk/t95.html

William James Gilchrist

Sergeant William James Gilchrist RAFVR (1824389) was the son of William and Mary Gilchrist of Greenburns, between Coupar Angus and Kettins and at the time of his death, they were staying at Crossgates, Fife. William was employed at Carmichaels Farm just north of Longforgan before joining the RAF during WW2.

Shortly after arriving in London on 15 January 1944 to assume duties as Supreme Allied Commander, US General Dwight D. Eisenhower had agreed to RAF Air Chief Marshall Sir Arthur Tedder's 'Transportation Plan' using the air assets of the Allies to bomb French roads, bridges, rail lines and marshalling yards to slow the movement of German forces and supplies to the D-Day invasion areas. In March 1944, Eisenhower directed the RAF and the USAAF to begin high intensity striking of a long list of targets in France such as the major transportation centres at Noisy-le-Sec, Tergnier, Juvisy, and Rouen, with the intention of making roads, bridges, and railroads unusable for the Germans.

On 18 April 1944, less than two months before D-Day, Sergeant William James Gilchrist was the upper air gunner in Handley Page Halifax Mk III, LW522, MH-J of RAF 51 Squadron on a bombing mission to Tergnier, in the Aisne department, Hauts-de-France. Tergnier had a large railway marshalling yard, where the Creil-Jeumont railway joins, and it located on the Canal de Saint-Quentin where it also joins with the Canal de la Sambre à l'Oise.

Take off was at 21.20 hours from RAF Snaith, east of Goole in the East Riding of Yorkshire. The bomb load was 7 x 1,000 lb and 6 x 500 lb high explosives. On board Halifax Mk III LW522 were:

Sergeant Charles CHRISTIE (1049057) RAFVR Flight Engineer

Sergeant William James GILCHRIST (1824389) RAFVR Air Gunner

Sergeant Desmond William KENNEDY (1620864) RAFVR Air Bomber

Sergeant Philip LATCHFORD (1038622) RAFVR Wireless Operator

Flight Sergeant Colin SHACKLETON (1398483) RAFVR Pilot

Flight Sergeant Fred TAYLOR (1549593) RAFVR Air Gunner

Flight Sergeant Eric Oscar Downing YORKE (1439296) RAFVR Navigator

Handley Page Halifax Mk III LW522 collided in the air with RAF 158 Squadron Halifax LV946, both aircraft crashing at Seraucourt-le-Grand, a commune in the Aisne department in Hauts-de-France, northern France. Sergeant William James Gilchrist was 26 years old, and all the crew are buried at Grand-Seraucourt British Cemetery, about 8 kilometres southwest of St. Quentin on the east side of the river Somme.

NOTES: On the night of 18/19 April 1944, Bomber Command aircraft made many heavy attacks on railway-yards and workshops at Noisy-le-Sec and Juvisy, near Paris, and at Rouen and Tergnier, with more than 4,000 tons of bombs being dropped; 14 aircraft were reported missing that night.

Wilfred Owen, officer, and poet was killed as he crossed the Sambre–Oise Canal at the head of a raiding party: Owen's death occurred only a week before the armistice.

Handley Page Halifax LW522 was delivered by the English Electric Company (Preston/Samlesbury) between 22 December 1943 and 20 January 1944. Samlesbury would go on to produce 700 Handley Page Hampdens and 3,000 Handley Page Halifax Bombers for the Royal Air Force. By the end of the Second World War, the site had five main hangars and three runways.

Under the protection of Lichtenstein night fighter radar and Benito (ground station) night fighter interception control of Luftwaffe 4. JD (Jagdgeschwader), at least 18 aircraft of NJG1 and NJG4 (Nachtjagdgeschwader), Messerschmitt Bf 110's operated against the 18 April 1944 raids between 22.43 and 01.18 hrs. These fighters tallied four Halifax abschüsse (kills) over France. Between 22.47 and 22.55 hours. Nine Bf110 G-4s of II. /NJG1 were scrambled from St. Dizier for ungeführte Zahme Sau (Tame Boar tactic) duties. Oberleutnant Hager, the Kapitän of the 6. Staffel downed a Halifax of the Tergnier force with Schräge Musik (upward-firing autocannon or machine gun) armament.

Luftwaffe Feldwebel Erich Handke later recalled: *'We took-off for a Wilde Sau sortie and flew a long way to the west to get into the returning Tergnier raiders near St. Quentin. We simply flew without any ground information towards the target markers until I gained a single contact heading west. We had to climb to 5,000 metres before we slowly caught up. At 500 metres range we saw the enemy. As it was on a homeward course, we fired into the fuselage with the Schräge weapons and wiggled the rudder a bit as he did so, at which the Lancaster immediately caught fire in the fuselage and both wings. It then went down in great spirals with a monstrous shower of sparks (2-300 metres) trailing behind, which looked like a comet. It crashed NE of Rouen.*

In the meantime, I'd gained more contacts. We pursued one, and again saw the enemy at a range of 500 metres. At first it looked like a Lancaster, but to judge by the tail it must have been a new Halifax. After a burst from 50 metres below it was burning as nicely as the previous one and went down immediately, SW of Dieppe. I then gained a lot of contacts which were already out over the sea, but they were all going very quickly whilst losing height. We were now only 2,500 metres up. If we had been able to catch up to them at all, it would only have been at the English coast, in the light ack-ack belt. As our Radar could under no circumstances be allowed to fall into enemy hands, we were only permitted to chase the English to our own coast. In addition, we also didn't have a single life vest with us. As a result, we flew 30 km inland, against the remaining home-bound bombers, then turned in behind them, however we were soon over the sea again, barely catching them up, and only 1,500 metres up. As the return flights had just ended, we gave up and flew home. Behind us another attack on Rouen had started, but we had too little fuel to be able to do anything more.'

The crew returned to Laon-Athies at 01.22 hrs. Both, abschüsse were officially anerkannt (accepted) on 6 July 1944.

The earlier short lived night fighter tactic mentioned above was known as Wilde Sau (Wild Boar or Sow), it was used until developments in German radar equipment made it more immune to the allied bomber tactic of using Window/Düppel (chaff -thin pieces of aluminium dropped to confuse radar).

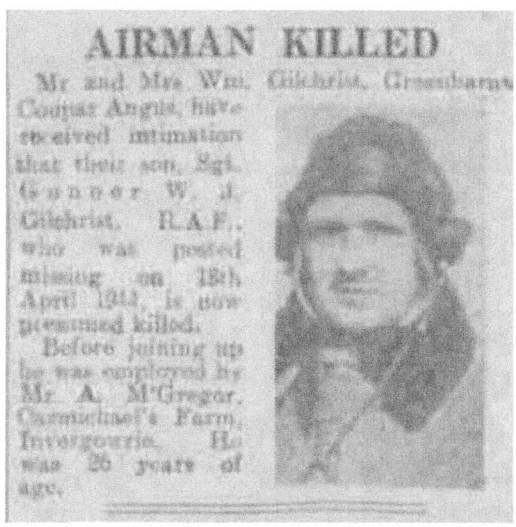

Dundee Courier and Advertiser 20 January 1945

THE STRATEGIC BOMBING OF GERMANY, 1942-1945 (CH 12598) Squadron Leader Peter Hill, briefs crews of No. 51 Squadron RAF on the forthcoming raid to Nuremberg, Germany in the Operations Room at Snaith, Yorkshire, 30 March 1944. The Station Commander, Group Captain N H Fresson, sits third from the left in the front row. No. 51 Squadron lost six Handley Page Halifaxes that night (30/31 March 1944), suffering 35 men killed (including Sqn Ldr Hill) and seven... Copyright: © IWM.

Denholm Gow

Leading Aircraftman Denholm Gow RAF (532923) was the son of John Boyd and Margaret Reoch Gow, Winterpark, Muirton of Ardblair, Blairgowrie. He was born at 33 William Street, Blairgowrie, had two brothers and two sisters and was married to Joan (neé Carter).

Gow was reported missing after an engagement with the enemy on 21 June 1940. He was a crew member of a Bristol Beaufort L4501, twin-engine torpedo bomber tasked with attacking the Pocket Battleship *Scharnhorst* which was anchored in Trondheim Harbour in Norway.

Bristol Beaufort L4501, RAF Coastal Command, 42 Squadron took off at 14.25 hours from RAF Wick, along with eight other Bristol Beaufort's to bomb the *Scharnhorst*. The Beaufort's were all armed with armour piercing bombs.

On the way, Bristol Beaufort L9810 was attacked by two Messerschmitt Bf 109s from 11. /JG77 but managed to catch up with the formation. Suddenly it's landing gear dropped, and an engine burst into flames and L9810 crashed into the sea.

The rest of the squadron successfully hit the *Scharnhorst* at Trondheim with three bombs. It was forced it to return to Kiel for six months of repairs.

The squadron was then attacked again on the return journey by Luftwaffe Messerschmitt Bf 109s from Jagdgeschwader 77 (JG 77) Herz As ('Ace of Hearts') based at an airfield at Værnes, about 20 miles west of Trondheim. A pilot of II/JG 77 later submitted a claim that he had shot down L4501 into the sea off the coast of Bergen approximately 400 miles further south.

The Bristol Beaufort L4501 crew killed in action:

Pilot Officer Alan George Rigg, RAF (41067), pilot, age 19

Pilot Officer Marcel Adrian Phillips, RAF (44259), observer, age 27

Aircraftman 1st Class George Edward Tanner, RAF (625471), wireless operator/air gunner, age 19

Aircraftman Denholm Gow, RAF (532923), wireless operator/air gunner, age 19

The other Beauforts lost from RAF 42 Squadron that day:

Bristol Beaufort L9810, flown by Flying Officer William Barrie-Smith – lost with all crew.

Bristol Beaufort L4486, flown by Flying Officer Herbert John Seagrim – lost with all crew.

Beaufort L4486 was attacked by two Messerschmitt Bf 109s of II. /JG 77: an engine burst into flames and the aircraft crashed into the sea off Bergen, Norway. Only the body of one of the crew was ever found, with the other three posted as 'missing, presumed killed in action'.

Denholm Gow was married in England just a fortnight before. He was previously employed on various farms in the Blairgowrie area. His father served in World War One and his brother was in The Black Watch. Denholm Gow is remembered on panel 23 of the Runnymede Memorial, in Englefield Green, near Egham, Surrey.

NOTES: Oberfeldwebel Hans-Jakob Arnoldy from the Luftwaffe 77 Jagdgeschwader was one of the pilots defending the Scharnhorst on that day, the same pilot who later shot down Acting Sergeant David Ferguson Sharpe Campbell from Perth on 25 June 1940. He is not listed as having shot down any RAF aircraft on 21 June 1940. The day before he shot down a Lockheed Hudson and the day after, two Blackburn Skua's (8 out 15 were shot down). Arnoldy was part of Luftwaffe 4. /JG77 Squadron in Norway at the time. He was later injured in a crash landing following aerial combat near Bergen on 26 October 1940. He ended up with seven victories before his death in Greece on 15 April 1941.

Norway had surrendered to the Germans on 10 June 1940. Off Norway, the British Aircraft carrier, HMS *Glorious* was sunk by the *Scharnhorst* and the *Gneisenau* on 8 June 1940. The *Scharnhorst* suffered some damage during the battle and sought refuge at Trondheim. RAF and Fleet Air Arm aircraft made attacks on the *Scharnhorst* from 11 June 1940, the Royal Navy also joined in with aircraft from HMS *Ark Royal*. The *Scharnhorst* retreated to the Deutsche Werke dockyard at Keil for shipyard repairs on 21 June 1940. The *Gneisenau* was also damaged in an engagement with the British Battleship HMS *Renown*. Two British escorting destroyers were sunk, HMS *Ardent* and HMS *Acasta*. On the same day, more than 10,000 soldiers from the 51st (Highland) Division were captured at Saint-Valéry-en-Caux and sent to POW camps.

Schlachtschiff "Gneisenau" *These images were provided to Wikimedia Commons by the German Federal Archive (Deutsches Bundesarchiv) as part of a cooperation project. The German Federal Archive guarantees an authentic representation only using the originals (negative and/or positive), resp. the digitalization of the originals as provided by the Digital Image Archive. The copyright is in the public domain because it has expired.*

Alastair Donald Mackintosh "Sandy" Gunn

Lieutenant Alastair Donald Mackintosh "Sandy" Gunn from Auchterarder and was a top-notch elite Spitfire pilot who flew on highly dangerous missions, including photographing the German pocket battleship Tirpitz in a Norwegian Fjord, he took part in the 'Great Escape' and was subsequently cruelly murdered on the orders of Adolf Hitler.

During its 22-week operational life, Sandy's Spitfire AA810, had at least 7 pilots, including the Welsh champion jockey and 1940 Grand National winner Mervyn Anthony Jones, and the Indian-born English motor racing star, Alfred Fane Peers Agabeg. Jones and Agabeg, both lost their lives flying missions for the RAF's Photographic Reconnaissance Unit (PRU). The Operation Record Book for 1 PRU shows that Spitfire AA810 flew for a total of 49 hours and 47 minutes. The PRU employed modified Supermarine Spitfires which were unarmed, stripped of armour plating, armoured windscreens, and even without a radio. They were also fitted with additional fuel tanks giving them 4 times the range of a conventional Spitfire. Some PRU Spitfires were designed to fly just under cloud cover, at sunset and sunrise, when the clouds took on a pinkish hue, so painting them pink rendered them almost invisible and gave them the nickname, 'Pink Spitfires'.

When Spitfire AA810 crashed in Norway, it was piloted for the PRU by Alistair Donald Mackintosh 'Sandy' Gunn, a native of Perthshire. Sandy Gunn was born on 27 September 1919 at 'Deansland', Auchterarder to the locally well-loved surgeon James Turner Gunn, MB, ChB, FRCS and Adelaide Lucy Frances Gunn. He was schooled at Cargilfield School and Fettes College (both Edinburgh) before undertaking an engineering apprenticeship at Harland and Wolff shipyard in Govan. He then went on to Pembroke College (University of Cambridge) to study Mechanical Sciences.

Sandy Gunn enlisted in the RAF on 22 February 1940 and commenced active service on 22 June 1940 as an aircrew candidate (airman second class). On 18 January 1941, he received his pilot's brevet (an honorary high rank that rewards merit or gallantry, but without authority) and was promoted to sergeant. He was commissioned as a pilot officer on 25 January 1941 and then promoted to flying officer on 25 January 1942. Much of Gunn's flying involved flying dangerous long-range PRU missions photographing German naval units along the Norwegian coast and in the North Atlantic. During one of these missions, he crashed in the North Atlantic after running out of fuel. Luckily, he was rescued and was soon back in the air.

At 08:07 hours on 5 March 1942, Spitfire AA810, piloted by Gunn, took off from RAF Wick. It flew 580 miles across the North Sea to Fættenfjord in the north of Norway. Gunn's mission was to photograph the German battleship *Tirpitz* which was sheltering in the Trondheim Fjord. This was the 113th PRU mission to try to monitor the German battleship and unfortunately for Gunn, the first to be successfully intercepted by the Luftwaffe, for AA810 was shot down by two Messerschmitt Bf109 E's undertaking air protection over the fjord. Sandy was unaware that the Germans had installed a new listening post at Kristiansund, to the west of the Trondheim Fjord and Luftwaffe pilots, Dieter Gerhardt and Heinz Knoke had been scrambled at 12.02pm from Lade airfield to wait high at 15,000 feet nine minutes later over Trondheim for Sandy to arrive.

Sandy was seen to be circling with an engine issue, he was trying to decide whether to risk returning home over the North Sea or head for neutral Sweden. Heinz fired first hitting the oil cooler on AA810. Then it was Dieter's turn, he peppered the Spitfire with hundreds of rounds. One of the cannon rounds hit Sandy's starboard wing tank, setting it on fire.

Sandy bailed out just before his Spitfire crashed. He was assisted by locals and tried to escape on skies but suffering facial injuries and other burns and unable to ski well, undertaking the 110-mile hike to the Swedish border was not a realistic option. He surrendered and became a prisoner of war. Surnadalsøra village lies over the river below the 'Troll Mountains' and being so remote it would also be his place of rest that evening as there was no way to get him to Trondheim that same day. A lorry arrived the next morning (*Note: see Heink Knocke account in Notes – flown by Fieseler Stroch*) and he was taken to Trondheim where he boarded a train for Oslo. Then he was flown to a Dulag Luft, (Durchgangslager der Luftwaffe, Transit Camp of the Airforce) for interrogation. The main Dulag Luft was at Oberursel near Frankfurt.

The German military believed Gunn had flown from a secret RAF airfield in northern Norway and interrogated him for some 3 weeks before sending him to Stalag Luft 3, a Luftwaffe-run POW camp in Poland immortalised by 2 break outs, that of October 1943 – the subject of the book (and subsequent film) by Eric Williams, The Wooden Horse – and that which became known as the 'Great Escape', on the night of 24-25 March 1944. This was a new camp and Sandy was the 5th prisoner to arrive.

Sandy found a place as a Security Officer, guarding Escape Committee conferences and as a tunneller. The tunnel he first worked on was discovered, his second was 'Harry' which was to become very well-known thought the world. The mastermind of the Great escape, Squadron Leader Roger Joyce Bushell (Big X) hand-picked the first 100 men that were to escape, priority given to those who had contributed the most. The tunnel they escaped through, Harry, was 100 metres long. The tunnel fell short of where it was supposed to end up, it was intended to go as far as into the woods. The weather was extremely cold that night and on the higher ground to the south snow lay up to six inches deep.

The men gathered in hut 104 and prepared to leave. Sandy was 68th on the list to escape. With the tunnel being too short, subsequent delays caused a backlog, and it suffered several collapses. Sandy Gunn was one of the 76 escapees who managed to get out and one of the 73 recaptured.

So furious was Adolf Hitler over the escape, he ordered the infamous "Sagan Befehl" execution of the escapees. It is said that due to the intervention of Herman Göring, this number was reduced to 50. Sandy Gunn was murdered on 6 April 1944 by members of the Gestapo along with 49 other RAF personnel, including 11 Spitfire pilots. Flight Lieutenant Alastair Donald MacIntosh 'Sandy' Gunn (60340) was but 24 years of age. He was buried at the time in Sagan. Subsequently, his ashes were re-interred in the Old Garrison Cemetery, Poznan.

From the Spitfire AA810 – Restoring Sandy's Spitfire Facebook page – *'Sandy was 68th on the list to escape, but the tunnel collapsed, between the half-way houses of Piccadilly and Leicester Square and had to be dug out by Cookie Long. Disappearing into the night with his escaper partner Mike Casey, with neither speaking German they headed for the Zagan train station to ride under the freight trains north. Their destination was the northern German port of Sassnitz where they would try and stow away on a boat to Stettin, Sweden. Sandy had photographed Stettin several times from his Spitfire. They managed to stay free through the entire day of the 25th.*

Once caught they were transported to the Gestapo HQ at 31 Augustastrasse, Görlitz, Germany where Sandy would be imprisoned and interrogated until 6th April.

Both Mike Casey (RAF 57 squadron) and Cookie Long (RAF 9 Squadron) were also murdered by the Gestapo.

Heink Knocke described the shooting down of Spitfire AA810 in his book, *'I Flew for the Führer'*, published 1953 in the UK by Evans Brothers Limited, London:

"5th March 1942. A shout from the operations room: "There he is again!" Out through the window and into the snow in one bound, twenty or thirty long strides, and I am in my aircraft. Seconds later I start rolling to take off.

12.02 hours: climbing steeply into the cloudless sky.

12.10 hours: altitude 15,000 feet. I adjust the oxygen mask. It is bitterly cold.

"Bandit in Cäsar-Ida–Hanni-seven-zero." (German Phonetic Language -Hanni, unknown, possibly meaning height or altitude as in the German word Höhe)

"Victor, victor; message understood," I reply.

Altitude 20,000 feet.

"Bandit now in *Cäsar*-Kurfürst

I shall climb to 25,000 feet. I simply must get him today.

"Bandit in Berta-Ludwig."

He seems to be sweeping round the northern tip of the Sound, heading up towards the anchorage of our *warships.*

I am now at 25000 feet, scanning the skies around and below. Ahead and to the left I discern a tiny dark speck in the sky against the unbroken white landscape below.

It is the Spitfire, leaving a short vapour trail behind. The Tommy comes round in a wide sweep, heading up the Inner fjord. I maintain altitude and study my prey. Now over his objective, the Tommy flies' round in two complete circles. He is taking photographs.

I make use of this opportunity to take up a position above him. Apparently, he is so intent on his task that he does not notice me. I am now about 3,000 feet above him.

Then he starts back a westerly course. I open my throttle wide and check my guns as I swoop down upon him. In a few seconds I am right on his tail. Fire!

My tracers vanish into his fuselage. And now he begins to twist and turn like a mad thing. Must not let him escape. Keep firing with everything I have.

He goes into a dive, then straightens out again. He begins trailing smoke, which gradually become denser. I fire yet again.

Then something suddenly splashes into my windshield. Oil. My engine? I have no visibility ahead and am no longer able to see the Spitfire. Blast!

My engine is still running smoothly. Apparently, the oil in front of my eyes must have come from the badly damaged Spitfire when its oil-cooler was shot to pieces.

I veer a little to the right, in order to be able to observe the Tommy farther through the side window. He is gradually losing speed but is still flying. The smoke-trail is becoming thinner.

Then another Messerschmitt comes into view climbing up on my left. It is Lieutenant Dieter Gerhardt, my old comrade, and I radio him to say that I am no longer able to fire.

He opens fire. The right wing of the Spitfire shears away. Like a dead autumn leaf, the plane flutters earthwards.

And the pilot? Is he still alive? My throat tightens. I had come to like that boy. If he is not dead, why does he not bail out?

The Spitfire goes down, a flaming torch now, hurtling towards the snowfield. It will crash there and be utterly destroyed. And with it the pilot.

I find myself shouting as if he could hear me: "Bail out, lad, bail out!" After all, he is human too; a soldier, too, and a pilot with the same love of the sky and clouds that I feel. Does he also have a wife, a girl like Lilo, perhaps?

"Bail out, lad, bail out!"

Then a body becomes detached from the flames and falls clear. A white parachute spreads open and drifts slowly down into the mountains.

A feeling of pure joy is in my heart now. This is my first combat victory in the air. I have got my man and he is alive."

Dieter and I share a bottle of brandy. We drink a toast to our own fighter pilots, and another to our Tommy.

Dieter brings him in, after landing in the mountains in a Fieseler Storch fitted with skies. He is a tall, slim Pilot Officer in the Royal Air Force. A stiff drink of brandy does him a lot of good. He joins in the laughter when I explain how the entire bottle was actually dedicated to him.

In 2018, Spitfire AA810 was discovered embedded in a mountainside peat bog in Norway – a remote area near Surnadal, Norway (Surnadalsøra). After careful excavation and meticulous on-site recording, its component pieces were carefully packed into boxes and driven back to the UK. The plane had been hit by over 200 machine-gun bullets and some 20 rounds of cannon fire. Before it hit the ground at an angle of about 20 degrees, its engine had stopped and its starboard side, nose, and cockpit were all ablaze. Unearthing, salvaging, and rebuilding the Spitfire is costing at least £2.5 million.

Work has begun on restoring Sandy's Spitfire; it is now being fully restored (image below) and will fly again as a memorial to the 305 known PRU pilots. Inside the top cowling of AA810 will be the names of all the PRU pilots, 77 who were killed, 19 made POW's and 74 who were missing in action. It is hoped to have AA810 back in the air in 2023/24. If you can support this restoration effort, please visit their website and you can honour them by adopting a name on the, For Those Who Served page. I personally hope one day to see Sandy's Spitfire flying over Auchterarder, what a tribute that would be to him.

Follow the restorers on Facebook: **Spitfire AA810 – Restoring Sandy's Spitfire** *@SpitfireAA810 or visit the website:*
https://www.spitfireaa810.co.uk/

NOTES:

Stalag Luft 3 also housed local former POW's Ernie Holmes DFC, who passed away in November 2021 at 100 years and Bill Reid VC who is buried at Crieff Cemetery.

Field Marshal Keitel, Major-General Westhoff and Major-General Graevenitz all argued against the "Sagan Befehl", the supreme command execution order, for it conflicted with the Geneva convention. Stalag Luft III was located near Sagan or Zágán, Silesia, in present day Poland.

In February 1944, the Stufe Römisch III Order is issued by OKW (Oberkommando der Wehrmacht), and it stated that, *'escaping POWs should not be automatically returned to their camps but held in special detention pending consideration of each individual case'.* In early March 1944, the Kugel or Bullet Order was issued. It stated that, *'all non-British or American recaptured escapers should be sent to Mauthausen concentration camp with a letter "K" appended to their name', this indicated that such prisoners should be immediately executed'.* Reichsführer of the Schutzstaffel (Protection Echelon), Heinrich Luitpold Himmler in mid-143 assumed control of Prisoner of War security.

Sandy Gunn was twice 'Mentioned in Despatches', 5 June 1942 for service as pilot officer and for conspicuous gallantry as a prisoner of war. On average, each PRU Spitfire had a life expectancy of just 14 weeks!

Sandy had also flown missions in January 1942 in Supermarine Spitfire AA790, 315983 Mk PRIV. It first flew on 12 September 1941 and was powered by a Merlin 46 engine. It looks like this Spitfire was produced in one of the small factories dotted around Henley-on-Thames and was probably first tested on a field grass strip aerodrome at the nearby Upper Culham Farm. Fortunately, following the bombing of the Supermarine factory at Southampton in September 1940, some of the precision machines, jigs and tooling that survived had already been dispersed to temporary facilities such as requisitioned car and bus garages, and furniture factories. Supermarine Spitfire production would continue in hundreds of different locations as well as at the Castle Bromwich Aircraft Factory (formerly Morris Motors).

AA790 was subsequently allocated, when it finished its PRU duties, to RAF 8 (Coastal) OTU (Operational Training Unit) based at RAF Fraserburgh. By a very strange and spooky coincidence, Spitfire AA790 crash landed due to engine failure on 15 December 1944 at Westburn Farm near Aberuthven, only three miles from Sandy's hometown of Auchterarder. The pilot, Flying Officer R. E. Ludman was undertaking a cross country flight at 19,000ft when the engine began to run rough, with a subsequent rise in radiator temperature and erratic boost reading. A sump oil tank in a wing had lost power and the aircraft had to belly land in a field near the farm. Westburn Farm is between Aberuthven and Dunning, near the Broadslap Farm Shop and Cafe.

Dubbed by Winston Churchill 'The Beast', *Tirpitz* was eventually sunk by Avro Lancaster bombers on 12 November 1944 using Barnes Wallis developed 'Tallboy' 12,000-pound bombs. There was a plan to use Wallis developed 'Highball' bouncing bombs against the *Tirpitz*. These were the follow up type to the

Dambuster 'Upkeep' bombs, used against the dams in Germany's Ruhr valley. Testing of the 'Highball's' was carried out by de Havilland Mosquito's on Loch Striven just north of Rothesay against the anchored former French Battleship *Courbet* and later the Battleship *HMS Malaya*.

Stalag Luft III housed 2,500 RAF officers, 7,500 USAF airmen and 900 officers from other Allied forces at its peak. Stalag Luft III was liberated by the Soviet army on 27 January 1945, the day before the prisoners with their German guards were marched to the city of Spremberg about 80 Km west. The three other Stalag Luft III tunnels were named, Tom, Dick, and George. Only 3 escapees managed not to be re-captured during the Great Escape, two Norwegians, Jens Müller and Per Bergsland and a Dutchman, Bram van der Stok.

The Sandy Gunn Aerospace Careers Programme (ACP) is a venture dedicated to inspiring and assisting those 15 – 18 years old into engineering and aviation. Website: https://www.acp-aa810.co.uk/

Heink Knocke on 14 February 1942 Knoke was detached to Jagdgruppe "Losigkeit" (Fritz Losigkeit), where he was charged with the air protection of the ships around the Norway coast. He returned to his squadron, JG 1 later in March 1941. In February 1942, Knoke participated with 3. /JG 1 in Operation *Donnerkeil*, the Channel Dash of the German battleships *Scharnhorst* and *Gneisenau* and heavy cruiser *Prinz Eugen*. By the end of the war, he was credited with 33 aerial victories and 19 unconfirmed kills and 1 shared (AA810), all in the western theatre of operations. His total included 19 bombers of the USAAF. After the war he went into politics in 1951, firstly as a member of the Socialist Reich Party. This party was declared illegal in 1952. Knoke remained in politics as a member of the parish council of the Gemeinde Schortens (Gemeindeparlament) from April 1954. He was elected in 1956, 1961,1964 and 1968 for his community/parish parliaments as a member of the Freie Demokratische Partei (FDP, Liberal Democratic Party). Knocke was born 24 March 1921 in Hamelin, Germany, best known for the tale of the Pied Piper of Hamelin. On 28 August 1941, Heinz married Elisabeth "Lilo" Makowski in Schieratz, Poland. He retired in 1972 and died 18 May 1993.

Dieter Gerhardt was killed in action on 18 March 1943, flying a Messerschmitt Bf 109 1/R.2 Werke number 14150, Schwarze 6. Gerhardt was downed by return fire from a Boeing B17 four-engine heavy bomber over Heligoland in the North Sea. He bailed out but died of his wounds in his dingy.

The Fieseler Fi 156 Storch was a small German liaison aircraft with a short take-off and landing (STOL) capability. 2,867 were built until 31 March 1945

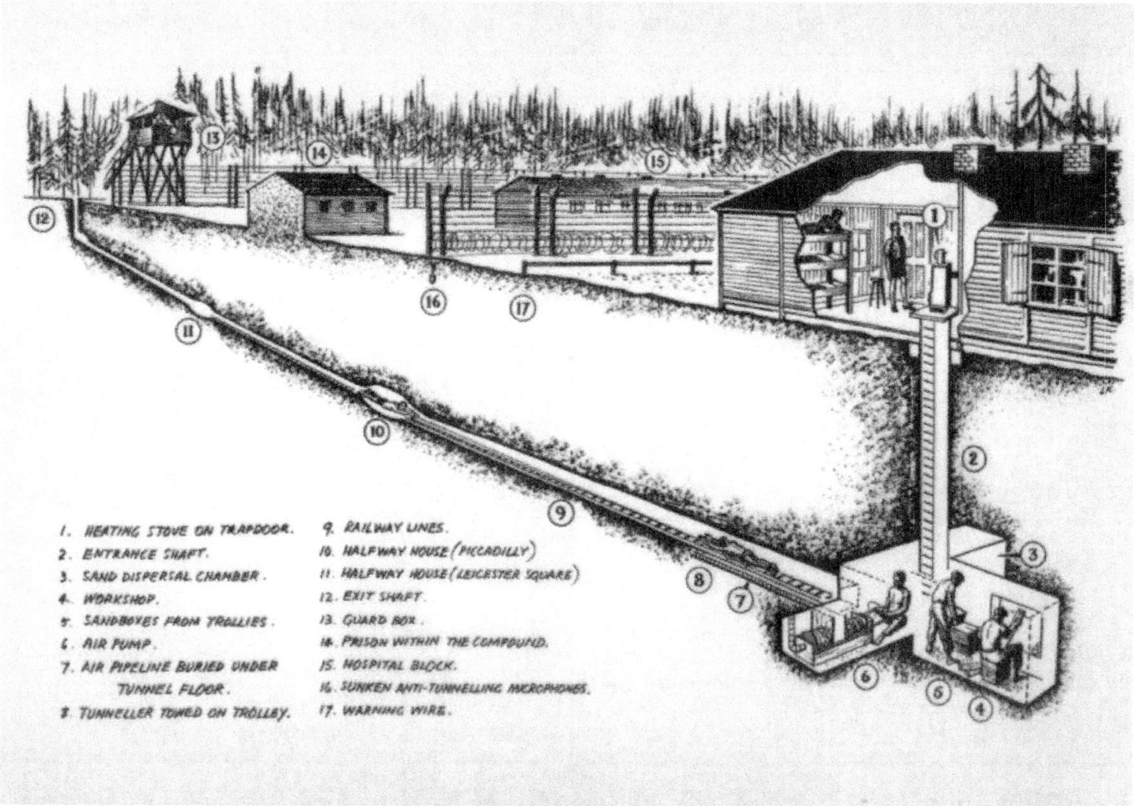

1. HEATING STOVE ON TRAPDOOR.
2. ENTRANCE SHAFT.
3. SAND DISPERSAL CHAMBER.
4. WORKSHOP.
5. SANDBOXES FROM TROLLIES.
6. AIR PUMP.
7. AIR PIPELINE BURIED UNDER TUNNEL FLOOR.
8. TUNNELLER TOWED ON TROLLEY.
9. RAILWAY LINES.
10. HALFWAY HOUSE (PICCADILLY).
11. HALFWAY HOUSE (LEICESTER SQUARE).
12. EXIT SHAFT.
13. GUARD BOX.
14. PRISON WITHIN THE COMPOUND.
15. HOSPITAL BLOCK.
16. SUNKEN ANTI-TUNNELLING MICROPHONES.
17. WARNING WIRE.

Sandy as a prisoner at the Stalag Luft 3 camp, back left in the doorway (Image: www.spitfireaa810.co.uk)

Sandy on the tail of Spitfire R7056 at RAF Benson, November 1941

This image of a PRU aircraft shows the light colour (intended to aid concealment against the sky) and lack of weapons.

Charles Grant

On Craigdootie Hill, just north of Dairsie in Fife, Bristol Beaufort L9834 crashed at 2.12 am on 30 August 1941, killing all the four crew. Charles Grant is buried in Wellshill Cemetery, Perth.

Squadron Leader Gerald Sebastian Patrick Rooney DFC, RAF (39245), pilot, age unknown

Flying Officer Charles Grant, RAFVR (78749), air gunner, age 29

Sergeant Lloyd Colley Mansell, RCAF (R/51633), air observer, age 32

Flight Sergeant Ronald Sidney Knott, RAF, (551646), wireless operator/air gunner, age 20

Charles Grant was the only son of Henry and Isabella Grant of 59 North Methven Street, Perth. He had just returned to his squadron at RAF Leuchars after a short period of leave. Grant had just attended a friend's wedding the previous Wednesday, left to return to Leuchars on the Thursday and his father was notified of his death the following Saturday.

Charles Grant attended Perth Academy and went on to Dundee College where he graduated. A series of scholarship successes enabled him to study on the Continent. Grant was the head of the textile department at the Glasgow College of Art and had been entrusted to design and decorate the tourist sitting rooms of the liner RMS *Queen Mary*.

Three days before the outbreak of war, Grant qualified as an RAFVR pilot at RAF No 11 EFRTS, RAF Perth. He was gazetted as acting pilot officer on 12 April 1940 and flying officer on 25 June 1940. He instead chose to enlist as a rear-gunner, giving up his career as an RAF pilot.

If Squadron Leader Rooney's crew was unchanged, then flying in Bristol Beaufort L4514, they took part in a famous strike against the German Heavy Cruiser *Lützow* (formerly the pocket battleship *Deutschland*) on 13 June 1941. The *Deutschland* had been heavily damaged by Norwegian coastal batteries during the German invasion of Norway on 8 April 1940. The British submarine HMS *Spearfish* attacked her on 11 April 1941, nearly destroying her stern. After about a year of repairs, the stern had been rebuilt and she was ready to sail on 10 June 1941 to commence commerce raiding in the Atlantic. 'Ultra' decrypts of German Enigma signals from the Government Code and Cypher School at Bletchley Park were sent to the Admiralty indicating that the *Deutschland*, now renamed the *Lützow*, was about to break-out into the Atlantic. On 12 June 1941, the battleship *King George V* and cruisers and destroyers of the home fleet set sail from Scapa Flow to intercept the *Lützow* and protect allied convoys. A force of five Bristol Beaufort Mk 1 torpedo bombers of RAF 22 Squadron at Wick and nine Bristol Beaufort Mk 1 torpedo bombers of RAF 42 Squadron at Leuchars took off just before midnight on 12 June 1941 to also attack the *Lützow*.

At 00.15 am, a patrolling Bristol Blenheim from RAF 114 Squadron sighted the *Lützow* and called in the Beaufort's. At 2.25 am, off the coast of Norway at Egersund, the Beaufort's attacked. One torpedo hit the *Lützow* on the port side, rendering her motionless and she took on a severe list to port. The German Destroyer, *Friedrich Eckodt* took the *Lützow* in tow whilst other destroyers screened her withdrawal to the south. The *Lützow* returned to Kiel for another six months of repairs.

From RAF No 42 Squadron Operations Record Book, 12.6.41 entry:

S/LDR. ROONEY and crew in BEAUFORT L4514, led BEAUFORTS X8929, on a strike against enemy shipping, with torpedoes. Course was set for LISTER (Lista, Norway), and at 01.25 hrs, a correct landfall was made, and light Flax was experienced. A search was made in the SKAGERRAK without result; at 02.18 hrs course was set northerly, coastwise, still accompanied by BEAUFORT L9938. BEAUFORT X8929 had broken formation in dense low cloud. At 02.22 hrs, an enemy force consisting of 1 CR (Cruiser) and 4 DR's (Destroyers) was sighted in position ZNEF 2145. They appeared to be stationary, and two torpedo attacks were made from the Port Beam at a range of 400 yards. The torpedo failed to drop. Moderate flak was experienced from the DRs, and smoke was seen coming from the CR, forward of the funnel – presumably the result of an earlier attack. At 02.40 hrs the aircraft set course for base, and landed at 05.20 hrs.

The *Friedrich Eckodt* was sunk by HMS *Sheffield* on 31 December 1942. The *Lützow* was eventually sunk by the RAF in the Piast Canal in April of 1945 and raised by the Soviet navy in 1947. She was again sunk by the Soviets as a target in the Baltic.

NOTES: Rooney was from Gibraltar.

The Queen Mary is now a tourist attraction, permanently moored at Long Beach, California, USA.

Later that year – 11 December 1941 – Flying Officer Oliver Philpot, MC, DFC and his Beaufort crew from RAF 42 Squadron at Leuchars were shot down by German anti-aircraft fire and ditched their aircraft in the North Sea. After two days, they were picked up by a German naval vessel and interned as prisoners of war. Philpot was one of three who successfully escaped from Stalag Luft III made famous by the book and later film The Wooden Horse. He made his way to Danzig and managed to smuggle himself onto a neutral Swedish ship. Philpot returned to Britain by the Christmas of that year.

Stalag Luft III also housed Sub-Lieutenant Peter William Shorrocks Butterworth RNAS (and Sandy Gunn from Auchterarder). Peter was involved in the 'Wooden Horse' escape at Stalag Luft III. Butterworth is better known for his appearances as an actor on television and in most of the Carry-On films. He applied but did not get the part in the Wooden Horse movie. They did however, it is said, name the main character Peter in homage to him. Butterworth was shot down by Messerschmitt BF109s on 21 June 1940 when he tried to attack an airfield at Den Helder in The Netherlands. He had to force-land on Texel Island, just to the north and was taken into captivity. Amazingly and very bravely he was flying a three-man, well-outclassed Fairy Albacore biplane. The Fairy Albacore was popularly known as the 'Applecore'. They were built at Fairey's Hayes factory and test flown at what is now Heathrow Airport.

Charles Grant, Perthshire Advertiser 3 September 1941

THE QUEEN MARY ON WAR SERVICE. 28 SEPTEMBER 1944, GREENOCK. THE 84000 TON CUNARD LINER QUEEN MARY IN HER GREY WHITE WAR PAINT AS SHE PREPARED TO MAKE ANOTHER ATLANTIC CROSSING TAKING WOUNDED US TROOPS BACK TO AMERICA. (A 25913) Port bow view of the QUEEN MARY at anchor. Copyright: © IWM.

James Crawford Halley

Squadron Leader James Crawford Halley DSO of RAF 502 (Ulster) Squadron was the son of the late Mr and Mrs Halley, Hay Street, Perth. James Halley was educated at Perth Academy and on leaving joined the RAF. He was granted a short service commission and later transferred to the RAFC (Royal Air Force College) at RAF Cranwell.

From 27 January 1941, RAF 502 Squadron were based at RAF Limavady near Derry in Northern Ireland with a detachment at RAF St Eval in Cornwall. They were part of RAF Coastal Command flying patrols in the Atlantic. In January 1939, they were equipped with Avro Ansons and from October 1940, the squadron flew Armstrong Whitworth Whitleys Mk. V and later Mk.VII.

In January 1942, they were stationed at RAF Bircham Newton, Norfolk, with detachments at RAF Docking (just a few miles away), RAF St Eval and RAF Holmsley South in Hampshire. After D-Day, on 14 September 1944, the Squadron was moved to RAF Stornoway.

Halley completed two tours of operational duty. It was reported in the Perthshire Advertiser, 13 November 1943, that 'officially, he is stated to have set a fine example by his work in the air, in addition to his heavy responsibilities on the ground. The high morale and work of the squadron, whose leadership he assumed, bear testimony to his energy and personality'.

RAF 502 Squadron, on 30 November 1941, possibly became the first Coastal Command unit to make a successful attack on a U-Boat – U-206 – with air-to-surface radar in the Bay of Biscay. Later, it was argued that U-206 had been sunk by the minefield 'Beech', laid by the British in August 1940. The U-Boat attacked was probably U-71, which managed to escape.

Halley was the brother of Sub-Lieutenant Robert Halley of the Royal Navy whose wife stayed with her parents, Mr and Mrs Buchan, 47 Wilson Street, Perth. Halley was also the nephew of Group Captain Robert Halley, see First World War Aviators.

ROYAL AIR FORCE 1939-1945: COASTAL COMMAND (CH 7043) The second pilot of a No 502 Squadron Whitley VII gives his skipper a helpful push as they climb aboard their aircraft, at the start of an anti-submarine patrol, August 1942. The camera just visible poking out of the hole in the fuselage was used to record the effectiveness of U-boat attacks – a standard F24 camera was mounted vertically and fitted with a mirror to give it a rear-facing view. Copyright: © IWM. Original Source: http://www.iwm.org.uk/collections/item/object/205218962

William John Henderson

Pilot Officer (Under Training) William John Henderson was undergoing training at RAF No 2 Air Observer School at RAF Millom in Cumbria. On 10 January 1942, at 0420 hours, Avro Anson Mk.1 AX536 crashed soon after hitting an obstruction during take-off. It crashed into the sea and all on board were killed. The accident report stated that the cause was primarily due to lack of control during take-off which caused the aircraft to swing. The undercarriage wheel had struck the flare cover which in turn tilted or threw it into the air where it possibly hit the tail plane of the aircraft.

The Anson crew:

Warrant Officer Frank George Ernest Tizard DFM RAF (564418) pilot, age unknown

Pilot Officer William John Henderson, RAFVR (106867) 2nd pilot (under training), age 19

Sergeant Henry Lincoln Gibson RAAF (40467) observer, age 22

Sergeant Maurice Henry Wadham RAAF (407740) observer, age 29

Flight Sergeant Joseph Lyon Roberts RAF (55191) wireless operator/air gunner, age 20

Henderson was the eldest son of Robert and Florence M Henderson, 3 James Street, Perth. He was educated at Guildtown and Balhousie Boys School. He had been in the RAF for 18 months. Before joining, he was employed by James Scott Electricians, Princess Street, Perth.

Tizard and Roberts have no known grave and but commemorated on the Runnymede Memorial. William John Henderson is buried in Wellshill Cemetery, Perth. A lectern in his memory was presented to St Martin's Parish Church, near Scone, by the 8th Perthshire, St Martin's Church Boy Scouts.

NOTES: The school at Millom trained night bomber aircrew – they used 79 Anson Mk.1's, along with Boulton Paul Sidestrand III, Boulton Paul Overstrand, Westland Wallace II, Hawker Hind, Handley Page Harrow I, Fairy Battle I, Blackburn Botha I, Airspeed Oxford I, II, Westland Lysander III, TT III, TT IIIa, and a de Havilland DH60 Moth aircraft.

ROYAL AIR FORCE BOMBER COMMAND, 1942-1945. (HU 54488) Avro Anson Mark 1, DJ104 'XF-K', and Armstrong Whitworth Whitley Mark V, N1369 'UO-U', both of No. 19 Operational Training Unit, after a night flying accident at Kinloss, Morayshire, on 19 October 1943, during which the Anson pilot mistook the airfield controller's signal and landed on top of the Whitley as the latter was starting to take off. Neither crew was injured and, although the Whitley was... Copyright: © IWM

David Hodge

On the night of 2/3 August 1941, Bomber Command sent 80 bombers to Hamburg, 53 to Berlin and 50 to Kiel, alongside 25 other operations. Eleven bombers were lost that night.

David Hodge of RAF 104 Squadron was onboard Vickers Wellington W5580 (EP-K) when it was lost over the North Sea and ditched off the coast of the Isle of Sylt, Germany. Two of the crew managed to get in their dingy but died from exposure.

Pilot Officer Robert Hugh McGlashan RAFVR (103491) pilot, age 24

Sergeant David Gall Hodge RAFVR (1152494) 2nd pilot, age 20

Sergeant Arthur Ernest Simpkin RAFVR (957726) wireless operator, age 21

Flying Officer Peter Bernard Verver RAFVR (43380) observer, age unknown

Sergeant Earle John Stevenson RCAF (R/59110) air gunner, age 20

Sergeant Hugh Peter Stuart White RAFVR (1253786) position unknown, age 19

Hodge was the son of William and Davina Hodge, Craigie, Perth, and is commemorated at the Runnymede Memorial in Surrey.

McGlashan and Simpkin were in the dingy which washed up onshore on 10 August 1941. Verver's body washed up on 17 August 1941. They were buried in Sylt, and later re-interred in war graves at Kiel.

Hodge was also the observer on Vickers Wellington Mk. II, W5331 of RAF 104 Squadron on the earlier night of 14/15 July 1941. The aircraft and crew undertook an operational flight to bomb Hannover in Germany. Take off was from RAF Driffield, west of York. They took off at 2245 hours and successfully released their bombs over the target from a height of 7,500 feet. Approximately 30 miles south of Hamburg on the return journey, they were attacked by what they believed was a Heinkel He111 night fighter. Damage was caused to both the Wellington's turrets, a wing was struck which holed fuel tanks and that caused a main undercarriage leg to drop down.

Despite this, the crew were able to bring the aircraft back to the skies over Yorkshire. The pilot ordered the crew to bail–out at 5,000 feet when it was discovered that the undercarriage legs would not lock into position. Despite thinking that he was making a belly landing, the pilot managed to land the aircraft safely – at 0535 hours. It was later assessed that electrical sensing equipment for the landing gear was damaged, it was in fact locked down correctly.

Ernie 'Sherl-E' Holmes

Originally formed during the Great War, No. 35 Squadron RAF was an elite squadron within No. 8 (Pathfinder) Group RAF. Along with Nos 79, 98, 99, 234, and 264 Squadrons RAF, No. 35 Squadron RAF was known as 'Madras Presidency' as the funding for the squadrons came from the Madras Province, then an administrative subdivision of British India. Equipped with cutting-edge navigation aids and flares, the Pathfinders were charged with providing target marking ahead of (and during) bombing missions. Trained at RAF Perth in 1941, Flying Officer Ernie Holmes was a pilot with No. 35 Squadron RAF. He was shot down over Holland in May 1944.

At 10:47 hours, on Monday, 22 May 1944, Holmes's Avro Lancaster Mk III (ND762) lifted off from RAF Graveley, Cambridgeshire. It was equipped with state-of-the-art technology including Gee, Nav Aid Y (H2S – airborne ground-scanning radar system developed during the Second World War that remained in use until 1993), IFF (Identification, Friend or Foe), GPI (Ground Position Indicator), Fishpond (display unit) and Carpet, and carried 2 x LB TI (Target Indicator coloured sky marking flare) Green, 2 x TI Green, and 6 x 1,000-pound, 2 x 500 pound and 1 x 4,000-pound munitions. Its designated Pathfinder role was as a 'Visual Centrer' offering back-up targeting within the main bomber stream.

That night, 361 Lancaster's and 14 Mosquitos of 1, 3, 6 and 8 Groups, were carrying out the first large raid on Dortmund (and Brunswick) for over a year and the last until after D-Day. The route was to Flamborough, 5315N 0330E, 5307N 0445E, 5212N 0715E, Target, 5110N 0734E, 5100N 0625E, 5143N 0450E, Orfordness. The raid concentrated on the south-eastern residential districts of Dortmund.

Eighteen Avro Lancasters were lost on the Dortmund raid, about 5 per cent of the total bombing force including that piloted by Holmes. On board ND762 was an 8-man crew, which had flown many missions together, always in the spirit of the squadron's motto, 'Uno Animo Agimus' ('We Act with One Accord'):

- *Ernie 'Sherl-E' Holmes (22) – pilot.*

- *John Kennedy Stewart (33) – navigator.*

- *Derrick Ernest Coleman (19) – air bomber.*

- *Frank Joseph Tudor (21) – wireless operator.*

- *Albert William Cox, age 21- air gunner.*

- *Alistair Stuart McLaren (37) – air gunner (a former Metropolitan Police officer).*

- *John Robert Cursiter (20) – flight engineer.*

The standard Avro Lancaster Mk III 7-man crew was complemented by Flying Officer Harold Thomas Maskell (35) – reserve air bomber and wireless operator.

The Lancaster was homeward bound, flying at 16,000 feet, when it was engaged by a German night fighter. A brief attack ended at 01:29 hours when the Lancaster exploded, killing 5 of the crew members, throwing out 3 of the crew with their parachutes, all of whom reached the ground alive. The debris from the bomber fell between Middelbeers (Noord Brabant) and Vessem, 14 km west of the centre of Eindhoven in Holland killing the 5 other crew members.

Luftwaffe night fighter pilot, Oberleutnant Heinz-Wolfgang Schnaufer claimed that he shot down 4-engine ND762 3 km northwest of Eindhoven at 01:15 hours. Schnaufer, known as the 'Spook of St. Trond' after his unit's Belgian headquarters, became the most successful night fighter pilot of all time. In total, he claimed 121 shot down during the Second World War – most of his kills were RAF 4-engine bombers.

Holmes and Coleman initially evaded capture and aided by Dutch locals went underground. They were both captured in Antwerp on 17 June 1944, interrogated by the Gestapo and confined in a POW camp until the end of the war.

Warrant Officer Frank Tudor, the other survivor, collided with a tree during his descent suffering concussion and a broken leg, which necessitated urgent medical assistance. Tudor, whose DFM had been gazetted on 15 February 1944, received treatment at Oirschot. Subsequently, he surrendered to the police post in Middelbeers and thereafter was transferred (the same day) to the Feldgendarmerie (military police unit) in Eindhoven. From Eindhoven he was taken to the Luftwaffe hospital in Amsterdam where he was nursed until 31 May 1944 before being interned in a POW camp.

As the Allies and the Red Army advanced into Axis held territories, prisoners were force marched to other POW camps. In the bitter cold winter of 1944, Holmes and his fellow prisoners were made to walk hundreds of miles. In their 'Liberation Questionnaires', which were completed as part of the POW repatriation process at 106 Personnel Reception Centre (RAF Cosford) in 1945, Holmes and Coleman shared the following information:

- *E. Holmes/D. E. Colman*

- *Evaded – 22.5.1944 to 17.6.1944 – betrayed.*

- *Captured – Antwerp 17.6.1944.*

- *Imprisoned – Stalag Luft III, Sagan July 1944-January 1945.*

- *Imprisoned – Marlag und Milag Nord, Westertimke (Tarmstedt) February 1945-April 1945.*

- *Repatriated – May 1945.*

Commonwealth War Graves Commission records detail that the remains of Stewart, Maskell, Cox, McLaren, and Cursiter were concentrated (reinterred) at Eindhoven (Woensel) General Cemetery:

- *McLaren, Alistair Stuart – sergeant (1891777) – plot KK, grave 55.*

- *Cox, Albert William – flight sergeant (1314241) – plot KK, grave 56.*

- *Stewart, John Kennedy – flight lieutenant (129742) – plot KK, grave 57.*

- *Maskell, Harold Thomas – flying officer (139295)– plot KK, grave 58.*

- *Cursiter, John Robert – sergeant (1570690) plot KK, grave 70.*

During Flight Lieutenant Ernie 'Sherl-E' Holmes was training at RAF Perth, he met a local woman, Irene Spinks. The couple married at the West Church (today St Matthew's Church) in 1946. The early years of their married life were spent on various RAF bases. They returned to Perth in 1954 when Holmes became a flight instructor for the University of Glasgow Air Squadron, and later joined the air squadron of the University of St Andrews. Holmes left the RAF in 1962 to join Airwork Services at Scone Aerodrome as a civilian flight instructor, after which he and his wife moved to Nairobi, Kenya (and then Soroti, Uganda), where Holmes worked for East African Airways.

During this time, Holmes started having significant troubles with his vision and had to give up flying. On returning to Perth, he qualified as a social worker working, in the main, in HMP Perth. Irene became Registrar of the Aberdeen Angus Association. The platinum wedding anniversary couple moved into Kincarrathie House (residential care home), Perth, in 2016. Despite being registered as blind due to his deteriorating eyesight, a week after moving into the care home, Holmes was treated to a flight from Scone Aerodrome by Donal Foley, a former student.

NOTES:

Ernie was an Avro Lancaster pilot during WW2. Not just any pilot, he was one of the best, an elite Pathfinder in RAF 35 Squadron and he is immensely proud of that accomplishment. Pathfinders located and marked the targets with flares, guiding in the main bomber force. They were also later referred to as the "master bomber".

Ernie's nickname was "Sherl-E" (Sherlock Holmes), this was given to him as a compliment to his skill in finding the target.

Ernie's DFC (= Distinguished Flying Cross) was awarded to him the day before his last bombing mission in 1944.

Ernie was awarded, Membership as a Chevalier of the Légion d'Honneur, this was given on his 99th Birthday.

Stalag Luft III where he was a POW, is the same camp that had the earlier Great and the Wooden Horse Escapes. Sandy Gunn from Auchterarder was also there, (killed by the Gestapo after the Great Escape) and Bill Reid VC from Crieff was imprisoned there as well.

Sergeant Alistair Stuart McLaren, who was Ernie's Air Gunner on Avro Lancaster ND762 and killed that day in 1944, was born at 14 Robertson's Buildings, Perth (opposite the Police Station). Ernie visited the family I believe after the war.

After the war, Ernie became a flying instructor and miraculously survived two further aircraft crashes. (Ernie survived aircraft crashes every 10 years, in 1944, 1954 and 1964)

Ernie and his pupil Cadet Pilot J. Mustarde from Campbelltown "bailed out" by parachute of a Chipmunk aircraft on 23 September 1954. The aircraft crashed in a field near Errol. It came down with such force much of it was buried. An eyewitness and first on the scene, was a 29-year-old German dairyman, Wolfgang Kosanetzki, oddly, he was a former Luftwaffe pilot during WW2.

Ernie was the instructor on 24 June 1964 in a twin-engine Cessna 310, which crashed shortly after take-off from Scone. Two trainee Iraq pupils were on-board – Kamil Aljarrah and Rayadh al-Freeig. The aircraft skimmed over the airfield boundary fence and ploughed into a field containing prize bulls. Ernie was admitted to Bridge of Earn Hospital with severe burns to face and hand. His condition was said to be "only fair". The others "fairly comfortable".

Memorial for the crashed Lancaster ND762

James Harper Greig Horne

Flying Officer James (Jimmie) Harper Greig Horne was the eldest son of Peter Bathie and Bessie Crichton Horne, 18 Breadalbane Terrace, Perth. James who was 23 years old at the time of his death. James was brought up in Laurencekirk being adopted by his uncle and aunt, Mr David Stewart Dakers and Mrs Eliza Dakers. He was educated at Laurencekirk School and MacKie Academy, Stonehaven, and was employed by the North of Scotland Bank in the branch at Auchinblae for four years before joining the RAF. He was secretary of the Laurencekirk Golf Club and took a keen interest in all local sports. On joining the Services, he went to the US and Canada for training as a navigator.

Flying from RAF Wick, Bristol Beaufighter LZ289 of RCAF 404 (Buffalo) Squadron crashed during a fighter affiliation training exercise near Stemster House, south of Scrabster. On the morning of 17 November 1943, the Beaufighter was observed by a Spitfire from the AFDU (Air Fighter Development Unit) to go into a spin to the right at approximately 5,000 feet. It failed to recover and stuck the ground between a farmhouse and a barn.

The two occupants of LZ289:

Flying Officer Norman Earl Long RCAF (J/20615) Pilot, age 23

Flying Officer James Harper Greig Horne RAFVR (132715) Navigator, age 23

Horne is buried at Laurencekirk Main Cemetery. The funeral was attended by the largest cortege seen in the burgh for years. His coffin was carried to the graveside by men of the Home Guard and was proceeded by a piper playing, 'The Flowers of the Forest'. A party of the ATC formed a guard of honour at the cemetery gate. Flying Officer Long from Toronto was buried at Wick Cemetery.

RCAF 404 Squadron was formed at RAF Thorney Island on 15 April 1941 as a Coastal Command long-range fighter unit. Flying out RAF Castletown, Skitten, Dyce & Sumburgh, they provided cover for convoys, flew shipping reconnaissance missions, and sometimes intercepted Focke-Wulf FW 200 Condor aircraft flying out of Norway. After a spell at RAF Chivenor in North Devon, they returned to Scotland in April 1943, operating from RAF Tain and RAF Wick.

Long had over 400 hours flying time and about 85 hours on Beaufighters. The inquiry faulted his handling of the aircraft. The pilot of the Spitfire involved was a Flight Lieutenant Virgin from the AFDU Squadron. The AFDU developed operational tactics and tested captured enemy aircraft. The unit carried out tests and evaluations on fighter aircraft, modifications, and new equipment prior to it being used by the RAF.

Flying Officer James Harper Greig Horne, Perthshire Advertiser 20 November 1943 & Flying Officer James Harper Greig Horne receiving his navigator's "Wing" at an RAF training Centre in Canada. Perthshire Advertiser 28 November 1942

Edward Peter William Hutton

Wing Commander Edward Peter William Hutton, DFC, AFC, DSO (37178) was born in Perth in 1916, educated at Perth Academy, Dollar Academy, Ross's (Perth) Commercial School and resided with his grandmother Mrs J. McLaren, 14 Robertson's Buildings, Dunkeld Road. Edward Hutton was the son of the late Edward and Mrs Hutton of Cockfosters, London. Edward's late father worked in Iraq for twenty years.

Edward played rugby for Perth Academy Former Pupils and Dollar Academy in 1934 and 1935. Edward married Freda Stamper and they lived together in Girvan, Ayrshire and Sands Close, Braintree Road, Felsted, Essex, England.

Edward Hutton joined the RAFVR in 1935 as a commissioned officer. His promotions:

Acting Pilot Officer 7 May 1935

Flying Officer 16 November 1938

Flight Lieutenant 16 November 1939 – Gazetted 21 November 1939

Posted to RAF 75 Squadron from RAF 9 Squadron (Squadron Leader) 19 January 1940

RAF 75 Squadron ceased to exist at Harwell, now New Zealand Squadron and assume new name, RAF 75 (New Zealand) Squadron, 4 April 1940

Squadron Leader 01 December 1940 – Gazetted 10 December 1940

Wing Commander 01 March 1942 – Gazetted 27 March 1942

Squadron Commanding Officer RAF 221 Squadron, October 1942 to June 1943

As Wing Commander with RAF 221 Squadron, he carried out 35 operational missions, involving mine laying, anti-submarine patrols, attacks on shipping and bombing sorties in the Mediterranean theatre. In January 1943, he was responsible for illuminating the harbour at Candia (modern day Heraklion, Crete), lighting up the target for the following bombers. RAF 221 Squadron at this time were based at RAF Shallufa near the Suez Canal, Egypt, with detachments at RAF St. Jean, Palestine, and RAF Gianaclis (Jiyanklis), Alexandria, Egypt. They flew at this time Vickers Wellington Mk XI and XII aircraft.

In February 1943 during an anti-shipping mission with RAF 221 Squadron, he spotted a medium sized merchant vessel, escorted by a destroyer. Wing Commander Edward P. W. Hutton immediately attacked the merchant ship, hitting it from close range with a torpedo. For the above actions he was awarded the Distinguished Flying Cross (DFC), gazetted on 23 April 1943.

Wing Commander Hutton continued flying many sorties, attacking enemy shipping. In September of 1944 he is reported by the Chelmsford Chronicle as having penetrated the narrow strip of water between the Helder (Den Helder) mainland and the island of Texel, Netherlands in the face of violent fire from ships and shore batteries. Wing Commander Hutton fired his canon shells into two auxiliary ships. He then noticed another Bristol Beaufighter in trouble, black smoke poured from its starboard engine which had been hit by flak. But he said the pilot did not waver and went straight through a convoy with his guns blazing. Hutton went to the assistance of the damaged Beaufighter and escorted it back to the nearest base.

On 3 May 1945, Wing Commander Hutton lead his Bristol Beaufighter wing to attack German naval and merchant ships attempting to escape to Norway (Germany surrendered on 12 May 1945). Following up on reconnaissance reports from Coastal Command of large numbers of ships stretching north from Kiel through the Little and Great Belts of Denmark. The vessels caught in the stampede included fishing boats, U-Boats and a 10,000-ton passenger liner. The wing immediately took off from bases in England for Denmark, escorted by RAF North American P-51 Mustangs. The Bristol Beaufighter of Coastal Command aircraft were armed with cannon, machine guns, torpedoes, and rockets. The weather was perfect, they first attacked 4 coastal vessels south of Sprogø, Denmark. Hutton detached one section from each of his formation to attend to it. Next the whole wing dived on a stationery merchant vessel with a tank landing craft and two motor launches. Initial claims revealed that two vessels were probably sunk with 38 more burning fiercely, smoking or otherwise damaged. This was reported as the Beaufighter biggest strike, three Coastal Command aircraft were lost.

The next day the attacks by the Second Tactical Air Force of the RAF continued. The weather was not so good, but ten ships were sunk and 61 damaged in the first 400 sorties flown. On land some 1200 vehicles were destroyed or damaged.

Awards:

AFC (Air Force Cross) 17 March 1941

Notification Only London Gazette No. 35107, Dated 1941-03-17.

DFC (Distinguished Flying Cross) 23 April 1943

Wing Commander Edward Peter William HUTTON, A.F.C. (37178), No. 221 Squadron. This officer has completed 35 operational missions, involving anti-submarine patrols, mine laying operations, attacks on shipping and bombing sorties. In January 1943, in extremely bad weather, he piloted an aircraft detailed to illuminate the harbour at Candia, preparatory to a bombing attack. Whilst over the target area, his aircraft was severely damaged but, displaying great skill and determination, Wing Commander Hutton flew it back to base. One night in February 1943, he captained an aircraft detailed to search for shipping. In the course of the flight a medium sized merchant vessel, escorted by a destroyer, was sighted. Wing Commander Hutton immediately attacked the merchant ship, obtaining a hit with a torpedo from close range. The vessel sank. By his skilful leadership, great courage and determination, this officer has contributed materially to the fine fighting spirit of the squadron he commands. London Gazette No. 35989, Dated 1943-04-23.

DSO (Distinguished Service Order) 13 July 1945

Wing Commander Hutton has completed a very large number of sorties involving many attacks on enemy shipping. He has consistently displayed outstanding devotion to duty and throughout has Shown courage and enthusiasm of a high standard. His efficiency was amply demonstrated in May 1945 when he led a successful low-level attack against enemy shipping in the Baltic, much damage being inflicted on the enemy. Wing Commander Hutton has set a fine example of keenness, determination, and gallantry London Gazette No. 37175, Dated 1945-07-13.

NOTES: Edward Hutton's grandmother's Mrs J. McLaren, 14 Robertson's Buildings, Dunkeld Road, Perth had a son who lost his life on 22 May 1944 – RAFVR **Sergeant Alistair McLaren** (189177) was an air gunner on-board Avro Lancaster ND762, piloted by another Perth resident Ernie 'Sherl-E' Holmes DFC.

RAF Shallufa was one of many overseas RAF Stations that had a Malcom Club. Wing Commander Hugh Gordon Malcolm, VC (2 May 1917 – 4 December 1942) was from Broughty Ferry and educated at Glenalmond College. The RAF's Malcolm Clubs were named in his honour. These were welfare clubs for RAF personnel, which operated in several countries mostly between 1943 and the early 1970s.

An earthquake located off the northern coast of Crete on 12 October 1856 destroyed most of the over 3,600 homes in the city of Heraklion. Only 18 homes were left intact. The disaster claimed 538 victims.

During the period of direct occupation of the island by the Great Powers (1898–1908), Candia was in part of the British zone.

In July 1945, RAF 75 Squadron began to train to join the Tiger Force, also known as the Very Long-Range Bomber Force of UK Squadrons to be deployed to the Pacific Theatre. They were scheduled to be deployed to Okinawa ready for the invasion of Japan. The colour scheme for Tiger Force aircraft was white upper surfaces with black undersides; this scheme, developed to reflect sunlight and thus lower the internal temperatures in the tropical heat. Flight refuelling was to be undertaken, if necessary, by equipment developed by Flight Refuelling Ltd, founded by Alan Cobham. Cobham's air circus visited Perth in 1934, using the fields at the top of Necessity Brae.

As early as 1943, the Avro Lancaster aircraft's name appeared on a US list of aircraft that could potentially carry a nuclear bomb internally. The highly advanced Boing B-29 was introduced for operational use in May 1944 and experienced many initial issues which required modifications. At the end of 1943, although almost 100 B-29 aircraft had been delivered, only 15 were airworthy, 150 aircraft were modified in the five weeks between 10 March and 15 April 1944. The Boeing B29 Superfortress had two bomb bays, neither large enough for the nuclear bombs, Little Boy or Fat Man. The B29 (Enola Gay) used to bomb Hiroshima and Nagasaki had to have it bomb bays modified and reinforced to carry nuclear bombs. The Enola Gay was the first of 15 from the initial production of Silverplate B-29s specification. Otherwise, the Enola Gay could have carried the nuclear bomb externally or the task given over to the Avro Lancaster's of Tiger Force. The forward bomb bay and forward wing spar required modification to accommodate a single bomb that would weigh around 10,000 pounds. They adopted the British Type G single-point attachments and Type F releases that the British used on the Avro Lancaster bomber to carry the 12,000-pound Tallboy earthquake bomb. Overall, the changes made enabled the modified B-29 bomber to carry an atomic bomb while cruising at 260 mph, at 30,000 feet.

Odense is the main city on the Island of Funen which lies between the Little Belt and Great Belt in Denmark. Canute IV of Denmark who had designs on the English throne and was considered to be the last Viking king, was murdered in 1086 by unruly peasants in St. Albans Priory, Odense. He was the grandnephew of Canute the Great, also known as Cnut the Great, who ruled England, Denmark and Norway until 1035.

William Joyce aka Lord Haw-Haw ("Germany calling, Germany calling") and other British propaganda broadcasters who broadcast Nazi Propaganda during the war left in a convoy for Denmark on 2 May 1945. He got as far as Kupfermühle, near Flensburg, right on the border of Germany and Denmark. Joyce was eventually captured by British soldiers as he cut a birch tree outside a cottage, he went for something in his pocket and was shot in the thigh. He had in his pocket pages of a manuscript in which he said he would be glad when he was caught as the suspense was getting on his nerves, and, anyway, he loved England. Back in England he was tried for treason, found guilty and hanged in Wandsworth jail, London in January 1946. Hitler's successor Admiral Karl Donitz had also taken refuge in Flensburg just before his arrest on 23 May 1945 to the Allies. Donitz died in 1980 at the age of 89.

Perthshire Advertiser 22 March 1941 & Perthshire Advertiser 18 July 1945

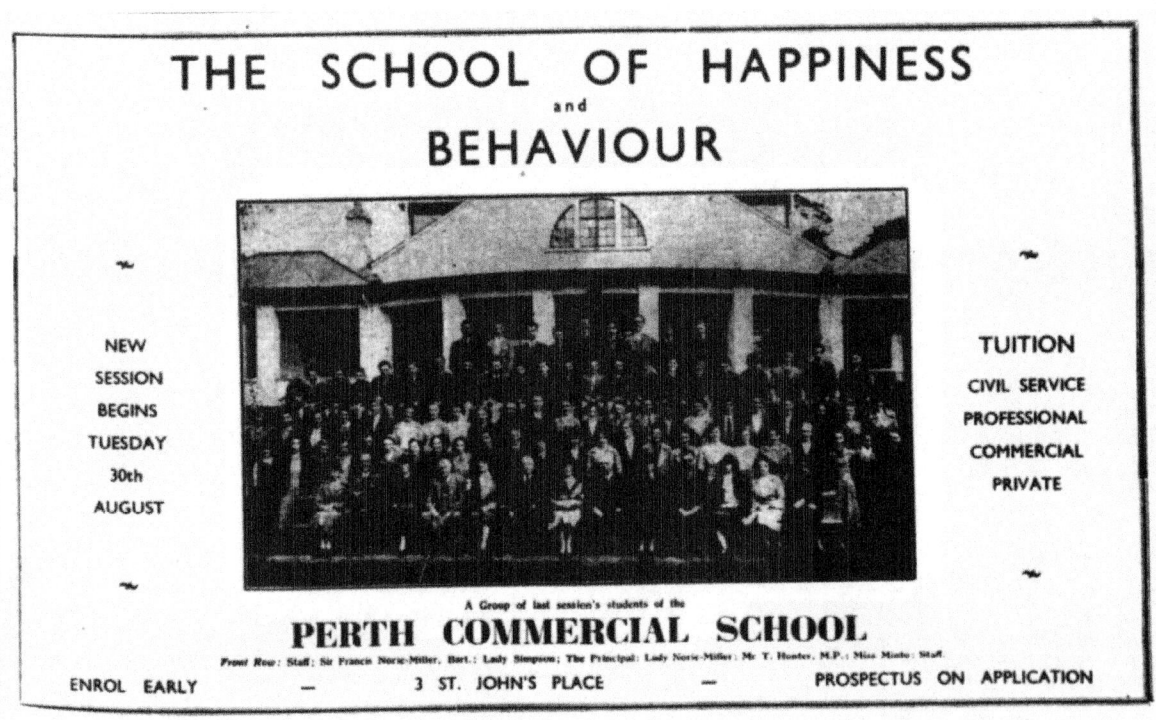

Perthshire Advertiser 13 August 1938 – (correction to advert address – the school was at 3 <u>South</u> St. John's Place)

Herome Alexander Innes

Flying Officer Herome Alexander Innes DFC, RAF 149 Squadron was the son of Colonel Sydney Armitage and Mrs (nee Blain) Innes, Fairmount, Barnhill, Perth. Herome was educated at Rugby and then joined the staff of the General Accident Fire and Life Assurance Corporation as a trainee at the Perth Head Office and the Cheltenham and Gloucester branches in England.

On 18 December 1939, Pilot Officer Herome Innes took part in the first named battle of the Second World War, The Battle of Heligoland Bight.

World War Two commenced on 1 September 1939 and the air campaign two days later. By January 1939, RAF 149 Squadron had been equipped with the new Vickers Wellington aircraft. The RAF mistakenly concluded from bombing raids during September, October, and November 1939 that German fighter aircraft were not a serious threat against modern bombers such as the Wellington.

A force of three RAF Squadrons totalling 24 Vickers Wellington bombers was launched on 18 December 1939 to attack German capital ships anchored in the Wilhelmshaven area. At the crew briefing the night before, it was said that there was a good chance of finding the German fleet in the Heligoland Bight.

Breakfast was at 4.30 am and the order to take off was given at 08.27 am. The weather was good, a fine day with a great deal of cloud. About ten miles from the German coast the cloud cleared, and the sun shown in a clear sky. Two Wellington's turned back due to engine issues before reaching German airspace. As they flew over Heligoland Bight they saw eight German Destroyers below, they were after bigger game.

The German reaction was slow, the first Messerschmitt Bf 109 came up to attack them over Wilhelmshaven which was met by a burst of fire and shot down. Flying at 18,000 feet in close formation they were met by a terrific barrage of anti-aircraft fire. As they were turning, they saw droves of enemy fighters coming up to meet them, at least 200 some thought, most were Messerschmitt Bf 110's. This was the start off a very confused and terrific air battle.

The battle started around midday and did not finish until after 1.00pm. They were attacked it is thought by 44 German fighter aircraft. Of the 22 Wellington's that made it to Wilhelmshaven, the Luftwaffe shot down 12 of them. (The Luftwaffe launched between 80 and 120 fighter aircraft to oppose this raid.)

Pilot Officer Herome Innes of RAF 149 Squadron was onboard Vickers Wellington, N2980, as second pilot. It took off from RAF Mildenhall at 09.27am for the Heligoland Bight. The full Wellington N2980 crew was, Squadron leader P L Harris, Pilot Officer H A Inness, Sergeant F H P Harris, AC2 G Watson, AC1 J J Mullineaux, and AC1 J A Doxsey.

Vickers Wellington N2980 was the lead aircraft in Formation 2, Section 1. Squadron Leader Harris and the overall leader of the attack, Wing Commander Richard Kellet were the only two with combat experience. They had orders to overfly the Heligoland Bight, attacking ships but avoiding civilian housing and merchant shipping.

On their return flight near Cromer Knoll, west of Skegness, they saw Wellington N2961 ditch in the sea. Herome's Wellington N2890 attempted to drop a dingy but this got fouled in the tail of their aircraft. They flew on with great difficulty and force landed at RAF Coltishall just north of Norwich. The Cromer lifeboat was launched but no survivors were found.

From the Operations Record Book of RAF 149 Squadron dated 18 December 1939:

Operation commenced with the take-off of nine Wellingtons led by Wing Commander R. Kellet AFC. No warships were in any of the naval anchorages, but at Wilhelmshaven, a pocket battleship (Deutschland?), a battle cruiser (Gneisenau?), the Tirpitz **ilding and a "K" class cruiser were seen lying in the inner basin. No bombs were therefore dropped. After Wilhelmshaven, the formation was attacked by a large number of fighters mostly Messerschmitt Me 109 and Me 110 – probably between 60 and 70 were involved. The ensuing battle lasted 40 minutes and proved to be the biggest to date in the history of the Royal Air Force. A number of enemy aircraft were claimed to have been shot down by the squadron. The squadron casualties were one aeroplane seen to go down in flames during action and one forced down in the sea on the return journey through petrol shortage due to the tanks being damaged in the fight.

Two others had been forced to turn back on the outward journey. Besides the fighter attacks, the enemy opposition included anti-aircraft from the land defences around Heligoland Bight but this fire, although heavy did not cause and casualties.

The failure of this raid led in part to the RAF abandoning daylight bombing missions and was one of the reasons which led the Luftwaffe to believe that Germany was invulnerable to enemy attack. At this time in the war the Netherlands and Belgium wished to remain neutral, they had refused the RAF permission to establish bases or to overfly their countries. The French had also refused to allow the RAF bombers to bomb German cities from French airfields, they were feeling secure behind the Maginot Line.

The military career of Herome Innes started as a Cadet Corporal with the Rugby School Contingent, then he joined the Territorial Army. On 2 June 1932, Herome was gazetted as being promoted to 2nd Lieutenant 6th/7th Black Watch (T.A.). On 24 October 1937 he was promoted to Acting Pilot Officer on probation becoming Pilot Officer on 23 August 1938. He was promoted to Flying Officer on 23 March 1940. Herome was gazetted on 20 February 1940 for his Distinguished Flying Cross obtained during the Battle of Heligoland Bight.

Pilot Officer Herome Alexander Innes was the captain of an aircraft carrying out reconnaissance duties and formation flying training on 27 March 1940. On 31 March 1940, He was piloting Wellington N2980, in formation with P9218 on a *'Special Sweep'* in the North Sea to a point roughly 60 miles west of Newcastle (possibly submarine spotting).

On 4 April 1940, two Vickers Wellington's from RAF 214 Squadron took off at 22.50 for night cross country flights to enable practice to be done using astronomical navigation. On their final flare path approach, the second aircraft to return at RAF Mildenhall, Vickers Type 416 Wellington Mark Ic, P9267 crashed one mile short of the runway, bursting into flames. Four members of the crew were instantly killed. Three of the crew were rescued from the crashed aircraft and were admitted to sick quarters in a serious condition, one later died just a few hours later from injuries sustained, AC2 L F Foster.

The Crew on 4 April 1940 of Vickers Wellington Ic P9267:

Flying Officer Herome Alexander Innes, 40227, age 27, Pilot, killed

Flying Officer Jack Patrick Majendie Hewitt, 39878, killed

Pilot Officer John Denton Hargreaves 77035, age 20, Air Gunner, killed

Sergeant Robert Melville Nelson 580853, age 22, Observer, killed

Aircraftman 2nd Class Leonard Frederick Foster, 630009, age 32, Wireless Operator, injured/killed

Flight Lieutenant John Martin Griffiths-Jones, 37734, Pilot

Acting Sergeant Harry Dean, 581276

Harry Dean was promoted to Warrant Officer and married in September 1942, Miss Margaret Kidd Powrie in the Trinity Church, Perth. Miss Margaret Kidd Powrie was the elder daughter of Mr. David M. Powrie, Rag and Metal Merchant, 5 Murray Street, a well-known businessman and Mrs Powrie, Davella, Burghmuir Road, Perth. Warrant Officer Dean was the only son of Mrs and Mrs Stephen dean, Dukes Brow, Blackburn, England. Harry Dean being one of the two that survived the crash became a member of the "Caterpillar Club", an informal association of people who have successfully used a parachute to bail out of a disabled aircraft.

Squadron Leader John Martin Griffiths-Jones DFC, RAF 7 Squadron was later killed on 3 March 1941. He was onboard Short Stirling I, N3653 which crashed in the English Channel, the cause unknown and his Stirling was the first of this four-engine bomber type to be lost on operations.

Sergeant Robert Melville Nelson was buried in Bathgate Cemetery, the others at West Row Baptist Chapelyard, Sussex, just south of RAF Mildenhall.

Major Berowald Innes, Herome's elder brother served as adjutant to the 6th Battalion of The Black Watch. His father Colonel Sydney Innes commanded the 9th Battalion, The Black Watch in the First World War during which he was awarded the Distinguished Service Award (DSO). Colonel Innes came out of retirement to take up an appointment at the Highland Area Headquarters at Perth. Colonel Innes previously had been the popular O.C. Depot. Miss Sylvia Innes, Herome's sister served as a mobile member of the Voluntary Aid Detachment engaged on nursing duties at Gleneagles Hotel.

NOTES: Five days later after Herome was killed, on 9 April 1940, Germany invaded Denmark and Norway.

Development of various aspects of the Vickers Wellington, such as the hydraulics and electrical systems, along with a revision of the ventral turret gun, led to the introduction of the Wellington Mk Ic. The Mark Ic also added waist guns and had a normal crew of six: pilot, radio operator, navigator/bomb aimer, observer/nose gunner, tail gunner, and waist gunner. A total of 2,685 of this type were built at Weybridge, Broughton in Flintshire and Blackpool.

Sergeant Gordon Downs Bushell (name is also recorded as George) in some sources as being in Herome's crash, he was not. Sergeant Gordon Downs Bushell, 745584 was age 24 years and a Hurricane Pilot. On 31 December 1940 he was killed whilst flying Hawker Hurricane P3267, RAF 213 (Ceylon) Squadron enroute from RAF Leconfield. Flying during a snowstorm with five other aircraft, P3267 made a violent turn to port and a short time later dived into the ground. Why it suddenly broke away was never understood, it was assumed that the pilot lost his bearings in the snow and flew into the ground.

During the last two weeks of March and the first two weeks of April 1941, the Wellington's and crew of RAF 149 Squadron were used for the making of the film *Target for Tonight*. It was filmed on location at RAF Mildenhall (using the fictitious name of Millerton Aerodrome).

PERTHSHIRE ADVERTISER 6 APRIL 1940

The Commanding Officer of No. 149 Squadron RAF talks to his aircrews in their Operations Room at Mildenhall, Suffolk, before they are briefed for the night's raid.

Wing Commander Richard Kellett, Commanding Officer of No. 149 Squadron RAF, seated at his desk at Mildenhall, Cambridgeshire. On 18 December 1939, Kellett led a force of 24 Vickers Wellingtons drawn from Nos. 9, 37 and 149 Squadrons to search for enemy shipping targets in the Schillig Roads off Wilhelmshaven, Germany. The Wellingtons were detected by a German radar station on Wangerooge Island while still on their approach flight and were subsequently intercepted by fighters. Nine Wellingtons were shot down, three ditched into the sea and a further three were forced to seek other landing grounds as they were too badly damaged to return. Kellett was one of those shot down and became a prisoner-of-war. In January 1940 (when this picture was released) he was awarded the Distinguished Flying Cross for his leadership during this disastrous raid which, together with that of 14 December, had a major effect on future British bombing policy.

Member of Caterpillar Club.

WARRANT Officer Harry Galloway Dean, R.A.F., who was married in Trinity Church, Perth, last week to Miss Margaret Kidd Powrie, elder daughter of Mr D. M. Powrie, well-known Perth business man, and of Mrs Powrie, Davelln, Burghmuir, is a member of the now famous "Caterpillar Club," membership of which is confined to airmen who have had to bale out on service. W. O. Dean, who is only son of Mr and Mrs Stephen Dean, Dukes Brow, Blackburn, was one of two survivors of the flying accident in which Pilot-Officer H. A. Innes, D.F.C., younger son of Col. S. A. Innes and Mrs Innes, Fairmount, lost his life in 1940.

WEDDING IN U.F. CHURCH of Miss Catherine Miller and L.A.C. Peter L. Greig, R.A.F., a city couple. Miss Christina Greig and L.A.C. M'Donald attended.

Sergeant Harry Dean of Vickers Wellington Ic P9267 married Miss Margaret Kidd Powrie, Burghmuir, Perth in Perth in September 1942 Perthshire Advertiser 12 September 1942

Join the R.A.F. or W.R.A.F.

IF you are a keen young man or woman desirous of highly specialised training while enjoying good pay, splendid living conditions, and an opportunity to travel overseas,

CONSULT THE R.A.F. INFORMATION BUREAU

Do not miss this unique opportunity of an interesting career in the Royal Air Force.

For further particulars apply to R.A.F. Recruiting Centre, 3 Atholl Place, Perth — Tel. 2560

Perthshire Advertiser 11 May 1949

Thomas Kaye

Sergeant Thomas Kaye RAFVR, (1051935), pilot, died age 22 in an accident at RAF North Coates, Lincolnshire on 31 August 1941. He was the pilot of Bristol Beaufort Mk. I AW213 of RAF 86 Squadron attached to Coastal Command. Kaye was killed when his Beaufort crashed into a parked Lockheed Hudson of RAF 407 Squadron during take-off.

In June 1941, RAF 86 squadron started to re-equip with the Bristol Beaufort Mark I. Initially, they performed mine-laying, reconnaissance, and air-sea rescue patrols but in October 1941, they undertook torpedo training, leading to torpedo bomber operations commencing on 11 November 1941.

Kaye was the son of Thomas and Helen Luna Kaye of Colintraive, 39 Queen Street, Craigie, Perth. He was educated at Perth Academy and went to St Andrews University. His studies were interrupted by the outbreak of war; he joined the RAF in June of 1940. Thomas Kaye is buried in Wellshill Cemetery, Perth.

ROYAL AIR FORCE COASTAL COMMAND, 1939-1945. (CH 7493) Three Bristol Beaufort Mark Is of No. 86 Squadron RAF Detachment based at St Eval, Cornwall, flying in formation over the sea... Copyright: © IWM.

Thomas Kennedy

On the night of 20/21 May 1940, Vickers Wellington Mk. Ic R3152 (KO-J) of RAF 115 squadron was lost on a combat tactical operation in support of the Allied armies in France, during an attack on the Meusse River Crossing at Dinant, Belguim, and German troop concentrations and transport about 100/150 km to the west in the Cambrai, Le Cateau-Cambrésis, Saint-Quentin triangle. Ten aircraft, five from each squadron flight took off at intervals. R3152 was the first away at 21.15 hours from RAF Marham, near King's Lynn, Norfolk.

The Germans invaded the Low Countries on 10 May 1940, the campaign plan, Fall Gelb (Case Yellow) had involved a decoy operation in The Netherlands and Belgium, with the main effort being made through the Ardennes, across the Meuse River, advance down to the Somme River valley, towards Amiens. The aim was to cut off the main French and British forces in the North of France.

The first French defeat was at the second Battle of Sedan, 12 to 15 May 1940, about 75 km south on Dinant. This led to another battle, the Battle of Arras on 21 May 1940, which was retaken by the Allies the following day. This delayed the Germans, which allowed more time for the evacuation of Allied troops at Dunkirk. The Dunkirk evacuation commenced on 26 May 1940 and lasted until 4 June 1940.

Vickers Wellington R3152 crashed near Le Havre (Seine-Maritime), France, on 21 May 1940; the crew all perished in the crash:

Pilot Officer Douglas William West Morris, RAF (41048), pilot, age 23

Sergeant Francis Williams, RAF (566298), 2nd pilot, age 24.

Sergeant Francis Alfred George Lowe, RAF (581516), observer, age 19

Leading Aircraftman Harold George Griffin, RAFVR (755893), wireless operator/air gunner, age 31

Aircraftman 2nd Class Thomas Kennedy, RAF (632947), wireless operator/air gunner, age 25

Aircraftman 2nd Class Allen Robinson, RAF (631370), wireless operator/air gunner, age 18

The crew are buried Cimetière Saint-Marie, Le Havre, France. Le Havre was one of the evacuation ports for the British Expeditionary Force in 1940. Unconfirmed reports suggest that Vickers Wellington R3152 was shot down by 'friendly fire' from a French anti-aircraft battery at (possibly), Octeville-sur-Mer, just to the north of Le Havre.

From the Operations Record Book of RAF 115 Squadron:

Ten of our aircraft, an equal number from No.38 Sqdn., and 12 from HOMINGTON with 12 250 lb. bombs D.A., attacked road targets in area – CAMBRAI – GUISE – HIRSON – ST. QUENTIN. Hits on enemy troops and concentrations obtained.

F/O GIBBES' aircraft was hit in front and rear turrets by A.A., and both gunners wounded, but not seriously, by shrapnel.

P/O MORRIS and F/S. MOORES did not return. The former received a first class bearing somewhere near LE HAVRE.

Thomas Kennedy was the second son of Harry and Winifred Kennedy, 18 Davie Park, Blairgowrie. He joined the RAF in 1937 as a wireless operator. In a letter sent to his mother a few days before he died, he stated that he expected to be home on leave for a few days that weekend. His father Harry served with the Scot's Guards in the Great War and his brothers Norman, Henry and William also served with the RAF. Flight Sergeant Henry Kennedy, the eldest son was awarded the DFM in 1941. He took part in many bombing raids over Germany. Henry was a slater by trade and learned to be a cinema operator in Quinn's Picture House in Blairgowrie. In 1936, he went to London to work as a cinema operator.

At the end of March 1939, RAF 115 squadron was re-equipped with Vickers Wellingtons. The first operation was to attack the German fleet off Norway on 8 October 1939, but no ships were sighted. The first successful raid was on 3 December 1939 when German shipping at Heligoland was bombed. Heligoland is a small archipelago in the North Sea, to the north of Bremerhaven. Until March 1940, the squadron undertook night-time 'Nickel' raids (dropping pamphlets). In April 1940, shortly after the German invasion of Norway they attacked the airfields at Stavanger/Sola.

AIRCRAFT OF THE ROYAL AIR FORCE 1939-1945: VICKERS WELLINGTON. (CH 16994) Wellington Mark III, X3662? KO-P?, of No. 115 Squadron RAF, at Marham, Norfolk. Copyright: © IWM.

William Knaggs

When Bill Knaggs retired at the age of 60, he moved to Stanley to spend the last 23 years of his life. Bill was shot down over Northern France in 1944, only one of two crew members of his Avro Lancaster bomber to survive; Knaggs not only survived the crash, but he also managed to reach safety with the help of the French Resistance.

Flight Sergeant William Knaggs was the bomb aimer on RAF 106 Squadron Avro Lancaster LL975 (ZN-H) on a mission to bomb a V-1 Rocket construction site at Pommeréval, south of Dieppe, France, on the night of 24/25 June 1944. The weather was fine and 17 aircraft from the squadron had been tasked to join over 700 aircraft attacking seven V-1 flying bomb sites. All aircraft were airborne by 22.23 hours and the good visibility allowed for accurate bombing from a height of 6,500 feet to 9,000 feet. Each aircraft dropped 18 500 lb bombs, two of which were Delayed Action fused.

Anti-aircraft flak was heavy, but no night fighters were seen, or so it was reported. From the bomber force, five Lancasters failed to return including LL975 which crashed in the target area.

A Messerschmitt BF 110 attacked and badly damaged LL975, the crew were ordered to bail-out, however, only Knaggs and Bill McPhail managed to escape.

Knaggs landed safely, despite having managed to get only but one arm in the straps of his parachute. He had a heavy landing but was safe, for the moment. His next move was to avoid being captured. For six nights and seven days, he headed towards Rouen where he thought he might find help, all the time distancing himself from any search party that might have found his discarded parachute.

Eventually, he was taken in by the French Resistance and found safe places to hide until the Allies, who had landed in Normandy on 6 June 1944, arrived. Troops arrived in Paris on 25 August 1944 and Bill met two Canadian officers the following morning in the village where he was being looked after.

Bill Knaggs' amazing story is told in full in a book, The Easy Trip, he wrote in 2001. It was published by Perth & Kinross Libraries, ISBN 0 905452 34 8.

The title of his book comes from the intelligence officer's assessment at his flight briefing, he advised *'little anti-aircraft fire anticipated in the target area and no night fighter opposition expected, adding that it would be a short, easy trip'*.

Bill Knaggs was born in Edinburgh and passed away in Perth Royal Infirmary on 21 January 2008 at the age of 85.

Note: Wing Commander Guy Penrose Gibson VC, DSO & Bar, DFC & Bar was commander of RAF 106 squadron at RAF Syerston, Nottinghamshire until he was posted 21 March 1943 to command the newly formed RAF 617 Squadron at RAF Scampton, better known as 'The Dambusters'.

John Laidlay

The only son of John Christopher and Maud Laidlay of Lindores, Fife and Perth, Pilot Officer John Laidlay RAFVR (79740) flew Bristol Blenheim's with RAF 254 Squadron. He attended Ardvreck School, Crieff and Malvern College, Worcestershire between 1930 and 1934, a public school where he was remembered in 1940: *'At school he was chiefly remarkable for his initiative and spirit of adventure, an ideal temperament for a Pilot Officer.'* (Malvernian, December 1940).

Laidlay was a member of RAF 254 Squadron. The squadron was reformed as a coastal fighter unit part of Coastal Command on 30 October 1939 at RAF Stradishall in Suffolk. The squadron moved to RAF Haston in the Orkneys on 24 April 1940 and then to RAF Sumburgh in the Shetlands on 16 May 1940. Sumburgh aerodrome was a grass field and tents and marquees. On 2 August 1940, they were on the move again, this time to RAF Dyce. The squadron was part of Coastal Command patrolling the North Sea on reconnaissance and convoy escort missions. They were equipped with Bristol Blenheim IV light bomber aircraft.

On Tuesday 3 September 1940 at 3 pm whilst practising attacks, Laidlay's aircraft, Bristol Blenheim Mk IV N3608 collided with Blenheim N3529 in the air at approximately 2,000-3,000 ft. It caught fire and ploughed into the ground. The main part of the fuselage with the engines were buried eight feet deep in ground eight miles north of RAF Dyce near Udny. Blenheim N3529 came down about a mile to the northwest at Cauldhame. The pilots were recent arrivals at the squadron and were being trained for operation duties. They had previously carried out attacks both singly and in formation.

There was according to eyewitness accounts no attempts to escape either aircraft by parachute; the wing tip fell off one aircraft and the other aircraft caught fire. Both aircraft burnt out with all the occupants killed:

Blenheim N3608

Pilot Officer John Reginald Laidlay, RAFVR (79740), pilot, age 23

Sergeant Ronald John Whiffen, RAFVR (747997), wireless operator/air gunner, age unknown

Aircraftman 1st Class Donald Campbell, RAF (638834), age 30

Blenheim N3259

Flight Sergeant Robert Charles Hanna, RAF (AAF) (816023), pilot, age 23

Aircraftman 2nd Class Joseph Edward Mangion, RAFVR (948167), age 21

Laidley had 261.5 hours flying time in a Blenheim, Hanna had 202.15 hours.

John Laidlay was a young laird, the heir of Lindores House and is buried in Abdie Old Churchyard near Grange of Lindores. Whiffen was from Bournemouth and Aircraftman Campbell was from Glasgow. Hanna was from Belfast and Aircraftman Joseph Mangion was from Malta. He was the son of Lorenzo and Carmela Mangion, of Pawla, Malta. The inscription on his war grave reads:

'Of Malta. Only Son of L. and C. Mangion who left his dear island to fight for the empire'.

NOTES: Bristol Blenheim N3608 was one of 100 delivered to the RAF from the manufacturer, A V Roe at Chadderton, Lancashire between March and June 1940 under Contract No 774679/38.

Four aircraft from RAF 254 Squadron were dispatched to RAF Detling in Kent on 28 May 1940 to operate on sea patrols covering the Dunkirk evacuation.

RAF Dyce is now Aberdeen airport.

Perthshire Advertiser 7 September 1940

David Maxwell Laing

On Monday, 6 April 1942, Sergeant David Laing took off for a mission to Essen in Germany from RAF Grimsby. Also known by locals as RAF Waltham or Waltham Grange Aerodrome, RAF Grimsby was built in the early 1930s. The airfield re-opened as RAF Grimsby in late 1941. RAF 142 Squadron soon arrived from RAF Binbrook, which was temporarily closed for the concreting of its runways.

Laing's aircraft was Vickers Wellington Mk IV, Z1205, code QT-W of RAF 142 squadron. It had departed on its mission at 00:14 hours, Tuesday, 7 April 1942. The aircraft was reported as being shot down by flak near the Hauptbahnhof (Train Station) in Köln, which is way too far south of their route to Essen. It is possible that this was another Wellington X3489 of RAF 75 Squadron which was lost the previous night. It is therefore not certain exactly where Z1205 was lost.

The crew are buried at the Rheinburg War Cemetery (Britischer Ehrenfriedhof) at Kamp-Lintfort in Germany, north-west of Duisburg.

Flight Sergeant George Henry Mays, RAFVR (963891), pilot, age 34

Sergeant Lawrence Ernest Taylor, RAFVR (1181905), pilot, age 20

Flight Sergeant Victor Reginald Dufton, RAFVR (920226), observer, age 24

Sergeant David Maxwell Laing, RAFVR (1003165), wireless operator/air gunner, age 23

Sergeant Francis Geoffrey Huntley, RAFVR (1165241), wireless operator/air gunner, age 21

Laing was the son of Thomas and Mary Maxwell Laing of 56 Darnhall Drive, Perth. In civilian life, Laing was a compositor employed by D Leslie Printers, Canal Street, Perth. He was a member of Pullar's Swimming Club and after finishing his apprenticeship joined the RAF (in 1940).

Prior to his death, Laing had been on 23 operational missions over enemy territory. He was due to be taken off flying duties for a short time after his last flight. One week before he was reported missing, he had been on leave at home.

Note: The British Cemetery of Honour, the Rheinburg War Cemetery is the largest Commonwealth war cemetery in Germany with 7,654 graves.

Alexander Little

Sergeant Alexander Little was the pilot of Armstrong Whitley V EB389 from RAF 24 OUT at RAF Honeybourne, between Redditch and Cheltenham in Worcestershire, England. RAF 24 Operational Training Unit was formed there on 15 March 1942 as part of RAF 7 Group Bomber Command to train night bomber crews using Armstrong Whitley's. During 1942, the unit carried out three normal bomber command operational sorties.

On the night of 2/3 January 1943, the aircraft and crew took off for a high-level bombing training sortie. It is believed that a Photoflash Flare exploded prematurely leading to a catastrophic crash at 00.05 hours. The aircraft came down near Cherington, three miles SSE of Shipstone-on-Stour, Warwickshire.

The crew on board Armstrong Whitley EB389:

Sergeant Alexander Little RAFVR (1365959) pilot, age 25

Pilot Officer Richard Patrick Mason RAFVR (129350) navigator, age 34

Sergeant John Davidson RAFVR (1369345) wireless operator/air gunner, age 32

Sergeant Kenneth John Fielding RAFVR (1332345) air gunner, age 19

Sergeant Douglas Bell RAFVR (1432116) air bomber, age 20

Little was born in Lanark and educated at Clunie School, Blairgowrie High School and then went to Edinburgh University where he graduated BSc in Agriculture in the summer of 1940. Alexander played for the Blairgowrie High School football team and was twice runner-up in the boys' sports championship.

In July 1940, whilst he was temporarily employed by the Department of Agriculture, Alexander Little received the King's commendation for his bravery in rescuing the pilot of an aircraft that had crashed on a farm where he was working. He received a letter from the Air Ministry, dated 27th February 1941:

'I am commanded by the Air Council to inform you that His majesty the King has been graciously pleased to approve the award to you of a commendation, in recognition of your brave conduct in rescuing the pilot of a Royal Air Force aircraft which crashed on July 20th, 1940. "The Air Council wish me to convey to you their warm congratulations on this mark of His Majesty's pleasure. "The award will be announced in a supplement of the London Gazette to be published on the evening of February 28th, 1941.'

During the summer of 1940, it was announced that he had won a Stevens Scholarship in Agriculture. Sergeant Alexander Little joined the RAF in October 1940 and was sent off to the United States to get his 'wings'.

Little was the youngest son of William and Nellie Little, Craigie, Clunie. He was buried on 9 January 1943 at Clunie Churchyard where he was a Sunday school teacher before joining up. Every home in the central Stormont area was represented in addition to mourners from Blairgowrie, Dunkeld and Birnam.

Note: A Photoflash device was dropped along with the bombs and would activate at a variable time-setting, based on the bombing height. A vertically mounted camera on the aircraft would expose the film for up to eight seconds to allow for the correct timing of the flash illuminating the appropriate bombing area. On the aircrafts return, this film was interpreted, and the results of the raid was plotted and analysed.

WITH A WHITLEY SQUADRON OF THE BOMBER COMMAND (CH 689) Original wartime caption: [For story see CH.674] A hangar filled with Whitley Is undergoing overhaul. Copyright: © IWM.

John Littlejohn

Member for three years of the Third Ward, Perth Town Council, Councillor John (Jack) Littlejohn was a pilot officer with the RAFVR. Littlejohn served in the First World War at the age of 18 with the Royal Flying Corp. At the outbreak of Second World War, he was granted a leave of absence from the council to take up his commission in the RAF.

Littlejohn was an airman of wide experience, a member of the Scottish Gliding Club and one of the first members of the Strathtay Aero Club. He was 41 years of age, married with two children and resided at 6 Charlotte Street, Perth. He was in business in Perth as a tea merchant. Littlejohn had worked in India for some years as a tea-planter.

In the operational record books for RAF 37 Squadron, in the 'Summary of Events' throughout the month of September 1940, several squadron Wellington aircraft were on standby in case of invasion. Operation Sea Lion (Unternehmen Seelöwe) was the German plan for the invasion of Britain. Hitler indefinitely postponed the German invasion on 17 September 1940 after the Battle of Britain. The entry for 16 September 1940 states:

Perthshire Advertiser 2 October 1940

Stand By, 8 aircraft stood by at 3 hours during the day and night on September 9th, 1940, also 2 aircraft stood by during the same period at 5 hours' notice for the attack of a possible sea borne invasion force.

On the night of Sunday 29 September 1940 Vickers Wellington Mk. Ic, R3150 took off from RAF Feltwell in Norfolk, England. It was one of 11 Vickers Wellingtons from RAF 37 Squadron on an operation to bomb targets in Germany and The Netherlands.

> 8 aircraft were assigned to Primary Target, L86 Aluminium Works at Bitterfeld, north of Leipzig, Secondary Target, Z29 Fokker Works, Amsterdam.
>
> 1 aircraft was assigned to Primary Target, M.480 Marshalling Yard at Erhang (probably Ehrang/Quint (Trier)). Secondary Target 60 Z40 2,000 yards.
>
> 1 aircraft was assigned to Primary Target, M431 Marshalling Yard at Osnabrück, Secondary Target, Z29 Fokker Works, Amsterdam.
>
> 1 aircraft was assigned to Primary Target M482 Marshalling Yard at Mannheim, Secondary Target, M469 Marshalling Yard at Coblenz.

As a last resort, the aircraft could target SEMO (self-evident military objectives) or MOPA (military objectives previously attacked).

On the outward journey, aircraft attacking L86 were ordering to cross the coast at Lowestoft, those attacking M480 and M482 at Ordford Ness and the aircraft attacking M482, at Yarmouth. Around Liepzig and in the vicinity of Bitterfeld, 9/10-10/10 cloud made identification of the target impossible. Heavy clouds in the vicinity of Erhang, Mannheim and Osnabrück prevented location of these targets.

Of the eight aircraft ordered to attack the Aluminium Factory at Bitterfeld one, owing to engine trouble, was forced to attack the alternative target, the Fokker Works at Amsterdam. Despite dropping four flares, they were unable to identify their target at Bitterfeld. On the return journey, an attack was observed on a highly explosive target. A further attack was therefore carried out from 10,000 feet, which caused an addition of two fires. Explosions from the previous attacks were very violent and were observed still taking place for a considerable time after the aircraft had left the target. It is estimated that the position of the objective was ten miles southwest of Magdeburg.

Another aircraft on its return journey bombed Hamelin aerodrome and an adjacent railway. Bombs were seen to straddle the target and caused heavy explosions. Another aircraft returning saw a flare path five miles east of the Dümmer See. An attack was carried out from 10,000 feet, the stick of bombs falling across the flare path causing large fires. Another attacked the Fokker Works at Amsterdam from 8,000 feet. Bursts were observed in the southern position of the target area causing several fires, which were visible for a considerable distance. One Wellington bombed an unidentified aerodrome from 12,000 feet causing three large fires. Lastly, another Wellington observed flying taking place at Aschersleben. An attack was carried out from 5,000 feet which caused three big explosions and fires.

Varying amounts of heavy and moderate flak were encountered by crews over targets. Searchlight activity appeared to be rather more intense than usual, which it is thought indicates that fighter patrols were active. This was borne out by the fact that red lights were fired from the ground into the path of approaching aircraft. Searchlights then opened–up on the position of these lights.

Vickers Wellington Mk. Ic, R3150 failed to return from this operation. Several other crews reported having seen an aircraft shot down in flames in the vicinity of Osnabrück. Wellington Mk. Ic, R3150 crashed at Malgarten, north of Bramsche, Germany.

On board the aircraft were:

Flying Officer Arthur Collins Dingle RAFVR (72148), pilot, age 30

Pilot Officer Gerald Percy Turner RAFVR (79576), observer, age 24

Sergeant George Henry Taylor RAF (644896), wireless operator/air gunner, age 21

Sergeant Peter Archibald Young RAF (650682), wireless operator/air gunner, age 19

Pilot Officer John Littlejohn RAFVR (79207) air gunner, age 41

The crew initially were buried in the Epe/Malgarten Cemetery (northeast of Bramsche); later, they were reinterred and buried in the Reichswald Forest War Cemetery.

NOTES: The first night of the London Blitz was 7 September 1940. Some 348 German bombers escorted by 617 fighters pounded London until 6.00 am. A second group attacked two hours later guided by the fires lit by incendiary bombs. The Blitz lasted 79 days, eight days later, Britain was considering celebrating the winning of the Battle of Britain. The Battle of Britain day is celebrated annually on 15 September, that day the RAF shot down 56 German aircraft in what was an overwhelming and decisive defeat for the Luftwaffe. On 10 September 1940, considering the destruction and terror inflicted on civilians by the German bombing, the British War Cabinet instructed British bombers to drop their bombs 'anywhere' if unable to reach their targets.

RAF BOMBER COMMAND (CH 469) Vickers Wellington Mk IA, L7779, 'LF-P' of No. No. 37 Squadron in flight, June 1940. Copyright: © IWM.

Ian Neil MacDougall & David Ormond MacDougall

Both Ian and David were born 1920 Georgetown British Guiana, and both attended Morrisons Academy, Crieff.

Pilots who had not completed their courses at RAF Cranwell were enlisted in the regular RAF as airmen under training. Ian MacDougall passed out on 21 October 1939 with a permanent commission and was posted to RAF 141 Squadron, which was reforming at RAF Turnhouse.

His squadron moved to RAF West Malling, near Maidstone, Kent, on 12 July 1940. On 19 July 1940, 12 Bolton Paul Defiants from the squadron were moved forward to RAF Hawkinge and at 12.23 hours they took off on an offensive patrol 20 miles south of Folkestone. Three aircraft did not take off due to engine trouble.

The nine remaining Defiants were attacked by Messerschmitt BF 109s of Luftwaffe Gruppe III, Jadgeschwader 51. Ian MacDougall's Defiant L6983 was hit in the engine. He ordered Sergeant J F Wise, his turret air gunner to bail-out, then managed to get the aircraft back to West Malling. Wise did not survive.

Ian MacDougall was posted to RAF 260 Squadron (Hurricanes) at RAF Drem on 2 May 1941 and they left for the Middle East, later that month. They were based at Haifa with detachments at Beirut (Lebanon) and El Bassa (Palestine), moving on to bases such as Sidi Rezegh (near Tobruk), Gazala (west of Tobruk), Msus (south-east of Benghazi), Antelat (south of Benghazi), Benina (east of Benghazi), Martuba (south of Derna). He was promoted to flight commander at the end of 1941. On 5 April 1942, he had a share in the destruction of a Junkers JU88 and was awarded the DFC on 15 May 1942.

'This officer has been engaged in operational flying since October 1939 and took part in numerous sorties by day and night whilst operating from this country. In the Middle East, he has performed much valuable work leading his flight with great skill and zeal on low-level machine-gunning attacks. Throughout he has displayed tremendous keenness and set a high standard.'

Ian commanded RAF 94 Squadron in the Western Desert from February to May 1942 (Hawker Hurricane's and Curtiss P-40s) then returned to Britain. His next posting was to Malta in May 1943 where he joined RAF 1435 Squadron, equipped with Spitfires. In June 1943, he was given command of RAF 94 Squadron at RAF Kendri (Malta). Flying a Spitfire on 8 July 1943, he damaged a Messerschmitt BF109 and on 20 August 1943, he shared in the destruction of a Cant Z.506 Airone triple-engine floatplane of the Italian Regia Aeronautica. In January 1944, he returned to Britain and commanded RAF 131 Squadron from May to October 1944. Ian stayed in the RAF after the war becoming Chief Flying Instructor at RAF Cranwell and a War Studies lecturer at the USAF Academy in Colorado. In 1965, he was Chief Air Staff Officer at RAF 38 Group and went on to be Air Defence Commander in Zambia. He was made CBE in 1967 and was Air Attaché in Paris until retiring on 27 December 1969 as Air Commodore. He passed away in August 1987.

A fortnight before Ian's DFC, David his older brother was awarded an immediate DFC for the part he played in the offensive operations from the island of Malta. Since October of 1941, Pilot Officer David MacDougall, RAF 355 Squadron, flew hundreds of hours on night operations. Many were undertaken in severe weather – he distinguished himself on a night operation during February 1942 where he obtained three hits on an enemy convoy of cruisers and destroyers. This may have been the attack on the night of 15/16 February 1942: from RAF Hal Far on Malta, five Fairey Albacore single-engine biplane torpedo bombers of RAF 828 squadron attacked an enemy force of four cruisers and eight destroyers – hits were observed on two cruisers and one destroyer.

David joined the RAF in 1940 and was gazetted on 30 March 1945 as acting Squadron Leader of RAF 355 Squadron. From 18 August 1943 until they disbanded 31 May 1946, the squadron was equipped with Consolidated Liberator III, VI and VIII long-range four-engine bomber aircraft. They carried out operations against the Japanese during the Burma Campaign flying out of RAF Salbini (Bengal), RAF Digri (Bengal) and RAF Pegu (Burma). The squadron mounted numerous raids on the Burma–Siam railway along with other important targets such as bridges, airfields, port facilities, supply dumps, gun positions, and marshalling yards.

Ian and David were the sons of Councillor Archibald and Mrs MacDougall, Barima Villa, Cawdor Crescent, Dunblane (a reference stated that David was from Taynuilt, Argyll.)

NOTES: Luftwaffe JG51 was commanded by Theodor 'Theo' Osterkamp. The unit lost 68 pilots during the Battle of Britain. Osterkamp was a First World War fighter ace, holder of the Pour le Mérite (Blue Max), with 32 victories achieved; he scored a further six victories during the second World War. He survived the war and died in 1975.

The Curtiss P-40 Warhawk was known as the Kittyhawk in RAF service.

On the island of Malta, on the night of 15/16 February 1942 during 20 hours of constant air raids, one bomb from a Junkers JU88 hit a cinema and killed 15 civilians and 26 servicemen, with at least 29 others wounded. A total of 30,000 buildings suffered destruction or damage during the siege. During 1941 and 1942, there were 3,000 air raids, making Malta the most bombed location in the whole theatre of war. The George Cross was awarded to the island of Malta by King George VI on 15 April 1942.

ROYAL AIR FORCE OPERATIONS IN THE MIDDLE EAST AND NORTH AFRICA, 1939-1943. (ME(RAF) 7299) Curtiss Kittyhawk Mark IIIs of No. 260 Squadron RAF, lined up at Marble Arch landing ground, Libya. HS-X in the foreground was the personal aircraft of the squadron commander, Squadron Leader O V? Pedro? Hanbury: at this time, it retained its US serial number 42-45798. FR350? HS-B? was flown by Flight Lieutenant J F Edwards RCAF, the most successful Kittyhawk pilot in the Western Desert... Copyright: © IWM.

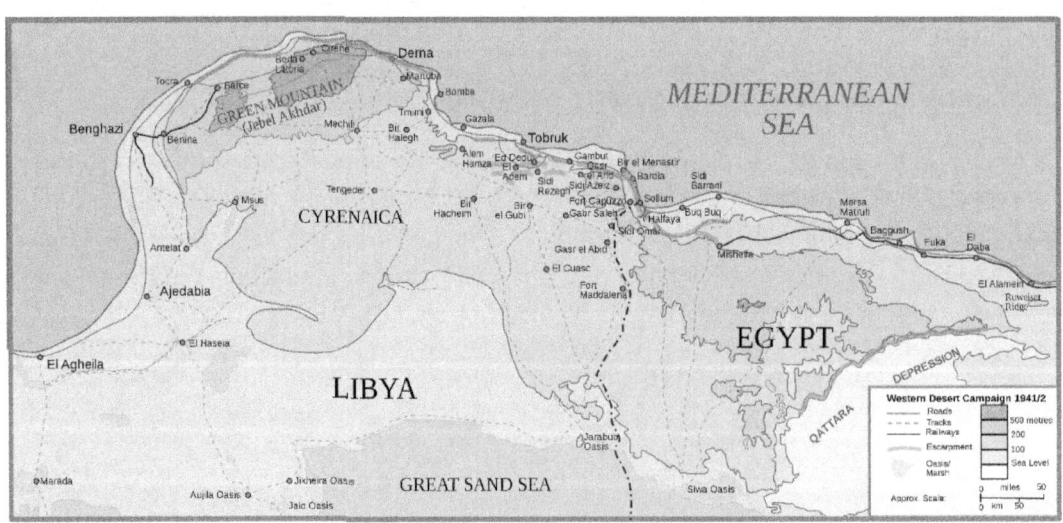

This image/file is licensed under the Creative Commons Attribution-Share Alike 3.0 Unported, 2.5 Generic, 2.0 Generic and 1.0 Generic license. Free to share – to copy, distribute and transmit the work. Author Stephen Kirrage 14 October 2007.

Charles MacFarlane

Sergeant Charles MacFarlane DFM was the only son of the MacFarlane's, 27 Campbells Buildings, Dunkeld Road, Perth. He was educated at the Northern District School and worked as a waiter at the Salutation Hotel in Perth. MacFarlane joined the RAF in 1940 at the age of 20.

On the night of the 12/13 May 1943 Handley Page HP 59 Halifax II DT776 from RAF 10 Squadron took off at 2329 hours from RAF Melbourne, southwest of Plockloington in Yorkshire to bomb Duisburg in Germany. One of the four engines became unserviceable en route, some height was lost but they flew on. At 0207 hours and at 17,000 feet, they bombed the target. While still over the target area, the aircraft was slightly damaged (close to the bomb doors) by a burst from a flak gun.

The crew managed to fly the aircraft safely back and landed at the nearest airfield at 0435 hours, despite it rapidly losing height as the English coast was crossed.

PERTHSHIRE ADVERTISER 17 NOVEMBER 1943

Flight Sergeant Gordon Roger Hewlett RNZAF (NZ415847) – pilot

Sergeant D McClelland RAFVR – navigator

Sergeant Kenneth Hamilton Dempster RAFVR (1451840) – bomb aimer

Pilot Officer Leslie Victor Williams RAFVR (126738) – wireless operator/air gunner

Sergeant Ronald Stanley Minnett RAFVR (1702041) – air gunner

Sergeant Tom Leonard Thackeray RAF (648457) – flight engineer

Sergeant Charles MacFarlane RAFVR (993788) – air gunner

Sergeant Frederick John Hands Heathfield RAFVR (1235550) – 2nd pilot

Many of the crew were later awarded Distinguished Flying Cross or Distinguished Flying Medal for service with RAF 10 Squadron. MacFarlane was mentioned in the Supplement to the London Gazette on 16 November 1943 as having been awarded the DFM. He was officially described as an *'outstanding air gunner'*.

NOTES:

Handley Page Halifax DT776 was in service with RAF 466 Squadron from September 1943. It was later damaged beyond repair on the night of 29/30 November 1943. A crew from 1658 Heavy Conversion Unit (HCU) were carrying out basic night circuits and landings exercises at RAF Riccall in Yorkshire. The aircraft flew a circuit and five minutes after taking off at 2301 hours, upon landing, possibly a tyre burst. They swung off the runway and an undercarriage collapsed. The crew were unharmed.

In total at five factories, 6,176 Halifax's were built during the Second World War. During 1939, English Electric constructed a 'shadow factory' and a new airfield at Samlesbury, near Blackburn, Lancashire. From 1940 onwards, a total of 2,145 Halifax's (including DT776) was built by English Electric with a peak delivery rate of 81 aircraft a month (achieved in February 1944).

This image is probably of some of the Hewlett crew standing on the wing of Halifax HR691. Taken in September 1943. This work created by the United Kingdom Government is in the public domain. UK Copyright contended to have lapsed 50 years after publication.

Left to right: Pilot: G. Hewlett NZAF, Nav: G. McClelland RAFVR, MU: R. Minnett RAFVR, W/OP: L. Williams RAFVR, B/A: J. R. Hulley RAFVR, FE: T. Thackray RAFVR, RG: C. MacFarlane RAFVR

John George Mackay

John George Mackay was the first pilot of the Civil Air Guard at Newlands (Scone) Aerodrome to fly solo. He received his commission on Christmas Day 1939 and was posted to France to join RAF 26 Squadron. The squadron had been equipped with Westland Lysander Mk III aircraft in February 1939.

RAF 26 Squadron moved off from RAF Catterick at 0545 hours to the port of embarkation for France on 25 September 1939 to join the British Expeditionary Force (BEF). Early breakfast was provided for the road party at 0500 hours and halts for short periods were made every three hours, with an average speed to be maintained of 15 mph.

From 3 October 1939, they were stationed at Abbeville. Mackay was listed as being the orderly officer at Abbeville on 12 April 1940. On 4 May 1940, Mackay is noted as reporting for operational duty with the squadron at Dieppe, France. On 6 May 1940, he was flying in the observer/gunner position along with Pilot Officer MacPhail in Lysander N1275 doing circuits of the airfield for 40 minutes. The next day with Halliday in the cockpit of Lysander N1290 they took off at 1005 hours and returned at 1235 hours providing anti-aircraft cooperation.

Perthshire Advertiser, 27 January 1941

On 8 May 1940, along with Pilot Officer Smith in Lysander L6854, he flew in a contact patrol from 1650 hours to 1825 hours. He was not flying on 9 May 1940 but on 10 May 1940, the day the Germans invaded the Netherlands and the Low Countries he was on Standing Patrol from 1430 hours to 1600 hours along with Pilot Officer Dixon in Lysander L4777.

On 12 May 1940, along with Pilot Officer Wheller in Lysander N1275, the duty was to fly to Arras and return. On 17 May 1940, in Lysander N1275 with Flight Lieutenant Hill they took off at 1130 hours on a bombing operation, returning at 11.50 hours. They were back in the air at 1455 hours until hours reconnoitring the situation. In the early hours of 19 May 1940 at 0430 hours, Halliday and LAC Church failed to return. At 1410 hours to 1530, Mackay with Hill were tasked with another reconnoitring mission.

On 20 May, the first batch of squadron aircraft was flown back to England, to Hawkinge, Blixbourne, Lympne and Canterbury. Mackay along with Hill left for Hawkinge in Lysander N1253 on 26 May 1940. Lysanders N1243 and L6863 did not make it and were reported missing the following day.

From 27 May 1940, flying from Hawkinge and Lympne, the squadron undertook bombing reconnaissance, and supply operations over the Dunkirk pocket. Hill and Mackay in Lysander N1283 took off at 1340 hours, returning at 1510 hours. Lysander L4782 failed to return that day.

Pilot Officer John George Mackay, RAFVR (76919) is not listed in the squadron records from June 1940 onwards. He sustained multiple injuries in a mishap which occurred while he was on duty in the middle of June 1940. John Mackay was admitted to RAF Hospital Halton on 30 November 1940, then transferred to the Radcliffe Infirmary, Oxford where he died of lymphatic leukaemia on 11 December 1940.

Mackay was the son of Donald and Christina Sutherland Mackay of Caithness, husband of Olga Alexandra Ritchie Mackay. He was educated at Thurso Academy and Aberdeen University. Pilot Officer John George Mackay was the father of four sons and three daughters and resided at Errolbank, Perth Road, Scone. He died age 44 and is buried at Scone Cemetery.

NOTES:

Lysander N1253 was lost on 1 June 1940, it had taken off from RAF Lympe, Kent at 06:00 hrs, possibly damaged by Flak/AAA, and crashed on landing at RAF Hawkinge, Folkestone, Kent. Both its crew were killed.

Flight Lieutenant Bryant and Pilot Officer Stone in Lysander P1689 were shot down off the coast at Dunkirk on 29 May 1940. Bryant was slightly injured, and Stone was uninjured, they were evacuated and returned to England the following day.

The Operations Record Book for April 1940 was lost in France during the evacuation of the BEF. The squadron at the time consisted of 23 officers, 2 warrant officers and 274 NCO's, airmen, and soldiers.

On 13 May 1940, the daily orders for the squadron reported that *'the enemy has dropped poisoned chocolate. They might attempt dropping poisoned food or shaving brushes.'*

After a period of training in October 1941, RAF 26 Squadron's Lysanders Mk I, II & IIIs were replaced by Curtiss Tomahawk (P40) Mk I & IIa aircraft.

From five Lysander squadrons a total of 174 Westland Lysanders were sent to France between September 1939 and May 1940:

– 88 were shot down in air combat

– 30 were destroyed on the ground

– 120 crews were lost, all in about three weeks.

The grave of Pilot Officer J G Mackay. New Scone in the background.

RAF 26 Squadron Lysander Mk. II N1290 P/O Christopher I. D. Halliday, Crash Site West of Authie (Somme) France 19 May 1940 © 2012 – 2020 Aircrew Remembered

Colin Mackenzie

Corporal Colin Mackenzie died in Perth Royal Infirmary on 25 November 1942, he was 22 years old. Mackenzie served as an aircraft fitter with RAF 222 (Natal) Squadron. The squadron was initially formed on 5 October 1939 at RAF Duxford to act in a shipping protection role. They were equipped with Bristol Blenheim's. In March of 1940, the squadron was re-equipped with Supermarine Spitfires and became a day fighter unit helping to cover the Dunkirk evacuation. RAF 222 Squadron fought in the Battle of Britain. Based at RAF Hornchurch the squadron suffered heavy losses during the battle.

Mackenzie was working on an aircraft when someone started the engine and he fell off. This was the start of a long illness that caused his death. He was the only son of Colin and Jane Mackenzie, Perth Road, Scone. Colin Mackenzie is buried in Scone Cemetery.

NOTES: Douglas Bader was a member of RAF 222 Squadron at the time of the Dunkirk evacuation, notably at the time shooting down a Messerschmitt Bf 109 and a Heinkel He 111. In August 1942, the squadron helped cover the Dieppe operation (Operation Jubilee). In April 1944, they moved to Selsey Bill (RAF Selsey) to provide cover for the convoys and invasion beaches on D-Day. The first German aircraft shot down on D-Day was a Spitfire from RAF Selsey.

The squadron motto was, 'Pambili bo' (Zulu) ('Go straight ahead').

ROYAL AIR FORCE SQUADRON CRESTS (CH 9094) Original wartime caption: This picture is one of a series showing R.A.F. Squadron crests and mottoes. (Picture issued 1943). No.222 (Natal) Squadron: 'PAMBILI BO' 'Go straight ahead'. Copyright: © IWM.

James McCash

Pilot Officer James McCash, RAFVR (78977) was the son of David and Ruby McCash, Waverley Bank, Viewlands Road, Perth. David McCash was a well-known businessman – a junior member of J McCash & Sons, Feus Road, Perth.

The former Perth Academy pupil started flying training at Perth (Newlands) Aerodrome, gaining his wings at the end of November 1938 having trained for 18 months. He became an instructor at RNAS Evanton (also known as HMS Fieldfare) on the shore of the Cromarty Firth in Ross & Cromarty. In 1937, the aerodrome was expanded to become a flight and bombing training school. The airfield was shared with the RAF to which it was known as RAF Evanton.

McCash was commissioned on probation for the duration of the war on 28 May 1940 as a No. 4 (Continental) Ferry Pilot Pool pilot at RAF Kemble, Gloucestershire where his task was to transfer aircraft to wherever they were needed. By 1944, there were 16 ferry pools of pilots – they were part of the Air Transport Auxiliary (ATA). It consisted of 1,152 male pilots and 168 female pilots. Ferry pilots delivered new aircraft and took away damaged ones for repair. They flew service personnel on urgent duty and even carried out some air ambulance work.

Crucially, they freed up the frontline combat pilots to spend as much as possible of their time fighting the enemy.

On 18 June 1940, McCash's formation of 12 Bristol Blenheim's and 12 Hawker Hurricanes took off between 06.30 am and 06.45 am. McCash was piloting Bristol Blenheim Mk. V, L9315. The planes were on route from RAF Tangmere, via France and Tunisia to Malta. They became split up in a severe storm with thick cloud about 60 miles south of the Loire River. Five of the Blenheim's crashed; L9315 crashed at Prunières, about 150 miles north of Nice on the Mediterranean Coast. The crew comprised:

Pilot Officer James McCash, RAFVR (78977), pilot, age 23

Aircraftman 1st Class George Harris, RAF (626479), observer, age 23

Sergeant Ronald Micklethwaite, RAF (636876), wireless operator/air gunner, age 19

All three are buried at the Hiesse Communal Cemetery about 40 miles south of Poitiers in the region of Charente, France. McCash is commemorated on the North Church War Memorial, Perth.

Perthshire Advertiser, 29th June 1940

"War Casualties "Perth Pilot Believed Killed: "Observer Missing

"Mr and Mrs D. N. McCash, Waverley Bank, Viewlands Road, Perth, were notified by the Air Ministry yesterday that their only son, Pilot Officer James McCash (23), was reported missing but believed to have lost his life in an aircraft accident on June 18.

"Pilot Officer McCash, whose father is a well-known Perth businessman, was a junior member of J. McCash & Sons, grain merchants, Feus Road.

"A former pupil of Perth Academy, he received his flying training at Perth Aerodrome.

"Recently, after a spell as instructor at Evanton, Rossshire, he was transferred south to the Ferry Pilot Corps."

That day, 15 crew members were lost from the five Blenheims that crashed in France, L9315, L9351, L9317, L9318 and L9314. Blenheim L9263 due to engine failure struck the airfield boundary on take-off from Marignane, near Marseille, on the start of the second leg of the journey. The crew were safe, but the aircraft was abandoned. Another aircraft was later lost, L9334 escorted by five Hurricanes it crashed in the sea near Bizerte, Tunisia, killing all the crew. A Hurricane Mk.1 flown by Pilot Officer A G Maycock also crashed near the commune of Parigné l'Evêque, Loudon, Maycock survived the crash.

Possibly at least two crew that crashed in France may have survived and became POWs – research information is contradictory. This was a time of great confusion, and this is as near to what happened as can be determined.

NOTES: McCash gained his wings on the same day as Pilot Officer David Wood, Pilot Officer John Robertson McLaren, and Sergeant Jack Norwell, who were all first posted to RAF/RNAS Evanton in 1939.

Seven days after the crash, France capitulated, officially surrendered to the Germans at 01.35. On the 18th, the day of the crash, General DeGaulle formed the Comité Français de la Libération Nationale, the French government in exile.

The airfield in Tunisia was just north of the town of Menzel Bourghiba, in the Bizerte Governorate. It was known as Ferryville during World War II (after the war and Tunisian independence from France, the town was renamed in honour of Tunisia's first president).

Beaverbrook, the World War II Minister of Aircraft Production, gave an appropriate tribute at the closing ceremony disbanding the ATA at RAF White Waltham on 30 November 1945:

"Without the ATA the days and nights of the Battle of Britain would have been conducted under conditions quite different from the actual events. They carried out the delivery of aircraft from the factories to the RAF, thus relieving countless numbers of RAF pilots for duty in the battle. Just as the Battle of Britain is the accomplishment and achievement of the RAF, likewise it can be declared that the ATA sustained and supported them in the battle. They were soldiers fighting in the struggle just as completely as if they had been engaged on the battlefront."

AIRCRAFT OF THE ROYAL AIR FORCE 1939-1945: BRISTOL BLENHEIM. (ATP 10479E) Blenheim Mark V: pilot's controls and instrument panel on the port side of the cockpit. Copyright: © IWM

William J J McDougall

Twin-engine, medium bomber, Avro Manchester 679 L7303 EM-P of RAF 207 Squadron from RAF Waddington took off at 19.30 hours on a mission to attack Düsseldorf, Germany on the night of 27/28 March 1941. At around 22.30 hours, they bombed the target, making two approaches and dropping a stick of bombs on each run. Flak was intense, one shell burst jolted the starboard wing up in the air.

The pilot was Flight Lieutenant John Aloysius Siebert DFC RAAF (36155). Siebert, aged 23, was the son of Francis Joseph and Ella Mary Siebert, of Kingswood, South Australia. He was the first Allied airman to be buried in Eindhoven after his Avro Manchester, was shot down on the night of 27/28 March 1941. The aircraft came down at a farm between Roessel and Bakel, Noord west of Eindhoven, The Netherlands. Siebert was the last to bail-out, the aircraft was side-slipping, and it is though he hit one of the main wheels, his body was later recovered; his parachute was unopened.

PERTHSHIRE ADVERTISER 16 APRIL 1941

The rest of the crew successfully bailed out and were captured:

2nd Pilot, Sergeant Peter C Robson RAF (754584)

Observer, Sergeant George T J Fomison RAF (580649)

Wireless Operator/Air Gunner Sergeant James A Taylor RAF (619199)

Middle Upper Air Gunner, Sergeant William J J McDougall RAF (749440)

Rear Air Gunner, Peter Gurnell RAF (566980)

Avro Manchester L7303 was shot down at 23.30 hours by Oberfeldwebel Gerhard Herzog of NachtJagd Geschwader 1 (III. /NJGI) flying a Messerschmitt BF 110. Twenty-five minutes before, he had shot down an Armstrong Whitely from RAF 78 Squadron. Herzog himself was later killed in action on 20 October 1943 having shot down between 9 and 12 aircraft.

Siebert was from Adelaide, Australia. He was awarded the DFC late in 1940 for successfully carrying out 200 hours of operational flying, many being made in adverse weather conditions. His courage and determination in attacking the enemy had been outstanding, and he had a long record of consistently good work.

McDougall was the only son of the McDougall family, 29 Whitefriars Street, Dovecotland, Perth. William McDougall was brought up in Dundee and was educated at Morgan Academy – the family came to live in Perth nine years previous.

McDougall served his time as a butcher with William Oake, Gowrie Street, Bridgend, Perth. In May 1939, he started a course to train as a wireless operator with the RAFVR at Perth. He was called up to serve at the outbreak of war. His father was employed at the Perth Abattoir.

NOTES: The Avro Manchester 679 did not last long in production; it was terminated in 1941. Its operational failure was primarily because of its Rolls Royce Vulture engines, which were underdeveloped, underpowered and unreliable. The Manchester was redesigned, it became the four-engine Avro Lancaster, powered by Rolls Royce Merlin engines.

L7303 was delivered to RAF 207 Squadron and subsequently transferred to the AFDU (Air Fighting Development Unit) for trials in early March 1941.

Stalag Luft I also housed wireless operator Donald Henry Pleasence of RAF 166 Squadron. He was shot down during an attack on Agenville, Northern France on 31 August 1944. Pleasance returned to acting after the war and starred in many roles such as Ernst Stavro Blofeld in the 1967 James Bond movie - You Only live Twice. One of his most memorable roles was when he played Flight Lieutenant Colin Blythe in the 1963 movie, The Great Escape. He played the forger in Stalag Luft III who was slowly going blind. Another star of that film, Angus Lennie, spent time treading the boards of Perth Theatre, along with Donald Pleasance and Gordon Jackson.

Sergeant William McDougall, third from right, in front. Picture taken in Stalag Luft I. Perthshire Advertiser 7 January 1942.

William Henderson McDougall

On 9 July 1941, seven Bristol Blenheim's from RAF 110 (Hyderabad) Squadron took off from RAF Luga in Malta to attack Axis shipping in the harbour of Tripoli, Libya. The Blenheim's claimed several direct hits on four merchant vessels. One vessel was estimated at 12,000 tons, two at 10,000 tons and one at 7,000 tons. During the raid, the Blenheim's were attacked by Reggia Aeronautica Fiat G.50 bis and Fiat Cr.42 fighter aircraft. The Italians of 366 squadron, 151 Gruppe CT, claimed to have intercepted five British aircraft, scrambling at 1600 hours (Axis Time). Four of the Bristol Blenheim's failed to return to Malta.

According to the Italian record book:

Pilot Sergente Maggiore Aldo Buvoli (Fiat G.50) shot down the Blenheim formation leader (Z6449) and another Blenheim. Pilot M.llo (Maresciallo) Paolo Montanari (Fiat Cr.42) claimed one enemy aircraft and Sergente Ottorino Ambrosi (Fiat CR.42) claimed a Blenheim shot down.

A bulletin issued by the Italian Armed Forces Head Quarters stated that two British aircraft were shot down by fighters and two others by anti-aircraft (flak).

The four aircraft that failed to return:

Bristol Blenheim Mk. IV Z6449

Squadron Leader Douglas Holland Seale RAF (45689) pilot, age 24

Sgt Frederick Bertie Mulford RAF (580522) observer, age unknown

Flight Sergeant William Henderson McDougall RAF (625871) wireless operator, age 25

Bristol Blenheim Mk. IV Z9533

Sergeant W. H. Twist pilot. POW

Sergeant D. W. Allen Observer. POW

Sergeant S. W. Taylor wireless operator/air gunner. POW

Bristol Blenheim Mk. IV Z9537

Flight Lieutenant Michael Ernest Potier pilot, age 20, KIA

Flight Lieutenant T. Griffith-Jones observer, POW

Sergeant D. H. Wythe, Wireless operator/air gunner, POW

Z9578 Blenheim Mk. IV

Pilot Officer Walter Hugh Lowe pilot, age 25, KIA

Sergeant Ronald Ernest Baird observer, age 20, KIA

Sergeant Harold Lummus wireless operator/air gunner, age unknown, KIA

Blenheim Z6449 was seen to have force-landed into the sea north of Tripoli after a long chase. The other aircraft were shot down a few miles north of Tripoli. Later a Martin Model 167 (Maryland) light bomber from RAF 69 Squadron seeking to ascertain the result of the attack was damaged but managed to escape. The Maryland's gunner claimed to have shot down a Macchi Mc.200 Saetta (Lightning) fighter.

William Henderson McDougall, 11 Arklay Street, Dundee, was the eldest son of William Menzies McDougall and Jean McDougall, Pitheavlis Farm, Perth; and husband of Edna McDougall, 20 James Street, Perth.

McDougall was home on leave towards the end of June 1941 and later wrote to his wife informing her that his Blenheim squadron was leaving for the East. No news was heard of him after that.

All who died in are commemorated on the Runnymede Memorial in Surrey.

Note: The rank, M.llo (Maresciallo) is a Marshall, the equivalent of Corporal, a lower grade officer.

Flight Sergeant William Henderson McDougall, Perthshire Advertiser 18 March 1942

Alistair Stuart McLaren

Former Metropolitan Police officer, Sergeant Alistair Stuart McLaren RAFVR (1891777) was the youngest son of the late John and Margaret McLaren, 14 Robertson's Buildings, Dunkeld Road, Perth.

McLaren was an air gunner on board Avro Lancaster ND762 on 22 May 1944 piloted by another Perth resident - See Second World War Aviators - Ernie 'Sherl-E' Holmes DFC.

Wing Commander Edward Peter William Hutton was also brought up by Mrs J McLaren at 14 Robertson's Buildings

A memorial to the crew in Vessem, Holland was unveiled by E Holmes on 29th September 2018 © Heemkundevereniging De Hooge Dorpen

Ian (Graham) Miller

Flight Sergeant Ian (Graham) Miller was an air gunner on an Avro Lancaster Mk1, LM127, KO-H with RAF 115 Squadron. He was the son of Kathleen Graham Miller (née Lipp) of 51 Priory Place, Craigie, Perth.

Avro Lancaster Mk.1, LM127, code KO-H, took off from RAF Witchford in Cambridgeshire, at 20.27 hrs on 26 August 1944. They were on an operation to bomb Keil in northern Germany a major naval port and shipbuilding centre of the German Reich. Lancaster LM 127 carried a bomb load of 1 x 4000 lb High Explosive (blockbuster or cookie), 900 x 4 lb incendiaries, and 96 x 30 lb incendiaries. The aircraft was fitted with HS2 (Fishpond), a ground scanning radar system that identified the targets on the ground during bad weather and at night.

The Pathfinder aircraft were hampered finding the target by smoke screens, but a successful raid was carried out. There was heavy bombing in the town centre and surrounding area with widespread fires that were fanned by a strong wind. The Rathaus (Town Hall) and many public buildings were destroyed or damaged. In total 372 Avro Lancaster's and 10 de Haviland Mosquitoes of RAF Nos 1, 3 and 8 Groups attacked Keil that night. RAF 115 Squadron lost three Lancaster's and 19 aircrew were killed, in total 17 Lancaster's were lost.

Avro Lancaster Mk.1, LM127, crashed into the North Sea, on board were:

Flying Officer James Edward Morgan, RAFVR (182018) pilot, age 29

Sergeant Kenneth Percy Coote RAFVR (3000114) flight engineer, age 19

Flight Sergeant Eric Young RAFVR (1487006) navigator, age 23

Flying Officer Desmond Francis O'Sullivan RAFVR (151430) bomb aimer, age 27

Sergeant Maurice Bell RAFVR (1621754) wireless operator, age 21

Flight Sergeant Ian Graham Campbell Miller, RAFVR (1552376) air (mid-upper) gunner, age 22

Pilot Officer Tom Yates RCAF (J/95439) air (rear) gunner, age 26

Flying Officer James Edward Morgan and Flying Officer Desmond Francis O'Sullivan are buried at Esbjerg (Fovfeld Gravlund) Cemetery in Denmark. Pilot Officer Tom Yates is buried at Bergen-Op-Zoom Canadian War Cemetery in the Netherlands. Flying Officer James Morgan's body was washed ashore near Vester Vedsted, Denmark, and was buried by the Wehrmacht where he was found. His remains were disinterred on 7 November 1945 and laid to rest in the Fovfeld cemetery. The Runnymede Memorial perpetuates the names of the rest of the crew whose bodies were not found.

Ian Miller had left for Canada with his father and sister in 1927. When he returned is not known. The ship, they departed for Canada in was the S. S. Athenia, this was the first UK ship to be sunk by the Germany military during World War II.

NOTES: A Blockbuster bomb exploding in conjunction with the incendiary bombs could destroy an entire street. The minimum drop height for a Blockbuster bomb was 6,000 feet to avoid damage to the aircraft from the shock wave of the explosion.

H2S radar remained in service for nearly 50 years with the RAF until 1993. It was last employed in military conflict during the Falklands War in 1982 on the Avro Vulcan bombers.

AIRCRAFT OF THE ROYAL AIR FORCE: AVRO 683 LANCASTER. (ZZZ 2954D) Annotated view of the instrument panel and flying controls of an Avro Lancaster B Mark I. Copyright: © IWM. Original Source: http://www.iwm.org.uk/collections/item/object/205207925

John William Charlton Moffat

Lieutenant Commander John William Charlton Moffat as a RNFAA pilot is generally recognised as responsible for torpedoing the Kreigsmarine (Nazi Germany's navy) battleship Bismarck. Flying a Fairey Swordfish biplane, on 26 May 1941, Moffat succeeded in crippling the battleship sufficiently that the Royal Navy could pursue and sink it. Moffat's bold action had a most important impact during Operation Rheinübung – the Bismarck's Atlantic manoeuvres.

Moffat was born within the Scottish Borders, in the village of Swinton, on 17 June 1919. In December 1939, he attended a flying school in Belfast. By June 1940, France had fallen, and Moffat had concluded his flying instruction and been posted to No. 759 Squadron, located at Eastleigh.

Moffat's air combat experience soon began in earnest. The first occurred while he was flying a Gloster Gladiator – a flight that involved testing a new improvised oxygen delivery mechanism. After an ascent to 29,000 feet, Moffat began to descend at which point he was set upon by several Luftwaffe Messerschmitt Bf 109s. Fortunately, Moffat managed to utilise cloud cover to evade his attackers. Another test flight, this time in an unarmed Blackburn Skua, resulted in a close call with a Heinkel He. 111.

It was his role in the sinking of the Bismarck that earned Moffat a place in military aviation history. On 24 May 1941, after the sinking of HMS Hood (Royal Navy flagship) and the damaging of HMS Prince of Wales by the Bismarck, the Royal Navy were determined to hunt down and destroy the German battleship, which though seaworthy had suffered damage that required its return to the safety of a port.

As part of what was called Force H, the aircraft carrier HMS Ark Royal was ordered to pursue and destroy the Bismarck. Despite high winds and low visibility, on 26 May 1941, just after 21:00 hours, a squadron of Swordfish torpedo bombers (RAF No. 820) from the Ark Royal including that piloted by Moffat alongside his crew – T/S-Lt (A) J. D. 'Dusty' Miller, observer, and LA A. J. Hayman, telegraphist/air gunner – spotted the Bismarck. Their squadron of open cockpit bombers attacked the ship receiving concentrated anti-aircraft fire. Two of the launched torpedoes hit the Bismarck – one amidships and the other (from Moffat's plane) in the rudder-steering area. It was the latter that resulted in the battleship losing its ability to steer.

With the Bismarck directionless despite maintaining good speed, Force H and ships from the Home Fleet pursued and destroyed the battleship. This attack was immortalised in the 1960s film *Sink the Bismarck!* which used Moffat's actual Swordfish (NF389) for the movie's flying sequence.

Remarkably after a 4-decade hiatus, Moffat began flying again in his sixties going on to be a member of the Scottish Aero Club for 30 years, flying a plane appropriately registered G-ARK. The Aero Club organised a special event for the war hero when he was aged 95. A year later, Moffat was still in the skies. In 2013, Moffat piloted his own plane to Sherburn-in-Elmet, North Yorkshire, where Fairey Swordfish biplanes were built, as part of a Royal Navy 'Historic Flight Event'.

In an interview to the BBC in 2016, Lt-Cdr Moffat, now ninety-six, recalled his first sight of the giant German warship as he descended through the clouds.

"The first sight I had was over my right shoulder. I could see it belching fire from the side of the ship. It's guns. They couldn't fire fast enough." With his observer hanging out of the open cockpit, communicating with him through their headphones, Moffat flew low towards the Bismarck to keep below its guns. *"He kept saying 'Not yet not yet'. And then eventually he said, 'Let her go'. "I pressed the firing pin on my throttle and the torpedo dropped into the sea." And it was him who said, 'We've got a runner, Jock'!*

"When Churchill gave the order to sink the Bismarck, we knew we just had to stop her trail of devastation at all costs! We dived in through the murk, into a lethal storm of shells and bullets. Bismarck's guns erupted and in the hail of hot bullets and tracer, I couldn't see any of the other Swordfish. I thought the closer we were to the water the better chance we had of surviving, so we flew in bouncing off the tops of the waves – and it worked."

That torpedo that disabled Bismarck's rudder. Unable to flee, it was caught by the pursuing Royal Navy force and shelled before it was scuttled. John Moffat, on a second attack of the giant battleship, saw it happen. He said: "The Bismarck turned on its side, and all the sailors seemed to be in the water. It's lived with me for a long time."

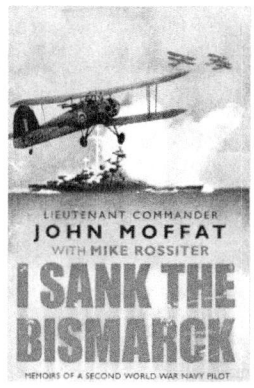

I Sank the Bismarck (2010), Moffat's autobiographical account of his time as a Second World War navy pilot was published in 2010. On 11 December 2016, Lieutenant Commander John William Charlton Moffat who had resided in Dunkeld for several years passed away in Viewlands House care home in Perth, aged 97.

The picture is of the three legendary naval heroes, John Moffat, Lt. Cdr. Edgar Lee who survived the suicidal attack, the "Channel Dash". When six Swordfish took on the battleships Scharnhorst and Gneisenau and the heavy cruiser Prinz Eugen in the English Channel. Only 5 Swordfish crew out of 18 survived. The third is the greatest flyer ever, Eric 'Winkle' Brown who was born in Leith. Eric Brown also died in 2016.

The story of Eric 'Winkle' Brown is a remarkable tale indeed well worthy of a read. He was at the 1936 Olympics in Berlin, was on an aircraft carrier when it was torpedoed, was the first man to land a jet on a carrier, interviewed Goring and many other Nazi's, was at Belsen, should have been the first man to break the sound barrier and was so well loved, that on 3 or 4 occasions when he was recovering from serious injuries, it is said that Winston Churchill was at his bedside. To say that he had an incredible life is no understatement. A statue in honour of Eric "Winkle" Brown has been erected outside the arrival's hall at Edinburgh Airport

Note: The Scottish Aero Club was founded in 1927 and is the oldest and largest flying club in Scotland.

Logbook of John Moffat, page showing attack on the Bismark, on display at Scottish Aero Club, Scone

Signed by the pilot.

John Alexander Morrison

On 6 June 1944, D-Day, the largest amphibious invasion in military history took place. It was officially called 'Operation Overlord'. It involved 156,115 troops, 6,939 ships and 2,395 aircraft along with 867 gliders. At the beginning of the invasion, RAF 575 Squadron dropped around a thousand airborne troops from the 1st Canadian and 9th Parachute Battalions, part of 3rd Parachute Brigade. They also towed 21 Airspeed Horsa gliders carrying troops into the battle. Daily they carried supplies and personal to Normandy and brought back the wounded for urgent medical treatment.

On 2 June 1944, the order was given to 'seal' RAF Broadwell at 14.00 hrs. The following day approval was given to close the Alvescot to Shilton Road in Oxfordshire. On 5th June 1944, RAF Regiment Squadrons were in pace to guard the marshalled aircraft. All 59 crews (6 spare) attended lectures during the day and the final briefing at 20.00 hrs in the 'War Room' at RAF Broadwell. here in the run up to D-Day was a tented village which housed both the 8th and 9th Parachute Regiments along with the 1st Battalion Royal Ulster Rifles. Security was very tight and the signal to prepare for the invasion was given by a Spitfire circling the airfield three times.

John Morrison was the navigator aboard Douglas C-47 'Dakota' KG326, RAF 575 Transport Squadron which took off at 23.30 on 5th June 1944. A total of 21 Dakotas from RAF Broadwell departed to drop Paratroopers and equipment of the 3rd Paratroop Brigade on landing zone, DZ-N (East of the River Orne between the villages of Ranville, Amfreville and Le Mariquet). The squadron was over the drop zone at approximately 00.57 to 01.12 hours on D-Day 6th June 1944. All troops were dropped successfully.

Dakota KG326 landed back at base at 02.45. Some enemy opposition had been encountered, and five aircraft were damaged by enemy flak, but all returned safely. Weather was 10/10 Cloud at 2,000 feet and visibility, 10 miles.

Crew on KG326:

Flying Officer Peter Carl Hakansson, RAFVR (152699)

Flight Lieutenant John Alexander Morrison, RAFVR (131804)

Sergeant E. F Guy

Pilot Officer W. Lomas

Douglas C-47 'Dakota' KG326 with the same crew took off again at 18.55 on 6th June 1944, part of Operation Mallard. This mission's objective was to tow the gliders containing the infantry of the 6th Airlanding Brigade and divisional troops to reinforce the 6th Airborne Division on the left flank of the British Invasion Beaches. Nineteen aircraft were detailed to land troops and equipment on Landing Zone DZ-N. The Horsa Gliders towed behind the Dakota's were over the Landing Zone at approximately 20.57. All gliders were released successfully. After turning to starboard on release of the gliders, three aircraft were hit by small arms fire from a wood to the west near the bank of the river Orne, southeast of Bénouville. Three hundred and four troops were carried, plus kit and equipment, including Jeeps, Cycles, Trailers, and Motorcycles. One aircraft crashed on initial take-off. KG326 landed back safely at 22.35. Weather was: – Visibility 10 Miles, Cloud 10/10 Medium and Wind 290/25 at 2,000.

On 10 July 1944, the same crew were back over Normandy, flying this time in Dakota FZ674. They conveyed 4023 lbs of general equipment to Advanced Landing Ground (ALG) B 14, returning with 18 stretcher cases and 4 walking casualties. A new flying corridor was used, Christchurch to Barfluer to north of the river Vire. Take off was at 0800 and they returned at 12.36.

On 17 June 1944, just 11 days after D-Day, 15 Dakotas from RAF Broadwell made the first landing on the advanced landing ground, B-2 at Bazenville, near the Normandy beachheads. On this day alone they evacuated over 200 wounded men.

On 5 August 1944, Flight Lieutenant John Morrison was now the navigator on a Douglas C-47 'Dakota' FZ674 detailed to evacuate casualties from the fighting in France. The Allies had air supremacy over this area, but flights over the Channel were still risky. They were heading for ALG, B-5 at Le Fresne-Camilly when they crashed into a field near ALG B-14, at Amblie.

These ALG landing strips were just south of Juno Beach and north of Caen. The weather was foggy, and visibility was down to zero. Take off was at 08.59 with 4522 lbs of freight. FZ674 was reported as struck ground and crashed.

On board Douglas Dakota FZ674 were:

Flying Officer Peter Carl Hakansson, RAFVR (152699), pilot, age 20

Flying Officer Norman Lomas, RAFVR (154352), navigator, age 32

Flight Lieutenant John Alexander Morrison, RAFVR (131804), navigator (bomber), age 26

Flight Sergeant Ernest Francis Guy, RAFVR (1317603), wireless operator, age unknown

Corporal William Edward Brennen, RAF (Auxiliary Air Force) (867113), age unknown

All the crew were killed. They are buried at Ryes War Cemetery, Bazenville.

John Morrison was the son of the late Captain George James Morrison, MC, Seaforth Highlanders, and of Aenea Kate Morrison, 2 Brunswick Terrace, Perth (2 Brunswick Terrace is now 23 St Magdelene's Road).

On 11 April 1918, the newly promoted, Captain G J Morrison died from wounds received at the Battle of the Lys. The Initial battle from 9 to 11 April 1918 was known as the Battle of Estaires, south of Dunkirk and north of Lens. George Morrison was gazetted 2nd Lieutenant 6th Seaforth Highlanders in January 1916. He was promoted to Lieutenant in October 1917 and Acting Captain in April 1918. He was posthumously awarded the Military Cross for conspicuous gallantry. He enlisted in May 1915 and in December 1916 was invalided home with trench fever. He re-joined his battalion in May 1917.

Before enlisting the Morrison family stayed at Station House, Blair Atholl, where George was a junior clerk at Blair Castle. He is buried at Lapugnoy Military Cemetery, Lapugnoy, Departement du Pas-de-Calais, Nord-Pas-de-Calais, France. Aenea Morrison, a teacher, only married for two years to George never remarried. She died in 1978 in Dunkeld.

Perthshire Advertiser, 9th August 1944

"DEATHS – On Active Service

"MORRISON – Lost his life on operations in August 1944, F.-Lieut. JOHN ALEXANDER MORRISON, R.A.F., dearly beloved only son of the late Capt. George J. Morrison, M.C., Seaforth Highlanders, and of Mrs A. K. Morrison, Seaforth, 2 Brunswick Terrace, Perth."

Perthshire Advertiser, 12th August 1944

"COUNTY AND CITY WAR CASUALTIES

"PERTH AIRMAN LOST IN FRANCE

"Mrs A. K. Morrison, 2 Brunswick Terrace, Perth, wife of the late Capt. George Morrison, M.C., who died of wounds in the last war, has received official word that her son, Flight Lieutenant John A. Morrison, has lost his life on air operations over France.

"Ft./Lt. Morrison, who was aged 26, joined the R.A.F. in 1940, and after completing his training about nine months later, served with Coastal Command in Britain, the Middle East, and the Far East, eventually being transferred to Transport Command, to a post which he was holding at the time of his death. He was pilot in one of the first waves of paratroop planes over Caen and was also connected with glider operations in this sector.

"Educated at Perth Academy and Skerry's College, Edinburgh, Ft./Lt. Morrison was a native of Blair Atholl, and previous to joining up he was employed with the Customs and Excise."

John Morrison is also commemorated on the Perth (West) Church War Memorial.

NOTES: The British military cemetery at Bazenville contains 979 war dead: 630 British, 326 Germans, 21 Canadians, 1 Australian and 1 Polish.

Bazenville was not under British control until the evening of 7 June 1944. The airfield, B-2 at Bazenville was fully operational, just eight days after D-Day.

RAF Broadwell saw the arrival of two squadrons of Dakotas from RAF Hendon on 24 January 1944. These were 512 and 575 squadrons. During the 6th of June 1944 initial assault, 32 Dakotas of 512 and 21 Dakotas of 575 dropped 952 paratroopers on two drop zones in Normandy.

No. 575 Squadron was later involved in operations at Arnhem where the squadron suffered severe casualties. They took part in Operation Market (Garden) during the period 17-23 September 1944. Operation Market Garden 17-25 September 1944 consisted of two sub-operations:

Market: an airborne assault to seize key bridges, and **Garden**: a ground attack moving over the seized bridges creating a salient.

It is possible that Corporal Brennen was on board the Dakota FZ674 just to care for the wounded.

Flight Lieutenant John Alexander Morrison, Perthshire Advertiser 12 August 1944

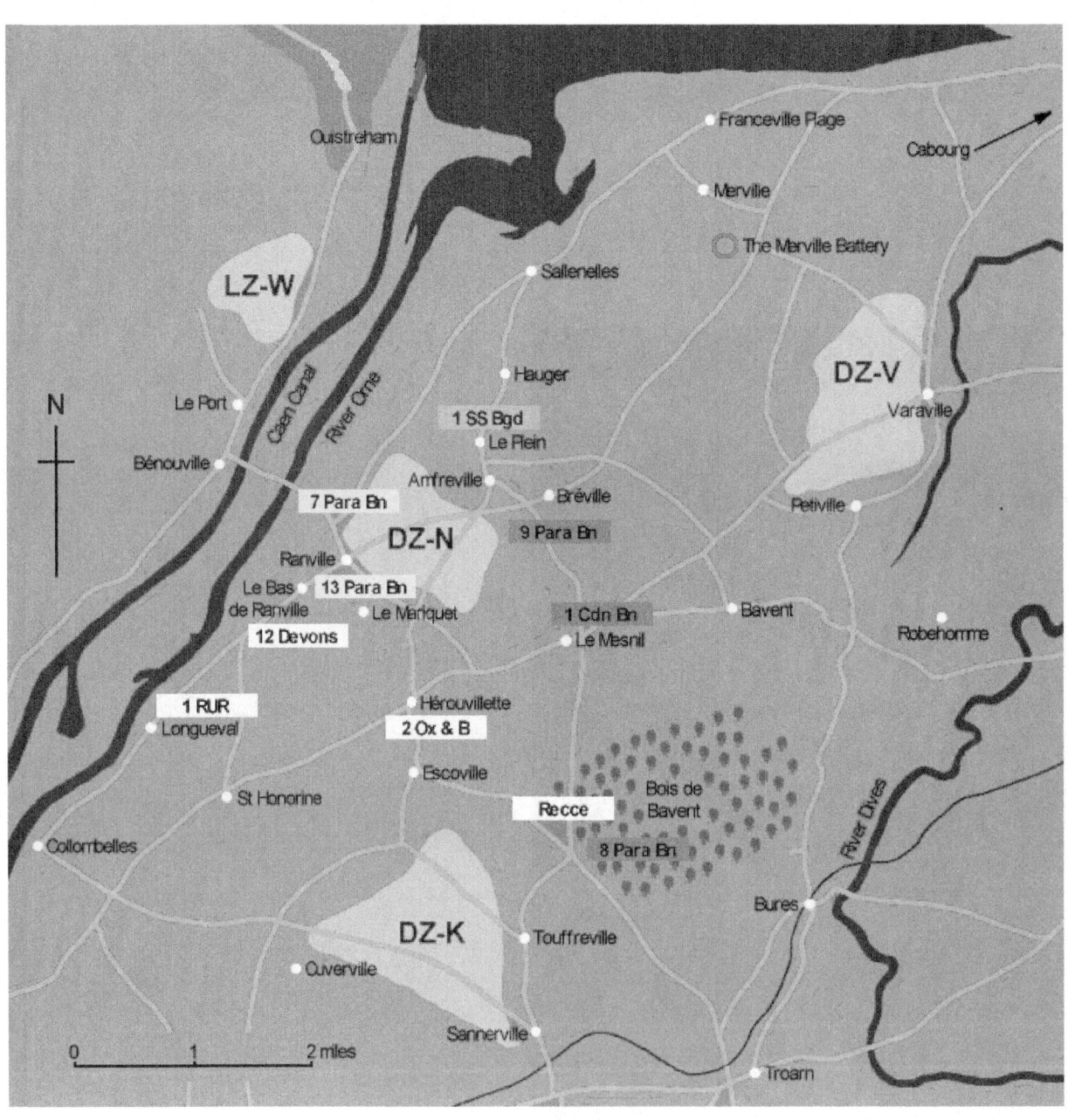

Positions of the 6th Airborne Division from 7 June 1944 by Jim Sweeney – Own work, CC BY-SA 3.0

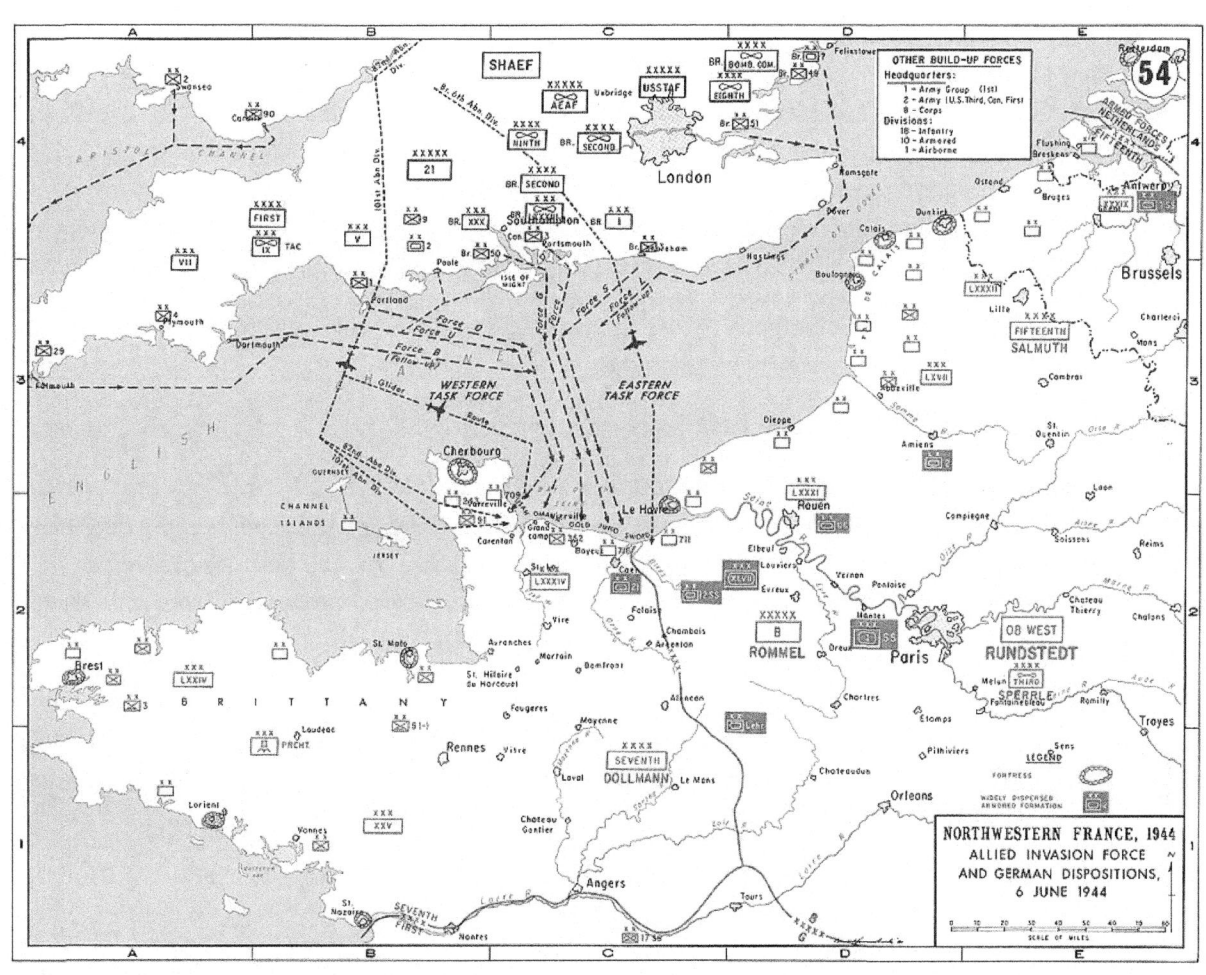

D-Day assault map of the Normandy region and the north-western coast of France. Source: http://www.dean.usma.edu/history/Atlases/WorldWarTwoEurope/EuropeanTheaterGIF/WWIIEurope54.gif, Public Domain

William Blair Morrison

In Perth High Court on 2 June 1942, the case was heard against Charles Robinson White, age 21. He was charged with the culpable homicide of Aircraftman 1st Class William Blair Morrison RAFVR (1104142), age 29. The incident happened at RAF Dunino in Fife, at 9.30 am on 11 May 1941. White presented a loaded rifle at Morrison and culpably and recklessly discharged it, shooting him in the head whereby he died immediately.

In the defence of White, a special defence of insanity was tendered. The view was put forward that White was suffering from schizophrenia or split mind.

From the **Perthshire Advertiser, 3 June 1942:**

Dr. W. D. Chambers, medical superintendent of Murray Royal hospital, Perth told the court that when he first examined White, the prisoner told him he was "controlled" and did not know what came over him. At a later interview he said he had been worried about his Morse Code training and volunteered a statement that he had heard voices in his head, one of them saying, "why don't you kill that man?".

Dr. Chambers then revealed that when he first saw White in hospital, the accused was suffering from a self-inflicted gunshot wound in the chest. Dr. Chambers said he was told that after shooting Morrison, the accused fired at another man but missed him. White informed him that he escaped from Guernsey in a coal boat during the German occupation, and that his parents were still there. Before leaving he had a breakdown and tried to commit suicide by gas.

White was ordered by Lord Moncrieff to be detained in prison during at His Majesty's pleasure. The proceeding was concluded within an hour.

Morrison was the son of David Lyall and Agnes Morrison, Perth, the husband of Mary Morrison of Perth. He is buried in Wellshill Cemetery, Perth.

Thomas Ralph Morton

On 23 August 1940, Leading Aircraftman Thomas Ralph Morton RAFVR (1005871) died age 20 on active service. He served with No. 3, Radio Maintenance Unit (RMU). Morton was the son of Andrew Gray Morton and Grace Hood Morton, 31 Muirton Place, Perth. He is buried in Perth Wellshill Cemetery.

Thomas Morton is commemorated on the Perth (West) Church war memorial. Thomas is one of ten per cent or so airmen whose cause of death is unknown or due to natural causes.

Perthshire Advertiser, 24 August 1940

'Perth Airman's Death

Was expected Home on Leave on Monday

Leading – Aircraftman Thomas Ralph Morton, the only son of Mr and Mrs Andrew G. Morton, 31 Muirton Place, has died at an R.A.F. station in England.

It is understood that Leading-Aircraftman Morton was hoping to be home on leave on Monday first. He was aged 20. His parents received news of his death by wire.'

Perthshire Constitutional and Journal, 31st August 1940

'CITY AIRMAN'S DEATH

WAS EXPECTED HOME ON LEAVE

On Monday, the day he was expected home on his first leave, the funeral took place of Leading Aircraftman Thomas Ralph Morton, the only son of Mr and Mrs Andrew G. Morton, 31 Muirton Place, Perth.

L./A. Morton, 20 years of age, joined the R.A.F. recently. He was stationed in the North of England, and only two days before his death his parents had a cheery letter telling how he was looking forward to his holiday.

The official communication indicated that Morton had died suddenly and unexpectedly. He appeared to be in the best of health a few hours before he passed away.

Mr Andrew Morton, his father who travelled south to arrange for the funeral taking place in Perth, was informed that a post-mortem had established that death was due to natural causes.

Before joining up deceased was employed with a city firm of electricians, and it was into this branch of the R.A.F. he graduated.'

Andrew McKenzie Munn

The situation in Europe in the summer of 1939 was deteriorating and as a prudent measure, Leslie Hore-Belisha, Secretary of State for War, persuaded the cabinet of Neville Chamberlain to introduce a limited form of conscription on 27 April 1939. The Military Training Act being passed the following month. Only single men 20 to 22 years old were liable to be called up, and they were to be known as "militiamen" to distinguish them from the regular army. National conscription had ended in 1920. Each man was to be given six months of training before being allowed to return home on an active reserve status. Andrew McKenzie Munn was called up on 15 July 1939 and posted to join the Seaforth Highlanders at Fort George, northwest of Inverness. War was declared on 1 September 1939.

Sergeant Andrew McKenzie Munn was a hero twice over, he fought with the British Expeditionary Force (BEF) in France at the start of the War, and was evacuated, wounded, from Dunkirk. He subsequently transferred to the RAF as an Air Gunner on Avro Lancaster bombers with RAF 103 Squadron. Later in this role on Avro Lancaster W8428 while on an operation to bomb the docks at La Spezia in northern Italy, he and all the crew on board were killed.

RAF 103 Squadron had allocated 20 aircraft for the attack on La Spezia. The overall force consisted of 208 Avro Lancaster's and 3 Handley Page Halifax aircraft. Three of RAF 103 Squadrons aircraft returned due to mechanical issues, one aircraft failed to reach the target owing to an unserviceable d/r (distance reading) compass, another ditched in the English Channel and Lancaster W8428 failed to return. Bombing height was between 7,000 and 12,000 feet with Pathfinder aircraft going in first to light up the target with flares.

The goal was to cause the maximum possible damage to the target area, each aircraft had a bomb load of 5 x 1000 lbs G P, T D (General Purpose, Time Delay), 2 x 90 x 4 lbs (incendiaries) and 2 x 8 x 30 lbs (incendiaries). In addition, all aircraft carried cameras and nickels (leaflets). Take off on 13 April 1943 was at 2019 hours, the route taken was directly south from RAF Elsham Wolds to Selsey Bill, Cabourg (France), Lac du Bourget (France) and on to La Spezia in northern Italy, southeast of Genoa.

There was no cloud cover over the target, the anti-aircraft flack was intense at first but soon died down. A dozen searchlights were in operation and a smoke screen was being used to cover the target area. The Pathfinder Force lit up the target with white flares so that each aircraft could pin-point the target individually and bomb from a lower height than usual. Bombing height was between 7,000 and 12,000 feet. The raid, judging by the fires observed was a great success, but the battleships anchored at the port were not visible due to smoke. The bombing force after their long journey, returned to the UK landing between 0545 hours and 0700 hours. Only one aircraft managed to return to base, the others were diverted for an unknown reason to RAF airfields at Westcott, Tangmere, Wyton, Exeter, and Middle Wallop.

Munn and the crew onboard Avro Lancaster W8428 were posted to the War Casualties Non-Effective Accounts Department, as non-effective missing. Their aircraft most probably crashed following a mid-air collision with RAF 12 Squadron Lancaster ED714, over Saint-Mars-d'Outillé, south of Le Mans in France.

The crew of Avro Lancaster W8428 who died on 14 April 1943:

Flight Lieutenant Edward Claude Lee-Brown RAFVR (125695) pilot, age 20

Pilot Officer James Smart RAFVR (144753) navigator, age 19

Sergeant George Watson Houliston RAFVR (974219) flight engineer, age 31

Flight Sergeant James Joseph O'Brien DFM RAF (551549) wireless operator, age unknown

Sergeant Stanley Moseley RAFVR (1351789) air gunner, age 20

Sergeant Andrew McKenzie Munn RAF (657170) air gunner, age 24

Warrant Officer Class 1 James Willis Toon RCAF (R74721) air observer, age 23

The crew were all interred at Le Mans West Cemetery.

Andrew McKenzie Munn was the son of William L Munn and Helen Munn, Coul Lodge, Auchterarder, Perthshire (late of Barnhill, Perth).

Prior Missions:

Edward Lee-Brown and his crew were posted to RAF 103 Squadron at RAF Elsham Wolds from RAF 1656 Heavy Conversion Unit on the 29 December 1942.

Their tour of 16 operations is shown below:

04-Feb-43 – Lorient – Lancaster – W4828 – P/O EC Lee-Brown

18-Feb-43 – Wilhelmshaven – Lancaster – W4828 – F/O EC Lee-Brown

21-Feb-43 – Bremen – Lancaster – W4828 – F/O EC Lee-Brown

25-Feb-43 – Nuremberg – Lancaster – W4828 – P/O EC Lee-Brown

26-Feb-43 – Cologne – Lancaster – W4828 – P/O EC Lee-Brown – Early return – MU gunner became unconscious because of failure of oxygen.

08-Mar-43 – Nuremberg – Lancaster – W4828 – F/O EC Lee-Brown

09-Mar-43 – Munich – Lancaster – ED528 – F/O EC Lee-Brown

11-Mar-43 – Stuttgart – Lancaster – ED612 – F/O EC Lee-Brown

12-Mar-43 – Essen – Lancaster – ED612 – F/O EC Lee-Brown

27-Mar-43 – Berlin – Lancaster – W4828 – F/O EC Lee-Brown

29-Mar-43 – Berlin – Lancaster – W4828 – F/L EC Lee-Brown – Did not take off – Passed take off deadline after runway change.

03-Apr-43 – Essen – Lancaster – W4828 – F/L EC Lee-Brown – Had to evade searchlights in the target area. Bombs fell short as a result.

04-Apr-43 – Kiel – Lancaster – W4828 – F/L EC Lee-Brown

08-Apr-43 – Duisburg – Lancaster – W4828 – F/L EC Lee-Brown

09-Apr-43 – Duisburg – Lancaster – ED612 – F/L EC Lee-Brown

13-Apr-43 – La Spezia – Lancaster – W4828 – F/L EC Lee-Brown – FTR – Crashed near Le Mans, France.

Before joining the RAF, Andrew Munn served with the Seaforth Highlanders and was evacuated from France at Dunkirk.

Andrew McKenzie Munn British Expeditionary Force - Dunkirk Personal Account

The following is a personal account, written by Alexander McKenzie Munn about his experiences with the British Expeditionary Force in France 1939/1940. The original personal notes are held by the Seaforth Highlanders Museum.

(Notes in square brackets for clarification by Ken Bruce)

Advanced into Belgium by way of Tournai [west of Lille] travelling in dark, pretty tough going driving without lights – hide out most of the next day in orchard close to Albert Canal where Battalion dug in to take position (about 190kms). Got my first shot at enemy aircraft out on reconnaissance, fired a couple of magazines on the Bren (better luck next time). A few hours later they came back and made a raid on a convoy coming up. Fifteen of them swooped down from the cloud on the tail of the first, dropping their death dealing pills, very exciting to watch, but hell to be near them when they explode. They all got clear despite machine gun and AA fire. That night we took up flank action with the Battalion. Using our Bren Gun Carriers. About 2 am we had just about enough – Gerrie shelled us out despite heavy fire from our own artillery in the rear. It would have been suicide to stay and so we returned with a few losses. It really was very aggravating as we could see precious little to fire at. We lost two of the Bren Gun Carriers, one broke down, and the other was ditched in the darkness, so we scuttled them.

We then stayed two days on the Franco Belgium border at Hal [Halle]. Discovered a chocolate factory that had been evacuated, Boko chocolate for soldier [much chocolate]. I carried a store in carrier only the heat of the engine and the weather did not help much. The worst sight was the poor people flying (fleeing) from their homes. Old men, women and children al on the trek with just one thing in mind – to get as far away from the fighting area as possible. The roads were packed with them, with their few personal belongings flung over their shoulders. That day I got a beautiful view of a battle between a Messerschmitt and a Spitfire, but sorry to relate the Spitfire bit the dust. The Messerschmitt managed to double round and follow the Spitfire up on the tail and gave it a few bursts with the machine-gun. The British pilot made a jump for it and his parachute, and his machine made a perfect nosedive and hit the ground about 500 yards from me, bursting into flames – You talk about 'Hell's Angel', it never had a look in. Shortly after this, we were called away to the region of Arras as we discovered Gerrie was there. How the hell he managed it I could not tell but it sure was an eye-opener for us.

[*The Spitfire was most likely a Hawker Hurricane, Spitfires were not sent to France/Belgium with the BEF. The BEF was pulled back to the line of the river Dyle, to the west of Halle, but the Germans had broken through to the south at Sedan, France. There was a counterattack at Arras, France, but the BEF, French and Belgian forces north of the Somme retreated to Dunkirk soon after.]*

The first night we arrived there after being hindered with refugees on the road all day, we were subject to another air raid in a wood which we rested in for the night. I like the word 'rested'. We did not know what it was to rest. There were quite a few boys cracking up under the strain. No wonder when you see the black buggers [Stuka Ju 87 Dive Bombers], about fifty of them screaming overhead, dropping eggs wherever they pleased despite the barrage put up against them. We shot down a few but they still came on. If I was telling a fishy story, I would say they were a 1,000 strong. The burning question with everyone was, 'Where is the famous RAF?' We were beginning to think there was none. After two days of dodging shells, bombs and bullets from the Gerrie Infantry, we were shifted to Ypres [Belgium], what for? Well, you better ask the War Office, but this sure was the hottest spot yet. Gerrie accounted for a few of our trucks, but we brought down two of their birds and took one crew alive. They were quite posh looking chaps with heir black tunics, breeches and leggings. Two of them had a few medals on their chest. There must be a Woolworth's in Germany too. They could speak English to a fair extent, their excuse being they might need it one day. You can take that crack both ways. Some of the boys were for lynching them but the officers said they were more useful the way they were, maybe so, I don't know.

We took up defensive positions that night and we were not there for more than two hours when we contacted Gerrie. After a night of popping at them or should I say any black object that moved, dawn broke and then came fireworks? He started shoving his trench mortar, 100 to the minute or so it seemed like anyway. All you could hear was the whistling over your head and exploding in the close vicinity. It was not so bad when they did whistle overhead, you knew at least you were safe anyway. Between the snipes and flying shrapnel, it was sure no paradise, so we decide to advance. The boys fixed their bayonets and pushed forward, boy did Gerrie retreat? I'll say he did. He could not stand the cold steel. Quite a few tried to give themselves up but the 'Jocks' were so het up they gave them all they had. We advanced alright but the Bat. On our right flank did not so we were in a hotter spot than ever. Between front and side fire, not so healthy I may tell you. The boys began to suffer pretty heavy casualties and it was then a nicely placed shell found my carrier which were hidden in a hollow. I was lucky to be out of it all the time. When I saw it go up, I was not feeling in too happy a position, nor was my crew, the officer and sergeant. The only thing I had on me was my rifle and fifty rounds of ammunition.

At that point, the Bat. Decided to retire back a bit as Gerrie was pressing us, it was then some lucky guy drew a bead on me. By God, it fairly stung, so I dropped into a ditch and lay there for I think about one and a half hours. I could hear one or two Gerrie's shouting to each other in guttural tones, but I just lay there still hoping they would pass by. It must have been a patrol because for the next hour I could hear nothing, so I decide to crawl along the ditch hoping I was making the right way. Somehow or other I managed to come in contact with a party of RA's [Royal Artillery] in a small truck by the side of a deserted farmhouse. They were just ready to make a dash for it across an open piece of country to where one of their guns were, so I got in the truck and lay down hoping for the best. Glad to say we only encountered a few stray shots, none of whom hit us, but they were too close to be healthy.

I then arrived at a dressing station behind our lines and had my leg dressed. From there we were put into Red Cross trucks and transported to the coast. We were thirty hours on the road, and we only travelled about 100 miles. What with air raids from Gerrie's and the road blocked with traffic, it was a nightmare of a journey. We arrived at our destination, Dunkirk, everything was in chaos. I shall always remember it; the plane was burning all over and the smell and smoke was terrific. Cars, lorries and everything imaginable was left lying around. I managed to salvage myself a new battle dress and a few pieces of new clothing out of a salvaged RASC [Royal Army Service Corps] truck as my own was in a horrible state what with mud and blood on them.

After a few nerve-racking air raids, we managed to get on a ship. Four of them were lying at the end of the pier. I got into a first-class cabin on the 3rd deck, so feeling quite comfortable, I changed into my new togs and had a wash, the first for four days. I head there was tea ready upstairs, so I managed to limp up for some. While we were up there, the sky seemed to be alive with Nazi planes circling away up above, so we knew we were about to get it hot. Down they came one after the other, whining and roaring like the devil, and dropped some of their heavy bombs despite heavy fire from our ships. 'Oh, where is the RAF? Some of their bombs went wild but our ship 'Crested Eagle', and the next one, were hit direct. I can still feel the blast of that bomb. I thought I could write 'finish' to my career. The next minute we got word to leave the ship, which was all very well, but there, was no pier or gangway left, so we were in a bit of a fix? I do not know how some of the wounded manged, but I slid down a rope on to the broken pier and made for the other boat. My leg was fairly giving me hell all the time. After getting as much as possible on board, we cast off 'toot sweet'. The ship was packed tight with men, but everything was not so bad for a while. About five miles out the vultures returned circling round about us. The ship's crew put up a heavy barrage with AA gun and a couple of Lewis machine guns, but the aircraft seemed to be blessed by Lady Luck because though a few of the shells burst very near them, they seemed to live a charmed life.

They repeated the same tactics as at the pier, diving at full speed and letting go with two or three bombs at a time sometimes the planes were only about 500 feet up before they brought them out of the dive and boy did those engines whine! I'll say they did, it was really nerve racking the noise they made.

Well as you understand we could not stand that bombardment, so the ship shook from bow to stern as the bombs contacted. What a hell of a din, the blast of hot air smote me across the face about one a second. After Gerrie did as much damage as possible, he drew off leaving the ship just totally wrecked, but still afloat and very surprisingly the engines were still running. How they made it I do not know. The cry went round the ship for fire extinguishers as the damn thing went up in flames. The noise was terrible, between the noise of the dying men and the cracking of burning wood as the fire was getting really desperate. Some of the men broke into song. I mind they sang 'Loch Lomond' and 'Tipperary' at the top of their voices. It made me think of a picture I once saw of the 'Lusitania' before it went down. Everything just looked the same. The heat and smoke were something terrible by now as the ship had turned back and was making for land, we thought we still had a ghost of a chance of life, at least what was left of us. She grounded about two miles out, but a destroyer could be seen steaming to our aid. There was magazine on board and the captain gave orders to jump for it. We were all pretty glad to get away from the heat and smoke which was suffocating us, so I made a bee-line for the side and like a mug dived off instead of jumping – I forgot at the time I was wearing a lifebelt around my neck. The distance to the water was about 15 feet and the impact as I hit the water nearly broke my neck. It was pretty sore for a day or two. When I stuck the water, I started swimming for the shore which now seemed an awful distance away. Too far for my liking. I noticed the destroyer had arrived and lowered a big flat pontoon boat to pick up the unfortunate ones who could not swim. I also noticed Gerrie still floating around way up in the sky. Surprising to relate I felt quite confident when I started swimming for the shore although after a bit the shore still seemed a long distance off. You make slow progress with the lifebelt and of course the salt water in my wound was giving me jip.

I limped up the beach to the sand dunes in front of me and discovered that we were not the only ones to be marooned. There was quite a large number of British soldiers there. I managed to scrape up dry shirt and underpants and I got an old leather coat from a French soldier. By gum – I needed it as the evening was wearing on and I was shivering like a leak. During the night between 2 and 3 thousand troops turned up on the shore and I discovered this was the first of the crowd that was on the retreat. They were to be loaded on to the ships, which were anchored out from the shore. They had come across the channel under cover of darkness. The troops were loaded on small boats, which held only about 10 men a trip, so you can imagine it was a painful night before we managed to get loaded again. Some of the soldiers got fed up waiting and waded out as far as possible and swam the rest, but this was soon stopped as the ships could not cope with them trying to get on board out of the water. It was dawn before I managed to bag a small pleasure boat, which was being used for loading purposes, and would you believe it – it stuck on a sandbank not far out, talk about luck! After about an hour of rugging and tugging, we managed to free it and we embarked safely on a destroyer, from there I fell asleep from pure exhaustion and was awakened at Dover sometime in the afternoon. I landed on English soil with nothing but a shirt, pullover, *underpants and a leather coat, which had seen better days, no boots or stockings just like an African native, dressed up. Such is life!*

I managed to get equipped on shore, so I made for the hospital train which I boarded and landed in Sheffield and then life was a bed of roses, good food, nice nurses and of all things a good bed.

Very nice reading, but Hell to be in!

(Signed) Andrew McKenzie Munn

6 Battalion Seaforth Highlanders

Dunkirk 1940

Transferred RAF 1941

Tail Gunner Aircrew (Lancaster's)

Killed in Action April 1943

Buried Le Mans Paris

NOTES:

The Lee-Brown crew were involved in an incident during a fighter affiliation demonstration on 27 February 1943 when they were forced to bail-out, the instructor, Flight Lieutenant Richard Noel Stubbs RAFVR, DFC DFM was sadly killed. At a height of 6000 ft, F/L Stubbs was demonstrating violent evasive action in Avro Lancaster W4857. During this the port fin collapsed inward and struck the port elevator which became detached. F/L Stubbs headed the aircraft back to base and ordered the crew to bail-out. Stubbs attempted to land at RAF Elsham Wolds, aborted and then climbed steeply during which the starboard fin and elevator collapsed. The aircraft dived into the ground and burst into flames killing the pilot.

F/L Stubbs was a very experienced pilot who had completed 2 tours with RAF 75 Squadron and RAF 9 Squadron. At the time of the crash, he was attached to the Air Fighting Development Unit.

Flight Sergeant James Joseph O'Brien was awarded the Distinguished Flying Medal on 25 April 1941 whilst serving with RAF 77 Squadron. He joined the RAF in 1937 at RAF Cranwell as a boy entrant.

A German night fighter flown by Lt Josef Pützkuhl (10/NJG 5) flying from Morlaix Airfield in Brittany, France claimed to have shot down a Lancaster over northern France – possibly it was a Lancaster that ditched in the English Channel.

Leslie Hore-Belisha is still widely associated in the UK with the amber "Belisha beacons" which were installed at pedestrian crossings while he was Minister for Transport.

ROYAL AIR FORCE BOMBER COMMAND, 1942-1945. (C 3697) Annotated section of a vertical aerial photograph taken during a night raid on the docks at La Spezia, Italy. An Avro Lancaster is silhouetted over the target area as a photoflash bomb (centre right) illuminates the docks below, revealing a 'Littorio' class battleship lying in harbour ('A'). Copyright: © IWM.

Thomas Nicholson

RAF 620 Squadron was formed at RAF Chedburgh, near Bury St Edmonds, Suffolk, on 17 June 1943. The squadron was part of No 3 Group of RAF Bomber Command flying 20 Short Stirling four-engine heavy bombers. It served not only as a bomber squadron, but was also used for airborne parachute forces, towing gliders and as a transport squadron. Within days, it was pressed into service as part of the strategic bombing campaign against the Ruhr area in Germany – the 'Battle of the Ruhr'.

On the night of 21/22 June 1943, RAF 620 Squadron flew to attack targets at Krefeld, northwest of Düsseldorf on the River Rhine. Eleven identified factories and 12 small industrial areas were destroyed or severely damaged. The raid destroyed large parts of the east of the city and a firestorm consumed most of the city centre (apart from the central train station, which remained intact apart from minor damage). The RAF and RCAF lost 44 lost that night from a force of 717 aircraft.

Short Stirling Mk. III, EE-875, call sign QS-A took off from RAF Chedburgh at 2335 hours on 22 June 1943. The mission, to attack Mülheim an der Ruhr, just east of Duisburg. The RAF dispatched 557 aircraft on this raid which destroyed 64% of the town. The entire industrial production capability was severely affected.

At 0230 hours, Short Stirling EE-875 was presumed to have crashed into the North Sea 20 kilometres west of The Netherlands province of Walcheren, north of Zeebrugge – all the crew were lost.

Sergeant Thomas Nicholson RAF (658284) pilot, age 23

Flying Officer William Henry Boundy RAFVR (134161) bomb aimer, age 29

Sergeant Ralph Owen Jasper RAFVR (1316326) flight engineer, age 22

Sergeant Kenneth William Read RAFVR (1394386) navigator, age 21.

Sergeant Amos Alfred Thomas Woodard RAFVR (1384980) wireless operator/air gunner, age 23

Sergeant Roy Jackson RAFVR (1098586) air gunner, age unknown

Sergeant Harold James Wells RAFVR (1304641) air gunner, age 22

Harold Wells body washed ashore on 8 July 1943. He is buried in Bergen-op-Zoom War Cemetery, Noord-Brabant, The Netherlands. The rest of the crew who were recorded as missing in action are remembered on the Runnymede War Memorial.

Nicholson was the son of Thomas and Elizabeth Nicholson (née Sanderson) of Brae Cottage, Fairies Road, Perth.

Perthshire Advertiser, 26th January 1944

'WAR CASUALTIES

BELIEVED LOST ON NIGHT OPERATIONS

Sergt. T. Nicholson, R.A.F., son of Mrs Reid, Brae Cottage, Fairies Road, Burghmuir, Perth, who was reported missing from night operations in June, is now presumed to have lost his life.

Called up at the outbreak of war, he a Territorial, he was then a driver in the R.A.S.C. and served in France, being posted missing at the evacuation of St. Valery. He transferred to the R.A.F. in July 1941, and trained in England and Canada, where he gained his wings. Twenty-three years of age, he was a skilful skater, having won many prizes, and a keen follower of the Panthers Ice Hockey team and Jeanfield Swifts F.C. He was educated at Cherrybank and Perth Academy, and was serving his apprenticeship with J. Johnstone, joiner, Craigie, when called up.'

Amazingly, Nicholson had earlier survived capture, being posted missing at St Valery en Caux whilst with the 51st Highland Division in June 1940. More than 10,0000 ended up as prisoners of war.

NOTES: The 'Battle of the Ruhr' was a five-month long campaign of strategic bombing of the Ruhr area in Germany (March 1943-July 1943). During the campaign, Bomber Command estimated that 70% of its losses were due to night fighters. By July 1943, the German air force's night-fighter force totalled 550 aircraft.

To man the anti-aircraft defences in Germany, 600,000 personnel were required. There were 1,000 large flak and 1,500 lighter guns in the Ruhr area, roughly about 1/3rd of all the flak guns in Germany. Whilst the RAF were bombing at night, the USAF continued the concentrated attacks on the Ruhr during the day.

Krefeld contained chemical works, large textile factories which made parachutes, and steel plants making crankshafts and armour plate. It was also an important railway centre.

Ronald Staples Ogg

Sergeant Ronald Staples Ogg, RAFVR 1557938 was the son of John and Helen A. Ogg of 13 Kenmore Street, Aberfeldy and the husband of Madge Eunice Ogg, Glenfield, Leicestershire.

Ronald was posted to RAF Transport Command and went on to further training and conversion courses, culminating at RAF Bramcote near Nuneaton with RAF 105 OTU (Operational Training Unit). Here the crews were prepared for flying the twin-engine Wellington aircraft, especially in readiness for the D-Day invasion and the campaign that would follow.

On the night of 28/29 April 1944, in Vickers Wellington T2968, they were practicing night take-offs and landings from the nearby satellite airfield at Nuneaton. The plane had been fully checked and passed fit for night flying. Gerald Toller, the pilot had logged 241 hours flying time with 38 hours at night.

The crew members of Vickers Wellington IC T2968 were:

Pilot, Flying Officer Gerald Stark Toller, RAFVR 74747

Wireless Operator/Air Gunner, Sergeant Ronald Ogg, RAFVR 1557938

Navigator, Sergeant Stanley Reed.

Vickers Wellington IC T2968 had completed five circuits and landings and took off for the sixth time, heading North. The plane failed to gain sufficient height, the flaps were not retracted and after three miles the starboard wing struck a tree and the plane crashed and burst into flames at Manor Farm, Upton, Nuneaton, 8 miles north. Gerald Toller and Ronald Ogg were killed, Stanley Reed was thrown clear with slight injuries and burns to his face and hands.

Sergeant Ronald Staples Ogg was 23 years of age and is buried in Aberfeldy Cemetery.

NOTES: Gerald Toller was born in 1912 in Shantou (also known as Swatow) on the eastern coast of Guangdong, China. At the start of WW2, he joined the RAF and at some point, was an Intelligence Officer working undercover in France.

RAF Bramcote after WW2 became HMS Gamecock and then Gamecock Barracks.

The satellite airfield near RAF Bramcote was also known as Fenny Drayton, Lindley, MIRA and RAF Nuneaton

The Vickers Wellington development was led by Vickers-Armstrong's' chief designer Rex Pierson; a key feature of the aircraft is its geodetic airframe fuselage structure, which was principally designed by Barnes Wallis (the bouncing bomb inventor).

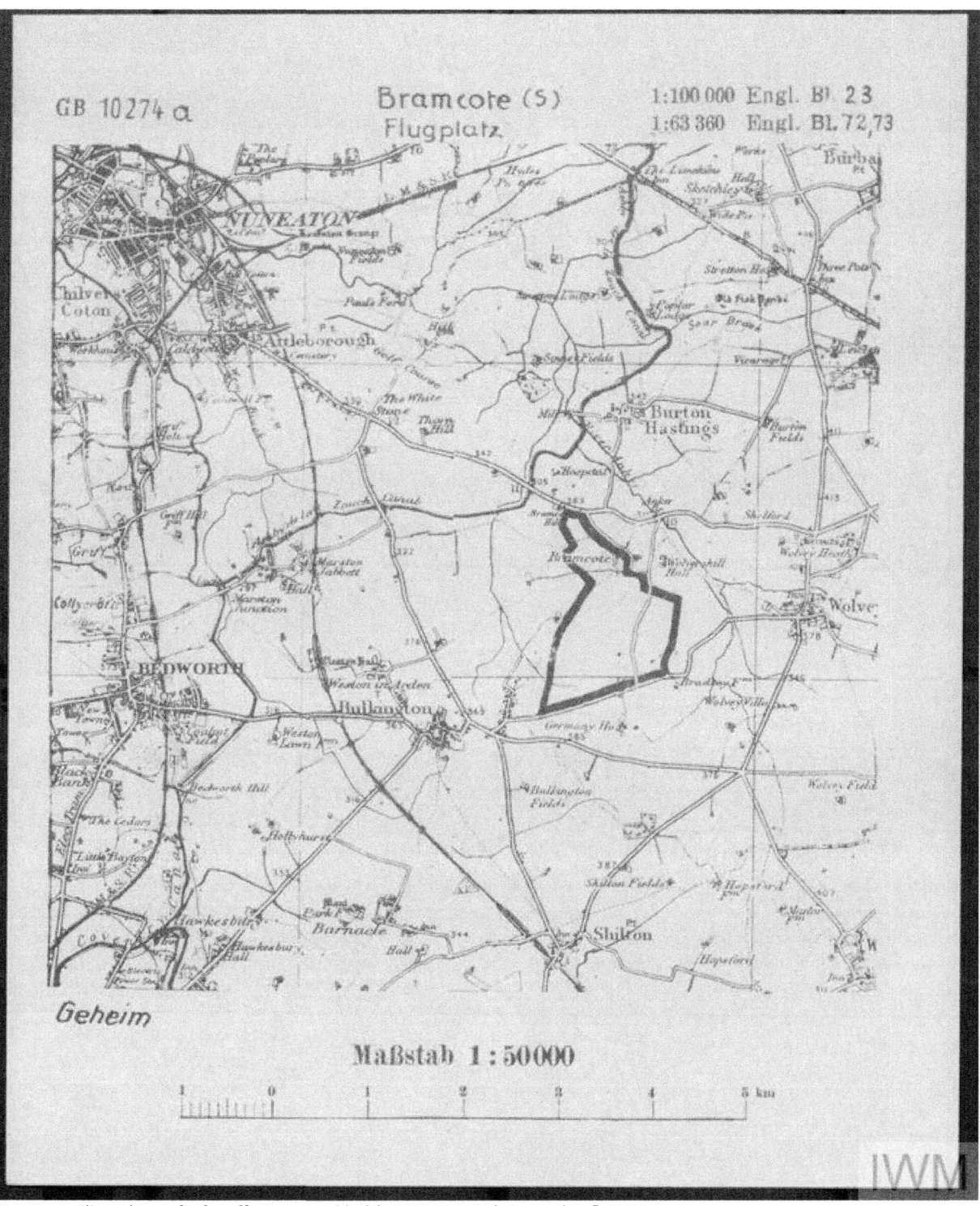

Bramcote Fliegerhorst: [Luftwaffe Target Folder] (LBY LUFT 1174) Copyright: © IWM.:

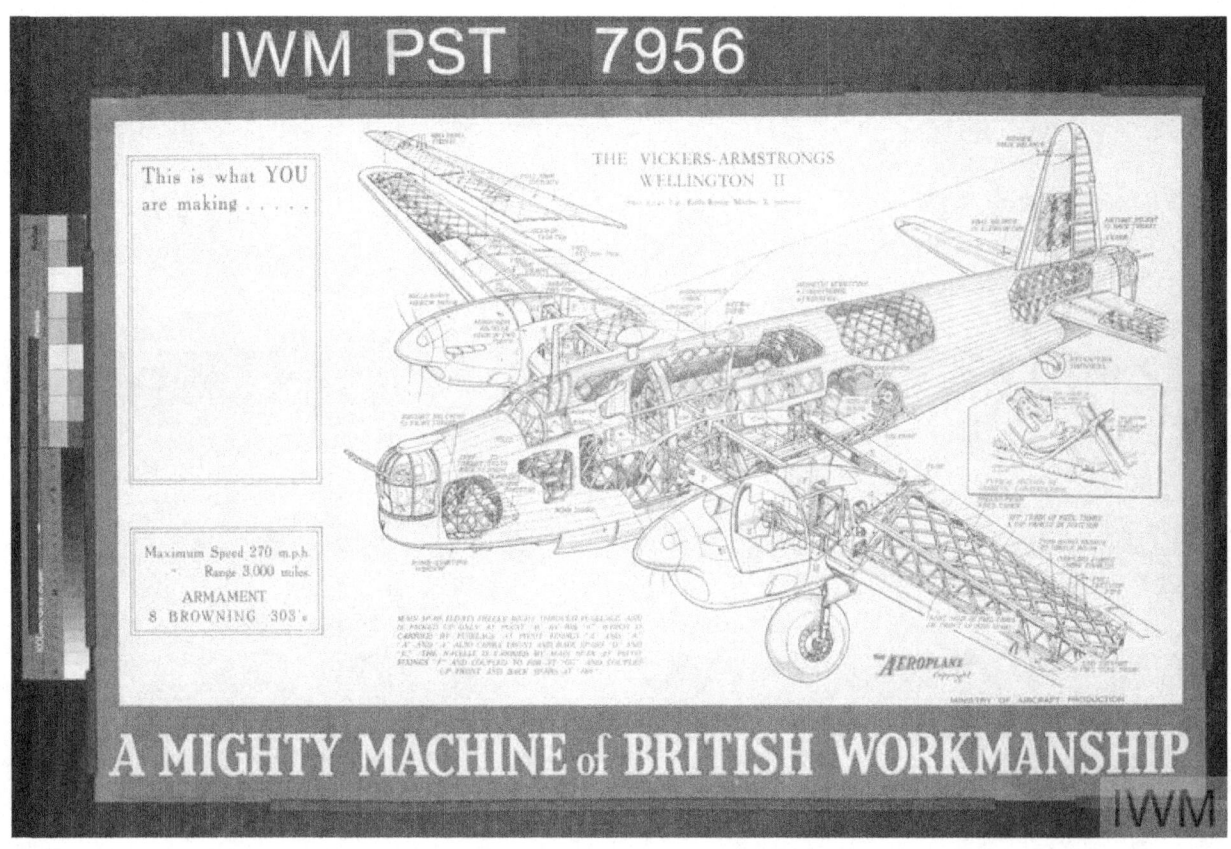

A Mighty Machine of British Workmanship – The Vickers-Armstrongs Wellington II (Art.IWM PST 7956) whole: the image occupies the majority, set against a white background. The title is separate and positioned across the bottom edge, in white. The subtitle and text are integrated and occupy the majority, in black. All held within a red border. image: a drawing of a Vickers-Armstrongs Wellington II aircraft, with cut-away sections to show the internal components. text: THE VICKERS-ARMSTRONGS WELLI... Copyright: © IWM.

Alex Thomson Patterson

During World War Two, more than 30,000 men served with the Airfield Construction (AC) Wings of the RAF (also known as Works Squadrons). An AC Squadron member consisted of every known trade and profession from the construction industry and their task was to repair bomb-damaged airfields and build new ones. As the war progressed, there was a requirement for longer and heavier runways as the RAF expanded and the USSAF 8th & 9th joined the battle.

Alex Thomson Patterson served with the RAF 5051 Bomb Disposal Squadron which spent most of the early part of 1943 in Malta preparing the island's airfields for their role in the invasion of Sicily of 9 July 1943.

Leading Aircraftman Alex Thomson Paterson RAFVR (1369874) died age 21, on 25 May 1944. He was the nephew of Margaret Paterson from Perth and is buried in Wellshill Cemetery.

It is not known how Alex died but given that he is buried at Wellshill it is likely it happened somewhere in the UK. In the early months of 1944, Airfield Construction Squadrons were involved in the major task of constructing 23 Advanced Landing Grounds in Kent, Sussex, and Hampshire. From which the RAF and USAAF fighter and fighter bomber squadrons would be able to effectively operate during Operation Overlord in northern France and over the D-Day beachhead. Security at military installations and camps was increased on 25 May 1944. Camps were sealed with no one allowed out and patrolled by military police until D-Day on 6 June 1944.

Note: In Italy on 2 May 1944, 1,500 Allied artillery pieces at the beach at Anzio commenced bombardment of the German forces as they started their breakout. The drive inland was underway on 25 May 1944.

BOMB DAMAGE AND LIFE IN VALLETTA, MALTA. 1942. (A 8553) Open air market carrying on among the wreckage. Copyright: © IWM.

Charles Duncan Powrie

Sergeant Charles Duncan Powrie took off from RAF Stradishall on board Vickers Wellington Mk. Ic T2476 at 17.09 hours on 7 December 1940. The mission was to bomb Düsseldorf in Germany.

Powrie was the son of Robert Powrie and Katherine Powrie, Homewood, 131 Glasgow Road, Perth. He was a former pupil of Perth Academy and before joining the RAFVR, six months before the war, he assisted his father in their fishmonger business at 62 South Methven Street, Perth.

Powrie's aircraft was one of three aircraft despatched 30 minutes ahead of the main force from RAF 214 Squadron. They were to act as Pathfinders, locating and marking the target for the rest of the force to bomb. The weather was atrocious, and the lead Pathfinder lost both engines. It fell several thousand feet before being able to restart them. The other two Pathfinders, including Sergeant Powrie's aircraft, were both lost, probably due to enemy action, but the weather may have played a part. It was thought that Wellington T2476 crashed into the North Sea.

PERTHSHIRE ADVERTISER 21 JUNE 1941

On board RAF Squadron 214 (Federated Malay States) Vickers Wellington T2476 was:

Flying Officer David Allan Dadswell RAF (40367) pilot, age 26

Sergeant Francis Thomas Buckingham RAFVR (758023) pilot, age unknown

Sergeant Charles Duncan Powrie RAFVR (745352) observer, age 24

Sergeant William Henry James RAFVR (972478) wireless operator/air gunner, age unknown

Sergeant Edward Cooper Lee RAFVR (969132) air gunner, age 28

Sergeant John Cunningham Macaskie RAFVR (936778) wireless operator/air gunner, age 25

Powrie had taken part in over two dozen bomber raids over enemy territory. The crew are commemorated on the Runnymede Memorial in Surrey.

NOTES:

RAF 214 Squadron's real-life Second World War bomber missions formed the basis for the 1948/9 BBC Radio drama 'I Shan't Be Home For Dinner', written by the wife of one of 214 Squadron observers. It also toured as a theatre play in the UK during 1949/50.

RAF 214 (Federated Malay States) Squadron lost 45 Vickers Wellington, 17 Flying Fortress, 54 Short Stirling and an unknown number of Handley Page Harrow's during the war. The highest percentage losses in RAF 3 Group, RAF Bomber Command.

Flight Sergeant William Alistair McLaren also served with RAF 214 Squadron.

David Douglas Pryde, George Pryde, William Symington Pryde, John Marshall Pryde

Squadron Leader **David Douglas Pryde** DFC was born in Crieff on 17 April 1918 and was one of four brothers, of which 3, David, George and William all joined the RAF and died during the early years of World War Two. The fourth brother, Captain John Marshall (Jack) Pryde also served with the RAF on a short service commission and then joined the Argyll and Sutherland Highlanders, served in the Middle East during World War Two.

The brothers were the sons of the Reverend John Marshall Pryde, B.D. and Jean Marshall Pryde, at the time of his death they were residing at Kilrenny Manse, Anstruther.

During World War One, whilst the Reverend John Marshall Pryde was on active service as a Chaplain, the family stayed in Crieff. David, his older brother, and his sister spent several years being educated at Morrisons Academy in Crieff.

Brothers, Squadron Leader George A.M. Pryde, D.F.C. and Flying Officer William S. Pryde, also died in service. Squadron Leader George Pryde won his DFC for an operational flight over Belgium in 1940.

On 9 June 1942 **Squadron Leader David Douglas Pryde** was piloting Armstrong Whitely V, BD195, of RAF 77 Squadron over the Bay of Biscay, just southwest of Brest.

The crew comprised:

Squadron Leader David Douglas Pryde (39564) RAF Age 24

Flight Sergeant William Carmichael (1252018) RAFVR

Sergeant John William Cook (922612)

Flight Lieutenant Robert Gordon Nicholas Laidlaw (J/5319) RCAF

Flight Lieutenant Alan Peter Tyson (123994)

They had taken off from RAF Chivenor, near Barnstaple on the north coast of Devon in England, tasked with an anti-submarine patrol. Over the Bay of Biscay, 60 kms southwest of Brest, France, at 12.30 hours they were attacked by enemy aircraft and shot down.

Squadron Leader Pryde, Flight Sergeant Carmichael and Sergeant Cook were reported missing, believed killed. They are all remembered on the Runnymede Memorial and Squadron Leader Pryde is also remembered at the family plot in Anstruther, his name is included on his parent's headstone and on the Waid Academy, War memorial, Anstruther.

Flight Lieutenant Laidlaw survived, was rescued, and became a prisoner of war at Stalag Luft3, Sagan and Beleria, near Żagań in Western Poland. Flight Lieutenant Tyson was also rescued and became a prisoner of war at Stalag 357, Kopernikus near Toruń in Poland.

Squadron Leader David Douglas Pryde had joined the RAF in 1937 at the age of 19. He was appointed Acting Pilot Officer on Probation 8 March 1937. Then graded as Pilot Officer on 21 December 1937 and promoted to Flying Officer on 8 September 1939. On the 20 May 1940 he was awarded the

Distinguished Flying Cross (DFC). When still a Flying Officer, on 20 May 1940 was detailed for a collaboration operation involving an attack on the communication centre at Hannapes, 100 km east of Amiens. (The German army had invaded France on 10 May 1940, making a surprise attack through the Ardennes Forest (50 kms west of Hannapes), code named – operation *Fall Gelb* ("Case Yellow")). (See also Aircraftman 2nd Class Thomas Kennedy)

Taking off from RAF Driffield in North Yorkshire in RAF 77 Squadron. Armstrong Whitworth Whitley Mk. V N1384 (KN-G) at 20.36 pm they were reported to have force landed near Abbeville, France. The Whitley was severely damaged by flak (anti-aircraft fire) and was set on fire. All the crew were uninjured and soon returned to RAF Driffield to resume their operational duties.

The official Air Ministry file on the incident: *"Whitley N1384 crashed at Beauvais, France, 21 May 1940. Warrant Officer A C Thompson, Pilot Officer A C Meigh, Flying Officer D D Pryde, Pilot Officer A W Dunn, Aircraftman 1st Class T B Kenny and Aircraftman 1st Class F Crawford, safe"*

Report on Flying Officer David Douglas Pryde's in Whitley N1384, 20 May 1940 mission:

'The example he set that day of courage and determination, that came at the end of six months of war flying during which he had completed 16 operational flights, both as a second pilot and as captain, showed courage and dash. And the spirit in which he tackles his flights is an infectious stimulant to all who work with him.'

This was further refined for the Air Ministry Honours and Awards Committee to read as follows: *'London Gazette No. 34870, Dated 11 June 1940. On 20th May 1940, this officer was detailed for a collaboration operation involving an attack on the communication centre at Hannapes, France. Despite difficult conditions, he succeeded in identifying the target from a very low altitude. Although his aircraft was hit heavily, Flying Officer Pryde climbed to 3,000 feet and executed a successful bombing attack. His aircraft subsequently caught fire, but he continued flying and when height could no longer be maintained, the entire crew landed by parachute. Flying Officer Pryde has completed sixteen operational flights during six months of war flying and has displayed considerable courage and determination of a high order.'*

Later, on the night of 19/20 June 1940, Squadron Leader David Douglas Pryde, RAF 77 piloting Armstrong Whitely, N3171 was undertaking an operational flight to attack marshalling yards at Wanne-Eickel, Germany (between Essen and Dortmund), when it was hit by flak and sustained some damage. It was able to make a safe return to land at RAF Driffield at 03.40hrs and the damage was soon repaired on site.

RAF Flying Officer **William Symington Pryde** (37690) died on 24 September 1939, age 22 years. William Pryde was piloting North American Harvard Mk. I, N7067 from RAF Grantham, No.12 Flying Training School when it went out of control, spun out of cloud into the ground at Newton, North Kesteven, Lincolnshire (10 miles west of Grantham). Flying Officer William Symington Pryde (37690), and Leading Aircraftman Albert Bernard Hayes (219069), aged 49, were both killed.

Flying Officer William Symington Pryde is buried in Anstruther New Cemetery. (In 1944, RAF Grantham was renamed RAF Spitalgate)

RAF Squadron Leader **George Archibald Marshall Pryde** (32232) (ex RAF 21 squadron) was killed on 19 June 1940 in an aircraft accident at Tunis, Tunisia, North Africa. The aircraft he was killed in was Bristol Blenheim Mk. IV, L9334. He was piloting it on a delivery flight, one of twelve Bristol Blenheim's going to Malta for 4 (Continental) Ferry Pilots Pool. Taking off from RAF Tangmere between 6.30 and 6.45 hours on 18 June 1940 in Bristol Blenheim Mk. IV, L9263 an engine cut-off at Mariganne (Marseille) in the south of France. The Blenheim L9263 struck the boundary and was abandoned there.

The next day they took off 1730 hrs from Marignane (Marseille) in Blenheim L9334 on the next leg of the flight to Malta. They overshot the island of Malta and on approaching the Tunisian coast they crashed into the sea. The pilot, Squadron Leader Pryde, age 30 and Sergeant Alexander Scott RAFVR (759142), RAF 500 Squadron, age 19, the Wireless operator/Air Gunner were killed instantly. Sergeant Leslie Arthur Hibbett RAF (58116), age 19, died two days later. Sergeant Scott is buried in Medjez-el-Bab War Cemetery. The others are commemorated on the Runnymede Memorial. George Pryde was born in St. Machar in Aberdeen city.

Before that, Squadron Leader George Pryde flew with RAF 21 Squadron on operations over France during the German Blitzkrieg (Battle of France (10/05/1940-22/06/1940). On 11 May 1940, Squadron leader George Pryde took off at midday from RAF Watton, Norfolk. They overflew the Netherlands and Belgium at 15,000 feet. George Pryde then led his RAF 21 Squadron to attack German forces in and around the Albert Canal bridges near Maastricht, Netherlands. Their Bristol Blenheim's bombers shallow dive-bombed vehicles on a road. A dense curtain of flak was put up in response, one air gunner was killed by shrapnel. The next morning no less than eight of the Squadron's aircraft were unserviceable.

George Pryde also attended Morrisons Academy, Crieff during the closing years of the Great War when his father was on active service as a Chaplain.

Captain **John Marshall Pryde** joined the RAF on 1 July 1937 on a short service commission. His commission was terminated on 3 December 1937. It was speculated that Sergeant John Pryde was involved in an air accident crash and left the RAF due to his injuries. John Pryde later joined the Argyll and Sutherland Highlanders as a 2nd Lieutenant in August 1940. He rose to the rank of Captain and was known to have served at some point in the middle east. He appears to have survived the war and emigrated to Arizona, USA.

NOTES:

During World War II, the Albert Canal functioned as a defence line. The Albert Canal that connects Antwerp with Liège. The crossing of the Albert Canal by the German forces and the destruction of Fort Eben-Emael (south of Maastricht) on 11 May 1940 was a milestone in the German invasion of Belgium. (See also Sergeant Andrew Mackenzie Munn)

In German, Stalag was a term used for prisoner-of-war camps. Stalag is a contraction of "Stammlager", itself short for Kriegsgefangenen-Mannschaftsstammlager.

On 20 May 1940, the day Squadron leader Pryde won the DFC, the first prisoners arrived at a new concentration camp, Auschwitz and German General Guderian's tanks captured Amiens at 0900 hours,

Abbeville at 1900 hours, and Noyelles-sur-Mer at 2000 hours (70 kms); they had reached the English Channel.

In 1872, the newly created School Board of Anstruther Easter approached the Trustees of the will of Andrew Waid, to set up his Academy and on Monday 6th September 1886 at 2pm, the Board of Governors opened the Waid Academy, Anstruther, to 75 pupils who had passed the entrance examination. Andrew Waid was born on 18th June 1736, and when the American War of Independence started in 1776, Waid was actively engaged on the Loyalist side. He lost his ship *"Thrifty Lass" to the rebels* shortly after the war started. He returned to his native homeland by 1781. His loyalty was rewarded with him being made a Lieutenant in the Royal Navy and served *"with distinction, especially in the North Seas"* till he retired on half pay. In 1795 he was given the freedom of the City of Perth, shortly followed by a similar honour by the Burgh of Anstruther Easter.

RAF 21 Squadron was formed in 1915 and was disbanded for the last time in 1979. The squadron is famous for Operation Jericho on 18 February 1944, when the crews of de Havilland Mosquitoes breached the walls of a Gestapo prison at Amiens, France, allowing members of the French Resistance to escape.

Squadron Leader David Douglas Pryde

Charles Rankin

On the night of 20/21 October 1943, Avro Lancaster DS726 of RAF 408 Squadron flown by Pilot Officer Charles Rankin took off from RAF Linton On Ouse to bomb the city of Leipzig in Germany. The crew successfully bombed the target and returned to base. Whilst DS726 was taxing around the perimeter track, its starboard wing stuck Lancaster DS771 that had landed earlier with flak damage. DS 726 received damage to the starboard outer engine and starboard wing tip.

On the night of 21/22 January 1944, Rankin was flying in Lancaster II, DS790, call sign EQ-B. They took off on an operation to bomb Magdeburg on the River Elbe, Germany.

Lancaster DS790 was attacked by a German night-fighter seconds before they were about to release their bomb-load. Both port engines and the wing were set ablaze. The aircraft went into a spin, was corrected, and then spun again, wildly. It dived and broke up, throwing clear only three survivors.

The crew of DS790 were:

Pilot Officer John Bleecker Mill RCAF, Pilot (of Watson Lake, Yukon), prisoner of war

Flight Lieutenant JB Dinning RCAF, 2nd Pilot, Prisoner of War

Sergeant William Johnston RAFVR (656566) Bomb Aimer, Prisoner of War

Sergeant Albert Edward Elliott RAFVR (1211502) flight, age unknown, KIA

Flying Officer Gilmour Murray Reid RAFVR (127268) navigator, KIA

Pilot Officer Charles Rankin RAFVR (171474) wireless operator/air gunner, age 30, KIA

Sergeant Howard Dennis Jones RAFVR (1413674) flight engineer, KIA

Pilot Officer Gordon Currie, RCAF (J/88815) age 31, (of Saskatoon, Saskatchewan) KIA

Reid, Currie, Elliot, and Jones have no known grave and are commemorated on the Runnymede Memorial. Rankin rests in Rheinberg War Cemetery, Nordrhein-Westfalen, Germany.

Rankin was the son of John and Barbara Rankin of Giffnock, Renfrewshire. John Rankin was the stationmaster at Perth and Charles attended Perth Academy. Charles Rankin was gazetted on 16 January 1944, six days before he was killed in action. He was commissioned as a pilot officer on probation (emergency).

Perthshire Advertiser, 18 November 1944

'DEATH OF P.O. CHARLIE RANKIN

The death is now presumed of Pilot Officer Charlie Rankin, R.A.F., son of Mr John Rankin, former stationmaster at Perth and Glasgow Central.

Charlie was reported missing from air operations over Germany on 21st January 1944. He was in the railway service as a clerk before going to the R.A.F., starting at Perth and going to Glasgow in 1937. He was very popular and well-known in the Perth district, and all will regret his untimely passing.'

Three interrogation reports from the three survivors who became prisoners of war:

NUMBER. J-19284, RANK. F/O, NAME. Mill J. B, SQUADRON. 408, AIRCRAFT. DS-790 EQ-B, TYPE OF AIRCRAFT. Lancaster II, DATE OF LOSS. 21/22.1.1944, TARGET. Magdeburg, HOW MANY OPS. 16 DUTY. Pilot

DATE OF INTERROGATION. 17.5.1945

INFORMATION EXTRACTED FROM. POW REPORT

NARRATIVE OF EVENTS FROM TAKEOFF TO LANDING.

Trip uneventful from take-off at Linton on Ouse till the target. We were in the last wave and on time. We started a normal bombing run, opened the bomb doors with two or three seconds to go when the fighter attacked (no warning from the gunners). The trace seemed to be coming from a little below and slightly to port. Straightened out by which time the two port engines and wing section from the port inner to the fuselage were blazing. After feathering etc and jettisoning bomb load, I saw the fire was increasing and told the crew to bail out. the 2nd pilot clipped on my chute and went into the nose. The stick seemed to tighten up and then the aircraft went into a spin and flew up after about two complete circles. There was an ear-splitting noise and then everything went black. I regained consciousness in an already opened chute and soon realized that I was drifting away from the target. There was 10/10 th's cloud at about 8,000 feet in the area. Twisted knee on landing.

NUMBER. J-3713, RANK. F/Lt, NAME. Dinning J., SQUADRON. 408/425, AIRCRAFT. DS-790 EQ-B, TYPE OF AIRCRAFT. Lancaster II, DATE OF LOSS. 21/22.1.1944, TARGET. Magdeburg, HOW MANY OPS. 0, DUTY. 2nd pilot

DATE OF INTERROGATION. 10.5.1945

INFORMATION EXTRACTED FROM. POW REPORT

NARRATIVE OF EVENTS FROM TAKEOFF TO LANDING.

No fighters were seen as we approached the target. There was plenty of flak and just as we started the bombing run (well out) the flt/engineer called out "look to port". As he said that, the fighter raked us from stem to stern in the port side. No warning came from the gunners. The aircraft caught fire immediately, also the 2 port engines. We spun and then it was corrected. The rear gunner was screaming for help as he was jammed in the turret. This was after the bail out order had been given. Attempts were made to feather the engines and put out the fire with no success. I put on the pilot's chute and then my own and moved down front. The bomb aimer was unable to get the hatch open. We spun violently and I was thrown up to the nose where I lay watching the bomb aimer still trying to hang on and open the hatch. I couldn't get near to help him as the aircraft was spinning with all 4 engines running wild. The next thing I knew I was about 100 feet off the ground and then landed. I figure the aircraft must have blown up at approximately 9,000 feet.

NUMBER. 162546, RANK. P/O, NAME. Johnston W., SQUADRON. 408, AIRCRAFT. DS-790 EQ-B, TYPE OF AIRCRAFT. Lancaster II, DATE OF LOSS. 21/22.1.1944, TARGET. Magdeburg, HOW MANY OPS. 20 DUTY. Bomb aimer

DATE OF INTERROGATION. 8.5.1945

INFORMATION EXTRACTED FROM. POW REPORT

NARRATIVE OF EVENTS FROM TAKEOFF TO LANDING.

We took off from Linton on the night of the 21st in a spare aircraft to bomb Magdeburg. The night was dark, about half-moon. We climbed over the North Sea to about 18,000 feet. Near to the German coast the navigator reported us well south of track. We aircraft immediately and came in between Bremen and Hamburg almost on track. We reached our last turning point on ETA. Ran up and saw our green flares going down slightly to south. We were in the stream running up. Before the target I ordered bomb doors open. Steady over target. And about to release bombs when we were attacked from behind and level. The fighter was not seen by our gunners, and he got in a long burst before the pilot could dive and turn to starboard. I released the bombs in the dive. We straightened out for about a minute, height 18,000 feet. The pilot feathered his port engines. Saw extent of damage and ordered us to bail out. During the elapsing minute I put on my chute and endeavoured to open the escape hatch. The second pilot put on pilot's chute for him and came to assist me to open the door. The plane went into a spin (left hand), and I was thrown against the Perspex at the end of the first complete spin. I felt a terrific crash of an explosion. The Perspex broke into little pieces, and I fell out. I was unconscious for a few seconds. Woke up to find the ground near, opened my chute and landed safely.

INTERROGATOR'S NOTES

Aircraft exploded as informant left, so some of crew were blown out and landed okay. Others were carried down in aircraft and killed in crash. Aircraft crashed near where informant landed.

NOTES: Lancaster DS790 was delivered to the squadron in November of 1943. Lancaster DS 726 was shot down over Cambrai on the night of 12/13 June 1944. Lancaster DS 771, transferred to RAF 426 Squadron, was reported missing over Stuttgart on the night of 15/16 March 1944. DS790 flew ten operations, including four to Berlin during this time.

Magdeburg was the main force target for 648 aircraft on 21/22 January 1944, 421 Lancaster's, 224 Halifax's and three Mosquitos. A small number of 12 Mosquitos and 22 Lancaster's attacked Berlin as a diversionary raid.

RCAF No 408 Squadron was the second of many Royal Canadian Air Force bomber squadrons which served overseas in the Second World War. They began operations with Halifax Hampdens in 1941, the squadron was equipped with the Handley Page Halifax towards the end of 1942, and Avro Lancasters in August 1943. They flew 4,610 sorties and dropped 11,340 tons of bombs. A total of 170 aircraft were lost and 933 personnel were killed. No 408 Squadron members won two hundred decorations, and 11 battle honours for its wartime operations.

RCAF No 408 Squadron (Goose Squadron as it was to become known), was formed at RAF Lindholme, east of Doncaster, Yorkshire, on 24 June 1941. They moved to RAF Syerston, near Newark, Nottinghamshire in July 1941 to begin operations. When the squadron converted to Avro Lancasters in August 1943 they moved to RAF Linton-on-Ouse and became part of No 6 Group RCAF.

The Lancaster crews were incredibly brave, heroic, 55,573 lost their lives (44.4%) out of 125,000 aircrew under Bomber Command defending our countries and so many of them were so young. They were up against a determined, ideologically driven, politically far-right fascist enemy. As an example, Heinz-Wolfgang Schnaufer was a German night-fighter ace flying a Messerschmitt Bf-110, credited with 121 victories, 114 of which were 'Viermots' (short in German for 'four-motors'). His most successful day occurred 21 February 1945 when he shot down nine bombers in a single day. His first night-fighter victory came on 2 June 1942 when he shot down a Handley Page Halifax of RAF 76 Squadron during Bomber Commands second 'Thousand Bomber Raid' against Essen. On 13 June 1944, operating above Cambrai in Northern France, 0031 hours at a height of 1,200 m, Schnaufer of Stab IV. /NJG1, damaged Charles Rankin's earlier Avro Lancaster II, DS726 of RAF 408 Squadron.

Schnaufer returned after the war to the family wine business and was on wine-buying trip to France on 13 July 1950. He was driving towards Biarritz when a lorry loaded with gas cylinders pulled out from a side road and collided with his sports car. It is believed that one of the cylinders was dislodged and struck the 28-year-old on the back of his head. He was taken to a hospital in Bordeaux with a fractured skull and died there two days later. Schnaufer was also responsible for shooting down Ernie 'Sherl-E' Holmes on 23 May 1944.

Colin 'Robbie' Robertson

Colin 'Robbie' Robertson RAF (33412) was a distinguished fighter pilot who as a member of RAF 603 (City of Edinburgh) Squadron engaged the first World War Two German aircraft to attack Great Britain – 16 October 1939. This and subsequent actions led him to be awarded the Distinguished Flying Cross (DFC).

ROBERTSON, Colin, P/O (33412, Royal Air Force) – No.603 Squadron – Distinguished Flying Cross – awarded as per London Gazette dated 31 May 1940. Public Record Office Air 2/9413 has recommendation and the following citation which is a digest of the original submission.

PERTHSHIRE ADVERTISER 18 DECEMBER 1943

'This officer has consistently shown skill and coolness in attacks on enemy aircraft, often in bad weather and always without Direction Finding facilities. On three occasions in October, he was a member of sections which shot down an enemy aircraft in each engagement. On the 7th of March he took part in an action in which an enemy aircraft was shot down and he also succeeded in closing in and reading its lettering which proved the aircraft to be one of the groups operating directly under the German High Command. On 17th March, in poor visibility, he intercepted enemy aircraft which, however, escaped into low cloud.'

In October of 1942, Agnes McAndrew Black, the second daughter of D. Black, GrayBank House, Perth, married RAF Squadron Leader Colin Robertson. Colin, the second son of the Robertsons, Roseneuk, Falkirk was educated at Falkirk High School and entered the RAF as an aircraft apprentice. He was promoted sergeant two years later. As the leading cadet at RAF College Cranwell, he graduated 17 December 1938 as a pilot officer.

Before the war started, Robertson was with RAF 41 Squadron at RAF Catterick in North Yorkshire. Here on 23 May 1939, he stalled and crashed during a night landing, Supermarine Spitfire Mk 1, K9842. The aircraft was 'Struck Off Charge' on 14 June 1939 as damaged beyond economic repair. It had first been flown at the Supermarine factory at Eastleigh, Southampton on 12 January 1939 and was delivered to the squadron on 16 January 1939. Total flying hours for Colin in a Spitfire was 97.15 at that time. He was then posted to RAF 603 Squadron at RAF Turnhouse, Edinburgh.

Robertson suffered a fractured skull in a horse-riding accident in June 1940. As a result, he was stood down from flying. This was just before the Battle of Britain (10 July 1940 to 31 October 1940) and means he does not count as one of the pilots who flew operationally in the battle. He was promoted to flying officer in June 1940, to flight lieutenant on 17 June 1941 and squadron leader on 1 July 1943. After serving some time in Canada, he returned to the UK and for two years flew de Haviland DH.98 Mosquitos, recording 365 flying hours' time in the type.

On 12 December 1943, Robertson of RAF 25 Squadron was flying in his Mosquito DH.98 NF MkII, DD754. Two Mosquito aircraft were carrying out a non-operational flight. Being a night fighter squadron, they were not used to fighting during the day, and were practising mock combats in pairs. His squadron was training to provide fighter cover for bomber aircraft returning the following day from an attack on the V-2 development and production facilities at Peenemünde, near the Baltic Sea in Germany.

His aircraft pitched up in a steep climbing turn without warning. It made a couple of spins before diving into marshy ground near West Flotmanby, west of Filey in North Yorkshire.

The RAF Court of Enquiry into the crash noted that the horse-riding accident had changed 'Robbie' Robertson's character 'from debonnaire to foolhardy', as he had attempted a loop at low level. A bit harsh and unfair given that Robertson had a considerable grand total of 1,116 flying hours experience at the time of his death.

Flying Officer Ernest Bartholomew RAFVR, the navigator and radar operator was also killed in the crash. Bartholomew received his commission of pilot officer on 13 April 1943 and had just been promoted to flying officer on 13 October 1943. He was (likely) aged around 28 years.

Robertson was a prominent athlete and won honours playing rugby, running events and in a sabre championship at RAF College Cranwell. S Robertson is buried at the Camelon Cemetery at Falkirk. He was aged 26 years. On 25 June 1944, a daughter was born to Agnes and the late Colin at St Johnstoun Nursing Home, Perth.

NOTES: Mosquito DH.98 NF MkII, DD754 was involved in an earlier crash on 28 April 1943. DD754 assigned then to RAF 25 Squadron, took off from RAF Church Fenton on a night-time test flight. While in the air the aircraft was about to fly into cloud so the pilot, Sergeant John Richard Brockbank, made a tight turn to avoid it. A bang was heard, and the observer, Sergeant David McCausland, reported a hole in the starboard tailplane. The starboard undercarriage would not lock down nor would it retract. The observer was instructed to bail out and the pilot made a one-wheel landing back at RAF Church Fenton. When the speed reduced, the starboard wing dropped, and it came to rest with some damage. Both crew members were unharmed. The problem was later found to be a known issue with the undercarriage door catch. The starboard undercarriage leg had dropped down in flight causing the door to break off and strike the tail. The dropping down of the undercarriage leg had caused damage to its front spar and the hydraulic system. The same thing happened to another Mosquito, DD747 on 8 April 1943, but this time the door caused the tail of the aircraft to break off. DD747 crashed with the loss of both crew members.

Mosquito DH.98 NF MkII's were fitted with AI (Airborne Interception) Radar and Gee Navigation sets were installed.

V-2 rocket production at Peenemünde was eventually destroyed by allied bombing and was relocated to Nordhaussen, Thuringia. The Mittelbau-Dora Nazi concentration camp on the outskirts of Nordhaussen was established in 1943 to provide slave labour for the underground Mitelwerk V-2 rocket factory in the Kohnstein Hill. Of the 60,000 inmates, 20,000 died from bad working conditions, diseases, starvation or were murdered. Around 10,00 worked in several factories within the city. The Junkers aircraft factory interned 6,000 forced labour prisoners at Boelcke Kaserne, a subcamp of the Mittelbau-Dora concentration camp. When the work camps were liberated by the US Army, blueprints for the projected A-9/A-10 intercontinental missile were found in the factories. Work on the supersonic missile was carried out in late 1944 under the Projekt Amerika codename. Perhaps, capable of speeds of 6,300 miles per hour and 3,000 miles range, it could have reached a target in the United States in 35 minutes.

Wernher Magnus Maximilian Freiherr von Braun who worked at Peenemünde and Nordhaussen, helped design the V-2 rocket. He was secretly moved to the United States after the war and his later work led to the development of the Saturn V rocket, that propelled the Apollo spacecraft to the moon.

Mosquito DD752 production NOTES:

Serial: DD752, Build Type: F.II, Merlin 21/22 engines, Build Location: Hatfield, Contract Number: 555/C.23(a), Contract Date: 9-2-1941, Delivery Period: Between 25-2-1942 and 15-10-1942

THE R.A.F. MOSQUITO: MARK II (FIGHTER INTRUDER) (CH 9474) Original wartime caption: This picture shows the R.A.F, Mosquito, Mark II – a new version of the Mosquito light bomber, now in use as a fighter and an intruder. Mosquitos in formation. Copyright: © IWM

Gilbert Ferguson Sage

On the night of 13/14 February 1945, Bomber Command launched the infamous raid on Dresden. Two separate raids of 805 bombers led by RAF 7 Squadron as the Pathfinders, dropped more than 1,800 tons of bombs onto the target. US bombers attacked the marshalling yards and the city the following day. Civilian casualties exceeded 20,000, some figures claim 50,000 to 100,000, some even higher.

On 22 February 1945, it was the turn of the city of Worms, just north of Mannheim in Germany. A total of 349 aircraft attacked and dropped 1,116 tons of bombs on Worms and a further 177 aircraft attacked the Mittelland Canal near Hannover. The city of Worms was 39% destroyed, 239 were killed and 35,000 houses were destroyed. The population of Worms at the time was 58,000. The only German factory making sprocket wheels for tanks was destroyed in the raid.

RAF 7 Squadron, Pathfinder aircraft, Avro Lancaster PA978, call sign MG-O, flying from RAF Oakington, Cambridgeshire took off at 1713 hours. Its payload of bombs for this raid was most probably, 5 x 2000 lb H C (High Capacity) and 1 x 500 lb M C (Medium Capacity).

No more was heard of Avro Lancaster PA978 after it took off. It was subsequently declared missing – lost on the night of 21/22 February 1945. Two of the crew survived and became prisoners of war, those killed in action are buried at Dürnbach War Cemetery, south of München (Munich) in Germany:

Flight Lieutenant J B M Liddle, RAF, pilot, (POW)

Sergeant N H Clydesdale RAF, air gunner (mid-upper), (POW)

Sergeant William Edward Pickering RAFVR (112361) flight engineer, age 23 (KIA)

Flight Sergeant Gilbert Ferguson Sage, RAFVR (1566413) navigator, age 23 (KIA)

Flight Sergeant John Ronald Mears RAFVR (1395032) air bomber, age 23 (KIA)

Flight Sergeant Harold Munro Watson RAFVR (1555045) air bomber, age 21 (KIA)

Flying Officer Gordon Angus Robertson RAFVR (168782) wireless operator, age 19 (KIA)

Sergeant Peter Louis Wyndham Scott RAFVR (1804436), air gunner, age 22 (KIA)

Sage was the son of Robert and Isabella Ferguson Sage of 24 Gray Street, Perth. He married Isabella Smith of 4d Ruthven Place, Perth on 14 July 1944 at the York House, Perth.

Perthshire Advertiser, 8 March 1947

INTIMATIONS – DEATHS

SAGE. -*Missing since 21st February 1945, now notified killed while on Pathfinding duties over Germany, Flt. /Sgt. Gilbert F. Sage, navigator R.A.F., beloved husband of Isobel Smith, 4d Ruthven Place, and son of Mr and Mrs R. Sage, 24 Gray Street, aged 23.*

Perthshire Advertiser, 12 March 1947

LOST OVER GERMANY

Flight-Sergt. Gilbert F. Sage, Perth airman, whose relatives – as reported in our last issue – have been informed that he lost his life when his' plane crashed in flames near the German village of Horcheim in 1945, less than three months before the end of the European War. He had been listed as missing since then. His widow resides at 4 Ruthven Place, and his parents at 24 Gray Street, Perth.

AIRMAN'S FATE CONFIRMED AFTER TWO YEARS

Relatives of Flight-Sergeant Gilbert F. Sage, a 23-year-old Perth airman who was reported missing less than three months before the end of the European War, have now been informed that he lost his life when his plane crashed in flames near the German village of Horcheim.

Flt. Sgt. Sage was married in the summer of 1944 and his young widow resided at 4 Ruthven Place. His parents' home is at 24 Gray Street. Sage had been in the R.A.F. for three years and had completed his series of operational flights when he met his death. He had volunteered for path-finder duties prior to the bombing of an important German canal and was navigating a Lancaster when it received a direct hit.

Six of the crew were killed when the plane crashed. Only the pilot and one of the gunners succeeded in bailing out. Sgt. Sage's relatives were unaware that he was on 'ops.' until they received word that he was missing on February 22, 1945.

In a letter which Mrs Sage received on Wednesday, the Air Ministry state that officers of the R.A.F. Missing, Research and Enquiry Service have now visited the scene of the crash and identified the wreckage of the Lancaster. After enquiry, it was ascertained that the remains of the six crew members were recovered from the plane and buried in a cemetery at Weinsheim, near Worms, Western Germany.

'It was observed that the graves were well kept.' the letter states, 'and that each was marked with a cross indicating that it was the burial place of unknown English airmen killed on February 21, 1945.' It is also explained in the letter that it has been decided that the Fallen in Germany will not remain in isolated graves but shall be transferred to special cemeteries where their graves will always be reverently attended by the staff of the Imperial War Graves Commission.

NOTES: At the age of 19, Gordon Angus Robertson was one of the youngest officers to be killed on Bomber Command operations during 1945.

The final resting place of the crew who died is roughly 400 km southwest of their target.

Allied forces had breached the Siegfried Line, 200 km to the west and were entering Germany at that time.

Twelve RAF 7 Squadron Lancasters took part in the raid to Worms. All the others returned to RAF Oakington safely.

AVRO LANCASTER Mark III (CH 18683) Photographic negative Copyright: © IWM.

James Shaw

In November of 1941, James Shaw left his position as manager of Perth Aerodrome to serve with the RAF. In 1944, James was serving with RAF 17 OTU (Operational Training Unit) in 1944. The unit moved to RAF Silverstone in 1943 to train night bomber crews with the Vickers Wellington aircraft. OTU's were mainly training units, but they did on occasion take part in Bomber Command operational sorties as part of RAF No. 92 Group.

On 7 July 1944, Vickers Wellington Mk X, HE235 took off at 23.48 pm for RAF Turweston for a night exercise. They were given permission to land at 01.17 am. Vickers Wellington Mk III, BK272 from the same unit also took off at 01.22 am directly into a bright moon to take part in the same exercise. At 01.28 am, six minutes later the two aircraft collided at 1,000 feet and went down. Both burst into flames and 13 men were killed.

The controversial Court of Inquiry findings said that the pilots and crews failed to keep a good look out. Navigation lights would not show up in full moon. Weather fine, visibility excellent.

New evidence suggests that BK272 took off earlier, given permission at 01.14 am and took off at 01.17 am. It had already made a right-hand circuit of the airfield and was again at the end of the runway climbing to 1,000 feet. Wellington HE235 was turning to land on the same runway and hit BK272 side-on at 01.28 am. The brilliant bright moon that HE235 was perhaps dazzling and the extremely poor navigation lights on the Wellingtons, that were not visible to BK272, contributed to this tragic accident.

Crew of Vickers Wellington HE235:

Flight Lieutenant John (Jack) Shaw RAF (70617), Pilot, age 32

Sergeant William Niven Mitchell RAFVR (1290938), Navigator, age 36

Sergeant William Charles Edward Willett RAFVR (1603136), Air Bomber, age 31

Sergeant Leonard William Barker RAFVR (916712), Wireless Operator, age 28

Sergeant Charles Alfred Wyatt RAFVR (1596540), Air Gunner, age 19

Sergeant Harry Kinchin RAFVR (1596079), Air Gunner, age 20

Flight Lieutenant Shaw was a graduate of Caius College, Cambridge, the son of Geoffrey Turton Shaw and Mary Grace Shaw and the husband of Marjorie Catherine Helene Shaw of Knowehead, Coupar Angus.

NOTES:

RAF Silverstone is the motor racing circuit, the current home of the British Grand Prix. It is located next to the villages of Silverstone and Whittlebury in Northamptonshire.

This incident was covered in detail in the YESTERDAY (UKTV) TV series WWII Air Crash Detectives– Episode 3/6: 'Death in the Moonlight'.

Garth Barnard (Air Crash Detectives) with wreckage from the crash

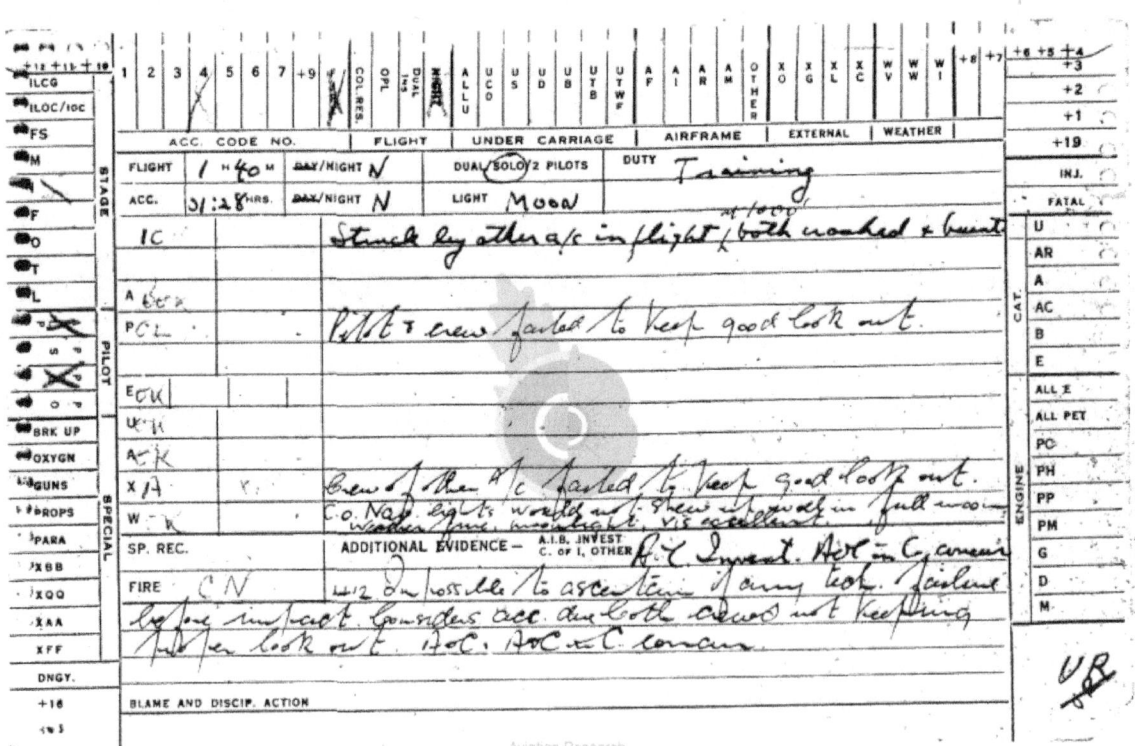

The accident report from the event.

Roderick Forbes Sim

Flight Sergeant Roderick Forbes Sim RAFVR 748347 of 1 Addison Crescent, Crieff was killed in action on 6 November 1941 and is buried in Crieff Cemetery. He was the elder son of Mrs Isabella Sim and the late Mr William Sim. Before joining the RAFVR Roderick was employed by S. Graham Mickel & Co, Solicitors, Crieff. Roderick was well known in Crieff and Comrie, where he was a member of the cricket club.

Roderick Sim was piloting a Douglas A-20 Havoc I DG555 of RAF 37 Maintenance Unit RAF Burtonwood Repair Depot, 15 miles east of Liverpool, north of Warrington. All that is known is that the aircraft crashed, and both occupants were killed. Also on board was a civilian, Mr. T. Butts. In one intimation it was suggested his first name was Percival, and from London. The Commonwealth Graves Commission only shows the death of T Butts, buried at Warrington Rural District Cemetery. Mr Butts was possibly testing equipment on the aircraft.

NOTES:

In the RAF, the Douglas A-20 Havoc bomber variants were known as the Boston for day bombers, while the night fighter and intruder variants were named Havoc. The exception was the Royal Australian Air Force, which used the name Boston for all variants. The USAAF used the P-70 designation to refer to the night fighter variants. In Interdiction raids, Havoc intruders caused considerable damage to German targets.

At RAF Burtonwood the RAF 37 MU was the RAF's centre for repair of aircraft built in the United States. The United States Army Air Force took over RAF Burtonwood in June 1942. Burtonwood was the largest airfield in Europe during WW2 with the most USAAF personnel and aircraft maintenance facilities.

AMERICAN AIRCRAFT IN ROYAL AIR FORCE SERVICE, 1939-1945: DOUGLAS DB-7 HAVOC. (ATP 10654C) Havoc Mark I (Turbinlite), AW400, on the ground at Burtonwood Repair Depot, Lancashire. This aircraft served with Nos. 1422 and 1454 (Turbinlite) Flights, and with 1459 (Turbinlite) Flight/No. 538 Squadron RAF, before transfer to the USAAF in April 1943. Copyright: © IWM.

Crieff Airman's Funeral

PILOT WHO WAS KILLED ON ACTIVE SERVICE.

The funeral of Sergeant-Pilot Roy Sim, R.A.F., V.R., killed on active service, took place on Monday afternoon from his home, 1 Addison Crescent, Crieff, to Crieff Cemetery. He was buried with R.A.F. honours.

There was a representative company of mourners, with a contingent of R.A.F. heading the cortege. A firing party was also present. The coffin, draped with the Union Jack, was borne on the shoulders of eight R.A.F. members to the graveside. A contingent of Morrison's Academy O.T.C., under Captain MacRae, was also present.

There were many floral tributes, including wreaths from the Commanding Officer and officers of the R.A.F. Depot to which deceased had been attached, from the Controller and friends, from the R.A.F. Motor Transport Section, and from the staff of Messrs S. Graham Mickel & Co., solicitors, Crieff, etc.

Pall-bearers were:—Messrs Donald Sim (brother), Alistair Gill, Crieff; Roderick Forbes, Leslie Forbes and David Forbes (uncles), Fraserburgh; Brebner Forbes (cousin), Rosehearty; George Brebner, Crieff; and Rev. George Martin, Strathaven.

Perthshire Advertiser 12 November 1941

son on the evils of intemperance. Mrs Walker sang very effectively a solo, "He will hide me." Miss Donald and Mrs Wilkinson proposed thanks. Mrs Rodger closed the meeting with prayer.

LOCAL AIRMAN KILLED. — Intimation was received at his home on Thursday night that Sergeant-Pilot Roderick Forbes Sim had died on active service. Roy Sim was 22 years of age, and the elder son of Mrs Isabella Sim and the late Mr William Sim, 1 Addison Crescent. Before joining the R.A.F., V.R., he was employed by the firm of S. Graham Mickel & Co. Roy was well known and liked in Crieff and in Comrie, where he was a keen member of the cricket club. The deepest sympathy of the whole community goes out to his widowed mother and his younger brother in their sad loss. It appears that Sergeant-Pilot Sim and a civilian named Percival Bulls, believed to belong to London, were flying from a north-west aerodrome when the 'plane crashed and burst into flames. Both occupants were killed instantly.

BUS ACCIDENT.—A Crieff driver and conductress were in charge of a bus belonging to Messrs Alexanders which met with an accident near Linlithgow

The Strathearn Herald 8 November 1941

Derrick Barrie Simpson

What happened to Sergeant Derrick Barrie Simpson RAFVR (755136), age 19, is a bit of a puzzle. He was recorded as killed along with Pilot Officer Matthew Roy Turnbull RAF (42915), age 19, and Sergeant Gilbert Peter Rowe RAFVR (751202), age 20, in the squadron operational record, but this is incorrect. Simpson was in fact killed along with Flying Officer Hugh Haswell RAFVR (72482), age 21 from South Africa, and Sergeant Raymond Bradshaw Martin RAFVR (751104), age 21, when Bristol Blenheim IV, L9473 was shot down over the English Channel on 25 July 1940.

Operational Record RAF 59 Squadron 26 July 1940

2 convoy patrols were carried out without incident. A reconnaissance flight was not completed owing to bad weather. One anti-invasion patrol carried out. Nothing unusual was observed. A formation of 9 a/c carried out a night bombing raid on oil tanks at CHERBOURG. 3 of these failed to locate target owing to bad visibility. Another experienced ice formation resulting in failure of instruments and returned to base without dropping bombs. 3 a/c dropped their bombs on target. 1 a/c was chased away, by fighters. One a/c, pilot P/O Turnbull, Sgt Roe and Sgt Simpson failed to return, and the crew are posted missing.

To add to the confusion, there is a memorial at Petit-Caux, Saint-Martin-en–Campagne (north-east of Dieppe) listing Haswell and Martin and a Sergeant D Wallace RAF (628797), age 38, as the third member of the L9473 crew. Wallace's body was the only one recovered and is buried at Criel-Sur-Mer Communal Cemetery (north-east of Dieppe) – he was from Crail, Fife.

Wallace was in fact onboard Bristol Blenheim IV T1801 along with Turnbull and Rowe. This was another RAF 59 Squadron, Blenheim that was lost the following day (26 July 1940).

The operation that Simpson was participating in when he was killed, involved one of the most infamous alleged German atrocities against neutral shipping during World War Two.

After the fall of France, the new 'Vichy' French Government insisted that French naval personnel in Britain be repatriated. Only those who volunteered to serve with the Free French under General Charles de Gaulle could stay. In accordance with the terms of the French Armistice with Germany, the Vichy government's representative, and the Red Cross, all had been informed in advance of the British intention to repatriate the personnel aboard the SS *Meknes*. Fifty-nine French ships, which had sought refuge in the harbours of Plymouth and Portsmouth had been seized by the British Royal Navy on 3 July 1940.

Great care had been taken to make the SS *Meknes* look like a neutral ship. She was flying the French Flag and had the French colours painted on her deck and sides. At night, she was fully illuminated and had her navigation lights on. On the night of 24 July 1940, at about 10.30 pm, the SS *Meknes* was stopped by two German motor torpedo boats (German: Schnellboot, or S-Boot, meaning "fast boat"), the S19 and the S27. Both S-Boots fired one torpedo each, both missing the SS *Meknes*. The French passenger ship stopped. Two more torpedoes were fired and again they flew wide of the mark. Every time the SS *Meknes* tried to signal to the S-Boot's its name and details, it was met with fire from S19's flak gun. The passengers and crew were given five minutes to take to their lifeboats. Fifteen minutes later when the S-boots had reloaded their torpedo's, a single torpedo was fired, and it hit the stern of the SS *Meknes*. The SS *Meknes* began to sink, and the S-boots retreated into the darkness.

The French passenger liner of 6,127 tons had left Southampton carrying 1,277 French naval personnel who were being repatriated as per their own choice. Some 383 Frenchmen were lost that night.

The RAF 59 Squadron Operational Record Book shows that that the mission of the Blenheim's the following day was to search for SS Meknes survivors. Of the three aircraft sent out, the only crew to report positive findings in the ORB (Operational Record Book) was that of Turnbull in Bristol Blenheim IV T1801 who guided Royal Navy destroyers to the survivor's location. Only one Blenheim appears to have returned safely and Luftwaffe daily situation reports confirm two Blenheim's shot down that day.

The squadron ORB also shows that Turnbull, Rowe, and Sergeant Henry Strickland flew their first sortie on 23 July. As was the custom for new crews in the squadron, their first sortie was a night patrol – *Time Up: 2155 – Time Down: 0235 – Nothing unusual seen*. Strickland was injured on the second mission by the dorsal turret glass exploding. It was thought it could have been a seagull hitting it. Three days later, on only their third mission, Turnbull, Rowe and Strickland's replacement, Sergeant Wallace were killed.

Simpson was the only son of the late James and Janet Stevenson Barrie Simpson, 18 Balvaird Place, Perth. James Simpson was a factor on the Scone Estates. Sergeant Simpson joined the R.A.F.V.R. while at Perth Academy and was called up on the out-break of war, being promoted sergeant the following May.

All those whose bodies were not recovered are commemorated on the Runnymede Memorial, Surrey. Sergeant Simpson is also commemorated on the Scone War Memorial, and the Scone Parish Church War Memorial.

Perthshire Advertiser, 10 May 1941

"INTIMATIONS – DEATHS – ON ACTIVE SERVICE

"SIMPSON – *Formerly reported missing, now officially presumed killed in action, Sergeant Derrick B. Simpson, R.A.F.V.R., aged 19 years, beloved son and only child of the late James Simpson, factor Scone Estates, and Mrs Simpson, 18 Balvaird Place, Perth.*"

"PERTH AIRMAN PRESUMED KILLED

"LOST ON FLIGHT FOR WHICH HE VOLUNTEERED: PILOT'S TRIBUTE – 'ONE OF THE BRAVEST PEOPLE I KNOW

"'*He was one of the bravest people I know,*' *is an R.A.F. pilot's tribute to a Perth wireless operator and air-gunner, Sergeant Derrick B. Simpson, R.A.F.V.R., who is now officially presumed killed in action after having been reported missing. Only son of the late Mr James Simpson, factor, Scone Estates, and of Mrs Simpson, 18 Balvaird Place, Perth. Sergt. Simpson was 19 years of age.*

"*He is presumed to have lost his life, it is learned, on a flight for which he volunteered. In a matter of urgency, he offered to take the place of another airman who had taken ill.*

"*Sgt. Simpson's own pilot has written of him this fine tribute:* –

'He was my gunner and wireless operator and one of the bravest people I know.

'It was always a reassuring thought to me to know that I had such a splendid fellow for a rear-gunner. When things were not looking too good, he would often give both my observer and me a feeling of absolute confidence by passing some cheery remark in the inter-communicating telephone.

'He was ready to do anything at any time and it was probably his courage and devotion to duty that led to his last flight."

NOTES: The E-boat was the Allied designation for the German Schnellboot, fast attack boats.

RAF 59 Squadron had been in combat action since the very first day of the German invasion of France and the Low Countries on 10 May 1940. On 19 May 1940, the squadron returned to Britain, resuming operations from RAF Hawkinge. The Battle of Dunkirk had just taken place (26 May 1940 and 4 June 1940) and RAF 59 Squadron operations at the time included observing the evacuation of the Allied troops including the British Expeditionary Force. The squadron moved to RAF Thorney Island, between Portsmouth and Chichester, on 3 July 1940.

RAF 59 Squadron was one of the squadrons denied the right to the 'Clasp' to the 1939/45-star award, the Battle of Britain bar (if they had flown at least one operational sortie during that time). On 9 November 1960, the RAF issued a revised list of those squadrons considered to qualify for the Battle of Britain bar, RAF 59 Squadron was no longer on it. Those airmen who previously had been issued this award were instructed to take down the bar immediately and return it to the RAF medals branch. RAF 59 Squadron was a Coastal Command Squadron but was under the control of Fighter Command during the Battle of Britain. RAF 235 Squadron, another Blenheim squadron, took part in similar operations and were recognised as Battle of Britain participants. As one 59 Squadron pilot later put it when writing of the withdrawal of the ward: '...the feelings about this change ran pretty high at the time, I can tell you!'

PERTHSHIRE ADVERTISER, *10 MAY 1941*

Alfie Smith

Squadron Leader Alfie Smith joined the RAFVR in 1937 and learned to fly at Scone with RAF No. 11 Elementary & Reserve Flying Training School. When war broke out, he was commissioned into the RAF. His first solo flight was made at Scone as was his first cross-country flight to Montrose (formerly the first operational military air station in the UK established in February 1913 as a Royal Flying Corps aerodrome, now an aviation museum). His advanced cross-country flight was in a Hawker Audax to Prestwick

Alfie's first duties were with the Air Ministry flying a Fairchild 24 Argus 4 seat light military transport monoplane from RAF Hendon. Then he was off to Canada on board the *Queen Mary* for advanced training. When he returned, he began conversion training in the Airspeed Oxford and Vickers Wellington. Finally, he qualified as an Avro Lancaster pilot and flew many operational sorties over Germany.

After the war Alfie, still in the RAF, flew Short Stirling's and Avro York's for Transport Command between the UK and India. The Avro York was developed as a transport aircraft from the Avro Lancaster bomber and shared many components.

Alfie is fondly remembered for his association, and as chairman, of the Scottish Flying Club at Scone Aerodrome. Alfie, after leaving the RAF and returning to Perth, set up in business as an accountant. Squadron Leader Alfie Smith passed away in 2002.

Note: Avro Yorks were used during the Berlin Air Lift and operated as the type used by the RAF in long range transport flights to the Middle East and India. Later, the British Overseas Aircraft Corporation (BOAC) and Dan Air both used the aircraft for carrying cargo and passengers.

Smith Drive at Scone Aerodrome was named after Alfie.

Crichton Alexander Smith

Pilot, Sergeant Crichton Alexander Smith, RAFVR 1368806 died on 10 March 1942 at RAF 61 Operational Training Unit (OTU), RAF Heston, Middlesex, England.

On 8 March 1942, in a Miles M.9A Master Mk. I T8504 taking off from RAF Heston, the aircraft swung 90% and crashed into four parked aircraft on the apron and burst into flames. Crichton died two days later from injuries sustained 10 March 1942.

Ground crew, Aircraftman (AC1) F. Waller was injured and de Havilland DH.87 Hornet Moth X9446 G-AFEC which was hit was written off.

Crichton Alexander Smith aged 21, was the eldest son of Mr and Mrs George Smith, 'Dyalla', Balmoral Road, Blairgowrie. Crichton attended Blairgowrie High School and worked at the Blairgowrie branch of the Union Bank before volunteering for the RAF in December 1940. He was a keen sportsman, cricket, golf, football, ice hockey and swimming, as well as angling. As a member of Blairgowrie Golf Club, he won the Druidesmere Cup in 1939.

Crichton gained quick promotion and was recommended for a commission a short time before his death. Sergeant Crichton Alexander Smith is buried in Blairgowrie Cemetery.

NOTES: 61 OTU was formed in June 1941 at RAF Heston to train single-seat fighter pilots. Supermarine Spitfires were allocated to the station.

61 Operational Training Unit (OTU) was formed at RAF Heston in June 1941 and moved to RAF Rednal in April 1942 and RAF Keevil in June 1945.

Hornet Moth X9446 G-AFEC was owned before being pressed into RAF service on 10 May 1940, by Captain Hugh Sale Ford, of Farrington, Berkshire.

PERTHSHIRE ADVERTISER 14 MARCH 1942

ROYAL AIR FORCE AIRCRAFT (CH 6455) Spitfire F Mk.2 about to touch down at 61 OTU Rednal, Shropshire. Copyright: © IWM.

BRITISH MILITARY AIRCRAFT: MILES MASTER I (CH 144) Original wartime caption: The Miles Master I, a two-seater low-wing cantilever monoplane, which is the most advanced and fastest training aircraft in service use throughout the world. Powered by one Rolls Royce Kestrel XXX engine developing 714 h.p. she attains a maximum speed of 300 m.p.h. at sea level.

Gavin Strang Smith

Gavin Strang Smith was the son of Robert and Marion Leiper Smith of Drumearn, Kincarrathie Crescent, Perth. He was educated at Sharp's Institution and Perth Academy (1933/1938). He served his law apprenticeship (trainee solicitor) between 1938 and 1940 with Messer's McCash & Hunter, Perth.

Gavin enlisted in the Royal Air Force Volunteer Reserve (RAFVR) on 10 September 1940 at RAF 9 Recruiting Centre, Blackpool, he was given the rank of Aircraftman Second Class (AC2). On 4 January 1941 he was promoted to Leading Aircraftman (LAC). His initial flying training was at RAF No. 19 Elementary Flying Training School (EFTS), RAF Sealand, (northeast Wales). 19 EFTS had just opened on 21 January 1941. On 31 September 1941 he was promoted to Temporary Sergeant. After training in Canada at RCAF 33 Flying Training School (southeast of Carberry, in the Municipality of North Cypress-Langford, Manitoba) under the Joint Air Training Plan, he was commissioned as Pilot Officer on probation on 13 September 1941 and was gazetted on 18 November 1941.

On 17 October 1941, Gavin was posted to RAF 16 Operational Training Unit (OTU) at RAF Upper Heyford. Training was carried out using the Handley Page H.P.52 Hampden and Handley Page H.P.53 Hereford. Upon completing that course, he was posted to RAF 142 Squadron on operational duties. Flying Vickers Wellington Mk. II and Mk. IV, they were based at what service personal and locals, referred to as Waltham, officially it was named RAF Grimbsy.

Gavin had a spell with RAF 28 OTU at RAF Wymeswold near Loughborough, from 25 May 1942, returning to RAF 142 Squadron on 18 August 1942. He was then posted on 30 November 1942 to RAF 1656 Heavy Conversion Unit as a Flying Instructor based at RAF Swinderby and RAF Wigsley. The unit's purpose was to convert medium bomber pilots to heavy bombers and used the Avro Manchester I, Avro Lancaster 1, Handley Page Halifax II & V, and Short Stirling III. During 1942 the unit flew twelve operational sorties with the loss of two aircraft. Gavin whilst at RAF 1656 was awarded the Distinguished Flying Cross (DFC) on 29 December 1942.

***Perthshire Advertiser*, 30 December 1942:**

In describing his exploits, the official statement says: As captain of aircraft Flying Officer Smith is always undeterred by the strongest enemy defences or adverse weather. By his fine offensive spirit this officer has inspired a high standard of morale in the squadron.

The statement also describes how, on one occasion, F/O Smith was detailed to make an attack on a factory in Northern France. On his first run over the target, technical trouble developed with the bombing panel. This was repaired and, although severely harassed by searchlights and anti-aircraft fire, he descended to 1500 feet before releasing his bombs.

On 17 August 1943, Gavin returned to operational duties with RAF 142 Squadron who were operating since 26 May 1943 out of RAF Kairouan, Tunisia. He was promoted to Flight Lieutenant on 13 September 1943, gazetted on 17 September 1943. The Squadron moved to RAF Oudna, Tunisia on 15 November 1943 and on 17 December 1943, on that same day Gavin was promoted to Squadron Leader and posted as a Flying Instructor to RAF 1 Group at RAF Lindholme. Gavin remained at Lindholme until 25 May 1944 when he was posted to RAF 550 Squadron at RAF North Killingholme.

Squadron Leader Gavin Strang Smith (pilot) and his crew onboard Avro Lancaster B Mk. I ME840, call sign BQ-V from RAF 550 Squadron took off from RAF North Killinghome at 23.05 on 16 June 1944 for a raid to Sterkrade, Oberhausen in Germany. Nineteen aircraft from the squadron took off without incident, but one aircraft was forced to abandon the mission when the port inner engine became unserviceable.

The targets for that night were factories creating oil products for the German war industry. When they arrived over the targets they were obscured in thick cloud. It was a cold night; some icing problems were encountered by the aircraft.

Ahead of the main bomber force, Pathfinder aircraft had dropped markers (target illuminators). Anti-Aircraft Flak at the target was moderate to intense and night fighters were active in the area.

Lancaster ME840 was late leaving the target and fell behind the rest of the bomber stream, losing any mutual protection from concentrated gunfire of the other aircraft, but also became exposed to enemy radar by losing the protection of 'window' dropped by other bombers. Somewhere near the Netherlands/German border, Lancaster ME840 was hit by a burst from a night fighter which hit their No 2 engine and petrol tank. No 1 petrol tank then caught fire.

Flying Officer Kay, the flight engineer, jettisoned the forward escape hatch, stopped No. 2 engine, and operated the extinguishers in vain. Smith ordered the crew to put on their parachutes, but before they could, the petrol tank exploded. The aircraft came down near Varssveld, northwest of Aalten in The Netherlands. It lost a tailpiece and part of a wing above Aalten and split into two pieces coming down, landing in a field behind a farm called "Oude Lieftink", in Varsseveld, in at the time, the Wisch municipality, since 2005 the Oude IJsselstreek municipality.

At 01.30 am, Kay was standing next to Smith when he was blown out of the aircraft. The next thing Kay knew was that he was falling. Regaining consciousness, he managed to pull his ripcord and open his parachute. Lancaster ME840 had exploded, he was the only survivor.

When he landed in an enclosed field, Kay was bleeding a from superficial wounds in the left arm and knee and his right boot had fallen off. Thinking he had landed further west than he did, he headed south, back towards the German border. On the morning of the 19th, he met a farmer who gave him food and put him in touch with the Dutch underground movement. He was then moved to The Hague where he stayed for 40 days before being transferred to the Belgian underground. Here he stayed until 19 September 1944 when the Americans overran the area.

Night fighter ace, Oberleutnant Josef Nabrich (3. /NJG1) flying a Heinkel He 219 Uhu ('Eagle-Owl'), from Venlo Airfield, claimed a four-engine aircraft flying at a height of 6,000 m at 01.49 am. This would be his 14th kill of 17. Josef Nabrich, then Staffelkapitän of 3. /NJG 1, was killed on 27 November 1944 when he was hit in the head by strafing fighter-bombers of RAF 2nd Tactical Air Force (TAF) whilst driving near Münster Handorf airfield.

Oberleutnant Josef Nabrich was buried at Münster-Lauheide war cemetery.

The crew of Avro Lancaster ME840:

Squadron Leader Gavin Strang Smith DFC, RAFVR (108543) – pilot, age 22 (KIA)

Flying Officer Roy Kay RAF (53358) – flight engineer, born 14 January 1921, (Evader) (died 23 March 2009)

Flying Officer John Joseph Berg DFC RAFVR (129551) – navigator, age 23 (KIA)

Flying Officer Leslie Pulfrey RAFVR (148869) – air bomber, age 29 (KIA)

Flight Sergeant Ralph Townsend DFM RAFVR (1078579 – wireless operator/air gunner (KIA)

Flight Lieutenant St. John Tizard RAFVR (112026) – air gunner, age unknown (KIA)

Flying Officer James Heath RCAF (J/20002) – air gunner, age 35 (KIA)

As the aircraft crashed Flying Officer Roy Kay jumped from the aircraft and managed to parachute safely to the ground. He escaped arrest, aided by the *'escapelijn'* (escape line) returning to the UK in September 1944. Flying Officer Leslie Pulfrey jumped from the burning aircraft above Aalten, his body was found the next morning by a farmer. His parachute was torn, damaged possibly by shrapnel and his head had become entangled in the parachute cords.

The remaining crew's bodies were found in the wreckage, they are all buried in Wisch (Varsseveld) General Cemetery, The Netherlands (Algemene Begraafplaats in Varsseveld). Gavin's death is recorded on the War Memorial of St. Leonards-in-the-Field and Trinty Church, Marshall Place, Perth.

Berg's DFC was gazetted 12 November 1943 for service with RAF 100 Squadron and Townsend's DFM was gazetted 10 December 1943 for service on RAF 460 Squadron.

A list of the crews last sorties, D-Day was 6 June 1944:

Battery near Calais, 2-3 June 44

Crisbecq, 5-6 June 44

Flers, 9-10 June 44

Le Havre, 14 June 44

Sterkrade, 16-17 June 44

NOTES: On Friday 6th May 2022 at 12 noon there was an unveiling of a memorial in Gendringen (close to the German border) to remember all (500+) casualties during WWII in the former municipalities of Gendringen and Wisch (nowadays: Oude IJsselstreek). These victims are, citizens, Dutch, Canadian, English, and German soldiers and RAF victims of the nine crashes in that area. The monument features a Canadian soldier in front and a Lancaster overhead.

In the late 1990's Police Sergeant Kemp of Western Division, Perth was tasked with trying to find the relatives of Gavin Strang Smith. Relatives of John Joseph Berg have been instrumental in memorialising the crew in the Netherlands. The locals in the area where Lancaster ME840 crashed have also been trying to find the relatives, they were the ones who contacted Sergeant Roy Kemp, (now retired) in the late 90's.

From the research of Sergeant Kemp: Gavin Strang Smith was in the same year at Perth Academy as another Perth flying legend, Neil Cameron. Neil Cameron rose to the highest rank in the RAF, Marshall of the Royal Air Force, he was also Chief of Defence Staff, and later became Lord Cameron of Balhousie.

Mr. Robertson, 199 Bute Drive, Perth worked on Moneydie Farm during the war. The farm was owned by a relation of Gavin. *Mr. Robertson stated, "that it was common for Gavin during training flights to 'buzz' the farm, and on one occasion just prior to his death flew so low over the farm that he lifted the hay from the stacks they were just constructing or had built and spread hay over the field.'*

A Mrs Simpson from Perth was one of the Met Officers (Meteorological) on 550 Squadron. Mrs Simpson and her fellow Met officers, shifts permitting, used to cycle out to the departure end of the runway and wave to each of the crews as they departed. She thinks she may well have done so on 16 June 1944.

Flying Officer Berg, DFC, the navigator in the crew was married just three weeks before the fatal crash. Tizard was the squadron's gunnery leader. The crew were very experienced, most, if not all were on their second operational tour (30+ missions).

Sterkrade is just north of Duisburg and Essen in the Ruhr area of Germany. The Ruhrchemie AG synthetic oil plant was an important bombing target whose bombing helped shorten the war by denying the Germans fuel and oils to power their war machine. There were 14 synthetic oil plants and 13 oil refineries in Germany and the occupied countries during the Second World War.

Of the 321 bombers that went to Sterkrade synthetic oil plant on 16/17 June 1944, 31 were shot down, nearly all by night fighters. RAF 550 Squadron from RAF North Killinghome lost three out of 18 Lancaster's.

RAF North Killinghome in North Lincolnshire opened in November of 1943, it became fully operational in January 1944 when RAF 550 Squadron moved there from RAF Waltham. They flew their first mission to Brunswick on 14th January 1944. Squadron Statistics: 194 raids, 3,485 take offs, 122 early returns, 188 'Ordered to Return', 3,175 successful sorties, 4,271-night operational hours flown, 4,988-day operational hours flown, 9,259 total operational hours flown, 16,195 tons of bombs dropped, 56 aircraft and crews 'missing', 14 aircraft crashed.

The Pathfinders were normally the first to receive the new blind bombing equipment, like Gee, Oboe and the H2S radar.

The German night fighters each defended a section in the so-called 'Kammhuber Line', a belt of anti-aircraft lights and night-hunting aircraft airfields stretching from Norway to France. Each zone or cell had a control centre known as a Himmelbett (canopy bed). The night fighters were supported by radar technology at the beginning of 1942.

Canada supplied more than 130,000 aircrew during the Second World War.

The Heinkel He 219 Uhu was Germany's most effective night fighter of the war. It was one of the few aircraft capable of engaging the de Havilland Mosquito on equal terms. It was armed with up to 4 × 20 mm MG 151 cannons in a detachable fairing under the fuselage, 300 rpg (rounds per gun), 2 × 20 mm MG 151s in wing roots, 300 rpg and 2 × 30 mm (1.18 in) MK 108 cannons, Schräge Musik (oriented 65° above horizontal), 100 rpg. Schräge Musik was the German term for upward-firing autocannon. The A-2 version from the summer of 1944 featured an updated, 90 MHz VHF-band Telefunken FuG 220 Lichtenstein SN-2 radar system, complete with high-drag 4 × 2-dipole element Hirschgeweih aerial. Had the Heinkel He 219 Uhu been produced in enough numbers it would have had a significant effect on the strategic bombing offensive of the Royal Air Force. The Uhu pilots claimed to have destroyed 20 RAF bombers during their initial six-night missions, Gruppen Kommandeur Major Werner Streib in a single sortie on the night of 11 June 1944, shot down five RAF Lancaster bombers. Streib was officially credited with shooting down 68 enemy aircraft, with 67 claimed at night.

On 19 December 1942, RAF 142 squadron were operating from RAF Blida in Alegria. Blida had just been captured from the Vichy French on 8 November 1942 by the British 11th Infantry brigade as part of Operation Torch, the allied invasion of French North Africa. An echelon of RAF 142 Squadron was retained in the UK at RAF Kirmington.

RAF 550 Squadron RAF was formed at Waltham, near Grimsby, November 1943, as a Lancaster heavy-bomber squadron in No. 1 Group and began operations that same month. Early in the New Year it moved to RAF North Killingholme also near Grimsby. It continued to play its part in the bomber offensive until late April 1945.

On 2 March 1945, when Varsseveld was still under control of the German Forces, a mass execution of 46 people took place on Rademakersbroek, a road just outside of the town. The victims had been chosen at random and had been taken from the Kruisberg prison in Doetinchem, where they had been imprisoned for numerous reasons, ranging from taking part in Resistance activities to unknowingly buying a stolen bike. The mass execution was a revenge attack in response to the earlier discovery of four dead Nazi officers in a semi-burnt vehicle near the village. Four weeks later, on 31 March 1945, the village was liberated by the English Allied Forces

Gavin Strang Smith, Perthshire Advertiser 30 December 1942

Memorial Plaque to the crew of Avro Lancaster ME840, Oude IJsselstreek, Netherlands. Credit Gary Begg, nephew of Flying Officer John Joseph Berg

Leonard Albert Soutar

Sergeant Leonard Albert Soutar RAFVR was the son of Albert Leonard and Agnes Soutar of Dundee and *Auchter Villa*, Clyde Place, Perth. He was a former pupil of Perth Academy and a member of staff in the Workmen's Department of the General Accident Fire & Life Assurance Corporation. He began training in his spare time with the RAF Volunteer Reserve in May 1939. Soutar was called up for service shortly after the outbreak of war.

Soutar served with RAF 44 Squadron at RAF Waddington who at the time were equipped with Handley Page Hampden twin-engine medium bombers. On 8 July 1941, his aircraft, Hampden, AD840 was sent on a mission to bomb the marshalling yards at Hamm, just west of Dortmund in Germany. They were initially reported as missing. It was later ascertained that they were hit by flak and crashed. None of the crew survived and they were all buried near Hamm. They were later re-interred in the Reichswald Forest Cemetery near the border with The Netherlands after the war ended.

Handley Page Hampden AD840 crew:

Sergeant Alfred William Wilson, RAFVR (970361), pilot, age 28

Sergeant Henry Douglas Makenzie, RAFVR (1000335), wireless operator/air gunner, age 19

Flight Sergeant Samuel John Lytle, RAF (619200), wireless operator/air gunner, age unknown

Sergeant Leonard Albert Soutar, RAFVR (748346), observer, age21

From the *Perthshire Advertiser*, 12 July 1941

'PERTH AIRMAN MISSING

TOOK PART IN R.A.F. RAIDS ON GERMANY

Mr and Mrs Albert L. Soutar, Auchter Villa, Clyde Place, Perth, were officially informed on Wednesday that their only son, Sgt.-Observer L. A. Soutar (21), R.A.F., is missing as a result of operations over enemy territory.

Sergt -Observer Soutar, who is attached to a bomber squadron, had been taking part in the recent heavy-scale attacks by the R.A.F. on Germany and on targets in enemy-occupied countries. The trip from which his machine failed to return was the fourth since he rejoined his squadron a fortnight ago after a spell of leave at home.

A former pupil of Perth Academy, he was a member of the staff in the Workmen's Department of the General Accident Fire and Life Assurance Corporation. He began training in his spare time with the R.A.F. Volunteer Reserve at Perth in May 1939 and was called up for service shortly after the outbreak of war.

"*His father, a former member of the Post Office staff at Perth, served in the Royal Navy throughout the last war. He was called up from the reserve, having previously served as a first-class petty officer.*'

Bomber Command Raids of 8/9 July 1941

A total of 171 aircraft took off from bases in England, ten aircraft were lost, 34 aircrew killed or missing, and nine aircrew taken prisoner.

Two Hampden aircraft were lost from RAF 44 Squadron.

RAF 9 Squadron (Munster) lost 1 aircraft.

RAF 10 squadron (Hamm) lost 1 aircraft.

RAF 35 Squadron (Merseburg) lost 1 aircraft.

RAF 58 Squadron (Hamm) lost 1 aircraft.

RAF 78 squadron – (Hamm) lost 3 aircraft.

RAF 83 Squadron (Hamm) lost 1 aircraft.

Mission Result

Hamm, 45 Hampdens and 28 Whitley's. Only 31 aircraft were able to bomb in the target area. 4 Whitley's and 3 Hampdens lost.

Munster, 51 Wellingtons. 1 lost. Large fires were claimed in the railway-station area. Munster recorded 15 people killed.

Bielfeld, 33 Wellingtons to attack a power-station. No losses.

Merseburg, 13 Halifax's and 1 Stirling to the Leuna oil plant. 1 Halifax lost.

In 1941, the Squadron was to be known as No 44 (Rhodesia) Squadron. The Squadron Motto, *Fulmina Regis Iusta* translates as 'The King's Thunderbolts are Righteous'.

The Squadron received its first Avro Lancaster in late 1941 and became the first squadron to convert completely to Lancasters. On 9 May 1941, a German raid on RAF Waddington saw ten killed including seven women from the NAAFI whose air raid shelter received a direct hit. RAF 44 squadron suffered third highest overall losses in Bomber Command during the Second World War, sharing this with No. 78 and 102 Squadrons. A total of 1,639 aircrew were killed in action and 309 became prisoners of war.

There were two RAF 44 squadron commanders who held the Victoria Cross, Wing Commanders Roderick Learoyd and John Nettleton. Squadron Leader R A B 'Babe' Learoyd VC led the attack on 8 July 1941 and between May and July 1941 he and his crew flew ten sorties, including Cologne four times, and bombing the German battleships *Scharnhorst* and *Gneisenau* and the U-Boat Pens at Lorient.

Leonard Albert Soutar, Perthshire Advertiser 12 July 1941

AIRCRAFT OF THE ROYAL AIR FORCE 1939-1945: HANDLEY PAGE HP.52 HAMPDEN AND HEREFORD. (CH 3478) Hampden Mark Is, AE257? KM-X? and AE202? KM-K?, of No. 44 Squadron RAF based at Waddington, Lincolnshire, in flight. Both aircraft were lost on raids over Germany, AE257 on the night of 21/22 October 1941 flying to Bremen, and AE202 over Hamburg on 26/27 July 1942. Copyright: © IWM.

Robert Stewart

RAF Corporal Robert Stewart 520472 was the son of John and Elizabeth Stewart of Luncarty. He was 30 years old when he was hit by a train at Inverlamond, just north of Perth.

The Perthshire Advertiser and the Dundee Courier reported on Monday 13 October 1941 that Corporal Robert Stewart was killed by a train at Inveralmond late on Saturday night. Stewart was believed to have been in Perth, missed his last bus home to Luncarty and decided to walk, apparently not seeing the approach of the train as he took a shortcut by the railway.

Corporal Robert Stewart had been in the RAF for 4½ years and had served in the Middle East. In civilian life he was a ploughman. His body was identified by his father and his brother at Perth Mortuary.

Corporal Robert Stewart is buried in Auchtergaven Parish Churchyard, Bankfoot.

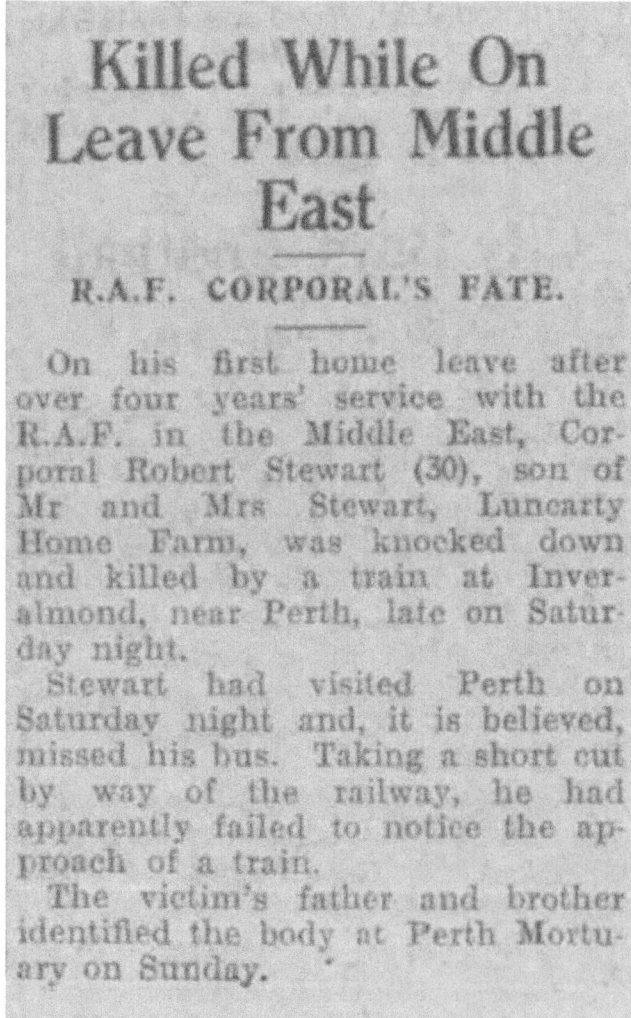

Perthshire Advertiser 15 October 1941

Peter Straiton

Sergeant Peter Straiton was the elder son of Peter and Janet Davidson Straiton of Cray Cottage, Glenshee. Educated at Blackwater School and Blairgowrie High School, he was then employed as a gardener at The Cairnies, Glenalmond. He was a member of a dance band, and the local ATC Straiton joined the RAF about 18 months before he was killed in an aircraft accident in Devon.

At 16.50 hours on 15 November 1944, Handley Page Halifax Mk. II JP201 of RAF 1666 HCU (Heavy Conversion Unit) took off from RAF Wombelton, north of York, to carry out a night cross-country flight exercise. Flying over Devon it collided with Handley Page Halifax LL137 of RAF 1664 HCU.

Both aircraft crashed near Morchard Bishop, between Exeter and Barnstable in Mid Devon. Only one of the crews survived: Sergeant Harold Pugh who was thrown clear when the aircraft crashed. Pugh was later killed during an air operation over the North Sea with RAF 640 Squadron six months later (18 April 1945).

The crew members of Halifax JP201 were:

Pilot Officer Harold Kenneth Pugh (415916), pilot, age 24

Sergeant Alfred Edwin Ackcral (RAFVR) (1595296), flight engineer, age 21

Flight Sergeant Ian O'Connor RAAF (29520), wireless operator/air gunner, age 28

Sergeant Bertram Eric Saunders (943666) (RAFVR), air bomber, age 26

Sergeant John Edward Loos Sherwin (1583794) (RAFVR), navigator, age 29

Sergeant Peter Straiton (1825366) (RAFVR), air gunner, age 19

Straiton is buried in Blairgowrie Cemetery. A permanent stone memorial to the crews that were killed was erected in November 1994 in the village square in Morchard Bishop, Devon.

Pugh was killed six days before RAF 640 Squadron's last mission. This mission – 18/19 April 1945 – was to bomb, Whitton, North Rhine-Westphalia, Germany, the home of the Ruhrstahl steelworks and Mannesmann tube factory.

Ian Taylor

Leading Aircraftman Ian Taylor RAF (649184) of RAF 113 squadron was stationed at Maaten Bagush, between Mersa Matruh and Alexandria in Egypt during August of 1942. In April of 1938, the squadron had moved the Middle East. Italy declared war in June of 1940 and the squadron started their campaign by attacking Italian forces in Libya. In March 1941, they were moved to Greece, but a month later they had to retreat to Crete. All of RAF 113 Squadron's Bristol Blenheim aircraft were lost in two days: to Junkers JU87 (Stuka) dive bombers (14 April 1941) and on the following day by strafing Messerschmitt Bf 109s. During this time, the squadron was equipped with Bristol Blenheim Mk I/IV/V light bombers and fighter types.

By June, they were back in Maaten Bagush. The squadron was quickly back in action in Egypt, they notably attacked a force of 100 tanks in Libya that month.

Taylor was on 8 August 1941, the first Caputh lad to pay the supreme sacrifice in the Second World War. It was reported that he died of burning injuries; he was 26. The squadron lost no aircraft on that day or previous days. His injuries may have been the result of an accident or happened during a Luftwaffe attack on the airfield.

The last squadron aircraft lost was on 8 July 1941: a Blenheim destroyed by raiding Messerschmitt Bf 110s.

Taylor was the eldest son of Raymond and Mary Elizabeth Taylor, Caputh, and is buried in the El Alamein War Cemetery, Egypt. He had joined the RAF before the outbreak of war and was posted to the Middle East early in 1940. Taylor attended Glendelvine School and Perth Academy. He served his apprenticeship with McMurray & Archibald, coach builders in Perth.

Perthshire Advertiser, 13th August 1941

"INTIMATIONS

"DEATHS

"TAYLOR. -On active service in the Middle East, as a result of burning injuries, on 8th August, L.A.C. Ian Taylor, R.A.F., eldest son of Mr and Mrs Raymond Taylor, Caputh. Deeply regretted."

"WAR CASUALTIES

"AIRMAN DIES FROM BURNING INJURIES

"The first Caputh lad to make the supreme sacrifice is Leading Aircraftman Ian Taylor.

"Intimation was received by his parents, Mr and Mrs Raymond Taylor, on Saturday to the effect that their son has died as a result of burning injuries on August 8th. Twenty-six years of age, he joined the R.A.F. be-fore the outbreak of war and was posted to a Middle East squadron early in 1940.

"He served his apprenticeship as a coach trimmer with the firm of McMurray and Archibald, Perth, in whose employment he was for six years. Eldest of the family of Mr and Mrs R. Taylor, of Caputh, he was born at Rattray, and educated at Glendelvine School.

"The passing of such a promising young man has occasioned feelings of deep regret in the district."

Ian Taylor is also commemorated on the Caputh War Memorial, and the Caputh Parish Church War Memorial.

RAF 113 Squadron mainly flew operations from Sidi Haneish airfield, this was regarded as a satellite of Maaten Bugush. RAF 113 Squadron records covering the period December 1940 to May 1941 were lost during the Greek campaign.

By November of 1942, the Africa Corps under General Erwin Rommel were losing about 70% of their supplies, sunk in the Mediterranean by Allied aircraft. As a result, more Luftwaffe aircraft were used to ferry in supplies. Sidi Haneish airfield was the scene of one of the most daring raids of the war, at the time, the airfield was under Luftwaffe control. The Special Air Service (SAS), detachment 'L' was ferried by members of the Long-Range Desert Patrol Group (LRDG) to attack the airfield in the evening of 26 July 1942. A convoy of 18 Jeeps destroyed 18 German aircraft and damaged many more. Each jeep was armed with four Vickers K machine guns, firing Buckingham rounds, .303 incendiary bullets.

Sir David Stirling, the founder of the SAS, was born in his family's ancestral home, Keir House, in the parish of Lecropt, west of Bridge of Allan (formerly in Perthshire). Stirling was captured by the Germans in January 1943, escaped, and was re-captured by the Italians. He made four more escape attempts before being sent to *Oflag IV-C*, better known as Colditz Castle, where he remained for the rest of the war. (See Alastair Cram)

Ian Taylor, Perthshire Advertiser 13 August 1941

Benjamin Thomas

The eldest son of W B Thomas, 4 County Place, Pitcairngreen, Leading Aircraftman Benjamin Thomas was on leave following his internment in Casablanca when he died 10 February 1943.

Thomas joined the RAF six years prior, and he was served in the Middle East from the outbreak of war. He was on his way home when his ship was torpedoed in September 1942. After swimming for some hours, he was picked up a lifeboat. The survivors were subsequently taken onboard a German U-Boat.

They were then transferred to a French vessel and taken to Casablanca where Benjamin spent two months in an internment camp. The Allied landings in North Africa in November 1942 brought his release. Thomas was put abroad a US relief ship and taken to an American port.

Following his return to the UK, he married Ann Horsburgh from Guardbridge, Fife. His best man was his brother. A second brother in the Royal marines won a DSM for distinguished conduct during the Battles of Narvik.

Mediouna Internment Camp, Casablanca: British subjects rescued at sea and detained by Vichy Government – sailors, soldiers, airmen and merchant seamen (Art.IWM ART LD 2887) image: View of an internment camp with figures standing around the huts Copyright: © IWM.

William Thomson

RAF 144 Squadron's was the first in WW2 to carry out an attack on German land objective on 6 March 1940. It involved attacking the German minelaying and seaplane base at Hornum, on the island of Sylt. Just over two months later, 10 May 1940, Germany invaded the Low Countries and France. On that same day, Winston Churchill succeeded Neville Chamberlain as Prime Minister of the United Kingdom. RAF Squadron 144 then shared in another notable "first", the first bombing attack on the German mainland. The squadron bombed the exits from the city of München-Gladbach on 11 May 1940. They were attempting to interdict German troop movements on roads, intersections, and rail lines, especially at the city's railyards. Only half of the thirty-six twin-engine RAF bombers sent on this bombing operation managed to hit their targets, three were shot down.

PERTHSHIRE ADVERTISER 5 APRIL 1941

On the night of 5/6 September 1940, Handley Page Hampden HP52 Mk. I P1172 (PL-J) of RAF 144 Squadron took off at 2200 hours from RAF Hemswell, east of Gainsborough in Lincolnshire. The mission was to bomb Hamburg in Germany.

At 0456 hours, P1172 reported that it was in difficulty and requested a bearing for home. The aircraft was asked for a call-sign, but that was the last contact from P1172, the signal faded out and then ceased. They are believed to have crashed in the North Sea.

The crew of Handley Page Hampden P1172:

Pilot Officer John Edward Newton–Clare RAF (33492) pilot, age 20

Sergeant Charles Owen Clarke RAFVR (745257), age 20

Sergeant William Thomson RAF (637247) wireless operator, age 18

Sergeant William Leslie Powell RAF (641379), age 19

William Thomson was the son of Thomas and Jessie Mitchell Thomson of 9 Dupplin Brae, Perth. He was employed with the motor engineers, Frew & Co, Ltd, Princess Street, Perth, and joined the RAF, six months before the outbreak of war.

William Thomson was survived by both his parents and all four of his siblings. Sergeant Thomson is commemorated on a memorial in St Matthew's Church (formerly West Church), Tay Street, Perth and commemorated on the Runnymede Memorial, Panel 20.

At the time, there had been a glimmer of hope, in the **Summary of Events** form of RAF 144 Squadron, for September 1940. The entry for Hamden P1172 was scored out, marked as cancelled. However subsequently in the left margin the Squadron Adjutant marked: *Advice of "Rescue" from Air Ministry "Proved False" 7.9.40.* No bodies of any crew members or any traces of wreckage were ever found. The crew were reported as "missing believed killed; failed to return from operational flight over Germany".

P1172 was one of two RAF 144 Squadron Hampdens that were lost on that operation: the other being P4378.

NOTES: Sergeant Thomson took part in an earlier operation on 3 June 1940. The duty was listed as 'widdling on the works at Wedel'. Widdling was not a standard or even non-standard term used in the RAF at the time, it was a colloquialism, a slang word best described as piddling (urinating). Wedel is located on the River Elbe in Germany, about seventeen miles West of Hamburg.

The operational report was made in the Operations Record Book, Form 541 by Pilot Officer Skehill, who was from Australia.

The **Detail of Work Carried Out** recorded provides an insight into a bombing operation carried out by the courageous RAF 144 Squadron crews:

Aircraft: Hampden L.4173

Crew: P/O. Bennet, P/O. Skehill, Sgt. Perritt, Sgt. Thomson

Duty: Widdling on the works at Wedel

Time Up: 21.02

Time Down: 03.20

Details of Sortie or Flight:

Aircraft L.4173 took off at 2102 hrs. on 3.6.40 and s/c (set course) from LINCOLN at 2114hrs. for SKEGNESS which was reached at 2129 hrs. From here we s/c for 55°N 6°E and turned-on E.T.A. at 2308 hrs. striking the German coast at WESTERHEVER. From this point we followed the course of the ELBE flying at 10,000' A few searchlights greeted us here plus an odd burst of H.E. A/A

The river and little else could be seen so we followed the course of the ELBE towards the target. Innumerable searchlights and tons of A/A. came into force halfway to target and in the glare of diffused light the river disappeared. Flying on a course of 147°M we failed to pick up the river or target and so returned to the river mouth and began yet again.

On our third run we picked up the straight stretch of river between SCHLAU and DOCKENHUDEN and, from 12,000' dropped 4 – 250's and a container of incendiaries at the target but could not observe the results of the bombing. Time 0043 hrs. while flying towards the mouth of the ELBE on the return journey we saw, in the neighbourhood of UTERSEN (Uetersen), tracers from medium A/A which had previously been hosepiping around a high elevation, suddenly swing down to a low elevation of fire and concentrate on a point several thousand feet below us. In the middle of this concentrated fire at 0046 hrs. we saw a bright yellow gush of flames and the A/A stopped. This blaze hovered for four or five seconds and then went earthwards sending up more bursts of flame on striking the deck. We presumed this episode to be the shooting down of an aircraft (S/Ldr. Field of Scampton?)

We flew NW, were popped at BRUNSBUTTELKOOG and set course for Corridor B at 0115 hrs. crossed the English Coast at MABLETHORPE 0258 hrs. and landed base at 0320hrs.

(Sgd) H. A. T. Skehill P/O.

Locations for RAF 144 Squadron were:

7 May 1938- 6 September 1939: RAF Hemswell

6-9 September 1939: RAF Speke (now Liverpool John Lennon Airport)

9 September 1939) -17 July 1941

Group and Duty RAF 144 Squadron:

From September 1939-April 1942 the squadron served in Bomber Squadron with No. 5 Group

RAF 144 Squadron was still equipped with Handley Page Hampden aircraft on the outbreak of the Second World War in September 1939, flying from Hemswell, Lincolnshire, but did not get an opportunity to do any operational work until the war was nearly three weeks old.

On 26th September 1939, its chance finally came when it was ordered to despatch 12 Hampdens to search for and attack enemy naval vessels which had been reported in the North Sea. Flying in two formations of six, the Hampdens approached to within about twelve miles of the German coast, but the only naval vessels sighted were two submarines of unknown nationality and the aircraft returned to base with their bomb loads intact.

The squadron's next mission, another armed reconnaissance over the North Sea on 29th September. Eleven Hampdens, split into two sections – a section of five led by Wing Commander JC Cunningham, the CO, and a section of six led by Squadron Leader WJH Lindley – were detailed to search part of the Heligoland Bight to within sight of the German coast. Cunningham's section left Hemswell at 4.50pm and was not heard from again. It has been reported that this second formation was intercepted by Luftwaffe Messerschmitt Bf 109 fighters, which shot down all five Hampdens.

Lindley's section found two enemy destroyers in the search area steaming east in line astern at 20 knots but, owing to the destroyers' manoeuvres and "flak" umbrella, only three Hampdens were able to attack; the results were not observed, although it has been reported elsewhere that neither of the two destroyers had been hit. All six Hampdens returned safely to base.

In the ensuing months, the squadron "stood to" for shipping searches on several occasions but only once – on 14th December 1939 – was it required to operate; the mission was uneventful.

The squadron started to fly night-time leaflet dropping raids (Nickel Raids) over Germany from February 1940. The first occasion on which 144 Squadron flew over the German mainland was the night of 24th – 25th February 1940, when propaganda leaflets (or 'Nickels') were dropped on Hamburg. By 6th March, by which time it had 'Nickelled' several other German towns and by had also flown several security patrols, the leaflets being distributed were replaced by bombs after the German invasion of Norway. The squadron spent the next two years operating with Bomber Command.

The Handley Page Hampden was designed by Gustav Victor Lachmann. Lachmann served as a lieutenant in the German Army cavalry during the First World War – joining the German Flying Corps in 1917. After working in Germany with the Schneider and Albatross aircraft works, he resigned in 1926 to join the Ishikawajima Aircraft Works in Tokyo as a technical adviser. In 1929, he joined Handley Page and in 1932 was its chief designer. On the outbreak of the Second World War, Lachmann was interned as an enemy alien in Quebec, Canada, and on the Isle of Man. Under pressure from his employers, he was allowed to continue his work from the 'Lingfield Cage', an internment camp on Lingfield Racecourse. In 1949, he became a British citizen.

Aircraft of RAF 144 Squadron supported the Arab Northern Army in 1918 by attacking Ottoman Forces in the Middle East. The Arab Revolt which began in June 1916 received help with their strategy by T. E. Lawrence, better known as Lawrence of Arabia.

The Royal Air Force Historical Society has outlined, in "Journal 50", the duties which would be undertaken by crew members such as Sgt Thomson. The Journal emphasises that a Bomber Command aircrew operated as a team. Each member, it states, was mutually dependent on the others and each had a vital part to play in ensuring that the aircraft reached its target, dropped its bombs, and safely returned to base. The crew all shared the same experiences and dangers.

Until 1942, each aircraft had two pilots and dual-role aircrew: an observer (or navigator) who also acted as bomb-aimer and a wireless operator who was also the air gunner. When the heavy bombers were introduced, a flight engineer replaced the second pilot and the other crew members were given single, specialised roles.

Wireless Operator

The wireless operator transmitted all messages to and from the aircraft to their base. He had fewer duties than the other crew members, as operations were generally conducted in wireless silence. However, he also served as the reserve gunner and addressed any minor emergencies in any part of the aircraft. If the aircraft got into difficulties, he would have to send out positional signals. Should the aircraft have to ditch into the sea, the Wireless Operator would have had to remain at his post to send out a distress signal to improve the crew's chance of being located and rescued.

Story by Ken Bruce and Sue Gibson.

Antony Verdon Verdon

Antony Verdon Verdon RAFVR (657777) was the husband of Phyliss Verdon, Perth, and the son of Reverend Everard and Mary Edith Dorothea Verdon. Verdon was born 1 July 1915 at the Caundle Marsh Rectory in Sherbourne, Dorset, England. In 1944, he married Phyliss Ella Impett of 12 Kinfauns Crescent, Perth. (Kinfauns Crescent is now 93 Needless Road)

Verdon was a day boy on the training ship TS *Mercury* in the mid-1920s. The *Mercury* was both a school and training ship – between 1885 and 1968, around 5,000 boys were prepared for a life at sea in conditions that were usually hard. Verdon then attended Sherborne School (day boy and Abbeylands) May 1929-July 1933. He joined Barclays Bank straight from school. At the outbreak of war, Verdon joined the army and was later evacuated from Dunkirk. He transferred to the RAF and trained as a pilot, joining RAF 612 Coastal Command Squadron.

For the second half of 1943 and the early months of 1944, the squadron concentrated on night missions over the Bay of Biscay, hoping to attack German U-boats. Several attacks were recorded and on 28 April 1944 they sank U-193 to the west of Nantes (Saint-Nazaire), France.

On the night of 17 March 1944, three of RAF 612 (County of Aberdeen) Squadron's aircraft were on operations that night, one being cancelled at the last-minute owing to unserviceability. At 21.49 pm, Vickers Wellington Mk.XIV, HF170 took off from RAF Chivenor, west of Barnstable in Devon for a 10-hour anti-submarine patrol over the Bay of Biscay.

Verdon and his crew did not return from this patrol. At 03.03 on 18 March 1944, they were recalled to base by RAF 19 Group, and they acknowledged this command. A subsequent call received no reply. No further signals were received from his aircraft, and at 10.30 hours overdue action was taken. The weather was clear and fine, with a small amount of cloud. It was recorded in 1949 that the missing crew had lost their lives at sea.

Vickers Wellington, code 'A' for apple was crewed by:

Flight Sergeant Antony Verdon Verdon RAFVR (657777) – pilot, age 28.

Flight Sergeant Raymond Charles Smith RAFVR (1338128) – 2nd pilot, age 21.

Warrant Officer Frank Esbert RAAF (405640) – navigator/bomb aimer, age 22

Sergeant Raymond Nash RAFVR (1575024) – wireless operator/air gunner, age unknown.

Sergeant Ronald Clewer RAFVR (1319660) Wireless Operator/Air Gunner, age 22.

Sergeant George Crabb RAFVR (1433134) – wireless operator/air gunner, age unknown.

All are commemorated on the Runnymede memorial in Surrey and Verdon is remembered on the war memorial at Sherbourne School.

NOTES: RAF 612 (County of Aberdeen) Squadron as a general reconnaissance unit served with Coastal Command throughout the Second World War. They were initially equipped with the Avro Anson's, but these were replaced from November 1940 with Armstrong Whitworth Whitley's, and from November 1942 (April 1943 – last Whitley left the squadron) these made way for various marks of specially-adapted General Reconnaissance (GR) versions of the Vickers Wellington (GR.Mk. VIII & Mk.XII & Mk.XIV). The squadron spent most of the war operating from Britain but for the first half of 1942, it was based in Iceland. They began coastal patrols at the outbreak of war in 1939 from Dyce, Aberdeen.

Several Vickers Wellingtons, Consolidated Catalina's and Consolidated Liberator's were fitted with a powerful searchlight, Leigh Light's. These were used to illuminate U-Boats recharging their batteries on the surface at night. Coastal Command Wellington's were fitted with a powerful 24-inch diameter, 22 million candela, carbon arc searchlight. U-Boats were forced to recharge during the day when at least they could see the aircraft approaching.

Verdon was the nephew of Humphrey Verdon Roe, the brother of Sir Edwin Alliot Verdon Roe who in December of 1933, changed his surname by deed poll to Verdon-Roe (with a hyphen) – following his knighthood in 1929 and in honour of his mother. During the war, two of his sons were killed in action whilst serving with the RAF: Squadron Leader Eric Alliott Verdon-Roe, aged 26, in 1941, and Squadron Leader Lighton Verdon-Roe DFC aged 22, in 1943.

Humphrey Verdon-Roe invested in Alliot's aeronautical inventions and in 1913, the firm of A V Roe & Company was formed – better known as Avro and went on to produce many of Britain's best military and civilian aircraft such as, the Avro Lancaster, Avro Vulcan, Avro Shackleton, Avro York, Avro Manchester, Avro Anson, and the Avro 504. Verdon-Roe was a prominent member of the British Union of Fascists formed in 1932 by Sir Oswald Ernald Mosley, 6th Baronet.

Humphrey Verdon-Roe was married to Marie Charlotte Carmichael Stopes. Born in Edinburgh, Marie Stopes was a family planning pioneer, author, palaeobotanist, campaigner for eugenics and women's rights. The Marie Stopes charity exists to this day and works in 37 countries throughout the world.

Flight Lieutenant William Walton DFC and Alexander McInnes

Acting Flight Lieutenant William M Walton from Guildtown, Perthshire, was awarded the DFC (Distinguished Flying Cross) during the Second world War. Walton, the son of Mr and Mrs Edward Walton, Mavisbank, Guildtown was educated at Guildtown School and Balhousie Boys' School. He was later employed at Newmiln Estates where his father was farm manager. He also worked as a ground mechanic at Scone Aerodrome for nearly two years.

Alexander McInnes, the son of the local police force Depute Chief Constable, Stanley Place, Perth, joined the RAF at the same time as Walton. They sailed together to the US where they trained in the same RAF training centres. They passed their examinations on the same day in November 1942 and were awarded the silver wings of the American Army Air Corps at the same ceremony. Alexander McInnes had been employed as a clerk by MacDonald Fraser & Co., Livestock Salesmen, Perth.

After the training in Canada, Alabama, and Georgia, William Walton passed out as a sergeant. He was later commissioned as a pilot officer and subsequently promoted to flight lieutenant.

William Alexander Watson

Flight Engineer William Alexander Watson (567222) joined the RAF straight from school in 1934 as an apprentice at RAF Halton, near Wendover in Buckinghamshire. Watson preferred to be known as Sandy. He trained as a fitter and by 1935 he was awarded the coveted Barrington-Kennett medal for his sporting achievements.

By 1938, Watson had been promoted to Aircraftman First Class. By 1941, he had been trained in air gunnery and he was posted to RAF 15 Squadron in June 1941. On 10 August 1941, William was promoted to sergeant on his return to the squadron following flight engineering training at Short Brothers.

Watson commenced operational flying as a flight engineer on 7 September 1941. During take-off on a mission to bomb Berlin, one wheel of the undercarriage of his Short Stirling heavy bomber would not retract. The pilot jettisoned the bomb load at a safe location and on the final attempt, the faulty undercarriage operated correctly. The aircraft and crew landed safely.

Watson started as a spare crew member. Flying Officer Peter Boggis, the pilot, was impressed by his ability and secured him as his regular flight engineer. He was now destined to fly in the most prestigious and historically important Short Stirling bomber.

Lady Rachel Workman MacRobert of Douneside in the County of Aberdeen donated £25,000 to buy a Short Stirling bomber in memory of her three sons killed in RAF service. It was given the serial number N6086 and had the MacRobert coat of arms painted on the nose. It was named, 'Reply' and presented to her crew at RAF Wyton on 10 October 1941. It was assigned to RAF 15 Squadron and given the code 'LS-F'.

The first operation flown by N6086 was on 12 October 1941, to bomb Nuremberg, Germany. On 28 October 1941, the 'MacRobert's Reply' sustained its first damage from anti-aircraft fire over Nieuport (Nieuwpoort), Belgium. On 18 December 1941, it took part in the attack on the German Pocket Battleship *Scharnhost* and Heavy Cruiser *Gneisenau* in the French harbour of Brest. This was their second visit, in four days, this time they successfully hit the dry dock where the *Gneisenau* was berthed and saw black smoke rising from the warship. They were attacked by Luftwaffe fighters and managed to damage one of them with their guns.

The 'MacRobert's Reply', captained by Flying Officer Peter Boggis flew on 12 operations from October 1941 to January 1942. On 7 February 1942, the aircraft veered during take-off at RAF Peterhead and collided with a damaged Supermarine Spitfire (Watson was not on board). It was repaired and flew again with conversion units before being written off in 1943.

On 26 January 1942, Watson had by now completed two tours of operations and was posted to RAF 15 Squadron Conversion Flight as an instructor. In August 1942, now an acting flight sergeant, he returned to RAF 15 Squadron where he took part in another eleven operations. He was then posted to RAF 90

Squadron where he took part in a further fourteen operations.

Watson teamed up with another former RAF 15 Squadron pilot, Hugh 'Wendle' Wilkie from New Zealand. On 11 June 1943, they lost a propeller due to friendly fire from another Short Stirling whilst over the target area – nonetheless, they returned safely.

On the night of 18 April 1944, Short Stirling EJ108 with Watson and Wilkie took off at 22.35 hours from RAF Grafton Underwood, east of Kettering, Northamptonshire, with a crew of nine onboard, most of whom were undergoing training. Watson was now a warrant officer and were now part of RAF 1657 HCU (Heavy Conversion Unit) which was based at RAF Stradishall, between Cambridge and Bury St Edmonds. They were on a training exercise, practising night take-offs and landings (circuits and bumps). RAF Polebrook which was being used by the USAAC (United States Army Air Corp) was clear that day of any operational flying.

During a practice landing and take-off at RAF Polebrook, they hit and killed three USAAC personnel who were cycling on a runway. With damage to an engine and the possibility of damage to the undercarriage of the aircraft, they were committed to continue the take-off. As they became airborne, they were advised to land at the emergency landing strip at RAF Woodbridge, Suffolk.

Shortly before reaching RAF Woodbridge, there was an internal explosion and control of the aircraft was lost, the aircraft went into a steep nose up attitude. Six of the crew bailed out successfully, the two others were killed at 22.30pm in the crash at Moat Farm near Little Glemham 7 miles NE of Woodbrige. Sergeant Atkins died as he had failed to attach his parachute harness correctly and slipped through the webbing, subsequently plunging to his death. Two civilians, a brother and sister, Mr. W Carter and Miss Carter, whose thatched cottage was hit by part of the aircraft emerged unscathed.

Crash Location: Little Glemham, Suffolk. The crew onboard EJ108:

Flight Lieutenant Hugh Charles Wilkie RNZAF (415397) DFC, pilot, age 21

Flight Sergeant Colin George Nairne RNZAF (42117) 2nd pilot, age 22, Survived.

Warrant Officer William (Sandy) Alexander Watson RAF (567222) DFM, fight engineer, age 25

Sergeant Frederick Thomas George Atkins RAFVR (1603538) flight engineer, age 20

Pilot Officer Lyndon Clifford Perry RNZAF (428925) air bomber, age 21, Survived.

Pilot Officer Frederick Gerald Rickard (429366) RNZAF wireless operator/air gunner, age 22, Survived.

Sergeant Alfred Richard Stannard RAFVR (1338510) wireless operator/air gunner, age 22. Survived

Sergeant Stanley Alfred George Woodford RAFVR (922095) air gunner, age 29, Survived.

Flight Sergeant Philip Falkiner RNZAF (425140) air gunner, age 21, Survived.

On the ground, the personnel from 545 Bomber Squadron, 384th Bomber Group, 8th Air Force. USAAC who were killed:

Staff Sergeant David K Ollre (6288183), age 23.

Corporal James A Moore, age 23

Corporal Teddy R Potocki (32141939), age 23

Watson was gazetted on 15 June 1943 with the Distinguished Flying Medal (DFM) for accruing 240 hours operational flying time whilst with RAF 90 Squadron. The recommendation for the medal read: 'The safe return of his aircraft on many occasions must be credited to his skill and knowledge'.

Five of the crew members who survived the crash at Little Glemham – Flight Sergeant Colin George Nairne, Pilot Officer Lyndon Clifford Perry, Sergeant Alfred Richard Stannard, Sergeant Stanley Alfred George Woodford – were tragically killed just three months later (30 July 1944). They were flying northwards over the English Channel in heavy low cloud on Lancaster Mk. I, HK558, AA-D (RAF 75 Squadron) when they collided with RAF 514 squadron Avro Lancaster, LL733. All the crews from both aircraft were lost. Pilot Officer Frederick Gerald Rickard was the only one to live through the war – he died in 1998.

Watson was the eldest son of William and Christina Watson, Isaville, Bankfoot, Perthshire. He is buried in Auchtergaven Parish Churchyard, Perthshire. He is also commemorated on the Auchtergaven War Memorial. A military funeral was accorded to Warrant Officer William (Sandy) Alexander Watson. In attendance were contingents of the RAF, Home Guard, and the Observer Corps along with many of the public. The coffin was draped in the Union Flag and was carried from the house to the churchyard by each of the services representatives. A salute of guns was fired at the graveside and a bugler sounded 'The Last Post'.

NOTES: Lady MacRobert also sponsored four Hawker Hurricanes, three named after her sons and the fourth honouring the fighting spirit of the Russian allies carried the inscription, 'MacRobert's Salute to Russia'. Through the years many RAF aircraft have been given the names 'MacRobert's Reply': a Hawker Siddeley Buccaneer and four Panavia Tornados. Her sons, Sir Iain, Sir Roderic and Sir Alasdair have had nine RAF aircraft named after them.

A second Short Stirling, 'MacRobert's Reply' (W7531) entered service in March 1942 and was lost on 18 May 1942, only one member of the crew survived. W7531 was carrying out a 'Gardening Daffodil' operation off the Danish coast, laying mines to sink enemy shipping. Take off was from RAF Wyton at 21.40 hours. On approaching the south entrance to the Øresund waterway via the Norwegian coast and Malmo, the Short Stirling dropped down to 200 feet as they closed in on their target area. The aircraft was suddenly lit up by the searchlights of their old adversary, the Hipper Class cruiser, *Prinz Eugen*. The *Prinz Eugen* had just survived the Channel Dash and was now heading towards the Kiel Canal. The cruiser opened up with anti-aircraft, scoring numerous hits, while her escorts and shore batteries also struck the Stirling with machine gun and anti-aircraft fire.

W7531 was badly damaged, and fires broke out, the pilot Squadron Leader John Hall DFC turned west and tried to guide the Stirling to open water, but anti-aircraft posts (3.lei Flak Abt. 844 II and IV Zugdealt) on the nearby Lille Bælt Bridge hit the aircraft several times with flak. The Short Stirling crashed at 02.10 hours into the Gals Klint Forest, approximately 2 km to the west of Middelfart. When the Short Stirling hit the ground, one of the remaining mines onboard exploded and the plane was totally wrecked. Among that blazing wreckage something stirred, it was Sergeant Donald Jeffs, although severly wounded, he would the only one to survive. Jeffs was taken by the Wehrmacht to the lazarett (hospital) in Fredericia, and later to the lazarett in Rendsburg. When he had recovered from his wounds, he was sent on to Stalag VIIIB / 344 Lamsdorf. After the war, a memorial stone was raised on the spot where W7531 crashed and every year on 5 May, the day of the liberation of Denmark, a ceremony is held at the site.

Grafton Underwood is the fictional childhood home of Bridget Jones in the novels by Helen Fielding, *Bridget Jones Diary*. During the Second World War, RAF Grafton Underwood was assigned to the USAF Eighth Air Force in 1942 as USAAF Station 106.

RAF Polebrook was the airfield from which the USAF's Eighth Air Force carried out its first heavy bomb group combat mission on 17 August 1942. Major Clark Gable the film star flew combat missions from here in 1943.

MACROBERT'S REPLY (CH 3945) Original wartime caption: 'MACROBERT'S REPLY' the bomber aircraft purchased by Lady MacRobert and presented to the R.A.F. in memory of her sons – is now in operation with Bomber Command and has already taken part in raids on enemy territory. The Wing Commander [W/Cdr.Ogilvie] commanding the squadron with which 'MacRobert's Reply' is operating, handing to the crew a letter from Lady MacRobert, Copyright: © IWM.

'MacROBERT'S REPLY (CH 3231) Original wartime caption: A recent portrait of Lady MacRobert. Copyright: © IWM.

MacROBERT'S REPLY (CH 3949) Original wartime caption: For story see CH.3945 Picture shows - 'MacRobert's Reply' in flight. Copyright: © IWM.

MacROBERT'S REPLY (CH 3952) Original wartime caption: For story see CH.3945 Picture shows -The navigator of 'MacRobert's Reply'. Copyright: © IWM.

The crew of the bomber plane "MacRobert's Reply" all ready to take off for a raid over enemy territory

In memory of William Prune of RAF 15 Squadron, he had his own logbook and undertook at least 14 flights, no one though would ever claim to have taken him aloft. His favourite pastime was chasing motorcycles, attempting to bite the front tyre. His career ended when he attempted to do this with a lorry.

Original wartime caption: Flight Lieutenant William Prune, bulldog mascot of a bomber squadron stationed in East Anglie, is dead. Born on 23rd May 1938 and named Bill of Bafford, he first served with an Army Unit. Bill granted a commission in the R.A.F.V.R. and, on 11th March 1942 posted to a bomber squadron for operational duties as a Pilot Officer. He immediately established himself as a firm favourite with all ranks. They all admired the tenacity with which Pilot Officer Prune followed his chief sports of chasing motor bicycles and petrol cans. On 1st October 1942, he was promoted to Flying Officer and on 17th June 1943 was Flight Lieutenant. Shortly after his last promotion Bill had a severe illness and was detained in hospital for four weeks. Fit once more he returned to duty and continued in excellent health under the care of an N.C.O. Then one day he chased a lorry with the same determination that enabled him to score so many victories over motor bicycles. Unfortunately, he was run over and died on the way to the veterinary surgeon. Flight Lieutenant William Prune was buried in front of the Squadron hangar. Picture (issued 1944) shows - Flight Lieutenant William Prune.

James Milton Whitehead

In November of 1999, a retired farmer of Staunton-in-the-Vale, Nottinghamshire, asked a friend if she could investigate and aircraft accident, he witnessed in possibly 1942. He thought it was a Wellington bomber, it had an engine on fire and disappeared into a valley and he next heard a loud bang. After much research it was found to be Avro Lancaster Mk I, W4270 (QR-T) that had crashed.

On 18 February 1943, the crew of the Lancaster from RAF 61 Squadron took off from RAF Syerston on a cross country training flight. After six hours and 45 minutes of flying, at 22.56 hours, a con-rod broke and smashed out of the starboard inner engine. This caused a fire and despite their best efforts it could not be put out. In addition, the aircraft landing gear and flaps were down, ready for a landing. They were diverted to land at the nearby RAF Bottesford. Their low altitude, the loss of control and it is possible that a fuel tank exploded, caused them to crash one mile from Staunton-in-the-Vale and about two miles from the airfield. None of the crew survived.

Perthshire Advertiser 03 March 1943

The crew of Avro Lancaster W4270:

Sergeant Thomas Herbert Warne RCAF (R/102085), pilot, age 23 (later a Warrant Officer Class II)

Sergeant George Arthur Hitchon RAF (576765), flight engineer, age 19

Sergeant Robert John Preece RAFVR (1174086), observer, age 22

Sergeant Thomas Raine Newton RAFVR (1119116), wireless operator/air gunner, age 21

Sergeant James Milton Whitehead RAFVR (975551), wireless operator/air gunner, age 22

Sergeant Edward John Loverock RAFVR (950159), air gunner, age 21

Sergeant John Coaker RAFVR (1276786), air gunner, age 22

Whitehead was born in Cambusnethan on 7 September 1920. He had two younger sisters. In September 1939, he attended an aircrew selection board and joined the RAFVR as a wireless operator. He first served in a Hawker Hurricane fighter squadron before moving on to aircrew in Bomber Command for further training as a wireless operator. In mid-1941, he retrained as an observer but failed the course. He finally passed out as a wireless operator/air gunner and joined Sergeant Warne's crew.

Avro Lancaster W4270 was delivered to RAF 61 Squadron in October 1942. These are the operations that the aircraft previously took part in:

Kiel 13/14 October 1942

Genoa 22 October 1942

Milan 24 October 1942

Genoa 7/8 November 1942

Genoa 13/14 November 1942

Gardening* 17/18 November 1942

Turin 18/19 November 1942

Turin 28/29 November 1942

Turin 8/9 December 1942

Gardening* 14/15 December 1942

Duisburg 20/21 December 1942, aborted.

Essen 7 January 1943

Berlin 16/17 January 1943

Essen 21 January 1943

Dusseldorf 23 January 1943

Hamburg 30/31 January 1943

Note: * Gardening = dropping mines into the sea

Whitehead was the son of Willie and Janet Reid Whitehead, Greenshields Whitehead of Riddrie, Glasgow. At the time, they were resident at HMP Perth Prison village and James had been educated in Peterhead and Perth Academy. (Riddrie is the area in Glasgow were HMP Barlinnie Prison is located.) Whitehead played for the Perth City boys' football team, Southend. He was buried in Cambusnethan Cemetery, Wishaw, Lanarkshire, the place where he was born.

Perthshire Advertiser, 3rd March 1943

'CITY AND COUNTY CASUALTIES

KILLED IN FLYING ACCIDENT

Official intimation has been received by Mr and Mrs W. Whitehead, H.M. Prison, Perth, that their only son, Sergeant-Observer James Whitehead, R.A.F., has been killed in a flying accident.

Sgt. Whitehead, who was 22½ years of age, had been in the R.A.F. for 3½ years. He received his education at Peterhead and Perth Academies, and prior to joining up he was employed temporarily in a Perth railway office.'

NOTES: RAF Syerston, their home base, was about seven miles northwest of the crash site.

Warrant Officer Class II Warne was the oldest and most experienced member of the crew despite only having 15 hours of night flying experience on the Lancaster.

Acting Flight Lieutenant Reid, who retired to live in Crieff, of RAF 61 Squadron, won a Victoria Cross on a mission flown from RAF Syerston.

ROYAL AIR FORCE BOMBER COMMAND, 1942-1945. (CH 10714) The crew of an Avro Lancaster B Mark I of No. 61 Squadron RAF walk towards their aircraft at Syerston, Nottinghamshire, before taking off for a raid on Hamburg, Germany. Copyright: © IWM.

David Wood

Pilot Officer David Wood was called up at the start of the Second World War. Wood was one of the first volunteers from the Reserve Force which was inaugurated at Scone Aerodrome in late 1938. He was the star pupil of the volunteer school and became flight commander of Perth 38F Squadron (3rd Scottish), Air Defence Cadet Corps (later renamed Air Training Corps) -the F in 38F Squadron stood for 'Founder Squadron'. Wood was one of the first two members of the volunteer school to take his commission as an officer in the RAF.

At the time of his death, Wood was attached to RAF No 8 Bombing and Gunnery School at RAF Evanton in Easter Ross, close to the shore of the Cromarty Firth (also known as HMS Fieldfare).

PERTHSHIRE ADVERTISER 04 MAY 1940

Within hours of each other, two RAF aircraft crashed within a few miles of each other, south of Huntly in Aberdeenshire. Armstrong Whitley Mk V, N1500 of RAF 102 Squadron, crashed during a transit flight at 10.59 hours on 1 May 1940 from RAF Kinloss to RAF Driffield (with an intended stop at RAF Leuchars). The aircraft stayed off course in extremely bad weather and went into the northern slope of the Hill of Foundland, southeast of Huntly. The four crew and of the two passengers were killed instantly, two passengers died later that month from their injuries; only one passenger survived. The crash site is often quoted as Bainshole on the north side of the Glens of Foundland.

Wood was flying in Hawker Henley Mk III, L3303 when it crashed near Rhynie, eight miles south of Huntly on Wednesday 1 May 1940. The Hawker Henley was a two-seat aircraft used as a fast target tug at RAF No 8 Bombing and Gunnery School.

Hawker Henley Mk III, L3303 crew: *Squadron Leader Wilfred John Francis Bull RAF (32042), Pilot Officer David Wood RAFVR (73016), age 23.*

Bull was from West Cults near Aberdeen and is buried at Allenvale Cemetery, Aberdeen. David Wood was the younger son of David Wood, partner in the firm of Wood & Son, printers, and booksellers and of Mrs Wood, Meadowbank, Pitheavlis, Perth. He was well known in rugby circles, formerly Secretary of Perthshire 'A' XV; and was a former pupil of Strathallan School, Forgandenny.

NOTES: RAF No 8 Bombing and Gunnery School had on strength the following aircraft: 9 Hawker Henley, 11 Armstrong Whitley, 64 Blackburn Botha, 47 Fairey Battle, 3 Westland Wallace, 21 Handley Page Harrow and a Miles Magister.

The Hawker Henley was conceived as a light bomber but was rejected and never saw any action. It was derived from the Hawker Hurricane and 200 were built as target tugs. During construction it shared the outer wing panel and tailplane jigs with the Hurricane. It also used the Rolls Royce Merlin 'F' engine and had a top speed of 300 mph.

James Currie Wood

RAF 100 Squadron, Avro Lancaster III, W4998, call sign, HW-J, took off from RAF Grimsby at 23.54 pm on Sunday 25 May 1943 on its way to bomb Düsseldorf in Germany. It marked the heaviest air raid in history, up to that time. The Royal Air Force dropped on that mission 2,000 tons of bombs on the Dortmund/Düsseldorf area, surpassing the previous amount on one target by 500 tons. Over 800 RAF bombers were involved, and 700 civilians would lose their lives that night.

Lancaster W4998 was hit by flak and crashed at 02.35 am near Horst – Melderslo in the province of Limburg, northwest of Venlo, The Netherlands. Just over the Nederland/Deutschland border, about 70 km on the return journey from their target. Five of the crew died and two survived and became prisoners of war:

Flight Sergeant Acel Theodore Walter Moore RNZAF (413106), pilot, age 29

Warrant Officer J S Wilkins RAF (940090), flight engineer, survived POW.

Sergeant David Campbell Stone RAFVR (1451978), navigator, age 21

Flight Lieutenant S W J Coventry, RAF, bomb aimer, survived POW.

Flight Sergeant James Currie Wood, RAFVR (755138), wireless operator/air gunner, age 24

Flight Sergeant Leslie Cormac Maunsell RNZAF (414318), air gunner, age 24

Sergeant Michael Keogh RAFVR (1586059), air gunner, age 19.

Wood and his fellow crew members are buried and remembered in the Jonkerbos War Cemetery and Memorial in the town of Nijmegen, The Netherlands.

James Currie Wood was the younger son of Charles Thornton and Flora Smith Wood, 69 George Street, Perth, and dearly be-loved husband of Jessie (Jennie) Ann Stewart, Lonsdale, Invergowrie (Longforgan). Wood's father was a fruiterer in St John's Street, Perth. Another son served in the Middle East, also with the RAF.

From the *Perthshire Advertiser*, 23 June 1943

'WAR CASUALTIES

PERTH AIRMAN REPORTED KILLED

Official information has been received that Flight Sgt. J. C. Wood, a Perth airman who was posted missing from a raid over Germany on May 26 this year, was killed.

He was the youngest son of Mr C. T. Wood, fruiterer, St. John Street, and of Mrs Wood, 69 George Street, Perth and was aged 24. His wife and infant son reside at Lonsdale, Invergowrie.

F/Sgt. Wood, who was educated at Perth Academy, entered the R.A.F. as a volunteer on his 20th birthday in May 1939. he flew as a wireless operator-air gunner before being posted as a gunnery instructor and later to radiolocation. Going back on operations, he be-came a radio officer.

His brother, H. S. Wood, has been serving as a Flying Officer in the Middle East for the past year and was, in civilian life, a bank accountant in Clydesdale Bank, Crieff.'

Perthshire Advertiser, 8 December 1943

WOOD. -Previously reported missing, now officially confirmed killed on operations over Germany during May 1943, Flight-Sergeant J. C. Wood, younger son of Mr and Mrs C. T. Wood, Perth, and dearly be-loved husband of Jennie Stewart, Lonsdale, Invergowrie.'

NOTES: Coventry initially evaded capture: he was caught in Paris on 6 June 1943.

This operation was the third consecutive night of large bombing raids over Germany by the RAF. Aircrews reported fires still burning from the previous nights.

RAF 100 Squadron aircrews and ground crews had performed heroic deeds in carrying the war to Germany in the only way possible in Europe at that point in the Second World War. Between their first mission in March 1943 and the end of the war in 1945, 100 Squadron flew 3,984 individual sorties (dropping just over 18,000 tons of bombs). The squadron's losses totalled 92 aircraft lost (an additional 21 were lost in crashes) and 593 crew killed. RAF No. 100 Squadron held second place in No. 1 Group for the number of successful missions completed, and first place for the lowest number of losses. Such attainments, including a spell of 700 sorties without loss during 1944, gave 100 Squadron the reputation of being a 'lucky squadron'. The RAF 100 squadron motto is: *Sarang tebuan jangan dijolok* (Malay for – *Never stir up a hornet's nest*).

Fearing a last stand, a Nazi national redoubt, the squadron took part in the last day of Lancaster operations on 25 April 1945, when it provided 16 aircraft for a devastating attack on Berchtesgaden where Adolf Hitler had his mountain retreat in the Obersalzberg, above the town in the Kehlsteinhaus (the Eagle's Nest).

On 9 November 1939, two British Intelligence Service agents were kidnapped by the German SD (*Sicherheitsdienst des Reichsführers-SS (Security Service of the Reichsführer-SS))* in what became known as the Venlo Incident. The incident was used by the Nazis to link Britain to the Georg Elser failed assassination of Hitler and other high ranking Nazi leaders on 8 November 1940 at the Bürgerbräukeller in Munich, and to justify their later invasion of The Netherlands, a neutral country, on 10 May 1940.

James Currie Wood, Perthshire Advertiser 2 June 1943

Lancaster MK-III W-4998 crashed here on 5/26/1943. Crossing Meldersloseweg / Vlasvenstraat Melderslo. Nell Verlinden was 16 years old when the Lancaster came to a halt a few meters in front of the bomb shelter. Antoon Spreeuwenberg saw the plane come to a stop a few meters ahead of him, he was smoking a cigarette. Copyright Edietomroy, this file is licensed under the Creative Commons Attribution-Share Alike 3.0 Netherlands license. Free to share, to copy, distribute and transmit the work.

William James Young

Pilot Officer William James Young RAFVR (179795) was the son of Arthur and Jeannie Barron Young, Broomhall, Coupar Angus. William attended Coupar Angus Public School and Perth Academy where he was the sports champion in 1940. He was a member of Coupar Angus Tennis Club and a boy scout. Before enlisting in the RAF, he was employed at Perth Employment Exchange, Alexandra Street, Perth.

William Young started his flying training as a member of Coupar Angus Air Training Corps (ATC) and then in Canada with the RAF where he obtained his wings. He was commissioned as Pilot Officer in July 1944, although his squadron service records show him as Flight Sergeant throughout July and August 1944.

From May 1944 to May 1945, William's squadron, RAF 77, was based at RAF Full Sutton, two miles south of Stamford Bridge, East Riding of Yorkshire. Prior to D-Day, 6 June 1944, Flight Sergeant Young flew at least 4 missions in May 1944 with RAF 77 squadron from RAF Full Sutton.

On the night of 5/6 June 1944 Flight Sergeant W J Young was the pilot of Handley Page Halifax Mk III MZ702 assigned to target Maisy, on the coast of Normandy, France. The town Maisy (or the commune of Grandcamp-les-Bains, now Grandcamp-Maisy) was on the west side of the Omaha invasion beach. Maisy is about 2 km inland was the site of a hidden German heavy artillery battery, and the German headquarters for the sector. Take off was at 01.30 and touch down at 06.15.

Sgt (later P/O) William J Young 77 Squadron (Halifaxes) 1943 missing August 1944, presumed killed; son of Mr,Mrs Arthur Young Coupar Angus Perthshire.

6 June 1944, Flight Sergeant W J Young and crew report: Target was identified by red and green T. I's (Target Indicator Flares), cloud was tops 7/8,000 feet. Bombs released from 11,000 feet on cluster of reds inside a triangle of three red clusters. There was also a cluster of greens in a triangle of reds about 200 yards south of the MPI (Mean Point of Impact) of the reds. The whole marked area was less than a square mile. First reds were seen as a glow in cloud at 03.28 hours. Several sticks of bombs were seen falling around the markers.

Later that same day 6 June 1944, Handley Page Halifax Mk III, MZ702 piloted by Flight Sergeant Young took off at 22.30 to bomb Saint-Lô, the capital of the Manche department in the region of Normandy. Saint-Lô housed the headquarters of the 84th German Army Corps (LXXXIV. Armeekorps). The bombing was aimed at the railway station and power station. Every day for a week the air raids continued bombing Saint-Lô; nearly 800 inhabitants were killed on the night of 6/7 June 1944. Halifax MZ702 returned at 03.15.

6 June 1944, Flight Sergeant W J Young and crew report: The primary target was identified, and bombs were dropped from 5,00 feet, white T.I. in bomb sight. Many bombs were seen bursting in the town area.

On 11 June 1944 the next target was the Massy-Palaiseau area which is in the southern suburbs of Paris. Massy-Palaiseau was a strategic railway transport node and marshalling yard where many tracks converge and allowed military reinforcement through passage towards Normandy. Flight Sergeant Young was this time piloting Handley Page Halifax Mk III, MK715; take off at 21.50 and down at 03.10.

11 June 1944, Flight Sergeant W J Young and crew report: Target could not be identified owing to 10/10ths cloud, so bombs (5 x 500lb GP 'Safe' and 1 x 500ln GP 'Live') were jettisoned in position 50.23N 00.33E, from 8,000 feet at 00.53 hours. 9 x 500lb GP, brought back.

On 12 June 1944 Flight Sergeant Young was assigned to bomb Amiens in northern France. Handley Page Halifax Mk III, NA351 took off was at 23.20, returning at 03.40. The target was the rail facilities at Amiens. Over 671 allied aircraft took part in this and other raids that night. On the night of 12 June 1940 RAF Bomber Command loses were 30 aircraft, 140 aircrew killed, 22 were made POW and 31 were to evade capture.

12 June 1944, Flight Sergeant W J Young and crew report: Target was identified, and attack made at 01.31 hours from 11,700 feet, fires burning in target area in bombsight. A big red fire was burning, with smoke rising to 1,500 feet. Bombing seemed generally well concentrated.

The night of 14/15 June 1944 Flight Sergeant Young took off at 00.50 hours in Handley Page Halifax Mk III, NA351 to bomb Évrecy in the Calvados department of the Normandy region. Between 3.00 hours and 3.20 hours, the Allies bombed the village of Évrecy, the air raid transformed the town into a heap of ruins. At that time, the 3rd squadron of the German 101st Heavy SS Panzer Battalion (Schwere SS-Panzerabteilung 101) was in the area. Halifax NA351 touched down at base at 06.00 hours.

15 June 1944, Flight Sergeant W J Young and crew report: The target was identified, and an attack was made from 5,800 feet, at 03.01 hours, bombs being dropped on fires burning in the target area. Bombing appeared well concentrated.

At 23.20 on the night of 16/17 June 1944, Flight Sergeant Young piloted Handley Page Halifax Mk III, MZ735 to the nights target of Sterkrade, a district of Oberhausen to the northwest of Duisburg, Germany. The mission was to attack the synthetic-oil plant at Sterkrade/Holten despite a poor weather forecast. The target was found to be covered by thick cloud and the Pathfinder markers quickly disappeared. The main air force crews could do little but bomb on to the diminishing glow of the markers in the cloud. The crew returned at 03.45. RAF 77 Squadron lost seven of its 23 Halifax's taking part in this raid. The route of the bomber stream passed near a German night-fighter beacon at Bocholt, only 50 km from Sterkrade. On this same night, another Perth son and former Perth Academy pupil, Squadron Leader Gavin Strang Smith DFC RAF 550 Squadron (Avro Lancaster ME840), formerly of Kincarrathie Crescent, was lost on the same bombing mission to Sterkrake.

17 June 1944, Flight Sergeant W J Young and crew report: Cloud was 10/10ths, and no markers were seen. Bomb dropped on E.T.A. (Estimated Time of Arrival), at 01.25½ hours from 20,000 feet.

Target for the night of 19 June 1944, was the V-1 flying bomb (Vergeltungswaffe 1 "Vengeance Weapon 1") supply depot at Domléger-Longvillers, a commune in the Somme department in Hauts-de-France in northern France. In the Hauts-de-France region, ten supply depots were built. The first missiles arrived in early 1944 and depots quickly began to fill up. The first V-1 bombs were dropped on London on 13 June 1944. RAF 77 Squadron were recalled immediately after take-off and bombs were jettisoned.

19 June 1944, Flight Sergeant W J Young and crew report: Handley Page Halifax Mk III, NA532. Take off 22.35, touch down 0025 hours. 7 x 500lb MC TD 0.025 brought back, remainder of load jettisoned 'Safe' at 53.32N 02.09E, at 23.49 hours.

On 24 June 1944 flying in Handley Page Halifax Mk III, NA531, the target was probably a V-1 Flying bomb launch ramp at Noyelles-en-Chaussée, a commune in the Somme department in Hauts-de-France, northern France. Take off was at 15.35 and they landed back at base at 19.20 hours.

24 June 1944, Flight Sergeant W J Young and crew report: Target was identified, and attacked at 17.20½ hours from 17,400 feet, on Red T.I.'s, which appeared to be the aiming point, from orders received from Master Bombers.

It seems likely that Flight Sergeant Young was given leave at this point.

On 6 July 1944 Flight Sergeant Young was piloting a Handley Page Halifax Mk III (marking unknown), the target was at Marquise Mimoyecques between Boulogne and Calais, France. The specific target was the fortress complex of Mimoyecques (Fortress of Mimoyecques), an underground military complex built between September 1943 and 1944. It was intended to house a battery of V-3 cannons Vergeltungswaffe 3, ("Vengeance Weapon 3") aimed at London. The V-3 was also known as Hochdruckpumpe ("High Pressure Pump") and Fleißiges Lieschen ("Busy Lizzie"). It was constructed by a mostly German workforce recruited from major engineering and mining concerns, augmented by prisoner-of-war slave labour. The project intended to use two cannon batteries to crush London under a barrage of hundreds of shells per hour, shells of 140 kilograms (310 lb) with an explosive charge of 25 kilograms (55 lb). The site was put out of commission that day, 6 July 1944. Bombers of RAF 617 Squadron (the famous "Dambusters") completed the attack using 5,400 kg (11,900 lb) Barnes Wallis developed "Tallboy" deep-penetration earthquake bombs. Sixteen aircraft from RAF 77 Squadron took off, one returned due to engine trouble. Visibility good at target.

6 July 1944, Flight Sergeant W J Young and crew report: Take off 06.25, down 10.20 – Target attacked on red T.I., (target Indicator) and by visual identification, from 15,600 feet at 08.22 hours. Aircraft landed at Church Fenton on return, owing to mist over base.

The following day 7 July 1944 Flight Sergeant Young was the pilot of Handley Page Halifax Mk III NA351.

The target was the city of Caen in support of the D-Day Normandy landings. This was part of *Operation Charnwood,* 8-11 July 1944 and saw the Allied forces eventually enter the city of Caen on 9 July 1944. Nineteen aircraft of RAF 77 Squadron attacked the target, none returned early, none reported missing. Visibility at target was excellent. A message of appreciation was received from the Commander in Chief Second Army Corps.

7 July 1944, Flight Sergeant W J Young and crew report: Take off 20.00 hours, touch down 23.35 hours. The target was identified visually and by T. I's, which seemed to be on the aiming point, and attack was made at 23.03 hours, from 6,300 feet, on what was believed to be the aiming point, as by time the bombing markers had become almost obscured by smoke.

On 17 July 1944, Flight Sergeant Young and his crew took off at 03.05 hours to bomb east of Caen. There was a preliminary artillery bombardment, then 2,077 heavy and medium bombers of the RAF) and USAAF attacked in three waves, in the largest air raid launched in direct support of ground forces so far. This was the start of *Operation Goodwood,* General Bernard Montgomery's massive British armoured attack to the east of Caen that he hoped would force the Germans to move reinforcements to the area and finally complete the liberation of Caen, but it failed to achieve the dramatic breakthrough that some had been expecting. For this daylight attack on Caen 25 aircraft took off. None returned early, none were reported missing. Four aircraft slightly damaged by flak. Visibility was not good, though there was little cloud.

17 July 1944, Flight Sergeant W J Young and crew report: Up 03.05, Down 08.15. The target was identified visually, and by red and yellow markers, and bombs were dropped at 05.51 hours, on MPI (Mean Point of Impact) of reds, from 6,800 feet. However, avoiding action had to be taken just as bombs were released, so aim may have been affected. The Master Bomber was heard to praise the backers up for dropping the T.I.'s "spot on". Bombing was very well concentrated. A mass of flames was seen in the direction of Caen A1 target. Flames seemed to be coming from the canal (Caen).

The target for 20 July 1944, was Bombing Chappelle – Notre–Dame; take off 14.20 and down at 17.35. (Target probably between La Chapelle L'Épée and Eglise Notre-Dame, 4 to 6 km west of Lisieux, Normandy.) Flight Sergeant Young and his crew were in Handley Page Halifax Mk III, MZ347. The operation report shows that 24 aircraft took off, none returned early. None were reported missing. Cloud 4/10ths over target with ground haze.

20 July 1944, Flight Sergeant W J Young and crew report: The target was identified, and attacked at 15.50½ hours, from 15,000 feet in red T.I.'s. Bombing appeared to be well concentrated in the target area.

On the night of 23 July 1944, the bombing target changed back to one in Germany, this time the city of Stuttgart. Take off was 21.40 and touch down at 06.00. Fifteen aircraft took off. Three aircraft jettisoned bombs owing to technical trouble, and returned early, none were reported missing. A small amount of cloud covered the target.

23 July 1944, Flight Sergeant Young, and crew report: *The target was identified by Wanganui flares, (Wanganui – target marking by blind-dropped sky markers when ground concealed by cloud) and attacked at 01.56 hours from 18,000 feet on MPI (Mean Point of Impact) of two of these flares, as instructed by the Master Bomber. Flares were being shot out by flak.*

The target for 25 July 1944 was the German city district of Wanne-Eickel in the northern Ruhr area (between Essen and Dortmund – now Herne). Wanne Eickel had a large railway station and marshalling yards, and a "fuel works" producing synthetic gasoline. Take off was at 22.50 and down at 03.30. Nineteen aircraft took off. Four aircraft returned early due to technical trouble, two bringing bombs back, and two jettisoning. The weather at target was clear.

25 July 1944, Flight Sergeant W J Young and crew report: *The target was identified and attacked at 01.16 hours from 17,000 feet on newly dropped T.I. greens. A reddish glow was seen through the haze covering the target area.*

A return to supporting the ground offensive saw a change in the target type for 28 July 1944 from industrial to a forest location, the Forêt de Nieppe in the Morbecque Nord commune of northern France. Forêt de Nieppe is a national ancient forest, the largest in French Flanders. The Germans built fortified blockhouses there, some of which were intended to prepare V-2 rockets before launching towards London, England. Sixteen aircraft took off, but one bombed an alternative aiming point in error. Visibility good target clear of cloud. Take off was 16.45, down at 20.30. A further seven aircraft from RAF 77 Squadron took off around 22.00 hours and bombed Forêt de Nieppe.

28 July 1944, Flight Sergeant W J Young and crew report: *Target was attacked on visual identification of aiming point at 18.37 hours from 16,000 feet. Bombing appeared generally rather scattered.*

Battle Area "G" was the target for 30 July 1944, Flight Sergeant Young flew Handley Page Halifax Mk III, MZ347. Take off 05.45, down at 07.35. Thirteen aircraft took off, but the sortie was abandoned on instruction from Master Bomber owing to low cloud and bad visibility. All aircraft jettisoned bombs, MZ347 in position shown below.

30 July 1944, Flight Sergeant W J Young and crew report: *50.23N 00.34E from 8,00 feet at 07.55 hours.*

On 7 August 1944, Pilot Officer William James Young piloted Halifax MZ347 to the nights target which was part of *Operation Totalize*. For the RAF it was to attack the German defences south of Caen on the eastern flank of the Allied positions in Normandy. At 23:00, RAF Bomber Command commenced the bombardment of German positions along the Caen front. At 23:30, the armoured columns began their advance behind a rolling barrage.

7 August 1944 Pilot Officer William James Young and his crew reported: *The target was identified by*

green and yellow T.I.'s (Target Indicator Flares) and star shells, and attack was made at 23.01 hours from 7,900 feet on centre of greens as instructed. No results seen.

On 9 August 1944 Pilot Officer Young's crew were listed as assigned to Halifax Mk III MZ809 for a bombing mission to Forêt de Mormal, Parc naturel régional de l'Avesnois, France. This was an attack on a fuel dump in Mormal forest. All aircraft returned safely, and all crews were enthusiastic about the results. Halifax MZ809 did not take-off.

On the night of 12 August 1944, 12 aircraft took off; 11 successfully night attacked Rüsselsheim, southwest of Frankfurt. Another eight aircraft including Flight Sergeant Young piloting Handley Page Halifax Mk.III MZ347 (KN-X). Take off was at 21.20 from RAF Full Sutton to bomb Brunswick, west of Hanover.

Flight Sergeant William James Young and his crew failed to return from this operation. The cause of loss and crash-site were not established.

Target: *Brunswick*

Route: *– Base – Hornsea – 53.55N 04.30E – 54.10N 06.50E – Enemy Coast – 53.00N 08.00E – 52.00N 09,20E – Target – 52.19N 10.43E – Enemy Coast – 54.00N 08.00E – 53.50N – Hornsea – Base*

Bomb Load: *All Aircraft: 7 x 500lb GP TD 0.025, 6 x 1000lb USA M59 TD 0.025, 1 x 500lb GP LD.37 6hrs*

Camera: *All Aircraft, colour film & flashes. Aircraft "N" Day Camera*

Opposition & General Remarks:

Moderate barrage heavy flak below bombing height of our aircraft. Flak from Celle area. Searchlights obscured by cloud at target but tended to silhouette aircraft above. Numerous searchlights immediately west of target, also at Bremen, Bremerhaven & Wesermünder. Numerous sightings of enemy fighters. Rocket projectiles reported again, described as fired from ground to about height of aircraft, then travelling at a high speed horizontally emitting yellow or red sparks which increased in intensity every few seconds.

The crew of Handley Page Halifax Mk III, MZ347 KN-A:

Pilot Officer William James Young RAFVR (179795) Pilot, age 22

Pilot Officer Charles Victor Ross Wigley RCAF (J/89966) Mid Upper Gunner, age 19

Flying Officer Colin Clifton Smith RAFVR (152042), Navigator, age 21

Sergeant Thomas Victor Parsons RAFVR (1836455), Flight Engineer, age 26

Sergeant David William Hughes RAFVR (982845), Rear Gunner, age 24

Flying Officer Ernest Norman Calvert RAFVR (151583), Air Bomber, age 23

Warrant Officer Norman Brook RAFVR (1379465), Wireless Operator, age 22

The crew of Handley Page Halifax Mk III, MZ347 are commemorated on the Runnymede Memorial.

NOTES: Full Sutton is now the location of a Category A and B men's prison, HMP Full Sutton. The prison has a unit, the Close Supervision Centre, which is referred to as a "prison inside a prison". This is used to house prisoners who are a high risk to the public and national security.

Grandcamp-Maisy is about 4 km west of La Pointe du Hoc where the US Army Ranger Assault Group attacked and captured the German bunkers and machine gun posts. The 6 June 1944 D-Day Omaha beach landing was memorably portrayed in the movies, *Saving Private Ryan* and the *Longest Day*. Omaha Beach was far more heavily defended than anticipated, with the full strength of the battle-hardened German 325th Infantry Division raining down fire from the cliffs above. By 12 June 1944 at midnight, 18 allied divisions (8 US divisions, 10 British and Canadian divisions) were present in Normandy, representing a total of 326,547 soldiers, 54,186 vehicles and 104,428 tons of equipment.

Of the German 101st Heavy SS Panzer Battalion 45 Tigers, 37 were operational and eight more were under repair. With the D-Day landings on 6 June 1944, it was ordered to Normandy where it arrived on 12 and 13 June 1944. Fighting its first battle on 13 June 1944, Kompanie 2, led by SS-Obersturmführer Michael Wittmann inflicted severe damage on the British in Villers-Bocage. The 101st Battalion had lost 15 of its 45 Tigers by 5 July 1944. The battalion lost virtually all its remaining Tigers in the Falaise pocket during the German retreat from France. Michael Wittmann is most famous for his action on 13 June 1944. Whilst in command of a Tiger I tank, Wittmann destroyed up to 14 tanks, 15 personnel carriers and two anti-tank guns within 15 minutes for the loss of his own tank.

Flight Sergeant Young did not take part in this operation, but on 1 July 1944, RAF 77 Squadron bombed Saint-Martin-l'Hortier, 33 kms southeast of Dieppe in the Normandy region of Northern France. At Saint-Martin-l'Hortier the Germans, from August 1943 were constructing a V-1 rocket storage depot. This and other storage sites were not completed because they were destroyed by Allied forces bombing.

Forêt de Mormal is best known to the British for its role in the WW1 retreat from Mons in August 1914.

Field Marshall Johannes Erwin Eugen Rommel was injured on 17 July 1944 after his staff car crashed after being strafed by allied fighter aircraft near Sainte-Foy-de-Montgommery, Normandy. He was replaced by Field Marshal Günther von Kluge.

On 20 July 1944, an attempt was made by German officers to assassinate Adolf Hitler *(Operation Valkyrie)*. Count Claus Philip Maria Schenk von Stauffenberg, Chief-of-Staff to General Friedrich Fromm, planted a bomb near Hitler in a conference room at the Nazi leader's East Prussian headquarters, The Wolf's Lair (German: Wolfsschanze; Polish: Wilczy Szaniec) at Rastenburg (now Kętrzyn, Poland – formerly East Prussia). The bomb exploded at 12.42 hours, after von Stauffenberg has left. The bomb failed to kill Hitler and the conspiracy fell apart. Field Marshall Rommel was implicated in the plot.

Because of Rommel's status as a national hero, Hitler desired to eliminate him quietly instead of immediately executing him. Rommel was given a choice between committing suicide, in return for assurances that his reputation would remain intact and that his family would not be persecuted following his death or facing a trial that would result in his disgrace and execution; he chose the former and committed suicide using a cyanide pill.

Chester Wilmot, the Australian war correspondent who reported for the BBC and the ABC (Australian Broadcasting Corporation) during the Second World War, described the opening of Operation Goodwood: "For forty-five minutes the procession of bombers came on unbroken and when they'd gone, the thunder of the guns swelled up and filled the air, as the artillery carried on the bombardment".

Perthshire Advertiser 1 June 1940 – William Young 3rd from left. Nellie Grassie 2nd left, is Helen Ann Taylor (Nicky) Grassie who was killed in the Bourne End Rail Crash in September 1945 and is buried in Wellshill Cemetery

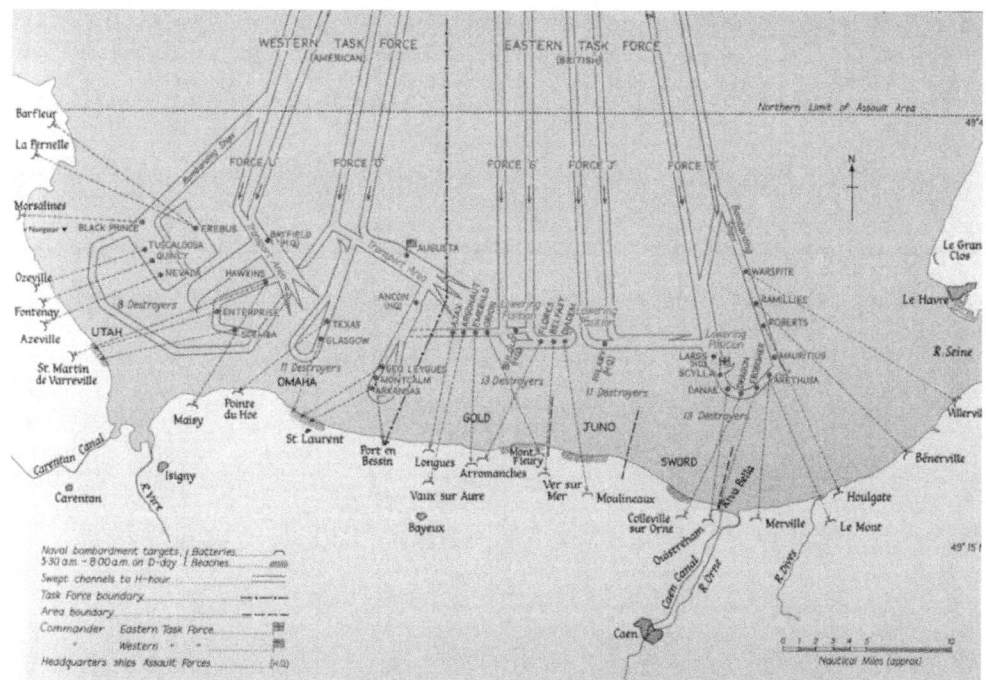

Naval Bombardments on D-Day – HM Government. Post-Work: User: W. Wolny, this work is created by the United Kingdom Government is in the public domain, via Wikimedia Commons

AIRCRAFT OF THE ROYAL AIR FORCE 1939-1945: HANDLEY PAGE HP.57 HALIFAX. (CH 12532) Halifax B Mark III of No. 77 Squadron RAF, taking off from Elvington, Yorkshire. Note the censor?s attempt to obliterate the H2S radome under the fuselage Copyright: © IWM.

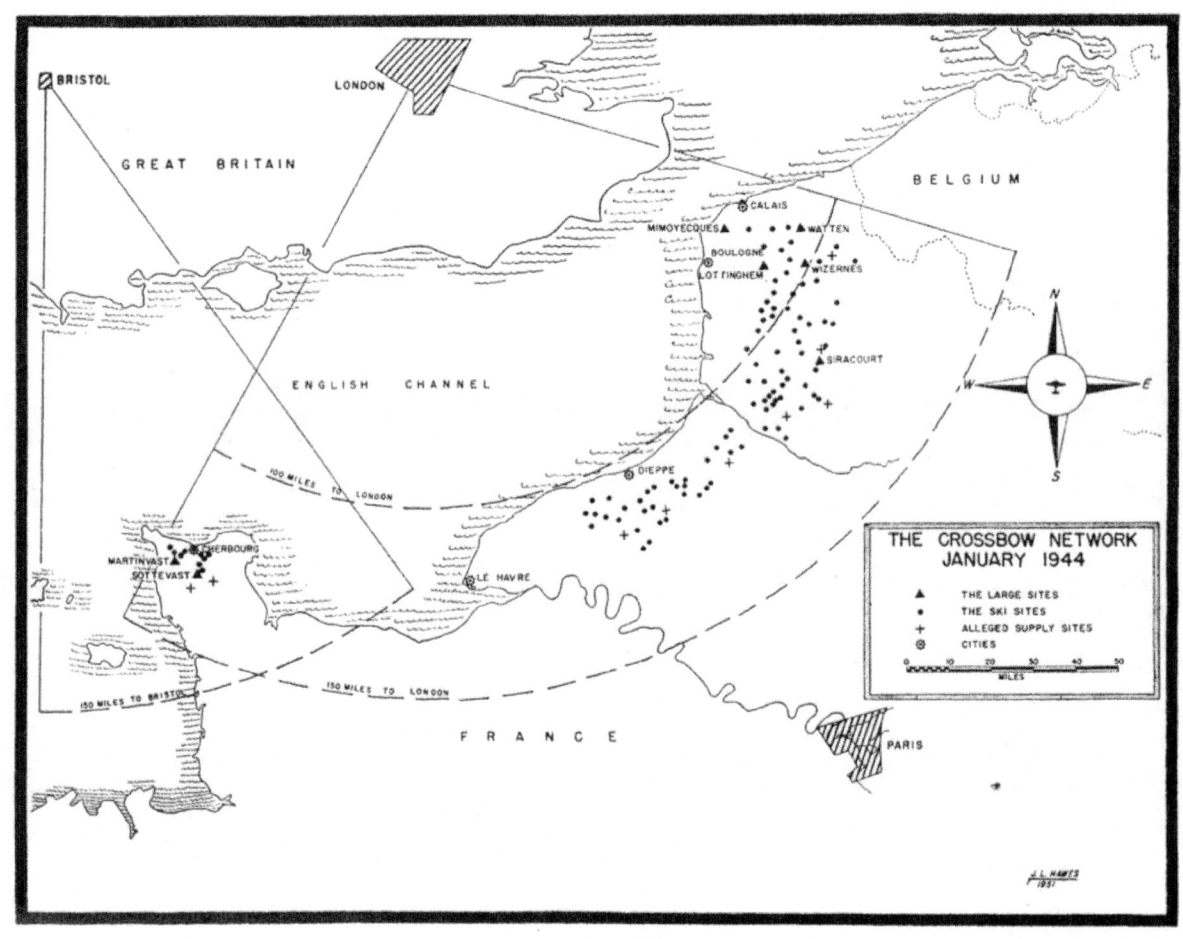

A World War II map shows the two areas where the Germans were setting up their secret "V" weapons to bombard England (right, center). These are the areas in which the Royal Air Force and 8th Air Force heavy bombers concentrated their bombs to knock out the weapons — part of the pre-invasion plan. This event was given the operational code name Crossbow during World War II. The grouping (left, centre) is the site of the Invasion of Normandy. By J.L. Hawes – This image was released by the United States Air Force with the ID 060421-F-0000S-001 (next). Public Domain

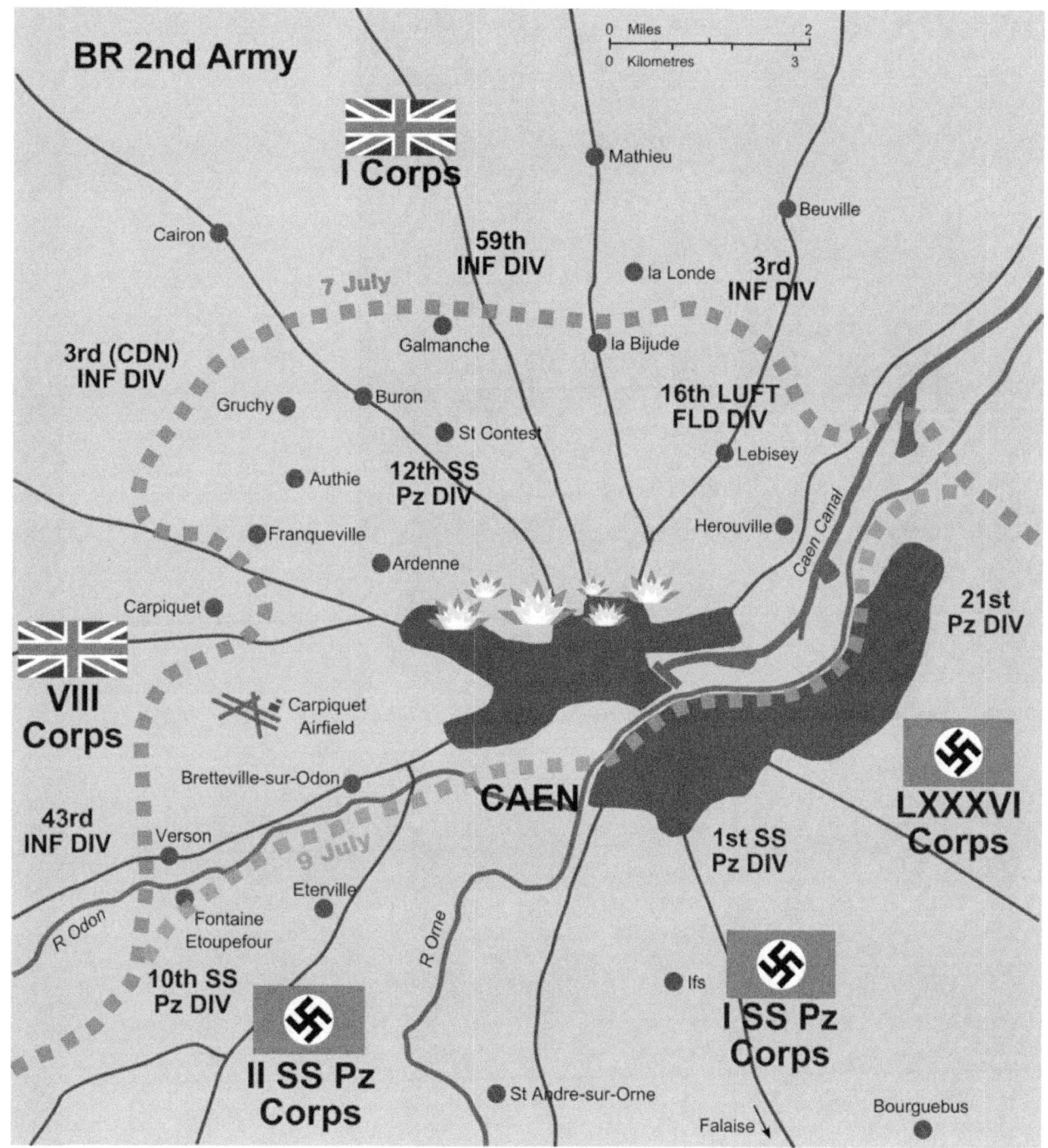

Anglo-Canadian and German positions prior to and after Operation Charnwood, 7-9 July 1944, showing the target zone of RAF Bomber Command's heavy bombers. The northern half of Caen was captured in the offensive. Attribution – EyeSerene, CC BY-SA 3.0 via Wikimedia Commons

Launch Ramp for Fieseler Fi-103 (V1) 'Flying Bomb (MUN 5785) ramp Launch ramp Copyright: © IWM.

V1 FLYING BOMB (CL 3430) Fiesler Fi 103 flying bombs being manhandled at a launching site. The bomb on the left has been placed on a conveyor trolley following servicing and is awaiting its move to the non-magnetic building for course setting. The bomb on the right has been secured for transport on a site-handling bogie. The background of the photograph has been obliterated by the German censor. Copyright: © IWM.

ROYAL AIR FORCE BOMBER COMMAND, 1942-1945. (C 4458) Vertical aerial photograph taken during the daylight attack on the German secret weapon (V3) site at Mimoyecques, near Marquise, France, showing a Handley Page Halifax flying over the target as exploding bombs send smoke and clouds of dust into the air.

Victoria Crosses

The highest and most prestigious award for valour *"in the presence of the enemy"* to members of the British Armed Forces. The Victoria Cross was introduced on 29 January 1856 to honour acts of valour during the Crimean War. Since then, the medal has been awarded 1,358 times to 1,355 individual recipients.

I am aware of, **eight Perthshire connected Victoria Cross Winners**, for conspicuous gallantry in the face of the enemy; two during World War Two, two during World War One, and three during the Indian Mutiny. One VC was awarded posthumously, and two were awarded for actions during the same battle, on the same day. Three VCs were awarded to RAF aviators.

John Manson Craig VC

John Manson Craig was born on 5 March 1896 to a family residing at Innergeldie in Glen Lednock, northwest of Comrie. After attending Morrisons Academy, an independent school in Crieff (est. 1850), he went up to Cambridge to study science. After graduating, Craig joined the Cameron Highlanders (6 April 1915) and went on to take part in September/October of that year in the Battle of Loos (France). In the summer of 1917, Craig, by then a lieutenant in the 1/5th Battalion, Royal Scots Fusiliers took part in the Second Battle of Gaza (Palestine) in which he won a VC on 5 June 1917 for bravery under fire – an action which involved Craig in the recovery of dead and wounded comrades and led to his own wounding.

John Manson Craig had already proven his bravery on 3 separate occasions including being wounded in May 1917 (he had only just returned to the battalion after recovering from this wounding when he won the VC), and had survived the torpedoing of the troop ship, the SS *Invernia*, which had carried him and the battalion out to Alexandria.

As the Great War moved to a close, Craig enrolled in the RFC, (Royal Flying Corp) and it is likely that he underwent flying training at El Rimal (later named RAF El Amiriya) with No. 19 Training Depot Station (TDS) and was possibly an instructor at Heliopolis (Crete) with No. 5 Fighter Training School.

During the Second World War, Craig re-enlisted in the RAF, and was assigned as Deputy Assistant Provost Marshal, RAF Police, based in Dundee. Craig's wartime duties included acting as escort to Vyacheslav Molotov, the Minister of Foreign Affairs of the Soviet Union during the latter's visit to Britain in May 1942 (see RAF Tealing).

By the end of the war, Craig had the rank of wing commander and had added several medals to sit alongside his VC including:

1914-15 Star, British War Medal (1914-20), Victory Medal (1914-19), King George VI Coronation Medal (1937), Defence Medal (1939-45), and the Queen Elizabeth II Coronation Medal (1953).

John Manson Craig VC died on 19 February 1970 at Crieff Cottage Hospital. He was cremated at Perth Crematorium and his ashes are interred in his family vault at Comrie Cemetery.

Vyacheslav Molotov May 1942 RAF Tealing (John Manson Craig possibly one of the three RAF Officers in the image)

2nd Lt. John Manson Craig, R. Sc. Fus.

For most conspicuous bravery on the occasion of an advanced post being rushed by a large party of the enemy. This officer immediately organised a rescue party, and the enemy was tracked over broken country back to his trenches. 2nd Lt. Craig then set his party to work removing the dead and wounded.

During the course of this operation his men came under heavy rifle and machine gun fire. An N.C.O. was wounded, and the Medical Officer who went out to his aid was also severely wounded. 2nd Lt. Craig at once went to their assistance and succeeded in taking the N.C.O. under cover. He then returned for the Medical Officer, and whilst taking him to shelter was himself wounded.

Nevertheless, by great perseverance, he succeeded in rescuing him also.

As the enemy continued a heavy fire and in addition turned on shrapnel and high explosives, 2nd Lt. Craig scooped cover for the wounded and thus was the means of saving their lives.

These latter acts of bravery occurred in broad daylight, under full observation of the enemy and within close range.

On three previous occasions this officer has behaved in a conspicuously brave manner, and has shown an exceptional example of courage and resource.

Hugh Gordon Malcolm

Glenalmond College (founded by W. E. Gladstone in 1847) sits amid 300-acres of beautiful Perthshire countryside, 8 miles to the west of Perth. Three of its alumni have been awarded the VC, the highest award for gallantry in the face of the enemy that can be conferred to British and Commonwealth forces. One of the awardees is Broughty Ferry born, Wing Commander Hugh Gordon Malcolm, VC.

Born on 2 May 1917, Malcolm attended Glenalmond College, 1931-5. On 9 January 1936, he began training at RAF College Cranwell (Lincolnshire) and by 4 March 1936 was appointed Air Liaison Officer on Lieutenant General Montgomery's general staff. By the end of 1941, Malcolm had been promoted to the rank of squadron leader. Hugh Malcolm was posthumously awarded the VC on 27 April 1943, the first RAF VC to be won in North Africa. In recognition of his valour, the RAF named its welfare clubs after him – the 'Malcolm Clubs' – these were to be found in many parts of the world and existed on some RAF bases (including RAF Brüggen (West Germany) and RAF Wittering, (Cambridgeshire)) into the 1980s and 1990s. Malcolm is buried in the Beja War Cemetery in Tunisia. To this day, he is remembered at Glenalmond College which maintains a memorial in the college cemetery.

"IN PROUD AND HONOURED MEMORY OF WING COMMANDER HUGH GORDON MALCOLM V.C. GLENALMOND 1931 – 1935 WHO WAS KILLED IN ACTION IN NORTH AFRICA ON 4TH DECR. 1941 AND AWARDED THE VICTORIA CROSS FOR HIS GREAT GALLANTRY ON THAT DAY."

A citation in the *London Gazette* of 28 April 1943 details the action in which Hugh Malcolm lost his life.

"On 17 November 1942, Wing-Comdr. Malcolm was ordered to carry out with his light bomber squadron a low-level formation attack on Bizerta airfield. In spite of fierce opposition, all the squadron's bombs were dropped on the airfield. Two enemy machines were shot down and others damaged on the ground.

On 28 November 1942, he again led his squadron against Bizerta airfield and though it was heavily defended he successfully attacked it with bombs and machine-gun fire.

On 4th December 1942, Wing-Comdr. Malcolm, while giving close support to the First Army, received an urgent request to attack an enemy fighter airfield. The attack of 10 Bristol Blenheim's, made without fighter escort, was successful, but the squadron was intercepted by an overwhelming force of enemy fighters. Although Wing-Comdr. Malcolm fought back, the aircraft in his formation were shot down one by one, in the end his own machine, the last one was shot down in flames fifteen miles from the target.

Throughout his service in command of a light bomber squadron in North Africa Wing-Comdr. Malcolm's leadership, skill and daring were of the highest order. His last exploit was the finest example of the valour and unswerving devotion to duty which he constantly displayed."

Flight Lieutenant William Reid VC

William Reid was born in Baillieston in Glasgow on 21 December 1921, the son of a blacksmith. He attended Swinton Primary and Coatbridge Secondary School. After training with the RAF in Canada, Reid gained his wings and was commissioned on 19 June 1942 as a pilot officer on probation in the RAF Volunteer Reserve (RAFVR). At RAF Little Rissington, west of Cheltenham, he trained on twin-engine Airspeed Oxfords. Moving on to the Operational Training Unit (OTU) No. 29 at RAF North Luffenham, he was selected as an instructor flying Vickers Wellingtons. He was promoted to flying officer on 19 December 1942.

His first operational mission was with RAF 1654 Conversion Unit at RAF Wigsley, he flew as second pilot in an Avro Lancaster belonging to RAF 9 Squadron to bomb Mönchengladbach. In September 1943, he was posted to RAF 61 Squadron at RAF Syerston where he flew seven sorties attacking various German cities, before his famous raid on Düsseldorf.

At the age of 22 Reid was awarded the Victoria Cross following a raid on Düsseldorf on 3 November 1943: the front of his cockpit was shot away just after crossing the Dutch coast. He was injured in the head, shoulders, and hands, in a fight with a Messerschmitt BF 110. The rear gunner could not fire as the heating circuit had failed, and his hands were too cold to press the trigger or operate his microphone to give warning. After a short delay he managed to return fire and the Messerschmitt was driven off.

A second fighter then attacked his RAF 51 Squadron Avro Lancaster, *'O for Oboe'*, the navigator was killed, the wireless operator was fatally wounded, and the flight engineer although injured in the arm gave Reid oxygen and assistance. The rear turret was badly damaged, the communications system and the compasses were put out of action. The windscreen was shattered, and blood was flowing down his face and Reid could feel the taste of it in his mouth. It soon froze because of the intense cold. Reid revived sufficiently to give the thumbs-up' sign and carry on with the mission and they managed to accurately bomb the target and return to base.

Image -VICTORIA CROSS WINNERS: 1939-1945. (CHP 794) Portrait of William Reid RAF, awarded the Victoria Cross: Germany, 3 November 1940. Copyright: © IWM.

Reid had memorised the course to the target and could therefore carry on with the mission without the compasses, Düsseldorf was still some 50 minutes away. After dropping the plane's bomb load, Reid flew back as best he could, navigating by the stars and the moon. The elevators trimming tabs had been shot away making control difficult, they had to always hold the stick with both hands, with the help of the engineer and the bomb aimer who was called on to help. The exertion started Reid's head bleeding again. They kept the Lancaster going and got through despite being caught in searchlights and heavy anti-aircraft fire over The Netherlands coast. At times Reid lapsed into semi-consciousness. (The flight engineer, Sergeant J Norris was later awarded the Conspicuous Gallantry Medal.)

Reid stated that: *'Then I saw a drome beneath us. I flashed the distress signal with the landing lamp. Just as we touched down the undercarriage collapsed. It had been shot through and we went on our tummy for about 50 yards. No one was hurt in the crash'.*

Convalescing in hospital, Reid recounted his experience: *'I just saw a blinding flash, and I lost about 2,000 feet before I could pull out again. I felt as if my head had been blown off – just the sort of feeling you get at the time. Other members of the crew shouted: 'Are you alright?' I felt alright. I resumed course and managed to get my goggles on. My shoulder was a bit stiff, and it felt as if someone had hit me with a hammer'.*

From the Operations Record Book of 61 Squadron, November 1943:

3/4th, Lancaster LM 360

F/L. W. Reid. Captain, Sgt J. W. Norris, Flt. Eng., F/S J. S. Jeffries. Nav., Sgt. L. G. Rolton. A.B., F/S. J. J. Mann. WT/AG., F/S. S. G. Baldwin. A.G.1., F/S. A.F. Emerson. A.G.2.

Up Time 16.59, Down Time 22.01

F/L Reid was attacked by enemy night fighters on the way out, but although he and Flight Engineer were wounded, and the Navigator killed outright he proceeded on to bomb the target. On returning a crash landing was made at RAF Shipman. (USAAF operated air base in Norfolk.)

Lena, Reid's mother, was busy feeding the children at Baillieston School when a reporter walked in and asked her for some details about her son. She asked: *Why, what's he done? I knew about my son's bomber being badly damaged on one trip, but I never guessed this would be the result'.* This was the first she had heard that he had won the VC: *'When I saw him in hospital after he was wounded, he did not want to tell me anything about the raid'.* At that time, Helena Murdoch Reid, 97 Swinton Crescent, Baillieston, had lost her husband, William, and in July 1940 her eldest son, Sergeant George Reid, 28, air gunner with RAF 15 Squadron had been shot down over Belgium.

Reid was visited in hospital by Air Vice Marshal Cochrane, who asked him why he didn't turn back. Reid said that he thought it safer to go on rather than turning back among all the other planes all flying in the same direction. Cochrane then added: *'It's as if they all said, "That bugger, Jock, he went on even though he was badly wounded, so we can't turn back just because of a faulty altimeter, or something like that'.*

In July of the following year, 1944, Reid was shot down and captured whilst bombing a V-1 rocket site at Rilly-la-Montagnes, near Reims, France. He had been posted to the second flight of RAF 617 Squadron, the famous 'Dambusters'. They had just released a massive 'Tallboy' earthquake bomb at 12,000 feet when they were struck by bombs from an aircraft above them. The bomb ploughed through his aeroplane's fuselage, severing all the control cables, and weakening its structure. Reid gave the order to bail-out and later recalled his Lancaster going into a spin. He was pinned to his seat but managed to reach overhead and release the escape hatch panel. He then recalled being outside the aircraft with the wireless operator, the two of them being the only survivors. Bill landed heavily by parachute, breaking one of his arms in the fall. Within an hour they were made prisoners of war, eventually ending up in Stalag Luft III at Luckenwalde, southwest of Berlin. He was released after ten months by Soviet troops, whilst they were on a forced march to a new pow camp.

From the Operations Record Book of RAF 617 Squadron:

Woodhall Spa. 31 July 1944

16 Lancaster's and 2 Mosquito aircraft were detailed for operations. All aircraft took off successfully, the target being a railway tunnel at Rilly-la-Montagne. The operation was successful, several bombs being seen to burst close to the aiming point. "S" (P/L. Reid) bail out, but it could not be confirmed that they were members of his crew, which consisted of F/L. Reid V.C. (124438) (Pilot), 909536 F/Sgt. Stewart D.G.W. (F/Eng), F/O. J.O. Peltier (J.17546) (Nav), P/O L.G. Rolton (171066) (A/B.), F/O D. Luker (134635?) (W/Op), Holt A.A. (M.U.) and 1378696 W/O. Hutton J.W. (R.G.). The weather at base was cloudy with poor visibility at first, becoming moderate. Fair early, in evening, becoming cloudy.

RAF 617 Operations Summary.

During the month 107 operational sorties were despatched, comprising 234 hrs. 45 mins operational day flying and 129 hrs. 35 mins night operational flying. Of these, 1 aircraft was lost and 29 failed to complete missions. A total of 256 hrs. 25 mins flying day was carried out on training. A total of 431.5 tons of bombs was dropped operationally.

Holt A A was Flight Sergeant Albert Arthur Holt (1159886). F/O D. Luker is not listed as being killed and may have survived. The crew who died are buried at Clichy Northern Cemetery, just north of the city of Paris, 150 km to the west.

In a postcard to his mother in Baillieston, Reid wrote: 'Again I tell you not to worry about me, mother, and you had better have another holiday. It will do no good moping about me'.

After the war, Reid was an agricultural degree student at Glasgow University, Then in Hertfordshire; he was the national cattle and sheep adviser to the Spillers company; later director of MacRobert Farms (Douneside) Ltd., and eventually manager of Douneside Group Farms, Tarland. In 1987, he was one of the successful applicants for the Freedom of the City of London. Reid was president of the British Legion in Crieff and honorary life president of the Air Crew Association. Coatbridge Secondary School affectionately referred to Wiliam Reid as 'Weelum or Whelam'. A second brother of Reid was killed during the war.

Reid and his wife Violet retired to Crieff for the last 20 years of his life. He passed away on 28 November 2001 aged 79 and is buried in the Ford Road Cemetery, Crieff. The couple had a son Graeme and a daughter Susan. Violet died on 25 September 2019.

Bill Reid always claimed that he had done no more than his duty. He was well known as a modest, kindly, family man. His wife Violet Gallagher was unaware that he was a VC holder until they were married in 1952, she was, he confessed, "a wee bit impressed". Bill's VC was sold at auction in London in November 2009 for £348.000.

With precision timing, four Tornado aircraft of Reid's famous 617 Squadron based at RAF Lossiemouth approached at low level at 1.30 pm over Crieff, overflying the church in diamond formation. Precisely as they passed over the church, the rearmost aircraft peeled off into a vertical climb and powered upwards into the clouds, the 'Missing Man' formation.

Act Flt Lt William REID RAFVR

"The KING has been graciously pleased to confer the VICTORIA CROSS on the undermentioned officer in recognition of most conspicuous bravery: —

Acting Flight Lieutenant William REID (124438), Royal Air Force Volunteer Reserve, No. 61 Squadron.

On the night of November 3rd, 1943, Flight Lieutenant Reid was Pilot, and Captain of a Lancaster aircraft detailed to attack Dusseldorf.

Shortly after crossing the Dutch coast, the pilot's windscreen was shattered by fire from a Messerschmitt no. Owing to a failure in the heating circuit, the rear gunner's hands were too cold for him to open fire immediately or to operate his microphone and so give warning of danger; but after a brief delay he managed to return the Messerschmitt's fire and it was driven off.

During the fight with the Messerschmitt, Flight Lieutenant Reid was wounded in the head, shoulders, and hands. The elevator trimming tabs of the aircraft were damaged and it became difficult to control. The rear turret, too, was badly damaged and the communications system and compasses were put out of action. Flight Lieutenant Reid ascertained that his crew were unscathed and, saying nothing about his own injuries, he continued his mission.

Soon afterwards, the Lancaster was attacked by a Focke Wulf 190. This time, the enemy's fire raked the bomber from stem to stern. The rear gunner replied with his only serviceable gun, but the state of his turret made accurate aiming impossible. The navigator was killed, and the wireless operator fatally injured. The mid-upper turret was hit, and the oxygen system put out of action. Flight Lieutenant Reid was again wounded and the flight engineer, though hit in the forearm, supplied him with oxygen from a portable supply.

Flight Lieutenant Reid refused to be turned from his objective and Dusseldorf was reached some 50 minutes later. He had memorised his course to the target and had continued in such a normal manner that the bomb-aimer, who was cut off by the failure of the communications system, knew nothing of his captain's injuries or of the casualties to his comrades. Photographs show that, when the bombs were released, the aircraft was right over the centre of the target.

Steering by the pole star and the moon, Flight Lieutenant Reid then set course for home. He was growing weak from loss of blood. The emergency oxygen supply had given out. With the windscreen shattered, the cold was intense. He lapsed into semi-consciousness. The flight engineer, with some help from the bomb-aimer, kept the Lancaster in the air despite heavy anti-aircraft fire over the Dutch coast.

The North Sea crossing was accomplished. An airfield was sighted. The captain revived, resumed control, and made ready to land. Ground mist partially obscured the runway lights. The captain was also much bothered by blood from his head wound getting into his eyes. But he made a safe landing although one leg of the damaged undercarriage collapsed when the load came on.

Wounded in two attacks, without oxygen, suffering severely from cold, his navigator dead, his wireless operator fatally wounded, his aircraft crippled and defenceless, Flight Lieutenant Reid showed superb courage and leadership in penetrating a further 200 miles into enemy territory to attack one of the most strongly defended targets in Germany, every additional mile increasing the hazards of the long and perilous journey home. His tenacity and devotion to duty were beyond praise."

Medal entitlement of Flight Lieutenant William Reid, 61 Squadron, Royal Air Force Volunteer Reserve:

Victoria Cross

1939-45 Star

Air Crew Europe Star – clasp: 'France & Germany'

War Medal (1939-45)

Queen Elizabeth II Coronation Medal (1953)

Queen Elizabeth II Silver Jubilee Medal (1977)

NOTES: Battle of Britain pilot, Flying Officer Donald Ballantine Hardy McHardy, a friend of Reid was also in Stalag Luft III with him. McHardy helped dig that camp's famous escape tunnels and was due to be in the second batch of escapees. This attempt was abandoned after 50 of the first batch were murdered by the Gestapo.

RAF 617 Squadron at the time of Reid's VC was led by Wing Commander Leonard Cheshire, who would later also win the VC to add to his DSO and DFC. Reid was invested with his VC by King George VI at Buckingham Palace on 11 June 1944.

William Reid Daily Record Wednesday 15 December 1943

Aberdeen Press and Journal 3 August 1950

Flight Sergeant George Thomson VC

George Thomson was born 23 October 1920 at Borestone Cottage, Trinity Gask, about 12 miles west of Perth. At the age of 15, after schooling at Portmoak Public School and Kinross Higher Grades School, Thomson began an apprenticeship with a Kinross grocer.

During the Second World War, Thomson volunteered with the Local Defence Volunteers (later known as the Home Guard) and applied to join the RAF but was given 'deferred service'. A second application in late 1940 resulted in an appearance at an 'aircrew selection board'. This too ended unsuccessfully. Undeterred, Thomson enlisted as RAF ground crew and went on to serve in Iraq for a year and a half. A third application for flying duties in mid-August 1943 resulted in Thomson being accepted for training as an air wireless operator (bomber crew) at No. 14 OTU RAF at Market Harborough (22 May 1944). Upon completion of training, Thomson joined No. 9 Squadron RAF at Bardney (Lincolnshire) on 29 September 1944. Thomson's first operational mission was a bombing run in an Avro Lancaster, 4-engine heavy bomber over Bremen on 6 October 1944. The following month (30 November 1944), he was promoted to the rank of flight sergeant.

On 31 December 1944, Thomson took part in a mission that saw him posthumously receive a VC. He was the wireless operator for Lancaster PD377 (call sign 'U' for 'Uncle'), one of 10 Lancaster bombers taking part in a dawn bombing raid on the Dortmund-Ems Canal, Germany. While over the target, having released its payload, PD377 was hit twice, and an intense fire took hold. Despite the personal danger, Thomson made his way through the smoke-filled plane to help the mid-upper gunner, Ernie Potts, whose turret was on fire. He dragged the gunner to a safer position and bare handed extinguished the gunner's burning clothing receiving consequently severe burns to his face, hands, and legs. Without further consideration of himself, Thomson repeated this act of bravery in rescuing the rear gunner, Haydn Price. After this, he made his way to the cockpit where the pilot, Flying Officer Ron Goebel, and the Lancaster's engineer Wilf Hartshorn had made the decision to land the plane – the option to bail out was not available due to parachute damage.

The damaged plane was manoeuvred to come down over a liberated part of the Netherlands where a successful landing was made near to the village of Heesch. Luckily, the fighter escort for the bombing run spotted the crash site and informed RAF Bomber Command, which arranged for medical services (an ambulance and 2 doctors) to be on hand at the village. The survivors were taken to Eindhoven Catholic

Hospital. Of the 2 gunners rescued by Thomson, Potts died after 18 hours, and Price needed plastic surgery but recovered. Sadly, Thomson who had begun to recover from his wounds succumbed to pneumonia. He died at No. 50 Military Field Hospital on 23 January 1945 and is buried in the Brussels Town Cemetery, Evere.

George Thompson was posthumously awarded the VC on 20 February 1945. The medal alongside Thomson's other medals is housed in the National War Museum of Scotland, Edinburgh Castle. A replica of Thompson's medal is on display in the Jackson Block at the Royal Air Force College, Cranwell. In addition, his name features on the Portmoak war memorial.

Polish 309 Squadron

Despite being the first to bear the brunt of Hitler's Blitzkrieg, Poland's martial resistance lasted longer than that of France, Norway, Holland, and Belgium. After the fall of Poland and France, elements of the Polish military were reconstituted in the west (under Western Allied command) and separately in the east (under the command of the Soviet Union). Many Poles answered Churchill's call to arms of "blood, sweat and tears" by continuing the fight against Nazi tyranny under British command. Notably, the call was fulfilled by the pilots of No. 303 Squadron RAF, who shot down the highest tally of German aircraft in the Battle of Britain; and the personnel of Anders 2nd Corps who were heavily involved in the liberation of Monte Cassino. Polish mathematicians and scientists were also critical to cracking the German Ultra codes and providing intelligence on the V1 and V2 rocket programme threatening the British population on the Home Front.

After deployment to Scotland to regroup its ground forces, a section of the former Polish army was recreated as the 1st Polish Army Corps (28 September 1940) under the command of Generals Stanisław Maczek and Marian Kukiel. Under the authority of the British Army's Scottish (district) Command, the Corps was headquartered at Moncreiffe House, near Bridge of Earn. It comprised 3,498 officers and 10,884 soldiers. Polish troops formed the fourth largest contingent among the Allied forces after the USSR, the USA, and the UK.

1st Polish Army Corps

Polish 1st Armoured Division. *(The division was the largest armoured formation among the Western Allies.)*

Polish Independent Parachute Brigade. *(The 1st (Polish) Independent Parachute Brigade, which fought in the Battle of Arnhem (1944), was trained mainly in the grounds of Largo House near Upper Largo in Fife.)* Polish 4th Infantry Division.

Polish 16th Independent Armoured Brigade.

Many Scottish cities, towns, and villages became very accustomed to seeing Polish soldiers with their distinctive 'POLAND' shoulder flash. Several of the Polish Army units based in Scotland adopted unit badges which included a Scottish motif and some Scottish towns presented standards to Polish units. There was a Polish reconnaissance battalion stationed in Perth as well as troops from the 1st Polish Armoured Division billeted in Pullars of Perth's Tulloch (dye) Works, which had undergone requisition by the Secretary of War. In November 1940, President Władysław Raczkiewicz visited his country's troops at the Tulloch Works.

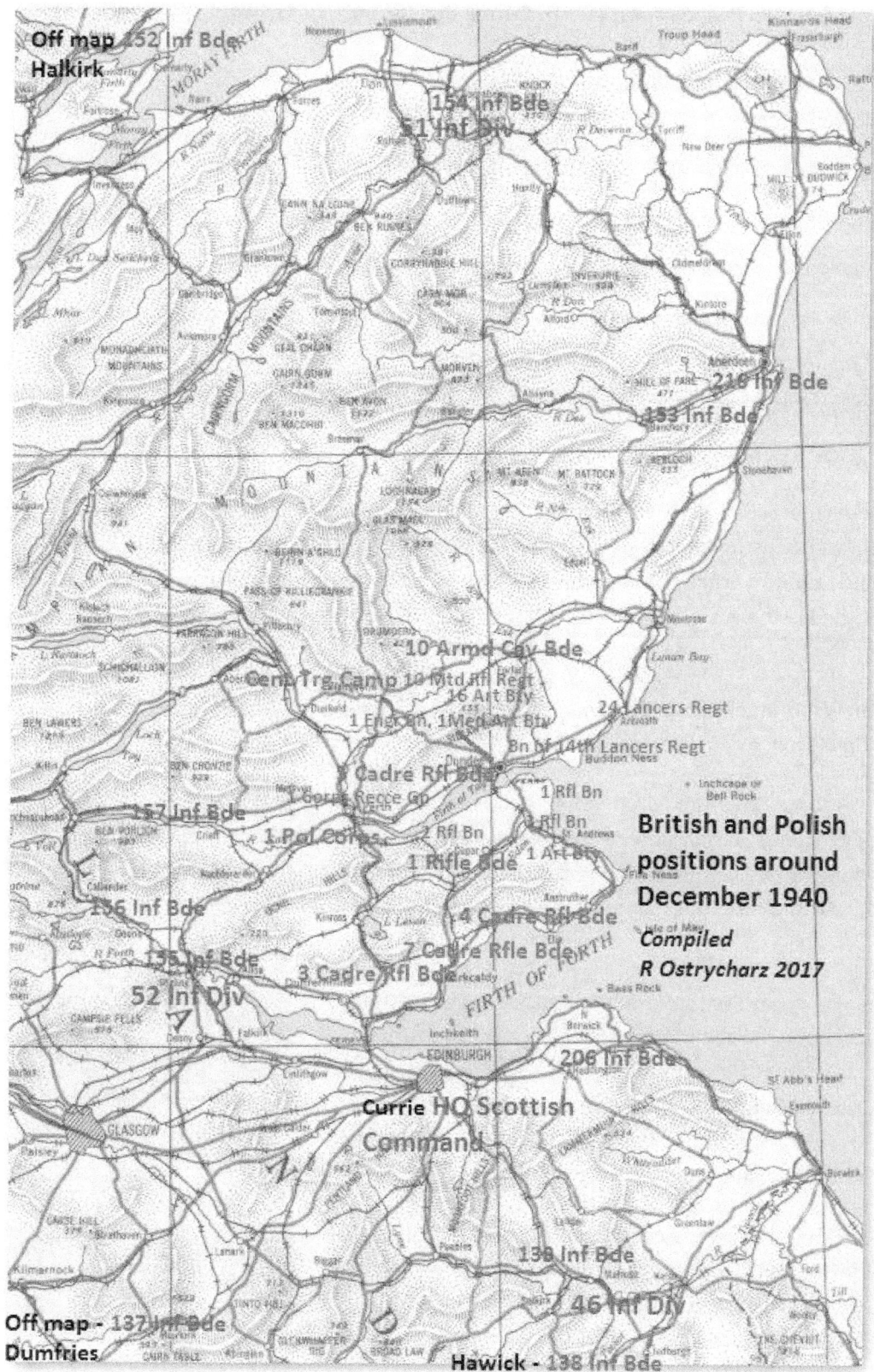

Polish Military Units Located in and Around Perth During the Second World War

HQ 1st Polish Army Corps – near Bridge of Earn.

Armoured Train Group – Perth.

Corps Recce Group – Perth.

Signals Unit – Bridge of Earn.

Central Training Camp HQ – Alyth.

Specialist Troops Centres – Blairgowrie, Dundee, Dunfermline, Alyth/Meigle, Alyth, and Coupar Angus.

Tank/A-Tk Units Training Battalion – Crieff.

1st Grenadier Brigade – Coupar Angus.

1st Polish Armoured Division – Blairgowrie.

Over 120,000 Polish veterans settled in Britain after the war, unable to return home due to political circumstance. Whilst they assimilated well into British society and were grateful for the safe haven offered, their contribution to Britain's freedom seemed to be soon forgotten. Sadly, when over 130 allied nations marched in the great 1946 'Victory Parade' in London, Polish veterans based in Britain were excluded.

No. 309 (Dywizjon Współpracy 'Ziemi Czerwien´skiej' ('Land of Czerwien´)) Polish Fighter-Reconnaissance Squadron

Formed as an army co-operation squadron at RAF Abbotsinch (now Glasgow Airport) in October 1940, No. 309 (Land of Czerwie´n) Polish Fighter Reconnaissance Squadron became one of 16 Polish squadrons flying from Britain during the Second World War. From 6 November 1940, the squadron was headquartered at RAF Renfrew. The squadron took its name from an area in Western Poland just north of Zielona Góra.

The Polish fighter squadrons (No. 309 Squadron included) were staffed with pilots who had obtained combat experience against the Luftwaffe, firstly in Poland and later with the French air force. During the Second World War, they proved themselves excellent fighter pilots. No. 303 Squadron was the top-scoring fighter squadron of all the RAF squadrons involved in the Battle of Britain.

During March of 1941, the Luftwaffe conducted a series of night raids on Glasgow and RAF Renfrew, which resulted in casualties among No. 309 Squadron. Consequently, the squadron was moved to RAF Dunino (by St Andrews) on 15 May 1941.

309 Squadron maintained a 'fighter' flight of aircraft at RAF Perth in 1941 with the mission to destroy German bombers taking a flight path in the skies above Perth. Flying outdated and slow Westland Lysander Mk IIIs, the squadron had little chance to accomplish the task.

Spring 1942 saw several of the squadron undergoing conversion training to Mk I North American P-51 Mustangs at RAF Gatwick (London). When fitted with Rolls Royce 2-speed supercharged Merlin 66 engines (early versions of the Mustang employed the Alison V-1710 engine which suffered from severe engine knocking at higher altitudes), the Mustang was one of the finest fighter aircraft of the Second World War. Additional under-wing fuel drop-tanks allowed Mustangs to fly alongside bombers as far as Berlin (and beyond) in Germany maintaining protection throughout their bombing run.

Within a few months, the entire squadron were trained to fly Mustangs. The squadron's first mission with the new planes was a reconnaissance flight over France (21 May 1942). The pilot of that mission was (most likely) Flight Lieutenant M. Piotrowski. In December 1942, No. 309 Squadron was returned to Findo Gask. This was a short-term relocation, Findo Gask was unsuitable for P-51 Mustangs – the runways were short and soggy, and before long the squadron was operational in the south of England. A subsequent move saw them at RAF Peterhead running defensive cover above the North Sea for convoys heading to Russia.

Four victories have been confirmed for No. 309 Squadron pilots flying Mustang IIIs: a Focke-Wulf Fw 190 and 3 Messerschmitt ME 262 jet-powered fighters.

No. 309 Squadron Commanders
25 November 1940 – Z. Pistl.

14 February 1943 – J. Piotrowski.

15 October 1943 – M. Piotrowski. 3 April 1944 – J. Golko.

9 September 1944 – A. Glowacki.

17 July 1945 – H. Pietrzak.

No. 309: Squadron Operational Locations
7 October 1940 – 6 November 1940 – RAF Abbotsinch.

6 November 1940 – 8 May 1941 – RAF Renfrew.

8 May 1941 – 26 November 1942 – RAF Dunino.

26 November 1942 –?

10 March 1943 – RAF Findo Gask (Perthshire) – Flights 'A' and 'C'.

15 November 1942 – RAF Gatwick – Flight 'B'.

10 January 1943 – RAF Peterhead – Flight 'B'.

10 March 1943 – 3 June 1943 – RAF Kirknewton (West Lothian).

23 April 1943 – RAF Acklington (Northumberland) – Flight 'A'.

3 June 1943 – 6 November 1943 – RAF Snailwell (Cambridgeshire).

6 November 1943 – 24 November 1943 – RAF Wellingore (near Lincoln).

24 November 1943 – 23 April 1944 – RAF Snailwell.

23 April 1944 – 14 November 1944 – RAF Drem (East Lothian).

14 November 1944 – 14 December 1944 – RAF Peterhead.

14 December 1944 – 10 August 1945 – RAF Andrews Field (Essex).

No. 309: Squadron Aircraft Flown

25 November 1940 – March 1943 – Westland Lysander II and III.

August 1942 – February 1944 – North American Mustang I – possibly Flight 'B'.

February 1944 – April 1944 – Hawker Hurricane IV.

23 April 1944 – September 1944 – Hawker Hurricane IIC.

1 September 1944 – November 1944 – North American Mustang I.

20 October 1944 – December 1946 – North American Mustang III.

Note: *"We should remember that, during the turning point of history, Polish airmen were almost the only allies – apart from Commonwealth nations – who fought in strength at our side. In the Battle of Britain alone Polish Airmen brought down or crippled over two hundred enemy aircraft."* The Right Honourable Lord Vansittart.

Pilots of the 309 Squadron, standing from the left: Lieutenant Stanisław Zajchowski, Lieutenant Jan Mozołowski, unrecognized, Lieutenant Franciszek Kubica, Plut.Mech. Zygmunt Janke, Lieutenant Jerzy Mencel, 2nd lieutenant Jan Lewandowski, Lieutenant Eugeniusz Antolak, Corporal Egon Eisenbach, unrecognized, Second Lieutenant Zygmunt Jaeschke. Second Lieutenant Zygmunt Kawnik. (Kneeling) -Peterhead, November 8, 1944.

Polish Airforce Graves at Wellshill Cemetery, Perth

Wellshill Cemetery was chosen as a Polish war grave cemetery during the Second World War. Some 380 Polish war graves are situated there (about 50 per cent of all Polish war graves in Scotland) of which 354 Polish casualties are recorded by the Register of Commonwealth War Graves:

The history of these Polish military forces is not as widely known as it should be. At Perth's Wellshill Cemetery a substantial monument stands testament to the contribution and sacrifice of these Polish military personnel. The graves and memorial are at the south end of the cemetery, near its Jeanfield Road entrance.

Army (339).

Airforce (9). Navy (4).

Nursing (1). Civilian (1).

And 26 are listed as British casualties (Polish Resettlement Corps).

The Polish War graves are at the Jeanfield Road entrance and the madeinperth.org website has a list of all the Polish War Graves names.

Among the graves to visit at Wellshill are those of:

The first Polish war casualty who was buried in Wellshill Cemetery, Officer Cadet Janusz Ulrych-Uleneski (37) who died in Bridge of Earn Hospital.

Father Karol BiK served with the 14th Jazlowiecki Lancers Regiment was the "beloved" chaplain of some of the first Polish troops sent to Scotland. He was first stationed in the Arbroath area, then shortly after Father Karol was moved inland with reservist troops to Newtyle, about 19 miles Northwest of Perth. Quickly adjusting to his new surrounds, the chaplain is said to have taken to the woods and hills surrounding the village for "each free moment" he had. One day, Father Karol never returned, his whereabouts unknown for several days. Among the trees at Newtyle stands a simple soldier's cross on the spot where the priest was founded dead. He was aged 54 and most likely suffered a heart attack. A second related tragedy for the regiment was the death 24 hours later of Aspirant Ignacy Brak who had served Father Karol at Mass, in a motorcycle accident in Perth. Both men were buried in the Polish war grave section of Wellshill cemetery. The funeral service was carried out by the Field Bishop of the Polish Army.

Ludwik Zasada was born in Potok Złoty, Poland on 7 October 1907. After the attack on Poland by Nazi Germany, in September 1939, Zasada was evacuated alongside other Polish Air Force personnel based at Warsaw-Oke͵cie air base to the rear of the German advance. At the start of October, Zasada took part in the Battle of Kock (2-5 October 1939) as part of the Polesie Independent Operational Group, an army corps created but a few weeks earlier and commanded by General Franciszek Kleeberg. The battle ended in a victory for the German 14th Motorised Corps. Zasada  subsequently escaped to Hungary and then to France where he joined Polish Air Force units forming there. With the capitulation of France, Zasada relocated once more, taking himself across the Channel to begin the fight anew. He died of natural causes on 17 November 1941 and is buried in Wellshill Cemetery.

Lieutenant Colonel Gwido Karol Langer, OOP (Grand Cross), was the Chief of the Polish General Staff's Intelligence Bureau (and later the Cipher Bureau), which had made a breakthrough into the German military 'Enigma' code in December 1932. Just before the German invasion of Poland, the Polish Intelligence agency shared its knowledge with the British and French Intelligence and the work unlocking the secret code continued at the British Government's Code & Cypher School, Bletchley Park. Langer and his deputy were captured attempting to cross the Spanish border in March 1943. He provided German Intelligence with disinformation that meant they believed 'Enigma' was secure. After the war, Langer lived in Scotland. He died in 1948 and was buried in Wellshill Cemetery, Perth. In 2010, his body was exhumed and taken to Poland for reburial at Cieszyn with a full military funeral. Langer was posthumously awarded the Grand Cross of the Order of Polonia Restituta.

If it were not for the work of the team of the Polish codebreakers at the Polish Cypher Bureau, Alan Turing and his team at Bletchley Park would have faced a far more daunting task in deciphering the German Enigma code. The Poles knew 95% of the Germans' order of battle before the invasion of Poland on the 1st of September 1939. Marion Rejewski, one of the most important code breakers at Bletchley Park was born 16 August 1905 in Bromberg in the Prussian Province of Posen (now Bydgoszcz, Poland). Bydgoszcz is twinned with Perth.(See Jean Millar Valentine)

The next time you visit Wellshill after you have read this, pause for a minute, and remember the Polish soldiers buried there. The inscription on the large granite stone, states - *Eternal Glory to the Polish Soldiers who died in 1939 – 1945, For our Freedom and Yours.*

A selection of RAF jargon

Anti-Diver - diving on the V-1 'Doodlebug'

Bogey – aircraft identified as foe

Balloonatic - member of Balloon Command

Beer Barrel - Brewster Buffalo aircraft

Belinda - nickname of barrage balloons

Bomphleteers - airman dropping pamphlets (see Nickel)

Brolly – parachute

Buster – go to full throttle

Bus Driver - bomber pilot

Cabbage - bomb

Channel Stop – sortie to hinder enemy shipping in the Strait of Dover

Circus - bombers heavily escorted in order to bring enemy fighters into combat

Cockrell – signal sent from aircraft radio, plotters could use it to indicate positions, sector controllers would ask "is your Cockerel crowing?" (pilots referred to it as Pip-Squeak)

Daisy Cutter - faultless landing

Dust up - heated action / fight

Flaming Onions - anti-aircraft tracers

Gardening - mine laying at sea by aircraft (the first British magnetic mine was codename 'Vegetable')

Kipper - fishing boat North Sea protection patrols

Noball - attacking V-1 flying bomb, storage, manufacturing, or launch sites

Mandolin – attacking ground targets and railways

Nickel - leaflet dropping operation

Pancake – instruction to land

Popular - photo-reconnaissance sortie

Rhubarb - small scale freelance fighter sortie against ground targets

Rover - armed reconnaissance against targets behind enemy lines

About the Author

I was born in Cluny Terrace in the Letham area of Perth. Educated at Carntyne Primary (Glasgow), Letham Primary, Goodlyburn Junior Secondary, Perth High School (Muirton), Perth College of Further Education and the Open University.

I was the Chair of Perth United Cycling Club and a founder of the Tay Titans Cycling Club.

After retirement, I began researching several local history topics, specialising in aviation and military history. I am the author of **Where Sky and Summit Meet**, published by Tippermuir Books Ltd. Perth (sold out).

I also research and write local aviation and military history stories on the **madeinperth.org** website and the Perthshire Advertiser newspaper.

Ken Bruce

Printed in Great Britain
by Amazon